# A LIFE
## AT
# THE CENTRE

# A LIFE
# AT
# THE CENTRE

## ROY JENKINS

**MACMILLAN
LONDON**

First published 1991 by
MACMILLAN LONDON LIMITED
a division of Pan Macmillan Publishers Limited
Cavaye Place London SW10 9PG
and Basingstoke

Reprinted 1991

Associated companies in Auckland, Budapest, Dublin, Gaborone,
Harare, Hong Kong, Kampala, Kuala Lumpur, Lagos, Madras,
Manzini, Melbourne, Mexico City, Nairobi, New York,
Singapore, Sydney, Tokyo and Windhoek

ISBN 0-333-55164-8

A CIP catalogue record for this book is available from
the British Library

Typeset by Macmillan Production Limited

Printed by Billing and Sons Limited, Worcester

For Jennifer,
a first dedication, but the most appropriate one,
after fifteen books and fifty-one years

# Contents

vii

# Contents

# List of Illustrations

# Preface

I approached the writing of an autobiography with some reluctance. This was for at least two reasons. First, I felt intimidated by the prospect of finding a tone of voice in which to write about myself. It seemed much easier to go on writing appraisals of other people, particularly in the form of the short biographies (of Truman and Baldwin) into which I had settled in the 1980s. Second, while to leave an autobiography too long is obviously fatal to the enterprise, to do it too early also has disadvantages, not only for the book, but also for one's own state of mind. There is, inevitably, a touch of 'ending up' about it.

However, by the summer of 1988 I decided that the time for getting over such hesitations had come. Accordingly, one August morning, staying in a house in Liguria and looking down on the narrow cove of Parragi, I started to write, and twenty-six months and many writing places later, I finished the perhaps too substantial text. I did not start at the beginning. I thought that the 'tone of voice' problem might be best overcome if I tuned in to a period of my life which was more public than childhood, and one for which I also had fuller records. I therefore began at the point when I first became a minister in 1964 and wrote in the course of the next twelve months Parts Two and Three which covered my period as a Labour front-bencher. For these twelve years I had available substantial chunks of memoir raw material, which I had dictated fairly close to the events described.

This middle section complete, I then had the choice of going on to the end through my Brussels and SDP years, or going back to do my early life. Both presented something in the way of cliff faces. In 1989 my period as President of the European Community was unexciting for me to write about because I had just published *European Diary 1977–80*, which, although different in perspective from memoirs (because written in a hurry close to the events described), nonetheless made me uneager to cover the same ground immediately. Even more forbidding was the fact that the wounds from the break-up of the SDP were still raw.

So I swallowed twice and got down to Part One, beginning with the dreaded childhood chapter but also including Oxford, the army and sixteen years as a back-bench MP, although one increasingly involved with activities outside parliamentary politics. For this section I had no material specifically created for memoir purposes. What I did have were my father's semi-narrative diaries until his death in 1946 and my own more sketchy but memory-jogging and memory-checking engagement diaries from approximately that date onwards. In addition I had a mounting volume of published writing, although this is mostly of as little use for autobiographical purposes as are Cabinet papers.

When I came to Part Four, on the other hand, I had a full narrative journal for the Brussels period, but decided, in view of *European Diary*, to use it sparingly, concentrating almost exclusively on the creation of the European Monetary System and the budgetary dispute which led to the estrangement of the government of Mrs Thatcher from the European commitment of Edward Heath. These were the two most pregnant issues with which I had to deal as President of the Commission. For the return to British politics in the 1980s I was again more dependent on engagement diaries and published sources, but fortified this time by recent and vivid memory.

In all sections of the book I have endeavoured to get the confirmation of independent witnesses for my memories and records. They have been invaluable, but of course bear no responsibility for my opinions of individuals or treatment of issues, only for my recollection of the sequence of events where it was within their knowledge. I am particularly indebted to Lord Allen of Abbeydale (formerly Sir Philip Allen, permanent under-secretary to the Home Office), to Lord Zuckerman, OM, to William Rodgers, my ally and political companion since 1957, and to Lord Harris of Greenwich, who from 1965 has been very close to all my public ventures. They read the whole manuscript, except for certain late additions. So did my wife (several times) and so did Lord Bonham-Carter, in spite of no longer being my publisher. John Kenneth Galbraith, Sir Nicholas Henderson and Robert Maclennan MP read large sections of it, and Hugh Brace read the early part. To all of them I am very grateful.

Bess Church, my secretary from 1955 to 1980, transcribed the memoir raw material soon after it was dictated, and Alexandra O'Bryan Tear and Juliet Wauchope (my current secretary) shared the typing of the manuscript of the book. Michael Sissons, my literary agent, was crucial in getting me to overcome the doubts expressed about autobiography at the beginning of this preface as well as being a great encouragement throughout, and Alan Gordon Walker and Roland Philipps have done more than everything which publishers could be expected to do, including the provision of Peter James as an exceptional freelance editor. Douglas Matthews was not prevented by the 150th anniversary celebrations of the London Library from compiling the big index with his incomparable speed and skill.

*Roy Jenkins*
*June, 1991*

# PART ONE

# 1920–1964

# CHAPTER ONE

# *A Late and Only Child*

My parents were very different from each other, although both were rather remarkable. They had been married in 1911, there had been one son, stillborn in 1915, after which there was only me, who did not appear until the end of 1920. The circumstances ensured that I received the maximum of parental attention.

My father, Arthur Jenkins, was born in 1882 in the remote mountainside village of Varteg, 1200 feet up and five miles from Pontypool, more or less in the middle of the old county of Monmouthshire, as Gwent was then more satisfactorily called. Monmouthshire was one of the forty counties of England, although it had enough Welsh characteristics that Acts of Parliament which treated Wales separately nearly always added Monmouthshire to it. But it had to be done specifically, and 'Wales and Monmouthshire' was a phrase as familiar as 'London and Home Counties' or 'Highlands and Islands'. In fact the ethnic divide ran down the middle of the county, as did a geological one which became of great social significance in the middle of the nineteenth century. The rich coal seams, which from about 1840 onwards transformed the valleys of South Wales from sylvan fastnesses into raw but renowned industrial communities, do not run east of the Afon Llwyd, the river which flows down the Eastern Valley from Blaenavon through Pontypool to join the Usk near Newport. Varteg (and Pontypool) was thus undisputedly, even if only just, in the Welsh, industrial and steep-valleyed part of the county.

To say it was Welsh did not mean that it was Welsh-speaking. None of my four grandparents could speak a word of maternal Welsh. (My father taught himself a little in middle life, but that was because he was interested in languages.) Nor were they unusual in their communities in this respect. There was a small north-west corner of Monmouthshire around the town of Rhymney which was Welsh-speaking, but in the rest of the county the main upholders of the language of eisteddfods

3

were school-teachers from Cardiganshire and other points west and north (of whom there seemed to be a large number in my childhood, just as there were a lot of Irish doctors, richer but less respectable than the school-teachers).

The lack of the language did not mean that the culture and way of life were not Welsh, any more than one would say that the same deficiency prevents Ecclefechan being Scottish. The place-names were Welsh, the surnames were Welsh (which meant there were not many of them), the accent was Welsh, and the depressing late-nineteenth-century nonconformist chapels, the Pisgahs and Bethanys and Ebenezers, were thick upon the ground. There are many things about Monmouthshire and Wales as a whole which clutch at my heartstrings, but the architecture of nonconformity (or indeed Welsh domestic building generally) is not amongst them. I am mystified that the religion of dissent should have produced such purity and elegance in New England and such lowering ugliness in Wales.

My father's father, in spite of his name, did not originate in Monmouthshire. He migrated from the old Somerset coalfield around Radstock and Midsomer Norton some time in the 1870s, when the demand for mining labour was growing enormously in South Wales and wages were higher than in Somerset. His wife came with him, so she was not obviously Welsh either. She died fairly young and played no part in my life. He died in 1929 at the age of seventy-three, the only one of my grandparents to live much beyond the age of fifty. I just remember him as a rather small man, a retired miner, living with one of my father's two sisters, who gave me gold sovereigns, already out of use as normal currency, on each of my last four or five birthdays of his life, which must have been an extraordinarily generous present for him.

My father left the Varteg village school at the age of twelve and went immediately to work underground at Viponds' Colliery. He was a miner (or collier as it was then more frequently called) for twenty-four years until 1918, two years before my birth, but with a significant break from 1908 to 1910, and I think he loathed every day underground. He was a great teller to me of imaginatively constructed children's stories, but few if any of them were to do with the 'romance' or excitement of life at the pit. Perhaps even more striking was that in the journals which he kept at least from 1912 to the end of his life in 1946, with entries of fifty to a hundred words for each day, he rarely failed to record the time at which he 'came up' after a shift at the coal face.

The menace of life underground in the great age of British coal is hardly imaginable today. As late as 1940 I was taken down a Blaenavon pit in which a twenty-one-inch seam was still being worked. To get to the coal face meant crawling up a slit less than two feet high for several hundred yards. I have never forgotten the claustrophobia induced by the knowledge that the only way out was to do the return crawl. I was at that coalface for about a quarter of an hour. The men who worked it were there for forty-eight hours a week. Nor were any fears aroused by such conditions irrational. The risks of being crushed or imprisoned by falls were substantial. For my seventieth birthday, fifty years after this Blaenavon visit, one of my former parliamentary private secretaries, Ian Wrigglesworth, gave me a reproduction copy of *The Times* for the day of my birth. The most riveting item in it was a small snippet announcing that 1919 had been a very good year for mining casualties. Only 1229 colliers had been killed, compared with 1487 in 1918. It was the first year in which the accident death-rate was less than one per thousand of those employed.

What did engage my father's interest in those years from 1894 to 1908 were the open air, the freedom of walking on the mountain (except for Sundays only a spring and summer pursuit, because in autumn and winter the hours of light were all spent in darkness below), reading, and, as time went on, trade union activity. In 1908 he won a union scholarship to Ruskin College, Oxford.

Ruskin, then as now, was almost in the centre of Oxford, between Worcester College and the University Press building, very conscious of the University, but not part of it. It had been founded nine years before, as a result of an initiative by two American philanthropists, and had been on this Walton Street site and in its own building only since 1903. It was named after John Ruskin, but more as a social reformer than as the aesthetic writer who so aroused Proust, and its teaching concentrated heavily on the social sciences. But the college was not class-conscious enough for some of the students or for the trade unions who were providing an increasing proportion of the funds. There was also an argument over the composition of the governing body, which was made up only of bourgeois dons and philanthropists. The Principal, Dennis Hird, took the radical side in the dispute over these issues, and was dismissed for his pains.

Some of the students, including my father and Frank Hodges, who was to be A. J. Cook's more moderate predecessor as general secretary of the Miners' Federation from 1918 to 1924 and who subsequently made the amazing transition (via junior office at the Admiralty) to coalowners' man by the end of the decade, gave a fierce support to Hird which led them first to go on strike in Oxford and then to move to London as part of a breakaway institution known as the Central Labour College, where they completed their course. It must have been an appalling conflict of loyalties for my father. He loved Oxford. I remember being encouraged in my later childhood to pore over a fine book of pictures acquired at this time which showed the last years

of the pre-Morris Motors city through evocative aquatints. And as I
advanced through my teens it became almost his central purpose that
I should go there as a full member of the University. Yet he appears
not to have hesitated about making the break in 1909.

He and Hodges then went to Paris for several months. Hodges says
in a sketchy autobiography published in 1925 that he was there for
three months, but I think that my father stayed longer. Quite how the
visit was financed I have never fully understood. Obviously they were
frugal, but the cost cannot have been non-existent, and they earned
nothing. They lived in a hostel called the Foyer de l'Ouvrier, situated
in a small street near the Place de la Bastille. It had fourteen places,
all the rest occupied by young Frenchmen from the provinces with
socialist connections. The warden or *directeur* was always referred to as
Monsieur Dupuis. I heard much about him (unlike life underground)
and indeed was taken on several street walks in the Paris of the 1930s
to try (unsuccessfully) to discover what had become of him, but I never
knew his Christian name. I always imagined him as looking like Jean
Jaurès, bearded, burly and benign.

Jaurès my father both met and heard speak in the Chamber during
these months, although his political connections were in general more
with the Guesdist or more Marxist wing of the French Socialist Party,
and were centred on Paul Lafarge, a prosperous deputy of Creole origin who had married Marx's eldest daughter, Laura. In the summer of
1910 the Lafarges appeared to be warm and relaxed hosts and invited
my father and Hodges for a memorable weekend in the Île-de-France
countryside near Juvisy; but the next year they both committed suicide.
My father also had contact with Jean Longuet, who was Marx's
grandson through his third daughter Jenny and was to be one of the
minority of French socialists who advocated re-establishing relations
with the Germans through the Second International in 1916.

All this, combined with an intensive immersion course in the
French language and still more intensive exploration of the streets
and monuments of Paris, as well as the palaces, parks and forests of
its environs, was obviously heady stuff for a young Welsh miner, and it
put a strongly francophil stamp on my father for the rest of his life. One
odd effect was that the editions of the great Russian novelists in his not
inconsiderable library with which I was brought up were translations
into French and not English.

The shock, physical and cultural, of going back to the pit at the
end of 1910 must have been shattering. I hope it was assuaged by the
fact that within a year he married my mother. She was called Hattie
Harris and had been born four years after him in 1886. She was the
youngest of three sisters who had been orphaned when their father,
the manager of the Bessemer plant of the Blaenavon Iron and Steel

Company, had died at the age of fifty-one in 1903. The account of his end, as it seeped through to me, assumed in my childhood imagination something of the quality of a medieval plague death. What he was suffering from I do not know, but it exhibited itself in an appallingly high fever which coincided with a period of unusually hot weather. With difficulty blocks of ice were procured from a Newport fishmonger and were put upon his forehead during a fluctuating few days. But it was unavailing.

My maternal grandmother had died twelve years before in the famous cold winter of 1890–1. My mother's only recollection of her was being held in her arms while she picked icicles off the top of the doorway of their solid stone house, isolated except for a little surrounding dell of trees on an otherwise bleak hillside two miles out of Blaenavon. It was a typical manager's house, half rural, half urban, of the South Wales industrial revolution. My grandfather had then married again, and the second wife seemed to possess all the bad qualities of a story-book stepmother. She produced one son who became for me a somewhat arm's-length 'Uncle Reg', mainly no doubt because she and he acquired all the possessions and such money as my grandfather left.

My mother was thus from a background several steps up in the valley social hierarchy (although South Wales was a relatively non-hierarchical society) from that of my father, but a combination of her stepmother's intervention and her father's death made her very much a fringe member of the middle class. She was left at the age of seventeen with no parent, no money, no obvious means of supporting herself and, in effect, no home. What she did for the next seven years was to work in the principal music shop in Pontypool (six miles from Blaenavon) and to live in lodgings in the town. Harmston's (for such was the name of the music shop) was a very respectable establishment, which I remember being taken to visit in the 1920s, when it still had cavernous rooms with polished floors devoted to the sale of pianos, and I have no doubt the lodgings were equally respectable.

After she and my father were married they moved first into a miner's cottage in Talywain and then, in March 1914, into a terraced house set on a steep bank twenty feet or so above the main road which ran up the valley from Pontypool to Abersychan and Blaenavon. It was just short of Abersychan and thus two or three miles from Varteg and five miles from the house beyond Blaenavon. It was in a much more lowland situation than either. It looked across the Afon Llwyd to a steep unspoilt hillside which was beyond the coal, on limestone and was known as Lasgarn Wood. The terraced houses were different from the stone-and-wash miners' cottages in one of which my father had been born. They had six rooms and were much uglier. They had probably been built in the 1890s, and were as devoted to the polychromatic use of brick as was Balliol chapel, but had not I think been designed by Butterfield.

Parts of the area had been developed earlier, for almost exactly opposite was a very basic alehouse called the Queen Adelaide, and I cannot believe that anyone would have wished so to honour King William IV's consort long after his death in 1837 or her own in 1849. I have never entered this pub, which was probably the first of which I ever knew the name, nor I am sure did either of my parents, although they were not teetotallers. 'Public houses', a less friendly title than 'pub', were regarded with considerable disapproval in industrial South Wales of that epoch and beyond. Even in my Oxford and army days I never went in one in the valley, unless the commercial travellers' AA one-star Clarence Hotel in Pontypool be counted in that category. 'In the country', that is towards and beyond Usk in the agricultural part of Monmouthshire, was a different matter. This was despite the fact that the not-very-long-surviving husband of one of my father's sisters was a licensee at Cwmavon, between Abersychan and Blaenavon. Visits to her were carefully timed so as not to take place during opening hours. Pubs were definitely not part of respectable culture in the South Wales of my childhood.

These first two houses were not much in comparison with my mother's Blaenavon house, but even the first was no doubt an improvement on the Pontypool lodgings, and marked the end of a fairly lonely time in her life. Those seven years cannot however have been too solitary, for she shared the lodgings with another assistant from the music shop, was naturally gregarious and was very pretty as a young girl with striking auburn hair and dark-brown eyes. What was lacking was a home-base.

Later, as I remember her from my childhood, she had become a little plump but no more, and was nearly always active and animated. And as I remember her in her third phase, as a member of Parliament's wife and widow, she was very much a figure in her own right with an active public life, although strongly feminine rather than feminist, very well turned out in her own style, good at giving a sense of occasion to every event, with a circle of close friends, but also on greeting terms with almost everyone she met in the street. She was chairman of a magistrates' court and of the governors' of the Pontypool Girls' School, and after my father's death she became a county councillor. When she died in 1953, still only sixty-seven, she had almost as big a funeral as my father had had seven and a half years before. On both occasions the streets were lined for most of the three-quarters of a mile from the house to St James's Church in the centre of Pontypool.

Leo Abse, my father's successor but one as MP for Pontypool, made a part-time occupation out of portraying my mother as a tremendously snobbish woman, alien to my father's beliefs and outlook on life, and a crucial influence on me. He worked from first principles rather than empirically, as he seems subsequently to have done in his book on Mrs Thatcher, for he met my mother on only one occasion. But by frequent repetition, as can often be achieved, he has succeeded in making his version the accepted wisdom so that few profiles or other journalistic descriptions of my early life do not bear heavy traces of Abse. To what extent have these traces relation to the truth? My mother did, I suppose, have some of the characteristics of a 'gracious lady' in later life. And her close friends were mostly, but not all, of the Pontypool middle middle class, a Latin mistress, the wives of a doctor, a dentist, a bank manager, a chemist, a builder, a council surveyor, a headmaster. But this came naturally to her, and fitted in with her, and my father's, way of life during my childhood. On the other hand I never had the slightest sense, by observation as opposed to what came to me as historical knowledge, that she was in any way the socially superior one. On the contrary my instinctive feeling was that, in spite of his Labour commitment, it was he who was the natural whig, reaching out to a wider world. This wider world was not only that of London politics and public service spilling over into international contacts, but also the local one of Cardiff shipowners and Monmouthshire gentry. If she was the more fond of the Pontypool middle class, it was he who more enjoyed occasional visits to the country houses of the eastern part of the county, provided that they were inhabited by people of public spirit (often on the county council) with whom he could mingle with unforced ease. If I developed a certain taste for still grander grandees of liberal outlook, the inheritance came, in my view, more from him than from her. She was less rational and less literary than he was, but more intuitive and more spontaneous. This should not give the impression that he was a grave figure. Nearly half a century after his death my wife, who first met him in 1941, remembers him not only as one of the most engaging companions she has ever encountered, but also as extremely funny.

This digression has taken me a long way on from the beginning of their marriage at the end of 1911 and their move to the terraced house in March 1914. They lived there in the last months before the extinction of the lights of Europe that August. But because not much of that refulgence had reached Abersychan and because my father did not join the army – he did not approve of the war and as a miner was in a reserved occupation – the contrast was nothing like as great as in more gilded lives. As the years of the First World War went by, he became increasingly occupied with Miners' Federation affairs and therefore less confined to a daily regime underground. More and more

his hitherto habitual diary entry of 'worked at colliery' was replaced
by 'did not work at colliery', followed by the explanation of 'Cardiff
conference' or 'insurance work' or some other union activity. Thus
in 1915 he worked underground for 204 days but in 1918 for only
99. The last day that I can discover that he 'worked at colliery' was
Saturday, 9 November 1918 immediately before the Armistice. This
did not mean that he did not subsequently spend many parts of days
underground, but thereafter he did so to investigate a grievance or
inspect the safety of a working, or visit the scene of an accident, but
not to hew coal. He became first an assistant agent and then in 1921 a
full miners' agent, a well-known coalfield term for a salaried Miners'
Federation official who covered a substantial geographical area and
perhaps a dozen pits.

Almost all the famous miners' leaders of the time when coal was king
graduated through the office of miners' agent, although in the case of
some, probably the majority, they did not ascend vertically through
the Miners' Federation, but spread their activities horizontally into
politics and other forms of public service so that they were often very
well-known local figures with an influence well beyond the members of
their union. Thus my father became a district councillor in 1918 and a
county councillor in 1919. He quickly evolved into very much a county
council man. He liked detailed committee work rather than polemics,
and was chairman of several, including for many years the finance
committee. He was also active in the affairs of the County Councils
Association, which owing to the balance of power across the shires
as a whole involved a cross-party approach. He continued with the
Association after he became a member of Parliament, and mainly for
this purpose he remained an alderman of the Monmouthshire County
Council until his death. In the 1920s he was also concerned with the
running of the Pontypool hospital, served for a time as a member
of the National Executive Committee of the Labour Party, and was
appointed to a Royal Commission (on licensing) in 1929. His activities
were a blend of the local and the national, and it would be an unusual
week if he did not go to Newport or Cardiff two or even three times,
and an unusual month if he did not go to London at least once or
maybe twice.

On 11 November 1920 I was born in the polychromatic house which
I have described. The date was easy to remember for, so soon after
the slaughter in Flanders, Armistice Day was a great national event,
with the silence observed all over the country and no question of the
ceremonies being shunted to the nearest Sunday. I therefore had a
vague childhood impression that my birthday was a very important
occasion, appropriately celebrated well outside the family. The house,
however, has no place in my memory for we moved in early 1923.

I know only its outside, from having frequently looked at it thereafter, although mostly without particular interest. The move was not a very sundering affair, for we went a mere 300 yards down the road, to the other side of it and more firmly into a neighbourhood known as Snatchwood. The house was not very different, was just as ugly, with the addition of a monkey-puzzle tree in the very small front garden, but it must have been thought better, probably because it had a bathroom and one extra room, and it had a good back garden which ran down to a low railway embankment. This brought an early introduction to railways and to the GWR in particular, with familiarity never breeding contempt, although the Eastern Valley line was not much frequented by the great expresses, which were what I really liked. Later on I developed a favourite, early and minor form of railway vandalism which involved placing a penny on the line before a train came and afterwards recovering its extended and flattened shape. Fortunately this led to no derailments. In the garden I had a swing from the age of about five, and spent endless hours upon it with my mind occupied with complicated rather than abstruse juggling with numbers. This gave me no great mathematical insights but did lead me to a continuing arithmetical obsession with exact measurements of time and distance.

Our neighbours in the new house were on the one side one of the Cardiganshire school-teachers, John Thomas, who was headmaster of a small mile-distant school which had the odd characteristic that it could hardly be approached except by paths which no motor could navigate; and on the other by a house-builder called A. C. Powell, who had recently constructed the whole terrace, and who had kept for himself a bigger house than ours and the others, embellished by a double garage, in which by the mid-1920s he had the appropriate complement of two motor cars. A figure of some dignity, he was almost universally called Alf, except by his wife, a lady of a little pretension, who preferred the sound or association of Charlie. Whether or not as a result of his habit of keeping his best product for himself, his business was in considerable financial trouble by the end of the decade and he closed it down, secured a job as clerk of works to the Monmouthshire County Council (with a bit of help from my father, I suspect), and moved to a still bigger house on the suburban heights above the railway station in Newport.

His son, Derek Powell, nonetheless remained the closest of my boyhood friends. He was a year older than me, good at all games, and became by his middle teens the finest swimmer for miles around, winning championships from Cardiff to Monte Carlo. He was also, I think, cleverer than I was, although perhaps with a little too much bombast. We did not go to the same schools, for at eleven he went off as a boarder to Monmouth School, twenty miles away, where he suffered for a time the most appalling Flashman-type bullying until he escaped first to a neutral position, and then probably to getting his own back (but on different people) as a prefect. He went to Merton College, Oxford, on the same day that I went to Balliol. We saw something of each other at Oxford, but more during the holidays in Pontypool or Newport, where our relationship remained very close until 1939. At the end of a successful war in the desert he got a dreadful disease which laid him low for five years, after which he almost miraculously recovered. He never quite regained his momentum, however, although he was headmaster of a Newport comprehensive school for the ten years or so before he died, after another great medical struggle, in 1976. He played a major role in an early fifteen years of my life (from four to nineteen), and some part for his remaining thirty-seven years.

The Cardiganshire schoolmaster also moved away from Snatchwood in the early 1930s, when he was promoted to a larger school in Pontypool, but we stayed until the end of 1937, by which time my father was an MP and I was almost grown up. These fifteen years in this house were a mixture – as I suppose is nearly everybody's life – of the routine and the dramatic. The routine mostly revolved around school. I did not go at all until I was almost seven, being allegedly taught at home (quite by whom I am not sure, but it must have had some reality, for when I eventually arrived I was more or less up to standard in reading and writing and certainly in arithmetic). Then I missed a good part of the next year, for in March 1928 I produced a burst appendix with an operation late at night (probably hazardous in those days with only general practitioners available to do the surgery and administer the anaesthetic), three weeks in hospital and six months off school.

As a result I did not settle down at Pentwyn, John Thomas's hillside school, until I was nearly eight. I then spent three years there, and can remember very little about the interior of the school or the content of its instruction, but a great deal about its approaches. These epitomised the intermingling of industrial scars and rugged rusticity which were the hallmark of the South Wales coalfield. In front of the school lay the open mountain, bare except for a couple of isolated colliery managers' houses and a few holes in which during the long coal strike of 1926 there had been some scraping for domestic coal. Behind the school a large coaltip ran out like the prow of a great ship. It was level with the school at one end, but 300 feet above the valley at the other.

An unorthodox way home was to walk out to the far end and then to slide or scramble down the precipitate black slurry. It did not make one as dirty as sounds likely. Even the orthodox approach, however, was interesting. This involved walking half a mile through what was known as 'the wood', although it was in fact a small, sharply tilted heath, with bushes about every twenty yards which made it wonderful territory for any sort of stalking game. Lower down it had two flat areas on which rough cricket could be played. Beyond the school end of the tip a disused colliery railway track ran another half-mile to a large brick structure known as Big Arch which was also I think out of use, although working coal trains could be seen in the light at the end of its cavernous tunnel. It was altogether a remarkable location for a school.

In 1931 I had to take the 'scholarship' examination for admission to a secondary or grammar school. My performance was thoroughly adequate, and I was placed third in the list. The year before, however, Derek Powell had come top, although rejecting the place in favour of the bullying dormitories of Monmouth, so there was no danger of the semi-success going to my head. What was more significant – and more mystifying – was the choice of school. Two miles away from us there was a good grammar school called Jones's West Monmouth School. It was a private foundation, with one boarding house but a great majority of day boys including some very poor ones, the school partly financed by the Haberdashers' Company, although with a board of governors on which the County Council was well represented. My father had no prejudice against the school on account of its hybrid nature. As early as 1924 he had been involved in ensuring that Ivor Thomas (now Ivor Bulmer-Thomas), the son of a brickyard worker in the lower part of the Eastern Valley and both a mathematical and a classical scholar of extraordinary facility, should proceed from the school to Oxford. Later, when Thomas had fought and nearly beaten John Simon in his Yorkshire seat at the general election of 1935, one of my father's favourite speaking arguments in favour of educational opportunity was to relate his spectacular early career, with this act of political fealty blending bizarrely but suitably for the purpose with his brilliant but highly traditionalist learning.

In the later 1930s the headmaster of West Mon (as it was known), a conventional schoolmaster who respected academic standards, his more striking Girtonian wife and their four Cheltenham Ladies' College-educated daughters, became about our most frequently visited and visiting neighbours. And in the early years of the war my father arranged for the sons of two of his parliamentary colleagues to escape from London by coming as boarders to West Mon.

Yet he did not send me there. I went to Abersychan Secondary School (or Grammar School as it later became), a newer establishment of less prestige, which was a short mile in the other direction. No doubt at the time I preferred it so. It was nearer home, involved only a walk, or later a bike ride, instead of a bus journey, and I knew more people who were going. Also it was mixed, which West Mon was not, but I do not think that was a factor one way or the other. My father was a governor there, chairman at one stage, but that again does not begin to amount to an adequate explanation. He was also a governor of West Mon, and in any event he was certainly not a member of the Hebdomadal Council of the University of Oxford, which he had already fixed upon as my ultimate academic destination.

It was this which made the lack of parental pressure towards the Pontypool school so surprising. It was clearly going to be much more difficult to get to Oxford from Abersychan than from West Mon, which frequently sent boys there or to Cambridge. Abersychan's higher educational outlets were largely confined to the Welsh university colleges, although there was one young man called Roger Keyes who was a research fellow of Balliol by the time I arrived and later became head of the Universities Department at UNESCO. He like me speaks English with hardly a trace of a Welsh accent, which in my case is sometimes commented upon with surprise. So does Ivor Bulmer-Thomas. So for that matter does Lord Chalfont, whom I did not know as a boy, but who was also an alumnus of West Mon. I think there must be something in the air or the water of the Eastern Valley of Monmouthshire which washes away deviations from 'standard' English more easily than do those of most other localities. But they do not do so completely. I am told that to a Professor Higgins (or even to his most newly joined assistant) my pronunciation of 'situation' is an immediate indication of Welsh origin. The odd thing is that I could observe this in the beautifully modulated voice of Lord Elwyn-Jones (although he came from fifty miles further west), but not in my own. My father had very little Welsh intonation, although his 'a's, as in chance or dance, were shorter than my own. My mother had more of an accent or lilt.

I was thoroughly happy at Abersychan, but I could not say that I was well taught, although I remember several masters and mistresses with affection. Apart from any question of the quality of the teaching, I was allowed to make a gross schematic error. After two years there was a choice between history and chemistry as a subject to be continued to School Certificate or 'matric' at the end of the fourth year. At the age of twelve I rather liked the smells and retorts and bunsen burners of the laboratory and chose chemistry. As a result, I have never been taught any pre-1760 history, although I have obviously picked up some. By the sixth form I had realised my mistake and took history (together with English and Geography) for Higher School Certificate (more or less the equivalent of today's A-levels) and slowly began a long-lasting immersion in nineteenth-century political history. But the damage had been done, or rather an unfillable gap had been created. As (much later) I got deeper into the minutiae of, say, the 1886 Home Rule split, so some elementary piece of ignorance about Cromwell remained liable to mar my perspective of Anglo-Irish history.

Perhaps all this is merely an excuse for my not doing particularly well at school. I was young for my year and therefore secured School Certificate with six or seven credits (but failing Latin and having to retake it) at the age of fourteen. Equally I got Higher School Certificate at sixteen. But my performance in neither of these examinations was distinguished, any more than was my position in the various forms through which I moved up the school. I was rarely near the top. I certainly showed none of the early academic gifts which Ivor Thomas had displayed two miles away a decade before. Despite the fact that I eventually (if narrowly) achieved the slightly more difficult goal of getting a first, I was not really a serious candidate for an Oxford scholarship. I would not have got there without my father's determination that I should do so, and his willingness to back this determination by devoting a remarkably high proportion of his income to achieving it.

The dramatic apogee of our life during those fifteen years in the house in Snatchwood Road was kept hidden from me. On 27 November 1926, when I was just six years old, my father was convicted of illicit assembly and sentenced to nine months' imprisonment at Monmouth assizes. On 30 August of that year, during the long-drawn-out miners' lock-out which continued for six months after the brief May General Strike, of which it had been the cause, there was an affray at a small mine-working known as Quarry Level close to the road between Pontypool and Crumlin. Fifteen 'blacklegs' were working there, and a mass picket was assembled. My father was undoubtedly involved in organising the picket, and he addressed the crowd. A contingent of fifteen police was already there under the command of one Superintendent Spendlove. Under his orders they launched a baton charge against the pickets.

What was in dispute, and long remained so, was whether there was adequate provocation to justify the baton charge and whether my father's role had been a pacifying or an inciting one. At the time and to the end of his life he quietly insisted that it was the former, which certainly seems more in keeping with his character. His brief diary entry for that day reads: 'At Quarry Level. Police batoned crowd very viciously. . . . Home at 7. Not out after. Bed midnight.'

It is impossible to tell from this and other laconic entries whether the incident was from the first a great trauma from which he could not subsequently divert his mind. Nominally he went on throughout the autumn with his normal life, going to London for two days the following morning, to Bournemouth the following week for the meeting of the National Executive of the Labour Party which habitually took place during the Trades Union Congress, and then to Margate at the beginning of October for the Labour Party conference, where he went for an hour's walk with Ramsay MacDonald, already a former Prime Minister. But interspersed with this routine there were more doom-laden entries. For 3 September: 'Got summons today re Quarry Level.' For 20 September: 'Was at Police Court from 10.30 to 5.30. The lies told by the police were appalling'; much the same without the comment for 21 and 22 September, and for 1 October: 'Was in Police Court all day. In witness box from 10.30 to 1.45. Did well I am told. Referred to Assizes.'

The trial began on 23 November and lasted five days before Mr Justice Swift, who did not enjoy a liberal reputation. He had been a Conservative MP before his appointment to the bench, and he ended the case with a eulogy of the highly controversial behaviour of the police. My father, however, did not seem to blame him. After the first day he wrote in his diary: 'Hopkins [another police officer] and Spendlove lied terribly. Seems to be a dead set against me. I fear I cannot hope for bare justice. The judge may be fair, but his picture is being coloured.' At the end of the second day he went into the witness box, but only for three-quarters of an hour. On the third day he recorded that 'Coldrick and Edwards [two of his co-defendants; Coldrick later became a Bristol MP and Edwards quickly emigrated to Canada] gave evidence splendidly.' On the fourth day he wrote: 'Our witnesses were not very good. Sir Joseph Bradney was very good.' (Bradney, a Monmouthshire country gentleman and former chairman of the County Council, gave character evidence on my father's behalf.) On the fifth day he concluded: 'about 5.00 p.m. sentences. Coldrick and Edwards got three months. I got nine months. To Cardiff by car. Got to Gaol alright [a curious way of putting it] at 7.00 p.m. What a night it was. And how was poor Hat?' Thereafter the diary stopped until 25 February 1927, the day on which he was released.

This was just short of three months after the date of his conviction, and was the result of an act of executive clemency by Birkenhead (F. E. Smith), who was acting as Home Secretary in the absence through illness of Joynson-Hicks. The pressure to remit had been strong and wide. The sentences, and my father's in particular, had caused outrage. Throughout his and Coldrick's (shorter) time in prison their seats in the council chamber in the Monmouthshire County Hall had been kept bedecked with flowers, and this had been accepted with approval by many of the Conservative or independent members of the council. The organiser of this was the chairman, Thomas Richards, a venerable miners' leader, a former MP and a Lloyd George-created privy councillor. Richards also took a powerful Labour delegation to see Birkenhead. But it was the cross-party pressure which was most effective. Two days after the sentence, Sir David Llewellyn, the leader of the South Wales coalowners, wrote to Tom Jones, Baldwin's *éminence grise*, to protest and ask for clemency. 'Arthur Jenkins is quite a moderate and sensible leader. . . . I always found him a man of strong character and fair minded.' Jones wrote back: 'I showed your letter at once to the P[rime] M[inister], and he undertook to put it before the Home Secretary.'[1]

For three months before this goodwill took practical effect I was scooped up with my mother and taken for a winter sojourn to a rather lavish long low bungalow, with fine views in both directions, on a ridgeway at the edge of Newport. It belonged to D. J. Vaughan, a Labour county councillor who had made money out of building and land speculation, was later briefly MP for the Forest of Dean, but was I fear something of a local and poor man's Oswald Mosley, enthusiastically committed to the Labour Party in Monmouthshire in the 1920s, a populist and bitter right-wing critic of it in the 1930s. But in 1926–7 he and his Northern Irish wife were generous and long-suffering hosts to my mother and me. My main recollections of the extended visit are playing the gramophone which my father's solicitor gave me for Christmas and running across what seemed to me the vast polished floor of the hall so fast that I skidded on a rug and shattered a large blue vase. It cannot I think have been Ming, but it possessed enough value to strain the Vaughans' otherwise unbroken goodwill.

Throughout this period I was successfully kept in complete ignorance of why I was there or why my father was away. I was told he was on an extended tour of inspection of the coalmines of Germany. I accepted this, and was not even suspicious on the day of joy when he returned to us at Newport and we proceeded after a few hours to Pontypool where we were greeted by an enthusiastic crowd of several thousand. I think I assumed they were merely as glad to see him back from Germany as I was.

Years went by before I knew the full story. I doubt whether this was a good idea. I suppose that the benign deceit having been invented it was difficult to know when to bring it to an end. The undesirable aspect was that I picked up the story almost surreptitiously, through the chance remarks of others, rather as is often the case with sex, and came as a result to regard it as a slightly embarrassing subject.

What long-term effect did all this have on my father and on me? The harshness with which he had been treated and the stoicism with which he had taken it won him wide local and national respect. But it also made him something of a spurious hero with the militant left.

They believed he had been quite right to cause a riot. He believed that he had been doing his best to prevent one, and had been unfairly convicted on false police evidence. This ambiguity meant that he was more anxious to put his experience behind him than to trade upon it. It did not leave him generally bitter towards the police or the judiciary. Spendlove he could not forgive, but he worked closely with several Chief Constables of Monmouthshire and was an active member of the standing joint committee, as police committees in counties were then called. One effect of his brush with the judiciary was that it made him determined to become a justice of the peace, although he had no time for the duties and would have done better to let my mother have the appointment straightaway (they could not both be JPs) rather than only after he had served for a few symbolic years.

I do not think that the trial or the prison sentence in any way complicated the relationship between him and me. It was I suppose lucky that, *mutatis mutandis*, our subsequent attitudes to those events of 1926–7 should have been so similar. Neither of us was remotely ashamed of what had occurred, or would have dreamed of denying it if the subject came up. Equally, however, neither of us wished to draw attention to it, to flaunt it as a special badge of virtue, or to make a *métier* out of being a victim (or the son of a victim) of a miscarriage of justice. I think it possible in retrospect that, having renounced occupational bitterness, it made him about 10 per cent more establishment-minded than he would otherwise have been. In our occasional political differences in the ten years between my becoming semi-adult and his death I was almost invariably, but not much, to the left of him. Whether this would have reversed itself had he lived for another thirty-five years over the key part of my political life, I cannot say.

During my two home secretaryships it was suggested from opposite directions that I might or should have been influenced by my father's experience. The *Sunday Express* claimed during my first tenure that it had left me with an anti-police bias which made me unsuitable for the office. This was not so. I on the whole had good relations with the police, and substantially improved their strength, organisation and equipment. Maybe it left me sceptical of the automatic guilt of those whose protestation of their own innocence is contradicted only by police evidence. There is I fear something in the police culture which can make the desire to secure conviction triumph over respect for the truth. But such a scepticism is in my view no bad thing for a Home Secretary.

The second issue, during the 1970s, concerned the so-called 'Shrewsbury Two' (see Chapter 21). Because they were gaoled for picketing offences there was a belief on the left that I should automatically release them on pietistic grounds. I did not however regard either the external circumstances or their behaviour as being in any way comparable with my father's case. Nor, I think, at the end of the day did the TUC. I believed that the 'Shrewsbury Two' were claiming to be above the law at a time of great trade union power, whereas my father's claim was not to be below the law and not to be discriminated against because of a climate of repression at a time when the miners were sinking into weakness as they lost a battle against wage reductions.

Oddly, an artificial three-months trip to Germany having been invented for my father while he was in prison, a real one of three weeks took place soon after he came out. It was organised by the Liberal newspaper the *Daily News*, a forerunner of the *News Chronicle*, and was no doubt intended as a sort of psychological convalescence. It was a kind thought, although I do not think that one was necessary, for there never was a time when his normally slightly downbeat diary comments ('Made a very bad speech' and 'What a wretched day' were quite common) were more euphoric. I am glad to say that for the Friday he came out he wrote: 'Glorious day. H. was lovely, and Roy too.' And for the Saturday: 'Another very happy day. Everybody is splendid.'

However, three weeks later he set off for the Ruhr, Berlin, Silesia, and Belgium on the way back, and my mother and I went to London for two days to see him off. It was during this London visit that a long-lasting family joke originated. On the morning of the second day we were to go to the Zoo. On the steps of the old Imperial Hotel in Russell Square, my father, searching his memory for bus numbers, said, 'I am not sure I know how to get there.' I, aged six years and four months, said, 'Easy, Daddy. Take a taxi.' This was held to foreshadow much of my future attitude to life and expenditure.

Looking back I have an impression of slightly greater family prosperity at the end of the 1920s and into the early 1930s. This may seem paradoxical as these were the years of general slump and of particular decline for the South Wales mining industry. But it was in fact entirely logical. To be employed in a sea of unemployment and to have a fixed income at a time of falling prices gave a little platform of advantage. From March 1929 we had a small motor car, and I think it was later in that same year that the 'live-in' maid arrived, a concept which has also excited some commentators on my mother and my early life. That year I was also taken abroad for the first time, a brief three-day July excursion to Brussels, occasioned by my father's visit to a Socialist International conference. Altogether, what with these changes and with the election of the second Labour Government at the end of May, it was a summer of expanding horizons.

The attachment of this Belgian visit to a political gathering was typical. We did not go on holidays in the sense of taking an August week or fortnight in a seaside hotel or boarding house. There were three or four such visits to Porthcawl or Weston-super-Mare, but they were widely spaced over ten years or more, involved only my mother and me, and were convalescent for one or other of us. On the other hand there was a fair amount of travel. Two-day expeditions to London were quite common, there was a Whitsun weekend in Oxford in 1929 and again in 1932, and a week in Paris in August 1931. In addition the annual conferences of the TUC and the Labour Party (particularly after the car came) provided the peg for long journeys with sight-seeing diversions, mostly to resorts in southern England (I was spared Blackpool until I went there under my own steam from 1945 onwards). Thus I was in Weymouth and Dorchester when the centenary of the Tolpuddle Martyrs was celebrated in 1934; in Margate when part of the fleet steamed round the North Foreland in 1935, on its way, according (inaccurately) to no less an authority than Sir Walter Citrine,\* to the Mediterranean for a possible Ethiopian-inspired conflict with Italy; in Norwich and Yarmouth in 1936 when Herbert Morrison (a great friend of my father's during these years) was the first man I had ever seen or heard order a dry martini; and in Bournemouth in 1937, and again in 1940, when Attlee and Greenwood first carried the conference for coalition and then left for London to join Churchill's War Cabinet.

This last example carries me on too far, for the period I am now writing about was essentially the first half of the 1930s. These longer trips were then buttressed by an immense amount of driving about South Wales, accompanying my father to engagements, quite often going in and listening if they were platform occasions, occupying myself by looking round whichever town we were in or reading in the car if they were committee meetings. These were most frequently in Newport or Cardiff, but there were also a lot of visits to the smaller valley towns, Tredegar or Pontypridd or Aberdare. We were also great motorists for pleasure on the empty if meandering roads of sixty years ago, and made frequent expeditions to the fine river valleys of the Usk

---

\* Lord Citrine, as he became in 1946, was a considerable figure of the period, general secretary of the Trades Union Congress 1926–46, chairman of the Central Electricity Authority 1947–57. He assured us of the destination when we met him during an evening walk on the promenade. I had a lot of seafront encounters in those years with figures who are now engraved in Labour history. I was presented to Arthur Henderson, who was sitting in a wicker chair in front of the Gloucester Hotel, Weymouth, in 1934, the year before his death. And I first met Ernest Bevin on another promenade walk in Sidmouth in 1937.

and the Wye, to the border castles which spattered the eastern half of Monmouthshire, often with tea, and occasionally more extravagantly lunch, at the little Trust House hotels (then a very different sort of hotel chain) of Abergavenny, Raglan, Monmouth, Tintern and Chepstow.

From the age of about fourteen I also became an enthusiastic bicyclist over much the same terrain. My principal companion was Hugh Brace, an Abersychan school contemporary, now a retired official of the Patent Office, with whom I maintain contact and who is now my longest-standing friend. He was a better long-distance performer than I was, and once got to Southampton in a day. Together we managed fifty- or sixty-mile round trips, Ross-on-Wye being I think our furthest destination. We also planned a number of more elaborate several-day expeditions which we never took. I was particularly good at working out the details of these.

Games played a moderate role in my early teenage life. I was a fast runner at ten or eleven and won several area championships. But I was going off by fourteen. Swimming was an actively pursued pleasure, although I was completely but not oppressively overshadowed by the prowess of Derek Powell. I was an adequate performer at cricket and rugby, although never more than on the fringe of the school teams. I was however a very good student of cricket. Its statistics suited my detail-accumulating mind, and I can still remember the names, initials and counties of every player of note of the period. I read all the daily scores avidly and occasionally went to first-class matches at Cardiff or Swansea. I was also taken to a number of memorable international rugger games at Cardiff Arms Park. But although my favourite sporting fantasy was the scoring of a great swerving centre three-quarter's try (I was nearly always in fact made to play in the less interesting position on the wing), rugger never occupied my mind in the way that cricket did.

The two years from November 1935 to November 1937 marked a gradual but considerable change in my life. At the end of 1935 my father became a member of Parliament. Pontypool had been a Labour seat since 1918, having previously (as North Monmouthshire) been represented since 1895 by Reginald McKenna, Home Secretary and Chancellor of the Exchequer under Asquith. McKenna had been beaten by Thomas Griffiths, a steelworkers' nominee, who sat silently in the House of Commons for seventeen years (he had the excuse of being a whip for six of them), and visited Pontypool as infrequently as McKenna had done. He lived in Neath, forty miles from Pontypool, where he spent much of his time contemplating his remarkable collection of Swansea porcelain. I remember being taken to see him during the 1931 election in his sitting room at the

Clarence Hotel in Pontypool. He had a fine but tobacco-stained moustache.

His position in relation to my father, who was a much better-known Labour figure, both locally and nationally, must always have been a little uncomfortable. But Griffiths was protected by the Labour habit of never turning anyone out of a job, by my father's natural loyalty and perhaps his ambiguity about whether he really wanted to go to the House of Commons, and above all by the fact that the miners had nearly every seat in South Wales and could not provoke a takeover of another one without being accused of intolerable territorial ambitions. But Griffiths reached the rigid Iron and Steel Workers' retiring age in 1932, and at the selection conference which then followed my father's support was sufficiently strong to sweep aside the complaints of that union. The trouble was that Griffiths's quiet but extended tenure had pushed my father to the age of nearly fifty-four when he entered the House of Commons, fourteen years older than Joseph Chamberlain said was the limit for the beginning of a fully effective parliamentary career.

Nevertheless the change threw our lives on to a more London-orientated track, and in particular, although this took a little time, removed us from the terraced house in the narrow valley, which apart from anything else the new miners' agent wished to occupy. This did not mean that we shifted our home to London, although a surprisingly high proportion, perhaps a third, of the South Wales Labour MPs of those days did precisely that. It merely involved moving two and a half miles down the valley to the lower edge of Pontypool, which was the centre of the constituency. But it made a considerable psychological difference. The valley opened out there, and there was a long perspective from the window of my father's study, in which I spent much time when he was in London, towards the direction, the south-east, in which there mostly seemed to be better weather and which always pointed to the outside world.

The house was also qualitatively different. It belonged to the Great Western Railway, from which we rented it, and had been built about 1900 for their area manager, who seemed no longer to exist, or perhaps merely no longer to justify a house. It stood on its own in half an acre of garden, had about twelve rooms and while not beautiful was inoffensively covered in stucco. My parents had always been great entertainers, both of local friends and of visitors from London who stayed one or several nights, and this new house greatly increased their capacity to receive both.

As gregarious as they were, I was very much the beneficiary of this change. A few years later we had a lot of my Oxford friends to stay. But for the moment it was mainly London politicians, a number of whom had indeed come to the smaller house in Abersychan, but not so frequently. I recall a lot of visits paid by Herbert Morrison (although there was a cooling of relations with him after 1937, when my father became parliamentary private secretary to Attlee, to whom Morrison was unforgiving for beating him in the leadership contest of 1935); then visits from Attlee himself, whose taciturnity I found intimidating, although I remember his telling me one rather good and mordant motoring anecdote; earlier visits from Hugh Dalton, later to be a closer friend of mine than of my father's, but who at that stage merely boomed at me like a scoutmaster; from that old poseur of a journalist Hannen Swaffer; from Ellen Wilkinson, who I thought made a very good speech; from D. N. Pritt, the fellow-travelling KC and MP; and from Wedgwood Benn (Tony Benn's father, later Lord Stansgate), who stayed three or four days and was a bright little man, full of rather quirky semi-jokes. The visitor who most dazzled me was Richard Crossman, not then an MP but a twenty-nine-year-old Oxford don on a political visit to South Wales. His blend of verve and paradox I found very exciting at sixteen. I remember him from that encounter as a bear of a man, with very thick ankles above suede shoes, and his bulk increased by a lavish camel-hair overcoat which, although already rather dirty, he claimed just to have bought out of the proceeds of some peculiarly provocative BBC talks.

After the 1935 election I became still keener than I had been before on visits to London. Even before that time I had a considerable childhood passion for what I saw as the romance of the metropolis. I collected a series of difficult jigsaw puzzles of London scenes, and completed them with the more determination because of what they depicted. I graduated from that to copying out with great meticulousness a street map of the whole of central London, which task at least had the advantage that it gave me (which I have half retained) something approaching a taxi-driver's knowledge. And one day when I was thirteen I succeeded in persuading my father to let me accompany him to London even though it was only for six hours. It was far from a first visit, just a day out. We had meals both ways in the restaurant cars of the trains, and in the afternoon while he attended his meeting, I, judged too young to cross busy streets, walked round and round St James's Park, identifying all the buildings visible from it, and counting the number of Rolls-Royces which passed. In 1934 there were a surprisingly large number, forty-seven I think. I regarded this as an eminently satisfactory day.

From the age of fifteen onwards, however, the House of Commons provided an additional incentive. I was an indefatigable listener to debates (a habit I fear I did not subsequently keep up), sat 'under the gallery' all one February night through a Labour filibuster on the

Unemployment Assistance Regulations of 1936, and heard at least once all the major figures of the 1930s who had gone from the House before I was elected in 1948: Lloyd George, Baldwin, MacDonald, Austen and Neville Chamberlain, Simon, Samuel, Lansbury, Maxton.

In the summer of 1937, when I was nearly seventeen and had just got my undistinguished Higher School Certificate results, it was suggested that I ought to move on from Abersychan. There was a tentative plan, much urged on my father by an HMI (inspector of schools), which was then regarded as a high rank in the education world, that I should go to a minor boarding school for a year or maybe two. Fortunately it came to nothing. I cannot think of anything I would have liked less at that late stage. What I did was to go young to University College, Cardiff, for six months or so. I mildly enjoyed it but did not take it seriously enough, for I always thought of it as a transitional stage to Oxford.

My most vivid memories from that interlude are of the hour's bus journeys to and from Pontypool (for I lived at home) and of a great deal of coffee-drinking in the Kardomah Café in the middle of Cardiff. I was privately tutored by a young assistant lecturer called Dorothy Marshall, who subsequently taught at Vassar and Wellesley and was the author of several good early-nineteenth-century biographies. I never encountered her again, although I read her books, but I think her teaching may have been crucial. I desperately needed coaching in the writing of Oxford-style history essays. Even she could not get me a scholarship, but with her help I secured in March 1938 my entry to Balliol, which was then the only Oxford men's college with competitive entry for commoners. (To the rest one just went if one could pay the fees and had the bare qualifications necessary to be matriculated.)

Once this was achieved I faded out from Cardiff. However, I read a lot that summer, made a visit to North Wales (memorable because I could drive for the first time), where my father taught a course at the adult education college at Harlech, and was then taken by him to Paris in mid-August and left there for a month, in a small *pension*, set in a courtyard off the Boulevard de Port-Royal.

I lived in an encapsulation of Third Republican Paris. The Boulevard's name was redolent of seventeenth-century Jansenism but its appearance was firmly nineteenth century, except for a scattering of black Citroëns, red Renaults and market trucks which rolled along the wide *pavé*, either up the gentle slope to the Carrefour de l'Observatoire and the Montparnasse of the Coupole and Dôme cafés a short way beyond, or down to join the Avenue des Gobelins which debouched into the Place d'Italie, the hub of the south-eastern and mainly working-class 13e arrondissement. The Boulevard de Port-Royal itself was flanked by oppressive public buildings, which seemed to me to have faintly sinister names, like Val-de-Grâce, which was a military hospital, or the Hôpital Cochin, or the Baudelocque lying-in hospital or the Hospice des Enfants Assistés. La Santé prison was just behind. I hoped I would not end up in any of them.

Inside the great wooden door of No. 85, controlled by the concierge, a *porte-cochère* led into a not very attractive gravelled garden, around which were several separate and 1830-ish three-storey buildings, one of which was my *pension*. It was presided over by Madame Vincent, who was probably not much more than fifty-five, but who looked severe and concentrated on accurate French and a Gallic but not luxurious diet at the communal table of fifteen or so at which we assembled for lunch or dinner. I was not really up to general conversation in a company that size, and I am ashamed to say that I did not then much like the rabbit stews or the salmis of pigeon which were typical dishes or even the *vin de table*, which most people diluted with water. My room was basic but had an adequate cloth-covered writing table which commanded a good view of the eastern sky, the direction of Germany I frequently thought, for both that summer, and the next one when I returned to the *pension*, were dominated by the threat of Hitler and the thought of Nuremberg Rallies taking place a few hundred miles away. I acquired some French but more knowledge of the topography of Paris – to match that of London – for which I had greater natural aptitude. I do not remember feeling apprehensive about the approach of Oxford. What I did feel apprehensive about was the approach of war.

# CHAPTER TWO

# *Balliol on the Brink*

The war, impending or actual, was a constant background to my years at Oxford. It created a vague overhang of apprehension, and in particular made any question of a future civilian occupation seem remote. After Oxford there would be the army (or some other service) and there was not much point in thinking beyond that thick barrier. Nevertheless it would be wrong to suggest that either fears about one's own fate or more elevated concern about the fate of the world dominated to the extent of making Oxford successes or failures seem irrelevant.

On the contrary I have often been shocked, looking back, to think that in June 1940 I was almost as cast down by defeat for the presidency of the Oxford Union as by the fall of France. And in June 1941 my desire to get a good Schools result was not diminished by the German attack on Russia. I remember that only three or four years before Oxford I had been surprised to hear some friends of my parents talking of what a good holiday they had taken in Aberystwyth in 1916. A holiday in 1916? It seemed almost unimaginable to me, who had never experienced 1914–18 and consequently imagined it as a time of continuous horror and squalor. In reality a great deal of normal life goes on in even the worst wars. In Oxford the running down of the University was only gradual and was never complete, so that there was still, say, a third of it left for Mrs Thatcher to go up to in 1943. More to the point for me were the facts that, once the shock of initial adjustment had been got over, 1939–40 was much more like a peacetime than a wartime year in Oxford, and that even 1940–1 was about halfway between the two.

What was true, however, was that a combination of external circumstances and my own interests at the time guaranteed that my life at Oxford was exceptionally dominated by outside political, or politico-military, events. On 18 September 1938, I scurried back from Paris to Pontypool, believing that the Czech crisis meant war within a few days. On 28 September this immediate fear dissolved in the uneasy relief of the Munich agreement. On 7 October I went to Oxford. On 13 October I attended my first debate in the Union and voted with the majority which, urged on by Edward Heath, who was to be President in the following term, Christopher Mayhew, already an ex-President, and A. G. Macdonell, author of the inimitable *England, Their England*, condemned Munich by a vote of 320 to 266. I thought all three speakers were good, but it was Mayhew's aphorisms about 'the peace which passeth all understanding' and a policy of 'reculer pour mieux reculer' which stick in my mind over fifty years. The Oxford 'Munich' bye-election, which Quintin Hogg won but the Master of Balliol (A. D. Lindsay) dominated, absorbed a good deal of the rest of that month.

Looking back on that last year of the peace I recall little difficulty about settling in to Balliol, but nor do I recall it as a period when I lived suffused in the golden glow of Oxford's mixture of medieval and baroque beauty. This may have been because I lived much more in nineteenth- and early-twentieth-century Oxford. Balliol was founded in 1263, but both its fame and the bulk of its buildings came from six hundred years or more later. My room at the top of Staircase XV above the Junior Common Room, which dated from 1912, was bleak, but in the style of an early Fabian hostel rather than of a monastery.

The Garden Quad, the centre of the life of the college, is a haphazard jumble more akin to a smaller Harvard Yard than to one of the quadrangle gems of Oxford, whether the medieval intimacy of Mob Quad at Merton on the one hand or the classical grandeur of Tom Quad at Christ Church and the Front Quad at Queen's on the other. Equally the Union Society, in which, beginning with that first debate, I was to spend a great deal of my Oxford time, eating, reading, talking, even debating there, was entirely a post-1850 collection of buildings. It was not that I and most of my contemporaries admired Victorian architecture. On the contrary we mocked it in a way that I find incomprehensible today. Butterfield's Keble, for instance, which I now regard as an exciting example of high Gothic revival, was thought of as a bad joke. It was just that my two most frequented Oxford locales were Balliol and the Union, and that I buttressed this by bicycling a lot past the uxorious villas of North Oxford, created after 1870 to meet the enthusiasm of some dons for their newly granted freedom to marry, and also along the canal and river towpaths, which fringed the lower Oxford parishes of St Ebbes and Jericho, roughly contemporary with those villas but more the haunt of Jude the Obscure than of Zuleika Dobson.

As a result my most vividly retained images of the 1938 University – those which unite time and place, rather like the stills outside the cinemas which played a surprisingly large part in our Oxford lives – are of unmonumental Oxford: the first morning's sight of the immense bulk of George Howard, scion of Castle Howard, later chairman of the BBC, waddling across the quad in a garish dressing gown on his way to his ten o'clock bath; canvassing for Lindsay in the Woodstock Road with fallen leaves swirling around the 'gabled Gothic houses'; Fuller's Tea Rooms in the Cornmarket with their walnut layer cake and the elegant green façade of the old Clarendon Hotel still standing opposite; more grandly the George Restaurant with its punkahs and semi-French menu; queues waiting to get into the Union debating hall in the evening gloom; and sharp late-October sunlight on the Balliol playing field in Jowett Walk, where for some extraordinary reason I took briefly to playing hockey, elaborately kitted out in college colours by Messrs Shepherd and Woodward. What is common to these mind pictures is that it is for ever autumn. Pre-war Oxford is for me not a clock stopped at ten to three but a calendar stuck at 20 October. But it is not paradise lost.

Paradoxically I think I enjoyed both of the next two wartime years more than the last year of the peace. This was partly because in 1938–9 I made a mess of Pass Mods, as the preliminary examinations for both History and Modern Greats (Philosophy, Politics and Economics) were then called. They were an irritating little examination, including two set-book language papers, one on Tocqueville's *Ancien Régime* and the other on the *Gesta Francorum*, a dog-Latin account of the First Crusade with Latin words arranged in a French order, and thus draining the language of all its neatness of construction. These papers could be dealt with after one term, although Balliol surprisingly preferred to take two, and I succeeded in sprawling them over three. As a result I did not properly get into the swing of PPE that year.

Nor did I emerge to rapid political prominence. I was a member of the strong Labour Club, then under light Communist dominance which did not oppressively obtrude so long as the Politburo was on a Popular Front line, but I held no office in it. At the Union I was a diligent attender at the Thursday evening debates. I listened for a term, made a maiden speech in January quickly followed by several others, was given the dizzy honour of being a teller (which involved dressing up in a tail coat and white tie) at the hugely attended conscription debate in April 1939 (although for the 'noes' I now regret to say), was given the more substantial award of a 'paper speech', that is a fifteen-minute speech opening a debate, later that term, and just before the end of the academic year, was elected a member of the Library Committee, the lowest of the rungs on the ladder which might or might not lead to the presidency.

The favour of the tellership and the opportunity of the paper speech were bestowed by courtesy of Hugh Fraser, who was to be an MP for forty years from 1945 and was President from Balliol in that Trinity (summer) term of 1939, just as Heath had been in the Hilary (spring) term, and a third Balliol figure (A. F. Giles, subsequently one of the last of the colonial governors) was elected for the Michaelmas term. Balliol was dominant in the Union, providing over a third of the inter-war presidents, although not on the basis of a phalanx of left-wing support, for the majority of prominent Labour Club figures, including Denis Healey, stood out from it as a piece of outdated bourgeois frippery with white ties and a subscription of thirty shillings a term, the rough equivalent of £40 today.

Balliol at that time was not so much a left-wing college as one which maintained the tradition of the 1870–93 mastership of Benjamin Jowett of training people for high-grade public service jobs – and seeing that they got them – combined with a determination not to be innovatively outflanked. Thus Balliol had taken enthusiastically to Rhodes Scholars, who in those days, according to the original provisions of Cecil Rhodes's will, came only from the ethnically 'pure' countries of North America, the old Dominions and Germany. But it supplemented them with a good non-Rhodes supply of Indians and so many Africans that when a film called *Sanders of the River* was shown in Oxford its scene of a native war canoe being vigorously paddled produced a cry of 'Well rowed, Balliol!', which convulsed the whole cinema.

The college took about a half of its entry from day schools where the fees were low or non-existent, which was then more unusual in Oxford than it is today. Unlike some of the other 'grammar school' colleges, however, it also had a sizeable contingent of Etonians. With a few exceptions the products of that academy then confined their patronage to Christ Church, Magdalen, New College (the nicer ones, it was sometimes said), Trinity (the stupider ones, it was sometimes also said) and Balliol. They (aided by clutches of Wykehamists and Harrovians) helped to give the college a leavening of peers (Landsdowne and Oxford and Asquith), other magnates such as Howard, and hereditary politicians (Julian Amery and Maurice Macmillan). There was also a stream which was in the tradition of T. H. Green and R. L. Nettleship and which practised a habit of low-living, social concern and high moral tone. Leading members of this group were Freddie Temple, nephew of the Archbishop and later a considerable cleric himself, and

Murray Maclehose, who became Governor of Hong Kong. I remember them as wearing rather thick grey flannel trousers with black shoes; they were often Rugbeians. I think the Master, in spite of his own somewhat more left-wing affiliations, liked them best of all of us.

I started with no Balliol friends (although two or three, including Derek Powell, in other colleges), but I quickly made some. From that first year there came (and have lasted) Ronald McIntosh, Madron Seligman and Neil Bruce. At the time there were also Cyril Stratton and Nigel Foulkes, but Stratton was killed and Foulkes and I never kept much contact after the war. None of these belonged to either the 'Etonian ruling class' or the 'Rugbeian pi' groups, although Seligman (an Harrovian) had some links with the latter, but not nearly as strong as those which bound him to Edward Heath, then a respected but somewhat solitary organ scholar and Union politician, to whom Seligman remained a devoted (and necessary) friend for decades.

The war had the effect of constantly taking people away from Oxford and consequently of producing a greater turnover of friends than might have been the case in peacetime. Thus McIntosh went into the merchant navy before Christmas 1939 (sailing to the River Plate from Barry Docks, where my parents saw him off, and subsequently surviving vicissitudes ranging from smallpox in Australia to torpedoes in the North Atlantic, to emerge with a master mariner's certificate in 1945), whereas I, because I was just over a year younger than him, was allowed to stay on until June 1941. He (and others) were replaced partly from the 1939 Balliol intake and partly by Tony Crosland. Crosland had come up to Trinity in 1937 as a classical scholar after a somewhat tumultuous career at Highgate School. He was a prominent, rather rakish Oxford figure, but I did not know him until nearly the end of that first autumn term of the war. Then, as I put it in a memoir written on his death in 1977, 'he came to my rooms, probably on some minor point of Labour Club business, and having settled it, remained uncertainly on the threshold, talking, but neither sitting down nor departing for nearly two hours. His character was more ambivalent than I had thought, but also more engaging.' Thereafter, I saw him nearly every day until he too left Oxford in the summer of 1940, for the army in his case, and eventually to land by parachute outside Cannes. Our friendship persisted on an intense but fluctuating basis for nearly four decades. Not only was his character engaging, his personality was dazzling and his intellect was of very high quality. He had maddening streaks of perversity, was in my view not at his best as a minister, but was the most exciting friend of my life.

The Balliol freshmen of 1939 produced close but less emotionally wearing friends in the shape of David Ginsburg, who became Labour

MP for Dewsbury in 1959, Isaiah Halévy and Anthony Elliott, who was drowned off the shore of Israel while serving as ambassador to that country in 1976. Ginsburg was the son of a refugee Russian merchant who had been an industrial scientist in St Petersburg until 1917. He came of a background remarkably similar to that of Isaiah Berlin, although they are not similar personalities. Halévy's father ran a Jewish school in Brighton, which he named Whittingehame College after the East Lothian country house of the author of the Balfour declaration. 'Shy' Halévy, who had great charm and more intelligence than application, in my third year shared the house in St John Street in which I had taken over Crosland's rooms. He was killed in 1944.

Elliott was a 'poor Etonian', colleger, son of a rather Attlee-like retired Indian Civil Servant baronet, who lived in an agreeably run-down house in the Woodstock Road and edited the Balliol Register for many years. Elliott, who had great if somewhat reclusive quality, brought into this circle two other unusual Etonians, who were both to be at Bletchley Park with me at the end of the war. Michael Ashcroft, a Magdalen undergraduate of high intelligence and bounding, almost naïve, political enthusiasm, was best man at my wedding in 1945, entered the Treasury in 1946 and died of a tragic disease in 1949. Peter Solomon-Benenson was the son of the marriage of Flora Benenson with Harold Solomon, a Jewish cavalry colonel who was briefly a Conservative parliamentary candidate. She combined being Kerensky's mistress with the promotion of staff welfare in Marks and Spencers and the early sponsorship of George Weidenfeld's career in London. Their son subsequently emerged as Peter Benenson but he functioned at Bletchley under the improbable rank and style of Regimental Sergeant-Major P. J. H. Solomon-Benenson. Later he founded Amnesty.

Rather analogously to Ashcroft and Benenson through Elliott, so Leo Pliatsky, a Corpus classicist from Russia via Manchester and the East End of London who became a powerful Whitehall permanent secretary, came into my life through Crosland. The three of us motored together in Crosland's low red MG through a bleak January landscape to a University Labour Federation Conference at Liverpool in 1940. They both stayed at Pontypool on the way to Merseyside; indeed, of the others mentioned, McIntosh, Bruce, Seligman, Elliott and Ashcroft all stayed there, and McIntosh, Bruce and above all Crosland, who during his army days sometimes went without me, were there for periods of a week or more.

There were of course many other amical acquaintances, both in Balliol and outside, particularly through the Union. Nicko Henderson, who became President when all four elected officers disappeared at the outbreak of the war, and Mark Bonham Carter, who came to Balliol in 1940, and who have both been amongst my closest friends for the past thirty-five years, were then in this category. Henderson moved in wider and more literary circles than I did, and Bonham Carter was grander, insofar as there was any grandeur left in Oxford by the time he got there.

Within these mixed although over-political Oxford circles I did not feel remotely socially inhibited by my South Wales mining background. Crosland was regarded as rather extravagant and dashing, and in Labour Club eyes I was probably thought of as an adjutant of his. In the Balliol Senior Common Room however, as I discovered many years later, at least one don put into currency for me the satirical sobriquet of 'nature's old Etonian'. Despite this doubtful tribute I do not think that in those days I would have been at home in the Gridiron or the Bullingdon, those differing pillars of self-consciously upper-class Oxford. Indeed I remember a fairly uneasy occasion in June 1939 when the recently succeeded Lord Faringdon, an acquaintance of my father's on some Labour Party committee, asked me to stay for a large social weekend at Buscot Park, twenty miles from Oxford. The Master of Balliol, whose permission I had to obtain to go away for two nights, looked fairly askance at the invitation, partly no doubt because Gavin Faringdon was a well-known homosexual, but probably more because he suspected that Buscot did not emulate the austere home life of the Master's Lodgings under the redoubtable but hardly Lucullan Mrs Lindsay. Buscot, which is a fine house with some remarkable things in it, was quite sensibly, even parsimoniously, run in the 1950s and 1960s. But in the 1930s it had been most elaborately done up after Gavin Faringdon succeeded his grandfather in 1934, complete with liveried footmen and pea-green Rolls-Royces to transport the guests. It was an abrupt introduction to country-house life.

I found less difficulty in entertaining my Oxford guests at Pontypool than Gavin Faringdon probably did in entertaining me. My parents enjoyed putting themselves out for them, and the surroundings and way of life for conventionally educated upper-middle-class boys from London or the Home Counties were sufficiently different to make it interesting. In the much less travelling world of the 1930s it was almost like being taken to visit a Druse stronghold in the Lebanon. There was pleasurable motoring with the contrast between the bare hillsides above the valleys and the benign landscape of the eastern part of the county, there was the strange experience of going down a coalmine, there were rather good meals which did not entirely conform to the London pattern of time or content, there was a mixed bag of people passing through the house, and there was a certain sense of local power, which was intriguing to, say, a civil servant's son living in Kensington. This reached its petty apogee one day when I drove in to the centre of Pontypool to collect my mother from the Magistrates' Court and parked in the most convenient and therefore most illegal-looking place. My companion was convinced that we were about to be removed, but when one or two constables passed they merely saluted. Then when a large officer decorated with the badges of a chief superintendent advanced and actually tapped on the window he thought his fears were at last to be vindicated. But when I wound it down the police dignitary merely said: 'Your mother asked me to pop out and say that we are just finishing the last case, and that she will be with you in ten minutes.' Perhaps they were all in a conspiracy to compensate for 1926.

The summer vacation of 1939 (which has been overtaken by my dissertation on Oxford friendships) I spent partly on a two weeks' tour of southern England with the Balliol Players. We took a production of Aristophanes' *Birds* (in English) around a dozen or so schools (Radley, Canford, Harrow, Raynes Park Secondary School and so on) and historic sites (Corfe Castle and Old Sarum in the open air and the Bath Pump Room indoors). It was organised that year by Madron Seligman and the company was recruited on a basis which did not pay much attention either to histrionic talent or to classical scholarship. It amused me subsequently to point out to Madron that he had not invited (Sir) Kenneth Dover, a Balliol undergraduate of my year, who subsequently became both President of Corpus Christi College and probably the greatest living expert on Aristophanes. However, the tour was a considerable financial success mainly because it was our habit to insure against rain at Corfe Castle, which had potentially the most lucrative box office. This could be done only on the basis that if a given quantity of rain fell on the nearest official rain gauge, which was at Swanage, the insurance company paid. At Swanage there was a cloudburst. At Corfe no drops fell, although references to the thunderbolts of Zeus were accompanied by appropriate flashes and crashes. It was very satisfactory.

Then I went to France for five weeks, and this time found a part-time occupation which was tailor-made for me. I was taken on by the Paris office of the Workers' Travel Association (an Ernest Bevin enterprise, run from Transport House) to meet parties of British visitors at the Gare du Nord or the Gare St Lazare and conduct them either to hotels or across Paris to the Gare de Lyon or the Gare d'Orsay. As I loved trains and great termini it was a treat and not a chore. I was not paid, but there was the perquisite of a first-class rail pass all over France. On one occasion I went to Biarritz and the Spanish frontier, then very forbidding, with the civil war barely six months over. On another I went to Toulon, just beyond the edge of which town Ronald McIntosh and I stayed in a villa rented by a rich girlfriend of John Biggs-Davison.* After a few days of swimming, drinking, reading and looking with hopeful respect at the grey shapes of the French Mediterranean fleet, we became frightened by the Nazi–Soviet Pact and, as in 1938, scurried back to England. But this time the journey took longer (over forty hours from Toulon to Pontypool) and the scare was not misplaced.

When war was declared a few days later none of us at first knew what to do. It was unlike 1914. No one stormed recruiting offices. They would send for us when they wanted us, and it soon became clear that unless we already belonged to a military unit that was not going to be for some time. Would there be an Oxford in which to wait? Slowly during September, a month during which I never left Monmouthshire and spent mostly in fatalistic discussions with Derek Powell, it became clear that there would.

On 8 October I returned to Oxford and found an ironic change in my circumstances. I was supposed to live that second year (having been in college for the first) in Holywell Manor, a recently acquired Balliol annexe which has now become its graduate centre. But a military hospital wanted St Hugh's College and St Hugh's was given Holywell Manor. In addition, Chatham House (Royal Institute of International Affairs), almost an honorary member of Balliol by virtue of Arnold Toynbee's key position there, was given refuge in several staircases in the middle of the college.

As a result I and most of the other Balliol second-year undergraduates were moved into the front quad of Trinity. For Balliol men to

* Sir John Biggs-Davison (1918–88), Conservative MP for Chigwell and later Epping Forest 1955–88, became almost a caricature of a back-bench right-wing Tory. In 1939, however, he was a straight-down-the-line fellow traveller with the Communist Party. When the Russian switch of allegiance made resistance to Hitler 'unprogressive' his belief followed the party line. But, equally typically, his sense of honour and patriotic duty made him accept immediate mobilisation into the Royal Marines. In the first autumn of the war he was almost the only one of my contemporaries who was already an officer. But, perhaps because of his views, the authorities gave him nothing to do. So he hung about Oxford, resplendent in his service dress, but complaining about the war (many of us did the reverse: we enthusiastically supported the war, but stayed at Oxford as long as we could).

Biggs-Davison was a close friend in those days. But when he changed his line (which was never mine) towards the end of the war and became a romantic Tory, I found him impossible to deal with, in a way that I never did Maurice Macmillan or Julian Amery or Hugh Fraser. He was like a reformed drunk (which he was not) who wished to obliterate the past. I had practically no contact with him during his three decades in the House of Commons.

move into Trinity was like Montagues fraternising with Capulets, but for me the arrangement worked out admirably. That front quadrangle (done in 1883–7 by T. G. Jackson) is not one of Jackson's best contributions to Oxford architecture, but I found two large rooms a great improvement on the bed-sitter at the top of Staircase XV which was what Balliol had given me in peacetime. Balliol had already gone in for gas fires and for all meals, save only tea supplied by the Junior Common Room, to be served in hall and not in undergraduate rooms. Trinity in wartime considerably improved on all that. In place of the oxygen-destroying qualities of gas there were great open fires, with hods of coal borne across the quadrangles by ancient servitors. In place of all meals in hall there were hot luncheons in the winter and lobster luncheons in the summer which were borne by the same old scouts, and could be eaten with guests in one's rooms. And on top of this there was the advantage in the second year of continuing Balliol tuition. A combination of Balliol teaching and Trinity living was the best of both worlds. It was reminiscent of Jack Kennedy's remark about a Harvard education and a Yale degree. For long afterwards, whenever anyone asked whether wartime Oxford had not been a sad decline from the splendours of peacetime, I said that, on the contrary, it had put my standard of living up by about a half.

It also greatly opened up my Union and Labour Club political prospects. In the former I was moved up from the Library to the Standing Committee for the Michaelmas term, and then for the Hilary term, when Madron Seligman succeeded to the presidency, I became Secretary. This was the junior of four offices, the intervening two in descending order being Librarian and Treasurer. The Librarian was Robin Edmonds, later to be a diplomat of liberal views and a writer of note, but at this time an unbending high Tory who achieved local fame with the remark, said to be a perfect hexameter and delivered in an undulating slightly nasal voice: 'The Spanish Republican Government, Mr President Sir, is hell's own indiscriminate fire let loose.' Crosland was Treasurer. We were all elected by each other, that is by the relatively small committee. For the next term, however, we decided to return to democracy, and in late February (1940) Edmonds beat Crosland for the presidency, while I was comfortably elected Librarian, although not against strong opposition.

This led on to my defeat for the presidency in the following term. It was only by five votes, which made it the more tantalising, and it was against the form. My side had won the presidential debate (measurably by votes cast and we hoped by argument) the night before the poll, when I was supported by Kingsley Martin, long-serving editor of the *New Statesman*, in favour of an uncompromising motion that 'without a great growth of socialism this war will have been fought in vain'. My successful rival was James Comyn, an engaging Irishman from New College, then at least nominally a Liberal, later a QC and (English) High Court judge. I stood again in the first term of the following academic year but, as can be the case with second attempts, was beaten by a more decisive margin, this time by I. J. Bahadur Singh, who became Indian Ambassador to Rome and Cairo and whom I last saw in Delhi in 1980, when I recorded him as being 'healthily free of Oxford *Schwärmerei*'.

These defeats were disappointing but they in no way turned me against Union life. That collection of red-brick neo-Gothic buildings off the Cornmarket remained very much the centre of my Oxford life. I continued to lunch there three or four times a week, to read much more in the Burne-Jones-decorated library than in either the Bodleian or the Radcliffe Camera, to attend most debates and speak occasionally in what I juvenilely imagined was an elder-statesman sort of way.

In the Labour Club I became the college secretary for Balliol in the first term of the war and was then elected to the executive committee in December. There, in the bitterly cold winter of 1940, three of us felt chilled and isolated by more than the weather. The others were Crosland and Ian Durham, a mature trade union student. We three were the only committee members not on the Communist Party line. Crosland, as recently as January, when he had organised some sort of anti-'aid to Finland' demonstration against the innocent head of Philip Noel-Baker, already a prominent Labour internationalist, had been pretty far to the left and certainly regarded himself as a Marxist. Nevertheless, he revolted against the Communist anti-war line, rather in the way that John Strachey did, and increasingly, despite the Noel-Baker incident, became nauseated with the rubric that the Red Army was fighting to liberate the Finnish people from the reactionary rule of Mannerheim. For all three of us these two issues of Finland and of support for or opposition to the war in the west which dominated politics at the time, made coexistence within an allegedly united left-wing club increasingly intolerable. It was different from the position a year previously when Communist manipulation was softened and shaded by the fact that on immediate policy there appeared to be substantial agreement.

During the Easter vacation we therefore decided to split the club, and so acted, thinking ourselves very bold, when we came back to Oxford at the end of April. To the breakaway organisation we gave the somewhat cumbersome title of Oxford University Democratic Socialist Club. Crosland was the natural leader and became the first chairman, Durham secretary and I treasurer. The main duty that I remember going with this office was that of engaging in a long and unrewarding correspondence with Iris Murdoch, my opposite number in the old club, about the sharing of its assets and/or liabilities. Both our different ideological positions and the arm's-length nature of our negotiations were indicated by our respective salutations. 'Dear Comrade Jenkins', she began. 'Dear Miss Murdoch', I replied. Forty-seven years later (see Chapter 32) I compensated by giving her an Oxford honorary degree.

The new club, rather to our surprise, was a runaway success. We quickly attracted over 400 members, which in a university then not much bigger than 3500 was a major breakthrough, and we well out-distanced the old club, which became a bunkered rump. There were a lot of resemblances to the early days of the SDP. Some time in the future there was reunification and then another split, and I believe the same thing over again before the mid-1960s when as Home Secretary I was elected (and remained for a decade) president of what had reverted to the title of the Oxford University Labour Club, but with an Oxford University Socialist Club outside it to the left. At the end of 1940 I became the third chairman of the new club, Durham having immediately followed Crosland, and was pleased to get a list of speakers which included Attlee and Dalton, although the former's name was more inspirational on the card than his address was in the hall, particularly as he showed reluctance to answer questions.

I also became chairman in 1941 of our attempt at a national university organisation which would scupper the equally Communist-controlled University Labour Federation (which had drawn Crosland, Pliatsky and me to Liverpool), but this was less successful. A good analogous club developed in Cambridge, where they were able to use the more natural title of Labour Club because the very strong Communist front organisation of the 1930s had there called itself the Cambridge University Socialist Club, but we did not get much of a foothold in the provincial universities, except for Nottingham, which emerged as an admirable hotbed of social democracy. There was something in a derisive remark which I remember from a speech of one of the hardliners: 'And where will you have your conferences – the first in Oxford, the second in Cambridge and the third at Bletchley?' (which was then most known for being a railway junction on the line between Oxford and Cambridge).

There was one other elective office for which I more successfully stood than for the presidency of the Union, and that was the presidency of the Balliol Junior Common Room. Unlike the university political offices it was for a year and not a term, and I served for 1940–1. Oxford JCR presidencies are now onerous, but at that time the Balliol one involved little more than presiding over plenary meetings of the junior members of the college twice a term, answering (not too seriously) entries in the suggestions book, and having occasional rather uneasy discussions with the Master about the state of the college. Perhaps the main retrospective interest of my holding this office was that it meant that, within four years, it had been occupied by Edward Heath, Denis Healey and me. The intervening figure was a Rhodes Scholar, Philip Kaiser, later American minister in London and ambassador in Budapest and Vienna. The pattern, while no doubt owing something to accident, also indicated what an extraordinarily concentrated political society Balliol, with its entry of no more than eighty a year, then was.

How did this semi-frenzy of undergraduate political activity fit in first with the war, and second with academic work, which must be regarded as the primary purpose of my being at Oxford, or at least of being allowed to stay for twenty-two wartime months? Private concerns can take a remarkable priority over public events. My memories of that 'hinge of fate' twelve months from June 1940 to June 1941 are surprisingly dominated by private events, even though played out against an unusually dramatic public backcloth. This private dominance was partly because on 3 August 1940 I met my wife. Late June and July, after the end of the Oxford term, I had divided between several weeks at Pontypool with Crosland, who departed from there to the army, and a fortnight at an Oxford-organised forestry camp in Shropshire with David Ginsburg and Anthony Elliott, which the Master of Balliol, seeing us lolling about on the mound in the Garden Quad had more or less decreed that we attend. Bicycling there from Craven Arms railway station on a perfect summer Sunday evening we stopped for supper at a pub at Lydbury North and heard one of the most famous of Churchill's 1940 broadcasts – 'we will defend every village, every town, every city . . .'. While we were at the forestry camp the most dramatic event was the arrival of a Black Maria from Shrewsbury (almost like a preparation for a Housman hanging) to arrest Ronald Grierson, Nuremberg-born and then called Griesmann, more recently chairman of the South Bank, as an enemy alien. I did not see him again until after the end of the war, by which time he, in spite of this unpropitious start, had with typical buoyancy achieved the rank of lieutenant-colonel as opposed to my humble captaincy.

Then I went to a week's Fabian summer school at Dartington Hall in South Devon. Summer schools were a traditional part of Fabian activity, dating back at least to the pre-1914 years when a fairly young H. G. Wells used them as amorous stalking grounds, a role which C. E. M. Joad later enthusiastically took over from him in the 1930s. Neither was however present in 1940. It was not scholastically strenuous, being more a holiday than a course. All that was involved in the latter aspect was attendance at a few lectures given by well-known political intellectuals and participation in subsequent discussions.

I had arranged to meet several Oxford friends at the School, but what turned out to be much more important was that I there encountered Jennifer Morris, who had come to Dartington with her Cambridge friend Jane Cole, the daughter of the king and queen of the Fabian court, Douglas (or G.D.H.) and Margaret Cole. She was at the end of her first year as a History scholar at Girton, by the winning of which award she had astonished St Mary's School, Calne, then a small and, she insists, as obscure a school as it is today a fashionable one, and was fair and rather tall, and I thought very attractive. We did not much entangle until the fifth day of the week's sojourn when a cricket match played some role at once surprising and obscure in our courtship. It was surprising because at the time I eschewed all organised games (except for bicycle polo on the Balliol field on Sunday afternoons) unless they were not serious (but that was I suppose true of a Fabian game), and she was certainly no intense lady cricketer. But, inspired by some exhilaration of attraction, I captained one side, performed unusually well and lost some inhibitions in the flush of victory. At any rate, when the School came to an end on the seventh morning, we left together and have been so for the subsequent half century.

This has not however precluded a lot of (mostly brief) physical separations, for although we travelled together by train through the West Country she went to a fruit-picking camp in Worcestershire (horticulture and silviculture seemed to play a great part in the life of those who were still outside the services in that summer when Britain was alone), and I returned to Pontypool. Then, after a couple of weeks we reassembled in London, where I did some research for the Fabian Society, and experienced the beginnings of the air raids until in early September I went to stay for a weekend with her and her parents* at Henley-on-Thames and then, for the last month of the long vacation, retreated to Monmouthshire, where she came to stay several times in the ensuing year.

Despite the sense of seriousness and acceptance conveyed by these family visits I do not think that we ever contemplated an immediate marriage. But I at least was even further from seriously contemplating separation, and our wedding eventually took place in the last months of the war in 1945. Even after that we approached the 1949 birth of our first child in a way that was leisurely enough to earn the serious disapproval of Mrs Attlee, who both took an excessive gynaecological interest in young couples and believed very literally that the state of

---

* (Sir) Parker Morris (1891–1972), Town Clerk of Chesterfield 1923–9 and of Westminster 1929–56, and Dorothy Morris (1892–1974), before her marriage in 1919 one of the earliest woman members of the staff of the *Manchester Guardian*.

holy matrimony was ordained for the procreation of the human race. But although these events were far ahead in the summer of 1940 there was no doubt that the Dartington encounter transformed my life and gave me a singularly well-timed injection of confidence and optimism. This produced an illusion of immunity from bombs and made me feel capable of solving most intellectual problems. I remember my mother for once getting the wrong end of the stick. She expressed considerable relief when she discovered that Miss Morris was at Cambridge, having previously believed her to be at Oxford, where she might have been a serious distraction to my work. That was not at all how my mental processes worked then, or have done since. Stimulus of one sort increases not diminishes activity in other fields.

Politics did however consume a vast amount of my time, and strictly academic work correspondingly little. I also spent a fair proportion of hours just enjoying myself, which then (as now) meant social meals, drinking and talking in other people's rooms, desultory reading, and being out and about, vaguely taking in buildings and landscape rather than systematically looking at them, bicycling (that, unlike the others, no longer an occupation) not only about the city but going for (mostly towpath) rides well out into the country. I think that what saved me academically was the substantial overlap between the current-affairs-orientated PPE school and many activities which I thought of as being political rather than scholastic. It is to the credit of the tone of Oxford politics that, while there was inevitably plenty of the manoeuvring for personal position and petty gossip which goes with it in any closed circle, there was also serious interest in the content of politics, both national and international.

Thus I acquired much of the knowledge necessary for the paper on comparative political institutions as a bye-product of my *political* interest in recent events in France and America (the two countries mainly covered). Equally the making of successful Union speeches required familiarity with historical allusion and quotation, and an even more dual-purpose discipline was provided by the Democratic Socialist Club habit (which we inherited from the Labour Club) of the officers addressing a series of college group meetings throughout the University on subjects which might be as quasi-academic as 'Why did the Weimar Republic fail?' or 'Can Keynes cure unemployment?' Preparing and delivering such talks fixed the subjects in one's mind and gave one arguable positions far more than just listening to any number of lectures.

I hardly put this issue to the test, however, for in my second and third years I do not think that I went to a single university lecture. In my first year I went to some dreary ones for Pass Mods and also to a few by the stars of the epoch, A. L. Rowse, David Cecil, Roy Harrod and, already, Isaiah Berlin. But I then decided that it was not the best use of an hour, and that I could read or write more productively. There was an element of fashionable bravado about this, and it was half contradicted by the fact that I spent many hours listening to political speeches. But whatever the sense or nonsense of the position, it was the one I adopted.

How then was I taught? The answer is that it was almost exclusively by the Oxford method of writing essays which were subsequently criticised in tutorials, sometimes alone with the tutor, sometimes with the addition of one other undergraduate. The austerities of war produced no worsening in the student/teacher ratio. What they did produce was an instability in the teaching body as fellows disappeared, sometimes into the army but more frequently to become temporary civil servants, and this meant that in my third year I was taught more outside Balliol than would have been the case a few years earlier. Thus I was taught for a paper entitled International Relations 1919–39 by Agnes Headlam-Morley of St Hugh's, later a professor but at that time anxious to become a Conservative MP; the History of Labour Movements 1815–1914 by G. D. H. Cole, then a fellow of University College and so successful a Left Book Club author that he could publish almost the same book several times over without the repetition impairing his sales; and European Diplomatic History 1870–1914, a ponderous subject at the best of times, by an elderly German who was himself so ponderous that I have forgotten his name and college.

Inside Balliol I was taught general philosophy by the Master (alone, of which more later), political philosophy by John Fulton, later the first Vice-Chancellor of Sussex University and the midwife of a not very good 1968 report on the civil service, nineteenth-century English political history by A. B. Rodger, who was a fellow of Balliol from 1923 to 1961 and Dean from 1933 to 1952, and economic theory by Thomas Balogh, who had only just arrived. Rodger was rather a comic figure with a clipped military speech which matched his appearance. When I was summoned to see him in my first term I thought he said, 'Won't you sit down,' murmured 'Thank you very much,' and subsided. 'I didn't say "Sit down",' he then spluttered, 'I said "Why aren't you wearing a gown?"' After this contretemps we got on well, and in the course of one tutorial he made a flattering remark of considerable confidence-giving importance to me. 'I am not sure how much you know,' he said, 'but you write it in a fine style, which I could not teach you, and which will be of more value to you than anything I could.'

Balogh had come from Hungary via Germany in 1931 and to Balliol in 1940. With David Ginsburg I was his first pupil. I was told that he later became a rather bored and fitful teacher, but at the beginning he was full of enthusiasm already mingled with a little perversity. He liked arranging for his tutorials to be interrupted by telephone calls from the famous, and if this could not be achieved he compensated by such simple exhibitionist devices as taking his temperature, sometimes lying on the floor to do so, during the reading of the essay. He was by far the best teacher I had, and the only one, although I admired Cole's fame and fastidious radicalism, who made my performance in a subject qualitatively different from what it would have been without him.

In general, however, I was a good example of the truth of the old Balliol adage that the dons did not much matter for the undergraduates taught each other. It was not an austere intellectual discipline which I absorbed. My natural critical tendencies were enhanced, and I imbibed the Oxford habit of liking to dispose of men and issues by sometimes flippant epigram. But I doubt if I emerged qualified to teach in any subject a rigorous sixth-form course at any school of leading academic quality. What my mind was opened to and what excited my intellectual enthusiasm was a desire to know what was happening in the world, to be able to put it in some sort of universal historical context, and to feel in a typical Balliol way, which combined self-confidence (or arrogance) with a sense of public service, that I ought to play some part in improving and not merely observing what happened in the future. Roosevelt and Keynes were my heroes, although this 'Anglo-Saxonism' was balanced by an interest in and affection for all things French, which was a stronger element in British culture of fifty years ago than it is today. I was infused by liberal optimism, tempered but not hobbled by a tendency to make mildly mocking jokes about the people and the institutions I most admired. That was essentially the cast of mind which Oxford, working on my natural proclivity, gave me.

To return to the more mundane details of Oxford teaching, the habit was to do two subjects a term and to write an essay for each of them in alternate weeks. I put a lot into these essays, often sitting up half the night before the day of the tutorial to finish them, and usually turning in two or three thousand words. But, apart from associated reading, I did virtually no other work. By a strict categorisation of time my weekly hours of work could barely have exceeded ten. As a not unnatural result I became somewhat panic-stricken as my chairmanship of the Democratic Socialist Club came to an end in mid-March 1941, and there was little left between me and the Final Honour School examination in three months' time. The disadvantage of the Oxford examination system is that, after the minor and unclassified Pass Mods, it puts all eggs in the single basket of nine three-hour papers spread over five days. If you do well this is very satisfactory, for examinations have not disfigured the rest of the time. But if you do badly you have little academically to show for three years of Oxford, and in those days there were not only the dismal depths of thirds but also the splendid starkness of a fourth class to be avoided.

It was obvious that my only hope of doing well was to change my habits completely and get down to an Easter vacation and a short Trinity term of unmitigated effort. I accordingly started to work eight hours a day seven days a week and kept up this average for the next eighty days. I did not do anything foolish like starting to attend lectures. I just worked over my essays, and Crosland's, which he had bequeathed to me, trying to fill in gaps in my knowledge which emerged between them, going back through the books which had had an impact on me, summarising their main points, and working out the lines of answers to possible questions. It was in a way easy work, which was the main reason I was able to do it for so many hours a day, often starting, which was contrary to my normal habits, with two hours before breakfast.

The desperate measures just worked. When the results came out in mid-July I got one of the four firsts (out of a total of about fifty taking the school) which were awarded in PPE that year. Oddly there were two in Balliol and two in New College and none anywhere else. I have no doubt that it was a damned close-run thing. To begin with I got it only after a long (forty minutes) *viva*, and the wartime habit was that only marginal cases were given these oral examinations, and that you could only improve and not worsen your position as a result of them. Mine was certainly not a 'congratulatory first'.

Then Balogh put it into wide circulation that when he heard that the results of his first year's teaching were out he had to have a large brandy to steady his nerves, and when he saw that I had got a first he had to have another to recover from his surprise. And the Master of Balliol, when he summoned me for a farewell interview, spoke in terms which were less than extravagant. 'You got the lowest mark in general philosophy', he said, 'of any undergraduate of this College who got a first since the Modern Greats school was established in 1924. That was singularly unfortunate,' he reproachfully continued, 'for if you remember I specially taught you the subject alone for a term.' However, he was kind enough to add that I had a remarkable run-through of alphas in the 'descriptive' history papers, the implication quite rightly being that descriptive skill was an inferior art to the analytical rigour which I had failed adequately to absorb from his tutorials.

My first has not subsequently made much practical difference to me. I have not pursued occupations in which appointments or promotions could be achieved on the basis of academic qualifications. But the cachet has been nice to have tucked away, and in particular it was a friendly little keepsake to have with one and occasionally to unwrap in private during the next four years in the army.

# CHAPTER THREE

# *Guns and Ciphers*

It was nearly eight months after Schools before the army decided that it had room for me. By a convoluted process of reasoning it first ordained that I should join the Oxford University Senior Training Corps (as it had become called) in my third year, and then, when I had passed an easy little test called Certificate A, that I should stay on and do the only slightly more difficult Certificate B in December, after which I could go straight to an Officer Cadet Training Unit in the New Year of 1942. This, they claimed, would save time and enable me to be commissioned at an earlier date, but they could not seem to assimilate that I had finished at the University, and that there was something ludicrous about being attached to Oxford in the middle of a war only for the purposes of doing part-time military training for two half-days a week.

However, that was how it worked out. I got an easy-going job in London, which was at once nepotic and glamorous, and travelled to Oxford twice a week to perform my military duties – and see friends, look in at Balliol and lunch at the Union. It was an almost idyllic existence, particularly as the job in London was at the American Embassy, just before Pearl Harbor but at the height of the 'westward, look, the land is bright' period. It was entirely due to the ambassador, John Gilbert Winant, who had become a considerable friend of my father's, and very good it was of that strange silent man who, partly because he looked like a twentieth-century version of Abraham Lincoln and partly because he was such a contrast to his predecessor Joseph P. Kennedy, was a highly effective symbol of American wartime friendship. But I have always thought that the subject on which I was set to work was a curious one to give to an Englishman, or even a Welshman. I was asked to analyse the distorting effects of the Ottawa imperial preference agreements on the Anglo-American trade in the 1930s. I doubt if I provided much extra ammunition for the Bretton Woods and subsequent assaults on the Commonwealth as a trading bloc, but the assignment makes it clear how much of an American policy interest, even in the darkest days of the war, was the build-up of *matériel* for this purpose.

Eventually, in the middle of a very cold February (1942), I was summoned to an artillery OCTU at Alton Towers in the hills of North Staffordshire. Despite the practice dips of the forestry camp and the STC, the full immersion into permanent battle-dress, the frozen parade ground (which did not thaw for six weeks) and the contrasting fug of Nissen huts accompanied by mess-tin meals and NAAFI tea was a considerable shock. However, I survived it perfectly easily, as did nearly everybody else, and emerged after six months as a very junior commissioned officer. I was a little better than average at the theory of gunnery, and a little worse than average at anything which required muscular co-ordination in response to orders. But there was not much in it either way. I was an adequate but not distinguished cadet.

What the shock of immersion did was to imprint on my mind with peculiar indelibility some physical images of those first few months. Alton Towers was a Gothic extravaganza set in a precipitate countryside of wooded ravines, which had been created for an Earl of Shrewsbury a hundred years before. Already in the 1930s it had become a public pleasure park, although of a gentler kind than is provided by the present 'Luna Park' facilities. Thus there were almost hidden rope-walks and elegant little footbridges which brought one unexpectedly upon tearooms disguised as Swiss chalets with an air of being unpatronised since 1939, but which were nonetheless prepared to serve such delicacies as poached eggs and cucumber sandwiches. In addition the ravine outside the park contained a temporary branch of Messrs Bernard Weatherill, the family tailoring firm of Mr Speaker Weatherill. It naturally did a brisk business in the making of officers' uniforms, particularly as it hit on the good psychological device of encouraging early ordering, followed by slow making and frequent fittings, so that these became like milestones on the road to a state of commissioned bliss. There was a danger of tempting fate by this procedure, but I believe that Weatherills recycled the service dresses of those who, in the dread phrase, were 'returned to unit' and did not add tailors' dunning to their other troubles.

After the first couple of months we were allowed to go away for two weekends out of three. These exeats were frequent but brief, from noon on Saturday to Sunday night, and it was generally assumed not much use to those who did not live locally. However, with my addiction to trains and their timetables, I worked out that with a taxi (which others would normally share) waiting almost with its engine running it was possible (just) to catch the 1.02 from Stafford (the time remains unforgotten) which would get me to Euston, or via Bletchley to Cambridge, where Jennifer still was, by the end of the afternoon. For the return it was necessary to get the 9.30 Sunday evening train from St Pancras to Derby. The bonus was that the 1.02 steamed into Stafford, even on a Saturday and two and a half years into the war, reliably bearing the most comfortable restaurant car. There were extraordinary contrasts in wartime England. Exactly an hour away from the bleak Alton parade ground one could be lunching with the pre-war napery and china of the London, Midland and Scottish Railway and watching the three spires of Lichfield cathedral slip by, the view then being across water meadows and not as now a housing estate. It was a moment to look forward to throughout the week.

After the six months I was posted to the 55th Field Regiment, Royal Artillery, which had been the West Somerset Yeomanry and still bore that subsidiary title. This posting was for no obvious geographical reason, unless it was an arcane tribute to my paternal grandfather's county of origin, and indeed the regiment always seemed to me oddly named for it had been based not on Dulverton or Minehead, which is what I would call West Somerset, but on Shepton Mallet, forty miles to the east of these towns. A lot of the officers were Bristol bank clerks, an occupation group which, as Anthony Powell brings out in his autobiography and in the *Valley of Bones* volume of *Dance to the Music of Time*, were great joiners of the Territorial Army. It counted as a good posting, for the West Somerset Yeomanry, together with the more fashionable Leicestershire Yeomanry, which had recruited its officers more through fox-hunting than through the hosiery trade, provided the artillery support for the Guards Armoured Division.

I joined this regiment on the northern edge of Salisbury Plain, just above West Lavington, where it was concentrated and entirely under canvas. It was held to be fully trained (although I certainly was not), and the atmosphere when I arrived was one of expecting early action. When the Dieppe raid took place two weeks later we thought this might be the beginning of a wider assault in which we would be involved. I remember on a clear night at the time of the raid walking a mile or so away from the camp across the open turf and having the impression of moving lights in all directions. The whole Plain seemed a hive of animated preparation.

When nothing happened this state of readiness meant that there was nothing to do. There was no training programme, and except on a very few days when we were allowed to fire the twenty-five-pounders on the Larkhill range or swoop up and down the undulations of the Plain in a Bren carrier or a light tank, officers just walked up and down the lines allegedly inspecting the routine maintenance work that was endlessly done on guns and vehicles. As summer moved into autumn the tension relaxed and the desultory life was made worse by the increasing cold and decreasing light. We stayed under canvas until early November, and shaving and half-bathing outside a tent (which I at least had to myself) was a distinct trial in the darkness of late-October dawns. Yet this was the peak of my strictly military career. Afterwards it was downhill all the way from this state of expectancy in a major fighting formation.

It began by being literally so. We moved down off Salisbury Plain to a hutted camp at Upton Lovell and spent the second half of the autumn in the melancholy river scenery of the Wylye Valley. We were taken off a state of readiness and settled down to a training programme. Then at Christmas it was decided that more field artillery regiments were needed and that we and the Leicestershire Yeomanry must between us produce a third by parturition. One battery from each was accordingly hived off and ours was sent to Clevedon, almost a seaside suburb of Bristol where fine Victorian villas climbed up the hill behind the even finer pier and commanded a good view across to the South Wales coast. I do not think we were being punished for incompetence or some dereliction of duty – although it felt as though we were. It was just that we were C Battery, and one had to go.

We then spent a cosy winter. We were billeted in the empty Victorian houses, we absorbed a lot of new recruits, and drilled and even deployed guns in the hilly residential streets. We seemed to have the town almost to ourselves and nobody bothered us. Even our regimental headquarters was some distance away, and was so unobtrusive that I cannot remember where it was or who was the colonel. But we were down to very basic training and were in no state to do much more than repel a Welsh rugby assault on Clevedon pier.

In the spring we were judged to have improved sufficiently to be integrated into a division and deployed on coastal defence in a more exposed part of the country, although nobody was seriously expecting an invasion by 1943. At the end of April we were moved to Sussex, first for a few weeks to a tennis club at the back of Brighton, on one wall of which Rex Whistler had recently painted one of his last pastiches, and then for an equally short time to a pub in the picturesque and tearoom-studded village of Bramber. From there I was suddenly transferred to what we still thought of as the Leicestershire Yeomanry battery, which was in a kitsch housing estate, thatched, mock-Elizabethan and clustered around a golf course at Angmering-on-Sea. It had everything to make it a caricature of 1930s Sussex seaside suburbia, the Southern Railway station at the edge and many of the inhabitants connected with West End show business. The Dolly sisters, who had not been evacuated, were the most famous residents.

The Leicestershire Yeomanry in exile still maintained a higher style than we had been used to in our battery. Several of the officers occasionally turned up in top boots and breeches and there was more wine in the mess. The battery commander was Robin Wilson, a grandson of the Arthur Wilson who had been King Edward VII's host at Tranby Croft when the great baccarat scandal of 1890 erupted from there. He was pursuing both the Conservative nomination for Dover, where Colonel J. J. Astor, the proprietor of *The Times*, was not standing again, and the Countess of Jersey, a famous beauty of Australian origin who subsequently married Major-General Robert Laycock. Wilson had more success with Lady Jersey, to whom he was briefly married before Laycock, than with Dover, but this was because he was killed in a jeep accident in Italy before the 1945 election. He was not altogether an easy man, but he was clever with some rather reluctant intellectual tastes, and we got along well enough on a basis of mutual wariness.

Our relations were well illustrated by a little farce which we played out that autumn. The commanding officer (of the regiment), who was in fact useless himself, told Major Wilson, who was thoroughly efficient, that his battery was slack. Wilson rather wearily ordered early-morning physical training on the golf course for all ranks below captain. I, who was by then the senior subaltern, had no intention of subjecting myself to this discomfort and indignity. Nor did Wilson care whether I did or not. The difficulty was that he and I shared one of the bijou residences and indeed a bathroom. Normally I came out of it in my pyjamas as he went in, well after the time of the PT. A continuance of this pattern would clearly be provocative. So I hit upon a happy compromise. Each morning when I got out of bed I replaced my pyjamas with PT kit, not to go on to the golf course but to go into the bathroom. This act of minor obeisance, which involved no deceit for he knew perfectly well that I had not been near the golf course, held the position for six weeks or so until morning darkness killed the whole exercise.

The Sussex summer had been enjoyable. We spent a lot of time out on two- or three-day exercises, the weather was not bad and once away from Angmering the scenery in an area not hitherto well known to me was a constant pleasure. Belloc's 'great hills of the south country', even if 'great' was a bit strong for the height of the Downs, provided magnificent views of both the Weald and the sea. Then for six weeks in September and October I was sent off to Staplefield, near Hayward's Heath, to be temporary ADC to the general commanding our division. The regular one, Arthur Corbett (now Lord Rowallan), who later achieved fame by marrying a former able seaman who had changed his or her sex, was ill. The general was not a notable one (although he lived until 1987 and the age of ninety-two), but we were not a notable division, and there were other compensations. We lived in remarkable comfort in a mock-Jacobean country house which had retained most of its peacetime furniture. The captain in charge of catering, who was the only officer in A Mess other than me below the rank of colonel, had been manager of the Imperial Hotel at Torquay and was determined to provide the same standard of food and service. The life was also satisfactorily idle and I read a lot, but it was lonely as well, and I was quite glad when Corbett recovered.

Back at Angmering, however, any enchantment which the 192nd Field Regiment, RA, and B Battery within it had possessed for me began rapidly to wither. It was partly because I fell ill in miserable conditions. On the eve of the battery going out on a week's major exercise I got the worst flu I have ever had. I was left alone with nobody except my soldier servant. He was solicitous, but he was neither a nurse nor a doctor. In his absence Robin Wilson's disadvantage as a house-sharer became more obvious than at the time of the bathroom farce. He kept sacks of oats in the house for his horse, which then, unlike four years before in the Leicestershire Yeomanry, was recreational rather than operational. The oats attracted a lot of rats. I had been used to them coming secretly down from the attic and nibbling my chocolate and my soap, both then scarce possessions. But I had not been used to hearing them gambolling about above me like small dogs during the days that I lay on a bed of fever. It was a depressing week, although I was lucky enough to be able to stagger off on leave to Pontypool on the day after the battery returned. I remember even my normally beloved train journeys being a great effort. As soon as I got there I was diagnosed as having jaundice, that epidemic officers' disease of wartime Britain. (It was alleged that other ranks did not catch it because they used their own mess tins and cutlery.) I was at home for nearly four weeks, and went back just before Christmas still in a fairly feeble condition.

There I was greeted with the news of instructions from the War Office that I was required for special intelligence work and that I was to proceed at the beginning of January to an unspecified 'course' at Bedford. I was destined for cryptography at Bletchley Park and work on the messages sent out by the German High Command in Berlin to the various commanders in the field, Rundstedt, Kesselring, Mannstein, Rommel and several others. A. D. Lindsay had been involved and had decided that the traditional role of Masters of Balliol, at least since Jowett, of placing Balliol men in what they regarded as appropriate jobs outweighed any irritation with my poor philosophy mark. Why he thought I would be a better cryptographer than a philosopher I do not know, but the fact that he did appeared to be decisive.

I cannot pretend that I hesitated over accepting the change. I would not in any event have had much choice. I half enjoyed my two years of field soldiering, even though I fired no shots in anger, and look back upon it with some nostalgia. But I had grown bored with the routine of always training for something that did not happen – although I would be hypocritical if I pretended that I was longing to hurl myself against the enemy. I had become eager for something different and I left Angmering and set off for Bedford without much regret. However, I did not shake off the dust of regimental life with distaste. It now arouses a glow of recollection in my mind, although that can, of course, be a form of retrospective self-deceit. I was at the time sorry to leave a number of companions, on the whole formed easy friendships with officers with whom I was suddenly thrown into propinquity (although finding it difficult on subsequent meetings, as many others have done, to maintain the intimacy without the prop of a shared daily life), and liked and was even quite tolerably good at commanding my little unit.

Those on the Bedford course gave the impression of having been incongruously gathered in from the hedgerows. There was Charles Beckingham, erudite curator from the British Museum who wore private's uniform and has since become a professor of Islamic Studies, there was Francis Dashwood of West Wycombe Park, who was a civilian recruited straight from school, there was a very unglossy university-educated North Midlands second lieutenant who shared a civilian billet with me, there was a sophisticated Etonian other rank who lived in Sloane Street, and about ten others I cannot remember distinctly. We sat at desks in a house by the river and played intellectual parlour games for twelve weeks. The object was to give us a basic knowledge of the different types of codes and ciphers, as well as some simple idea of the possible methods of breaking them (letter frequencies, word patterns, etc.) and to test whether we had any aptitude in that direction.

I also worked hard at German, by an unorthodox but appropriate method of my own devising. I did not need to be able to speak or write German. For the purposes of cryptography I merely needed to know what was a German word and what was not, and once I thought I saw one what were likely companions for it. Grammar was not therefore important, but vocabulary was. I read every article in *Die Zeitung*, a little weekly newspaper published by and for refugees, underlined every word I did not know, looked it up in the dictionary and made voluminous lists. Ten weeks of this proved effective, although knowledge acquired so superficially quickly slipped away again.

I was judged to have adequate aptitude and was moved to Bletchley in April. Bletchley was shrouded in secrecy at the time and remained so for thirty or so years subsequently, but has more recently been deluged with publicity. It assembled strange personalities, one of whom, Ralph Turing, has been made the central figure of a successful mathematical/homosexual stage play. It constructed vast calculating machines out of which by a great but miniaturising leap from valve to solid-state technology the whole computer dynasty has developed. And according to some commentators such as Martin Gilbert, who interleaves his *Second World War* with Ultra extracts like the comments of a Greek chorus, it more or less won the war.

This fanfare of trumpets at least avoids the need for me to try to wrap my mind around distant intricacies to produce a detailed account of exactly what we did. I give it only in probably incomprehensible outline. There were two sections which worked on the German military cipher known as Fish. One was called Dr Newman's section and consisted mainly of civilian mathematicians assisted by Wrens and by the embryonic computers. Their task was to strip the first layer of disguise off the intercepted messages. This they did purely by the techniques of probability mathematics, for their product had no more obvious meaning than their raw material. Both were a stream of five rows of noughts and crosses (or positives and negatives). Each vertical row of five represented a letter of the alphabet or a figure or a conventional sign.

Having got this far they sent the half-deciphered messages over to us in Major Tester's section. (The major existed, but was always a shadowy figure, neither much encouraging nor admonishing, nor indeed performing great feats of cryptography himself.) We were a more mixed bag, army officers if we were already so, RSMs (Warrant Officer Class I) if not (this saved time; the rank, at least equally well paid, could be conferred without officer training), one American lieutenant, and a few civilians who were nominally on the strength of some section of the Foreign Office. We were assisted by ATS girls, but by no machines, for our task was the more intuitive one of seeing the clear German (or at least German obscured only by Wehrmacht jargon) under the second layer of cipher, and this was thought to be beyond the help of machines. I would guess however that what we did could now be easily computerised. Another retrospective reflection from the perspective of half a century on is that it was very odd that in both sections, despite the fact that the processes called for no strength of physique or even exercise of authority, the question of giving women other than subordinate jobs simply never arose.

Tester's section was divided into two parts. There were the 'breakers' and the 'setters'. The breakers were obviously the elite. They were like matadors compared with picadors, except that they did their work first. Setting was relatively routine. You had to know all the properties of the cipher which had been discovered during the past three years or so, and work with logic and precision. But, if you did this, output for any individual was more or less predictable.

After about six weeks as a setter I was allowed to become a breaker, or at least a would-be breaker. Sometimes nothing would happen at all. It is the night shifts which remain engraved on my mind. We worked three shifts, for there was great urgency about the need to get the intelligence, and changed shifts within a compass of three weeks, one week of days, one of evenings and one of nights. The night shift for some strange reason was the longest – nine hours – as it was certainly the bleakest. I remember quite a few absolutely blank nights, when nothing gave and I went to a dismal breakfast having played with a dozen or more messages and completely failed with all of them. It was the most frustrating mental experience I have ever had, particularly as the act of trying almost physically hurt one's brain, which became distinctly raw if it was not relieved by the catharsis of achievement.

On the other hand there could be nights when a cornucopia of success was upended on one's head. I remember one shift when I made thirteen separate breaks. They just fell into my lap like ripe apples. I thought it was too good to be true, and grew rather superstitious towards morning, particularly when it became clear what the exact score was going to be. I was going to London immediately I came off duty, a journey which at the time was accomplished by walking down to Bletchley Junction and getting on the first night train from Scotland which heaved into the station. They were often two or three hours late and contained some fairly exhausted passengers. There were then a lot of flying bombs arriving in London by day as well as by night, and the thought crossed my mind that the unnatural success of the night might be a fine apotheosis before being caught by one.

Our ability to break depended crucially on the quality of the work sent over by the probability mathematicians. No one could break a transcript if the first process was wrongly done. The majority of their efforts they confidently and rightly marked 'certain'. Some they marked 'probable' or even 'possible'. These were hardly worth bothering with. But the mathematicians also invented a category to which they gave the interesting label of 'morally certain'. One lesson I took away is that there is a great difference between 'morally certain' and 'certain'. Once 'certain' is qualified it loses its meaning.

In September (1944) I went seriously off form for several weeks and was rightly returned to the setting room. It was a considerable blow, which ironically coincided with my being promoted to captain, a good indication of how indifferent the whole operation was to rank. It took any gilt off my third pip. Fortunately, I was judged to have recovered form after a couple of months (I am not sure how anyone could tell without trying me out, but perhaps such insight was Major Tester's special contribution), and was allowed back.

Bletchley exhausted the mind, and to some extent, with the difficulty of adjustment to a frequent change of shift, the body. We tried extremely hard, feeling that it was the least that we could do as we sat there in safety while the assault on the European mainland was launched and V-1s and V-2s descended on London. And trying hard meant straining to get the last ounce of convoluted ingenuity out of one's brain, rather like a gymnast who tries to bend his bones into positions more unnatural than he had ever achieved before. It also meant doing everything as quickly as possible for, the break having been secured, messages had to be set, then decoded by machine and then sent in their entirety to what was known as Hut Three, where their intelligence value was appraised and decisions were made as to which commanders should be informed of what. And a lot of the information was of value only if it could be passed on within a day or so. Despite the intense secrecy we were encouraged if so minded, presumably on morale grounds, to read any of the decodes which we had helped to produce. But I never much did so. I think it was partly that an approach of professional detachment developed. The surgery completed or the case pleaded, one did not dwell too much on the fate of the patient or the prisoner. But partly it was just brain fatigue, at least for anything to do with ciphers.

I did however retain adequate energy for general reading and for politics. Throughout my time in the army I had kept up both political interest and contacts. I attended, not as a delegate but as a visitor, two of the wartime Labour Party conferences in Central Hall, Westminster, one in May 1943 and the other in December 1944. By the time of the latter I was anxious to be selected as a parliamentary candidate. Adoptions had begun actively to take place during that last autumn of the war. My hopes fastened on the West Midlands, because the regional organiser there was friendlily disposed. The Aston division of Birmingham was the first serious prospect. It had been won by John Strachey in 1929, although lost by Labour in 1931 and 1935, but looked hopeful for 1945. Woodrow Wyatt and I were the two main contestants during a foggy weekend in November. He won. He attributes his victory largely to the fact that he stayed with the secretary of the local party in a back-to-back house without indoor sanitation, whereas I stayed in the Queen's Hotel, the old LMS railway hotel which was pulled down to make the modern New Street Station in the 1960s but was then famous for the opulence of its chandeliers. He may well be right, and if so it was a considerable feat to lose to Woodrow Wyatt on the ground of being too sybaritic. But it was not fair to see me as seeking only luxury. I had stayed with the secretary on a previous visit, and my reason for preferring a hotel on this occasion was that Jennifer was able to come for a rare weekend. Nor should Woodrow underestimate the attraction of the more militantly socialist appeal which he addressed to the selection conference.

Two months after that, on 20 January 1945, Jennifer and I were married. It was an elaborate occasion by wartime standards, with the wedding in the Savoy Chapel and a Savoy Hotel reception afterwards. It was naturally arranged by Jennifer's parents, and Parker Morris's City of Westminster base accounted for the location. But there was a strong Jenkins presence, both of my friends, perhaps a third of whom were in England at the time, and of my parents', with a contingent of about thirty from Pontypool. Attlee came and made an appropriately laconic principal speech.

Michael Ashcroft was best man, and the ushers were the oddly assorted trio (as it now seems to me) of Asa Briggs, David Ginsburg and Ivor Bulmer-Thomas. My parents and I lunched with them at Boulestin beforehand. The festivities were partly to be explained by the fact that it was almost a celebration of the end of the war. Yet that was a dangerous thing to do prematurely. London was being battered by V-2s, the silent (until they exploded) rockets. One very loud one went off while we were signing the register. It had landed at the Elephant and Castle, which was barely a mile away and at the heart, as it turned out, of my 1948 constituency. Another arrived disagreeably close when I went in the early evening to get some clothes from the house in Markham Street, Chelsea, in which Jennifer lived. We stayed the night in a grand suite in the Savoy which looked out on a snowy Embankment and South Bank and cost us only twelve guineas, which I suppose may have been a spin-off from having the reception in the hotel. The next day we went to Cambridge and stayed a night in the University Arms Hotel, and then on for a week to Edinburgh, where we stayed first in the Roxburghe Hotel in Charlotte Square until it was gutted by fire, and then in the Caledonian. Eastern Britain was lightly snowbound throughout.

My next Birmingham political foray was at Sparkbrook in February 1945. There I was beaten by one vote by a local alderman called Percy Shurmer. Had that one vote gone the other way that solidly 'Brummagem' working- and lower-middle-class division (no multi-racialism in Sparkbrook in 1945) would have had an all-Balliol election, for the other two candidates were Leo Amery, the sitting Conservative, and Rajani Palme Dutt, the Eurasian Communist theoretician, and I would have had a fairly safe Birmingham seat five years before Stechford.

Despite these defeats I continued to seek a constituency and eventually found one in Solihull in late April. There I avenged Sparkbrook by beating Eddie Shackleton on the casting vote of the chairman. It does not sound a famous victory, but as Shackleton (now a former leader of the House of Lords and Knight of the Garter) was a wing commander with a famous name and ten years older than me it was something to have won at all. There was however one important difference between Solihull and Sparkbrook. Sparkbrook was one of the most vulnerable Tory seats in the area and Solihull was one of the safest. It had a small tail on the east which stuck up into the City of Birmingham and was mostly inhabited by factory workers. But for the rest it was a solidly middle-class outer suburb, centred on Birmingham but very pleased with its detachment from it.

At the end of April 1945, however, I was in no way disposed to look the gift horse of Solihull in the mouth and quibble about its Tory propensities. After five or six attempts, I was delighted to have a constituency of any sort to fight. At twenty-four, the age at which Pitt had been Prime Minister, my aspirations were more easily satisfied. It seemed a fine thing to be an adopted candidate. I remember making some rather self-important remarks along the lines of 'I must ring up my agent and settle a few campaign details.'

The campaign went well in every respect except the result. I had five weeks before polling day off from Bletchley, and three weeks of pure leisure afterwards while the assembling of the forces' vote postponed the day of the count. We arranged a lot of small schoolroom meetings, which turned out to be very well attended, typically with 150 sitting and another 80–100 standing around the edges. It is an almost ideal shape and size of meeting before which to learn to speak to audiences less self-consciously precious than the Oxford Union, and I had an educative few weeks. I argued with mechanistic certainty that the detailed planning which had been necessary to win the war was essential to make a success of the peace. My fluency and even persuasiveness grew. I also recall two or three twilight open-air meetings outside pubs which had just closed, when great seas of faces looked up seeking a message appropriate to that June of relief, exhaustion and hope.

The response was such that, unused to sophisticated psephological analysis, I thought that, whatever might have happened elsewhere in the country, the Conservative walls of Solihull had surely been made to crumble. On 26 July I discovered my error. The Labour Party swept the country, but the fortifications of Solihull remained impregnable. I did respectably but lost by 26,000 to 21,000. I then began to suffer from disappointment. Nearly all the other candidates I knew had been swept into the House of Commons. I returned to Bletchley Park, where I settled down to five months which were a combination of public uselessness and private utility.

The public uselessness stemmed from our work no longer seeming of primary importance, from our failure to do what there was and from my singularly inglorious role in it. When the Russians got to Berlin they took over the Fish machines in the War Ministry, somewhat changed the settings, and proceeded to use them for sending signals traffic to Belgrade and other capitals in their new empire. We continued to get the intercepts and played around with trying to break the messages. We never succeeded. I think it was a combination of the new settings being more secure (which raises the question of how much the Russians had found out about our previous success) and the edge of tension having gone off our effort. During this phase I was transferred for a few weeks to the Newman section, from which many of the star mathematicians had already gone. There I never really understood what I was trying to do. I would give random instructions to the Wrens who worked the machines. They would come back with reams of tape at which I would look uncomprehendingly while they waited to be told what to do next. Eventually I would give another equally random instruction. Fortunately it did not greatly matter. But there are few things more demoralising than pretending you understand something when you do not. I learned from this lesson nineteen years later when I first became a minister in a fairly technical department (see Chapter 8).

The private utility came from the fact that when I retired hurt from this excursion beyond my intellectual capacity I acquired a room to myself in a remote part of Major Tester's section. There no one disturbed me with work or anything else for days on end (night shifts had happily been abandoned). I settled down to read the 'tombstone' volumes which then formed the core of English modern political biography. I read in rapid succession the three volumes of Morley's *Gladstone*, the four of Garvin's *Joseph Chamberlain* and of Lady Gwendoline Cecil's *Salisbury*, and the two each of Churchill's *Lord Randolph Churchill*, of Crewe's *Rosebery*, of Gardiner's *Harcourt*, of Spender's *Campbell-Bannerman*, of Spender and Asquith's *Asquith*, of Petrie's *Austen Chamberlain* and Ronaldshay's *Curzon*, topped off by the single volumes (almost biographically insulting in those days) of Newton's *Lansdowne* and Trevelyan's *Edward Grey*. I read all day, apart from getting up for a few minutes every one and a half hours or so and playing a ball game with arcane rules of my own devising against a wall of my solitary room.

This immersion course transformed my knowledge of and interest in the lives and careers of British political figures of the previous hundred years. At the end of my time at Oxford I was still weak on such detail. In my Schools *viva*, K. C. Wheare, later Gladstone Professor of Government and Rector of Exeter, had strangely asked me if I knew who was Foreign Secretary in 1869. When I hazarded

'Granville,' he sadly said, 'No, Clarendon,' and I thought that my chance of a first had gone. After that autumn of 1945 at Bletchley I would certainly have got that right, and my mass of new knowledge gave me a framework into which I have over the decades since been able to fit and remember more recondite but often trivial and even useless facts.

Altogether the army did not do badly for my education. During more active periods I had read a lot of fiction, the whole of Jane Austen and Proust, most of Trollope, Hardy, Dostoevsky and Tolstoy, as well as a clutch of inter-war writers of varying quality but including the disparate geniuses of Virginia Woolf and Evelyn Waugh. Looking back I was remarkably ill-read when I got my Oxford degree, but significantly less so when I emerged from the army. This, like my childhood birthdays, was on a date that was easy to remember. It was 1 January 1946.

# CHAPTER FOUR

# *A Politician Without a Profession*

January 1946 was an early date at which to get out of the army. A very cautious programme of demobilisation had been worked out in Ernest Bevin's Ministry of Labour, partly to avoid servicemen coming home to unemployment (there was no confident assumption that the war had set full employment on its throne for a quarter of a century), and partly to sustain for Britain the role of a great power. The twin themes of the Attlee Government – welfare concern at home and splendid but exhausting commitment abroad – were neatly epitomised in the stateliness of the march back to civilian life which Bevin had planned in the final phase of the wartime coalition. A year to eighteen months in the post-war army looked a likely prospect for a young 1942 recruit such as I was.

There were, however, devices known as 'Class B releases'. For a limited range of jobs the quick demobilisation of the nearly time-expired soldier could be procured. A few months earlier the Industrial and Commercial Finance Corporation (which, following the modern corporate passion for initials as titles, has since evolved into the investment banking house known as 3 I's), had been established under Bank of England auspices with the joint-stock banks as conscripted rather than enthusiastic shareholders. The new institution was intended to fill the 'Macmillan gap'. This had been identified by a committee of inquiry under a Scottish law lord which had been set up by the second MacDonald Government and included both Maynard Keynes and Ernest Bevin among its members. The 'gap' related to the difficulty of access to long-term capital experienced by small to medium-sized business.

William Piercy, just ennobled as the first baron in those hereditary days, had been nominated as the founding chairman. He was an impressive but elusive man, then in his late fifties, with one foot in the City and one in the London School of Economics. In provenance and

59

outlook he was not dissimilar to Lionel Robbins, although he did not achieve the repercussions of the latter's Report on Higher Education. Piercy had worked for Attlee some part of the time the latter was in the War Cabinet, and it was by virtue of this link that he knew me. As a result he offered me a job with ICFC, which surprisingly commanded the right to obtain Class B releases for the staff it was assembling from scratch.

The offer was irresistible, particularly as I had nothing to do in the army except go on reading political biography and, Solihull having voted as it had, no settled alternative occupational bent. So, on Tuesday, 22 January 1946, I took myself to 7 Drapers Gardens, Throgmorton Avenue, just on the northern edge of the heart of the City of London, and began my first (and almost my last) proper job as a very junior banker. The trouble was that I was a banker by accident rather than by vocation. A member of Parliament was what I wanted to be. It was the Class B release rather than the interest of the job which had ensnared me.

As a natural result I was not very good at it, except at best in spasmodic bursts. I had been recruited as an economist, which a product of the Oxford PPE school with no further specialist training hardly was, but I was quickly moved to more general work: to assist in a very junior way in analysis of a company's prospects and in negotiation with it. There were four 'controllers' who handled serious applications. I became an assistant to a controller. I was moved round between three in the first year, which was not a compliment to the success of my performance. The first was a smooth City go-getter who was ill at ease in an organisation to which Lord Piercy gave a high moral tone and which was at least partly based on a concept of public service. The second was a very gentlemanly figure of unassertive manner, fair ability and highly critical mind, who might have reminded me of Waugh's Guy Crouchback had it not been six years before even the first volume of *Sword of Honour* was published.

I was not really a success under the aegis of either of them. The first I distrusted, and the second rather disapproved of me. I remember his complaining that I had spent almost the whole of one office day drafting and redrafting 'a political letter'. It was true, and was in fact to the *New Statesman*, which was then well worth spending a day's work upon, although it should perhaps not have been in my employers' time. Although I rather admired this controller's style, working for him did not engage my mind.

After two failures, chairman's patronage was probably necessary for my survival. No doubt in desperation, I was transferred to work for the most senior controller, John Kinross, who became first the guiding spirit and then the patron saint of the organisation until he died at the age of eighty-five. He and I were totally unalike (much more so than I was with either of the other two) but we got on splendidly. When I found another election to fight (in 1948) he insisted on 'putting on his hat' (a phrase he much liked) and walking across London Bridge to canvass for me in Southwark. In 1989 I gave an address at his memorial service and commented on the difference, *inter alia*, in our attitude to money. He had an extraordinary gift for making it, and practically no desire to spend it, except for his munificent charitable bequests. I then and subsequently had no feel at all for making it, but a considerable desire to spend it.

During my ICFC years, however, I did not have much to spend. Once, after I had been engaged in my biggest deal there, under Kinross's supervision – this was to lend £168,000 to Lord Forte (as he was not then), which was the equivalent of about £3 million today and was of considerable significance in setting him on the road from milk bars to caravanserai – I was swept away by the glamour of high finance and wrote to my bank manager in Pontypool saying that I was enclosing a cheque for £25,000. He wrote back and pointed out that it was in fact for £25.

A sum of £25,000 would have been distinctly useful, for at ICFC I was paid only £500 a year, which rose hesitantly to £650 over two years. Jennifer was working, first in the Ministry of Labour, where she had been a wartime assistant principal engaged with the retraining schemes which were the reverse side of the coin of Bevin's slow demobilisation, and then at Political and Economic Planning (PEP), where she assisted Angus Maude, later Paymaster-General at the beginning of the Thatcher Government, to produce a survey of highly qualified manpower needs, and earned about £400 a year.

That left us short, but by no means catastrophically so. Our basic living costs were low. For the first few weeks after I came out of the army we were in a dreary bed-sitting room in Allen Street, Kensington, but by the early spring we were installed together with some utility furniture in a flat of three small rooms and a kitchen combined with a bathroom above a snack-bar in Marsham Street, Westminster. The location was impressively central, within three minutes of the Abbey in one direction and of Transport House (then Labour Party headquarters) in the other, as well as the Houses of Parliament within five. The building, which has been taken over and converted by the Westminster City Council, was however less elegant than was the district, and its immediate surroundings consisted of bomb sites adorned with weeds. It stuck up like a blackened tooth in an otherwise empty mouth. Sharing this tooth with us, in flats above and below, were two newly elected MPs, the Conservative Commander Maitland (he never seemed to have a Christian name) from Horncastle and John Freeman, the very model of a modern Labour major, who was there with the first of his several wives and fresh from his triumph in moving the Address at the beginning of the new Parliament and proclaiming the occasion as 'D-day in the battle for the new Britain'. We did not see much of either of them.

We stayed in Marsham Street for nearly three years until December 1948, and then perversely, I having just become a member of Parliament, moved out of division-bell range to a cavernous seven-roomed apartment on the two top floors of a post-Great Exhibition stucco mansion in Cornwall Gardens, South Kensington. Even there the rent was only £240 a year, so that with one room let out to a friend of Jennifer's, our housing costs were almost negligible by SW7 (or indeed most) standards. We stayed in Cornwall Gardens for five and a half years until we acquired 33 Ladbroke Square in Notting Hill, where we spent a quarter of a century; but that moves events well on into the area of later chapters.

Apart from rents, the prices of day-to-day items were in the immediate post-war years not nearly as different from pre-war ones as they were from those of today. Indeed our need for money was less than it would have been had we been a young married couple in 1938, for there was a shortage of household goods and severe restrictions on both the cost of restaurant meals and the money which could be taken abroad for holidays. Nevertheless I seem to have had a mild money obsession in 1946–7, which took the form not so much of a desire to make it (I might have done better in the City had this been so), as of uncharacteristic care in noting what I spent. For these two years, my diaries are disappointingly uninformative about what I did, but full of the minutiae of petty-cash transactions. These at least have the charm of recalling the precision of old denominations and the lowness of old prices. Thus one Monday in March 1946 I spent 3s on a taxi (having arrived back at Paddington from a weekend away), 5s 8¹/2d on lunch, 2s 4d on cigarettes, 3d on bus fares, 2d on newspapers, and 2s 1d (mysteriously) on telegrams.

We lived modestly, but we were not greatly inhibited by shortage of cash in doing the things that we wished to do. In the summer of 1946 we went to Ascona at the Swiss end of Lake Maggiore for our first post-war foreign holiday, and combined it with a day's swoop down into a chaotic Milan. In 1947 we went to France in June and to Lake Garda and Venice in September. In London we went to the theatre more than we do now, occasionally to Covent Garden when it reopened at the end of 1946, and frequently to the cinema, both to the relatively expensive palaces of Leicester Square and to local Gaumonts, Odeons and Classics. We ate out a good deal, both in Soho and in neighbourhood restaurants. On the other hand we did not own a motor car until 1953, five years after I had become an MP.

Our standard of living was subsidised by the fact that we had family houses available for weekends and for longer periods at Christmas, Easter and in the summer. It was Pontypool that we used mainly for these longer periods and the Morris houses for ordinary weekends. During 1946 the Morrises were at Henley-on-Thames, where they had moved early in the war, but at the end of that year they came back to their pre-war house in the Hampstead Garden Suburb, and we took to suburban weekends. I remember with particular vividness that in the great freeze-up (and fuel shortage) of early 1947 we had four or five successive Saturdays and Sundays of intensive tobogganning on Hampstead Heath. There were much-used hard-packed pistes down in various directions from near the Whitestone Pond, and the north London landscape improbably assumed a Breughel-like appearance.

I was continuously restive in my City job, but this was more because of a lack of vocation than because of inadequacy of salary. I thought there must be other things that I could do better. Above all, of course, this applied to being a member of Parliament, but while I could not be that my eye roved in various other directions. I played hard with the idea of reading for the bar, which I almost certainly would have done had the army not intervened when I left Oxford. But by 1946, although I took a number of preliminary steps, I was ultimately disinclined to get reinvolved in examinations followed by pupillage.

I applied for two university teaching jobs. One was an assistant lectureship in philosophy at Manchester under the redoubtable Professor Dorothy Emmet. Once again the Master of Balliol, recently ennobled as Lord Lindsay of Birker, was the agent. He probably thought it would be good for me to live in Manchester, and this outweighed what ought to have been his better judgement that, while he could just make a cryptographer out of me, he could not make a philosopher. Professor Emmet was more realistic. She took one look at me – in Manchester – decided that I wanted neither to live there nor to teach philosophy, and wisely appointed someone else. It was a lucky escape, probably by a large margin.

The other escape was narrower. After a brief period as an economics lecturer there, Tony Crosland became a fellow of Trinity College, Oxford, in 1947. That created a vacancy for the lectureship, for which at his suggestion I applied. At the time I did (mistakenly) want that job very much, but the governing body, I think narrowly, preferred (Sir) Fred Atkinson, subsequently assistant secretary-general of OECD and chief economic adviser to the Treasury. He was a better economist than I, but even more importantly it would have been a great mistake for me to have worked directly under Crosland, close and on the whole happy though our relationship was in those days. What I cannot understand, looking back, is why of the three prongs of Philosophy, Politics and Economics I never applied for a job teaching the one (Politics) which I might have done well, but only for the two at which I was less well qualified. Perhaps in those days there were fewer politics jobs available.

I also applied for a BBC post as a talks producer. I cannot remember what happened to that application, except that it foundered at some stage. My other and more effective response to the frustrations of being a low-paid financier was to begin to learn to write. In the six years or so following the 1940 encouraging remark of the Dean of Balliol I had written little and published practically nothing except for my election address in June 1945. Then, by acts of almost inexplicable generosity not obviously stemming from his detached character, the Prime Minister launched me on a writing career. First Attlee threw to me the editorship of a volume of his speeches delivered between May 1945 and November 1946. I selected them and wrote a few linking passages and an introduction of five hundred words. For this I was paid £50, which was in itself welcome, being worth £1000 today. Typical of both of us was what then followed. He sent me the cheque himself. I was slow to acknowledge. About five days later I received one of his famous self-typed pungent missives:

> Dear Roy,　I sent! you　　a
> cheque　　　fOR £50 a week　ago. I
> (have　not had?　an acknowleDgment.
> You'Rs　eVer,
> *C. R. Attlee.*

What other Prime Minister would ever have produced such a letter on his own typewriter? However, his acerbity did not hold out against my hasty letter of apology. Moreover there continued intact an arrangement made at the end of 1945 by which I should write a short (85,000 words it turned out) interim biography of him, and have a free run in his 10 Downing Street study of his fairly exiguous private papers in order to do so. This remarkable forthcomingness was really a tribute to my father (which became a posthumous one, for he died in April 1946), to whom Attlee felt deeply indebted for eight years of exceptional service as parliamentary private secretary. Apart from anything else the arrangement guaranteed me a publisher.

I wrote the book over the year from November 1946 to November 1947, and Heinemann published it in April 1948. It was all written in snatches, an evening or at best a weekend. In contrast with my subsequent habit, I never managed a continuous period of a few weeks when it was my central occupation. In these circumstances, and given my complete lack of experience, it was not a bad book. It was not a major work of scholarship or a profound analysis of character, but it was a cool and succinct account of the life up to 1945 of a cool and succinct man, and it reads unembarrassingly today. It did not sell enough to bring much in the way of direct financial reward, but it got a lot of review space, most of it favourable, and it gave me a certain position as a writer, which meant that I had no difficulty in publishing two more books with Heinemann before I switched to Collins in 1955.

Nonetheless, although I am in no way ashamed of the book itself, I am faintly ashamed of having written *Mr Attlee*. I do not much approve in principle of writing biographies of living persons, and I have never since contemplated doing one. Much more strongly, however, do I disapprove of books about a subject with whom the author is in a client relationship. And that I overwhelmingly was vis-à-vis Attlee. I was obviously bound to him by close family ties. He had been at our wedding and he was to become a godfather to our first child a year after the book – and in addition my main objective in life at the time was to become a member of his party in the House of Commons. Had I discovered some damaging facts or formed some hostile opinions about him (as it happened I did not), I could not possibly have expressed them without inhibition. Paradoxically, I had less trouble with Attlee or any other member of his family over this book than I have had with the relicts of almost all my other biographical subjects, but the principle nonetheless holds. I would not write another 'living' biography, although I might well be tempted to return to Attlee and attempt a short reappraisal from the very different perspective of the 1990s.

My father had become ill in the spring of 1945 and had got through the general election campaign of that summer only with considerable difficulty. For the last few months of the Churchill coalition he had been a junior minister, parliamentary secretary under W. S. Morrison at the Ministry of Town and Country Planning, and when the Labour Government was formed he had been transferred, in the same rank, to the Ministry of Education under Ellen Wilkinson. I think that Attlee might have put him higher had he not been sadly aware of how much his health was impaired. As it was this appointment proved an unhappy end to his career. He was hardly able to engage with the duties before he had to go into St Thomas's Hospital and face a hazardous operation. A neglected prostate gland enlargement had gravely infected his kidneys. When he had narrowly survived the relieving operation he resigned and returned to Pontypool for the winter. He then had a difficult choice, for a second and in those days still more risky operation was necessary if he was not to be a permanent invalid. He decided to take the chance and returned to St Thomas's in early April. It did not work and he died there on 26 April 1946 at the age of sixty-four.

I was shattered by his death. Measured either by intent or by result (and the two often fail to go together) he had been an almost perfect father to me. He was devoted, mind-awakening and enjoyable to be with. By political standards he was not very ambitious, but he had exceptional charm which long kept his memory alive amongst a range of sometimes surprising people, and he had a capacity, comparable oddly enough in my experience only with that of Anthony Crosland, to infuse a small gathering with either exhilaration or gloom according to his mood. Happily benignity was about five times as prevalent with him as with Crosland, and social sulkiness was almost wholly absent. His private impact was greater than his public fame, although that was not negligible.

On the evening that he died we were gathered up by the Attlees (again a surprisingly warm and spontaneous gesture for such a cool couple) and installed in 10 Downing Street for the night. On the following afternoon I took my mother back to Newport by train. Paddington Station was a hall of memories. It was the hinge of my father's life between Monmouthshire and Westminster, and he must have passed through it several thousand times, often with one or other of us. Three days later there was a public funeral in Pontypool, with crowds lining the streets. There was a lot of public grief, particularly but not exclusively there. A memorial clock tower was subscribed for and erected in Pontypool Park. Such physical commemoration was more frequent in the nineteenth century, and is a rare twentieth-century tribute to a local MP.

His death was an even greater deprivation for my mother than for me, and although she subsequently engaged in a lot of public activity she was I think never wholly happy for the remaining seven and a half years of her life. One odd effect was that she ceased abruptly to go to the Calvinist chapel to which I had been persuaded reluctantly to accompany her in my childhood and early adolescence. I never asked her why, but I think she must have thought that God had let her down. It was not that she could not bring herself to go unaccompanied by my father, for he, although devoted to hymn-singing, did not go to church or chapel unless he was committed to address the Brotherhood or perform some other public act. He was not hostile to religion or clergymen, but quietly agnostic.

His death also created a vacancy in Parliament for a very safe Labour seat. Within a few weeks the question of whether I should seek the nomination arose. Encouraged by some but by no means overwhelming local pressure, my mother and I were persuaded that I should do so. For me, any quick route to the House of Commons was at the time irresistible, for her it offered the immediate solace of something to lift her mind from her loss, and the longer-term one of the prospect of some continuity in the pattern of her life. It was a mistake, not because we lost, but because it was divisive, with friends and admirers of my father's going in different directions, and because it would have been much worse had we won, which we nearly did.

Throughout the second half of May and the whole of June one of the nearest British approaches to an American primary campaign was waged in Pontypool and the surrounding urban areas which made up the parliamentary division. I must have addressed at least twenty meetings of local Labour parties, miners' lodges and other trades union branches, as well as spending many hours calling on individuals who were thought to be influential.

There were a lot of candidates for this honey-pot of a seat, and there was no short-listing. As a result twelve of us turned up for the selection conference on the early evening of Saturday, 29 June. We all made speeches and answered a few questions, which put us well into the late evening. Then we waited in an adjacent room. Those whom I remember being present were Granville West, of whom more later, Eirene White (Tom Jones's daughter, later a middle-rank minister, now a life peer), Ernest Fernyhough (Harold Wilson's parliamentary private secretary in 1964–7) and Brinley Thomas, an attractive professor of economics at Cardiff, who mistakenly thought he might be of more use in the House of Commons and with whom I formed a sort of hospital-waiting-room friendship, intense but feverish.

There was a long delay after the last of us had spoken. We could not understand what was happening. Eventually an embarrassed regional official of the Labour Party appeared and said, 'Ladies and Gentlemen, there has been an unfortunate development. There are 220 delegates present in the room [an enormous number for any Labour Party selection conference], but only 208 credentials were received at the door, and, to make matters worse, 226 votes were cast on the first ballot. We have no alternative but to adjourn the conference until tomorrow afternoon when we hope you will all come back.' The primary atmosphere had produced too much of a Tammany touch, and tension dissolved into farce. We shuffled off to our houses or hotels in a mood of discontented anticlimax.

The next afternoon they ordered things better. However, it took a long time to go through six or seven eliminating ballots. Eventually only Granville West and I were left in for the final vote, in which he proceeded to beat me by 134 to 76. I was not surprised, although a little low, as I trundled back to London sitting up in a night train, thinking that I had been so long away from ICFC that the least I could do was to get back for 9.30 on the Monday morning.

It was a lucky miss, as at one level of consciousness I knew perfectly well. I cannot think exactly how the future would have worked out had I won, but I am sure it would have done so uneasily. Living when I was in Pontypool in the house which had been his, with my mother actively present, I would inevitably have been seen as a surrogate for my father, would have always been measured against him, and would have been found wanting in a whole range of ways, of which the difference in the balance we struck between local and national politics would have been only the most obvious. One hereditary chamber (which the House of Lords wholly was in those days) was more than enough.

At the bye-election Granville West was duly elected by a large majority. I had earned the plaudits of the Welsh Labour Party office by going to speak for him, but I am afraid that he never became a Jenkins family favourite. He was a successful local magistrates' court solicitor (although I doubt if he scored his greatest triumphs when my mother was presiding over the bench) of somewhat glossy appearance. Indeed Professor Thomas constantly referred to him as 'old striped pants' (although he was little older than the professor) during our long selection-conference vigils. But he never made any impact in the House of Commons. He sat there until 1958, when Gaitskell (without telling me, despite our closeness at the time) unaccountably made him one of the first batch of Labour life peers, and he was replaced by Leo Abse, another solicitor, who was more colourful even if he had other disadvantages. Lord Granville-West, as he became, made Gaitskell's action even more surprising by subsiding completely on ennoblement, hardly ever going to the Lords during the twenty-four years he was a peer. I suppose we reacted with typical and not very admirable family jealousy of a 'usurper'. I ought to have been more grateful to him for my escape from imprisonment in a family tower.

The unsuccessful Pontypool campaign in no way stilled my desire for engagement in another part of the political battlefield. But no opportunity arose for nearly two years. There were plenty of bye-elections, but I did not get near to any of them except for being conscripted by the London Labour Party to go and assist Harold Nicolson, who was an improbable and unsuccessful sixty-one-year-old Labour candidate in North Croydon in March 1948. It was very cold and that distinguished literary figure walked round looking depressed in a black homburg hat and an overcoat with an astrakhan collar. I was easily conscriptable because I had my eye on another possible bye-election in Central Southwark and wished to keep on good terms with the London Labour bureaucracy.

Why, it may be asked, had my life been so preoccupied for the previous three years by desire to get into the House of Commons? It was not just family piety. I was not a natural follower in parental grooves. Had my father remained a miner my lack of desire to follow him would have been as passionate as his own resolve that I should not do so. Even had he continued as primarily a local government luminary, I do not think that I would have sought fulfilment as a councillor or an alderman. I was, I suppose, too ambitious for that, although I did not see myself for nearly another twenty years as a major player on the political stage. But I had come to regard the Palace of Westminster, and in particular the chamber of the House of Commons, as the centre of national life. From the age of fifteen onwards I loved visiting it. My over-political university life made me see the Oxford Union as an ante-chamber of Westminster. In the University political coterie we not only pursued our own little careers but also followed form in the real arena, scanning Hansard and looking out for rising MPs to ask down. Then, during my army years, the House of Commons became even more of a London mecca, eagerly visited whenever a leave made it possible. In addition my interest in the classical period of British parliamentary politics gave me the view that the House of Commons was a place to go to young, fortified by a feeling that my father, with too much self-effacement, had allowed the silent Tom Griffiths to keep him out until it was almost too late.

So I became a young man in a hurry. There was of course an element of simple self-advancement about it. I was hardly seeking great financial rewards at a time when MPs' salaries moved hesitantly up from £600 to £1000 a year. From that point of view I would have done much better to have concentrated on the City. But I was seeking prestige and opportunity. However, there was more to it than that. I was a deeply committed supporter of the Attlee Government and a devotee of traditional British politics. I believed that the measured development of the welfare state and of a planned framework for the economy enhanced civilisation. And I thought it all could and should be done within the framework of the Gladstonian and Asquithian political system. This combination of views made the House of Commons of the late 1940s an infinitely desirable institution to which to belong.

There was nothing new about taking this starry-eyed view of it. Anthony Trollope, eighty years before, would probably have rather belonged to it than have written the Barchester novels. And Harold Nicolson, whose trudging round the streets of Croydon provoked this piece of introspection, could not see the light shining over Big Ben without wishing he were sitting under it. Neither of them had time to be disillusioned by Westminster: Trollope no time at all and Nicolson only ten years, whereas I, without comparable literary talents, have had more than four decades in one House or the other in which to grow cynical. Yet I do not find it difficult today, despite considerable changes in my beliefs and ambitions, to understand that eagerness of 1945–8.

Nor should I discount the sense of public service which my family background, accompanied by Balliol and fortified by Jennifer's even stronger feeling that this was what counted in life, created in me. The liberal optimism, which I described in Chapter 2 as being Balliol's main imprint on me, meant that, if accompanied by a reasonable self-confidence, the House of Commons was the natural place in which to try to exercise it.

The Southwark election, which came a few weeks after Croydon, was an odd affair from several points of view. First, the seat was represented by a reclusive rather upper-class figure called John Martin, who had surprisingly become a Labour MP at the age of nearly fifty in 1939. In 1948 he announced that he must resign urgently on grounds of ill-health. Perhaps he had some false medical diagnosis, for I believe he quickly came to regret his decision, and he lived another thirty-eight years until the age of ninety-four. During this long twilight he was glimpsed only fleetingly, like the Scholar Gypsy, but in the bar of Brooks's club rather than in some lone alehouse.

Second, the constituency was very small in area, being made up of two triangles, each with a hypotenuse of about three-quarters of a mile, the points of which met at the Elephant and Castle. Third, its electorate had shrunk from a respectable pre-war figure to about 25,000. The old Metropolitan Borough of Southwark, much smaller in area than the present London Borough of Southwark, had declined from an earlier population of nearly 200,000 to one of not much more than 80,000. Three seats were about to go into one at the pending redistribution. Since then a further three seats have been poured in, so that the present not over-large Southwark and Bermondsey constituency covers six pre-war divisions.

In 1948 the other two Southwark seats were represented by printing workers' trades union nominees. For the North division there was George Isaacs, the Minister of Labour in the Attlee Cabinet, then aged sixty-five but anxious to continue to serve in future Parliaments, which he did until 1959, and then survived another twenty years to the age of ninety-six. The member for the South-east division presented no problem, for he was already eighty and willing to retire, although he also survived into his nineties. (Southwark in 1939, although a foetid slum area, had a remarkably preservative effect upon its MPs; the three then sitting for the borough attained an average age of ninety-three and a half.)

A new man coming in for the Central division might however present

Isaacs, who was not a dominating or a demagogic personality, with an uncertain prospect of selection for the amalgamated constituency. He therefore persuaded the authoritatively minded and hierarchically impressed London Labour Party to insist that whoever was selected as candidate for the bye-election should give an undertaking not to contest the nomination to the combined seat. This made Central Southwark unattractive to many aspiring Labour MPs. To go through the travail of fighting a bye-election for the sake of twenty-one months of an unrenewable lease struck most people as a pretty bad bargain. Only someone as crazed as I was to get into the House of Commons, and also, in a curious way, as confident of his ability ultimately to fall on his feet, was likely to be attracted. Few were. At the selection conference on 23 March there was supposed to be one other outside candidate. He did not turn up. I was therefore left with a straight run against an able, rather sardonic local alderman, who had some friends but more enemies. I won by twenty votes to eight, was overjoyed by my luck, and prepared for the bye-election in five weeks' time.

John Martin had won in the bumper year of 1945 by 9300 to 3600. Three years later, with the Government not unnaturally in a mid-term trough, my problem was to prevent this reflecting itself in a massive abstention or, worse still, a big swing to the Tories. We fought a short (ten-day) but, for a moribund area, vigorous campaign. Even in that postage-stamp-size constituency we fitted in nine public meetings (and filled them all, with audiences of between a hundred and a thousand). The most successful speakers were Hannen Swaffer, the old charlatan of a journalist whom I mentioned earlier, and Bob Mellish, then a young MP for the adjoining constituency of Bermondsey. Southwark hardly counted as a needle contest, but it was near enough to Fleet Street to attract a fair amount of newspaper coverage, although I have no recollection of holding press conferences such as are the daily and central feature of modern bye-elections. The journalists actually came to the meetings and even reported the speeches.

The result was satisfactory rather than inspiring. Although polling little more than 40 per cent of my losing Solihull vote I nevertheless won by just under two-to-one. The constituency produced a better turn-out than at the 1945 general election, although it remained well within the bracket of inner-city apathy, and also registered a distinct but containable swing against the Government. My reported comment after the declaration was: 'The result shows that, despite the present national difficulties, the majority of people do appreciate the way the Labour Government is trying to solve our problems.' It could be regarded as suitably restrained and determinedly loyal. I was naturally labelled by the press as a complete Attlee supporter, although in fact the campaign I had fought had been more Crippsian than Attleean, with great emphasis on the responsible management of the economy so that Marshall Aid should be a springboard and not just a subsidy.

In any event I was an MP by the early afternoon of Friday, 30 April 1948, and remember feeling at a loose end, although contentedly so, as I waited to take my seat on the following Tuesday. I was moreover the youngest MP, displacing Edward Carson, MP for Thanet and the son of the old leader of the Ulster revolt, in this mildly enviable but necessarily impermanent role, for which at twenty-seven and a half I was in any event rather old. I nevertheless held the 'baby of the House' title until I was superseded in November 1950 by Edward Boyle, who after two weeks was himself replaced by Anthony Wedgwood Benn.

On the Tuesday afternoon I was introduced by the incongruous combination of the London area whip (which was normal) and the Prime Minister (which was not). I think it may have been the first time that a bye-election victor had been brought in by a Prime Minister since Lloyd George (and Balfour) introduced Nancy Astor when she became the first woman to take her seat in 1919. It was an over-egged custard, and it was unlike Attlee's culinary style to have produced it. Yet it was entirely his doing. It was certainly not my suggestion, and the whips I think were against. It was too rich a diet for my own good, although the dyspepsia was produced mainly in others who not unnaturally thought my silver spoon was too much in evidence.

I made my maiden speech a month later. It was about 4.30 on a Thursday afternoon during the committee stage of the Finance Bill, which was then taken entirely on the floor of the House, and was thus at a good time with divisions impending and a lot of people about, but was not remotely a great occasion. It was in a quiet way a success. I had carefully prepared a taut little essay which talked briefly about the bye-election campaign and the constituency of Central Southwark, but which turned quickly to a general defence of Cripps's budget of that year and in particular of his 'special contribution', a small non-recurring capital tax on individuals. It was a fiscal device of which I was twenty years later to use a near copy, again on a non-recurring basis. This could be held to point to a certain consistency, although my views on capital taxation had in fact substantially moderated over the two decades. The 1948 speech lasted just under a quarter of an hour and had been learned by heart so that I delivered it apparently spontaneously but almost word perfectly in accordance with my text. It was a feat which I never again repeated in the House of Commons.

I came after David Eccles, who had opened the debate, and was followed by Arthur Salter, the former Gladstone Professor at All Souls who was then MP for Oxford University and in general a crusty old thing, although on this occasion noticeably generous, while choosing his words in a way which neatly captured the minor-key impact which my speech had achieved: 'I can say with complete sincerity that I have hardly ever heard an honourable member speaking for the first time in this House, and without notes, who has spoken so charmingly and with such clarity as the honourable member for Central Southwark. I say that with no less sincerity because I take a diametrically opposite view from him.'

Later a more practised payer of compliments in the shape of Oliver Stanley, something of a Prince Rupert of debate until his premature death in 1950, made an obvious but gracious point: 'The honourable member made a most admirable maiden speech which we all enjoyed enormously, with a pleasure which was not diminished by the affectionate remembrance in which many of us hold his father,' and then, being as practised an inserter of stilettos as a payer of compliments, praised me above all for my 'candour', which he claimed had blown sky-high Cripps's excuses and exposed his real motives.[1]

Although the speech was on a divisive subject about which in substance if not in manner I had spoken more controversially than is normally considered appropriate for maiden speeches, it was more complimented from the Conservative than from the Labour side of the House. Looking back I think this may have been because, combined with the Attlee patronage, it was too much of a 'little Jack Horner speech'. It was too perfectly in line with Government policy. I was a tremendous loyalist during my first years in the House. I stuck closely to an economic policy last, and I defended, sometimes with original arguments and with growing debating skill, the Government position. Thus, in my second speech in July, I praised both Marshall Aid and the Government's response to it; in the autumn I argued strongly in favour of the Iron and Steel (Nationalisation) Bill and eagerly served and spoke frequently in the committee which sat for several months upon it; and in the spring of 1949 I was as faithful an auxiliary of Cripps and his Treasury team in support of his second Budget as I had been of his first, but more loquaciously so.

I was useful, but too much like an advocate with a brief for what I said to be interesting. I waited to see what the Government was going to do and then devoted my speeches to defending decisions made rather than attempting to influence those which were still to be taken. Maybe it was all right for a young member cutting his parliamentary teeth, but it would not have done for long, and fortunately it did not have to do so. By my late thirties, as opposed to my late twenties, I had become almost excessively devoted to trying to push particular policies which commanded my conviction, with indifference to whether or not they accorded with the party line. But that was all in the future in 1948–9.

I found being an MP in the late 1940s an easy life. There was still an enormous Labour majority, which had been elected in 1945, so that whipping was mostly light. Southwark was undemanding. I went there often – it was only a ten-minute and one-penny tramcar-ride away – and tried to find non- or quasi-political organisations to address. But no one seemed to expect this. Neither of the other members did it, nor had my predecessor. Constituency correspondence was negligible. Advice bureaux were more popular, but not much. It was one of the last of the pocket boroughs.

The trouble was that its 1832 was approaching fast, and unless I was going to balance becoming an MP at twenty-seven by ceasing to be one at twenty-nine, I had to find another constituency during 1949. In 1948, however, that did not greatly oppress, and I remember a sense of freedom which I had not experienced since leaving Oxford. ICFC had involved working office hours for five and a half days a week (the City still worked Saturday mornings) and fitting all holiday plans into three weeks plus bank holidays. It was the only time in my life when I was formally so constricted. In various subsequent offices I worked much harder, most notably when I was Chancellor, and, as I record in Chapter 12, once went four and a half months without having a single day free from pressing work. But the allocation of time was then my own decision. Had I judged it wise I could have taken any day or week or even a month in the summer off, and no one would have gainsaid me. I was therefore delighted to be free of ICFC restrictions, light though they were, and remember taking particular pleasure in walking round an open-air sculpture exhibition in Battersea Park one Thursday morning in June, and in going first to Pontypool for ten days and then, after a few Southwark engagements, to France and Italy for four weeks in the summer recess. It was not that I wanted to do nothing. I was already beginning to work on what became a book called *Mr Balfour's Poodle*. But I wanted to do things in my own time, and was lucky to have permanently achieved this happy state before I was thirty.

In January 1949 I made my first and last expedition abroad as part of an official parliamentary delegation. It was to Italy, and was memorable as well as enjoyable, mainly because it stands in my mind poised on two frontiers, both that between a Europe at war and the Europe of the Community, and that between the travel habits of the 1920s and 1930s and those of the modern world.

The delegation did not emulate Randolph Churchill, who when asked by an Italian immigration officer a couple of years before in what capacity he was visiting the country was reputed to have replied, 'as a conqueror.' Nonetheless it was less than four years from the end of the war, and when we were unwisely given an over-lavish luncheon in a restaurant with a glasshouse-style front extension on the waterfront at Anzio, around which there clustered a good proportion of the idle population of the still-(British)-damaged town, curiosity, envy of the food, and resentment at the damage seemed to be present in about equal proportions.

On the other hand we were enthusiastically received by all the leading figures of the nascent Italian Republic, which compensated for its own youth by having venerable leaders. De Gasperi was not only the most notable, but also, at sixty-seven, the youngest. Einaudi (seventy-four) was President of the Republic, Bonomi (seventy-five) President of the Senate, and Sforza (seventy-five) Foreign Minister. At one banquet I even sat next to Orlando (eighty-eight) who had been the fourth side of the quadrilateral with Wilson, Lloyd George and Clemenceau at the Paris Peace Conference in 1919. All these old men were full of an enthusiasm for a united Europe of the future which they mistakenly hoped would be shared by the British. Pope Pius XII (Pacelli) also received us at length and with courtesy, but perhaps with more reserve. He had survived the war without endearing himself to either side, and reserve had no doubt become habitual. Furthermore he was the first of several Popes I was to meet who spoke English convincingly while hardly understanding it, which made conversation confusing.

The travelling was fascinating because it must have been one of the last occasions when a full-scale parliamentary delegation crossed Europe by train. We went to Paris by Golden Arrow, dined at the Embassy, and proceeded by the Simplon Express from the Gare de Lyon. It was like Harold Nicolson's description of Lord Curzon's journey to the Lausanne Conference in 1922. At Milan we transferred to two saloons of the royal train of the House of Savoy which had been taken over by the Republic, and so proceeded to Rome. They remained with us until we returned to Milan. From London to our hotel in the Via Veneto we took over forty hours in a stately and (for me) never repeated progress.

Rab Butler was the leader of the delegation and taught me that whenever confronted with a guard of honour, an uncertain *huissier*, an hotel manager or a papal chamberlain, the best thing to do was silently but graciously to incline one's head and move firmly forward in the direction in which one thought one ought to be going. He also regaled me with constant back-handed remarks, the one which has most stuck in my mind being 'The trouble with Anthony [Eden] is that he has no intellectual interests.'

We also had Mr Speaker Clifton-Brown as a rather surprising participant, particularly as he appeared not much to like 'abroad', and, amongst others, John Boyd-Carpenter, Lords Beatty (the son of the Admiral) and Holden (a Labour *bon vivant* who had written an evocative pre-war book called *The Land of France*) and my old family friend, Ivor Bulmer-Thomas. During a day trip to Naples Thomas and I escaped after lunch and he took me to see Benedetto Croce, then aged eighty-two, in a fine book-lined apartment set like a pearl in the mud of a Neapolitan slum. I remember Croce's library better than his words.

In February, Philip Noel-Baker, Secretary of State for Commonwealth Relations, asked me to be his parliamentary private secretary, and although the functions of this department were distant from the bent of my parliamentary interests, I accepted without much hesitation. I was keen to have a foot even on the lowest rung of the ladder of office, and there were some advantages in the split between Noel-Baker's portfolio and my interests. The rules were that PPSs should not speak too critically of the Government on any subject (not a problem for me), certainly never vote against it and not speak at all (in the House) on anything to do with the department to which they were accredited.

I did this job for a year, until Noel-Baker was shunted to be Minister of Fuel and Power, outside the Cabinet, and sensibly thought that he ought to have a miners' MP as his PPS. I did not make a great deal of the opportunity, partly because, although I liked him, I did not find Noel-Baker easy to work for. He was clever, high-minded and even inspirational (although mainly with women), but he was unco-ordinated, lacked critical judgement and was a weak minister. He also had the misfortune both to irritate Ernest Bevin and to be frightened of him. He had been his Minister of State at the Foreign Office for the first year of the Government, after which Bevin had insisted on having him moved and Attlee had rather cruelly made the old disarmer Secretary of State for Air. Noel-Baker had escaped from there to the Commonwealth Relations Office in 1947, but his relations with Bevin, who dominated the whole external policy of the Government, were a fatal bar to his full effectiveness as Commonwealth Secretary. The Prime Ministers and High Commissioners of the old Dominions and of Ireland, India, Pakistan and Ceylon, which was all the Commonwealth was in those days, knew perfectly well where power lay and that it was not in the Commonwealth Relations Office.

However, I had the advantage of seeing the inside of a department of state, which I would not otherwise have done for another seventeen years, and enjoyed observing the appurtenances of power, including in particular attending meetings in the Secretary of State's great room, with its huge imperial globe, which had improbably descended from Joseph Chamberlain to Philip Baker. Also, in those still austere days, I enjoyed the frequent government hospitality meals over which Noel-Baker presided with grace. But I never visited a dominion, not even Ireland, if that was a proper name for it at that stage, and my PPS-ship never became the centre of my political life. I shed no tears when it came to an end after a year, and when a short time later G. R. Strauss, then Minister of Supply, asked me if I would work for him in a similar capacity I declined, although I think that he and I would have got on easily.

It was in the summer of 1949 that, provoked by a prolonged bout of the imprecise, lowering, although never disabling psychosomatic pains which have occasionally afflicted me throughout my adult life, I went to see a psychiatrist. He was an impressive man who subsequently enjoyed a distinguished medical career and died only a few years ago. After a long consultation he pronounced a mixture of diagnosis and prognosis. He took my condition seriously, but thought that I might nonetheless survive for a normal span provided that I led a quiet life. Subjecting myself to any degree of strain or nervous pressure would however be unwise and even dangerous. I took notice of his prescription to the extent of being depressed by it for about three months, but not to that of allowing it to disrupt any present or future activities. I have occasionally wondered whether he recalled this consultation when I became Chancellor of the Exchequer or President of the European Commission or founded a new political party. I cite this not so much to cause medical scepticism as to amuse myself and perhaps to encourage some others cast down by sombre prognoses.

What was central to my political life at that time was the search for another constituency. A major redistribution (the first since 1918) came into effect in 1949, so there was a considerable state of flux about candidatures and a number of difficult judgements to be made about the winnability of seats. I turned down two, one wisely and the other foolishly, two turned me down at the selection-conference stage, and I was finally adopted for the one which I probably most wanted from the beginning. The one I rejected wisely was Poole. The one I rejected unwisely was Hammersmith North, where D. N. Pritt, near-Communist King's Counsel, looked impregnable as an Independent Labour member, but was not. The two constituencies which rejected me were Eton and Slough, which preferred the already sixty-one-year-old Fenner Brockway, and, being more Slough than Eton, duly elected him by a 4000 majority, but failed in 1964, which would have been inconvenient for me, and Ogmore, a Glamorgan valley seat, where Walter Padley, an ILP (that is, left-wing but anti-Communist figure like Brockway), narrowly beat me and then proceeded to beat his Conservative opponent by 26,000.

With the Parliament four and a half years old at the time of this last defeat I was becoming dismayed and even a little desperate. I had one last shot in my locker, which was the Stechford division of

Birmingham, where the selection conference was due to take place the week after Ogmore. It was late because, although it was a new constituency with a name which had never previously appeared on the parliamentary map, it was substantially the successor to the old Yardley division, the 1945-elected Labour member for which could not make up his mind whether he wanted to continue in Parliament or go to a full-time job with his union. He was called Wesley Perrins, had one of the broadest Black Country accents (he came from Stourbridge) ever heard in the House of Commons and was a popular local member, despite or because of the fact that his heart was never in the House of Commons. The Stechford Labour Party was therefore prepared to wait for his slow decision. But I could not wait without trying elsewhere, for there was no guarantee of what Perrins would decide, or that I would get the nomination if he decided to withdraw. There was a strong local candidate who was currently chairman of the constituency Labour Party.

I had the active and powerful backing of Alderman (later Sir) Joseph Balmer, who was to be an outstanding Lord Mayor of Birmingham in 1955–6, and who was already the most buoyant and influential figure in the constituency. I owe my adoption for Stechford, and the twenty-seven years of secure and largely untroubled constituency life which it gave me, more to him than to anyone else. The selection conference was far from being a walk-over, however. It was, indeed, much the most difficult hurdle, with one possible exception in 1954 (see Chapter 5), which I ever had to surmount in Stechford.

It took place on the afternoon of Sunday, 16 October 1949, and was attended by about seventy delegates, a more modest and normal number than the 200-plus of Pontypool. There were two other aspirants remaining at this stage, Ron Tranter, the local chairman, and Fred Mulley, then a fellow of St Catharine's College, Cambridge, who had fought Sutton Coldfield in 1945 immediately after being a prisoner-of-war in Germany for five years. They were both slightly older than me. On the first ballot Tranter was a few votes ahead of me, while Mulley was clearly third with eleven votes. I got nearly the whole of these as second preferences and went to a small but decisive lead of six votes.

As is often the case in politics this narrow edge made a great difference to our futures. Tranter behaved well personally. He was far to the left of me, and would sometimes make trouble politically, but he showed no personal animosity. He never came again near another public office, not even as a councillor, and he gradually dropped out of politics soon after he was forty. Mulley became member for a still safer seat in Sheffield, which he represented for thirty-three years and was Secretary of State for both Education and Defence.

The successful outcome at Stechford transformed my morale over that autumn of 1949. Apart from anything else, I began to look forward to the general election which had to come in 1950, instead of disliking its approach as I had done while I had no seat to fight. I went enthusiastically to Birmingham five or six times in that November and December, but I also continued to make frequent short excursions to the Elephant and Castle and the Walworth Road. Indeed being adopted for Stechford slightly increased my attentiveness towards Southwark. Any resentment which I had about not being allowed to try for the combined Southwark seat was dissipated, and my general zest was also increased. Even after I was elected for Stechford I continued for many years to pay once- or twice-yearly visits to the Southwark Labour Party and give them extremely hardline Gaitskellite appraisals of the general political situation. This hardness they liked, for 80 per cent of them were just as hard-line themselves.

Stechford, of course, got much more attention, both before and after my first election there. But there was never any question of my going to live in Birmingham, or even acquiring the smallest *pied-à-terre* there. The issue simply never arose. For the first year or so I stayed with a variety of hospitable but by no means rich or lavishly housed party members, with occasionally a night or so in a central Birmingham hotel. At the 1950 election I stayed for most of the three-week campaign in the George Hotel, Solihull, about two miles from the southern edge of the constituency, where I had also stayed throughout the 1945 campaign. Then, during 1951, I began to stay more and more with a couple called Austin and Dink Hitchman. I was with them for the whole of the campaign leading up to the election in October of that year, and the arrangement worked so easily that I repeated this at each of the next six general elections. Only in October 1974, the last election which I fought in Stechford, and when I was in any event away from the constituency a good deal, did I campaign from a Birmingham hotel.

The Hitchmans lived in a small but comfortably furnished semi-detached 1930s house on the border between the nucleus of Old Stechford and the large council estates of Glebe Farm and Lea Village, and thus in the heart of the constituency both geographically and psychologically. Stechford had a limited amount of rather neat middle-class property and some socially indeterminate older housing, although hardly a single building which was there before 1870, but almost no professional class, except for a minimal scattering of doctors and clergymen. It could not have been more different in this respect from the Hillhead division of Glasgow for which I was to become member thirty-two years later. This difference was reflected in the contrasting place of higher education in the two constituencies. Hillhead is dominated by Glasgow's two universities, its major teachers' training college, its medical schools, its School of Art and other specialised institutions, supplemented at the secondary stage by a quiverful of notable academies and high schools.

Stechford was mostly remote from higher learning. It was essentially a skilled manual workers' constituency. But it was not poor. Birmingham at that period, with a booming British motor industry, was relatively a very prosperous city. In 1954, amazing though it seems today, Leicester was placed on some reputable scale of measurement as having the highest income per head of any European city. Birmingham must have been close, probably only statistically behind because, without a hosiery trade, it then had fewer women working.

Stechford itself did not contain many factories. Metropolitan-Cammell (which had made *wagons-lits*, including one I once stepped into in Belgrade, and was currently making 'blue' Pullman trains for British Rail), Wolseley Motors, Booth Aluminium (a subsidiary of Alcan) and Southalls (a subsidiary of Smith and Nephew, which made surgical dressings and sanitary towels and employed almost exclusively women) were about all there was. These firms could have employed barely a fifth of the manufacturing population of Stechford. The rest went out of the constituency to work, principally to a ring of great factories with resonant Midlands names which surrounded it like grandstands round a football pitch: Dunlop Rubber, Fisher and Ludlow, BSA, Lucas Industries, Rover Motors and, a little further away, Imperial Metals and the Austin works at Longbridge. Stechford in 1950 was a highly paid (which then meant about £15 a week) manual workers' residential district, with about half the population in council houses (the flats had hardly begun), exporting its male population during the day just as much as did a middle-class suburb of London like Sutton or Surbiton. Commonwealth immigrants barely existed, although there were quite a lot of Welsh from the 1930s and Irish from the 1940s. The Roman Catholic influence was significant.

Austin Hitchman, although he did not work in a Birmingham factory, was a representative Stechford figure. He was employed by Baker Perkins of Peterborough, and went round the country, although without a motor car, servicing and repairing the bakery ovens which they made. He was a skilled and well-paid craftsman, only moderately interested in politics. His wife was then the activist, although as the 1950s and still more the 1960s went on she too became a passive and only semi-committed Labour voter, whose link with the local party was only through me. Sometimes more vigorous Labour supporters expressed surprise and even impatience that I did not press the Hitchmans into more active party work. I countered firmly by saying that the service they performed (and the burden they accepted) by having me to stay was far greater than any amount of canvassing or attendance at meetings. It in fact suited me very well to have hosts who were uninvolved in any local party faction fights. I also thought there was a lot to be said for being kept in touch with that segment of Stechford voters which mostly voted Labour but was quite capable of floating.

Both the Hitchmans and their two daughters (aged eleven and four when I first went to their house) became close family friends, and often stayed with us in London and in various houses which we took for Augusts. In 1965 Austin Hitchman died suddenly in his mid-fifties, but Dink Hitchman remained a welcoming hostess as long as I was in Stechford. They contributed greatly to the ease of my constituency life, which was a helpful factor in the unexpectedly successful way in which, at least up to 1976, my political career developed.

Looking back I suppose that I was by modern standards (particularly those now applying in the Conservative Party) an old-style member. I descended on the constituency for what was at first a weekend a month (although it latterly became more like a day a month), with one or sometimes two supplementary visits to fulfil specific engagements, and for a week in each September. But I was always careful not to cancel an engagement once it was accepted and never to give a blank refusal to a request for a visit, although frequently to juggle it into a time which suited me. I dealt meticulously by correspondence and in advice-bureaux interviews with individual cases, but I hardly ever raised constituency issues on the floor of the House of Commons. I rarely asked parliamentary questions (except for an occasional supplementary to the Prime Minister or some other senior minister) or used adjournment debates. But I sometimes (and successfully) went to see ministers on constituency issues, and made perhaps ten House of Commons speeches a year on national issues. I never had any personal quarrels in Stechford (one advantage of semi-detachment) and the political hiccups, as will be seen, were almost all confined to the first few years. And the Stechford electorate, while it proved more than averagely 'swingy' (in both directions), never got near to putting me out of Parliament.

It began even better than it mostly continued. The February 1950 election gave me a majority of 12,400, and made Stechford look the second or third safest of the thirteen Birmingham seats. The great Labour majority of 1945 had disappeared and the Attlee Government, already tired, had to get used to living with a majority of only six. But I, at the age of twenty-nine, had for the first time a secure parliamentary prospect ahead, as well as two years of parliamentary experience behind me, and hoped that I was at last free of trudging round the country looking for a constituency, an experience at once nerve-racking and mildly humiliating, of which I had had more than enough since the autumn of 1944.

# CHAPTER FIVE

# *The Evolution of a Gaitskellite*

During my first three years in the House of Commons I was not particularly identified with either the right or the left of the Labour Party. I was regarded as an Attlee man – up to a point correctly – and Attlee was always careful not to get himself committed to tribal loyalties. But although I was given an Attlee label, the two senior ministers who attracted something like hero-worship from me were Stafford Cripps and Aneurin Bevan. The one I talked to most was Hugh Dalton, who had re-entered the Cabinet six months after his accidental budget leak and dramatic fall from the Exchequer, but as Chancellor, this time, only of the Duchy of Lancaster. I did not exactly admire him, although I enjoyed his company and was flattered by his indiscretions. Ernest Bevin's foreign policy mostly commanded my support, for my left/right ambiguity never made me doubt the need for American commitment in Europe, through both NATO and Marshall Aid, but I was not perceptive enough at that stage fully to appreciate through the elephantine pedestrianism of his parliamentary speeches the massive quality of his personality and achievement. Herbert Morrison I thought of as a party-machine boss, skilled at his trade, but operating a little below the level of events. Gaitskell, although I supported him as Chancellor, I hardly knew until after the fall of the Government.

Cripps and Bevan were vastly different from each other. Cripps was a remote god. He strode along the corridors of the Palace of Westminster with at best a frosty nod of recognition, and his speeches were masterpieces of disdainful lucidity. Bevan was not nearly so physically remote, although in a more florid way he was just as disdainful. He must have been very quick in the discharge of official business (and he was by no means a bad administrator), for he sat in the smoking room nearly every parliamentary day from 5.30 until 7.30 or 8.00 expatiating to a large circle of intimates and would-be intimates on politics and life. I, for a time, joined the category of would-be intimates. He also made spectacular debating speeches, devoted at this stage to the discomfiture of the Tories rather than to that of the other half of the Labour Party.

While I cherished these parliamentary 'crushes' I could not possibly be categorised as a man of the hard right, for my heroes were the traditional leaders of the left, although in Cripps's case this had become little more than an ancient affiliation, but not one which he wished to deny. However, both my enthusiasms were to be dissipated during my third year in the House, one by the sad collapse of Cripps's health and his disappearance to a Swiss clinic, and the other by what I regarded as the intolerable nature of Bevan's behaviour towards Gaitskell (Cripps's successor as Chancellor) and towards the Government generally when he (Bevan) resigned in April 1951.

Gaitskell's replacement of Cripps in October 1950 meant that a new man had leaped over Bevan to become one of the inner circle of the Government. But at least he had leaped into an office for which Bevan, apart from a general belief in his own ability to seize the essentials of any job, probably did not consider himself particularly suited. When Morrison replaced Ernest Bevin at the Foreign Office six months later it was a different matter. Not only did the grievance become cumulative, but Bevan considered that he would have been an excellent Foreign Secretary, whereas Morrison proved a hopeless one. Even the displaced Bevin grumpily agreed with the preference. 'I'd sooner have had Nye than 'Erbert,' he is reported to have said.[1] It was Attlee's one major failure of deftness in his Cabinet dispositions. Even so, it did not justify Aneurin Bevan's surprisingly successful attempt to make an ideology and found a major faction on the basis of a personal grievance.

At a level of politics well down the mountainside from these elevated events, the ways in which I endeavoured to make a mark were just as 'broad church' Labour as was my choice of ministerial heroes. I continued to speak mainly in economic debates and to take a responsible line on wage restraint, public expenditure control and priority for the balance of payments. But I was a believer in further nationalisation. I have already described how eagerly I had supported the 1949 Steel Bill in committee, and my public/private frontier did not stop at steel. In 1950 I wrote an article for *Tribune*,* to which journal of the left I was

---

*\*Tribune*, founded by Cripps, George Strauss and Bevan in 1937, had been Bevan's organ for his campaign of criticism of Churchill during the war, but by the late 1940s, with Bevan in the Government and his faithful henchman Michael Foot in the editorial chair, it was regarded as quite respectable in ministerial circles, more so than the *New Statesman*, which was seen as unsound on the Soviet threat and on NATO. *Tribune* swung into a more factious position with Bevan's resignation.

for eighteen months or so a frequent contributor, advocating the public ownership of at least one of the five major motor manufacturers.

In the autumn of 1949 I had written there arguing for the harder-line approach to the House of Lords: no reform of composition, because that was a Tory trap leading into the quicksands of a more influential but still reactionary second chamber, but a concentration upon the restriction of powers. As a piece of radical doctrine this was not to the left of Campbell-Bannerman, but it was opposed to the thinking of Addison and Jowitt, the Labour leaders in the Lords, and of Morrison in the Commons. My knowledge of and interest in it stemmed from my involvement in the early stages of writing *Mr Balfour's Poodle*, a short book on the constitutional struggle of 1909–11. This was my first venture into early-twentieth-century or late-nineteenth-century history. It did not see the light of publisher's day for nearly another five years.

Then in the spring of 1951 I produced a *Tribune* pamphlet of about 7000 words advocating a stringent programme of capital taxation and satirically entitled, I think at the suggestion of Michael Foot, *Fair Shares for the Rich*. That marked the apogee of my excursion to the left, not particularly because of the *Tribune* association, but much more because of the almost Robespierrean nature of the contents. It was a harsh and rigid doctrine which I preached, and one which now seems to me (as it would have for at least three decades past) to pay little or no regard to historical continuity or to the organic relationships of society, let alone to that now overworked concept of incentive. Nevertheless this doctrine continued to be central to my political thought, although expressed in a less crudely mechanistic way, at least up to the publication of *New Fabian Essays* in May 1952.

This was a collection of eight papers, presumptuously modelled upon the original *Fabian Essays in Socialism*, which Shaw, Webb, Graham Wallas, Annie Besant and five others had produced in 1889. We had the excuse that our essays were no less authentically produced under the auspices of the Fabian Society and sprang out of an intensive series of small conferences which had assembled at Buscot Park (both the pea-green Rolls-Royces and the swallow-tailed footmen of 1939 had gone) and occasionally at University College, Oxford, over the previous two and three-quarter years. We were also blessed by a preface from Attlee. Richard Crossman was the editor and wrote one essay. The other contributors, apart from me, were Anthony Crosland, Margaret Cole, Austen Albu, Ian Mikardo, Denis Healey and John Strachey.

My essay was entitled 'Equality',[2] and began with the unequivocal statement that 'The desire for greater equality has been part of the inspiration of all socialist thinkers and of all socialist movements.' But it was revisionist in what came to be thought of as the Gaitskell/Crosland sense of the late 1950s in that it treated nationalisation as a secondary question, unimportant for its own sake, although probably a necessary concomitant of a further advance to equality. The essay was also incipiently Gaitskellite by virtue of its dismissal of Communism as having nothing to do with equality either in theory or in practice. Marxism–Leninism had always 'been more interested in capitalist maldistribution as a flaw to be used for the overthrow of the system than as an evil to be rectified for its own sake'. 'Uninterested in individuals', Communism had not surprisingly produced less equality in the Soviet Union than in 'any of the welfare states of the West, and less even than [in] some of the more purely capitalist countries'.

The essay also recognised a possible conflict between equality and liberty. 'Obviously there are ways in which it is easier to tyrannize over a society of equals, in which nobody enjoys prestige or power except in so far as he earns it by his contribution to society (the value of which must be judged by those who at the time exercise the dominating influence), than over a society in which certain individuals enjoy undeserved but almost inalienable hereditary rights of wealth or influence.' But I then proceeded to resolve the dilemma in what now strikes me as at once a sophistical and naïve way. 'Equally obviously, a society which destroys these privileges and yet escapes tyranny will have achieved a more complete freedom than one which can only defend liberty by restricting many of its benefits to a few. How high the sights should be set must depend upon the stage of development of the particular society. The fact that Whiggery was necessary to the creation of English political liberty in the seventeenth and eighteenth centuries does not mean that it is necessary to its maintenance in the second half of the twentieth century.'

Here, while protesting too much that I was not going to use it for the time being, there were signs that I had at least spotted the emergency exit which might lead me thirty-five years later to proclaim, with my tongue not far in my cheek, that four of the best bastions against Thatcherism were the monarchy, the House of Lords, the Church of England and the ancient universities. I would never deny that my political positions have changed a good deal over the decades. I would regard it as a sign of a dead mind if they had not. But I like to believe that the movement has been in a straight line or at least along a steady curve rather than in a series of irrational or opportunistic zigzags. A rereading of *New Fabian Essays* gave me partial reassurance on this point.

The outbreak of the Korean War in June 1950 was an important stage in the evolution of my position in the Labour Party spectrum. As befitted a future biographer of Harry Truman I had no doubt that the United States was right to resist this Communist act of aggression and that the British Government was right to support the resistance. It followed from this that I supported the substantial, perhaps excessive, British rearmament programme which was announced in the early autumn of that year and which dominated Gaitskell's thirteen months as Chancellor of the Exchequer. I also supported the immediate measures of sending troops to Korea and calling up some reserve forces to mount a show of strength in Britain against possible Soviet moves in the West to balance their cat's-paw strike in the east.

What was called the Z Reserve was to be mobilised on a lottery basis that summer and autumn for two or three weeks of fitting into formations and refresher training. Those of us who had been demobilised fairly young at the end of the war were liable for inclusion in the draw. But as many fewer than the numbers available were required the War Office was only too willing to exempt certain categories, which needless to say included members of Parliament. Tony Crosland, Woodrow Wyatt and I, who were close friends, conceived a late-night idea of rejecting the exemption and renewing our soldiering experience, which was then only four and a half years distant. We thought it would give practical expression to our commitment to Western defence, and maybe enable us to deal more easily with constituents who showed less enthusiasm for being re-embodied.

We got as far as applying to the War Office, which reluctantly accepted our requests. Then we got cold feet. First, it became apparent that the last thing the army wanted was to have a lot of young Labour MPs monitoring the mobilisation. Second, we were going to have to serve in ranks well below those from which we had been demobilised. Third, there was of course no question of our serving together; that rather took the fun out of the prospect. Fourth, the three weeks were going to be extraordinarily difficult to reconcile with constituency and other commitments. So we humiliatingly withdrew. The humiliation was mitigated by the almost audible sigh of relief which emerged from the War Office.

This foolish little episode did however illustrate that we were eagerly if ineffectively committed to a strong British response. At first that did not separate me from my Bevanite friends. Bevan allowed himself to be shifted from the Ministry of Health to the Ministry of Labour in January 1951 on the ground that his new department was closer to the rearmament effort. As late as 15 February he made a notable defence of the Government and of the full rearmament programme of £4700 million. 'We shall carry it through; we shall fulfil our obligations to our friends and allies,' he concluded. It was an exceptionally powerful speech, wholly commanding the House with its range and passion.

Three weeks later Morrison replaced Ernest Bevin at the Foreign

Office, and six weeks after that Bevan (with Harold Wilson and John Freeman) resigned from the Government in protest against the charges on false teeth and spectacles in Gaitskell's Budget, and immediately broadened the issue to include an attack on the rearmament programme and on the subordination of British foreign policy to American leadership. So Bevanism was born, and I became disenchanted with Aneurin Bevan.

It was by no means inevitable that I came down on the side that I did, but once I had done so I was voluntarily swept almost out of hailing distance with friendly acquaintances of the previous years. The Labour Party entered a period of tribal warfare which was to last for most of the decade. Within the areas controlled by each tribe there was order and even rational government. But each faction was dedicated to the fight against the other, and on the border where the two areas joined there were bitter skirmishes interspersed with periods of hostile watchfulness. Each faction would claim that they were the better at fighting the enemy across the floor of the House of Commons, but in reality their minds were occupied with hostility more to each other than to the Conservatives.

The years of Bevanism were not quite so bad for the Labour Party as the descent into lunacy of 1979–83. This was partly because the personalities were bigger in the 1950s than in the early 1980s and neither side embraced such foolish policies. But the degree of separation and bitterness after 1951 was dramatic. *New Fabian Essays* published a year after Bevan's resignation could be cited as evidence to the contrary, but the project was far advanced at the time of the split, would never have been mounted after it, and only involved Crossman and Mikardo from the other side. With Crossman, who was a Bevanite more because he did not get on with either Attlee or Gaitskell than because of ideology or temperament, I always maintained wary but talkative relations. And Mikardo, although a dedicated tactician of the left (with views far beyond Bevan's own), liked operating behind enemy lines, which his sardonic restraint enabled him to do well.

With more central figures relations quickly became non-existent. Bevan and I hardly addressed a word to each other throughout the decade. He would stalk past scowling in a corridor. He once deliberately turned his back on Jennifer, who should have been innocent enough in his eyes, except on an extreme and very male-chauvinist theory of uxorious guilt, and did it in Buckingham Palace of all improbable places for both of us. I would not have dreamed of trying to join his circle in the smoking room or his table in the dining room. His wife, Jennie Lee, was even more resentfully sharp-clawed. Looking back, it all appears very childish. Bevan was petulant and vain, but he was on the frontier of being a great man, and he was certainly a great talker and a considerable wit. To shut oneself off from any concourse with him was like forgoing the opportunity to talk to Fox or Disraeli. It would have been difficult to break through, for he was prickly with politicians who were not acolytes, but it could be done, as one or two who were not his supporters, notably Reggie Paget, the fox-hunting QC from Northamptonshire, succeeded in showing.

I do not admire my narrowness of this period, and am reminded by it of one of the characters in Harold Nicolson's *Some People*. Jacques de Chaumont, a rather ludicrous French aristocrat, when asked why he rejected some overture from Proust, whom he had once known well, said: 'Then there is moy aunt de Maubize [he spoke Cockney]. She 'ates Jews.' I might have said 'Then there is my friend Hugh Gaitskell. He hates Bevanites.' Chaumont shut himself off from the greatest novelist of the twentieth century. I shut myself off (or at any rate was shut off), not from the greatest politician of the twentieth century, for Bevan was far from that, but from the second most striking personality of my early years in the House of Commons.

It would have been easy enough for me to have become a Bevanite, and might indeed have been politically profitable. My constituency party at that time would certainly have preferred it. Later in that summer of 1951, in spite of my move the other way, Stechford was to carry by a large majority an extreme Bevanite resolution which was published on the agenda for the annual Labour Party conference and caused me considerable embarrassment. Furthermore, Tony Crosland, who had got into the House in February 1950, was closer at that time to Gaitskell than I was, and was also very much the apple of the eye of Hugh Dalton, that old talent promoter of the Labour right. (Dalton was always friendly and helpful provided a choice did not have to be made between Crosland and me; when it did, I was nowhere with him.) There was also Douglas Jay as a more senior and equally academically talented economic adjutant of Gaitskell's. Where there was a vacancy for a young MP with economic credentials was much more amongst the Bevanites than amongst the Gaitskellites. The Bevanites had Harold Wilson, but although he had been the youngest Cabinet minister since Palmerston he was not then very highly regarded. He was still a dull speaker, although he was fairly soon to transform himself into a master of public wit, and was widely thought of as a bureaucrat who had turned opportunist. Dalton's cruel reference to him as 'Nye's little dog' was a sobriquet which stuck and damaged.

I also knew quite well those who were to become the recruiting sergeants of Bevanism. Michael Foot had become a friendly acquaintance as a result of his commissioning my various contributions to *Tribune*, and we retained good relations, wisely talking about books rather than politics, throughout the 1950s and early 1960s. (One of my favourite

teases of Hugh Gaitskell was to tell him how much I liked Michael
Foot, to which he never failed to rise.) Then there was Donald Bruce,
in 1951 aged thirty-eight but remarkably the same as he is forty years
on in the House of Lords, gruff, diligent, committed. He had kindly
taken me under his wing between 1948 and losing his seat in 1950.

In a less workaday way I had some though not wholly easy social
relationships with both John Freeman, the third of the resigning trio,
and Tom Driberg, whose cynicism was such that his political beliefs
were difficult to place, but who was as determined not to be outflanked
to the left in politics as he was not to be exceeded in the alpine
nature of his Anglo-Catholicism. As Driberg knew he was a bit of
a fraud he did not take his politics wholly seriously (unlike many
local Labour stalwarts who consistently elected him to the National
Executive on the basis of his articles in *Reynolds' News*, the Sunday
newspaper owned by the Co-operative Society). He could therefore
be as generously tolerant of Gaitskellites as he was of heterosexuals.
Freeman was different, although a very close friend of Driberg's, but
of such apparently controlled and ice-cold a temperament that it did
not make much difference to relations whether one agreed with him
or not.

The basis of my relationship with these two was the surprising one
(as it now seems to me for I have hardly played any card game for the
past forty years) that, together with Crosland and Wyatt, I formed part
of a canasta school of which Freeman was the host and Driberg the
croupier. The circumstances out of which this arose were that canasta
had just become a popular and/or fashionable game and that, with the
wafer-thin majority and the militant opposition of 1950–1, we were all
incarcerated in the House of Commons night after night and often well
towards dawn. Card games were against some standing order of the
House, so we had to play *in camera* and it was the provision of the
*camera* which made Freeman the host. As a junior minister he had a
tiny room in the vaults into which we could just fit. When the frequent
votes were called it was the duty of the policeman to fling open the
doors of such rooms and bellow 'Division!' This presented a problem,
for we were clearly liable to be caught *in flagrante*. Although Driberg
claimed to be an expert at bribing policemen, he chose to solve the
problem not by this method but by sitting with his broad back against
the door so that it would not open by more than a few inches and in a
direction which gave no view. This frequent resistance might have been
expected to arouse suspicion over a period, but it did not appear to do
so. Perhaps he combined the two methods, even though we provided
him with no resources to do so, for the stakes were either low or
non-existent. Nonetheless we all became addicted, Crosland perhaps
less so than the other four of us.

In the summer of 1951 Driberg was married, a bizarre event which was celebrated in an appropriately bizarre way, with a high nuptial mass at St Mary's, Graham Terrace, and a large guest list, which included a substantial contingent of his Essex constituents, most of the Eastern European ambassadors in London, and a sprinkling of high literary society. The canasta school was paraded for the wedding. Freeman 'gave away' the bride, and Wyatt, Crosland and I were ushers, supplemented by an attractive Bevanite MP with the designation of Captain Hugh Delargy, which made him sound as though he might have been a rakish Irish Nationalist of the Parnell era. I found some difficulty in allocating the church seating. Driberg, typically, thought that the constituents could stand at the back and the diplomats and others occupy the preferred positions. But the constituents, in charabancs hired by Driberg, predictably arrived well in advance, and proved impossible to keep standing behind rows of empty chairs. So I had to try to explain to po-faced diplomats why it was they who had to stand. The whole occasion would have made Waugh, who was a close friend of the bridegroom but in France at the time, a most appropriate guest.

The canasta school deployed itself less unitedly on the Bevan resignation. Freeman and Driberg were of course for the messiah. The position of the other three of us was less predictable. Wyatt had been a signatory of the Keep Left manifesto in 1949 and he had been on the staff of *Tribune* in 1948 and 1949. But he was moving to the right by 1951, although then and for long afterwards perfectly acceptably so from my point of view, and he was to enter the Government within two weeks. He was unaware of this impending promotion on the night of Thursday, 19 April, when I told him I had just received news from Dalton that Bevan was certainly going, and we both reeled with dismay as we walked out through New Palace Yard together. I recall the physical circumstances with a clarity undimmed by the passage of forty years. We thought it was likely to be a mortal blow, although maybe with delayed effects, to an already weak Labour Government, about the survival of which we then both greatly cared, and we searched for points of certainty to which to cling. We agreed, as I also did with Crosland at some time that evening, that Bevan was wrong and that we could not support him.

The factors which most weighed with me were: a mounting admiration (although still from a distance) for Gaitskell's handling of the Exchequer over the previous six months and culminating in his Budget and its presentation; a belief that Bevan had acted more out of personal pique than political principle; and a fear that the thrust of Bevanism would quickly be towards a weakening of the whole Western position at a time when the Korean War was still at a critical stage and

st/West divide in Europe was still raw from the Berlin
...any rate the die was cast and my political orientation,
...a decade, perhaps for my remaining twenty-six years in
...our Party, was determined on that night. A few days later I
...e a speech in Birmingham which received considerable local – and
...little national – publicity, and turned my private commitment into a
public one.

Ten days later there was a strong rumour that I would be offered
the parliamentary secretaryship at the Ministry of Supply vacated by
Freeman's resignation. It did not happen. Michael Stewart was moved
there from the War Office, with Woodrow Wyatt taking his place in
that department. I felt little disappointment. It would have been nice
to be the youngest member of the Government at the age of thirty, but
I was not desperate for office. I thought I had plenty of time, and this
thought, fortified by my subsequently becoming the youngest member
of the Cabinet in 1965, was with me in varying circumstances until well
into the 1970s. Then in the 1980s I suddenly found that I had stepped
over a divide. I was much the oldest member of the Gang of Four, and
in 1983 was in danger of becoming the oldest leader of any party.

In 1951, however, in spite of my fear that the Government was
fatally wounded, it never occurred to me that, thanks largely to
the continuing activities of the flawed genius from whom, at several
removes, the petty vacancy essentially stemmed, it would be nearly
fourteen years before I again had a chance of office of any sort. I
subconsciously thought that Attlee was right in relation to me. I had
enjoyed enough patronage from him and would be better off in the
long run for having to wait a few more years.

That autumn our fears about the mortal blow to Labour in office
proved well founded and a general election on 25 October turned
a Labour majority of six into a Conservative one of seventeen.
Considering the vicissitudes which the Government had suffered,
with the loss of Cripps, Bevin and Bevan, the exhaustion of nearly
everybody else except for Gaitskell, and an election date chosen more
in response to that exhaustion than to any tactical game-plan, it was a
surprisingly narrow defeat. Stechford held up well, and the decline in
the majority to a shade under 11,000 owed more to the disappearance
of a Liberal candidate than to any weakening of my support. In that
great national plebiscite of a general election, when 83 per cent voted
and the bulldozers of the two great party machines razed both regional
differences and candidates' merits into the ground, my vote floated up
by 1300 to 33,000, the highest I ever polled in any constituency.

The election for me was not otherwise remarkable. I worked hard
in Stechford and spoke around in the West Midlands a good deal,
but not outside, except for one visit to Tony Crosland in South

Gloucester. I was without Jennifer for the only time in the fifteen parliamentary elections which I fought. Our first child, Charles, had been born in March 1949, and (an indication of how straight-line a politician I was in those days) christened in the Crypt Chapel of the Palace of Westminster with the Prime Minister as one godparent and Crosland as the other and the loaf only somewhat leavened by having a Yorkshire millowner's wife who was a schoolfriend of Jennifer's as the third. Of his two godfathers, Attlee proved diligent but inevitably not very long-lasting (and his wife, who was the present-buyer, even less so), and Crosland fitful at best.

Then our daughter Cynthia was born in June 1951. She had a cast for her christening which was less political although, by accident, equally distinguished. The Crypt Chapel was closed for repairs, so we had the ceremony at St Stephen's, Gloucester Road, our Cornwall Gardens local church. When we arrived T. S. Eliot, as churchwarden, was sweeping out the porch. He came and joined us round the font. One child aged ten months had not prevented Jennifer from being active in Birmingham during the 1950 election, but two, with the younger only three months old, was a different matter, and she stayed away in 1951. The strain for her of these two was increased by the fact that they lived their first five and three years respectively at the top of seventy-nine steps in Cornwall Gardens. Edward, the third, came in July 1954, but he never had to be carried up the stairs, except in the womb, for we had by then moved to Ladbroke Square, although only a month before.

The new Parliament assembled on 31 October, and the shock of moving on to the opposition benches, which I had never previously experienced, was considerable. It was only twenty months since we had all adjusted ourselves to coming from the ornate House of Lords chamber (for it was there that I had made my maiden speech and all subsequent ones as member for Southwark) to the reconstructed Commons one. But the change of sides took more getting used to, although once I had done so the opposition benches became only too familiar to me. I was to spend twenty-two of my remaining thirty years in the House of Commons on them. This change leading to stability was reflected in a range of other aspects of life over the next five or six years. My life in 1951 was an extension of those immediate post-war years which now seem very remote. But by 1956 or 1957 it had, without any violent change, gone through a series of mutations which brought it broadly into a pattern which has since persisted.

There were a number of ways in which this occurred. The first and most formative was that I moved from being a politician without a profession to being a writer/politician. Writing is not exactly a profession. Its practice demands the taking of no examinations and requires no qualifications. It has no controlling governing body, although for what

had become a member of the Committee of Management
of Authors by 1956. But the transition from being an
pened to have written a book (*Mr Attlee*), which was my
in 1951, to being on the borderline between an author who
also an MP and an MP who was also an author to which I had
moved by 1956 was nonetheless a significant one.

Paradoxically, I achieved it by writing a wholly political book. After
the defeat of 1951 I interrupted writing *Mr Balfour's Poodle* and
spent the first half of 1952 writing *Pursuit of Progress*. This was
a very short (55,000 words) 'critical analysis [in the terms of its
subtitle] of the achievement and prospect of the Labour Party'.
It was essentially an attempt to show, drawing mainly on Labour
Party history, that any left-wing party was necessarily a potential
battleground between impatient utopianism and practical reformism,
but that effective advance was achieved only when the utopians, having
had a necessary and even useful fling, allowed the conflict to ebb. It
was thus an attempt to contain Bevanism while understanding rather
than denouncing its springs.

Needless to say it had no effect at all on Bevanism, but it got quite
a lot of interested and on the whole friendly reviews (although less
so than did either *Mr Attlee* or *Mr Balfour's Poodle*), provided some
soft-sell ammunition for Gaitskellites and created the expectation for
the future that I must soon be about to publish another book. 'What
are you writing now?' people always thereafter asked me when they
could think of nothing else to say. And I always had a positive answer.
In particular I very quickly followed up *Pursuit of Progress* (April
1953) with *Mr Balfour's Poodle* (February 1954), mainly because it
was mostly written in advance.

This was a different sort of book. *Pursuit of Progress* was ephemeral,
propagandist and on a typical subject for an MP. *Mr Balfour's Poodle*
was supposed to be objective, although permitting itself an occasional
partisan joke, has not proved ephemeral (its third edition was published in 1989) and was on a type of subject about which no other MP,
and indeed hardly anybody at all, was writing at the time. Its aim was
to give a narrative account of a linked series of historical events with
enough scholarship not to offend the specialist reader with inaccuracy,
but not so much as to bog down the general reader in excessive detail.
Other books of this type were Cecil Woodham-Smith's *The Reason
Why* (which came a little earlier), Elizabeth Longford's *Jameson's
Raid* and Frances Donaldson's *The Marconi Scandal*. It seemed rather
a female genre.

The title was perhaps a mistake. I took it from a fine piece of
derisory invective by Lloyd George. 'The House of Lords', he said
in 1908, 'is not the watch-dog of the constitution; it is Mr Balfour's

poodle.' But the naming of books may be too serious a matter for trying to be witty. In any event, I was rebuked for frivolity by as authoritative an arbiter of gravitas as Randolph Churchill, there was persistent ambiguity as to whether or not I had written a biography of Balfour, and some bookshops allegedly had difficulty in categorising the book, although there was no evidence from the sales that I came near to breaking into the dog-lovers' market.

Randolph Churchill's mild complaint apart, *Poodle* (as literary conceit might abbreviate it) had wonderful critical acclaim. The cover of the most recent edition quotes from reviews by R. C. K. Ensor, Leonard Woolf and A. J. P. Taylor, and manages to find immensely warming and flattering sentences from each of those sharp pens. However, by far the most memorable joy came not from any of these three pundits, whose praise had faded in my mind into a general glow until resurrected by William Collins and Sons, but from a private letter from Harold Nicolson, who also wrote a good *Observer* review, although the detail of this too has faded. His letter has not. I remember opening it as vividly as I remember walking out of New Palace Yard on the night when Bevan's resignation became known. It was the Saturday evening a week or so before publication and I had come downstairs in Cornwall Gardens on my way to a cinema and there found Nicolson's letter. (Both the cinema visit, then quite frequent for me, and a mail delivery on a Saturday afternoon set the incident in its 1950s context.) He said he had read the book, would review it and went on through several typewritten paragraphs to praise it extravagantly. He hardly knew me, and it was an immensely generous and reassuring letter to receive before publication from one of the two or three most esteemed general reviewers of the period. My heart almost literally leaped.

After the publication party for *Mr Balfour's Poodle* Jennifer and I dined in the House of Commons with Anthony and Caroline Wedgwood Benn, with whom we were then on close and friendly terms; he had a particular interest in constitutional issues affecting the House of Lords, of which he saw membership looming. In the course of dinner, Mark Bonham Carter, whom I had known since Balliol but not at all well and who was dining with Jo Grimond, came across to our table and suggested that I wrote my next book about Sir Charles Dilke, the late-nineteenth-century radical politician who had been ruined by a divorce case which retained several elements of mystery.

The next day I looked up *The Times* reports of the case and over the following week or so read the two-volume 'tombstone' life of Dilke by Stephen Gwynn and Gertrude Tuckwell. The biography was reticent, but Dilke was obviously a fascinating subject. So, as a result of an almost casual remark and without a pause from one book to the next,

ˢ my book-writing work for the next four years was set.
ˎone off in another direction. In 1952 Arthur Deakin,
ˏe of a right-wing trade union boss and Ernest Bevin's
ˏˢ general secretary of the Transport and General Workers'
ˏ, had asked me to write a commissioned life of his illustrious
ˏedecessor. I was flattered and excited, perhaps too much so to
consider coolly whether Bevin was the ideal subject for me. We began
excellently with a planning lunch at the Hyde Park Hotel. A. S. Frere,
the chairman of Heinemann, who had been Bevin's public relations
adviser at the Ministry of Labour during the war, was also present.
The book was to be a big project in several volumes, and financed by
a good deal of TGWU money.

In subsequent discussions it emerged that the union money was to
be balanced by an equal amount of union interference. There was
even a suggestion that I should have Herbert Tracey, an in-house
TUC journalist, whom I regarded as a Transport House hack, as
an adviser on union affairs and possible writer of certain chapters.
I began to find Deakin difficult to deal with, and thought that Frere
stood up inadequately for the rights of one of his authors. The real
trouble was that some time after our first encounter Deakin had
been greatly impressed by Alan Bullock's *Hitler* and began to wish
he had commissioned him and not me. So he negotiated to an impasse.
Eventually he got what he wanted, and I think he was probably right
to do so. Apart from anything else, I had come in the course of the
proceedings considerably to dislike Deakin, whose style if not his name
made him just as entitled to the sobriquet of Bullying-Manner as was
the then Solicitor-General, Sir Reginald Manningham-Buller. I had
to keep reminding myself that Deakin was not Bevin, even though
there was a marked resemblance of physical shape, and that I must
not visit the sins of the organiser of the biography on to its much more
considerable subject.

Bullock eventually wrote three excellent volumes, which showed no
signs of any interference. He did, however, take until 1983 (mainly
because of the thirty-year restriction on Foreign Office papers) to
produce the most important third volume on Bevin as Foreign
Secretary. As Deakin had died twenty-eight years before this, and
five years before the appearance of even the first volume, it was not
surprising that he did not maintain any tight control. Nevertheless I
now have no regrets that I did not get involved in this massive project
– although I most certainly did at the time. Bullock was a better choice
for Bevin.

The episode left me disenchanted with Heinemann, and Bonham
Carter was a publisher, one of the few senior people who was not a
Collins in the very successful and then wholly family-controlled firm

of William Collins and Sons. Its general publishing division, at the fashionable address of St James's Place, SW1, was part of a great iceberg which lurked deep in bibles and dictionaries in Cathedral Street, Glasgow. Bonham Carter did not for a moment claim that because he had suggested Dilke I ought to publish it with Collins. But he made it clear that an invitation was there. I saw no reason not to accept. He would be very interested in the book. We clinched the matter at a lunch two months later. Collins became, and remained for thirty-five years, my mainline publisher, and Mark Bonham Carter, only partially as a result, moved over five years or so from being an old amicable acquaintance to being probably my closest all-round friend.

There were two other effects of my becoming a more or less professional author. I was asked to do a certain amount of paid general journalism, although it would be an exaggeration to say that this amounted to a great deal in the five middle years of the 1950s about which I am now writing. The next quinquennium was to be quite different, but up to 1956 or 1957 I was doing no regular book reviewing, and regarded an invitation to write a series of 3000-word articles on English provincial cities for an illustrated paper called *The Sphere* as distinctly attractive. I did Birmingham, Bristol, Nottingham and Coventry, and was I think paid £40 plus the expenses of a visit for each of them. From 1951 to 1956 I wrote even less remuneratively a weekly London letter for the *Current*, the Bombay journal edited by D. K. Karaka, my cousin by marriage. This commitment was a mixture of the amateur and the professional. I was paid only £5 a week. The copy had to be posted airmail, which from the viewpoint of the fax era sounds incredibly archaic. Yet, with a reliability now unknown, it invariably arrived within three if not two days. The discipline of a weekly commitment was good for me, and also broadened my range, for fifty columns a year meant that I had to go well outside politics.

I also began to get involved in literary politics. During 1954 there were five separate prosecutions of highly reputable publishers for putting allegedly obscene books on the market. Heinemann, Hutchinson, Secker and Warburg, Arthur Barker and Werner Laurie, each in the shape of their chairman or managing director, were literally put in the dock on criminal charges for publishing novels which would not have aroused the slightest tremor in this or any other Western country during the past twenty-five years. Those who fulminate against 1960s liberalism (although happily doing nothing to repeal its measures even when they enjoy over ten years of unfettered power) should remember just how obscurantist were many aspects of British laws and the Home Office regime which administered them in the years before evil began in 1965.

The mid-fifties were amongst the worst of these years. This parade

before the criminal courts was surrounded by a crop of
ded upon with incredible insensitivity by the two Home
o divided the period and who between them drove
s into the coffin of the death penalty. A thirty-year-old
who had shot her lover in a fit of jealousy was hanged, so was
an who manifestly had not done it, so was a youth of nineteen
who never touched the gun which fired the shot. By comparison
the tribulations of the publishers were minor, but they had more
capacity for hitting back. A committee under the chairmanship of
A. P. Herbert, former MP for Oxford University, whose Divorce
Bill had given him a formidable reforming reputation, was set up
and I became the only parliamentary member. Amongst the others
were the publishers William Collins and Rupert Hart-Davis, Norman
St John-Stevas, ten years short of becoming an MP but an ingenious
drafter of liberalising clauses, and C. H. Rolph, ex-chief inspector in
the City of London police and *New Statesman* writer on questions of
life and liberty. This committee led to the Obscene Publications Bill
of 1959 and my part in the *Lady Chatterley* trial in 1960.

My growing involvement in authorship from 1951 onwards did not,
at least at first, lead to any diminution of my political energies. On
the contrary I engaged in more detailed parliamentary drudgery in the
spring and summer of 1952 than I had ever done before or was ever
to do again. Rab Butler's first Budget contained a number of simple
measures such as a cutting of food subsidies and a reduction in the
standard rate of income tax, but it also contained a complicated piece
of window dressing known as the Excess Profits Levy. It was there
because Churchill had given an undertaking during the 1951 election
campaign that there would be some creaming off of rearmament-boom
profits. It was window dressing because its impact upon broad social
distribution was negligible compared with the contrary effect of the
food subsidies or income tax measure. And it was complicated because
that is always the way with new forms of company taxation. It was also
liable to have perverse effects on overseas mining companies and on
companies' investment decisions generally.

The opposition finance team, which was composed, amongst others,
of Gaitskell, Frank Soskice QC (former Attorney-General), Douglas
Jay, G. R. Mitchison QC, Crosland, Austen Albu and me, decided to
take the strategically bold and somewhat bewildering step of opposing
the whole scheme. I was the foremost instigator of this decision, which
attacked Butler on a flank where he thought he was secure against
the opposition. Having helped to set us on this adventurous course
I obviously had to take some responsibility for sustaining it, and this
I did with enthusiasm. I devoted the whole of April and May to the
issue. I attended endless group meetings, I organised briefings from

interested parties outside, I devised amendments and with the help of the two QCs got them properly drafted. I wrote notes on clauses and on amendments for the use of myself and others. When this part of the Finance Bill came to be debated I think I understood it more completely than did the then Chancellor and more completely too than I ever was to understand any complicated part of a Finance Bill which I was myself to introduce nearly two decades later. Crosland understood it too, and spoke very well, but was a little less diligent than I was in organising the work of others. As a result, with some help from the front bench, we were able to provide an heroically boring opposition. We had eight full days on the floor of the House for the committee stage and managed to keep the House going far into the night on several of them. In one sitting I made nine speeches before going home in a summer dawn. Whether we achieved any political purpose is doubtful, but at least I taught myself to make informal unprepared interventions in the House. Most of the parliamentary Labour Party were surprisingly tolerant of our antics, which made them troop through the division lobby at all hours of the day and night. When at the end of the committee stage I asked the chief whip, Willie Whiteley (an elderly Durham miner not to be confused with his near namesake who had not then arrived on the Conservative benches), whether I could be away, lecturing in Berlin, for the first week after the Whitsun recess, he acceded at once. 'If anyone deserves a week off it is you,' he said with perhaps even more relief than gratitude.

This marathon performance marked an important stage in the development of my relations with Hugh Gaitskell. While he was Chancellor of the Exchequer, as I recorded earlier, I admired him but hardly knew him. But, by 1953 at the latest, I was a fully fledged Gaitskellite, a member of the XYZ dining club, a core participant (in spite of living in Kensington) in the 'Hampstead Set' insofar as it existed, and on the road to becoming more intimate with the man we were all dedicated to making Attlee's successor than was any other member of it except for Crosland. Although I do not recollect any particular incident which brought Gaitskell and me close, the timing strongly suggests that that Finance Bill co-operation must have been central to the process. This was in a way strange for we were both on the threshold of wanting to escape from being too politically obsessed and too narrowly economically specialised.

Nineteen fifty-three was a very different year for me from 1952. It was dominated by extra-parliamentary events. I played no comparable role in the Finance Bill of that year because I was almost continuously ill from the third week in April to the third week in July. It was the only period when I was significantly unwell between my 1928 appendicitis and 1984. I had glandular fever, and lay in bed in Cornwall Gardens for a month with a violently but predictably fluctuating temperature, then retreated to Pontypool for two weeks of convalescence over the period of the Coronation, then managed in June a hesitant return to engagements, and then had my tonsils removed in mid-July. This was painful at the age of thirty-two, but proved well worthwhile as it drove away the threatened reappearance of the glandular fever. But the operation consumed another fortnight and meant that I was able to do nothing much before the end of July except indulge in a week of social engagements, of which the most enjoyable at the time as well as a great precursor for the future was a dinner at the Lowndes Place house of a young French Embassy couple called Beaumarchais.

After another three weeks of Pontypool convalescence, interspersed by three brief Birmingham visits, I set off on my first visit to America. Just over the watershed of the century, I went like a traveller of the first rather than the second half, crossing the Atlantic in the *Queen Mary*. That increased the impact upon me of arrival in New York. In the fierce glow of a late August dawn I watched the then vast navy yard and commercial docks of Brooklyn slip past my porthole before going on deck as we came past the Statue of Liberty into the Hudson River and were manoeuvred into the Cunard pier at West 50th Street. It seemed one of the strangest prospects I had ever seen, paradoxically made more bizarre by the great freight cars which penetrated to the quays being labelled in English, even if with such exotic names as Chesapeake and Ohio and Erie-Lackawanna, and by the Western Union telegraph agents, who came thronging on to the ship the moment we were tied up, also appearing to speak a version of that language. The scene now seems to me very remote in time and feel, almost as far away as was then the Washington, 'still the city in which Lincoln had just been shot and into which the rebel forces had so nearly advanced', of which I was soon to write when describing Dilke's arrival there in July 1866. In sober fact the first gap was eighty-seven years and the second has now been only thirty-eight, but it is nonetheless the case that the America of the early Eisenhower years was a vastly different country from that of today.

The whole trip made a big impact on me. It lasted two months and I not only spent a good deal of time in New York, Washington and Boston, but also did a wide circle of Pittsburg, Detroit, Minneapolis, Kansas City, San Francisco, New Orleans and Atlanta. It gave me a certain geographical grip on the whole United States, and included one or two places to which I have never since returned. I went under a US Government scheme known as the Smith–Mundt programme, Smith being a Congressman and Mundt a Senator, both of right-wing views, who had promoted it to bring 'young leaders', as I think we were called, to America. We were given first-class passages across the

Atlantic (a pleasant but unnecessary luxury) and free travel anywhere in the United States, but only $12 a day on which to live, which even at 1953 prices was not much. It was just all right if, as was frequently the case, I had free hospitality, but not in an hotel, although quite tolerable ones could then be stayed in for between $4.50 and $8.00 a night. I remember being distinctly pleased when I opened a Gideon's Bible in Pittsburg and a $20 bill fell out. I debated whether to hand it in to the management but decided that it was a divine gift and that anyway it belonged to me as much as to them.

However, there was no inhibition on earning money by an occasional lecture, and still more important there was not the slightest attempt, despite Smith and Mundt, in the second year of the Eisenhower presidency, and with McCarthyism still rampant, to give a Republican stamp to my visit and contacts. I was escorted to a Democratic tea party in St Paul by Senator Hubert Humphrey, I called on ex-President Truman in Kansas City, and in Cambridge, Massachusetts, through the good offices of Professor Seymour Harris, the most dedicated of American Keynesians, I was introduced to John Kenneth Galbraith and Arthur Schlesinger, who became, and have remained, not only the most academically distinguished but amongst my closest American friends. From this trip there also dates my continuing friendship with Irwin Ross, New York journalist, and Douglass Cater, then Washington-based but since more peripatetic as commentator and as academic administrator, to both of whom references will be found at several later stages in this book. Stewart and Joseph Alsop, the first alas dead in 1971 and the second in 1989, also date for me from this visit.

Altogether it was a brilliant piece of unforced propaganda by the United States Information Services. It transformed my thinking and my emotions about the United States. Hitherto it had been an important but remote place, its geography vague, its politics fascinating but difficult to comprehend, like a lot of Tammany braves dancing around a wigwam. Since 1953 I have believed (probably falsely) that I understood America, and have felt very engaged with it. And the impressions gained in that first and longest visit have reverberated through the sixty or seventy subsequent visits which I have paid to North America. August to October 1953 was a major formative influence in my life; it could also be regarded as a fairly sound investment of not much more than $3000 by the US Government.

There was, however, a great sadness associated with the visit. On 7 September in Washington I received news that my mother was in hospital following a stroke. There was said to be no immediate danger. This proved false reassurance. On 11 September in Detroit I was told first of a heavy deterioration and then of her death. I got back to Pontypool on Monday the 14th (journeys from Michigan to Monmouthshire were not as easy as today), attended the massive funeral on the Tuesday and decided, after many hesitations, to go back to America for my remaining five weeks on the Wednesday afternoon.

She was only sixty-seven, and had passed the seven and a half years since my father's death in a mixture of continuing grief and loneliness, indomitable determination to remain busily active and neglected threats to her health. The circumstances in which I heard about her death inevitably made it a shock, although at a different level of comprehension it was not exactly a surprise. It was a great blow, not only to me, but also to her elder grandchild, then aged four and a half, with whom there had been mutual devotion, and who went around in deep gloom for a short time.

In addition, it marked another change in our lives. It was the end of Pontypool, not as a place of origin to which I make nostalgic returns and sometimes take friends on visits of inspection, but as a family house and residual place of retreat when I did not have to be in London and there was no exotic alternative. I was very glad that I had spent five weeks there that summer. But there was no way in which we could sensibly keep it on. So a dimension of our lives disappeared.

On the other hand the winding up of Pontypool made possible the move to Ladbroke Square. We bought a house there four or five months later and moved in at midsummer 1954. Although Notting Hill was not then nearly as sought after as it has since become, 33 Ladbroke Square was a fine family house on the edge of central London for a young and fairly impecunious Labour MP. It had been built at the end of the 1840s, and was not altogether easy to run, for it was on four floors plus a basement, which was mostly let as a self-contained flat. There were six bedrooms, and a large ground-floor dining room which could seat twelve or even fourteen. The first floor was entirely taken up with an L-shaped drawing room, one-third of which could be shut off by folding doors and served as my study. There was a small paved garden at the back, and in front the largest square garden in London, the nine acres of which provided both tennis court and cricket pitch. We bought the house freehold but in poor condition for £5250, and had to spend another £1750 on it. We stayed there for twenty-three years and then sold it rather badly – for sixteen times what we paid for it! Had we kept it until the peak of the 1988 boom we probably would have got nearly 150 times the 1954 figure. It was altogether a very satisfactory house, although now sadly less attractive, for the 1977 company purchasers celebrated their bargain by destroying the mouldings and filling the garden with a too big swimming pool which made it look like a fish farm.

Encouraged by Ladbroke Square we began gradually to have quite a lot of people to dinner, not merely old, mostly Oxford friends whom we had always had to Marsham Street and Cornwall Gardens, but a range of newer ones as well. My 1955 engagement diary shows about a dozen such parties during the year. Two random entries show that on 8 February the Beaumarchais (already mentioned), Solly and Joan Zuckerman, Barley Alison (just beginning her thirty-year career as a small publisher with a brilliant eye for launching hitherto unknown fiction writers), Woodrow Wyatt (I think between wives), Thea Elliott (wife of my Oxford and by then Foreign Office friend Anthony) and Thomas Balogh, my old Balliol tutor, were there; and on 5 October J. K. Galbraith, the Charles Wintours (the then editor of the *Evening Standard*), the Kenneth Youngers (he still MP for Grimsby) and Caroline Benn. The Gaitskells came frequently and other MPs who appeared with or without wives during that year were Douglas Jay, Dick Crossman, Denis Healey and Austen Albu. We had already decided that, close though we were, it was better to see Crosland only on his own. Famous for his flounces and his unconcealed disapproval of those he might be asked to meet, he was too hazardous a guest for dinner parties.

Apart from the Beaumarchais, who in any event were not in London after that summer of 1955 until they returned to head the Embassy in 1972 (although we remained in close touch), there was always from 1953 on a strong French diplomatic element in our dinner parties, both those we gave and those we went to. We did not aspire to deal with ambassadors until the 1960s, but Jacques and Helena Tiné, who were here from 1955 to 1961, he as counsellor, became considerable friends of ours, as did Gérard André, who between 1946 and 1969, when he departed to become ambassador first in Finland and then in Thailand, seemed to have become permanent interpreter of Britain to France, and indeed of France to Britain. His fellow bachelor, Vincent Labouret, was more a bird of passage, although one of bright plumage, and was also a friend. In addition, we had continuing social relations at counsellor level with the Italian, American and German embassies, broadly in that order, although the French link was much the strongest.

This probably had some effect on the evolution of my European commitment. In the early and mid-1950s I was in no way a foreign affairs expert. I lacked confidence on the subject and never dared to open my mouth in the House of Commons throughout the Suez crisis of 1956. I spoke outside on the issue, but not in Parliament, where I hardly made any sort of external affairs speech during my first ten years of membership. Nor was I a 'premature European'. In my first month in the House of Commons in 1948 there took place the famous Hague Congress, which effectively launched the post-war European Movement and for the fortieth anniversary of which I went to Holland in 1988 to make a commemorative speech. I wished I had been able to tell that anniversary gathering how much I had fretted at the Labour Party's narrow-minded ban on attendance in 1948, which had been defied by only a very few bold spirits. But it would not have been true. I meekly accepted the party line, just as I found no difficulty in voting against the Schuman Plan in 1950. In 1951 I had gone to a European Movement weekend conference in Brussels, but I remember being cautious enough to telephone Healey, then the Labour Party international secretary at Transport House, to secure his *nihil obstat*, and when I got there argued the boring old case of Britain's special need to protect her full employment and her welfare state by import and exchange controls.

In 1955 I was appointed a delegate to the Consultative Assembly of the Council of Europe at Strasbourg. This was only for a two-year term, for the Labour Party, unlike both the continental socialist parties and the British Tories, believed that a longer spell carried the risk of members contracting European fever. In fact the incubation period was sufficiently short for this precaution to prove not merely ineffective but counter-productive. All it did was to spread the infection more widely. A high proportion of the Labour Europeans of the 1960s and 1970s had been through a brief Strasbourg induction course. So it proved with me. I spent a total of about seven weeks in Strasbourg or at committee meetings from Palermo to Berlin between the summer of 1955 and the spring of 1957, the period between the Messina Conference and the Treaty of Rome, and I have no doubt that those experiences sowed the seeds of my subsequently persistent conviction.

The seeds did not immediately sprout. I was made rapporteur of some committee, the presentation of the report of which enabled me to make a successful speech to the whole Assembly in October 1956. It was the first significant speech I had made to an international and multilingual audience, and I was much congratulated upon it. It was full of goodwill about what had been started in Messina and Britain's need and desire to be closely associated with it, but it also contained all the fallacies which were to bedevil our relations with the Europe of the Community for most of the next thirty-five years. Our position would need to be special and somewhat disengaged so that we would not have to choose between a Commonwealth and a European connection. I did at least avoid the old canard that we must also be careful not to imperil the special relationship with the United States, for in spite of my post-1953 enthusiasm for a lot of things American I always saw that, so far from there being a contradiction between this and a

European commitment, Britain's conviction that we were not as other European nations were was an exacerbating factor in our relations with Washington. But this benign omission apart, that Strasbourg speech contained little clear-sighted rejection of the conventional British wisdom on Europe.

This was however a last burst of obfuscation. I learned a lot from those two years of watching Britain throw away its opportunity to play a formative role in the shaping of the Common Market, and when in 1958 the Macmillan Government came up with the halfway house of the European Free Trade Association I opposed it as a foolish attempt to organise a weak periphery against a strong core, which could provide no satisfactory European strategy for Britain. This indeed quickly proved to be the case, for as soon as Macmillan moved to applying for full membership of the Community, EFTA became an embarrassment, and we eventually had to split our own creation. In 1959 I published another short political book (see Chapter 6) which expressed a full European commitment, mainly on the ground that it would enable us to escape from our 'great-power complex' which made us play at being in the same league as the United States and Russia while in reality being rapidly overtaken by the German and other lesser European economies. And, at the beginning of 1961, six months before the belated conversion of the Macmillan Government, I was instrumental in setting up the all-party Common Market Campaign. I got Lord Gladwyn, just retired as ambassador in Paris, to become chairman, and became deputy chairman myself. Thereafter my European commitment was steady and at most times dominant in my life. By the standards of the pioneers I was a latter-day convert, although one well before the bulk of, say, Foreign Office, City or Conservative Party opinion. When eventually enlightened I remained so, and with some fervour.

The European excursion has taken me on well past the general election of 1955 and without a mention of it. This is partly because it was the dullest of all those that I fought. Winning it, and putting the Conservative majority up from seventeen to fifty-five was the one bright spot of Eden's disastrous premiership, and there was throughout a sense of inevitability about the outcome. Attlee was still leader, but unzestful at the age of seventy-two, and was portrayed with some success as having become no more than a figurehead behind whom lurked the much more sinister power of Bevan. Stechford was considerably reduced in size, one-third of it having been lopped off in a redistribution. The majority came down to 6700, which was only a little more than proportional, but made it look a less safe seat.

A more dramatic and important episode in my relations with the constituency had occurred in the year before that flat campaign. It was the only occasion when I came near to serious constituency trouble. The issue was German rearmament, whether the Federal Republic should make a much needed contribution to the greatly outnumbered land forces of NATO. The Americans were insistent on the need, the German Government (but not the opposition SPD) were eager for reasons of international rehabilitation that they should be allowed to do so. The British Government was also in favour, and the Labour Party leadership in the shape of Attlee, Morrison and Gaitskell felt committed by undertakings they had given to the Americans in 1950–1, and probably on the merits too. The left made opposition to this line into their great issue of the year and were joined by the pacifists, as well as some (mostly First World War) German-haters, of whom Dalton was the most dedicated. Together they constituted a formidable coalition, and when a vote was taken in a packed parliamentary Labour Party meeting on the evening of 23 February 1954, the leadership was supported only by a majority of two.

By a singular misfortune the Management Committee of the Stechford Constituency Labour Party met on the same evening and carried a directly contrary resolution by a vote of thirty-four to nil. The newspapers the next day were full of the wafer-thin majority in the PLP. It naturally occurred to some of the most eager and politically motivated proponents of the Stechford resolution that I had almost certainly voted 'wrong', and that had I done otherwise it would have been a tie and a great triumph for the left. There was no question of dissimulation. My Gaitskellite affinities joined with my belief that Germany must be brought into the full comity of Western nations made me want my position to be publicly on the record.

A motion was then put down in Stechford that a special meeting should be called 'to discuss the relations of the member with the constituency'. This phrase was obviously well chosen to sound menacing without being too specific. Most of my Stechford friends thought we should let the meeting take place in a leisurely way and hope, as they confidently predicted, that the criticism would then dissolve in confusion. I insisted that we had to resolve the issue more quickly and more clearly. We should contest the motion at the next regular meeting. I accordingly went to Birmingham in a state of some tension on the evening of 3 March, and after the motion had been moved and seconded made a substantial speech devoted in about equal parts to the case for German rearmament and to my right to act as I had done even if they did not agree with me. The motion for a special meeting was then defeated by thirty votes to two, with about four abstentions, and a nasty corner had been turned.

It was a useful catharsis, buttressed by the luck that the 1955 redistribution took most of the awkward people out of the constituency, and I never subsequently had difficulty in Stechford on any policy issue. On the great unilateralist argument of 1960–1 they supported my Gaitskellite position on the merits, and when I subsequently divided first from Gaitskell and then a decade later from Wilson on the European issue they also agreed with me. But even had they not it was by then firmly established that I would listen to them but always make my own decisions. That 1954 meeting was also a watershed. Before it, I had been rather nervous of the Stechford party; after it I was not.

At about this time I began my only long-term commercial association. Spedan Lewis was the son of a successful draper who had established himself in Oxford Street. When he inherited he turned the business into the John Lewis Partnership, which had by then expanded into a group of about fifteen department stores plus the Waitrose food chain. He had written to me in the summer of 1953 saying that he had read *Pursuit of Progress* and wished me to join the firm. In July Jennifer and I went to lunch with him near Stockbridge in the Test Valley, where he was living in semi-retirement and pouring out memoranda interspersed with occasional not very readable books. He was an eccentric autocrat of strong personality. He believed that in the Partnership he had created a unique instrument of industrial democracy. This was not so, for strong central control remained with the self-perpetuating management. But what he had genuinely done was to give away to his employees the equity of a major business, and done so in such a way as not to impair its continuing competitive efficiency. He believed in recruiting a highly educated management, paying them only moderately, forbidding commissions and kick-backs for buyers from suppliers, giving them a share in the profits but only to the same proportion of their salaries as junior staff received, and encouraging them to apply ratiocination to the buying of fancy goods and even to shop-walking. It was a formula which worked. The mathematicians and philosophers stood up very well against the street-wise traders more favoured by some other chains.

His proposition was that I should join in either an executive or an advisory capacity. When I hesitated he thought that I was nervous about the reaction of my constituency party, and offered himself to come and address them about the glories of the Partnership. I hastily assured him that this was not necessary, and that I would decide as soon as I came back from America in the autumn. I then agreed to join for about one and a half days a week, giving economic and general advice. For this I was paid £1000 a year, which with MPs' salaries at the same amount and my writing earnings still fairly limited until the beginning of the

1960s made a considerable difference. I stayed with the Partnership for eleven years, until I entered the Government in 1964, for the last two years taking somewhat more financial responsibility and earning more money. I did not subsequently see much of Spedan Lewis, although I used to visit him occasionally in the country during the remaining ten years of his life. I got on amiably with the largely Oxonian top management team that he had recruited. Eddie Shackleton joined on a nearly full-time basis after his defeat at the 1955 election, and that was a bonus both for John Lewis's and for me. So, in a variety of ways, my life by the mid-1950s had become substantially different from and wider than what it had been in the late 1940s and very early 1950s.

# CHAPTER SIX

# *A Semi-Detached MP*

The seven years or so from the aftermath of Suez to the beginning of the Wilson Government in 1964 was the period of all my thirty-four years of membership when I was most detached from the House of Commons. In spite of or perhaps because of this, it was a time of considerable and surprising success for me, with as much sense of opening windows as was brought by the subsequent six years of ministerial ascent. Yet in 1957–64 my position in the political hierarchy hardly advanced at all. I was elected neither to the shadow Cabinet nor to the National Executive Committee of the Labour Party. I occupied a very minor front-bench position for a few months or so, but resigned from it in irritation at a suggestion that it should inhibit me from speaking unequivocally (from a back bench) about Britain's membership of the Common Market.

This was not the only paradox of this period. Although I was a resigner who regressed rather than advanced in the hierarchy my link to mainline politics was a close relationship with Hugh Gaitskell, the leader of the party from December 1955, who believed in discipline, at least against those he regarded as his enemies within the party, but whose friendship with me was substantially based on the fact that he thought I had many interests and friends outside politics, for he had come to feel that the pressures of full-time politics made him miss many things in life. As a result, he was enthusiastic about my non-political successes, half respected my political advice, but did not feel any great need to promote my conventional political career.

I admired and indeed loved him more than anyone else with whom I have ever worked in politics. When unexpectedly asked twenty-seven years after his death on *Desert Island Discs* who was my political hero I unhesitatingly answered, 'Hugh Gaitskell.' Yet, to compound the paradoxes, I split from him on a major political issue in the last six months of his life, and then, when I had in spite of this been desolated

109

by his death, found that my straight political prospects were enhanced by the transfer of power to his successor with and for whom I had little contact or regard.

Gaitskell was fourteen and a half years older than I was, which was a wide enough gap for the thought of rivalry never to cross my mind. Our relationship was thus untouched by jealousy or envy, those banes of political friendships and associations. His triumphs (apart from the last anti-European one at the 1962 Brighton conference) were almost as satisfying as if they were my own, and his failures gave me no malicious pleasure. The only marginal exceptions I recall had a ludicrous flavour. Charlie Pannell, the Amalgamated Engineering Union-sponsored MP for Leeds West, was a combative right-winger who was as staunch a supporter of Gaitskell as he was later to be of me. He was also as unencumbered by aspirates as Ernest Bevin had been. On several occasions he came up to me and said, 'I thought 'Ugh [which sounded like 'you'] made a brilliant speech last week.' Each time I involuntarily preened myself as I searched for what utterance of mine had so commanded his approval, only to realise two seconds later that it had been our beloved leader to whom he had been loyally referring.*

On the other hand the age gap with Gaitskell was narrow enough for it to place no inhibitions on the content or style of our conversation. On matters of substance (until the European crunch) I accepted his ultimate authority without question, but I would drop into his room unannounced whenever I wanted a talk with him, which was often as much social and literary gossip as politics, and could mock and tease him fairly relentlessly if so disposed. I did not go quite as far in this respect as Tony Crosland, who made a fetish of constantly reproving, sometimes for frivolity, sometimes for simple lack of intellectual quality, his political seniors who were fond of him (Dalton suffered much more than Gaitskell). Crosland knew Gaitskell at least as well as I did, although on a slightly different basis. In my retrospective view, with both of them long dead, Gaitskell was more excited by the idea of Crosland than he was by the idea of me, but found me rather easier to be with. As a result he saw about an equal amount of one as of the other, but mostly although not always separately.

Crosland and I, however, were by no means separated in other ways. We saw at least as much of each other as either did of Gaitskell, and

*The classical example of confusion produced by unaspirated diction was Hugh Dalton's story of a meeting of a small group early in the war presided over by Ernest Bevin and also attended by Dalton, Nye Bevan and Dai Grenfell (Secretary of Mines, 1940–2). Bevin at the end said, 'That's settled then, 'Ugh [you] and I [Nye, Dai] will deal with it,' which, as Dalton pointed out, left open every possible ambiguity within the four of them.

when one of us disagreed with him we were mostly united. This was true of our view that he put too much reliance on 'discipline' exercised through the National Executive Committee or by the withdrawal of the whip in combating Bevanism, that he led himself into a quagmire in the famous Clause Four dispute* of 1959–60, and that he was wrong about Europe in 1961–2. Crosland in those days was almost as committed a European as was I. It was only in the 1970s that we differed on this. On the other hand there was no division at all over the unilateralist issue of 1960–1. We thought Gaitskell had no option but to stand and fight, and that he did so with courage and skill. And even on the other issues, up to the European one, it was only in private that we criticised. In public we always supported.

Immediately after the 1955 election we were both convinced that the essential aim was to make Gaitskell leader of the Labour Party at the earliest possible moment, a strategy of the merits of which our prospective candidate took a good deal of convincing. He thought that Herbert Morrison, with whom he had worked in close alliance for the previous three or four years, should first have a turn. We believed this would be a near disaster for the Labour right. We had never thought a great deal of Morrison, and we were convinced by 1955 that he was well past his best. Furthermore, Attlee was dedicated to Morrison not being his successor. If he could not be confident that this skilled, half-admirable but limited politician would be defeated, he might postpone his own resignation almost indefinitely. And we believed the time had come when the party would be better off with a replacement for Attlee. So did Attlee, provided it was not Morrison. Furthermore we were by no means sure that Morrison would beat Bevan in a straight fight. And even if he did, we did not believe that after a Morrison turn there would be an assured inheritance for Gaitskell. We feared that an inept Morrison leadership (and his House of Commons performances had become appallingly so) would use up the credit of the whole Labour right and leave the road wide open for Bevan.

This was the argument which convinced Gaitskell. I first put it to him with all the force I could command on 7 June, when the Gaitskells dined with us alone. Gradually it worked. In the autumn he said that he would tell Morrison that he felt he could no longer refrain from being

---

*After the 1959 election defeat the analysis of all the Gaitskellites was that the Labour Party had presented an out-of-date and doctrinaire aspect. It was thought that this might be symbolically corrected by amending Clause Four of the party's constitution which nominally committed it to the public ownership of 'the means of production, distribution and exchange'. However, changing a sacred text proved more trouble than it was worth. Crosland and I thought Gaitskell ought to have cut his losses earlier.

a candidate and that his previous offer of support no longer stood. Courageously he did this at a lunch with no one else present. He dreaded the occasion, and I remember asking him with apprehension how it had gone. He said, 'Remarkably well,' for Morrison, with incredible complacency, had not been particularly worried, and had more or less patted him on the head and said that he was right to cut his teeth by having a go.

I fear, however, that Morrison may reasonably have attributed his change of plan to pressure from me (and no doubt from Crosland too), for when the contest took place, in December 1955, and the result was Gaitskell 157, Bevan 70, Morrison 40, Morrison did not speak to me for the next seven years. It was a period of his life when he was sour with most people (which was a pity, for his career had been a notable one and his bitterness contrasted sharply with Dalton's generous bonhomie in old age), but he probably felt an hereditary grievance against Jenkinses. My father, he believed, had let him down by becoming PPS to Attlee in 1936, and I had compounded the betrayal by urging Gaitskell to stand against him in 1955. In 1962, however, when he took a firmly pro-European position (inspired a little by the fact that both Attlee and Gaitskell had gone in the other direction) we had a reconciliation. I presided over a Fabian lecture which he gave and he presented me with a copy of his autobiography, inscribed with a mixture of old resentment and new forgiveness.

When Gaitskell's victory was announced I was in Paris attending a meeting of the Western European Union Assembly (membership of which went with that of the Council of Europe Assembly), and suffering for the only time in my life from oyster poisoning. The news was enough to lift me out of even the depression induced by that condition. Apart from my joy at his triumph, I felt that for the first time I had influenced major events.

The result was a remarkable personal triumph for Gaitskell. He had been in the House of Commons for only ten years, and both as Chancellor and in opposition he had taken a very hard social democratic line. Some would say he had been unnecessarily intransigent: certainly no one could accuse him of having trimmed. Furthermore he had no natural political base within the Labour Party. Morrison had the bastion of the LCC and the London Labour Party and years on the National Executive Committee. Bevan had the left and most of the constituency parties, and ought to have had the Welsh and the miners, although by 1955 he had alienated many in both these categories. Gaitskell was a quintessential bourgeois intellectual in politics, a Sidney Webb with fire in his belly, a Léon Blum without the aestheticism, a Ferdinand Lassalle without the Marxism. Despite this provenance he had achieved respectful support from the bellicose right-wing trade union leaders. But he was nowhere with the constituency parties. As recently as 1953 he had failed to be elected for one of their seven places on the National Executive. Yet in the parliamentary Labour Party the strength of his performance had carried him through to a massive single-stroke victory over the forces of both the old right and the new left. For those of us who were still young and his committed supporters there was an almost Wordsworthian quality about our reaction to his achievement, but unlike Wordsworth with the French Revolution, we did not become disillusioned. Eight years later and six months after Gaitskell's death, I wrote that his life was 'a standing contradiction of the cynical and depressing view that only those with cold hearts and twisted tongues can succeed in politics'.

At the time of his election Gaitskell was stronger on a cross-party basis than he was within the Labour Party outside the parliamentary party. He was the hero of the political journalists and the fashionable flavour amongst the chattering classes, extending well into the Conservative Party. By comparison Morrison was seen as dowdy and Bevan as loud-mouthed. Given the vagaries of political and newspaper taste, that view would probably have swung round in any event. But the change was hastened and accentuated by Suez.

That seismic controversy extended over six months from July 1956 to January 1957, when Eden's premiership collapsed. Gaitskell was alleged both to have reneged on the anti-Nasser line he took in July, before he comprehended that Eden envisaged the use of force, and to have struck too shrill a note of opposition at the crunch. I see no validity in the former point and little in the latter. The Tories became sour towards him because they were raw from failure and even a little guilty. Moreover it is easier to admire a man when he is number two or three in the opposition than when he has become your principal opponent. In any event one result of Suez was that Gaitskell lost his cross-party respect, even found considerable difficulty in getting a hearing in the House of Commons for the next year or two (which was peculiarly upsetting to the cumulative logic of his style of parliamentary speaking), and saw Aneurin Bevan acclaimed as having been more restrained, subtle and statesmanlike in his Suez criticism. Bevan became the flavour of the year, and Gaitskell became the dowdy one (Morrison had rather dropped out). To some extent this persisted until Bevan died in July 1960, and Gaitskell then again swam into fashion with his anti-unilateralist stand of 1960–1.

Bevan's swing to favour was compounded by his own anti-unilateralist 'naked into the conference chamber' speech at the Brighton Labour Party conference of 1957. The speech effectively announced the winding up of the Bevanite revolt, which had plagued the Labour Party like a civil war for the previous six and a half years.

This was not because Bevan capitulated to Gaitskell. On the contrary, his idea of reconciliation was to try to patronise Gaitskell as though he were Charles James Fox dealing with Lord North. The reason this revolt was over was that Bevan by this speech left most of his followers, and notably Michael Foot, stranded and dismayed. What disgraceful behaviour, it is tempting to say, typical of the man whom we had so rightly opposed, until one remembers that by an extraordinary coincidence Gaitskell, in the same hall five years later, was to put most of the old-guard Gaitskellites in an almost exactly similar position with his 'thousand years of history' anti-Common Market speech. The only sad difference was that, in my view, Bevan was as right in 1957 as Gaitskell was wrong in 1962. So perhaps it is best to settle for saying that there are a lot of paradoxes in politics.

In 1956–7, Gaitskell being safely elected, the balance of my interests moved away from Parliament. One of Gaitskell's first actions, quite rightly, was to detach Wilson from Bevan by making him his own replacement as shadow Chancellor. A minor side-effect of this however was that it made me less eager to devote time to the minutiae of Finance Bills than I had been, particularly in 1952 and again in the autumn of 1955, when we had so tormented Rab Butler for taking back in an autumn Budget what he had given in a pre-election one in the spring that he agreed to be replaced as Chancellor by Macmillan at the turn of the year.

In politics outside Parliament the Fabian Society became a focus of interest for me. My association with this venerable (and in the 1920s and early 1930s somewhat moribund) organisation went back at least to 1940 when its summer school had made an unforgettable impact on my life. In 1949 I had become a member of its executive committee, and in 1957–8 I became its chairman. There was a considerable element of 'Buggins' turn' about my succession to this position, but it nonetheless gave me pleasure (partly perhaps because of 1940), and I applied myself with more than average vigour to the office, paying particular attention to the organisation outside London of this traditionally metropolitan Society, and addressing Fabian gatherings in Norwich, Durham, Newcastle, Glasgow and Aberfoyle. These tours were significant for two reasons. First, they brought me into close contact with Bill Rodgers, who after two years as assistant secretary had become general secretary of the Society in 1953. As he was to become my single most important political associate of a younger generation, just as Tony Crosland was of my own generation and Hugh Gaitskell of an older one, this made the journeys more than worthwhile for that alone. Second, they provided the occasion for my first visit to Glasgow, which cast equally long shadows into the future.

In work outside politics a great part of my effort was put into the writing of *Sir Charles Dilke*. This book, as I indicated in the previous chapter, was conceived on the evening of the publication party for *Mr Balfour's Poodle* in 1954, it was seriously worked on (mainly in the Manuscript Room of the British Museum, where the Dilke papers were kept) in 1955 and the first half of 1956, written in the second half and in 1957, and published in October 1958. I again got good reviews, and in addition sold a lot more copies, in hardback and paperback, in Britain and in America, than had been the case with either *Mr Attlee* or *Mr Balfour's Poodle*.

It also generated more secondary activity than any other book of mine has done. Granada made a television drama a year or so after publication, to which I contributed a short introductory commentary. Then in May 1964 a full-scale play with the slightly mocking title of *Right Honourable Gentleman* was put on in the West End. The lead parts of Dilke and Mrs Crawford were played by Anthony Quayle and Anna Massey. This play was a considerable success, and ran at a big theatre (Her Majesty's in the Haymarket) for more than a year. Afterwards it went to New York, and although markedly less successful there managed about three months. Unfortunately the playwright, I think mainly instigated by the impresario (Emile Littler, who also claimed part authorship), took the view that the play was not based on my book and that no cash nexus between us was therefore necessary. They were right to the extent that all the papers I had used were in the public domain, and that the play *could* have been written without the existence of my book. Whether it *would* have been was a different matter, and was made less likely by the fact that a minor factual error which I had made in the book was duly repeated in the play.

An action for plagiary was however judged to be both heavy-handed and hazardous, and I even decided to roll with the punch to the extent of accepting Littler's invitation to the first night. I asked him if I might have two extra tickets in order to take my publisher and his wife (Mark Bonham Carter had not merely commissioned but invented the book) and he answered certainly, provided that I paid for them as he did not own the theatre (his brother did). I then decided that parsimony was as important as flamboyance in the make-up of a great impresario. For many years thereafter Emile Littler used to send the biggest Christmas card of any which we received. They were appropriately sent from Angmering-on-Sea, my old 1943 theatrical housing estate stamping-ground. I never opened their envelopes without the ungracious thought crossing my mind that a modest royalty might have been even more welcome.

In 1968 I encountered a different sort of impresario. Sam Spiegel, the Hollywood mogul who had achieved such triumphs as *The Bridge On the River Kwai* and *African Queen*, decided that he might be able to do almost as well with my unfortunate Victorian politician. He also decided, as a sort of angel of justice, that he would prefer to buy my book rather than Littler's play. I hope it had nothing to do with the fact that I had become Chancellor of the Exchequer by then. He paid £40,000 for the film rights, which was a substantial sum before my great inflationary successors as Chancellor had got to work. He must have taken the project seriously to begin with, for he brought no less a director than George Cukor to see me in 11 Downing Street and they talked about a dazzling cast, which might have seemed a piece of braggadocio had it not been exactly the sort of list they were used to commanding. Alec Guinness was I think their favourite for Dilke, and Julie Christie for Mrs Crawford.

Alas, they never made the film, and I never got any benefit out of the money. There was no reason at all why as Chancellor I should not receive some sterling for myself and some dollars for the country as a belated reward for a lot of hard work done over ten years before. But there was every reason why I should not attempt to exploit the various loopholes which made high tax rates less oppressive for authors with overseas earnings. I just received a cheque and paid it in. It subsequently turned out, by an almost supreme irony, that had I waited a few weeks until ten years after first publication I would have benefited substantially under 'spreading' provisions introduced in one of James Callaghan's Finance Bills, of which I remained blissfully ignorant, although then spending my life surrounded by the Treasury officials who had worked on this. Worse was to follow. The money was routinely invested (without my being told how or where, which was appropriate for someone holding my office) while awaiting the tax demand for about 90 per cent of it. By the time the demand came in, the stock exchange had declined sufficiently, no doubt partly due to my stringent management of the economy, that the margin of 10 per cent which might have been left to me had more than disappeared. The whole episode had turned out a real handful of dust: no film, and no money for me, despite the fact that Spiegel, who remained a friendly acquaintance until the end of his life in 1986, had paid up promptly and without complaint.

Nevertheless *Dilke* brought many rewards, material and non-material. Its success, I think, was due to the fact that it was half a serious biography of an intriguing political figure and half a detective story with some titillating sexual quirks. Dilke's downfall was important. Had his career not been ruined by the scandal, he *might* have changed the course of British politics. He *might* have kept Joseph Chamberlain in a social-reform-orientated Liberal Party and so have avoided the twenty years of semi-impotence to which Gladstone's last-phase obsession with Ireland condemned it, and which gave the Labour Party the opportunity to make its 1900–6 breakthrough; and this breakthrough contained the seeds of the death of the Gladstone/Asquith governing tradition.

As a detective story it was unusual in that the mystery was unsolved at the end of the book. After several years of work I remained uncertain of the exact truth. I thought that Dilke was almost certainly not guilty as charged by Mrs Crawford, the errant wife, but that there was enough murk in his life to make him an unconvincing rebutter of calumny. Cardinal Manning, as I believed and as indeed he claimed, was the man nearest to knowing the full truth, but he left no record which I could discover. And I doubt whether more will ever now be revealed.

The success of *Dilke* was a further notch in my movement towards being a professional writer. Once it was done I automatically thought of what my next biography was to be. I also undertook to write as a Penguin Special a short campaign book for the general election of 1959. It was to balance books by Quintin Hailsham for the Conservative Party and by Roger Fulford for the Liberal Party, was entitled *The Labour Case*, was completed by Easter 1959 and was published in July, just in time for the October election.

In addition I wrote frequently for the *Spectator* in those years of the late 1950s. In 1954 Ian Gilmour had bought this old-established journal of fluctuating repute and began a five-year spell as editor as well as proprietor which was as innovative and sparkling as any in its 185 years of existence. Its general tone was libertarian/iconoclastic. It was also pro-European and had been vehemently anti-Suez. It was not pro-Labour (and indeed got involved in a messy 1957 libel action with Bevan, Crossman and Morgan Phillips, the general secretary of the party). But it was friendly towards Gaitskell, and above all was against pomposity and an air of complacency in politics, which made its principal target the Government of Harold Macmillan, with I fear a special corner of it reserved for the Wirral woodenness of Selwyn Lloyd. Bernard Levin, who under the pseudonym of Taper both invented a new style of parliamentary commentary and made his own reputation on the paper, specialised in the loyal but hapless Foreign Secretary, to whom he mostly referred as 'Mr Hoylake, UDC', on the somewhat inadequate ground that Lloyd had once been chairman of that now long since abolished local authority. Altogether the *Spectator* became both more exciting and of more interest to the moderate left than the *New Statesman*, which it had certainly not been in the 1930s and 1940s, the prime of Kingsley Martin's editorship of the latter journal.

I wish I could claim to have been a key agent of this remarkable blossoming of the *Spectator*, but this is not chronologically sustainable. During the first few years of its transformation I had no connection with the paper beyond being an enthusiastic reader. I do not think that I met Ian Gilmour until February 1957, although he and his wife became considerable friends over that summer and remained so both in the next few years and in the long run. We went on a French holiday together in August 1958 and to America in October 1960 for the Kennedy/Nixon presidential contest. The first article for the *Spectator* which I wrote was in March 1957 and must have stemmed directly from that first meeting with Gilmour. But the spate of my *Spectator* writing came after he had handed over the editorship to Brian Inglis. John Campbell, my 1983 biographer, records that in 1960 I wrote eight articles of political commentary and no less than fourteen full-scale book reviews for the paper. This was the first fairly regular book reviewing that I had done, and it gave me a habit with which I have since persisted, except between 1964 and 1970 (when the pressures of office were too novel and too strong), although gradually transferring to the *Observer* as my main outlet from about 1962 onwards.

I also wrote for *Encounter* during these years and, although I did not specifically know it at the time, was not particularly shocked when it subsequently emerged that the magazine was partly CIA-financed. We had all known that it had been heavily subsidised from American sources, and it did not seem to me to be worse that these should turn out to be a US Government agency rather than, as I had vaguely understood, a Cincinnati gin distiller. There was never the slightest interference with what I wanted to write, and *Encounter* was happy to commission Crossman and Strachey as well as more hard-line social democrats like Crosland and me. No doubt had we tried to urge a Soviet or fellow-travelling line our invitations would have dried up, but we had no such desire and were left perfectly free to advocate positions which were miles away from the Eisenhower/Dulles ones.

I also wrote occasional pieces for a variety of newspapers, the *Daily Telegraph*, the *Sunday Times*, the *Evening Standard*, even the *Sunday Express*. But I did not command space. I waited to be asked, almost invariably agreed and gratefully accepted whatever fee was offered. A good indication of my journalistic status was that when in 1958 I went for a three weeks' tour of a Middle East which was still in a very raw post-Suez state I did a series of politico/topographical articles for the *Birmingham Mail*. It obviously made more sense from a constituency point of view to publish them there than in another provincial newspaper, but I would have preferred to write them for, say, the *Observer* or the old *News Chronicle* (which still existed).

In addition, I accepted whatever broadcasting and television invitations came my way. Here too I was on the fringe of being amongst the small minority of MPs who (to the great envy of their colleagues) were showered with invitations. There were many fewer outlets in those days. In November 1958 I did my first BBC *Any Questions* programme, and was thereafter asked about once a year. In April 1959, I began to do a Sunday television programme called *Free Speech*. It had begun life on the BBC and under the name of *In the News* but it had run into trouble with the political parties for employing its own favourite mavericks rather than party spokesmen. The original mavericks were Robert Boothby, Michael Foot, A. J. P. Taylor and W. J. Brown. The BBC, I fear, weakened under pressure, and agreed to a considerable dilution. I did one *In the News* myself in 1956, rather badly I thought. So with the coming of independent television the original team reassembled itself and migrated. The new title of *Free Speech* really meant free choice of participants. But Associated Rediffusion, which was the producing company, must have weakened in turn, for by 1959 there were practically never more than two of the famous four. To fill the other slots, there was recruited a sort of reserve team, of which I became a part. I did about a dozen of these programmes over the two years after my first appearance. The invitations then ceased abruptly, whether because the programme was wound up or because I was dropped I cannot now remember.

*Free Speech* thought it was the flagship of political television, and was self-consciously pleased with itself about it. The producer (John Irwin) and the chairman (Edgar Lustgarten) believed in turning each performance into a beanfeast. We assembled at 11.30 on Sunday mornings in Lustgarten's flat in Albany for a preliminary discussion and a ceremonial uncorking of champagne bottles. Then we proceeded in a fleet of Daimlers to a disused music hall, either in Holloway or in Bethnal Green, where we did a technical rehearsal of camera angles. Then we adjourned to a private room in an adjacent gin palace, where the most gargantuan lunch, specially brought from a West End caterer's, was served. (The idea that those old working-class inner suburbs of north-east London could have produced a decent meal of their own was considered preposterous in those days.) It was accompanied by rich hock, fine claret or burgundy and liberal supplies of port and brandy. Only thus, was presumably the theory, could an adequate level of wit be generated for the programme and (considered almost more important) at the lunch itself. Then we staggered back to the theatre and performed live.

After a bit it was decided by higher management that, while we could continue with our indulgent luncheons, the programme must be recorded beforehand. It was probably a wise decision, provoked, it was thought, by one or two particularly fruity performances from Boothby. We were paid in crisp white five-pound notes – seven of them, although we players from the substitutes' bench always suspected that the old regulars got more – handed to one in an envelope before dispersal. At a time when a good meal for two rarely cost more than £4 this provided a cash supply for several weeks ahead. It also provided an interesting experience of British political television, if not in its childhood at least in its adolescence.

My other extra-parliamentary activity of these years of the late 1950s was to represent the British European Airways pilots in negotiations with their management, and eventually (in 1960 and again in 1963) before the Industrial Court. They were part of the British Airline Pilots Association, in which organisation Norman Tebbit had not then emerged to prominence, but they were significantly less well paid than the BOAC long-haul pilots (the two Corporations were not merged until 1974), felt a considerable sense of grievance about this and wanted independent representation in negotiating or arbitral proceedings. Why they picked on me is (in retrospect at any rate) shrouded in mystery. I have a vague feeling it was based on a suggestion of Aidan Crawley's. I was telephoned out of the blue, saw their emissary and accepted light consultancy duties, partly out of curiosity and partly for the money. These duties escalated considerably (but so did the pay), and right through until 1963 the pilots' problems kept bubbling away. Whenever I felt I had finally disposed of them they always got involved in some fresh dispute and came back to me. I also represented the independent pilots (that is, those employed by private airlines) in one negotiation and hearing.

In bursts the pilots occupied about a quarter of my time. They were on the whole a nice lot, although a bit gloomy, partly because they mostly much disliked 'abroad', which was a pity in view of their occupation. I was totally unconvinced by the conventional aviation wisdom that a pilot deserved higher pay per hour for sitting quietly at the controls for long stretches across the Atlantic Ocean or the African continent than for dodging in and out of the busiest airports of Europe. I enjoyed refuting this, and indeed generally enjoyed my single experience of presenting a case before a court, even if it was only in the informal atmosphere of the Industrial Court, where first Lord Forster of Harraby and then Sir Roy Wilson presided with sympathetic courtesy. The pilots also gave me the opportunity to make my first excursion into the rather self-consciously separate world of aviation.

In the House of Commons I was much concerned in 1957, 1958 and 1959 in pursuing the single and non-party issue of the reform of the law of censorship. My closest parliamentary collaborator became Tony Lambton. In March 1957, Lambton, who had won a good place in the ballot for private members' bills, introduced the draft statute which had been prepared (largely by Norman St John-Stevas) for the Herbert Committee. The Government did not oppose the second reading, although fifteen months before the under-secretary at the Home Office had himself 'talked out' (an unusual proceeding, for the dirty work is normally left to back-benchers) a similar bill which Hugh Fraser had brought forward on our behalf. In the meantime there had been a change of regime at the Home Office. Rab Butler had replaced Gwilym Lloyd George, who had been a remarkably illiberal Home Secretary, not only for one bearing his radical name, but for anybody; and J. E. S. Simon (later President of the Probate, Divorce and Admiralty division of the High Court and now Lord Simon of Glaisdale), who had seconded Fraser's bill, became under-secretary.

Butler, as befitted the President of the Royal Society of Literature, had more respect for the views of the literary establishment than did either of his predecessors (David Maxwell Fyfe, later Lord Chancellor Kilmuir, had been the Secretary of State before Lloyd George), but he sometimes expressed it in rather crablike action. At this stage he offered us the suggestion that Lambton's bill should go to a select committee of the House rather than a standing committee. A select committee can brood on the subject at large and call evidence, but it does not lead directly to the statute book in the way that a standing committee can do. It would take Lambton's bill off into a bourn from which no traveller returns, and we would have to start again in the following session.

On the other hand the only standing committee which dealt with private members' bills was hopelessly blocked. There was not much prospect of progress that way either. We therefore decided to accept the select committee with its enjoyable prospect of the examining on literary censorship of such dignitaries as the permanent under-secretary of the Home Office (then Sir Frank Newsam), the Commissioner of Metropolitan Police, the Director of Public Prosecutions and the head of Customs and Excise, and the hope that if we could persuade the committee to produce an agreed bill the Government would feel committed to give us parliamentary time in the following session.

The select committee took a year. Its high point was the day that I got T. S. Eliot and E. M. Forster to make a joint appearance as witnesses for liberty. They sat together, like birds on a bough, at a small table surrounded by a semi-circle of the fourteen members of the committee, and answered questions for nearly two hours. The committee's achievement, however, was to produce an agreed report which, while there were substantial elements of compromise in it, was sufficiently libertarian to satisfy the reformers. The key point which made it so, the admission of 'expert evidence' on literary merit, was carried only on the casting vote of the chairman, a somewhat bemused Yorkshire squire. But, once it was in, no one voted against the compromise as a whole.

Having climbed up this ladder we next found ourselves, in the vivid metaphor of A. P. Herbert, at the bottom of a very large snake. At the beginning of the session of 1958–9 none of the twenty members who drew places in the ballot showed the slightest interest in introducing our measure, ripe though it was for plucking. I therefore reverted to the forlorn device of introducing a Ten Minute Rule bill, which was exactly where I had been three and a half years before. This time, however, we hoped that the Government would assist a formal second reading and thus put the bill early in the queue for the standing committee. On the contrary the Government whips organised a few back-benchers to cry the necessary 'object' at the appropriate time on two Friday afternoons.

A. P. Herbert retaliated by announcing his intention to stand in an impending bye-election and thus split the Tory vote in that Government-held constituency. He got as far as printing and selling (nationally) many copies of his election address, appropriately entitled 'I Object' and addressed to the electors of Harrow East. Quite why it was thought that mixture of flat suburbia and sometimes philistine school on the hill would rise up for literary freedom was not clear; perhaps we placed too much reliance on the Harrovian spirit of Byron, Gerald Gardiner and John Mortimer. In any event the effect on the Government was dramatic. Within a week the whips offered us a debate and an unopposed second reading.

Then there was another snake. It became apparent through some truculent growlings of Manningham-Buller, currently Attorney-General, that the Government saw the second reading as a preliminary not to passing the bill as it stood but to a substantial rewriting of it in committee, with provisions for increased police powers left in, but most of the liberalising provisions struck out; the compromise of the select committee was to be largely destroyed. The only hope was to by-pass Manningham-Buller and other obstructive ministers and officials and get into direct negotiations with Butler. This I succeeded in doing in three meetings, two in the Home Office and one in the House of Commons, over the month between mid-January and mid-February 1959. I first had to make it clear that if the Manningham-Buller position remained that of the Government I would withdraw the bill (which was under my control because under my name), that we would all denounce the Government not only for illiberalism but for trickery, and that Alan Herbert would be back on the bye-election campaign trail. Rab Butler's reaction to this was not to be affronted but to conduct a serious negotiation which led to our regaining about 40 per cent of what we were threatened with losing. This left us prepared to go into committee, but still uncertain whether we would want to go on with the bill which emerged.

Beyond this result, worthwhile but limited, the process was a fascinating insight into the methods of operation of that most ambiguous of politicians. Rab Butler was friendly and flexible, although not ingratiating, and always retained an air of authority. He commanded the officials who were present and he had a complete grasp of the points at issue. Then, when the business of one meeting was over and the officials had gone, he held me back and gave an unforgettable display of irreverence and indiscretion. He launched into an exposition of the breadth of the duties of a Home Secretary, gazed wistfully out of the window of the large and gloomy room (it was the first time I had ever seen this traditional seat of the senior Secretary of State which I was later to occupy for a total of four and a half years) and said, 'If the Prime Minister were arrested in the park [which had just happened to an under-secretary] it would come to me to deal with, you know.' Then the fantasy evaporated, for he saw the precipice ahead and said sadly and inconsequentially: 'But I couldn't do anything. I would have to leave it to the law.'

Fortified by this negotiation I took the bill through four Wednesday mornings of standing committee in March. To our amazement we discovered that in practice although not in theory we had a majority. This was because most of the Tory members did not turn up. Whether the organisation of this was the final ploy in Butler's crablike attempt to assist us I rather doubt. In any event it had the effect of leaving almost isolated the Solicitor-General, Harry Hylton-Foster. (He was however compensated for his punishment by being made Speaker of the House of Commons six months later.) We defeated him in seven out of the ten divisions called in the committee. In the most crucial one, on admissibility of expert evidence of 'literary, or artistic, scientific or other merit', he was supported by five of the eighteen Conservative back-benchers on the committee, while we won by the votes of eight Labour members plus Lord Lambton and Mark Bonham Carter, then briefly Liberal MP for Torrington. The need for the Attorney-General's consent to a prosecution we carried by twelve votes to five.

We decided to use our unexpected majority with some restraint and only put back about another 40 per cent (making a total of 80 per cent) of what the Government had been threatening to take away from the select committee report. We hoped that leaving them with 20 per cent would encourage them not to be vindictive and try to 'talk out' the report stage on the floor of the House. We could still lose the bill through lack of time. They wanted us to give up both expert evidence and the need for the Attorney's consent in return for a smooth passage. We decided to hold firm on the former and give on the latter. On the evening before the crucial day Manningham-Buller, who seemed to have assumed command of the retreating Government forces, summoned me to his room and announced that he would accept the bargain. He did so with all the graciousness of a dog-hater throwing a bone at an importunate animal. Dealing with him compared with dealing with Butler was like moving from an Oxbridge common room to an army parade ground.

We still had to get the bill through the House of Lords, a substantially less liberal chamber then than it has subsequently become. This task was undertaken with skill and eloquence by Norman Birkett, recently ennobled after a career as one of the most golden-tongued KCs of the 1930s and 1940s. He reduced the mauling to a minimum, but he could not avoid it altogether. We were back to perhaps 70 per cent, but we had become more worried about the efflux of time than about a small retreat of substance. We dealt with the Lords' amendments in the Commons on 22 July and got royal assent on 29 July. It was another damned close-run thing, for that was within two days not merely of the end of the session but, as it turned out, of the end of the Parliament. Private members' legislation requires a great deal of luck. We had just enough, as well as a number of other assets. At our Herbert Committee celebratory party that evening we emitted even more sighs of relief than cries of triumph.

# CHAPTER SEVEN

## *Almost Out of Politics*

The 1959 election result was a sad disappointment for the whole Labour Party, and above all for Hugh Gaitskell. None of us realised at the time that it was his only chance of becoming Prime Minister. But even without that knowledge it meant that, instead of the period of constructive power for which at the age of fifty-three he seemed to be almost perfectly poised, a three-times defeated party was condemned to a splurge of bickering.

What is more difficult to say is whether the result was a shock as well as a disappointment. Nearly three years before, when Macmillan had taken over a government which was on the verge of post-Suez collapse, there were very few who believed that the new Prime Minister had the remotest chance of winning the next general election. The more relevant question was whether he could survive the next three months. Macmillan's formidable feat was to bring the Conservative Party back to a position from which it could grasp at victory. He achieved it by a rare combination of nerve and opportunism.

Gaitskell, however, had always been amongst the least complacent. I remember three conversations in which he was very hesitant about the prospects. The first was as early as May 1957, and was occasioned by his own special post-Suez difficulty of getting a hearing in the House of Commons. It was in a little Russian restaurant, long since disappeared, in Draycott Avenue, South Kensington. Gaitskell always liked the nostalgic melancholy of White Russian establishments; he had once made several of us accompany him to dine at a 'balalaika' semi-nightclub in Paris when we wanted to go to a serious French restaurant. That May lunchtime in Draycott Avenue he doubted how much longer he could continue as leader of the opposition if he was hardly allowed to get out a single coherent sentence. It was half serious and half just a blowing off of his own dismay. The second was just over a year later when I drove him to a train from a Fabian weekend school near Steyning in Sussex, and on a sunny Saturday evening in that not very good July of 1958 he expressed his private view that the election prospect was evenly balanced. The third was in late August 1959, on the threshold of the campaign itself. We had rented a holiday house near Chichester, as we did (in varying places) for every August between 1954 and 1960. It was part of a small preparatory school, which was also part of a pattern, for a cricket pitch was demanded by our elder son (then aged ten). The Gaitskells came down for a day. There was no cricket, in contrast with the days of other visitors, for that was not Hugh's style, but we walked on the downs near Goodwood and then spent a lot of time looking for a deeply concealed pub/restaurant called the Black Rabbit, which when eventually unearthed turned out to be not very good, but of which he had faintly romantic memories of having visited twenty years or so before. That was very much his style. There he expressed a mixture of hope and apprehension about the outcome of the campaign, a sensible approach for the private thoughts of a leader on the eve of an election.

The next week he went to Russia with Bevan and Healey. That trip cannot have been a boost for him, for the Soviet leaders gave him noticeably less in the way of an election fillip than they had given to Macmillan in the spring, and the internal events of the visit also somewhat weakened his position in relation to Bevan, with whom his partnership was inevitably fragile. He got back to London hurriedly, after Macmillan had announced the election, and slightly on the wrong foot. But he then proceeded to fight a brilliant campaign for two weeks. He did everything which a challenging candidate of the moderate left could be expected to do. He united and invigorated his party. He raised the level of the campaign and cut deep into uncommitted voters who cared about principle, but he did not disappear into the clouds. He got as good a synthesis between conscience and reform, between liberal values and 'jobs, pensions, homes and schools' (Bill Rodgers' loudspeaker phrase in much later days) as anyone is ever likely to achieve.

Then, ten days before polling day, he made the most terrible mistake. At least it was widely regarded as the most terrible mistake, not least by Gaitskell himself, but also by those in the Labour Party who wanted ammunition, not for immediate use, because they had been swept along by the surge of Gaitskell's campaign, but for a reserve armoury. He promised that in normal peacetime circumstances a Labour Government would not increase the rate of income tax. As Harold Wilson was campaigning on a reduction in purchase tax and Labour had an expensive social programme it sounded irresponsible. The Conservatives exploited the 'a promise a day' gambit as hard as they could.

I incline to the view, subsequently expressed by Rab Butler and a lot of level-headed Conservatives, that it did not make much difference to the result. But it was unwise, out of character, and had the undesirable effect of putting Gaitskell on the defensive for the rest of the campaign. It checked the onrush of his assault. But it did not affect the more important underlying current of the election, which was that the hidden mood of the country was against the Labour Party. There was a strong latent satisfaction with the new affluence of the previous few years. This satisfaction was not paraded. But it was there, and was well exploited by the deft materialism of Macmillan's campaign. In the circumstances no radical leader could have won. Gaitskell did at least as well as anyone else could have done.

In a way he did much better than this. The 1959 election campaign at once lost Gaitskell the premiership and made him a public figure of fame and high repute. Before it he was just another upper-rank politician. After it he was in a category with Macmillan and with no one else, and while Macmillan was slightly ahead on fame Gaitskell was slightly ahead on repute.

In Stechford, in a minor way, I had an equally mixed election. The campaign seemed to go smoothly enough. The weather was spectacular, day after day of high pressure and misty early-autumn sun. I did not exert myself unduly. I went outside the West Midlands only on a strictly personal basis, to Bosworth for Woodrow Wyatt, to Dewsbury for David Ginsburg and to Grimsby for Tony Crosland. All three were fighting these constituencies for the first time. On the way to Dewsbury I had to put up the hood of my open Morris Minor while driving through Sheffield, not because it was cold or wet or windy, but because the smuts were insufferable. Thanks to the Clean Air Act I have never since had a comparable experience.

I also had the solace, for the first time during a Birmingham campaign, of the Zuckerman house in Edgbaston. I did not stay there, I remained faithful to the Hitchmans and to Stechford, but the Zuckermans provided a lot of meals and high-quality wine. Solly was then Professor of Anatomy at the University of Birmingham as well as Macmillan's chief adviser on the science of weaponry, but did not find the latter role incompatible with providing me with hospitality and encouragement in Birmingham. Jennifer and I were indeed at the Zuckermans' on the evening of polling day and heard the first and gloomily decisive results before we went down to the Council House for our own count.

Birmingham counting was normally slow, but on this occasion it was a bit too fast for us. The process was far advanced and my supporters were looking baleful, whether about our lateness or about what had come out of the ballot boxes was not clear. One or two of them

even suggested we might have lost. I moved hastily round the tables
trying to form my own view, and while doing so was calmed by the
Conservative agent, a detached professional who later claimed to be
a fan of my *Spectator* articles. He said, 'I can assure you that you've
won, but I don't know what's happened to your majority.' In fact it
had gone down to 2900, which while not exactly knife-edge was not
glorious. Birmingham as a whole was bad – we lost three of the nine
seats we had previously held in the city – but the outer constituencies
with large new housing estates were the worst. They contained a
lot of beneficiaries of the Macmillan consumer-durables boom. The
Stechford result was worse than the Birmingham average and much
worse than the national average, but better than its two neighbouring
constituencies.

I think it was genuinely the case that my disappointment was more
for Gaitskell than for myself. I would have liked office, but was not
burning for it, and thought that in any case, in spite of (or perhaps
because of) our immensely close relationship, he was not likely to give
me any very exciting job. He on the other hand was eager without
reservation for the premiership, and was convinced by the success of
his campaign that it was within his grasp. The last time I had seen him
had been at supper in the Queen's Hotel after his Birmingham meeting
twelve days before the poll. He was then more optimistic than I had
ever known him. And he cannot have greatly changed as a result of
his income tax gaffe, for on the last Sunday evening he wrote out his
Cabinet list. The result was therefore an immediate shock as well as
a longer-term deprivation for him, and he had to absorb it under the
public gaze of the television cameras at his own count in the Leeds
City Hall. He did so with notable grace, which was one of the reasons
why the lost election enhanced his national standing.

I next saw him for an hour on the evening of the Friday on
which we all returned to London and then at what became the
much written-about and even notorious meeting at his Hampstead
house on the Sunday morning following the defeat (11 October).
Philip Williams's biography of Gaitskell says that this originated
as a farewell party for Hugh Dalton, who had not stood at the
election. I have no recollection of that being the motive, and think
it inherently implausible. Dalton was certainly there (indeed I drove
him back and lunched with him afterwards), but there was no occasion
for hurriedly arranging a post-election party at which to say goodbye.
We had known he was going from the House of Commons for months
if not years, and he soon became a peer. Furthermore, Patrick Gordon
Walker and Herbert Bowden (then chief whip, now Lord Aylestone),
who were both present, were not particular friends of his. Nor was
John Harris, whom he met for the first time and whom he referred

to in his diary as a 'nice looking young man' whom he must meet again.[1] Tony Crosland (above all), Douglas Jay, Jennifer and I were his friends but we were all seeing Dalton frequently at that time. I think we just came together because Gaitskell thought we were people with whom he could lick his wounds at ease.

Once we were together however we inevitably got down to a sort of inquest, and at one stage we sat in a circle and each expressed our view as though at a seminar. Dalton recorded that Jay took the lead and advocated dropping further nationalisation, loosening the link with the trade unions, changing the name from 'Labour' (as too class-conscious) and making an alliance and perhaps even a merger with the Liberal Party. My retrospective impression is that the talk was less taut than this and I have no recollection of the last point being raised. Dalton was in general a witness of the truth, but I think he must have been wrong on this, particularly as it is strongly denied by Jay himself.[2] I agree, however, with Dalton's statement that Gaitskell 'said little'; what he did was to encourage the most free-ranging discussion with no sacred cows. Dalton's account has led other commentators to believe that this was a decisive meeting rather than the casual beginning of a series of rolling discussions. He himself, for instance, had the Callaghans to dine that evening, and listened to reports from Cardiff which were just as damaging to Labour traditionalism as any of Jay's premises. We dined with the Wyatts, who also had Crosland and the Gaitskells, and there too the discussion naturally continued.

I had been due to go to America for a month on Tuesday, 13 October, for the first time since 1953, to stay with the Galbraiths and deliver four or five lectures at New England universities which Kenneth Galbraith had arranged so as to cover Jennifer's and my travelling expenses. At Gaitskell's request I telephoned on the Saturday (10 October) and told Galbraith with considerable embarrassment that the political situation at home made this impossible. This is a clear indication that Gaitskell intended to strike while the iron was hot in an attempt to reform the Labour Party, and wanted to have the members of his praetorian guard around, both for moral sustenance and in order to prospect the ground over which he might or might not advance. I also arranged with Galbraith that I would start the visit four weeks later and that he would (very tolerantly) reset up as many of the lectures as he could. This meant both that I was completely locked in from 10 November, as I could not possibly cancel for a second time, and that I had an incentive to use the intervening four weeks intensively so as to justify my change of plan.

This I on the whole did. At first it was a case of war 'to the knife and fork' as were mockingly described the Liberal battles at the end of the South African War, when competing banquets to Campbell-Bannerman and Asquith were organised. In the two weeks following the election, apart from the Wyatt dinner already mentioned, we dined with the Daltons, the Jays and the Cronins (Labour MP for Loughborough), as well as the Benns (no Hampstead set plotting there), and had Crosland, the Healeys, the Gordon Walkers, the Mayhews and the Denis Howells (defeated in Birmingham; they stayed for two nights) to dine with us. But it was not all incestuous plotting over dinner tables. On the first Monday I did a *Panorama* interview and trailed the anti-nationalisation and trade union link-loosening line which four days later Jay was to set out more fully in an article in *Forward* (an old ILP weekly which had been brought under Gaitskellite control). I went to two parliamentary Labour Party meetings, and spoke at one, where Jay and I took the brunt of the attack from those who wished to defend the citadel of Labour traditionalism. I went four times to Birmingham, where I tried to sweep the Stechford activists into the movement for reform, and at least gave them full notice of what I was up to. I delivered a Fabian lecture on the causes of defeat which was subsequently published, and I wrote a *Spectator* article on the sort of Labour Party (I did not share Jay's view about the change of name) which I thought could win in the future.

This set out seven 'great issues of today and tomorrow', which were those:

(1) of Britain accepting her new place in the world;

(2) of colonial freedom;

(3) of whether, as we grow richer, this new wealth is used exclusively for individual selfishness or for the growth of necessary community services and whether, in consequence, we follow or escape the American precedent of great private affluence surrounding rotting public services;

(4) of whether we reverse the present anarchy in the use of land sufficiently quickly to prevent the permanent destruction of the amenity of life in this overcrowded island;

(5) of the right of the individual to live his private life free from the intolerant prejudices of others or the arrogant interference of the State and the Police;

(6) of whether we can expose and destroy the abuses and inefficiencies of contemporary private industry without offering only the sterile alternative of an indefinite extension of public monopoly;

(7) of whether, as existing class barriers break up, they are replaced by a new and nasty materialistic snobbery or by a fresher and more co-operative approach.

It was, in my view, rather a good radical programme, although, as my 1983 biographer John Campbell pointed out, not a socialist

My birthplace. 'As polychromatic as Balliol chapel but not I think by Butterfield.'

Beside the seaside at Weston-Super-Mare, 1933. My father, me, a Monmouthshire vicar's family with my cousin, later Pita Karaka, next to the vicar.

The day my father returned from Cardiff Gaol. He is standing on the right; next to him is his solicitor, Gordon Edwards, and on the left D. J. Vaughan, our Newport host. In front are (*left to right*) Mrs Vaughan, me (aged six) and my mother (aged forty).

A trio of politicians from the South Wales coalfield: James Griffiths, Aneurin Bevan,
Arthur Jenkins. London, September 1934.

The Oxford Union in the first autumn of the war: Nicko Henderson (later ambassador to nearly everywhere) in the centre of the front row, Madron Seligman ('friend to Heath' and to me, now MEP) on the far right, James Comyn (later Mr Justice Comyn), who beat me for the presidency two terms later, third from the left and next to me in the back row. Canon Claude Jenkins and Michael Maclagan (later Richmond Herald of Arms), one in the cloth the other in khaki, represent the senior members of the university.

Union debate, February 1940. Ex-President Beñes of Czechoslovakia is speaking, Madron Seligman presides flanked by Robin Edmonds, librarian, and Anthony Crosland, treasurer. I am in the secretary's chair. Edward Heath, ex-president, is on the committee bench to the right at the back.

Local dignitaries assembled outside our Pontypool house to greet the deputy Prime Minister, June 1941. Front row (*left to right*) Sir Henry Mather Jackson, Lord Lieutenant of Monmouthshire, my mother, Attlee, Mrs Attlee, my father, Mrs George Bailey, wife of a prominent Cardiff dry-dock owner, and me. Behind are Captain Geoffrey Crawshay, Monmouthshire country gentleman and Welsh public servant, John Roberts, junior museum curator who was assistant private secretary to Attlee before being killed in the later stages of the war, unknown, and Colonel Sir Gerald Bruce, later Lord Lieutenant of Glamorgan and then Civil Defence Regional Commissioner for Wales.

Our wedding in the Savoy Chapel, 20 January 1945.

With Denis Healey at the Blackpool Labour Party conference, May 1945.

Campaign in Southwark, April 1948. I look eager to please. They look only semi-sceptical.

*A summer and a winter christening.*

Charles in 1949: Attlee holds the baby while Jennifer and Philip Noel-Baker look on.

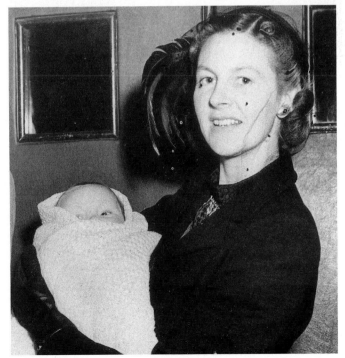

Cynthia in 1951 with Jennifer.

My mother arrives from Pontypool at the old Snow Hill Station, Birmingham, to assist in my 1950 election campaign, and is greeted by my chairman (later Sir) Joseph Balmer and my agent Sid Cooke.

With Anthony Crosland and his first wife, Hilary, July 1953. We all look very svelte.

one. I also made political speeches in both Oxford and Cambridge, addressed a *Socialist Commentary* lunch, and proselytised the French and Italian embassies as well as the *Time* magazine London bureau, the *Observer* newspaper and the editors of the Westminster Provincial Press group about the virtues of the new revisionism. All this was before my postponed departure for the United States. I was thus fully involved in the launch of what became the Clause Four battle in the Labour Party. I did not, as it happened, actively approve of the choice of this particular piece of ground on which to fight. To amend a ritualistic statement of aim did not seem to me to be worth the trouble of great argument. It would have been better to have concentrated on dropping specific offending nationalisation proposals and amending, not the party's dogma, but its working constitution so as, for example, to make the National Executive Committee less the creature of the trade unions and more that of the parliamentary Labour Party. But I was convinced that some battle had to be fought, and thought the choice of ground well within the prerogatives of a leader, on whom the main risks and brunt would necessarily fall. I therefore happily joined in.

Inevitably, however, my long visit cut me off from the second stage of the battle. (Although the Atlantic flight, in contrast with 1953, had been reduced to eight hours and – mostly – one hop, I still thought of America as somewhere one went to for a long time; it would not have occurred to me to go, as now, for an engagement and come straight back.) I missed the postponed and shortened Labour Party conference at Blackpool in the last days of November, which was a near disaster for Gaitskell and left Bevan for the first time (and last time, for he became ill immediately afterwards and died within eight months) in a commanding position with the centre of the party.

I was also away when the *Sunday Times* published a report that Gaitskell intended to shunt Harold Wilson from the shadow chancellorship and replace him with me. When I read it a few days late in New York I thought it was an agreeably flattering bit of nonsense. Not unnaturally it did not have the same effect on Wilson. He subsequently told Philip Williams that had it not been for the hostility aroused in his mind by these rumours he would not have been a candidate against Gaitskell for the leadership in 1960. And while his primary resentment was obviously against the bigger target, I suspect that the incident cast a shadow over his relations with me for several years. So it was an expensive piece of flattery. What I did not know at the time was that Gaitskell did contemplate replacing Wilson. But I still do not believe that he thought of putting me in. He had far too much sense to give such a senior post to someone who had not been elected to the shadow Cabinet. When in 1960 he did replace Wilson (but moving him sideways to the shadow foreign secretaryship) it was Callaghan, senior and not strictly Gaitskellite, whom he made shadow Chancellor. In 1959 he did bring me on to the front bench, but in a very junior Treasury position and accompanied by Anthony Wedgwood Benn, Roy Mason, Reg Prentice and George Thomson.

When I got back to London in early December I therefore found a Labour right in considerable disarray and the whole party rent by currents of bitterness which had not been seen for several years past. The edginess of the mood remains symbolised in my mind by a single trivial but unforgotten incident. On the afternoon of my early-morning return from New York I went into the House of Commons and stood beside the Speaker's chair. Gaitskell was sitting on the front bench half listening to a speech by Ellis Smith, a senior and honest if discontented and flat-footed member from Stoke-on-Trent whom Cripps had disposed of for incompetence as parliamentary secretary to the Board of Trade in 1946. Gaitskell immediately got up and came to talk to me, whom he had not seen for some time. Whereupon Smith stopped his speech and muttered something like: 'The leader prefers to greet someone who hasn't bothered to come to the House for a month than to listen to me.' It was *sotto voce* enough to escape printing, but I do not think it can have been a figment of my imagination, for when I consulted Hansard after a gap of thirty years Smith's speech was there at exactly the time that I recollect it. I quickly realised that the mood had got fairly rough.

From Christmas onwards the Clause Four battle increasingly became one within the National Executive of the Labour Party, in which I could play little part. It ground its way to a dreary draw in the spring, and I became diverted by a number of other activities. I reported back to the colours with enthusiasm but for short service when the unilateralist battle was joined over the summer and autumn of 1960, although never again in that Parliament of 1959–64 was I so absorbed by politics as I had been during that month of frenzy between the election and America. The BEA pilots became preoccupying in February and March 1960. I addressed the Industrial Court on their behalf in a four-hour speech on 21 March and fortified my respect for the bar by discovering how long it takes to prepare a quasi-legal submission of that sort.

I also began serious work on *Asquith*. As soon as *Sir Charles Dilke* was published in 1958 I had started looking for a new biographical subject. I wanted a late-nineteenth- or early-twentieth-century figure. I was radically partisan enough to want a Liberal rather than a Tory. And following Dilke, who achieved great interest by a quirk but did not attain the front rank of politics, I wanted a major rather than a minor figure. Asquith would almost have chosen himself by these criteria alone. In addition he was the grandfather of my publisher, Mark Bonham Carter, who was keen that I should undertake the work and able to obtain for me the remarkable cache of letters which Asquith had written to Venetia Stanley (later Mrs Edwin Montagu) between 1910 and 1915.

These letters had an adventurous history. They were physically in the possession of the daughter of the recipient, Judy Montagu (Mrs Milton Gendel). She had some years earlier allowed copies to get into the hands of Lord Beaverbrook. In the last part of his life Beaverbrook became a crazed Monopoly player with early-twentieth-century political papers. Moreover, in the main hobby of his old age – the refighting of the political battles of his youth – he was firmly anti-Asquith. However, he was inhibited from doing more than gossip about the letters by the fact that their copyright, which did not run out until 2015, did not go with their physical possession. It remained with the Asquith family, most forcefully represented by Mark's mother, Lady Violet Bonham Carter.

Beaverbrook had made a minor set at Jennifer and me in 1955 and 1956. We were several times bidden to Cherkley, near Leatherhead, or Arlington House in London and were regaled with jeroboams of champagne, reminiscent political gossip and private film showings. After a few years he dropped us, I think on anti-Common Market grounds. And then, in the last year of his life, we were retaken up in a way which was curious and revealing, as well as bearing upon the Asquith/Stanley letters. In 1963 he published *The Decline and Fall of Lloyd George*, the third of his trilogy about the premiership of the Welsh wizard, who had certainly cast a spell over Beaverbrook. I reviewed it in the *Observer*, half critically, half favourably: it had a compelling narrative, I said. On the Monday the *Daily Express* summarised the Sunday papers under the heading 'Acclaim for Lord Beaverbrook'. Every other review was quoted at length. The *Observer* was left shrouded in disregard. My review was obviously not considered nearly adulatory enough.

Beaverbrook however thought otherwise. On the Wednesday a letter written in the South of France came from him. 'Dear Mr Jenkins', it ran (he never called me anything else), 'I much appreciated your fine review. . . .' Then, even before I could get a letter back to him, three 'puffs' of me appeared, one in each of the Beaverbrook newspapers. Crossbencher in the *Sunday Express* wrote favourably about my political position (for the first time for several years), William Hickey in the *Daily Express* wrote some friendly piece of social gossip, and the Londoner's Diary in the *Evening Standard* praised my literary work. It was a fine example of independent editors working with the spontaneous agreement of Leibniz's clocks. Beaverbrook deserved some friendly acknowledgement and we went to a last dinner at Cherkley that summer. It was unlike the great parties of seven or eight years before. He had just married Lady Dunn, the widow of the Canadian steel millionaire, and there were only the four of us. She had a nursing fixation and regaled Jennifer with tales of bedpans and how she was much richer than Beaverbrook, while he regaled me with talk of Asquith and Venetia Stanley. With guttering candles between us and his face wreathed in mephistophelian mischief, he said, 'Lady Violet lets you have the letters because she knows how much more damaging would be the use I would make of them.' I never saw him again.

There were several reasons why his remarks did not make total sense, memorable though they were. First, whatever I did or did not do with the letters, he could not have used them until 2015, and with the intimations of mortality only too strongly upon him in 1963 he could hardly have expected even in his most optimistic moments to live until then. Second, my problem was that Lady Violet did not know I had the letters for the very good reason that she did not know they existed. This was a complication. When she eventually read my typescript four years later she claimed that the letters came as the most appalling shock to her. On the face of it this was unlikely. Venetia Stanley was her exact contemporary and close friend. She knew how much Venetia had been at Downing Street in the years before and at the beginning of the war of 1914. Nor was Lady Violet unworldly. However, the terms in which she denied knowledge tilted the probability back to her version. She did not say, 'It cannot be true. My father would never have done it,' which would have been a routine protest. What she said was, 'It cannot be true. Venetia was *so plain*,' which gave a ring of spontaneity and therefore of conviction to the denial.

The difficult encounter with Lady Violet, which took place on 6 April 1964, was however far ahead in the early months of 1960 when I began serious work on the book. Apart from the thousand or so Stanley letters (all written in the Prime Minister's hand over a period of little more than three years), copies of which were available for me 'to have and to hold', the more pedestrian general collection of Asquith papers was owned by Balliol and deposited in the Bodleian Library. I arranged to take six cardboard boxes of them away at a time and worked hard on these in 1960 and into 1961.

I started to write in the summer of 1961, and completed a 220,000-word manuscript in January 1964. It was by some margin the longest book that I had then written (Dilke was 160,000 words), and was the most substantial in other ways too. Its publication nine months later coincided with my becoming a minister, and partly perhaps for this reason it sold well: nearly twenty thousand copies in hardback, which involved several reprintings. The reviews, both in extent and in quality, were well up to *Mr Balfour's Poodle/Sir Charles Dilke* levels. Apart from America and paperbacks, there have been two subsequent editions in this country, one in 1978 and one in 1986. It has come near to being the standard work on Asquith, for the 1933 two-volume 'tombstone' life by J. A. Spender and Cyril Asquith (Asquith's fourth son who became a law lord) even when it was published seemed in the style of a biographical epoch which was ending, and the high-quality but fairly brief 1976 work by Stephen Koss, an American, did not supersede my book. Although I can see a lot of faults in *Asquith*, I still regard it as my central biographical work and would rather be judged by it than by anything before or since.

I wrote it mostly in the three long recesses of 1961, 1962 and 1963, supplemented by Christmas and Easter bursts. I was doing too much journalism in those years to have much time for it during the parliamentary terms, and in any event my method of writing meant that I could not much move a book along in the interstices of going to the House of Commons, attending a John Lewis meeting and thinking what I was going to say on a television programme. I needed a substantial but finite period (ideally about three weeks) away from London, during which I had little else on my mind, could write for four or five hours a day, and had a great incentive to get on because my morale depended centrally on whether or not I was making good progress. In these circumstances I could produce about 25,000 words at the rate of slightly more than a thousand a day. After that I felt written out, so that a fourth or a fifth week was not much good to me.

In 1961 I had a very good burst in the South of France. We took on an old mill set in olive groves about a mile from Grimaud and five miles behind St Tropez. It was a fine house with several terraces including one with good shade for pre-lunch writing (to which I devoted a solid four hours nearly every morning), and would now cost the world to hire for nearly a month. But it was then tolerably cheap. Moreover, the roads around St Tropez, even in August and in contrast with the immobilising congestion which developed a few years later, were uncluttered. The rest of the family went to the beach soon after nine. I was undisturbed, except for the mid-morning visit of the postman, who could be seen advancing on a bicycle and in a cloud of dust from half a mile away, until our German au-pair girl brought the car back to collect me for a picnic lunch on the long sandy sweep of Pampelonne. It was a last taste of this area while it still bore some traces of the provincial quietness of Third Republican France.

In these favourable circumstances I wrote four substantial early chapters. At the end we drove back to Lyon to put the car and ourselves on a train. We arrived too late for the car, but not for ourselves. Indeed unless we went on that night we would never resecure our *couchettes*. The car, we were promised, would come on the next night. We sadly abandoned it and the luggage. Then ten minutes before departure I suddenly remembered that the irreplaceable product of a month's work was in the boot, did not wholly trust the promise, insisted on going by taxi to retrieve it from its different loading point about half a mile away, and was within a minute of missing my second train deadline of the day.

This sojourn in the Var, which gave *Asquith* as near to a flying start as my slow composition could ever achieve, was buttressed on either side by several weeks at Hatley in west Cambridgeshire. Over the second half of the 1950s Jakie Astor had become no longer just a House of Commons 'pair' (indeed he ceased to be that at all, for in 1959, disenchanted by post-Suez bitterness towards the handful of Tories, including himself, who had opposed that foolish venture, he gave up his seat) but a close friend, which he had since remained. In July 1961 he very kindly offered us the use of his dower house in the park at Hatley. We had it for eighteen months until January 1963, then surrendered it to Jakie himself (because he was engaged in one of his favourite pastimes of pulling part of his big house down and wanted to move in), but went back again in October 1964, and used it until January 1966, by which time we had acquired East Hendred.

We went to Hatley for several weeks in the summers, two weeks or so over four Christmases, a week at Easter and about fifteen other weekends a year. It was an immense assistance to my writing. Most of the middle stretches of *Asquith* were done there. The surrounding countryside had a cabbage-field bleakness about it, but its wide landscape produced great open skies and the large park had splendid trees and contained a good tennis court, a handsome swimming pool and a lake. On the tennis court we played a lot, and on 27 August 1962 a most memorable game. Our elder son Charles, then aged thirteen and a half, and I played a single set which lasted an hour and forty minutes and went to a score of 18–16. He won. He had never beaten me before. I never beat him again. I am afraid the result was that a short time afterwards I gave up playing singles, although I continued for many years to play enjoyable doubles.

The lake came into its own in the cold Christmas holiday of 1962–3 when it froze hard from about 22 December and we began skating on Christmas afternoon and continued every day, graduating into ice-hockey parties, until the snow came on New Year's Eve. After dinner that evening we set off for Cambridge to celebrate the beginning of 1963 with Noël and Gabriele Annan in the Provost's Lodge at King's. We only got two miles before plunging into the deepest snowdrift I have ever encountered. My car at that time bore a sticker appropriately proclaiming: 'Forward Britain into Europe'. This gave Jakie Astor great pleasure when he had to come and dig out the totally immobilised chariot of advance.

Cambridge in general, and the Annans in particular, played a considerable part in our Hatley life. It was little more than twenty minutes' drive across the straight and empty roads of the East Anglian prairie, and it provided Jennifer with a nostalgic return and me with an excursion away from the more familiar and more intimate charms of Oxford. Christmas Eve carol services in King's chapel and emerging round the corner of Gibbs Building on to a freezing Back Lawn with a red ball of a sun just disappearing across the Cam remain fixed in my mind as a symbol of the more statuesque beauty of the junior university.

In the summer of 1962 we mostly stayed at Hatley, with no major foreign expedition, and *Asquith* progressed adequately. In the summer of 1963 we went to France for five weeks. We took a house a few hundred yards from one the Beaumarchais had recently acquired at Sare, behind St Jean-de-Luz in the foothills of the Pyrenees. I have paid many subsequent visits to Sare, several of them in spectacular, mostly autumnal, weather, but on this first extended visit it rained as I have never known it do before or since anywhere in the world – but I have never been in, say, Bombay in the monsoon, although I have spent a lot of time in Glasgow. There were only five August days on which no rain fell and on thirteen days of the month it rained without ceasing from morning till night. While less good for other forms of holiday activity this was splendid for *Asquith*. I spent up to six or seven hours a day sitting surrounded by piles of books at a small table in a bedroom window, smoking small bad cigars to which I was then addicted, listening to what music I could get from Radio Bordeaux or Radio Toulouse, passing much of the time just gazing at the sodden Basque meadows, but nonetheless producing a lot of words. I there managed most of the crucial chapters dealing with Asquith's declining authority in the First World War and his fall in December 1916.

I was then able to finish it off over the Christmas recess, mainly in ten early January days in Nicko and Mary Henderson's house at Combe near Hungerford. But the actual end was more curious and in a way more forced than that. As it got near I became desperate for finality, which was not surprising after four years of work, two and a half of writing, and with an election pending – the spring seemed more likely than the autumn at that stage. On the weekend of 17–19 January I had Birmingham engagements from Friday evening to late on Saturday afternoon. Then I had twenty-four hours free before returning to Birmingham for the necessary courtesy of sitting on the platform of the Town Hall for Harold Wilson's first appearance in the city as leader of the Labour Party. At six on the Saturday I escaped from Birmingham and drove as fast as I could to the Lygon Arms Hotel at Broadway.

In twenty-two hours, nearly all shut up in a fine panelled bedroom there, I wrote three thousand words and got Asquith through his decline and to the threshold of death. But to my intense frustration I could not quite finish him off, still less write a paragraph of appraisal and farewell, before I had to depart for the oratory of the Birmingham Town Hall. Having sat through that I got in my car and drove to London. In Ladbroke Square I wrote three or four hundred *nunc dimittis* words, inscribed a large THE END across the bottom of the page, and went contentedly to bed at about 3.00 a.m. *Asquith* still required a good deal of not very demanding work before the proofs were finally sealed up in August 1964, but at least there was no doubt after that January weekend that whenever the election came and whatever followed from it, I had a completed book to show for my long working holidays.

Between holidays I also wrote as well as politicised in those early 1960s years, but articles rather than books. A lot of the articles were book reviews (ten for the *Observer* in 1963) and some of the rest were just political ephemera. But some were more substantial projects. In February 1962, David Astor suggested that I should undertake for the *Observer* what was then a novel form of journalism about a fairly novel conjuncture of events. Imperial Chemical Industries was in the course of losing a takeover battle against Courtaulds. The spectacle of these two great firms, both of them giants in artificial fibres but ICI still more gargantuan because more widely based, locked in denunciatory conflict was then both a shocking and a riveting one to much of the British public. Astor proposed that I should write a detailed but (he hoped) vivid study of what was happening and why. He conceived of it on a grand scale. Three successive fronts of the review section were to be devoted to my investigation. The concept was entirely his, although the treatment was entirely mine. It was a very good illustration of why he was the greatest (mostly) non-writing editor/proprietor of the thirty post-war years. He had an exceptional capacity to inspire enthusiasm and point a general direction without bossily trying to dictate the way in which it should be carried out.

I worked for about a month on this project, which at the time was regarded as breaking new journalistic ground. It was unusual to write for the general reader such a detailed account, which nonetheless assumed no prior knowledge or expert understanding, of what had hitherto been regarded as a specialised field. If I did break new ground I did so almost unconsciously, and the idea was in any event David Astor's. But I got some acclaim, a Granada Award of the Year for innovative journalism, and a lot of offers (mainly from journals which could not afford to pay the costs of the electricity) to shine a similar searchlight into other corners.

The *Sunday Times* offered more serious counter-bidding, and in those years when the quality Sunday press was both flowering and competing upwards it was morale-boosting and remunerative to be sought after. I wrote a few shorter pieces for the *Sunday Times*, but I regarded anything which followed in the ICI/Courtaulds form as being an *Observer* copyright, although I did nothing more for them in that shape for over a year.

What I did immediately was to write and narrate a peculiar programme for Granada Television. This was directly based on the ICI/Courtaulds techniques (but I did not regard a television programme as being competitive with the *Observer*) and concerned the affair of the Royal Academy Leonardo cartoon of the Virgin and Child with St John and St Anne. The Academy had decided it wished to sell to the highest bidder unless the Government would give it 10 per cent less than the average of three independent valuations, in which case it could go to the National Gallery. Although the sums involved were small by recent standards (under £1 million) it was an early example of conflict between the pulls of the market and conservation of the national heritage. The programme was peculiar because it comprised nothing except a few shots of the cartoon and nearly thirty minutes of me reading my own script straight to camera. Commercial television franchises were soon coming up for renewal and I remember saying (privately, not to Granada) that the only explanation for the programme of which I could think was that Granada wished to show the IBA that no one could exceed their willingness to be boring for the sake of culture.

However, while it may have bored a lot of viewers it was quite a testing assignment, particularly as I had an engaging, energetic and critical young producer called Jeremy Isaacs. I did a lot of research and interviewing of the mandarins of the art world in May and June (1962), tried to write a taut script by the end of the second month, played about with it for several more weeks and finally recorded the programme in a five-hour session on 30 July. Whether many viewers watched it to the end I doubt, but it was not badly reviewed, and Granada kept their franchise.

In 1963 and 1964 I did three repeats of my first *Observer* series. At the end of 1962 I conceived with them the idea of doing a blow-by-blow inside story of the events of the Cuban missile crisis, which was then only a few weeks past. In January I went to America for four weeks, and was in Washington for half the time. Although I had a journalistically successful visit and talked to President Kennedy, McNamara, Stevenson, Bobby Kennedy, Rusk, Bundy, Acheson, Ball and nearly all the other key participants, I did not feel that the subject was ripe for writing about in a retrospective way. I therefore arranged that I would treat this as merely a first bite at the cherry and would return in October to finish my investigation and write my article in time for publication on the first anniversary.

The second 'club sandwich' that I actually published was in late June/early July and on the improbable subject of the papal election which followed the death of Pope John XXIII and resulted in the choice of Archbishop Montini of Milan as Pope Paul VI. It could certainly be said that I approached the subject with a fresh mind. I spent five days in Rome while the cardinals were assembling, but then had to make a brief return to London to vote (at the end of the Profumo debate when Macmillan's majority fell from its habitual hundred to sixty-nine) and speak on the Peerage Bill, which made renunciation possible and therefore opened the way for Alec Home to become Prime Minister four months later.

This break meant that I was lucky not to miss the end of the Conclave, which lasted from the Wednesday evening to the Friday morning. The Thursday ballots put up only black smoke, for the second release of which I was back in position in front of St Peter's. And on the Friday morning I was again in the great square to see the white smoke go up at 11.19. At that stage there was not a huge crowd, but in the fifty minutes between then and Cardinal Ottoviani, the head of the Holy Office (the Curial equivalent of a Cabinet Secretary), coming out on to the balcony, an estimated 100,000 had poured in between the arms of Bernini's colonnade. Ottoviani spoke with great clarity so that the syllables of the simple Latin, which even I could understand, each fell with the distinct plop of pebbles going into a still pool. 'Annuntio vobis gaudium magnum: habemus Papam, Eminentissimum ac Reverendissimum Dominum Cardinalem Ioannem Baptistam Montini: qui sibi nomen imposuit Paulem Sixtum.' Montini's choice of pontifical name seemed to arouse more enthusiasm than the revelation of his identity. Perhaps it was simply that his election was hardly a surprise, aided by the well-known antipathy of the Romans to the Milanese, which kept the crowd so restrained.

My writing approach was to describe some of the procedure, to analyse the pre-Conclave balance of forces within the Sacred College in a way that mingled geography and personality with superficial Church history, and to attempt a theory of the movement within this balance which produced such a decisive result in favour of the moderate reform candidate. My account paid more attention to the temporalities than to the spiritualities of the Church, but this was a week in its life when temporalities were prominent in the minds of its princes and prelates.

In Rome I acquired two unpaid 'stringers', both of whom were quasi-ducal, although they could hardly have been less like each other. The first was the young Sanche de Gramont, who was then *Time* magazine correspondent in Italy. He later went to America from where his mother came, changed his name to Ted Morgan, which although an anagram of de Gramont might be regarded as a rejection both of rank and of nationality, and wrote biographies of Roosevelt, Churchill, Somerset Maugham and William Burroughs. The second was the old Sir D'Arcy Osborne, who had been British minister to the Vatican throughout the war, and had retired to live an elegant bachelor old age in the via Giulia. He was an Anglican whose primary interest had become the affairs of the Church of Rome. A month later he became the twelfth Duke of Leeds, but only for nine months after which he and the title died. Both Osborne and Gramont were informed and helpful, and amongst other services put me in touch with a number of gossipy monsignori, who were delighted to accept invitations to small luncheon parties at Passeto's restaurant.

At a more elevated ecclesiastical level I achieved a few interviews with cardinals. Bea, the German Jesuit who was head of the Secretariat for the Promotion of Christian Unity, was the most impressive, but Cushing of Boston was the most memorable. His indiscretions in the course of an hour's meeting with someone whom he had never met before were on a scale which added Butler to Dalton and squared the sum. He was the diocesan of the whole Kennedy clan, so I thought that, as we walked out from his room in the American College and stood in the sunshine looking down at the view of Rome from the Janiculum Hill, I would cast a Kennedy fly over him. Was he, I asked, going to stay over for the President's visit (due in about a week's time)? 'No, I shan't bother,' he said with a dismissive sweep of his hand. 'I've christened them all, I've married them all, I've . . . [happily there were not many to have buried at that stage] I've seen enough. I have my reservations about Jack and Bobby. Jack's the sort of man who asks you out for a doughnut and leaves you to pick up the check [an extraordinary view by any standards of both J.F.K.'s eating and paying habits], and Bobby stirs up too much trouble. The two I really like are Teddy and the old man. If I had Joe Kennedy here working with me I reckon I could just about fix this papal election.'

I did not at all share Cardinal Cushing's view of Jack or Bobby and was delighted to be back in Kennedyland for two weeks in early October. It was both actually and metaphorically the last sunlit Indian days of the brief summer of the Kennedy presidency; when I left there were exactly five weeks to go before Dallas. And very splendid it all looked in those mid-autumn weeks. To be a young British member of Parliament (forty-two at least seems that to me now) in the city which was then even nearer to being the capital of the world than it is today, staying at the Embassy to which David Ormsby Gore (not then Harlech) had given a special gloss much aided by his intimacy with the President, rather taken up by the Kennedys and therefore by most of the top members of the Administration, and working in a leisurely way on what I hoped was going to be a major piece of journalism, was as enjoyable a way to pass two weeks as it is easy to imagine, and I look back at them with great nostalgia.

Not unnaturally in the circumstances I was a fan of Jack Kennedy. And I have not changed my mind since. I was subsequently close to Bobby, and I have remained on friendly terms with Jacqueline Kennedy and with other members of the family. In the aftermath of President Kennedy's assassination I wrote: 'Compared with the greatest presidents of American history, he inevitably leaves more promise and less achievement behind him. Yet, aided perhaps by the manner of his death, it is difficult to believe that his name will not live with theirs. He will be the great "might-have-been", the symbol of fate in its most vicious and retaliatory mood.' Although written within twenty-four hours of his death I would not retract it. I think he was the best president of the past four decades.

I returned from that American visit by sea, hoping that the comforts of the then new SS *France* would conduce to a fluent writing of the Cuba piece. It was a mistake. The weather was rough, I was lonely, particularly as I had to spend eighteen hours a day, partly sleeping and partly writing, shut up in a small cabin. I did my four thousand words (Cuba was published as a single long piece, not a series) but I got off in Southampton in distinctly worse condition than I had got on in New York. At that time Cunard had an advertisement showing a little man getting on the ship bent and haggard, and striding off it at the other end twirling his umbrella in ebullient health. I was exactly the reverse. I have never since been tempted to cross the Atlantic by boat.

My fourth and last *Observer* piece of this sort was published in two parts in July 1964, and was entitled 'How Not to Run a Public Corporation'. It was occasioned by a BOAC crisis arising out of their inability to combine buying British with operating commercially. The worthy but late piece of equipment over which battle was fought was the VC-10. 'Here was one of the nodal problems of BOAC's relationship with the British aircraft industry,' I wrote in the key paragraph. 'Orders are too big for the Corporation, too small for the manufacturers, or both at the same time. In America there are enough airlines to reduce the problem both for themselves and for the manufacturers.' These two articles may have made me Minister of Aviation. They appeared only three months before the general election and they set up in Harold Wilson's mind a relationship between flying machines and me. If so, it makes me doubly grateful to David Astor and the *Observer*, for I greatly enjoyed my first ministerial job.

Throughout 1961 and 1962 I was devoting my main political energy, and some appreciable part of my writing as well, to trying to get Britain into Europe. CIA-financed or not, *Encounter* provided an excellent outlet for my liberal internationalism. Just as in 1959 I had used it to set out the five-year history of the struggle to get the Obscene Publications Bill on the statute book, so in the summer of 1961 as the Macmillan Government teetered on the edge of Britain's first application to join the Europe of the Six, I wrote a long refutation of the case against entry and particularly of the Commonwealth argument which was then considerably used on both left and right in politics.

The next year, when it was hoped (vainly, thanks to General de Gaulle) that the Heath negotiations in Brussels were moving slowly towards their conclusion, *Encounter* encouraged me to go on a round-Europe trip, which comprised two legs, first Brussels, Bonn, Düsseldorf and Paris, which was an excursion through the heart of the Six, and second Copenhagen, Stockholm and Oslo, which enabled me to see how other EFTA countries, shivering on the northern fringe like ourselves, were approaching the problems of membership or non-membership. These visits, as well as being useful to me in the rolling argument inside and outside the Labour Party, produced a five-thousand word survey for *Encounter*, entitled 'Notes from the Brink'.

My third surviving piece of European journalism of those years was a June 1964 *Daily Telegraph* article which looked back on the lessons of the 1961–3 negotiations. I was surprised to find that this contained two bits of prescience. The first was that the French were crucial and that we would always be disappointed if we looked to Germany or to the other five as a whole to deal with the French for us. 'We must establish our own equilibrium with France. . . .' The validity of this point was demonstrated by Edward Heath's effective partnership with Pompidou in 1971, which was the key to the success of our third application for membership. The second was my guess that if a Labour government came in during the autumn it would make an attempt at closer Commonwealth unity, but that when this faltered it would be ready, improbable though this seemed in view of Harold Wilson's derogatory remarks about the effeteness of 'selling washing machines to Düsseldorf' (as opposed to the manliness of exporting hydro-electric equipment to the Great Snowy Mountains of Australia), to make another approach to Europe. This, I thought, might be 'about the beginning of 1966'. In fact it took until 1967.

In addition to these writing activities I was engaged before and over the eighteen months of the Macmillan Government's Brussels negotiations in a lot of European speaking, up and down the country as well as in the House and on television, and perhaps even more European caballing. I had the cross-party Common Market Campaign, of which Gladwyn was chairman and I was deputy chairman, and also the Labour Committee for Europe, of which I was chairman. Jack Diamond was treasurer of both. And the two organisations were vigorous during this period.

This commitment and activity did not seriously separate me from Gaitskell until the late summer of 1962. He did not pretend to share my enthusiasm, but nor did he take a line of clear hostility to British membership. Indeed he claimed that he would rather see it than not, provided the conditions were right. But I knew in my bones, not that he was deceiving himself or me, but that his lack of basic conviction was such that he would never have the pro-European momentum to get over the rough ground which inevitably lay ahead.

There were also occasional hiccups. In July 1960, when I resigned from the opposition front bench to which he had appointed me only seven months before, he was not pleased. While I was waiting (on a back bench) to speak in a European debate Patrick Gordon Walker (later to be not only an ill-fated Foreign Secretary but later still a staunch European) came and sat beside me and announced that Hugh thought that as a front-bencher I ought not to speak. I rather intemperately said: 'Tell him I will solve his problem by resigning.' It was not the answer Gaitskell wanted, but the job I held was so minor (which was no doubt part of the reason I was so ready to resign from it) that neither he nor I could get very excited. Furthermore Europe was not then the central issue of politics. The central issue was the unilateralist revolt, on which Gaitskell was about to be defeated at the Scarborough Labour Party conference in early October 1960, and on which he and I were absolutely united. In any event, there was no approach to a rupture and we lunched and dined together three or four times in the next six weeks. I was moved to tears and total commitment by the 'fight, fight and fight again' speech, and rushed back from my Kennedy-election October visit to the United States to give any help I could against the Harold Wilson challenge to Gaitskell's leadership.

That was satisfactorily seen off (by 166 votes to 81), but the issue was not closed, for until midsummer 1961 it looked as though there would be a second conference defeat that autumn, and Gaitskell did not believe that he could defy the conference for more than one year and remain leader. He was seriously contemplating resignation and withdrawal from British politics as late as March 1961. Then the union conferences began to swing over to his side (and some of the constituency parties as well) so that by July it was clear that the

1961 Blackpool conference was going to be as triumphant a victory for Gaitskell as the 1960 Scarborough one had been a triumphant defeat. I wrote a long and adulatory *Sunday Times* profile of him to celebrate the turnabout. For some reason the paper wished it to be anonymous, and few people at Blackpool guessed its authorship. Hugh however did, he said without hesitation, and was very pleased with it. This more than compensated for the fact that my little speech to the conference was a hard-line one on Europe, which was at least looking to next year's rather than to last year's controversy.

The next hiccup was in April 1962, when I organised one of the least successful evenings with which I have ever been concerned. I arranged for Jean Monnet to address a meeting of the XYZ dining club and made sure that Gaitskell would attend. I think I fondly imagined that Monnet would lucidly meet all Gaitskell's points and dissolve his doubts. I have never seen less of a meeting of minds. They were both at their worst. Monnet would not answer Gaitskell's detail and swept it aside as trivial against the grand historical view which the issue merited. Gaitskell was uncomprehending of Monnet's faith and got more and more stubbornly pedestrian. I drove Monnet back to the Hyde Park Hotel in deep depression.

Nonetheless relations continued to be thoroughly amicable over the summer and the Gaitskells came to stay with us for two days at Hatley in early August. I do not think we much discussed the European issue on that visit – it was supposed to be the beginning of the holidays – and on the basis of the few relevant words we exchanged I half deceived myself that Hugh's mind was still open on whether he might accept the terms which were emerging from the Heath negotiations in Brussels.

Then at the beginning of September he made a speech which dashed all hopes. Crosland came to Hatley the following week and fulminated against it even more strongly than I did. The following day I went to London specially for a serious talk with Gaitskell. He gave me lunch with the idea of making a last-minute attempt to find some common ground between us. We were in the small back dining room of the Garrick Club, which was not full to begin with, and everybody else had gone by the time we got to the crunch of the discussion. I remember Hugh pacing up and down the room. We went on until four o'clock, but it did not work. The more we talked the wider the gap became. We parted friendlily, but a temporary separation, personal as well as political, began that day. I did not see him again before the Brighton conference three weeks later, and there, in contrast with other conferences for ten years past, we were in different camps. So far from the habitual meal or two together we hardly exchanged a word. The one time when we did come face to face at the *Daily Mirror* party (always a great occasion for Labour Party encounters) Hugh, with uneasy and slightly obscure jocularity, said, 'Dr Livingstone, I presume,' but he did not attempt to linger.

I felt sad but not lonely, for the odd thing was that the majority of Gaitskell's closest supporters were in my camp and not in his. Dora Gaitskell's memorable remark to Charles Pannell during the standing ovation at the end of Hugh's 'a thousand years of history' speech ('Charlie, all the wrong people are cheering')[3] illuminated the new landscape like a flash of lightning. Unlike Bill Rodgers (the organiser of the Campaign for Democratic Socialism, which had done much to turn the unilateralist tide), who more courageously remained seated with his arms folded, I did stand but did not applaud. Probably only afterwards I worked out a sophistical theory that standing was a tribute to the man, whereas clapping would have been a tribute to the speech.

After that Brighton conference there was an estrangement. On the Tuesday of the following week I remember with shame that for the only time in my life I spoke about him with bitterness – to a very close friend during a restaurant dinner. It was more a blowing off than an expression of settled opinion, but I wish that I had not done it. For seven weeks following Brighton I did not exchange a proper word with him, although we must have nodded in the House of Commons. Then he took the initiative to restore personal relations. He asked Jennifer and me to Frognal Gardens on a Sunday evening, the ice broke easily, and together with Dora we all gossiped for several hours, at the end of which he and I arranged to meet in Paris where we were both due to be the following weekend. I was going as part of my pro-European *Encounter* tour. He was going to see de Gaulle and Couve de Murville and to do a little plotting against Macmillan and British entry. But we nonetheless wanted to see each other.

We dined together on that next Sunday evening, accompanied by the Beaumarchais and by Gerard André. Jacques de Beaumarchais and André had been involved in arranging his nefarious visit to the General. This did not prevent it being a very jolly party in a restaurant called La Méditerranée near the Odéon, where we ate a lot of shellfish and drank a lot of wine. The next morning Hugh telephoned me from the British Embassy, where he but not I was staying. He asked whether I felt all right and whether we had been poisoned the night before. I said that I was perfectly well. He said he felt awful, and added, 'But I never feel well these days.' It was the first hint I had of the collapse of his health.

Two weeks later I went on the second and Scandinavian leg of my *Encounter* tour. It was a sign of the total restoration of personal relations that I sent him a mocking postcard from Stockholm saying that I was sure he would approve of my being in a good EFTA country, discussing with a lot of boring and insular economic ministers the advantages of neutrality. I am not sure that he ever got it, for he was in hospital when I got back. I went to visit him at Manor House (the trade union hospital in Golders Green) for an hour on the morning of 21 December. Although he was low, there was no political shadow over our conversation.

It was the last time I saw him. I had two long telephone conversations with him after Christmas, when he was temporarily at home, and I went to America on 12 January. I was worried about his long and depressing illness, but it did not seriously occur to me that he was about to die. I regarded him as having something of the equivalent of my glandular fever of ten years before. Then, four days later, I was telephoned in the deep snows of Hanover, New Hampshire, and told that he was dying. Two days later, when I had moved down to the Douglass Caters' in Middletown, Connecticut, he did. He was reported in the next day's newspapers as having died at 9.10 p.m. British time, 4.10 Eastern American time. Just after 4.15 the telephone rang in Middletown and I was informed by the *Daily Express* in New York that it had happened. How they found me so quickly I cannot imagine; it at least pointed to high technical efficiency. What they wanted was a comment or tribute from me. I said I did not feel able to give them one. They expressed disapproving surprise. 'Harold Wilson, who is in New York, was able to give us a very moving one without difficulty,' they said. 'Yes,' I said bitterly, 'but you have to remember that he was very fond of Gaitskell,' and rang off. The silly little incident expressed both my shattered dismay and my revulsion from the prospect of a Wilson leadership, a succession to the man I loved and revered, in spite of one considerable but contained difference, by the man who had stood against him two years before, and whom, since 1951, I had deeply distrusted.

I stayed on in the United States for another two weeks. There seemed no particular point in going home. After a few days America half revived me, but when I got back to London in early February I felt the full bleakness of the deprivation. The savour of politics had been destroyed for me, and indeed I doubted (perhaps not in a very deep-seated way) whether I wanted to go on with them. The semi-rupture of the previous autumn in no way diminished my sense of loss. Paradoxically it rather heightened it.

I have often been asked whether I think Gaitskell would have changed his view on Europe had he lived another ten years. The answer is that I do not know, much though I would like to think so. I have always been hesitant about attributing posthumous views. But I think it at least possible that he would have done so, particularly as his main Commonwealth counter-argument is the one which crumbled most rapidly over that decade. What I am sure is that, if he had moved, he would have done so slowly, and then stuck with great tenacity.

At the end of those ten years I wrote a long biographical essay for *The Times* about Gaitskell, which represented my view of him well after the emotional dust had settled:

All his struggles illustrated some blemishes as well as exceptional strength. He would not have been a perfect Prime Minister. He was stubborn, rash, and could in a paradoxical way become too emotionally committed to an over-rational position which, once he had thought it rigorously through, he believed must be the final answer. He was only a moderately good judge of people. Yet when these faults are put in the scales and weighed against his qualities they shrivel away. He had purpose and direction, courage and humanity. He was a man for raising the sights of politics. He clashed on great issues. He avoided the petty bitterness of personal jealousy. He could raise a banner which men were proud to follow, but he never perverted his leadership ability: it was infused by sense and humour, and by a desire to change the world, not for his own satisfaction, but so that people might more enjoy living in it. He was rarely obsessed either by politics or by himself. He was that very rare phenomenon, a great politician who was also an unusually agreeable man.

That remains my view several decades later. I have not seen his like.

The immediate political issue after Gaitskell's death was the election of a successor. As is often the case following the disappearance of a great leader, the Gaitskellites split. The majority, including me, were for George Brown, but Crosland and George Thomson were for Callaghan. I was still away for the early stages of that campaign, and when consulted by telephone said that I was 'unenthusiastically but firmly for Brown', adding rather pompously that I wished equal weight to be put on both adverbs. This may now seem a strange judgement but in retrospect I think it was the tepidness which was inappropriate. It was largely occasioned by post-Gaitskellian indifference. Brown was certainly not a tepid character. He had great qualities both of intellect and of personality, although they were balanced by appalling faults. On the big issues he was almost invariably right and pursued his conviction with persistent courage. Whether, had he won, a different balance would have been struck between the qualities and the faults than that which ended his career is something that remains hidden. It was a gamble, but the winnings could have been great.

The split on the right of the party ensured that it was never put to the test. Maybe Harold Wilson would have won in any event. But Callaghan's intervention and his 41 first-ballot votes (as against Brown's 88 and Wilson's 115) ensured that Brown had lost momentum before he had a straight run with Wilson. Callaghan wrote in his autobiography that it was all for the best, and perhaps he was right.

In my view, and probably in his own, he was not himself nearly ready for the leadership at that stage. He required the adversity of the Exchequer and the nerve-testing of his 1969 quarrel with Wilson to harden and burnish him for the role. But whatever may be his or my retrospective judgement, I certainly did not welcome the result at the time. It merely increased my disillusion with and detachment from politics. I was not on positively hostile terms with Wilson. There was no question of our stalking past each other scowling as Bevan and I had done. But there was neither friendship nor trust. I can find no record of any contact in the first spring and summer of his leadership. In a slightly flat way, I just got on with *Asquith*, my other (mainly *Observer*) writing commitments, picking up the pieces from de Gaulle's veto in my Common Market Campaign and Labour Committee for Europe, looking after my pilots, advising John Lewis's and pursuing my over-active social life.

In these circumstances, disenchanted with politics, detached from my new leader, keeping too many balls in the air, I was an obvious sitting target for the offer of a job outside politics. On 5 July 1963 one duly came, and very attractive it at least superficially was. I lunched that day with Norman Macrae, the assistant editor of the *Economist*. There was an old joke that all members of the *Economist* staff were assistant editors, on the ground that they all tried to assist the editor. But Macrae was the real McCoy. Not only was he the one person indisputably entitled to the designation, but he was also the epitome of the internal spirit of the *Economist*, a Willie Whitelaw to the Conservative Party, a Gubby Allen to the MCC. Although intellectually didactic, he was personally modest. Donald Tyerman, who had followed Geoffrey Crowther, the modern refounding editor in 1956, ought to retire, he said. He did not think that he (Macrae) had the all-round qualities to replace him. His view and (he implied) that of the staff, and (he stated) that of Crowther, who was then chairman, was that I should do so.

I was surprised, flattered and excited. We were lunching at Quaglino's, an improbable rendezvous with such a craggy figure as Macrae, and I arrived preoccupied and low, as I had that morning been to an incompetent new doctor who had responded to minor symptoms by ordaining tests for leukaemia, which turned out to be totally negative, but took some time to do so. Although Macrae's offer would have been without interest had the tentative diagnosis been true it nonetheless succeeded in half jerking me out of my preoccupation. And when the doctor retracted I became distinctly interested. Macrae was right about Crowther, with whom we dined at the end of that month, and who pressed me hard to accept. The *Economist* in 1963 did not have the vast international circulation and popularity of today, but it perhaps had greater prestige and influence in Britain, maybe in New York and Washington, and quite enough money to go on with. I was offered over twice a Cabinet minister's salary (which is probably about the going ratio today), and more than expected perquisites. (There was a mention of an apartment in New York; I suppose they must have had one going.)

I was much tempted, and yet there was always some deep reservation somewhere between my heart and my stomach. I would of course have had to give up any prospect of office in a possible 1964 Labour government. That I did not mind very much, for I rated low my chances of a decent job. I would also have had to resign my seat in the House of Commons. That I minded more. It seemed very final, and I never passed what I have always found to be an important test of whether I want to do a job or not, which is whether my imagination embraces with enthusiasm the next practical step, which in this case was that of going to Birmingham and telling the Stechford Labour Party that they must get a new candidate.

So I told Crowther that I would think it over during the long French writing holiday that I had planned for that August. At the very end of that holiday (not in Sare, but in Paris on the way back) Marie-Alice de Beaumarchais made a crucial remark to me. I told her how much I was tempted to accept the *Economist*, partly because, in the event of a Labour government, I had absolutely no claims on Wilson. 'He will want you for your own sake,' she flatteringly said, 'but in any case why on earth don't you go and ask him instead of deciding in the dark?'

On 12 September I put this to the test and went to see Wilson in the old leader of the opposition's (now the Home Secretary's) room in the House of Commons. It was the first time I had seen him there, although I had known it well not only under Gaitskell but going back to the time when my father had become PPS to Attlee in 1936. And by a curious irony it was the first anniversary of my separating Garrick Club lunch with Hugh. At exactly that time the year before he had been pacing up and down the back dining room.

Wilson received me with immense consideration. I cannot pretend that Gaitskell would have been nearly as nice to, say, Barbara Castle in similar circumstances. I think he was genuinely impressed by the *Economist* offer, more than Hugh would have been, and more than he would have been had I told him that I had been asked to be editor of, say, *Horizon* at the height of its fame. It was exactly the sort of institution that he respected. But he did not give the impression that this was crucial to his consideration. He kept me for an hour. He said he was looking forward to forming a broad-based government (an aspiration which he fulfilled: fifteen out of nineteen Commons members of his first Cabinet would have voted for Gaitskell rather than for him in the 1960 leadership contest). He would certainly wish to find a worthwhile place for me. It could not be in the Cabinet to begin with, but the road to promotion would be wide open. He knew which departments (to be Minister of State in, I assumed) would interest me and which would not. He would understand if I accepted the *Economist* offer, but he would deeply regret it.

It was a masterly performance, made the more impressive by the fact that he promised less than he delivered a year later. When I next saw Crowther I was cooling. But so was he. It was rather the story of Arthur Deakin and the Bevin biography over again, except that there was no Bullock in the background. Crowther was chairman and patron saint of the *Economist*, but Lionel Robbins was chairman of the *Financial Times*, which was the principal shareholder in The Economist Newspaper Ltd. Perhaps to compensate for his current occupation of putting the finishing touches to one of the great 'state as provider' documents of the post-war consensus, Robbins's half-free-market soul was rather shocked by the idea of having a Labour MP as editor of Bagehot's journal. I backed off and so did Crowther. Although we were still in some sort of vestigial (and friendly) discussions as late as January 1964, they were never serious after 17 September 1963. Tyerman continued until 1965, and was then succeeded by Alastair Burnet, who in turn was succeeded by Andrew Knight. Had I said 'snap' in July, I have no doubt that Crowther would have done so too, or at least would have felt committed to resist Robbins. But again I had no regrets. Although it was beyond my wildest dreams in a Gaitskell Government let alone a Wilson one, I had been Home Secretary and was Chancellor of the Exchequer fifty months after the *Economist* offer fell away. It would have required a strong addiction to criticism as opposed to execution to have preferred editorship to chancellorship. But any form of office remained a bird in the bush for any Labour member for a year after my Wilson and Crowther encounters.

# PART TWO

# 1964–1970

# CHAPTER EIGHT

# *A Lucky Landing*

The general election campaign of 1964 was the last that I fought primarily on a constituency basis. I did my usual moderate quota of meetings outside Birmingham, although speaking mainly for pro-European candidates rather than at key points in the battlefront. I drove myself everywhere I went, and indeed on one expedition to do a television programme in Norwich nearly killed myself in an encounter with a lorry near Wisbech. I did no national television.

My expectation about the result I find difficult to recall. I think I regarded it as rather a toss-up, as indeed it turned out to be. Wilson seemed to be fighting effectively and was helped by increasingly bad news about the balance of payments. But his fate did not command my personal commitment and emotional loyalty in a way that Gaitskell's had done in 1959. My expectation about office was mostly predicated upon the conversation I had had with him about the *Economist* offer in September 1963. Some water had flowed under the bridge since then, one of the basic tenets of Gaitskellism was that Wilson was a tricky fellow, and my lack of instinctive loyalty towards him obviously meant that I had no claim on a reward from him above my going political rate.

By noon on the day after the poll – Friday, 16 October – it was clear that Wilson had won by a minuscule majority, and that after thirteen years there was to be a Labour government. After entertaining constituents to lunch in the Midland Hotel I motored down from Birmingham to London, arriving at Ladbroke Square about 6.00. That evening I went at short notice to Lime Grove to do a television programme with Crossman, Maudling and Boyle about the prospects for the Government. The programme was interrupted by an announcement of the first six Cabinet appointments. There were no surprises. Dyarchy was to be the order of the day on the

155

economic front, with George Brown given precedence as head of the
new Department of Economic Affairs, but Callaghan commanding
the truncated although seasoned timbers of the Treasury. Gordon
Walker (even though he had lost his seat at Smethwick) was Foreign
Secretary and Healey (the only near contemporary to make the first
list) Defence Secretary. Crossman had received no summons at that
stage, although I think he assumed he was going to be Secretary of
State for Education.

Thereafter, as far as I was concerned, a silence descended for many
hours. No bells rang for relevant telephone calls. At about noon on the
Saturday I went for an hour's drink with Tony Crosland, who was then
living at the far end of Chelsea in the house of his new wife, the highly
talented journalist Susan Barnes. We were at that time, as during most
of our adult lives, on very close terms, but it would nonetheless be
hypocritical to pretend that I, marooned in silence, was not relieved
to discover that he had heard nothing either, or that I was not a little
jumpy about the telephone calls he received when I was there.

The afternoon was punctuated by a short sleep, by Charles (our
elder son, then aged fifteen) coming in with the *Evening Standard*
which contained all the rest of the Cabinet appointments, which
had the effect of sending me into a considerable gloom (which was
irrational for I had not expected to be in the Cabinet), by a drive to and
around Richmond Park with Jennifer in a simulated *nolo episcopari*
mood, and by a return to be told by Edward (our younger son, then
aged ten) that there had been a message the moment we left to ring
10 Downing Street immediately. 'I expect it's too late now,' he added
cheerfully.

It was not, of course, and I was summoned for 10.30 the next
morning. Encouraged by this, I took the two boys to see the new
James Bond film *Goldfinger* at the Kensington Odeon. Bill and Silvia
Rodgers came to dinner, just before which George Brown telephoned
in a state of high excitement to summon us all to his Marble Arch
flat at 10.30 that evening and to inform me that it was the Ministry
of Aviation that Wilson was to offer me the next morning. This was
good news, for I was delighted to have a department of my own and not
be a subordinate minister, and I had become considerably interested
in both the aircraft industry and the airline corporations as a result of
the last of my big *Observer* features on BOAC and the VC-10 three
months before.

When we got to George Brown's the Croslands were already there
and it transpired that Tony was to be his Minister of State at the
DEA. I counted myself lucky to have escaped this, the prospect of
which Brown had pressed on me earlier in the year, thinking that

he was adding to its attractions by promising that I would be privy to all his decisions, and even offering, semi-farcically, that we could sit in the same room and 'work together like brothers'. High though was my regard for many aspects of Brown's brilliant but uncontrolled personality, I thought this would be more a recipe for emotional exhaustion than for calm ratiocination and effective decision-taking. He and Crosland were indeed already involved in a quarrelsome argument about devaluation, which had been foolishly ruled out at a meeting between Wilson, Brown and Callaghan that morning. I joined in on Crosland's side, but not as strongly as I should have done because I had temporarily succumbed to the infantile disease of departmentalism and had my mind too much on aircraft.

Forewarned by the intelligence provided by George Brown, the next morning's interview with Harold Wilson was something of an anticlimax, which was no doubt George's maybe subconscious intention. It was in the Cabinet room, and was the first time that I had been in 10 Downing Street since my work on the Attlee papers in 1946–7. The interview was remarkably circumlocutory. Wilson began with a long and unnecessary apology for not putting me in the Cabinet. Next he explained that, with a majority of only four and another election necessarily on the near horizon, this was a Cabinet intended to last in its present form for only a short time. Then he implied, and almost promised, that I would come into the Cabinet with this next round of changes. At last he said that what he was now proposing was what he called 'the poisoned chalice'.

By this time I was thanking God for George Brown, as I would otherwise have been on about a triple ration of tenterhooks. Nearly ten minutes into the interview, the Prime Minister brought himself to mention the words 'Ministry of Aviation' and explained that he equated them with 'poisoned chalice' because of the mess which had been created in military-aircraft procurement, and indeed in the aircraft industry in general. He spoke in terms of the clearing of this mess taking a year or so and of the Ministry then being wound up with its various functions dispersed in different directions and my coming into the Cabinet. I think that his reasons for reiterating this promotion prospect were, first, his general and genuine desire to be agreeable, and, second, a skilful wish not to frustrate his plan for structural change by putting a minister with a vested interest in the status quo in its path.

It emerged that his original intention was not to put me in charge of civil aviation – airports, BOAC and BEA, the licensing of independent companies, the Civil Aviation Authority and so on, as opposed to the production of both military and civil aircraft – but to run this loosely under the Board of Trade umbrella. However, when I told him that I would much rather this remained under the Ministry of Aviation (my mind influenced by interest aroused during my *Observer* investigation), he proved amenable and quickly agreed that this should be so, at any rate for the time being. On the question of a junior minister, he was less easy. He asked my views, but when I said perhaps a young trade unionist (having Tom Bradley in mind), he quickly countered with the names of John Stonehouse or Bruce Millan. This was left unresolved, with the implication that there could be further discussion. Three days later, however, he informed me by telephone of his decision in favour of Stonehouse, and (unusually brusquely for him) overruled my protests. Tom Bradley was left to become my parliamentary private secretary, a personal appointment.

Later that first Sunday morning the permanent secretary of the Ministry of Aviation telephoned me at home. Sir Richard (or Sam) Way turned out to be an admirable man, one of the two or three best amongst the twenty or more who had or subsequently attained that rank and served me, even though a number of them in my later departments were higher in the Whitehall hierarchy. Way was not a mandarin, had never been to a university (although he was to become Principal of King's College, London) and had been a boy entrant to the civil service. He was nevertheless a cut rather than a rough diamond. I think his primary object (apart from courtesy) in telephoning that Sunday morning was to discover whether or not I intended to rush into the office in the afternoon. I assured him that I did not propose to do so, and this put our relationship on a relaxed basis which subsequently persisted.

My official life therefore began only on the Monday morning, and not very early at that, for unlike my present habit I was not then at all matutinal and believed that I should start as I intended to go on. I think I had floating round in my mind both a precept which Hugh Dalton had tried to impress upon me to the effect that a minister who was to have any chance of success must make it clear to his department from the first day exactly how he wanted things done, and also some nostalgic ideas of Victorian and Edwardian political life, which came from my biographical writings and which were epitomised by Dilke fencing on his Sloane Street back terrace until he went into the Foreign Office at 11.30. I did not quite have the nerve for that, but it was 9.45 before the official car, a great whale of an Austin Princess, came to Ladbroke Square for the first time, and 10.00 before I arrived at the office in Horse Guards Avenue, the status of the Ministry of Aviation being suitably symbolised by its occupying a portion of the relatively new Ministry of Defence building.

I was met at the front door by the principal private secretary and conducted up to my room on the second floor and the waiting Way. It was all efficient and flattering. There was no question, as is recorded in a lot of political memoirs, of my arriving before they were ready for me and trying to convince sceptical doormen that I was the minister. The room on the second floor with a view over the Embankment and the river seemed agreeable enough. Its main feature was its almost oval shape with doors leading into it from various angles so that it faintly reminded me of a bull ring. This comparison was stamped on my mind when, fairly early on, George Brown paid me a storming unannounced visit (very unusual for a senior minister to visit one junior to himself), and so terrified the private office that they had just inserted him through one of the doors, whereupon he had charged round very like a young taurus fresh from the farms of the Castilian plateau.

Its second feature was that it had a long polished dining table in place of a desk. This was apparently an innovation of Duncan Sandys, who had passed it on to Peter Thorneycroft, who had passed it on to Julian Amery, who was now passing it on to me. I thought it was a good idea. It meant that there was plenty of room for private secretary or permanent secretary or any other official to sit down around one, and that bilateral exchanges could merge into small meetings or bigger ones or the receiving of a moderate-sized deputation without any move to more formal surroundings. When I went on to the Home Office and then to the Treasury the desk was banished and a long table installed. When I got back to the Home Office in 1974 after six and a half years away, the table had survived the three intervening Home Secretaries.

The first couple of days were occupied with a series of briefing sessions, some of them rather difficult to absorb both because, unlike many ministers, some of them very successful, I take things in more easily through reading than through listening, and because of my non-technical cast of mind. I was glad that I had retained the relatively easily comprehensible problems of civil aviation to dilute the intricacies of weapons systems, rocketry and space projects. I remember making an early resolve never to pretend that I understood something when I did not. This abnegation was based not on a moral imperative but on a fear that the consequences of pretence might ultimately be more damaging to self-esteem than the confession of incomprehension at the time. The Bletchley experience of August 1945, when I played uncomprehendingly with the embryonic computer, was also in my mind. The rule was intended to apply in the privacy of discussions with one's own officials. The House of Commons or foreign governments or even the Cabinet were a different matter. To none of these is it a good idea to confess ignorance.

I think that to the rule of not simulating understanding I nearly always succeeded in sticking, not only at the Ministry of Aviation, but at the Home Office and the Treasury, in both of which there were in any event fewer problems of technical comprehension. But I cannot pretend that it survived inviolate during my four years in Brussels. Having the problems of the interaction between the Euratom Treaty and INFCEP or the effect on the green lira of a choice between the grid and the basket systems of exchange-rate intervention explained to me in a language other than English sometimes produced a glazed nod of comprehension when none should have been given.

This period of aviation instruction without immediate purpose or urgency was sharply interrupted on the third day and I then spent a full month skidding down a political slalom course with no opportunity to do anything except to try to keep on my feet. This period of complete involvement began at lunchtime on Wednesday, 21 October. I had been to Buckingham Palace to be sworn in as a privy councillor at noon, and had been suitably impressed by the complications of the manoeuvres from one kneeling stool to another as well as by the fantastic archaism of the oath, and then went to Brooks's to entertain the John Lewis Partnership chairman to a farewell lunch. Sir Richard Way intercepted me in the hall of the club with the whispered information that he had just heard that the Government's emergency White Paper on the economic situation, which was to be taken in Cabinet the next morning and published on the following Monday, was in effect to announce a unilateral British decision to cancel the Concorde project.

There was a great deal to be said against Concord (in England we then spelt it without the 'e'). It involved the committal of a significant proportion of scarce research and development resources to the hazardous creation of a product which was certainly going to be very expensive (£10 million, which was the current estimate per unit, was then regarded as almost ludicrous for an aircraft) and which showed little prospect of gaining a market sufficient to produce a return on capital. The Anglo-French arrangements had been made in 1962 by my predecessor Julian Amery with a good deal of anti-American rodomontade, and the very tight treaty which he had signed with the French was more suited to a matter concerning a nation's honour than its commercial investment decisions. Furthermore, taken in conjunction with the military aircraft developments to which Amery had also committed us, it amounted to a heavy overloading of an aircraft industry in which at least one of the two big firms had been encouraged to pay too much attention to developing as opposed to making and selling aircraft.

On the other hand, while it was probably the case that no proper cost–benefit study had been done by Amery's Ministry of Aviation in 1962, it was certainly the case that no rational reappraisal in the circumstances of 1964 had been done since the previous Friday by or for the small group composed of Brown, Callaghan and Douglas Jay (President of the Board of Trade and mildly dissenting), which had apparently decided upon the crucial sentence. The treaty with the French, while it might have been unwisely drawn, was indisputably a binding treaty. It therefore seemed crassly foolish, from the point of view either of general good relations or of getting the French to agree that the project had lost its attraction, to present them without consultation with a unilateral declaration of intention to cancel. And, in any event, the issue was plumb within the responsibilities of the Minister of Aviation, and I had not been consulted.

I therefore had no difficulty in deciding that, independently of the merits of Concorde, this was a typical example of government by rushes of blood to the head, and that I must try to get the Cabinet to take the offending sentence out, unpromising a prospect although this was for a non-Cabinet minister summoned only to be in attendance for that one item. I thought I had better try to neutralise George Brown, although I suspected him of being the fount of the whole unfortunate exercise. Such indeed proved to be the case when I succeeded the next morning in getting ten minutes with him in his car on the way to his office. He agreed however that if I could swing the rest of the Cabinet he would not resist.

He was on safe ground as the task he had set me proved wholly impossible. The disadvantages suffered by a non-Cabinet minister in such circumstances are very considerable. I had to start speaking almost from the moment I first entered that august room – but not continuously, for Wilson constantly interrupted me, not hostilely but interrogatively, and I, instead of telling him politely but firmly to keep quiet, as I would have done a few years later, had to have three goes at deploying a coherent argument. However, none of this made much difference to the outcome. Teeth were bared, swords were girded, resolution not rationality was the order of the day. My officials had been told by the Foreign Office that we could look for strong support from the Foreign Secretary, but in fact Gordon Walker did the reverse, saying that the stringency of the economic position meant that we all had to make sacrifices and that he was prepared to sacrifice good relations with the French. Callaghan said that sterling could be sustained only by a White Paper with teeth, and this meant biting on specific projects. The fact that none other was mentioned did not seem to affect the force of the argument. Whenever an anti-Concorde point was made the left of the Cabinet (Barbara Castle, Frank Cousins, Fred Lee, Tony Greenwood) formed a little claque and said, 'Hear, hear.' Wilson seemed content with the mood.

So there was nothing to do except accept defeat. I could hardly resign from a government of which I had been a member for only four days, and in fact the thought or the desire never crossed my mind. I could not however just put my head down, for while decisions could be taken over the heads of non-Cabinet ministers, such inferior creatures had to be used for carrying them out. I was deputed to tell the Concorde airframe and aero-engine firms early on Monday, before the White Paper was published, and confront the French later in the week.

The meetings with the British Aircraft Corporation (Sir George Edwards, later OM) and with Bristol Siddeley (Sir Reginald Verdon-Smith) were not exactly joyous occasions, but dealing with a new minister who was their paymaster for most of their other projects they had little alternative but to accept the news with dismayed resignation. The dismay was genuine, but the resignation was feigned, for they had every intention, as was reasonable from their point of view, of organising as much opposition as they could muster, and shrewdly saw that, given the style and nature of the Wilson Government, the unions with whom they normally battled and the press offered the best foci. Furthermore, the fact that I insisted on putting the Government's position in semi-tentative terms ('a disposition to cancel'), for otherwise our position with the French would have been indefensible, meant that they had an unbolted door at which to push.

The French seemed likely to be a more intimidating proposition. The Government of General de Gaulle did not have a reputation for forgiving tolerance when British clumsiness exposed a flank. Also I obviously had to go and see them on their own ground. We could not issue a unilateral declaration and summon them to London to hear the explanation. Accordingly, and with a large party of officials, I set out for Paris on the morning of Tuesday, 29 October. Sitting in the plane on the tarmac at London Airport I was handed a Foreign Office telegram which contained the encouraging phrase: 'The Minister of Aviation should be prepared for the atmosphere of cold enmity with which he will be met in Paris.' This inspired me to spend the short journey working so hard at my opening statement for the afternoon meeting that I did not notice when the plane landed, and looked up only as we taxied to a halt. I then saw a great crowd of people, mostly photographers and journalists, assembled on the tarmac.

At that moment I realised more vividly than on any other occasion what was involved in being a minister. I had with me not only my permanent secretary and one or two other experienced general administrators but also aviation technicians of high quality. They all knew far more about Concorde than I did and were also more experienced in dealing with the French about it. But not one of them was going to get out of that plane before I did. Ministerial privilege and ministerial responsibility united to ensure that I had to walk down the steps alone and deal with the waiting crowd. After a few 'on the hoof' television and press comments we drove to the British Embassy, and had an hour's apprehensive respite over lunch.

Thereafter things began to pick up. The meeting with my Concorde vis-à-vis, Marc Jacquet, Minister of Transport and Public Works, was not nearly as bad as I had feared. He looked grave (although in general, as I discovered in our later dealings, he had a rather earthy humour) and gave absolutely nothing away from the French point of view, but he was perfectly courteous and even friendly throughout. Unlike my Cabinet experience with Wilson I had no difficulty in getting through my prepared statement of position without interruption. The other ministers, Pierre Messmer at Defence and Gaston Palewski at Science, on whom I called because our responsibilities overlapped, were equally urbane. Palewski, Nancy Mitford's old hero, even regaled me with some socio-literary gossip in his splendid room, from which we inappropriately looked over the Place de la Concorde.

The next stage in the Concorde battle was a House of Commons debate, arranged at very short notice, on the following Thursday. It was one of the days on the Address and had started by being about something else, but the opposition suddenly decided that Concorde was a subject to exploit and announced during the day that they were putting up Angus Maude, my new 'shadow', to wind up on this subject. I was therefore summoned to answer him in my first government front-bench performance without the opportunity for much more than sketchy preparation.

There could be no vote, but the subject was hot news, the Parliament and the Government were new, and the habit of attendance at debates was much greater in those days than it is now. So when I rose to reply at 9.30 p.m. the House was packed. In sixteen years on the back benches I had never previously addressed a completely full House. Two or three times I might have had one, largely by chance, of say 250. The test was therefore considerable. By the grace of God I passed it. Maude had been sour but dry. I do not think that my following speech contained any great prose or reached any oratorical heights (I was to make a much better-structured one on 9 February, when I opened a debate with a more prepared and schematic critique of the pretensions of the aircraft industry), but it held the full House unexpectedly, put the Tories on the defensive, was loudly cheered by the Labour side and widely praised in the press the next morning. Modern technology being still in the future, the newspapers had no difficulty in fully reporting and commenting on a speech finishing at 10.00 p.m., a feat which they would find impossible today.

Quite how this success happened, I do not know. I remember that Julian Amery unwittingly helped a great deal. He rolled in a little late, pushed his way along the front opposition bench to a position from which he could interrupt and soon got up to attempt a plummily delivered *ex cathedra* rebuke. I said, 'The right honourable gentleman must recognise that his administration of the Ministry of Aviation was not such that all his opinions are sacrosanct.' It was not argument. It was just an attempted put-down, and the fact that it worked is a classic illustration of the irrational way in which a full House of Commons operates. In the middle of a speech going badly, it could have been a disaster. In the middle of one going well, it was regarded as a crushing riposte. As a result of this and a few other pieces of luck I was thought to have had a triumph. Its effect on me was certainly comparable to that which I imagine big-game hunters felt when they were still allowed to shoot a tiger, or Grand National jockeys do when they not only survive but win.

The effect on other people was considerable too. What I had done said very little about my judgement or administrative ability as a minister, but according to the *victor ludorum* rules which applied to British parliamentary government in those days, just as much with a Labour as with a Conservative majority, it greatly increased my elbow room for trying to exercise these qualities. After 2 November I would not (for a time at any rate) have been treated in the Cabinet as I had been twelve days before. My authority in my department also increased perceptibly.

Several things followed from that evening of unexpected success. First I became and remained until 1976 a high-stake parliamentary player. I was in those days a much better speaker in the House of Commons than at party gatherings in the country, although I think the reverse became the case when I returned to British politics in the 1980s. In important debates I attracted large houses and tried very hard to win. If I did, it was splendid. But if I did not, as certainly sometimes happened, the let-down was the greater, and there were plenty of loyal colleagues as well as opponents to take pleasure in the event. On the whole, however, I was given credit for possessing a greater command over the House of Commons than did, say, Crosland or in those days

Healey, and this was undoubtedly a factor in certain promotions which I subsequently achieved.

Second, my pattern of work as a minister perhaps paid the price of too great a concentration upon debating success. I was never keen to appear too often in the parliamentary arena. I became like a prize fighter who would not risk his title except for a big purse. I was therefore mostly willing to give junior ministers the opportunity to gain practice by getting knocked about. And when I felt I had to speak I was likely to go into a two-day purdah when nothing much mattered except the preparation of the speech. To balance this I worked out a theory that, if one was lucky enough to have a triumph, the momentum of its slipstream should be used to take as many difficult decisions as possible. Both my own nerve and my departmental, Cabinet and parliamentary authority for doing so were temporarily improved. Of course all these powers and precepts did not spring ready made from that single debate at the beginning of the 1964 Parliament. It merely began a process.

Meanwhile the Concorde affair rumbled on for several months. The French, if they wished the project to continue, played their hand brilliantly. They did not get over-excited, reacted more in sorrow than in anger, implied that it was inconceivable we would actually cancel the contracts except in agreement with them, and always kept in hand, neither brandished nor discarded, the threat of suing us for damages in The Hague Court of International Justice. This was their trump card, particularly as the firm advice of our Law Officers (I wonder if the French knew this) was that if they did we would lose and might well have damages of the order of £200 million awarded against us.

This was the equivalent of about £2 billion in today's money and became a powerful influence on my mind, as I think it did on that of Wilson. (Brown and Callaghan remained more sceptical or more bold.) It was not only the size of the sum, although that was not negligible, which influenced me, but also the indignity of losing an action for breach of a treaty, the bad effect on our relations with Europe, and my conviction that the £200 million would become a major political factor and have at least as many lives as a cat. Whenever an awkward public expenditure issue subsequently arose we would always be taunted that if we had not thrown this money away on illegality we could easily have afforded X or Y. The damages would assume much more reality than the money we were saving by not building the plane.

Nevertheless I remember that when I went to Bristol on 11 December, where the British side of both the airframe and the engine work was being carried out, I still thought that the plane was on its death-bed. The visit therefore had few of the features of an early pre-Christmas party. I was struck by the remarkable constriction of the Concorde fuselage, which then existed only as a wooden mock-up, which is a quality it has not since lost.

By mid-January however a reprieve, or at any rate a temporary stay of execution, had become available. A Cabinet committee met to consider the recently received third formal French note on the issue, which sounded as firm as could be, and which taken in conjunction with the Law Officers' persistent croak of doom and the facts that we were on the point of cancelling two embryonic military aircraft projects (the P-1154 and the HS-681) and had a much bigger, because much more advanced, cancellation project (the TSR-II) lurking in the background, was sufficient to tip the balance and secure a reversal of the ill-judged October pronouncement.

This was ironical, for I subsequently received strong but not absolutely verifiable hints that this third note was the last French throw, and that, had we then persisted, they would have accepted that the project was dead, with a bad grace but without going to The Hague Court. What is certain is that when we made our brusque White Paper announcement there were deep French worries about Concorde, which our unilateralism temporarily suppressed. Hamfistedness therefore had the paradoxical effect of saving the project, for had we approached the French confidentially a quiet funeral could almost certainly have been arranged. Whether this would have been desirable is open to argument. Concorde has been a technical success and has brought some but not vast prestige to the British and French aircraft industries, as well as considerable convenience to a limited number of passengers. But it has cost a disproportionate amount of money, produced nil return on capital and been remarkably unseminal. It is also noticeable that the French in recent years have been less keen than have the British to keep Concorde services going. As in general the French disposition towards both continuity of policy and state subsidies is greater than is ours, this can be taken as further confirmation of the view that their 1964 attachment to Concorde was only skin-deep.

While the Concorde affair and other aviation alarms and excursions had been proceeding in the late autumn of 1964 I had managed to make a less reactive move than those I have been describing. It was one which I hoped would result in shining a beam of rational light on to what was becoming the smoke-obscured battleground of the too political aircraft industry. Soon after taking office I developed the idea of a small, fairly quick independent committee of inquiry into the industry. I thought it should have as chairman Edwin Plowden, former chief planner at the Treasury under Cripps, Gaitskell and Butler, later head of the Atomic Energy Authority and currently chairman of Tube Investments, and only two other members: Austen Albu and Aubrey Jones. I wanted Plowden because he had high sceptical intelligence and a unique British public service record. He had even been one of the three 'wise men' of the Western world, with Monnet and Harriman, who in 1951 were to smooth away the unfairnesses of the burden of rearmament. The two MPs might have seemed a contradiction in terms as part of a remedy for an over-politicised industry, but I thought that they were both peculiarly free of party dogma, that Albu had been foolishly left out of the Government and that Jones had the useful authority of being a Conservative ex-minister without any closed-minded loyalty. I had little doubt that Plowden with them could produce unanimous sense.

My trio held, although Albu was soon snatched away to a belated government job and was replaced by John Cronin, an engaging MP, but with a less rigorous approach to the aircraft industry. In addition, Cabinet pressure forced me to widen the committee so as to include at least one trade unionist, one industrialist and one scientist. In fact I ended up with a body whose distinction (actual or subsequent) astonished me when I came to look back at it for the purposes of these memoirs. Apart from those already mentioned, it was: Lord Penney OM, Admiral of the Fleet Sir Caspar John, Sir St John Elstub (chairman of ICI Metals), Sir David Barran (later chairman of Shell and of the Midland Bank), Sir Fred Hayday (the trade unionist and later a strong political ally of mine – see Chapter 19), and Sir Christopher McMahon (another future chairman of the Midland Bank). Their corporate weight did not prevent Lord Plowden producing a good report by early the following autumn.

A month after I had set up this committee, however, I myself was almost enticed away from the enjoyable and surprisingly politically rewarding problems of Aviation. So far from it proving the 'poisoned chalice' of which Wilson had warned me, its first autumn had given me more public exposure and parliamentary opportunity than had been the case with more than three or four of those in the Cabinet. I was therefore basically a satisfied minor power and contented member of the Government on the night of Thursday, 21 January 1965. The significance of that date was that it produced the result of the Leyton bye-election, the first of the Parliament. It was a disaster. The bye-election had been artificially created, which was perhaps part of the trouble, to make a seat for Patrick Gordon Walker, who had been a Foreign Secretary unable to speak in Parliament since his defeat at Smethwick in October. The result was that three months of government seemed to have destroyed the position of the Labour Party in one of the safest seats in East London (it had been comfortably Labour since 1935). A House of Commons majority of four had been reduced to one of two. An unwinnable general election loomed on the horizon. For Gordon Walker it was a crushing blow. He became with Charles Masterman and Arthur Griffith-Boscawen one of the only three politicians this century whose Cabinet career was irrevocably damaged by personal electoral failure. Although he comfortably won back Leyton at the 1966 general election (which showed the freakish nature of the 1965 result) it was too late. He had to resign the foreign secretaryship and, although he returned to lesser Cabinet offices for a couple of years, he never again came close to a great office of state.

After the news of Leyton, it did not at first occur to me that I might be involved in its repercussions. I was merely sad for Patrick Gordon Walker, an exceptionally nice man and an old friend, and depressed for the future of the Government. Next morning at breakfast however the thought did cross my mind that Denis Healey was the most likely Foreign Secretary, and that the vacancy at the Ministry of Defence might then involve me. This thought did not take root, and I went into the office with my mind on other things. At about 10.15 my private secretary said that Mr Shinwell was on the telephone and wished to speak to me. Emanuel Shinwell, already aged eighty, although with another twenty-two years to live, was then chairman of the parliamentary Labour Party and thought to have a powerful influence with Wilson. He was in no way a friend of mine, having been a bitter enemy of Gaitskell's and hostile to me on the Common Market. I was therefore amazed when, over a very bad line which made the conversation jerky but not incomprehensible, he said that Wilson had consulted him that morning about who should be Foreign Secretary and that he had told him that I should be. He asked for an undertaking that if offered I would not refuse, and this I had no difficulty in giving him, even though I found it difficult to take his agreeable intelligence seriously.

I then had to go across to 10 Downing Street for an hour's meeting of the Defence and Overseas Policy Committee of the Cabinet. As it was concerned with aircraft cancellations I was much engaged. Wilson presided but gave no indication of his intentions. Gordon Walker was not present and was understood to have resigned. When it was over I walked out of No. 10 and across to the Foreign Office courtyard where my car was waiting. There was a posse of photographers who ran round in front of me to take pictures. As soon as I got back to my own office, my second private secretary came in and said that there was a message asking me to go back to 10 Downing Street immediately. I must say that then, for the first time, I took Shinwell's telephone call wholly seriously and ingested the thought, unbelievable though it seemed on any previous basis, that Wilson was going to make me Foreign Secretary. To calm my nerves, clear my head or just bask in a moment of pleasure, I told my driver that I would walk across and that he was to follow. Accordingly, on a sunny not very cold January morning I walked round the back of the Banqueting Hall, across Whitehall and up Downing Street, Foreign Secretary for five minutes at the age of forty-four and only a few months away from being a fairly obscure back-bencher on doubtful terms with the Prime Minister-to-be and semi-tempted to abandon politics for a weekly editorship.

Outside No. 10 the photographers on this occasion seemed uninterested in me. Their intelligence was much more accurate and up to the minute than mine. I did not react to this, but when I got inside and was asked to wait in the little hall outside the Cabinet room, I began to smell a rat. Foreign Secretaries arriving for appointment, I instinctively felt, went straight in. (This instinct about ministers of such rank was confirmed thirty-four months later when I almost equally unexpectedly became Chancellor of the Exchequer and was indeed swept straight in.)

A moment later Callaghan walked by. He always liked being in on other people's appointments and resignations, rather like a breezy and over-eager attender of weddings and funerals. 'You know what you are here for, don't you?' he said. I shook my head. 'Well, if you knew who was inside, you would know what you were being offered,' he continued. 'Who is inside?' I rose to asking rather bad-temperedly. 'Michael Stewart,' he said with the self-satisfaction of one who was privy to all movements on the inner circle.

So the mystery was anticlimactically solved. Stewart was to be Foreign Secretary and I was to be offered his job as Education Secretary, with of course a place in the Cabinet. The next moment he came out and I went in. Foiled (although presumably unknowingly) for the second time in three months by one of his economic ministers from being able to deliver an offer with any element of surprise, Wilson was less circumlocutory than he had been in October. He was also very gracious. He made it clear that what he was essentially doing was offering me the first promotion to the Cabinet. The fact that it was Education was accidental, although he assured me that he thought I could do that job. He said that the Secretary of the Cabinet (then Burke Trend) had told him that I was the best minister in the Government. I was by no means clear what feat of bureaucratic good-behaviour had extracted this tribute from that frosty eminence, but it was nice to hear, even though I do not believe Trend's view persisted when he had longer and closer experience.

After my brief journey through the sky in the Foreign Office comet I was inevitably in a mood of let-down and disappointment. Independently of this, however, I was not vastly attracted by the Department of Education. My mind was not on its problems and I was not stimulated by the thought of them. Perhaps looking for an excuse, I said that all three of our children were at fee-paying schools and that this was surely an obstacle to being Minister of Education in a Labour government. Wilson brushed this aside as being of no importance. 'So were mine,' he said. I then asked him if I could think it over during lunch. Reluctantly he said that I could, provided it was a short lunch and that I gave him an answer in the House of Commons at two o'clock. (Had he said no I am as sure as I can be that I would have said yes, although with a torn mind and maybe even a heavy heart.)

As it was, I went back to my office, summoned Jennifer and pondered over a sandwich with her. I tried to consult Sam Way, but he had gone out to lunch and could not be found. I did not consult any private secretary or other official. By a supreme irony, David Dowler, who was to stay with me for five years and become my closest possible confidant, had arrived that morning to take over the principal private secretaryship, but as is I fear my habit with people I do not know when matters are critical, I kept him at bay all day, excluded and unspoken to in the private office.

Jennifer inclined towards acceptance, but as we talked it over my mind moved in the other direction. What I think decided me was that I tried to imagine how I would feel walking up the steps of the Department of Education the following Monday morning, and concluded that I would do so with more regret for Aviation than enthusiasm for Education. So I drove over to the House of Commons and beckoned to Wilson, who was sitting in the members' dining room. 'Let us go outside for ten seconds,' he said. 'No,' I said, 'it will take longer.' He looked mildly displeased, but not more, and said that in that case he would finish his lunch and meet me in his room in ten minutes. Waiting for him outside I apprehended for the first time that when I said no someone else would necessarily get Education and leapfrog over me into the Cabinet. It was an ignoble thought, and in any case too late to do anything about.

Wilson when he came took my decision remarkably well. Indeed he soon began to warm to it, and talking throughout on the assumption of an early election said that what happened at Aviation 'over the next thirteen weeks' could affect its outcome much more than what happened at Education. After it, if we won, I would have another opportunity to come into the Cabinet. If we lost, we would all be out. Trying to take some balm away with me, I asked him if my having stayed at Aviation would make it more difficult for me to get one of the four or five top jobs if one became available and I were otherwise considered suitable. He said no, perhaps even easier. He added that he had considered me for the Foreign Office, but as number three on a list which began with Stewart and had Herbert Bowden, leader of the House of Commons, second. We parted friendlily.

I got through the afternoon's work with verve, feeling rather pleased with myself. At about six I heard that Crosland had been appointed Secretary of State for Education, and experienced an inevitable stab of jealousy that I had surrendered my brief lead over this great friend but formidable rival. Fortified by a drink at Brooks's with Nicko Henderson, who was then the principal private secretary at the Foreign Office, and John Harris, who had also been working for poor Gordon Walker, I nevertheless went out to dinner in a buoyant enough mood. Next morning, however, I awoke in a deep gloom, convinced that I had made a horrible mistake. By Monday I had fortunately reverted to my Friday view and was glad that I did not have to go to a new ministry leaving the unsolved but temporarily glamorous problems of Aviation behind me. And that, with the exception of a few weeks in the autumn of 1965, has since remained my settled mind.

I did however have to be disabused of my foolish view that I ought to have the best of both worlds, that is to be treated like a Cabinet minister even though I had declined to become one. In the following week Churchill died and at his great state funeral in St Paul's the Cabinet had some sort of special *entrée* which was denied to lesser ministers and through which I saw the Croslands gliding. Equally, I recall that when I was next summoned to be 'in attendance' at a meeting of the Cabinet I was slow to leave when my item was over and half expected Wilson to invite me to stay on. Quite rightly, he did not.

Until the spring the 'problems of Aviation' mostly continued to revolve around aircraft cancellation. The big beast was the TSR-II, a swing-wing or variable-geometry fighter-bomber, with a powerful long-distance strike capacity which made it particularly suited to an East of Suez role. The British Aircraft Corporation, in conjunction this time with Rolls-Royce, had developed the plane to the stage of a few flying prototypes. Such an advanced weapons system was naturally a very expensive project. The essential trouble was that it showed no sign of achieving any market beyond the Royal Air Force. The Americans were producing a rival aircraft known in development as the TFX and in production as the F-111, which was a little further advanced. There was passionate debate about the respective merits of the two planes. I have never known an argument about military aircraft so engage lay attention. The TSR-II may have been a little better, but they both still had plenty of problems, and the Americans with a bigger home order and a better export prospect had far more resources with which to overcome them.

This was the view of all prospective customers. The Australian Air Force had in early 1964 delivered a nearly final blow to the TSR-II by opting for the F-111. By early 1965 the British Ministry of Defence, air marshals as much as ministers, wanted to do the same. The TSR-II, good plane though it was, had few friends outside the aircraft industry and the military chauvinist political lobby. I did not think that we should keep it going, although I was not convinced that the automatic alternative was to buy the F-111. My scepticism about a continuing British East of Suez role predisposed me in favour of doing without either. This divided me from Healey, who was determined to buy the American plane.

The Treasury were naturally in favour of saving money, although their voice was rendered uncertain by Callaghan's being as instinctive an East of Suez man as I was a sceptic. But he certainly wanted the TSR-II axed, and indeed evolved a tactic of needing to announce it in his Budget speech (due on 6 April) in order to provide one of those puffs for sterling without which that unsteady craft was always in danger of foundering. This meant a decision at a Cabinet meeting on Thursday, 1 April, a timetable which suited me badly. I was due to leave that morning, with Jennifer, on the inaugural flight of the VC-10 to New York and to speak the following day at a grand civil aviation luncheon to mark the creation of a separate BOAC terminal (the first for any foreign airline) at Idlewild, as Kennedy Airport was generally still called.

I let Jennifer go alone and booked myself on the Thursday-evening flight. This showed how inexperienced I then was in Harold Wilson's Cabinet tactics. Whenever he had a possibly divisive decision to take he believed in letting everyone talk themselves out, preferably over more than one meeting. He accordingly made no attempt to get the matter settled before he left to attend a minor royal memorial service at noon. There had not been time for much more than opening statements from Healey and me. The Cabinet, Wilson said, would meet again at 10.15 p.m. after the House of Commons division. He graciously added that, if I felt I ought to be in New York, I need not stay. What I felt was that, while I wanted to be in New York, I ought to be in London. I had not stayed at Aviation to be on jaunts across the Atlantic when key decisions were taken.

The night Cabinet took two and a half hours, Wilson marking down every individual's views, and eventually reached a unanimous decision to cancel, although with Douglas Jay and Frank Cousins the most reluctant, accompanied by a decision, with a minority of six, to take an option, available until the end of the year, on the F-111. Having got Healey to check on the telephone with McNamara that the option involved us in no moral or financial obligation, I supported the majority. I then went to New York at 11.15 the next morning by the second day's VC-10 and, having helicoptered to Manhattan during the most filthy hail storm, walked into the Waldorf at ten to one ready for my lunch speech. This was regarded as very good time in those days (although aided by April being a month with an unusual six-hour time difference), and I felt like a true aviator as well as a Francis Drake who had finished his game of bowls.

Back in London the unveiling of the decisions produced some high old parliamentary scenes. The Chancellor's bare announcement did not disrupt his Budget speech, although I am not sure it did much good to sterling, but a rather oddly timed intervention by Healey at seven that evening led to his being more or less shouted down. A week later we had a very noisy aviation debate, which Healey opened and I wound up. It was the most tumultuous and I thought the least satisfactory of a series of four or five major aviation clashes which had come near to dominating the House of Commons stage since November. But it also turned out to be the last of them. There were a few spurts of opposition anger when I refused to mount a flying programme for the three TSR-IIs which existed, or to maintain a sort of phantom production line which could have been reactivated with a change of government, but which would have been industrial nonsense. Nevertheless the ideological clash was on the wane. I began to feel I was no longer in the front line. At first this was a relief, then it became rather boring.

During the summer I devoted more time to civil aviation, although I did go to America in June to look sceptically at the F-111, which was being hatched out at Fort Worth. It was a very bad summer in Britain and my exaggerated recollection is of bumping endlessly up and down the country in the little tub of the Civil Aviation Authority Dove, which could never get above the thick cloud cover. We were putting through Parliament an airports bill, which set up the British Airports Authority and devolved the Ministry airports in one direction or another, either to the new body or to local authorities. I thought it a good idea to familiarise myself with the contrasting circumstances of British airports and visited them almost without exception. On one trip in a July depression (weather rather than personal) I went to all the strips and fields in the Scottish Highlands and Islands. I am not sure that it greatly helped the passage of the bill, which in any case John Stonehouse was mostly conducting, but it gave me a grid of geographical knowledge which became useful when I entered Scottish politics seventeen years later. I discovered on this and other journeys that aircraft bumping is only nerve-racking or sick-making if you sit in the passenger cabin. If you sit strapped in at the controls (fortified by a co-pilot, for I was far from having a licence), you can see the bumps coming and mind them no more than when driving a car on a rugged road. My officials therefore increasingly had the bumps while I had the view. My crabwise landing on the beach at Benbecula – it was the correct place to land there – remained engraved on the minds of Sir James Mackay (a deputy secretary, whose career became entangled with mine) and David Dowler (both, alas, now dead) for several years to come.

By the summer recess, however, with Wilson's 'thirteen weeks' more than twice over and no election in sight, and with the excitements of the winter six months well behind, Aviation was beginning to lose its charms. It was not unreasonable in view of my January conversations with the Prime Minister to cast my mind towards a high office, and the one which beckoned, for a variety of reasons, was the home secretaryship.

# CHAPTER NINE

# *A Young Home Secretary*

The Home Secretary at the beginning of the first Wilson Government was Sir Frank Soskice, later Lord Stow Hill. He was a man of legal skill, very good manners, considerable charm and unusual provenance. His father had been a Russian liberal and his mother was a grand-daughter of Ford Madox Brown, the pre-Raphaelite painter. Soskice appeared entirely English, had been at St Paul's School and Balliol, and had been first Solicitor-General and then Attorney-General in the Attlee Government. He had been a core member of Gaitskell's so-called Hampstead Set, living only 200 yards from the leader in a beautiful house in Church Row.

Despite these attributes, he was a remarkably bad Home Secretary. He had practically no political sense and an obsessive respect for legal precedent. In addition he was extremely indecisive. It was his habit, I was subsequently told, to proceed home each evening with ten or twelve brown pouches (he thought red boxes too flamboyant) stuffed with Home Office cases. Next morning he usually returned with all the cases worked on and none of them decided. He had got a rather restrictive immigration-control bill into trouble in committee, and the Race Relations Board which he set up was given very few teeth. The notable event of his period of office was the passage of a private member's bill abolishing the death penalty. He was the first Home Secretary never to hang anyone. For the rest he opened no more windows to relieve the internal stuffiness of the Home Office than had his well-meaning but not adept predecessor, Henry Brooke, whose penchant for falling into elephant traps of his own creation was notorious, but who in this respect too had a worthy successor in Soskice.

This was the man whose office I came to covet in the summer of 1965. It was not a heinous thing to do, for Soskice was said to be anxious to resign on health grounds. The struggle for the Obscene

175

Publications Bill in the late 1950s had led my mind on to Home Office questions beyond censorship, and in *The Labour Case*, my Penguin Special written for the 1959 general election, I had devoted one chapter, entitled 'Is Britain Civilized?', to producing what was in effect an unauthorised programme for Home Office reform. I was stimulated by the thought of the Home Secretary's work in a way that had not been so with Education. I was also perhaps attracted by the traditional grandeur of the office and by the thought that Asquith had achieved it in his fortieth year and that I had been able to entitle another chapter in a different book 'The Young Home Secretary'. At best I was going to be five years older than him, but it was something to be within that range. I might however also have reflected on the fact that no Home Secretary since Churchill had become Prime Minister, and that it had taken him thirty years and a very roundabout route to effect the transition.

On 15 September I had a chance encounter with Frank Longford at one of George Weidenfeld's many dinner parties. The third party to the conversation was Jakie Astor, who kindly asked Longford if he did not think that I ought to be in the Cabinet as Home Secretary. Longford replied that he was sure I would be in the Cabinet by the end of the year, but not as Home Secretary. He spoke with such certainty that I took him aside afterwards and asked him how he knew. He said that he had had a conversation with Wilson only that morning, and that the Prime Minister had spoken in precisely these terms, adding that 'horses for courses and courses for horses' he did not think it was my job. This phrase stamped the information with authenticity, for it was one which I had several times heard Wilson use.

This was vexing. It was of course more than possible that Wilson simply did not want me to be his Home Secretary. If so, there was nothing I could do about it. But it was also possible that, as he had expressed to me his own distaste for the job during our January reshuffle conversations, he thought that I would share it, and was merely acting under a misapprehension. On reflection I decided that the stakes were so high that I had better risk the rebuff which might be involved in trying to sort this out. I therefore went to see him five days later, having put together an agenda of a number of aviation points.

My last point, carefully sprung, was to ask him what were now his views about the future of my Ministry. He responded perfectly. That, he said, depended on my future, and his view on this was that I should come into the Cabinet as a result of a series of moves following Soskice's resignation as Home Secretary. 'As a result of a series of moves?' I asked, trying to get the right note of interrogative disappointment into my voice. He was walking about the room and turned round sharply. 'You surely wouldn't like to be Home Secretary, would you?' he said. I said that I would very much indeed: it was no moment for beating about the bush. 'Well, that makes it all much easier,' he said. I then told him some of my ideas about letting fresh air into the Home Office, about which he became enthusiastic. He had apparently been upset by an article by Jo Grimond in that morning's *Guardian* which had said the Government was competent but not radical. He thought my appointment might help to redress the balance. I hoped he meant by increasing the radicalism not reducing the competence.

On the timing of the change I told him that I was due to go on an eighteen-day world trip on 7 October. He said that there was no need to cancel it. I could accept by telegram while away, provided I did not wish to introduce any complications into my acceptance. I said there would certainly be no complications. There were some things about the future organisation of the Home Office I would want to talk to him about, but there would be no conditions *sine qua non*. He said, 'Surely *sine quis non*?' and looked frightfully pleased with himself. I was happy to assent.

This conversation ushered in a pleasurable few weeks. We went to see East Hendred for the first time, having noticed a newspaper advertisement for the house, and Jennifer bought it at an auction in Abingdon a week or so later. I paid a four-day visit to the Labour Party conference in Blackpool, which was relaxed because it was one of the rare occasions over twenty-five years when I felt no obligation to speak either from the platform or from the floor. On the Thursday morning I flew down to London in a small private plane, giving a lift to Roy Hattersley, then a thrusting back-bencher of whom I thought highly. I remember his intense and agreeably spontaneous pleasure at sharing in this piece of ministerial privilege. That evening, accompanied again by my now hardened fellow aviators of the Scottish tour, David Dowler and Sir James Mackay, I left London Airport on the first leg of my world trip. We had some moderately serious aviation business to transact, but it would be idle to pretend that the expedition had not assumed in my mind the guise of a rounding-off reward for a year's testing work as Minister of Aviation. A nice touch of interest was provided by the uncertainty about how far we would get before being summoned home to higher office.

There was no problem of being brought back before we had properly started. We proceeded to Bangkok, to Hong Kong, to Tokyo (for a British fair in which the aircraft industry was well represented), back to Hong Kong, to Manila, to Sydney, to Woomera (where our civilian space rocket, the first stage of which was all that we hoped to salvage from the collapse of the military Blue Streak, was being tested), to Melbourne, to Canberra, without a whisper from Downing Street. For the first few days we were followed by British press summaries which were full of confident predictions of an early reshuffle, of a break-up of the Ministry of Aviation, much of it going to Technology, a new (1964) department presided over by Frank Cousins with C. P. Snow as his improbable Sancho Panza, and of my translation to the Home Office. But even these rumours had ceased, rather like birds first accompanying and then falling away from a departing ship. So it was out of an empty sky that we got news in Canberra of a very minor change-around of junior ministers with the accompanying guidance that that was to be all for several months.

Mystification and disappointment jostled with each other for the dominant position in my mind. Neither Jennifer nor Sir Richard Way when telephoned in London was able to provide much in the way of explanation to assuage their confirmation that this was what had happened. So there was nothing to do except restrap on the aviation harness and proceed to New Zealand, Fiji, Mexico City, New York and London.

New Zealand I liked less than Australia, thinking it more claustro-phobic, and in Wellington found this prejudice perfectly confirmed, with some consolation for not being in a Cabinet provided as a side-wind. The Prime Minister (Keith Holyoake) kindly invited me to lunch with all his colleagues. 'How often do you have these Cabinet lunches?', I asked him. 'Every day,' he said. 'We always lunch together; only those abroad unfortunately miss it.' I decided that the social aspects of political life in New Zealand would not suit me. I preferred lunch in New York with Mrs Kennedy, then less than two years away from Dallas, and still well short of becoming Mrs Onassis.

Back in London I was able to attempt an explanation of the mystery of the 'mouse out of a mountain' government changes. Crosland told me with some pleasure that it was because Wilson had reacted against the spate of inspired press rumour. Sam Way, from the official net, confirmed this, although he added comfortingly that Cousins and not I was thought to be responsible for the leaks. Wilson (who showed no hurry for a meeting) neither accused nor exonerated me, was less forthcoming than in September, added the gloss that Soskice at the last moment had proved loath to go, but ended by saying that the operation could be reinstated for January, or perhaps even December.

This time he was better than his word. I eventually became Home Secretary on the evening of Wednesday, 22 December 1965. This time it was I and not Wilson who was subjected to the harassment of a prior press bombardment. The week before there had been a lot of stories (including some datelined New York, where Wilson was on a Rhodesian UN mission) saying that Soskice and Fraser (the Minister of Transport) were to go, but that I was to be left at Aviation to carry out the recommendations of the Plowden Report. This was nerve-racking, but if it enabled the Prime Minister to feel that he had had his tit-for-tat for October (even though I had not then been responsible), and could proceed according to plan, it was worth it.

As it happened I was once again abroad, in Bonn, to try to arrange some aircraft collaboration with the German Government. The confirmatory call came through to the ambassador there (Sir Frank Roberts), who was sitting beside me while I conducted a press conference at the end of the talks. I listened out of one ear to a conversation which settled the matter beyond peradventure while delivering my final aviation pronouncements. Barbara Castle became Minister of Transport at the same time.

The word was made flesh by two Special Branch detectives arriving to take charge of me as soon as I got to London. The next afternoon I was sworn in as Her Majesty's Principal Secretary of State for the Home Department, the senior secretaryship of state, for such has been its Court precedence, although by no means always its Cabinet precedence, since the office of Secretary of State was departmentalised, at first only into Home and Foreign, in 1782. (There had briefly been a Colonial Secretary from 1768, but his functions were absorbed in the Home Department in 1782.)

I then went to the Home Office, observed the immense gloominess of my room, which appeared to be illuminated (and perhaps heated as well) only by a half-size very old electric fire incongruously placed in the middle of the carpet, halfway between the desk and the empty fireplace. There I had a first encounter with the formidable permanent under-secretary of state, Sir Charles Cunningham. He welcomed me politely, but expressed little enthusiasm for my preliminary views about Home Office work. Nothing had to be resolved at that stage, however, so we wished each other a merry Christmas, and I departed for Hatley, where, East Hendred not being habitable, we spent ten days half with the Astors and half on our own, I going to London for two and a half of them, but devoting more time to quiet Home Office reading and planning.

I was in a buoyant mood during this Christmas holiday. I was delighted to be Home Secretary at the age of forty-five, the youngest in that grave office since Churchill in 1910. I have never replied with so much enthusiasm to letters of congratulation as I did over many Christmas hours sitting in my bedroom in the big house of Hatley. On Christmas morning we went to church in Cambridge at Great St Mary's, and I think it was during the Erastian 'Church and state' bits of the prayers that, with a more temporal than spiritual reaction, it was first fully borne in upon me what a position of at least nominal authority in the state (and even indeed, because of my role in the swearing in of bishops, in the Church), I had amazingly assumed.

Jean Monnet liked drawing a distinction between those who enjoyed 'being someone' and those who enjoyed 'doing something'. I cannot deny that on this occasion I enjoyed being someone. But I also had plans for doing something at the Home Office. I had the advantage, probably to a greater extent than when I took over any other office, the Ministry of Aviation in 1964, the Treasury in 1967, the Home Office for the second time in 1974 or the presidency of the European Commission in 1977, of having a published personal agenda of what I wanted to do.

I had begun my 'unauthorised programme' for the Home Office chapter in my 1959 book by stating flatly: 'First, there is the need for the State to do less to restrict personal freedom.' This required 'wholesale reform' in the Home Office field. 'The ghastly apparatus of the gallows', which made us 'one of the few advanced countries which retains the presumptuously final penalty', had to go. That was done by 1965, but it was an issue which has since required a continuing and vigorous defence against retrogression. So did the removal of flogging from the penal code, which never in that period failed to excite Conservative conferences against their Home Secretaries. I was also anxious to remove it from the prison discipline code. (This was done in 1967.)

'The law relating to homosexuality remains in the brutal and unfair state in which the House of Commons almost accidentally placed it in 1885,' was my next complaint. This was made worse by the fact that the clear recommendation of the Wolfenden Committee on the point had been ignored, while its much more vague proposals about prostitutes had been implemented in a way that considerably increased police power. Furthermore there was the hypocrisy that the leading members of previous governments applied no 'social disapproval to homosexual conduct which, for public consumption, they insist[ed] on keeping subject to the full rigours of the criminal law'. (The 1885 law was replaced in 1967.)

Next there was 'the fantastic position by which the Lord Chamberlain, a Court official who may exceptionally have an intelligent playgoer's knowledge of the stage but never has anything more, possesses powers of absolute censorship over all the public theatres of London'. (This was changed in 1968.) Then there were 'the licensing laws, which may have been necessary to cope with the mass drunkenness of the early part of this century, but are today an unnecessary restriction which would not be tolerated in any other European country'. (They, I regret to say, were left until the 1980s to be dealt with.)

The divorce laws, 'which involve both a great deal of unnecessary suffering and a great number of attempts (many of them successful) to deceive the courts', were in urgent need of reform. (This was done in 1969.) The 'harsh and archaic abortion laws' were also indefensible. (They were changed in 1967.) The 'administration of the immigration laws (affecting foreigners, not Commonwealth citizens)' – and therefore hardly touching any threat of mass immigration – 'would often be more suitable to a police state, terrified of infection from the outside world, than to a Britain which is the traditional refuge of the oppressed'. (I think I somewhat civilised the administration of these laws in 1966 but there is room for dispute here.) There were also references to the need for a reform of the laws of betting and suicide. The former had been liberalised between 1959 and 1964. About the latter I did no more than about licensing powers. A certain casualty rate of good intentions is inevitable, but the implementation rate is nonetheless respectable.

By Monday, 10 January, I felt that I was ready (if I was ever going to be) for my high-noon (it was actually 5.30 p.m.) shoot-out with Sir Charles Cunningham. It was at once the most difficult and the most crucial encounter that I have ever had with any high-ranking civil servant. Over the subsequent decades, despite a strong natural tendency to question my own judgement in retrospect, although happily not to falter much at the time, I have never varied in my view that on this occasion I was right. This is odd, for Cunningham was not only of the highest ability; he also had surprisingly liberal views and was rather a nice man. He had however become the guardian, not so much of particular Home Office policies, as of a certain Home Office approach to life which I was convinced had to be broken if future Home Secretaries were to avoid the St Sebastian-like fate of Brooke and Soskice. An air of dutiful defeat had become the most appropriate demeanour for a Home Secretary. 'Poor old Home Office,' Soskice had minuted on one file. 'We are not always wrong, but we always get the blame.'

I was determined both for my own good and for that of the Home Office not to be the third victim of this system. This meant changes in the organisation of the Department which would improve the chances first of my not taking stupid decisions, or of finding too late that they had been taken on my behalf, and second of the better public presentation of Home Office policies and announcements. This crystallised into a list of specific organisational demands which I put to Cunningham at this Monday evening meeting. I think there were altogether twenty-two of them, but I have forgotten more than a handful.

I wanted an immediate change of principal private secretary. The incumbent, despite the advantage of a frequently worn Balliol tie, did not seem to me to have adequate iconoclasm about the old Home Office. Furthermore, I wanted the replacement to be David Dowler, brought back from the Ministry of Aviation, and I wanted him promoted to assistant secretary, the rank occupied by a group of four of five private secretaries to senior ministers, but out of which group the Home Office had typically allowed itself to slip. In addition, I wanted John Harris, still at the Foreign Office but not equally at home with Michael Stewart as he had been with Gordon Walker and before that, in opposition, with Gaitskell, to come to me as a special adviser, concerned primarily but not exclusively with public relations, which was then his speciality. I also required a change at the head of the Home Office press and publicity department, with a new man of general Whitehall experience brought in. The ingrowingness of the Home Office was one of its special problems. It did little exporting to or importing from the rest of Whitehall. A typical successful career was that of my soon-to-be-replaced private secretary, who served in the Department without a break for thirty-five years, rising from assistant principal to deputy secretary. I indicated to Cunningham that the next promotion to deputy secretary ought to be from outside the Department.

None of this was welcome to him, although eventually it was all resignedly implemented, but the hostility it aroused was as nothing compared with that stemming from my central demand. Cunningham had introduced into the Home Office, of which he had become permanent secretary in 1957 after nine years as secretary of the Scottish Home Department, the most centralised system of submissions to the Secretary of State which can ever have been seen in Whitehall. Everything came on one or two sheets of thick blue paper, boiled down to a few hundred words of lucid explanation, concluding in a clear recommendation, and boldly initialled 'C.C.C.' It was a most formidable display of intellectual energy and control over the Department, economical of the Secretary of State's time, provided that the recommendations were accepted and did not too frequently blow up in his face. But it was certainly not a system designed to allow the Home Secretary to weigh up different courses of action. No other course was outlined, there were no background documents from which an alternative could be devised, there was no indication whether or not there had been dissenting opinions as the file had made its way up through the various ranks of the hierarchy. All wrinkles had been smoothed away by the firm and skilled hands of the permanent under-secretary.

It was an intensely hierarchical system and it was reflected in the hierarchical atmosphere, quite different as I came to discover later from the easy-going Whiggish equality within an elite of the Treasury, which pervaded the Home Office of those days. Nobody, except for one under-secretary on the verge of retirement who had entered the civil service on the same day, ever called Cunningham anything except 'Sir Charles'. It was difficult to get any discussion going at a meeting of officials and thus to hear a case argued. It was very much a case of *Sir Charles locutus est; causa finita est.*

This was an undesirable side-effect of the system. But it was not the core of the objection to it. The core was that it put the Secretary of State in the position of either having to hand his judgement over to the permanent secretary or have a major confrontation with him, equivalent to a client demanding to see his solicitor's books, every time he disagreed. How Rab Butler, the most illustrious of my 'Cunningham' predecessors, put up with the arrangement I cannot imagine. When I asked him about it several years later, his reply was sympathetic but opaque. 'I always meant to do something about it' was the burden of what he said.

I had no alternative to doing something about it. I trailed none of Rab's clouds of Whitehall glory. Nor did I have his gift of making a virtue out of ambiguity. I knew with more certainty than I have often commanded that if I and not Sir Charles Cunningham (who since Butler had ridden two less substantial horses to political death) was to make Home Office decisions the system had to go. Cunningham defended it with every weapon he could muster. He threw his whole authority and experience behind it. I remember that at one stage in that difficult Monday encounter his eyes filled with tears. I almost wavered. Was it right at the end of a distinguished public servant's long career to reduce him to such misery? It was only later that I realised that the tears were caused by rage and not by sadness.

Such a confrontation was legitimate enough on both sides, but he used one ploy which in my view was not legitimate and which prevented a full reconciliation on my side when the battle was won. He argued that a change to the submission of the whole file to me would mean that copies of what I saw could no longer go at the same time to junior ministers, who would thus be deprived of the opportunity to make timely observations, and he put this argument on paper and circulated it to the said junior ministers.

This was an odd action for an authoritative permanent under-secretary of state. The Whitehall tradition of those days was based on a one-to-one relationship between the head of the Department and his chief official. This was particularly so in the Home Office, where only they were informed of certain security matters, where only they had brooded together in lonely isolation over whether or not a death sentence should be carried out. Junior ministers were very much the fags of Whitehall, useful to run errands and do parliamentary chores, but not to be involved in serious discussions between housemaster and prefect (but which was which?). This relationship is illustrated by the fact that when a Secretary of State is away he can be deputised for over a large part of his functions only by another Secretary of State and not by one of the ministers in his department.

For Cunningham to attempt to enlist the junior ministers in a dispute about his own authority was therefore a fine example of *trahison des clercs*, as well as a nicely calculated attempt to stir up a distinguished but slightly prickly trio whom I had inherited from the previous regime. Lord Stonham, dedicated to penal reform, was nearly twenty years older than I. Alice Bacon, former Gaitskell supporter in Leeds and on the Labour Party National Executive Committee, was somewhat older too and had got used to the Soskice ways in the Home Office. Amazing though it now seems, the most junior in rank, although not in age, was George Thomas, the future Speaker and Viscount Tonypandy. Upstart though they must have thought me, they were all wise or loyal enough not to get much involved in Cunningham's dispute.

When this was over, with victory for me on almost all counts, as was inevitable given the respective weights of firepower, relations settled down reasonably. I respected most of Cunningham's views. But I was not prepared to endorse an arrangement provisionally agreed with my predecessor by which he would stay on as permanent secretary for a year or so after his sixtieth birthday, which was in May 1966. I thought that nine years was enough and that the Home Office needed a change. Accordingly Charles Cunningham retired early that summer (although he quickly became deputy chairman of the Atomic Energy Authority) and was replaced by Philip Allen, now Lord Allen of Abbeydale, who with Way and the other Allen (Douglas, now Lord Croham) formed a triangle of mandarin excellence with which I have been lucky enough to be served. Philip Allen had started in the Home Office and served most of his career there, but as he had also spent a full decade away from it, in the War Cabinet Office, the Ministry of Housing and Local Government and the Treasury, he did not count as a troglodyte.

At the farewell party for Cunningham I had little difficulty in patching together a speech which was both honest and complimentary, although I permitted myself to say that I was glad to have assembled for the occasion all four of the Home Secretaries (Butler, Brooke, Soskice and myself) who had served *under* Sir Charles. Twelve years later, when I was President of the European Commission, I gave a dinner in London for my former permanent secretaries. I hesitated whether to invite Charles Cunningham, but quickly decided to do so, put him on my right as the most senior, and greatly enjoyed our conversation.

Compared with these upheavals it was a relatively easy task, during those first weeks of 1966, to revamp my room. I had no desire to get away from a 'traditional' style, which seemed to me to be appropriate for the Home Secretary and was in any case necessary in the 1860s building, but merely to lift the atmosphere of inspissated gloom. The desk at which Soskice had sat with his back to the private secretaries' entrance was replaced by a long dining table in the Ministry of Aviation style from the middle of which I confronted the length of the room and the entrances. Almost everything else went except for the bookcases and the full-length portrait of Charles I, which was behind my chair and seemed to me vaguely apposite. It was a sufficient reminder of the decapitatory traditions of the Home Office and I had the indicator board in the corner alcove, on which the names of convicted prisoners had been moved towards the date of their execution, replaced by a refrigerator.

My most difficult refurbishing reform was to insist on reactivating the long-defunct open fireplace. It was the only hope of getting a glow of winter warmth into the ensemble. Smokeless fuel was procured with some delay, but thereafter made its impact. When Kosygin called on me a year later the fire was the main thing that he noticed. I had not been summoned to any of the Downing Street or other festivities (there was a temporary chill over my relations with Wilson), and it was not until nearly the last day of his visit that he encountered me. I think he was mystified by this hidden senior member of the Government who alone was allowed a coal fire, and half attributed to me a Beria-like position.

I also settled into the routine and ceremonial sides of the Home Secretary's life. I was at first appalled at the thought of permanent police protection, but soon became adjusted to it, particularly when I discovered that it was not heavy (my detectives did not have to come into houses with me and during weekends were merely present in the locality) and that my Special Branch detective sergeants were not heavy either. I think they were specially chosen for their liberal views and wide interests (but that showed discrimination at the top). One in particular (Ronald Rathbone, a considerable musicologist), who came back to me in 1974–6, has remained a friend. He explained to me early on that the chances of their preventing my being killed by a determined assassin were small. 'But,' he added comfortingly, 'we would write a very good report after the incident.' More to the point, he said that what they were really there for was to prevent my getting arrested, which would be embarrassing for everybody. I agreed, and found that this 'cushion against life' aspect of their presence grew on me, so that when I became Chancellor of the Exchequer, an office quaintly thought not to need police protection, I missed them.

In addition, I inherited a practice which had prevailed since Peel's time of a uniformed constable standing day and night outside the London house of the Home Secretary. I thought this was of doubtful utility, particularly as he was removed whenever I went away from London, even if my wife and/or children did not. The Commissioner of Police for the Metropolis was at first adamant against my desire to stop it. Nor was he attracted by my compromise suggestion that the officer should sit inside, preferably under an eighteenth-century looking hood, where he could at least double up as a footman and answer the door. However, the Notting Hill police rallied to my side. Two of them fainted on duty on closely adjacent winter mornings. Jennifer had to go down and make them 5.00 a.m. cups of tea. The Commissioner was undermined. The practice was then discontinued.

It was not only the police but the Palace which obtruded on a Home Secretary's life. He was not the senior Secretary of State for nothing. I obviously apprehended this in advance, for on my New Year's Eve visit to London from Hatley I ordered a new morning coat. I had previously made do with one inherited from my father, which could not be said to fit well. It was a wise purchase for I then proceeded to wear it at least once a fortnight until I became Chancellor of the Exchequer, and then did not put it on for two years. This difference between the sartorial demands of the two offices was symbolic. It stemmed from the fact that the Home Secretary was constantly in attendance on the Sovereign – swearing in bishops, dubbing knights, receiving foreign Monarchs and Presidents at Victoria Station – whereas the Chancellor, a much more workaday officer of state, hardly saw her except for the annual Budget audience.

At the end of February an election was announced, with polling day on 31 March. I played an intermediate role in the campaign, a sort of apprentice star, but definitely not a fully fledged one. I am surprised, looking back, at how much I was deployed in aircraft constituencies: Preston, Lancaster, Bristol. I also went, outside the West Midlands, to Portsmouth, Monmouth, south-east London and Leicester. I had a lucky start to the campaign, with exactly the sort of issue on which I had said I was going to put a new imprint on the Home Office breaking favourably on 4 March. A Surrey child had been instructed by its over-hygienic mother to wipe its cutlery at school. This was against some school regulations, from which stemmed a ridiculous escalation culminating in the child being taken away from the mother and placed in care. Vast publicity was building up. The Prime Minister with his night editor's eye exceptionally telephoned to inquire what we were doing, by which time we were able to tell him that we had settled the matter.

By summoning the Attorney-General, bullying the Home Office, slightly straining the law and speaking faithfully down the telephone to the chairman of the local children's committee, I got the child out of care and back to its mother within a few hours. This was obviously common sense and both press and public (as far as I could tell) applauded. It gave me a favourable wind for the whole campaign, the outcome of which was a Labour majority of ninety-seven and a more favourable swing in Stechford (8.9 per cent) than in any other constituency in Britain. (This paved the way for a substantial movement the other way in 1970.) My main reaction to the result was relief (although not surprise) that the Government had been confirmed in office and that I could continue as a minister, which I was for the moment greatly enjoying.

That mood continued over the spring and early summer. In the Department I was much engaged with three issues. First, the preparation, presentation and defence of a major scheme of police reorganisation. On 18 May I announced a reduction in the number of separate police forces from 117 to 49. This was operationally desirable and was well received by most police opinion, although greeted with predictable squeals by some of the chief constables who lost their independent commands and still more from the police committees of the amalgamated forces. The very small forces – sometimes with a strength of little more than twenty, had been got rid of by Chuter Ede soon after the Second World War, and Soskice had also done one or two amalgamations, running into a good deal of parliamentary trouble, particularly for his bringing together of Luton and Bedfordshire. I was however left with a clutch of forces with strengths of around 200. Lancashire was spattered with borough forces of about this size: Blackpool, Southport, Preston, Blackburn, Bolton, Barrow-in-Furness, Burnley, Oldham, St Helens, Warrington, Wigan. In forces of this size promotion could be completely blocked by the prejudice of a single senior officer or by one man staying too long in a particular rank. In addition technically well-equipped headquarters could not be afforded and would in any event have been top-heavy.

I decided that the best chance of avoiding impalement on the well-entrenched local opposition which had met Soskice in Luton was to announce advance on such a broad front that, first, everyone's breath would be taken away and, second, as the proposals were likely to be accepted in quite a lot of cases, those who attempted to stand out would look selfish and obscurantist. This tactic worked well. Under the Police Act of 1964, we could proceed without specific legislation provided we were prepared to face a quasi-judicial local inquiry. The Lancashire one was the test case, the result of which I awaited with considerable trepidation. I could have overturned it, but this would obviously have produced a lot of reaction. When the inspector (Mars-Jones QC, later and deservedly a High Court judge) reported favourably I heaved a sigh of relief. Cardiff also created a lot of trouble, mainly on the specious ground that the capital city of Wales needed an independent police force for ceremonial reasons. Eventually, however, the scheme went through intact. It left a few county forces – Wiltshire, Hertfordshire, Bedfordshire – smaller than I would have liked, with a strength of only about 600 or 700, but they did not fit conveniently with any other unit.

The only subsequent significant change in the police map of England and Wales (Scotland is outside the Home Secretary's responsibilities) followed from the creation of the metropolitan counties in 1973–4. The police results of that were not entirely beneficial. The removal of Coventry and Solihull from Warwickshire left that force sadly attenuated, and even Lancashire, deeply invaded by Merseyside and Greater Manchester, became a shadow of the very strong force of nearly 7000 which my abolition of the old borough constabularies had made it.

Second, I was resolved to strike a more upbeat note on race relations than had hitherto been forthcoming from the Home Office. I had recently announced the appointment of Mark Bonham Carter as chairman of the new Race Relations Board, set up under Frank Soskice's act. He was a close friend and it could have been regarded as a blatant piece of personal jobbery. My view was that it was the other way round and that he was doing me and the Government a favour by accepting a thankless job. He proved an outstanding chairman and confirmed my view that one should not be afraid of appointing friends provided that they are good enough.

I wanted to provide a favourable splash for the launching of his chairmanship, and chose a meeting of the National Committee for Commonwealth Immigrants on Monday, 23 May. Jennifer and I spent the preceding weekend, during which I remember being almost totally absorbed by the speech, with the Annans in the Provost's Lodge at King's College, Cambridge. On the Saturday evening we went to the Founder's Obit Service in the chapel during which, in the obscurity of the provostial stalls, I continued to scribble away and produced the following sentences, of which I was subsequently rather proud: 'Where in the world is there a university which could preserve its fame, or a cultural centre which could keep its eminence, or a metropolis which could hold its drawing power, if it were to turn inwards and serve only its own hinterland and its own racial group? To live apart, for a person, a city, a country, is to lead a life of declining intellectual stimulation.'

Even more remarkable than the preoccupation induced in King's chapel by the prospect of the speech was the shadow of amnesia which it cast over dinner later that evening. I see from my engagement diary that, in addition to the Annans and ourselves, there were present Mrs Ian Fleming (who was staying), Lord and Lady Rothschild and Sir (as he then was) Anthony Blunt. Yet I have no recollection of the occasion (which was the only one on which I met Blunt), only of the scribbling beforehand – and no doubt later that night too. This is doubly remarkable because a few months later I was informed by the permanent under-secretary of the Home Office and by MI5 of Blunt's guilt, assured both that prosecution had been decided against by the Attorney-General of the previous Government and that the Queen (because Blunt was the keeper of her pictures) had been told. I was asked, as previous informants had been, to remain silent because this was the best way of blowing other people's cover. This ought vividly to have recalled the Cambridge dinner encounter and imprinted it on my mind.

It did not. I claim to have a good memory for the sequence of events and the dates of particular happenings. Yet, had I in a witness box ten or fifteen years later but before I discovered this diary entry, been asked whether I had ever met Blunt when Home Secretary I would have answered unhesitatingly no. A hostile counsel in possession of my diary would then have devastated me. The thought has since made me sympathetic to those who have a bad time in front of a court.

The race-relations speech, insofar as it had impact, was more memorable for the words 'I define integration, therefore, not as a flattening process of assimilation but as equal opportunity, accompanied by cultural diversity, in an atmosphere of mutual tolerance' than for any immortal phrases concocted in King's College chapel, and also for the fact that it invited the audience to campaign for a new Race Relations Bill, to which I was able to commit the Government before leaving the Home Office at the end of 1967, but which fell to be carried through by my successor.

The third Home Office issue with which I was concerned was the preparation of a major Criminal Justice Bill. We did not have to complete it that summer for it was not published until the end of November, but we had to give it enough substance to secure a place as a 'main programme' bill. I had inherited from my predecessor a proposal for the introduction of a system of parole, and this formed an important part of the bill, although I eventually upended its form, mainly by giving greater independence to the Parole Board, from that which had been outlined in the 1965 White Paper on the Adult Offender. Parole in carefully judged cases, as well as being penologically desirable, also had the advantage of working against the pressures of a mounting prison population. (It had then reached 33,000 against 29,000 in 1964, which in those innocent days was regarded as an intolerably high level.) Other parts of the bill pointed in the same direction by encouraging the use of bail, by restricting the powers of magistrates' courts to imprison for default in the payment of fines, and by introducing suspended sentences, compulsory, with exceptions for violence, up to six months, discretionary up to two years.

There was also a batch of disparate but desirable measures: legal aid was improved; corporal punishment in prisons was ended; and the possession of shotguns without a certificate was prohibited. In addition there was a series of provisions aimed at creating criminal law procedures more directly concerned with discovering the truth – and convicting the guilty – than with preserving legal traditions. Committal proceedings before examining magistrates were considerably streamlined. The 'sprung alibi', that great instrument of drama and confusion in court, was banned (unless the judge decided otherwise). Alibis of course remained admissible, but notice of this line of defence had to be given by the accused's counsel. And, most controversial at the time, although it has since become wholly unchallenged, was the introduction of majority jury verdicts in criminal trials, which I discuss in more detail in the next chapter.

This period of home-secretarial honeymoon did not last into the summer holidays. First there was a sharp deterioration in the general political climate and then there sprang up the first of a series of Home Office squalls. The former had the effect not only of stripping the Government of any enchantment with which its electoral triumph had clothed it, but also of putting me at odds with the Prime Minister in a way that overtly damaged our relations for several months and probably left some permanently scarred tissue.

The issue was the perennial one of the weakness of sterling. So long as the rate of $2.80 was clung to as a symbol of national pride (although it must be said that things did not get much easier when that rate was at last reluctantly abandoned), there was hardly an event in the world which did not produce a British currency crisis. And the only way of dealing with such a crisis was a new package of hastily approved deflationary measures, which seemed bereft of any strategic framework. Thus the upheaval of July 1966 stemmed from a combination of bad trade figures for June (following a seamen's strike), the resignation of Frank Cousins as Minister of Technology (because he did not like the Government's prices and incomes policy) and some disobliging remarks of Georges Pompidou, then French Prime Minister (partly because he had been treated with hamfisted and most uncharacteristic discourtesy by Wilson during an official visit to London); and the measures eventually taken to deal with the squall destroyed (without putting anything in its place) the National Plan, which had been presented in 1965 as the centrepiece of the Government's economic policy for four years and which was the *raison d'être* of George Brown's Department of Economic Affairs.

The other characteristic of this fluctuating sterling fever was that its periods of remission produced moods of wild optimism. Thus I remember Callaghan assuring me in a long talk in the last week of June that everything looked set fair at least until the autumn, and he records in his memoirs that he took the same view at a meeting with Wilson and Brown on 1 July. He was in a very different mood by 12 July, when at the end of a Tuesday Cabinet he suddenly began talking, outside the agenda, about the appalling pressures on sterling and conveyed to his startled audience an impression both that the objective situation was desperate and that his own nerve had cracked. Wilson hushed him up and brought the meeting to an end rather like a policeman trying to get a blanket around a nude streaker.

I had several private talks with Callaghan in the next forty-eight hours, and found him very critical of the Prime Minister. He claimed that he had come round to devaluation, of which he knew I was in favour. And he expressed his desire to get out of the Treasury, perhaps out of the Government altogether, although his desire was probably more accurately represented by his remark that I could do his job and he would do mine. There was another Cabinet, this time specifically concerned with the economic situation, on Thursday, 14 July. There was no overt discussion of the devaluation option, for this, sometimes prudishly referred to as 'the unmentionable', was still barred by the Prime Minister, as it had been for the preceding eighteen months. The Cabinet accepted that some disagreeable measures would have to be taken in the following week and concluded with a tactically foolish decision that the Prime Minister should make a holding or 'I shall do such things, what they are I know not' statement in the House of Commons that afternoon, promising another one in a week or so.

The effect of this was predictably unfortunate. The pressure on sterling increased and the reserve losses mounted. I had a meeting with the Prime Minister at my request on the Friday evening. We were alone but he firmly confined the conversation to Home Office matters and avoided any discussion of the economy. He would by then have known the disastrous dollar losses by the Bank of England in that day's trading, and this reticence could be regarded as a sign either of good nerve or of a bunkered sullenness.

On the Saturday morning he departed for Moscow for a doubtfully necessary seventy-two-hour visit to a British trade fair, buttressed by talks with Kosygin. This was the weekend of the 'July plot', which Harold Wilson came to believe had almost led to his replacement as Prime Minister. In early August Callaghan recorded him as saying:

'I am in great trouble and I must tell you about the events of the last fortnight' [these do not strike me as *ipsissima verba*], and before I [Callaghan] could interrupt he swept on with a detailed account of how his own position as Prime Minister had been placed in great jeopardy during the weekend of his visit to the Moscow Trade Fair. He elaborated in great detail on the colleagues who were involved, but exonerated me of any knowledge of the so-called 'plot': 'You were on the side of the angels.'[1]

Barbara Castle, always an honest diarist and in general a good Wilson witness, recorded for 6 October:

the interesting thing was his obsession with 'plots' against him. At the ITN cocktail party on the last night [of the Labour conference] he dilated to me about Ministers who went a-whoring after society hostesses and was livid with Tommy Balogh for coming down specially [to the Labour Party conference at Brighton] to attend Pamela Berry's dinner party (which Ted and I refused)* . . . 'Mrs Ian Fleming is another one,' he said darkly. 'If any of you knew your job you would find out who attended that weekend meeting at her place last July when I was in Moscow. . . .' He said he knew what the ploy was – to make Jim Callaghan Prime Minister, Roy Jenkins Chancellor, and form a Coalition Government. Jim had lost his nerve during the crisis and badly wanted to change his job.[2]

What was the reality of that weekend as I saw it? After leaving Wilson I addressed a dinner of the Friends of Friendless Churches in the House of Lords (an innocuous enough occupation, one might have thought), and we then proceeded, picking up Mark and Leslie Bonham Carter in Kensington, on a late-night drive to Mrs Fleming's at Sevenhampton near Swindon, thereby illustrating that the castles of fantasy are mostly built on molehills of truth. There was indeed a certain allegorical quality about the behaviour of all of us that weekend. Callaghan, wounded and gloomy (quite why it was thought that he would choose a moment of nervous prostration to try to make himself Prime Minister I have never understood), went to ground in Sussex with his non-political future farming partner. Wilson, as we have seen, kept up his adrenalin by going on an unnecessary trip to Moscow. George Brown went berserk at the Durham Miners' Gala. And I went to stay with Mrs Fleming at Sevenhampton.

This dispersion did not preclude some contact. As soon as I arrived at the House of Lords dinner I received a message via David Dowler that Brown's office had said it was imperative I speak to him that evening, as he was on the verge of explosion and resignation. I did not think that I could both protect friendless churches and calm down frenzied First Secretaries at the same time, so I decided, perhaps mistakenly, to give priority to the former, and it was nearly one

* So did I.

o'clock in the morning before I had George Brown on the line for a dithyrambic half-hour from the County Hotel, Durham. The burden of what he had to say was that Wilson had decided on deflation not devaluation and that he (Brown) was going to resign rather than put up with this.

The next morning I had a briefer and less swirling but more fundamentally confused telephone conversation with Callaghan. I thought from my previous talks with him that he had moved in favour of devaluation, and my objective was to keep him and Brown in a solid front so that they could exercise the joint influence of the economic departments upon Wilson. I did not have the thought of a change of job for myself in my mind. As can be seen from previous (and subsequent) passages, I was by no means always immune to such sordid considerations. But they were quiescent at that time. I was primarily concerned about the stability of the Government, within which I was a minister wholly satisfied, for the time being at least, with my own job.

It turned out that Callaghan was pursuing a different line from me. He states his position fairly in his memoirs in a way that I ought to have understood at the time. He thought that inaction, that is the postponement of deflationary measures, was making devaluation inevitable. But once he had got deflation in the bag, he was against devaluation. I, on the other hand, was prepared to accept deflation only if an accompanying devaluation gave us a chance to *reculer pour mieux sauter*. (This was also Brown's position, except that he was more reluctant than I was to see the need for deflation even with devaluation.)

Callaghan said that he would send Robert Nield down to see me that afternoon. Nield was a Cambridge economist, later the holder of a senior chair there and as such the guardian of the traditions of that great school, well known to me, who had come into the Treasury in 1964 and won the equal trust of Chancellor and officials. I considered it better not to have him to Sevenhampton, but to drive over to Didcot, meet him off a train and take him to East Hendred. I thought that he was coming to discuss the modalities of devaluation. As we paced the croquet lawn there, I discovered that his brief was to sell me a three to six months' postponement of devaluation. I did not believe that harsh medicine could be swallowed except at a gulp. Disappointed, I dropped him at Swindon, but I think that this switch to a station further from London owed more to timetables than to disapproval.

This was the only 'secret' meeting that I had during the weekend. The Sevenhampton trail which Wilson was to invite his October audience of journalists to pursue would have proved a barren one. The only people who came there other than the Bonham Carters and ourselves were John Sparrow, right-wing Warden of All Souls, and Stuart Hampshire, left-wing philosopher and future Warden of Wadham. Even though Sparrow was then more sprightly than today, we would not have made a very convincing nucleus for a coalition or any other form of government.

I went back to London on the Sunday afternoon, saw Tony Crosland and found that our views were very close. Then I telephoned George Brown and discovered that, as was often the case, the storm had blown itself out and that he had become calm and friendly, although still set on resignation. I told him that I thought this was a mistake, and that while I would fully support him in the argument within the Cabinet I had no intention of going with him. Although he was disappointed by this, we arranged that he would dine with me at Brooks's club on the following evening.

This turned out to be an unfortunate arrangement. By ill chance I was late, and Brown had been early. The welcoming Brooks's habit of serving drinks to waiting guests for once rebounded, for George by the time I arrived had already managed to engage in several quarrels with casually present members, about which I had to write an abject letter of apology to the chairman of the managers. However, this was small stuff. What was more to the point was that he was still resigning and believed that Crossman and Mrs Castle would do so with him. Without being remotely offensive, he contrasted their promised behaviour with mine.

Later that night Crossman saw me on his initiative, and made it clear that while he and Mrs Castle were solid on the merits he had no more intention of resigning than I had. Indeed he raised one point of doubt on the merits, on which my recollection exactly tallies with his, so I give it in his words:

I then asked Roy about the European background to this affair. You know, I said, that Harold is working against you, telling us anti-Europeans that anyone who wants to devalue the pound is trying to do so as a practical way into Europe. 'Tell me, Roy,' I said, 'what have the two things really got to do with each other?' And he said, 'Plenty, of course. I mean we will have to do something about sterling in order to enter Europe. This might mean devaluation; but in my view a floating pound gives a certain freedom of action, either to enter Europe or to do anything else, and what we are trying to regain this week is freedom of action. If we go on as we are we remain prisoners of the situation and prisoners of our own weakness.'[3]

The next day, Tuesday, 19 July, was sunk in a trough of physical dismalness, with leaden skies and pouring rain. I went at noon to greet King Hussein on the platform at Victoria Station. The Prime Minister, unlike the Queen, did not turn up, although he was back from

Moscow. Michael Stewart and I were there from the Government, with various other plumed dignitaries. As the rain poured down around the assembled splendour I could not avoid the thought that this looked like the last act in a dreary imperial charade.

The Cabinet met that afternoon at 5.00 and sat for four and a half hours. The ban was taken off the open discussion of devaluation but the majority, led by Wilson, did just as good a job against it in result if not in argument. Those in favour were six and no more: Brown, Crossman, Crosland, Castle, Benn and me, a curious mixture it may be thought. Of the others, those with the most open minds appeared to be Gardiner, Healey, Greenwood and possibly Marsh. Frank Longford had originally been in favour of devaluation but had been persuaded by Douglas Jay on the previous evening that it was immoral.

The Cabinet met again for another four hours the following morning and agreed to the package of deflation and austerity. George Brown was present, but sat back taking no part so that it was impossible to tell whether he was resigning or not. That afternoon he did not come to the House of Commons for Wilson's crisis statement but skulked in his official residence in Carlton Gardens, deliberately creating a great press drama. Bill Rodgers tried to persuade me that we should go over together and see him, but I declined, feeling that I had done what I could and that Brown should now make his own decision. Late that night he decided not to resign. Two weeks later Wilson rescued him from the torpedoed Department of Economic Affairs and made him Foreign Secretary. It was probably a kindlier act than Wilson implied when he finished his previously quoted conversation with Barbara Castle by saying, 'by making George Brown Foreign Secretary, I have cornered him', particularly as he inconsequentially added, 'And George Brown was never the danger.'[4]

At that Wednesday morning Cabinet there were two issues which stuck in my mind. The first was whether the wage freeze, which was generally accepted, should be complete for the first six months or whether, as Wilson wanted, it should have loopholes for productivity increases and for the lower-paid. I was passionately against this, both because I thought loopholes would make a nonsense of the whole thing and on the more self-interested ground that my only hope of containing the police, who had an award due, was to have an absolute freeze for everybody. Rather to my surprise I carried the day against the Prime Minister.

The second issue related to the tourist allowance. The majority was thoroughly content to reduce it to £50. Healey, not untypically, said that it was perfectly possible for anyone to do anything they wanted anywhere on £50 – provided they camped. With Gardiner, Crosland, Crossman and Castle I tried to get a bigger allowance compensated for if necessary by the restriction applying to the sterling area as well as to other countries. The Treasury said this was impossible without breaking up the sterling area (which would have been a very good thing). I always hated this travel restriction, considering it an interference with human freedom in a quite different category from physical restrictions on the import of goods, which while mostly economically undesirable are not philosophically so. The tourist-allowance restriction was one of the first things I got rid of when the balance of payments had turned round in early 1970.

After Wednesday the week showed some signs of subsiding into relative calm. Friday brought the substantial bonus of a huge majority for the second reading of David Steel's Abortion Bill, on a free vote but with a strongly favourable ministerial speech from me. On the Saturday morning however there arose a great storm in the politicians' teacup. Callaghan, who always had a penchant for announcing appointments he did not control, proclaimed through William Davis, the City editor of the *Guardian*, who was then a well-known confidant of his, that he proposed to become Foreign Secretary in the autumn, that I could replace him at the Treasury, and that Stewart could go to the Home Office. (This was before George Brown's appointment to the Foreign Office, and may well have been one of Wilson's motives for making it.) This story reverberated through the Sunday and Monday papers and kept the Government in a state of high fever. It led both Callaghan and me (although neither had knowledge of the other's interview until many years later) to fix meetings with some difficulty to explain ourselves to the Prime Minister, and each to receive assurances of exoneration – Callaghan from the 'plot' of 16–17 July, I from the inspiring of the press of 23–25 July. In both cases, too, the assurances seem to have been accompanied by heavy hints that the other was to blame, although for differing sins. At the end of my talk with Wilson, which was on 27 July, I took the opportunity to ask him whether I should go ahead with an official American trip, postponed from June because of the seamen's strike and now scheduled for 17 September.* It clearly ran counter to his new instructions about ministerial visits overseas, which had just been put out. He was at pains to urge me to go ahead. Indeed the impression left on my mind after an otherwise perfectly amiable

---

* As it turned out this visit proved well worthwhile in terms of results. Following twenty-four hours with the impressively equipped Chicago Police Department, then presided over by a former professor of criminology at Berkeley, I put in hand a substantial programme for the improvement of British police technology. This led to the innovation of two-way radios for officers on the beat, command-and-control systems in police headquarters and ultimately to the establishment of the Police National Computer.

interview was that if I wanted to take a world trip lasting the whole of the autumn he would be happy to give me permission to do so.

After that meeting I had no direct contact with the Prime Minister until I went to Brighton for the Labour Party conference immediately after my return from the United States at the beginning of October. In the meantime he seemed to have reassembled all the rumours of the summer and beaten them into a fine lather of grievance. On the Tuesday evening when I walked into his suite at the Grand Hotel for a Cabinet which he had summoned in those most unusual surroundings, there was an atmosphere between him and me which could have been cut with a knife. Despite my long absence he offered no word of greeting or even sign of recognition. There was an equally frigid approach when I ran head on into him at a *Daily Mirror* party on the following evening. The only light relief had been at the *Socialist Commentary** tea meeting. Just as I was about to begin my speech, Marcia Williams and Gerald Kaufman (then on Wilson's staff) marched in looking like ill-disguised Special Branch officers at a subversive meeting, sat in the front row and opened their notebooks.

I thought this was all very tiresome and decided on the basis of previous experience that by far the best course was to have it out with Wilson. I had an hour's meeting with him on the following Tuesday afternoon (11 October). This meeting provided a remarkable display of both his niceness and his weakness. I had asked for the meeting and began with a fairly rough complaint that he had apparently believed some quite ridiculous stories without putting them to me direct. His obvious tactic was to be gruffly monosyllabic, which would probably have made me flap and gasp like a harpooned fish out of water. I tremble to think how an interview with Lord Attlee would have proceeded after such an opening. Instead he suffused me with the oxygen of words. He must have talked for fifty minutes out of the hour, devoting most of the time to exonerating me of sins of which I was hardly aware I had been accused, and eventually coming round to registering as his only complaint the alleged intrigues of John Harris and what he described as 'the young MPs around you'. This narrowed down to an argument about Hattersley. I said why did he not put him in the Government and keep him out of mischief? He looked slightly affronted, but in fact did so three months later.

As I hoped, this confrontation cleared the air. It did not apparently prevent the Prime Minister responding eleven days later to the news that George Blake, a major spy, had escaped from Wormwood Scrubs

* A good internationalist social democratic periodical which provided a beacon of light within the Labour Party from 1941 to 1978.

by turning to Crossman and saying: 'That will do our Home Secretary a great deal of good. He was getting too complacent and he needs taking down a peg.'[5] But this was a perfectly reasonable private reaction on his part to a buffeting for a sometimes unamenable colleague. What was more to the point was that from 11 October forward our dealings, whether alone together or in a group, were normally civil and thoroughly agreeable. This was a considerable advantage for I was running into a lot of rough weather from the outside and the last thing I wanted was to have a hostile Prime Minister on my inside flank.

# CHAPTER TEN

# *The Liberal Hour*

On Friday, 12 August 1966, the day after I had escaped from London at the end of a session which I felt had been going on much too long, three policemen were shot dead at Shepherd's Bush. I was due to go abroad on the Sunday but decided after consultation with the Commissioner of Police (then Sir Joseph Simpson) that I should return to London on the Saturday morning and visit both the Shepherd's Bush police station and the scene of the crime.

There was a small crowd outside the police station, and the atmosphere amongst both police and public was inevitably heavy. There were a few women screaming 'Bring back the rope!', but the others did not seem anxious to join in the demonstration, although they probably agreed with the sentiments. I obviously had to say something to the television cameras and had therefore prepared about 150 words in the train which I read out from the steps of the police station. The burden of them was that it would not be right to take a decision on a major point of policy in the light of one event, however horrible that might be.

When the oppressive visit was over I went to Ladbroke Square and wrote difficult letters to the widows of the murdered policemen before returning by train to Didcot. The journey had been right and necessary, but it could hardly be expected to satisfy hard-line opinion, either in the press or amongst the public, which had been greatly inflamed by the murders. I then spent eight days driving Charles and Cynthia down through France, from Dieppe to Nice Airport, before going on from there to Italy to join Jennifer and Edward, and was informed both at occasional news-stands and by reports gathered during my daily telephone call to my office of continuing hysteria in the British press. In addition, there was a Home Office postbag of approximately two thousand letters, of which all except ten demanded the return of capital punishment.

When I returned to England on 4 September (after a six-hour

199

crossing to Dover because it had been too rough to land earlier) there was still an unusual concentration of interest on crime and punishment, and I decided that I ought to attempt a steadying speech on the issue before going to America in the middle of the month. This was fixed for Hounslow in West London on the evening of 12 September, and just before setting off for the meeting I heard that another policeman had been murdered, this time in Co. Durham and by stabbing. This in no way represented a significant shift of statistical trend, and it was several years before another such incident took place. But it seemed to me to kill the chance of the speech getting any rational attention and to guarantee that the hysteria would be increased. Curiously, I was wrong. A combination of the media being much less interested in what happened in Hartlepool than in Shepherd's Bush and of the fact that this crime was committed by a fourteen-year-old boy who would not have been eligible for hanging much after the time of Judge Jeffreys meant that this incident hardly reverberated at all.

There were plenty of other issues which did. At the end of that same week a decision by the visiting magistrates of Maidstone Prison to order the birching of Maxwell, a young prisoner who had previously murdered an officer at Portland Borstal, was front-page news in every morning newspaper. The sentence had to be confirmed or overturned by me and, as I was proposing to include in the Criminal Justice Bill a provision to complete the abolition of corporal punishment in prisons, there was considerable interest in whether I would allow one or more last acts of what I regarded as useless barbarism to take place in the interim.

I probably ought to have grasped the nettle and set aside the magistrates' decision before leaving for America the following morning. But I judged it too cavalier to do this just before stepping on to a flight to New York and without awaiting the full medical reports, although there was already plenty of evidence that Maxwell was seriously deranged. This caution gave the story a run of nearly three weeks, and when my setting-aside decision was finally announced it stole the headlines from Wilson's main speech to the Labour Party conference and was thought by some to be an exacerbating factor in our bad relations at the time.

The next lurch in that autumn's crime and punishment roller-coaster ride was provided by the annual meeting of the Metropolitan Police Joint Branch Boards in the Central Hall, Westminster. This for no very clear reason had become an annual fixture for the Home Secretary, although I decided in both my periods of office that one year in two was enough. A tradition, perhaps starting only in 1966, has developed by which it is treated as an annual bacchanalia when the disciplines of the rest of the year are cast off and those present are allowed to

throw verbal missiles at their political master the Home Secretary or, if
they cannot get him, at their professional master the Commissioner of
Police. We had been warned a few days beforehand that trouble might
be expected and that in some police stations plans for a mass walk-out
were being laid. There were a lot of component causes: a certain
endemic bloody-mindedness, fortified by a sense of grievance about
the postponement of the pay award and brought to a combustible point
by the unwillingness of the Government to restore capital punishment
in the face of the police murders; the non-birching of Maxwell; the
posthumous free pardon for Timothy Evans (announced two days
before the meeting), who manifestly had not committed the 1949
Rillington Place murder of his wife despite the confession which the
Notting Hill police had extracted from him; and a few lesser similar
matters. In addition, there was a strong undercurrent of racial feeling.
In the chairman's inflammatory introductory speech the point which
evoked the most responsive howl of derision was his reference to my
having urged the police to seek some black recruits.

Fortunately in view of the atmosphere of the meeting I had not
prepared a script, and replied rumbustiously to the nine points which
the chairman had raised. With a great number of interruptions this
took me nearly an hour. Then I answered half an hour of questions.
There were about 1500 present and the walk-out came to little. At
one point about forty people shuffled towards the door. But it was
one of the roughest and most disagreeable meetings I have ever had,
not made easier by the knowledge that it would be a dominating news
story that night and the next morning. I think most of the noise came
from a couple of hundred policemen. At the end of my question
period perhaps twice as many applauded vigorously. The other 800
maintained a sullen silence. When it was over, I went to Brooks's with
David Dowler and John Harris and sat exhausted over a large drink.

Two days after that came the escape of George Blake. Blake was
serving forty-two years for espionage activities which had betrayed
a substantial number of British agents. He was a master spy and his
escape over the wall of a London prison was a serious matter. As
it happened the street from which he was wafted away was within a
few hundred yards of the scene of the Shepherd's Bush murders. The
proximity was irrelevant, but it could be used by those who wished to
point to a pattern of wet impotence. We thought Blake had probably
been taken out through London Airport on the run, but in fact he went
to ground in Paddington for several weeks. I consider that MI5 and the
Special Branch contributed little skill to the attempt to find him.

I heard the news when I got back to Hatley, where we were
endeavouring very unsuccessfully to spend a weekend (with the
Astors; we had East Hendred so we no longer used the Dower

House there). After a Friday evening in Birmingham, I had been away for a Saturday-long meeting of ministers at Chequers to discuss Europe. It had gone rather well and I was driven back to Hatley tired but content. I walked into the dining room there at about 8.30 and Jennifer gave me the glad tidings, just received from David Dowler. I telephoned Wilson amongst other people that evening. Whatever snide comment he may have made to Crossman, he behaved thoroughly well to me. He sounded calm, with no hint of recrimination, although not underestimating the seriousness of the event.

The next morning I went to London and held a fairly useless two-hour Home Office meeting before lunch. It was the only occasion in two years on which I had been into either the Ministry of Aviation or the Home Office on a Sunday, and little good it did. Overnight I came to the view we had better have an outside inquiry into the escape and prison security in general. As soon as I got into the office on Monday morning David Dowler suggested that we should ask Mountbatten to conduct it. This was a bold idea, which I accepted with some enthusiasm. With remarkable expedition we then settled the whole thing by one o'clock. We had to get clearance both from Wilson and from the Queen, then find Mountbatten, put the proposition to him cold on the telephone, to which at first he was resistant, and then in a further telephone call, just before lunch, secure his acquiescence, which was easier on the second go because he had become interested and even enthusiastic. Then the announcement of his appointment had to be put into the statement about the escape which I was required to make in the House of Commons that afternoon.

Despite these feats of imagination and expedition, the statement did not go at all well. The atmosphere was wrong before I came to the inquiry announcement, glacial on the opposition benches, uneasy on the Labour side, and Mountbatten appeared as more a gimmick than a coup. I was saved from a substantial parliamentary disaster only by ineptitude on Ted Heath's part. He got himself into a great state about the issue, wrote out a motion for the immediate adjournment of the House and made Quintin Hogg (then shadow Home Secretary) take it along the bench to the Speaker as though he were a messenger boy. When the Speaker predictably refused it the occasion concluded in a mild farce. Heath however had got the bit between his teeth, called a special meeting of the shadow Cabinet and resorted to the full panoply of a leader of the opposition's motion of censure. This was announced that evening, set down for the following Monday and hung over me for the week.

At the weekend Jennifer and I, accompanied by the Philip Allens, went on an official visit to Jersey, during which oppression really set in. The charms of the Channel Islands could not compete with it. I ineffectively scribbled odd sentences whenever I could get away from the Governor, the Bailiff and the States-General. But I had no real approach to a speech when I arrived back at Ladbroke Square at the end of the Sunday morning. I had David Dowler to lunch and then worked solidly at slowly writing half an hour's speech from 2.30 until 10.30 p.m. I paused only for a brief walk at 7.00 and an equally brief dinner at 8.30.

The next day David Dowler and John Harris and I messed about with the speech for most of the day until the debate began at 7.00 p.m. We checked every fact, pruned a few passages, toned down a few others, but made no fundamental changes of language or structure. Hogg opened the debate and Enoch Powell wound up for the opposition. Duncan Sandys intervened heavily from below the gangway. I had no Government opener and waited to reply until 9.30. The House had been full for most of the three hours and was then packed. It was a high-risk strategy which worked. Every London newspaper led with my speech the next morning and all proclaimed it a rout of the opposition and of Heath in particular. He had not spoken, but he was the instigator of the debate and sat broodily throughout it. I concluded: 'I believe that this problem will be met by the constructive measures we are taking, and taking quickly; but it will not be met by that combination of procedural incompetence and petty partisanship which is the constant characteristic of the [leader of the opposition's] parliamentary style.'

It was by far the greatest parliamentary triumph that I ever achieved. It provided most welcome and even glorious relief. Yet it was all rather ludicrous and showed that debating (for it was that rather than oratory) really is the harlot of the arts. The position was turned round by the debate. I, who had been against the ropes, was rampant. Heath and Hogg were flat on their backs. Yet nothing of substance had happened. I had merely effectively deployed the art of *tu quoque*: everything I had done Henry Brooke had done worse. Blake had still escaped and was as far as ever from being recaptured. I had not become a better Home Secretary as a result of the debate. In fact it was as foolish to pretend before the debate that I had any real responsibility for who got over a wall in W12 as it was to suggest that I had suddenly become a superman whose ability to deflate leaders of the opposition more than compensated for my inability to find absconding spies.

Ted Heath, I regret to say, took the outcome badly. Despite our then more than quarter of a century of relationship (now more than half a century) he wrote me a constituency-case letter later that week beginning, unbelievably, 'Dear Jenkins', and in the following week he flapped around like an affronted penguin in order to avoid speaking to me at the French Embassy. A year later, however, the death of Attlee led to his inserting into his House of Commons tribute a most generous reference to my father, through whom he had first met Attlee, which completely disarmed me, and since then Europe, fortified on my side by great respect for his grumpy integrity, has mostly kept us together, as I hope we will now always continue.

There then followed a period of relative calm. I even went on a two nights' holiday to the Wye Valley and my county of origin in the second week of November and last week of the autumn foliage. On 23 November we had a ten-minute-rule bill from Sandys for the restoration of capital punishment and defeated it decisively. A week later we published the Criminal Justice Bill, and secured its second reading, without a division, on Monday, 12 December. As I came out of the chamber after my speech and Quintin Hogg's reply, David Dowler, who was as experienced in delivering messages of doom as he was wise in advising what to do about them, was just getting news of the escape from Dartmoor of Frank Mitchell, a gentleman who subsequently became known as the 'mad axeman'.

This sobriquet overestimated his powers, for although a fully paid up member of the criminal classes he never killed anyone but was himself eventually chopped up and put in a London sewer. However, his escape was another piece of front-page news, which managed to run for the rest of that week and began an extended Christmas bonanza of prison escapes and abscondings. The distinction between the two categories, which was real (there was a vast difference between Blake's highly planned abseiling from Wormwood Scrubs and a minor offender walking off from an open prison or an outside working party, of which there had long been about ten a week), perhaps inevitably became totally blurred in news presentations.

The Mountbatten Report was published on 22 December, and while less critical of the Home Office than we had feared, its existence (but I was responsible for that) encouraged a press concentration upon prison escapes. It was not just the press. The BBC became equally obsessed and found that a picture of a prison gateway and a story of a few abscondings was an easy way to lead the news. This publicity, presumably watched in many a prison recreation room, seemed to feed on itself and led previously supine inmates of low-security establishments to think that no self-respecting prison should be without its quota of escapes. The Christmas holiday took on the air of a true festival of home-going. Five got out from Liverpool on the day before Christmas Eve, and another five from Dartmoor on Boxing Day. British prisons became something of an international joke, with cartoons by Faizant in the *Figaro* and columns by Art Buchwald in the *Herald Tribune*.

My nerve was a bit shaken. Prison business took me for a couple of day visits to the Home Office between Christmas and the New

Year, and on one of them I was almost as amazed as its other readers presumably were to see in the *Daily Mail* (of all papers) a major feature pointing out that prison escapes in 1966 had actually been slightly fewer than in 1965, when they had attracted hardly a flicker of interest. I used the opportunity to bring in to the Home Office a new outside deputy secretary in the shape of Sir James Mackay, my old Aviation adjutant, which was a good thing. But in general I overreacted to this ephemeral public (or press) hysteria about escapes, and tilted the emphasis of prison regimes too much towards security and away from training and work. I ought to have been steadier under fire, but it is easier to say this in retrospect than it was to sustain it during the barrage of daily bombardment.

Nineteen-sixty-seven was neither as fraught nor as exhilarating at the Home Office as 1966 had been. But it contained both its achievements and its alarums and excursions. The buffetings of the autumn, which had taken much of the gilt off the triumph of the Blake debate, meant that I was not as buoyantly self-confident at the beginning of 1967 as I had been during most of 1966. *The Times* commented amiably at the turn of the year that I faced the task of getting the Criminal Justice Bill through its committee stage with my authority distinctly on the wane. This task did not however prove too formidable and was completed in an orderly way on the last full parliamentary day before Easter. We had needed nineteen two-and-a-half-hour sessions of a standing committee which met every Tuesday and Wednesday at 4.30 p.m.

The difficult and controversial stage of this bill was the report stage on the floor of the House on 26–27 April, because this was when the majority-verdict provision was put to the test. My decision in favour of this change was very much a personal one. I think that Home Office opinion was mostly against. Robert Mark, whom I had made redundant as Chief Constable of Leicester by my police reorganisation, then employed as an assessor to the Mountbatten inquiry, and was in the process of appointing as Assistant Commissioner of the Metropolitan Police (with great difficulty because of the traditional mercantilism – plenty of exports but no imports – of that organisation), had a considerable influence on me on the issue. There was mounting evidence of criminal intimidation of one or occasionally two jurors in major trials. Three or more would be more difficult to do, and a move to accepting ten-to-two decisions might be expected significantly to increase the conviction rate for serious crime (as has indeed proved to be so). This fitted in well with my general approach to deterrence, which was to regard the likelihood of detection and conviction as more powerful factors than an enormity of punishment. On the other hand there was some presumption in seeking to end the unanimity role which had prevailed in England since the end of the fourteenth century, although in Scotland even an eight-to-seven majority had long been considered sufficient.

I thought that my Conservative flank ought to be secure on the issue. Quintin Hogg was firmly in favour, and fulminating for 'law and order' has long been part of the stock-in-trade of the right. I was more concerned about my liberal flank, although encouraged by the support of Gerald Gardiner, not only as Lord Chancellor but as a veteran of many a civil-liberties campaign. I decided that two other pieces of litmus paper should be tested. The first was Jeremy Hutchinson QC, who was rapidly becoming the leading defence counsel and who brought more of the attitudes and cadences of Bloomsbury than of those of Rumpole into the Central Criminal Court; and the other was Michael Foot. Hutchinson, who was later to arouse Robert Mark's ire as a much too effective destroyer of bad police evidence, was on balance in favour. The exchange with Foot I remember clearly. I deliberately made it casual, and sought from him only an indication that he would not automatically regard the provision as a *casus belli*. This he gave as we walked along the library corridor one evening after a division. He said that he had not thought much about the issue and therefore had no very strong views one way or another.

On this basis I decided to go ahead. By April however the clause looked in grave trouble. My appraisal of the Conservative Party proved quite wrong. Hogg failed to carry the majority, but himself remained unshakeably staunch. The others were more attracted by a combination of resistance to change, lawyers' pedanticism and opposition politics than by effective action against crime. They preferred to confine themselves to fulmination. Only twenty-two Conservatives voted for the clause against seventy-four, including Mrs Thatcher, who went into the lobby against the change, which has contributed more to the conviction of professional and dangerous criminals than any measure which was introduced by her four Home Secretaries.

The seventy-four were joined by eleven Government supporters. The libertarian left of the Labour Party mostly came out against; and Sydney Silverman and Leslie Hale made powerful hostile speeches during the difficult debate. It would have been a natural issue for Michael Foot, and it must have been tempting for him to join his friends. Yet he never moved. He must have regarded himself as bound by his casual and not very committing conversation with me in November. Since then, whatever my views about his political judgement, I have never doubted that Foot was a man of high honour. We carried the clause by 180 to 102, and also survived on 6 June an analogous division in the Lords, which had equally provoked a good deal of preliminary flurry, but ended up with only eight peers, headed by Lord Denning, voting against.

Between the committee and report stages of the bill I had the Easter agitation and diversion of the *Torrey Canyon* adventure. This encapsulated almost all of the characteristics of a typical Home Office affair. It blew up suddenly. It dominated press and television during a holiday period. It then went away almost as quickly as it had arisen. It was not as important as it seemed at the time. To deal with it required a good deal of improvisation and the taking of decisions in areas about which I previously knew nothing. It was nerve-racking, but at the same time rather fun. It was one of the experiences I had very much in mind when I subsequently contrasted the climate of the Home Office – sudden violent summer storms out of a clear sky – with the predictable long dark Arctic winter of the Treasury.

The *Torrey Canyon*, a vast oil tanker of American ownership sailing under a Liberian flag from Kuwait to Milford Haven, had impaled herself on some rocks off the Scillies on Saturday, 18 March. About 30,000 tons of crude oil were spilt as a result of the wreck and if she broke or blew up there were another 80,000 tons which might be spewed out. With the prevailing winds and tides the beaches of Cornwall and maybe of half the south coast of England were in danger of being fouled for the whole summer. There was also a considerable threat to marine life.

Six days later on Good Friday the Prime Minister helicoptered to the Scillies for his Easter holiday, and as a result of what he saw from the air and heard from old salts on the shore became a good deal more agitated. On the Sunday he summoned to Culdrose Naval Air Station, beyond St Ives, all the relevant ministers plus my old friend Sir Solly Zuckerman, who just as he switched from apes to bombs in the war now switched from nuclear missiles to the use of detergents in cleaning up beaches. The only surprising thing is that, particularly as a combined operation was envisaged, we did not reactivate Lord Mountbatten. David Dowler and I therefore ate our Easter Day lunch bumping over Devon in some curious antiquated plane which called for me at Abingdon and took us to this much publicised gathering.

The result of this meeting was that the Government at political level, as distinct from the technical services for the state, took on full responsibility for the battle of the beaches. It was further arranged that as chairman of the Cabinet Emergencies Committee and supplied with all appropriate scientific and operational advice supplemented by the unusual addition of a local observation post manned by the Prime Minister, I should assume the central responsibility.

The crucial decision we had to take was whether to bomb the wretched ship in the hope of setting it in flames and destroying the oil, but with the risk of releasing the oil for distribution along both the north and south coasts of the Cornish peninsula. We decided to do so on the Tuesday afternoon. I spoke to the Prime Minister, who was on the quayside at Tresco, and asked for his endorsement. He says he approved,[1] but my clear recollection is that, unusually, he was not supportive under stress, and rather coldly said, 'It is for you to decide.' Perhaps he was acting on the good precept of leaving it to the man on the spot, except that, paradoxically, he and not I was that, although I had all the relevant advice. He sounded better an hour or so later when the bombs had produced the flames and the operation had worked. We were lucky with the wind and weather, what damage had been done was fairly quickly cleared up and the threats of worse to come never materialised. I do not think that any beach had to be avoided that summer.

There then began a political inquest. The point on which we were most exposed to immediate criticism was why, if it was right to bomb when we did, we had not done so sooner. The answer that we were not ready before (the salvage team was still aboard, apart from anything else) and that this was rather like asking Montgomery why he had not won the Battle of Alamein in October instead of November 1942, did not seem wholly convincing. The Montgomery argument, which fortunately did not occur to me at the time, leads on to what could be a more fundamental criticism. Both Wilson and I were too inclined to be seized by a boy-scout enthusiasm and to play at being military commanders, whereas we might have done better to sit back and delegate to the experts.

The summer of 1967 saw the passage through the House of Commons of the two bills for which, with approval by some and disapproval by others, my first period as Home Secretary is probably best remembered: the Medical Termination of Pregnancy (or Abortion) Bill and the Sexual Offences Bill, the latter freeing homosexuals over twenty-one from the rigours of the criminal law. Neither was a Government bill, but they would not have got through had not I or someone of similar mind been Home Secretary. I could not have got the Cabinet to agree that they should bear the *imprimatur* of the Government. A substantial majority of ministers were in favour of both, but three or four were opposed, and another larger group wished the issues would go away. The minority were not the same people in both cases (Frank Longford for instance was as strongly in favour of homosexual reform as he was opposed to abortion), but the Secretary of State for Scotland (Willie Ross), who had my responsibility for these matters north of the border, was in each case intransigently part of it.

It was therefore necessary to proceed by stratagem, and the one which I adopted was that the Government, while nominally neutral, would free the back-bench sponsors of these measures of the normal bane of private members' bills, which is a shortage of parliamentary time. The Government would allow the House to sit for as long as was necessary to get the bills through. In addition, while members of the Cabinet would be free to *vote* against them, I would be free to *speak* (and vote, of course) in their favour from the despatch box and with all the briefing and such authority as I could command as Home Secretary.

These arrangements, accepted somewhat reluctantly by the Cabinet, gave the bills a virtual guarantee of passage, provided – and it was a big proviso – their supporters were sufficiently enthusiastic to stay, unwhipped, throughout long night sessions, for although I was able to offer limitless time I was not able to offer convenient time.

This condition was abundantly met. There was little difficulty in gathering enough members of the 1966 House of Commons to stay throughout three nights for non-party causes in which they believed. They were mostly young and mostly Labour, but there were some Tories and a high proportion of the few Liberals as well. We completed the Sexual Offences Bill between 10.00 p.m. and 6.00 a.m. on the night of the 3/4 July. I remember recuperating at a pre-luncheon American Embassy Independence Day party followed by an afternoon at Wimbledon.

The Abortion Bill was a higher fence, despite its nearly ten-to-one second reading majority the previous July. It had more skilful opposition, a large part of it provided by a couple from either side of the House – Leo Abse and Norman St John-Stevas – who were amongst the most committed supporters (Abse indeed the sponsor) of the Sexual Offences Bill. Ministers naturally work up a not very serious short-term hate against those who are getting in their parliamentary way, particularly by talking a lot in the middle of the night, and to have to treat this pair as heroes at one sitting and hobgoblins the next was distinctly confusing. We took the Abortion Bill from 10.15 p.m. on Thursday, 29 June, to 10.15 a.m. on Friday, 30 June, and then returned to it on Thursday/Friday, 13/14 July, starting at 10.15 p.m. and completing it only just before noon. In my third-reading speech I paid the first of what was to turn out to be a series of warm tributes to David Steel, although he had to wait nearly fifteen years for most of them. His steering of this difficult bill, at the age of twenty-nine, had been notably cool and courageous.* We aborted (if that is the

* 'He must have been under great pressure. I think that as a young member of the House with a marginal constituency and without a great party machine behind him he has shown exceptional courage in carrying on with the bill in these circumstances.' (Hansard, 14 July 1967)

appropriate phrase) the fourteen-hour filibuster only by making it clear that we were prepared if necessary to keep the House sitting throughout Friday night and Saturday to get the bill. The 120 people (against about 40 on the other side) who had already stayed voluntarily throughout two nights (following a whipped all-night sitting on a Prices and Incomes Bill on Tuesday/Wednesday, 11/12 July) were resolved to complete the job. It was indeed the liberal hour.

That day I recuperated by speaking at the Stanley Baldwin centenary luncheon which his old friend Lady Davidson had organised. I doubt if he would have marched through the lobbies by day, let alone by night, in support of either bill, but the occasion nonetheless began an interest in Baldwin on my part which was to culminate in my publishing a short life of him twenty years later.

The passage of these two bills was the culmination of my first period as Home Secretary. There were some similarities with my position at the Ministry of Aviation after the aircraft cancellations had been settled and defended. But there were also big differences. My specific remit at Aviation was to prepare the Ministry for winding up and myself for promotion. My task at the Home Office was certainly not to preside over the dissolution of that historic and august Department. Nor did I have any lively expectation of further early promotion. I was treated in a lot of press comment and also by a substantial group of Labour MPs, particularly amongst the large new 1966 intake, as an 'upwardly mobile' minister. This however was of doubtful benefit to my relations with the Prime Minister, and I had no reason to expect the reversion to Callaghan's job in the event of his failing to survive as Chancellor. He always looked potentially vulnerable in that office, not exactly fragile but more like a large guardsman who might suddenly come crashing down at a ceremonial parade. However, for what it was worth, the middle six months of 1967 seemed one of his more secure periods. The Budget was launched under the nautical motto of 'steady as she goes', and for the only year in the three of his chancellorship there was no July crisis.

The excitements of the Home Office may have been just over their zenith, but the Department continued to provide both opportunities for legislation and vulnerability to sudden storms. On 19 July Crossman recorded me as demanding time in the following session for a new Race Relations Bill as well as for a measure implementing a report of a select committee in favour of abolishing theatre censorship by the Lord Chamberlain. On the former he noted sadly (for his heart was never in race legislation) that I 'got [my] way easily'. On theatres, despite the fact that I was allegedly 'getting more imperious every day', he as leader of the House of Commons succeeded in blocking me for the time being.[2] (I think his irritability may have stemmed from the fact that he was acting on this issue somewhat against his real views and as an agent of the Prime Minister, whose enthusiasm for stage freedom was dimmed both by royal hesitations and by the impending theatre presentation of *Mrs Wilson's Diary*.) In the course of a few months the blockage dissolved and a Theatres Bill, private-member-sponsored but Government-assisted like the homosexuality and abortion legislation, got on to the statute book by July 1968. I was then eight months away from the Home Office, but the Lord Chamberlain of the day, Kim Cobbold, former Governor of the Bank of England, always held me responsible, was touchingly grateful for being relieved of a distasteful task and continued frequently to thank me until his death in 1987.

The Race Relations Bill discharged an implied promise to give some enforcement teeth to the Board, which I had made both to the chairman and to the public when setting it up in 1966. It was a Government bill, and was so far advanced before I left the Home Office that it carried my successor along with its own momentum, although I am not sure that he had more enthusiasm for it than did Crossman.

The summer storm of 1967 came out of the Surrey hills to the north of Redhill. A legal inquiry, set up following allegations and conducted by an eminent QC, into a voluntarily run but Home Office-financed approved school for delinquent boys disclosed an appalling regime of mismanagement and cruelty. At the beginning of August I decided, on advice, that the troubles were so deep-seated that a run-down to closure of the establishment, known as Court Lees, was the proper course. This unleashed a storm of protest, uniting the 'disciplinarians', the approved school masters, a few voluntary bodies and some local opinion. Eventually the official opposition took the matter up, although gingerly, suggesting that I was exceeding my powers. Whatever room there was for argument about my judgement, the *ultra vires* point was nonsense. The term 'approved schools' stemmed from the fact that they had to be approved by the Secretary of State for the Home Department. This one was manifestly no longer so. The suggestion that I had to pretend it was when it was not would make a mockery of the whole concept.

Despite this clear logic (as it appeared to me) Court Lees ran for most of that late summer and early autumn, although not with quite the vigour of the issues of 1966. It led to several difficult telephone conversations with my permanent under-secretary, Philip Allen, during my August holiday in the far south of Italy (difficult not because of his views but because of the connections in the days before automatic dialling), and in early November we still had a testing debate in the House of Commons with which to deal.

When we were preparing for this occasion it suddenly occurred to David Dowler, exercising a tactical sense beyond the call of his private secretary duties, that I might be vulnerable in the House of Commons if, in response to interruption, it were discovered that I had not as Home Secretary visited Court Lees or any other approved school. The point was in reality irrelevant, as Dowler of course knew. I had visited plenty of other penal establishments. And a careful study and discussion of the report of the legal inquiry with the assistance of skilled Home Office inspectors was more to the point than an on-the-spot instant decision. The purpose of ministerial visits is to raise morale, which was not going to be achieved in these circumstances, and secure a general acquaintanceship with problems, but not to dispense a sort of travelling justice.

The appearance of things is often different from the substance, however, and duly forewarned we set out for an uneasy visit to another (and satisfactory) voluntary approved school, only four miles from Court Lees, on the afternoon of Tuesday, 14 November. I have subsequently seen that day as neatly encapsulating my existing and future responsibilities. I lunched at 10 Downing Street for the Belgian Prime Minister (then Pierre Harmel), whom Harold Wilson was cultivating as part of his approach to Europe. We then hurried to Victoria Station for our *pro forma* visit to the North Downs. That mission accomplished, we were waiting at about 5.00 p.m. on Redhill Station platform when a comfortably filled and brightly illuminated Pullman train from London Bridge to the Sussex coast swept south. 'There go the City gents,' said David Dowler, whose mordant jokes rivalled his tactical sense. 'They've sold enough sterling short to be able to catch the four-thirty home with a good conscience.'

The incident was a tribute both to the superior service then provided by the Southern Region and to the short hours which in those days were a feature of City life. It was also an example of the prescience of Dowler as well as a marker beacon to a watershed in my ministerial life. In fact the anonymous travellers and their associates both at home and abroad had already sold enough sterling by the previous day finally to convince even such resolute defenders of the parity as Callaghan and Wilson that the battle was over. But I knew nothing about it until the Cabinet assembled on the morning of Thursday, 16 November. Ludicrously, in view of what was subsequently to happen, I had been kept off the Economic Committee of the Cabinet. The Home Secretary had no *ex officio* right to membership of this committee, but if there were even an outside chance of his becoming the next Chancellor it would seem the merest common sense to include him amongst the informed rather than the uninformed half of the Cabinet on these matters. The fact that a contrary view was taken could be regarded as *prima facie* evidence in the convoluted story which then followed of the Prime Minister's late conversion to the view that it should be I who succeeded Callaghan.

In Cabinet on the Thursday morning I received the news of the impending devaluation with satisfaction. I had regarded it as not merely inevitable but desirable for at least eighteen months. The pity was that the Government had allowed itself to be forced into it from weakness rather than embracing it with enthusiasm at a more favourable moment. Even then much punctilious attention was devoted to giving the $2.80 rate an appropriate state and imperial funeral, with the Americans as the principal non-family mourner allowed plenty of time to put on their crêpe. It was not to be announced until the Saturday evening.

This stately delay had a disastrous effect. On the Thursday afternoon in the House of Commons a well-informed Labour back-bencher, Robert Sheldon, insisted on asking the Chancellor a private notice question about his intentions. His desire was to get an assurance that the Government was not proposing to incur still further borrowings in defence of an indefensible rate. Strenuous but unavailing efforts were made to get him to desist or the Speaker to disallow the question. When it was asked, James Callaghan, exactly as I would have had to do in the circumstances, struck an equivocal note. The result was to clean out much of our remaining reserves. At the end of that Thursday afternoon and on the Friday we lost about $1500 million. It was a haemorrhage which left us debilitated and defenceless for nearly two years. It must have been by far the most expensive parliamentary question ever asked. The motives were as good as the effect was disastrous.

It ought at least to have killed the Court Lees debate which came on immediately afterwards. Surprisingly it did not. In a full and turbulent House, I replied for forty-five minutes in a much interrupted speech which struck me on rereading it for the purposes of this book long after the last glow had gone out of the embers of the controversy as reasonably convincing and surprisingly intransigent. I succeeded in quietening the House and perhaps even in sowing doubts in a few minds of the other side, but the speech was by no means a repeat of the Blake triumph. It turned out to be the last occasion that I spoke in the House as Home Secretary (in that incarnation).

# CHAPTER ELEVEN

# *The Long Dark Treasury Winter Begins*

The announcement of the devaluation went about as badly as it could have done. The Prime Minister made his unfortunate 'pound in your pocket' broadcast, and the general impression given was that a spuriously good face was being put on a major national defeat. What was in reality spurious however was not the good face but the national defeat. This was the penalty for having made the defence of the $2.80 rate into a sort of British Dien Bien Phu. In fact what had happened to sterling was about the equivalent of what happened to the dollar in what was regarded as the golden glow of the last three months of the Reagan presidency. But a long and desperate stand is not compatible with treating the subsequent retreat as being of little importance.

James Callaghan was as responsible as Harold Wilson for the Dien Bien Phu approach, but behaved with more sombre dignity when defeat came. It was generally assumed that he was determined to resign, at any rate from the Treasury, but there was no clear indication of exactly when. On the evening of Thursday, 23 November, I went to see him, at his request, in 11 Downing Street. He confirmed that he was definitely going, in about ten days' time and probably out of the Government altogether. Towards the end of the conversation he told me that he was sorry that, contrary to what he had assumed earlier, it was now unlikely that I would be his successor. Crosland was probable, although Healey was a possibility. He implied that his estimate was based on direct knowledge of Wilson's mind. It was bad luck for me that his resignation had come at a time when my relations with the Prime Minister were so strained.

All this was amiably presented and was presumably the purpose of his asking me to see him, although why on earth he took it upon himself to be the bearer of unwelcome (and as it turned out false) bad news I have never been able to understand. I did not doubt its authenticity. Crosland was obviously a strong candidate for the office. He had been

214

moved from the Department of Education to the Board of Trade at the end of August, which could be seen as a positioning approach to the Treasury, and he had opened for the Government the painful two-day inquest on the devaluation decision which Callaghan had wound up on the previous evening.

Over the following weekend the Government – and the Prime Minister in particular, Callaghan seeming to have passed into immunity – had an appalling press. A mood of doubt about its chances of survival was created. Throughout the Monday and indeed on the Tuesday morning I sensed, and commented to John Harris and David Dowler, that an unreal hush had descended on Whitehall. Government business seemed to be suspended, and the Home Office felt like an isolated bastion which had survived but been cut off by some dreadful attack. I suspected that something must be happening, but thought that we were definitely excluded from it.

Then just before lunch there came a call from 10 Downing Street to say that the Prime Minister would want to see me some time that evening in order to settle, so it was suggested, some unspecified item of Home Office business. The excuse was two-thirds plausible, although the penumbra of warning sounded a little elaborate in relation to the core of substance. At 4.00 p.m. I went to a session of the all-party conference on House of Lords reform in a room at the peers' end of the Palace of Westminster. At about 5.30 a note was passed in asking me to go immediately to see the Prime Minister in his room in the House of Commons, and to ensure that no one at the meeting should know why I was leaving or where I was going. The last instruction proved impossible to discharge, for Crossman sitting next to me read the note out of the corner of his eye, looked knowing and said something like 'good luck'. Outside the room I was greeted by one of the Prime Minister's junior private secretaries, who had come to conduct me. I think it was at that moment that I guessed that, against the odds, I was going to be Chancellor. Had the circumstances not been exceptional, the Prime Minister would hardly have thought it necessary to provide me with an escort in the Palace of Westminster. As I paced the long corridors with that to me anonymous young man (probably by now a permanent secretary) there was not quite the (misplaced) exhilaration of that walk from the Ministry of Aviation to 10 Downing Street in January 1965. Apart from anything else, the economic prospect was hardly encouraging. But there was nonetheless a sense of solid satisfaction, perhaps accentuated because of my conversation with Callaghan five days before.

I went straight in to see Wilson, who in contrast with some other occasions came to the point with singular directness. He said: 'Jim Callaghan is resigning tomorrow and I want you to go to the Treasury.'

I said, 'Thank you very much,' and accepted without question or reservation. We then talked for about three-quarters of an hour, during which I do not think I said anything of significance, being anxious, compatibly with a show of adequate interest and gratitude, to get away and commune with my own thoughts. Harold Wilson, on the other hand, said three things of import. First, he expressed the hope that we could have relations of much closer contact and mutual confidence in the future than we had had in the past. Second, he insisted that I had been his first choice for the Treasury. Callaghan would go to the Home Office, so the change would be a self-sealing operation. But he would have made me Chancellor independently of that. He did not say *when* I had become his first choice (my guess is that it was only the day before) but he spoke with conviction on the point of substance. Third, he asked for secrecy to be preserved until after the seals of office had been exchanged at 4.00 o'clock the following afternoon.

This was contrary to normal practice with reshuffles, which are announced as soon as they are arranged, and was due to some obscure view that negotiations with the International Monetary Fund for a post-devaluation stand-by credit were at such a delicate stage that there must never be a moment without a Chancellor. I observed Wilson's injunction with sufficient strictness (always believing in a degree of flexibility about secrecy) that I told only Harris and Dowler when I went back to the Home Office and Jennifer and the children when I went home an hour later. The next morning I told Sir Philip Allen.

I continued to work from the Home Office on that Wednesday, and made the afternoon visit to the Queen from there. After this the communicating doors through to the Treasury were opened and the Treasury permanent secretary (Sir William Armstrong) padded along with the so-called Letter of Intent to the IMF, which Callaghan had sent off, and a draft following letter from me, saying in effect that my appointment would make no difference, which I reluctantly signed. I was arrogant enough to hope that it would, but not in a way deleterious to the IMF.

At the end of the morning I had been surreptitiously to the Treasury for a hand-over talk with Callaghan. He was sad but friendly and claimed that he was pleased, although surprised, that things had worked out as they had. (Wilson, however, subsequently told me that he had strongly urged the Crosland candidature.) He gave no impression of turning his back on the Government, and indeed said that if by chance we did not want 11 Downing Street he would be happy to continue living there. I judged it unwise to accept this as a permanent arrangement but said that he could certainly stay until January.

Relations with Crosland presented a considerable problem. Apart from being by far my oldest friend in the Government, with whom I still had a strong emotional link, he was as President of the Board of Trade my most important economic colleague. Thanks partly to the busy-body activities of Callaghan, it was a devastating blow to him that I became Chancellor. As Susan Crosland recorded in her 1982 biography he had been led to believe that his appointment was 95 per cent certain. Then on the Wednesday he had been telephoned by Callaghan and told (1) that I was to be Chancellor and (2) that he was to go immediately to Paris and uphold the Government case at an OECD ministerial meeting, as neither the outgoing nor the incoming Chancellor was in a position to do so. It must have been one of the most thankless missions ever undertaken by a member of a Cabinet.

As a result of this we did not meet until the evening of Monday, 4 December. Crosland then expressed himself as both dismayed and depressed. Had he known the outcome he would never have agreed to go to the Board of Trade from Education, and he would now welcome any opportunity for a move away from an economic department. In these fields, he said, any achievements for the rest of the Parliament would inevitably redound to my credit and possibly to that of Wilson, but certainly not to him, who faced a prospect of gloom. In the circumstances, exacerbated by the fact that his two and a quarter years of seniority (very important at our 1939 ages) had set him on a nearly thirty-year course of regarding me as a junior partner, he behaved remarkably well. Nonetheless it would be idle to pretend that these events of November 1967 did not leave a scar on Crosland which had the effect of crucially damaging the cohesion of the Labour right over the next eight or nine years. Had he and I been able to work together as smoothly as did Gaitskell and Jay or Gaitskell and Gordon Walker a decade before it might have made a decisive difference to the balance of power within the Labour Party and hence to the politics of the early 1980s.

Crosland was compensated in 1976 (the last year of his life) when Callaghan, able for the first time to make appointments as opposed to announcing what they ought to be, preferred him to me as Foreign Secretary. And in the meantime he comforted himself with the belief that it was merely the ironic fact that Callaghan, much persuaded by Crosland himself, had decided to stay in the Government provided he could be Home Secretary which had deprived him of the Exchequer.

This explanation is plausible, but not I think true. Wilson by the weekend of 25–26 November was desperately worried about the survival of the Government and of his premiership. He regarded his choice of Chancellor as crucial to this. Callaghan he preferred to keep in the Government rather than risk the possibility that he could rehabilitate himself in the future to be a back-bench menace. But the first danger was present and urgent, the second was medium-term and hypothetical. Callaghan's reputation was very low at the end of 1967. Wilson would far rather have lost him than he would have appointed the wrong Chancellor.

Why would he have thought Crosland this? Crosland was cleverer than I was and substantially more skilled in economics. But Wilson could never get on with him. Perhaps oddly, Wilson and I, when not locked in a dispute which made him suspicious, could get on. We liked talking to each other about minutiae which Crosland regarded as puerile: railway timetables or Wisden-like political records. More important, however, was Wilson's belief (or so I have been led to understand) that I had a command over the House of Commons that eluded Crosland, and that I was the more decisive of the two. Whether this last edge was wholly beneficial may be open to argument, but I do not think its existence is open to doubt. Crosland indeed used to admonish me for it, saying in effect: 'What you are pleased to regard as your rational processes seem to me to be just a series of intuitive lurches. You pronounce on things on which I would not pretend to have a sensible view without turning them over in my mind for at least three days.' The implication, of course, was that my view was not sensible either. Had he known the story, he would have thought Birkenhead's description of Baldwin's method of government apposite to me: 'He takes one leap in the dark, looks around, and takes another.' The disadvantage of Crosland's impressively ratiocinative progress towards a view was that when the three days had gone by and he had come out of the dark the issue had often resolved itself. He had not so much taken a more rational decision as lost the opportunity to take one at all. In any event, I believe that Wilson's perception of this difference was a factor.

My surmise is that when he first had Callaghan's impending resignation on his plate he recoiled from the prospect of me, whose relatively good press he had come to find an irritation and whom he regarded as his most dangerous rival because of the support I had amongst the Labour MPs who were critical of his leadership. By the Sunday or Monday (26–27 November), as the Government began to look shakier, he decided, possibly substantially influenced by Marcia Williams (later Lady Falkender) that the best hope for safety and stability was that he and I should be bound together, if not by hoops of steel, at least by bonds of mutual self-interest.

So, at the age of forty-seven, there opened before me, not exactly a smiling and golden prospect, but one of the great opportunities of my life. Having accepted the new job almost insouciantly, I soon developed an oppressive sense of awe towards my responsibilities.

The weekend press following my appointment was frighteningly favourable. The *Observer* and the *Sunday Times* both had huge features about me, that in the latter supplemented by hyperbolic editorial comment: the whole future of the British economy and the Labour Party, it was suggested, with even parliamentary democracy thrown in for good measure, depended upon whether or not I succeeded at the Treasury.

I read these comments during a short weekend which was in a jumbled way illustrative of my life at that time. I did not go to East Hendred for it was closed (indeed let) from the end of September until the beginning of the Christmas holidays, but went from Ladbroke Square to look at 11 Downing Street with Jennifer in the afternoon (the Callaghans being away) and then caught a train to Nuneaton, preparatory to speaking at a Meriden constituency Labour Party dinner. It being a political engagement I had no private secretary with me, but John Harris was, and we subsequently drove to the north Buckinghamshire farmhouse of the recently ennobled Jack and Frankie Donaldson. On the Sunday morning I absorbed the heady press comments, then played tennis for an hour, then entertained to a drink Pamela Berry (later Hartwell), a ten-mile neighbour, then had a (fairly) relaxed lunch with the Donaldsons and John Harris, and was driven back to London, Jennifer and a mountain of work in mid-afternoon.

The higher the newspapers and others raised the stakes, the worse the prospects began to look. I became depressingly aware that there was no sign of the vital reserves we had lost on 'black Friday' (17 November) flowing back, that the mood in industry remained sour, and that there was a widespread impression in the City and amongst informed journalists that we would be forced into a second devaluation before long. The mechanics of our desperate vulnerability following the November haemorrhage were as follows. If the holders of sterling offer it for sale on the foreign exchange markets the rate will go down unless there is an equal volume of buying. This is unlikely to be forthcoming from private sources if sterling is under pressure and there is doubt about its future value. The Bank of England can fill the gap, but only to the extent that it has the reserves with which to do so. When they show signs of being exhausted the Government has no alternative but to let the rate take the strain. Under the Bretton Woods system, which prevailed until 1971, a dip of more than two cents below the central rate, that is below $2.38, triggered a formal devaluation. For several years after November 1967, we rarely had more than $2000 million of reserves, some of it held in gold. This amount, as 16–17 November showed, could almost all go in twenty-four hours of disastrous trading. A more normal pattern was that a bad day cost around $250 million. We were therefore always near to the edge of the cliff, with any gust of wind, or sudden stone in the path, or inattention to the steering, liable to send us over.

One December night at East Hendred I read a particularly frightening Treasury paper in bed before going to sleep. It outlined the likely consequences if we were forced into floating without having settled the future of the large overhanging sterling balances held by Australia, Hong Kong, Kuwait and other relics of empire. These balances remained a source of great worry until July 1968, when we made a satisfactory settlement (see Chapter 13). Until then the danger was that these sterling holders might suddenly and in unison decide that they wanted to convert their claims against Britain, as the banker of the sterling area, into dollars. Had they done so we could not have paid. So we would have had no alternative but to refuse, which we would have tried to disguise by calling it 'blocking the sterling balance'. But it would nonetheless have been a default, and would have been a signal to everyone else with a sterling claim to cash it into another currency as quickly as possible.

The conclusion of the paper was that in these circumstances the exchange rate might go spinning down in a free fall. A pit almost comparable with Arthur Balfour's nightmare of the decay of the solar system when 'all thoughts [of man] will perish' would open up. Certainly the British standard of living would crash to perdition – and it would be mainly my responsibility. I slept fitfully after that bedtime reading, and indeed began to develop a bad general habit of waking much earlier than my middle-age sleep requirement (since much reduced) made desirable, and contemplating the prospect with apprehension and gloom between 5.00 and 7.00 a.m.

No doubt it was desirable that there should not be a complacent Chancellor. That danger, thanks to circumstances and the Treasury, was avoided by a fairly wide margin. The Treasury at that time was less good at suggesting constructive action. I think the trouble was that they were exhausted and demoralised by the long and unavailing battle against devaluation. Whatever the reason, the one time in my ministerial career when I consider that I was badly advised on major questions was in my first two or three months as Chancellor.

It was an unfortunate time for this to happen, but I ought to have circumnavigated the deficiency with more self-reliance than I displayed. I was loath to recognise the deficiency, for I arrived with a considerable respect for the smooth-working Treasury machine, expecting it to be much better than even Philip Allen's Home Office or Richard Way's Ministry of Aviation. I was also hobbled by the fact that it took me several weeks to get my personal staff properly organised. The principal private secretary whom I inherited from Callaghan was (Sir) Peter Baldwin, later permanent secretary to the Department of Transport. He was a sympathetic and able man, but was due to go within a few weeks and could not be expected both to get used to a new Chancellor and to plan with him a major initiative. I wanted David Dowler once again to be imported as a replacement. This was even more of an affront to the Treasury than it had been to the Home Office, although the Treasury took it better. It was like a new Pope trying to import a lay Secretary of State – say Henry Kissinger – into the College of Cardinals. Eventually it was agreed that Dowler and Robert Armstrong (later Secretary of the Cabinet and now Lord Armstrong of Ilminster) should become joint principal private secretaries. They sat on either side of the same table, like two very senior airline captains both trying to fly the same plane. Amazingly it worked well for nine months (which was as long as it was intended to last), which was a tribute primarily to the balance of Armstrong's personality, for he had the more difficult row to hoe: he was the senior, and the fact that he knew the Department much better could have aggravated rather than assuaged the problem of Dowler (to begin with at any rate) knowing me much better. When Armstrong went on promotion in the autumn of 1968, Dowler moved into undisputed command and (Sir) David Hancock, later permanent secretary of the Department of Education, came as number-two private secretary.

The Armstrong/Dowler arrangement, however, took nearly six weeks to set up and during this interval I was dependent for an intimate 'no secrets barred' confidant, of which I have always had great need, upon John Harris, who had come immediately from the Home Office to the Treasury with me and whose political judgement was admirable, but who would not at that stage have claimed to have much economic expertise.

The Treasury's initial omission was that it never forcefully presented me with an urgent package of measures which would promote the diversion of resources into exports. Callaghan, it subsequently emerged, had been urged to put through such a programme immediately after devaluation, but had said (not unreasonably) that he was too much the used-up man for such an initiative. It ought manifestly to have been re-presented to me on almost my first day in my new office. It was not. Still worse than this, I half committed myself to a contrary policy in the House of Commons on 5 December. Michael Foot was waging a back-bench campaign against the danger that Callaghan's Letter of Intent to the IMF pinned us to deflation. He, and most of the Labour left, were oblivious of the fact that devaluation would not solve the balance of payments problem without a shift of resources away from home demand. I had to answer a private notice question on the issue within three hours of first getting to my Treasury desk (I am surprised to see from my engagement diary that I was so devoted to being non-obsessive about politics that I spent most of that short interval fulfilling a lunch-party engagement), and for the following Tuesday he secured an emergency 'standing order nine' (now ten) half-day debate on the issue.

True to my policy of always doing my own speeches for major House of Commons tests, I retreated to Ladbroke Square after the important and difficult pre-dinner talk with Crosland and wrote the speech until late on the Monday night. It refuted the 'Footite' argument that no measures against home demand were necessary, but sought to reassure the critics on timing. 'We do not want to dig a hole and leave it empty,' I said. 'We want it to be there only when the export demand is ready to fill it, and we think that the Budget is likely to be about the right time for this further excavation.' This was nonsense, and rather dangerous nonsense. It implied that you could control the allocation of resources in an economy with the precision of air-traffic controllers allowing planes on to a glide path. So far from waiting with this lofty assurance I ought to have been shovelling earth out like mad from the moment of my appointment.

The draft speech was seen by Treasury officials on the Tuesday morning, but they made no remonstrance that I can recall. Looking back, I guess that the reason was that we had not had time to establish a climate of mutual confidence in which it was easy for them to comment on a speech of mine without a fear of impertinence, or for me to accept a comment without feeling they were behaving like nursemaids. A few months later, with Armstrong and Dowler *in situ* and relations of easy mutual trust prevailing with the new permanent secretary, Douglas Allen (now Lord Croham), it would never have got through. It is a perfect example (by default) of the liaison role which a private secretary on easy terms with his minister can perform between him and the Department.

In any event the (mildly) heretical doctrine was propounded, and nothing was urgently undertaken for a week or so. I was working on a scheme of major expenditure cuts, which would have been necessary in any event, for the financial year 1968–9 was forecast to show a dangerous spending 'hump', but had been made more pressing by devaluation. These I thought would have to bear sharply on both overseas defence spending and on civil programmes at home. Preparing for the former (which I thought must involve the major change of a withdrawal from East of Suez), I had Denis Healey, a powerful Secretary of Defence with whom I needed good Cabinet relations, to a 'softening up' lunch in a private room at Brown's Hotel on Thursday, 14 December. I disclosed my broad thoughts, which he took in without fainting or blustering and we arranged to have a return luncheon on the following Tuesday.

I cite this to illustrate both the direction and the pace at which I was proceeding. The next day the pace was sharply increased as a result of an initiative which, it must be recorded, came neither from sagacious Treasury officials nor from the new and supposedly vigorous Chancellor of the Exchequer, but from the much maligned Prime Minister. At a special Cabinet on the Friday morning he had a peculiarly bruising time for a head of government, being shouldered around, not particularly by me but by what was sometimes then known as the 'junta' composed of Brown, Healey, Callaghan and Ray Gunter. He was alleged, with some justification, to have been playing politics against the Foreign Office and the Ministry of Defence over a tentative arms deal with South Africa.

His reaction to this buffeting was surprising but beneficial. He telephoned saying that he had cancelled his planned constituency visit for that afternoon and wished to have a long and major public expenditure discussion with me at 3.15 with a view to fixing a plan for action in mid-January. Insofar as this was a tactical response to the morning's troubles it was typically adept politics. If the lie of the cards looked menacing the best thing was to use his Prime Minister's privilege to reshuffle the pack and start another game. But insofar as his response was to the realities of the situation, it was wise and courageous.

We talked alone for about one and a half hours. I found that he accepted without much difficulty the direction in which my mind had been moving on the scale and shape of the cuts. Withdrawal from East of Suez should be brought forward to 1970–1, which would make easier the cancellation of the order for fifty American F-111 strike aircraft. At home there was to be a restoration of prescription charges, a postponement for four years of the raising of the school-leaving age to sixteen, and restrictions on both roads and housing expenditure. The only one of these proposals, some of them positively palatable to me (East of Suez) and some of them unpalatable (school-leaving age) but all of them necessary, to which the Prime Minister took any exception was the proposed housing cut. That I think was due primarily to his having used in the 1966 election one of his unfortunately mockable phrases about the construction of 500,000 houses a year being 'not a promise but a pledge'. It took him a few weeks to reconcile himself to eating these words, which was understandable, although he eventually accepted that there was no case on the merits for housing standing out as an accidentally protected enclave.

For the rest he accepted on that mid-December afternoon the controversial quadrilateral of East of Suez, F-111s, prescription charges

and the school-leaving age and did not retreat on any of them throughout the strenuous (and almost endless) Cabinet battles of January. I did
not admire the way in which he got the package through. He showed no
panache of leadership, and indeed left the advocacy almost all to me.
His own patience being apparently limitless he allowed the Cabinet to
bore itself into exhaustion. But his quiet almost resigned loyalty was
impeccable, when it came to votes and in other ways.

We agreed that I should seek a general mandate from the Cabinet
on 20 December, that intensive work would go on within and between
Departments over the Christmas recess, and that the House of
Commons must be presented with the results when it returned in
mid-January. I left the Wilson meeting in a state of some excitement,
indeed exhilaration. At least we were out of the trenches and into
a war of movement. I went to stay that weekend near Burford,
going to Kingham by the 6.15 train from Paddington. John Harris
came specially as far as Oxford with me, and I both impressed my
own memory and informed him by recounting what had passed with
Harold Wilson and appraising the political battles for which we had
to prepare.

During the weekend I played a lot of winter tennis and myself wrote
(a rare event for any minister) a Cabinet paper to be circulated for
the 20 December meeting. It began: 'The economic situation remains
extremely menacing.' This was wholly justified by the facts. Sterling
even at its devalued rate had become appallingly weak in the exchange
markets during the previous ten days. But the phrase and the paper
as a whole was motivated by the desire to create a suitable mood
of malleable apprehension. Up to a point it succeeded. My general
strategy of major and widely spread public expenditure cuts was not
seriously challenged in the Cabinet that morning.

In the afternoon I realised that general approval for economy
measures does not necessarily translate itself into the acceptance
of particular consequences. Foolishly I agreed to attend a meeting
with the three main overseas ministers in George Brown's room in
the House of Commons and consequently under his chairmanship. I
quickly learned that a Chancellor should never see together a group
of spending ministers with common interest, and is unwise to see them
even singly except on his own territory and with the initiative firmly in
his hands. I never made these simple mistakes again.

George Brown was flanked by Denis Healey as Defence Secretary
and George Thomson as Commonwealth Secretary. They were each
supported by several officials, Healey indeed by the collective presence
of the Chiefs of Staff. And they all proceeded to defend Britain's
worldwide role with an attachment to imperial commitments worthy
of a conclave of Joseph Chamberlain, Kitchener of Khartoum and

George Nathaniel Curzon – although it would be difficult to allocate the analogues. Oddly enough George Brown, in the interstices of a good deal of banging of the table, let through the most shafts of reason. At least equally surprising was the fact that George Thomson, although as usual the most agreeable, had the hardest line. Healey I knew from our two luncheons was prepared to be reasonable on at least some points, but on this occasion he was mainly engaged in speaking, or shouting, for the benefit of his Chiefs of Staff.

After about an hour of being knocked around like a squash ball I escaped, cursing my naïveté in agreeing to such a forum, feeling that I had signally failed to impose my authority, but comforting myself with the thought that a greater advocate than I, in the shape of the exigencies of our financial position, and a different jury in the form of the Cabinet as a whole would probably reverse that afternoon's verdict. The trouble was, however, that these three were amongst the members of the Cabinet with whom my general political affinity was greatest. I did not agree with them on keeping Britain over-committed in the world, and had not done so for long before I arrived at the Treasury, but I was by political habit and loyalty much closer to them than I was to the Prime Minister. It was part of the skill of Harold Wilson in making me Chancellor that I was now going to have to fall back on the support of him and his Cabinet 'tail' in order to defeat a substantial part of the old Labour right.

I went to East Hendred for six days at Christmas and then again for three days over the New Year. I was however working hard – at least six or seven hours a day – on every day of these holidays. I remember being particularly concerned, as have been subsequent Government financiers, with the search for a philosopher's stone which would make possible the saving of money on social security payments including family allowances without penalising the worst off or impairing incentive. Rather oddly, as it now appears to me, I believed that I was more likely to find it in solitary intellectual effort than were the officials of either the Treasury or the Ministry of National Insurance (as it then was), and devoted many hours, including a large part of Christmas Day, to the fruitless quest.

Harold Wilson long afterwards began to propagate the doctrine that I was not a hard-working Chancellor. He did it in mild and unobjectionable terms. My specific recollection is that when he came to campaign (not very enthusiastically) for my Labour opponent in the 1981 Warrington bye-election he was asked at his press conference whether I had not been a good Chancellor and he replied: 'Yes, up to seven p.m.' In the circumstances he had to give something other than a ringing endorsement, and he did so in markedly unwounding terms. Moreover, I think I know what caused the probably unprepared thought to flash into his mind over a gap of a decade and a half. He loved late-night meetings. His idea of recreation was to sit around with his kitchen cabinet and one or two congenial ministers mulling over the events of the day and the problems of the morrow. He never wanted to go out to dinner or even much to eat it at home, but he never seemed to want to go to bed, although he was nearly always fresh in the mornings. He never appeared to need periods of quiet ratiocination over his speeches, although they were mostly voluminously if loosely prepared.

My methods of operation were quite different. I liked general social life but not endless political gossip in a narrow circle. I kept my speeches (except for Budget ones) much shorter than Wilson's, but I needed a lot of uninterrupted time alone to put them together. And I did not like going to bed late for no purpose. One evening in my first few weeks as Chancellor, when the Callaghans were still living in 11 Downing Street and we were still in Ladbroke Square, Wilson's response to a minor difficulty which arose in the early evening was to suggest that we meet again at 11.00 p.m. It was before a heavy following day. I would have had to come in specially, and I knew it would not be for a taut little meeting but for an open-ended ramble round the ramparts of politics. I politely said no. Wilson amenably backed off, but no doubt tucked away the acorn of memory which subsequently sprouted.

In fact I worked as hard as I was capable of as Chancellor, and harder than I have ever done in any job before or since. On the simple matter of hours I habitually sat at my Treasury desk until 8.00 p.m., which was hard on the private secretaries, although I did then frequently go out to dinner, but worked again on boxes late at night and in the morning, as I did for five or six hours each Saturday and Sunday. I liked teasing Barbara Castle, who made a political virility test (if that is the right phrase) out of being continually on the brink of exhaustion, by pretending that I ran the Treasury in a much more easy-going way than was the case, and she, as her excellent *Diaries* frequently show, rarely failed to rise to my bait.

On Wednesday, 27 December, we had the first meeting of a curious *ad hoc* inner Cabinet of eleven which the Prime Minister thought would form a phalanx to ease the passage of the economy measures through the whole Cabinet. In fact it turned out to be split down the middle (and less favourably to the measures than the Cabinet as a whole proved to be). The main individual surprise was that Callaghan, whom Wilson confidently recruited because he had last seen him as a rigid economist, turned out to be a gamekeeper turned poacher, opposed us on three of the controversial issues and gave only grudging acquiescence on the fourth (prescription charges). As a result this unhelpful body was quickly put into limbo and was widely regarded, I am afraid, as a typically 'too clever by half' Wilson ploy.

I had more success with a series of bilateral meetings on the Tuesday. Kenneth Robinson (Health), Patrick Gordon Walker (Education) and Anthony Greenwood (Housing) all proved reasonably helpful. Barbara Castle, as determined to spend money at the Ministry of Transport as I was to save it, was ill. I was able to see her only by finding my way in the dark of New Year's Eve through narrow Oxfordshire lanes to her Chilterns cottage. When I got there I found her like a hoarse tiger greeting an intruder who had come to remove one of her cubs. We had a very gritty conversation. However, the expedition had served its purpose. I think she liked being both visited and confronted, and, although still a dogged defender of her empire, was more amenable when she returned to London.

There then began the marathon series of Cabinets on the cuts, which was Wilson's chosen tactics. Between Thursday, 4 January, and Monday, 15 January, we had eight separate meetings lasting a total of thirty-two hours. During them I must have spoken for an aggregate of at least eight hours and been unable to take my eye off the ball during the remaining twenty-four. The main time-swallowing issues were the quadrilateral I have already mentioned, although another round of complaint without action about the costs of Concorde and Mrs Castle's rearguard action on roads also consumed a good deal of time. Of the central four decisions three were secured only by very narrow majorities, Wilson pursuing his usual habit of counting heads around the table. The exception was prescription charges, which was ironic in view of the fact that this subsequently caused much the most trouble in the parliamentary Labour Party. All the discussion was about the details of exemptions, with the principle going through with only three or four ministers mildly dissenting.

The real cliff-hanger was the cancellation of the F-111. There we had two votes at an interval of about a week, for after the first vote had come out as eleven to ten in favour of cancellation Denis Healey not unreasonably asked for a pause for reflection. On the second occasion to the astonishment and chagrin of Healey the majority rose to three. He had swung one vote, that of Frank Longford, who announced to an amused Cabinet that the Secretary of State for Defence with exceptional courtesy had arranged for him to see a very high-ranking Air Force officer who had argued powerfully for the retention of the plane. Healey apparently believed that this feat of persuasion left him safe. It did not occur to him that others might lobby too. I had swung Patrick Gordon Walker and the Prime Minister had swung Cledwyn Hughes. Healey had threatened resignation during the discussion, but when I took him back to the downstairs study of 11 Downing Street (which I had managed to prise out of Callaghan at the beginning of the marathon, although it was 24 January before we replaced him upstairs) it was obvious that Denis drew a sharp distinction between the threat of resignation in argument and its reality when the battle was lost. Of this I was glad, for I would have regarded his loss as a major weakening of the Government and of the forces of sense within it.

The date of withdrawal from East of Suez was hotly contested, Lee Kuan Yew, then more popular with the left than he later became, arrived from Singapore and did some successful lobbying. On the Sunday evening before the final Cabinets there was a 10 Downing Street dinner for him, which I reluctantly returned from the country to attend. As the other ministers present were instinctive 'world role' men, I had no alternative but to take him head on and tell him that he must expect his devotion to political independence and economic self-interest to be matched by a similar approach from Britain. At the time he fulminated, but subsequently went out of his way to maintain a friendly contact with me, in London, Singapore and Brussels. However, his pressure plus a knife-edge balance in the Cabinet forced me to give nine months. The date of final withdrawal was moved from March 1971 to the end of that year. Even so, we got the proposition through the Cabinet only by a couple of votes.

The postponement of the raising of the school-leaving age (ROSLA as it was called) provoked an equal degree of opposition in the Cabinet – although the composition of the two groups overlapped rather than coincided – and caused me considerably more unease. This was increased by the fact that in the almost ludicrously Oxonian Cabinet of those days (twelve out of twenty-one, I think the highest score ever), it was those deprived of a university education – Brown, Callaghan, Gunter – who protested most. However, I considered that the measures had to be driven through in four columns abreast, and that if I weakened on one because of my personal predilections the exercise would be dead. I therefore rejected a bargain which Crosland had tried to strike on 8 January. He said that unless I gave way on ROSLA he might well switch his vote to Healey on the F-111. I could not understand the logic of this proposition and rejected it on the spot (thereby no doubt shocking Tony with his devotion to lengthy ratiocination), believing that if I started to make deals of this sort I would quickly be cut up like a salami sausage.

The problem of maintaining a fluctuating majority was however a nerve-racking one. There were only two members of the Cabinet who voted with me on all four issues. The first was Crossman, then Lord President of the Council and leader of the House of Commons, therefore not a spending minister, and temporarily in a mood of cataclysmic enthusiasm about economy cuts. The second was Harold Wilson, who was muted but reliable.

There was only one issue between Wilson and me during this exercise and that was played out back-stage and not in the Cabinet. It was the question of who should make the statement in the House of Commons on 16 January. Late at night on New Year's Day Crossman had come to see me at Ladbroke Square, arriving dramatically through thickly falling snow, in order to urge that I should do so. I would carry conviction, the Prime Minister would not, was the burden of his argument. Wilson was adamant the other way, which was a piece of perverse courage on his part. It was a thankless task for anyone, and for him would be made worse by his being portrayed as eating his words and expiating his past sins. I think he was influenced by a mixture of a wish to reassert himself over me (he was cartooned at the time as being very much my poodle) and by a certain nobility of feeling that as head of the Government he ought to expose himself to any punishment that was going.

I eventually decided to give way to him, influenced partly by a desire for good relations and partly by the knowledge that if I conceded here I could control the other dispositions, deliver the television broadcast that evening and open the debate the next day. This was a mistaken judgement on my part, although it would have been very bloody (but possible) to have insisted otherwise. It was a mistake because Wilson's statement went badly in the House, was ill received by the press, particularly by the *Daily Mirror*, which was then politically important, and, after all the travail, further depressed both the gilt-edged and the foreign exchange markets. This did not mean that the public expenditure exercise was ineffective: it was one blade of the scissors which led to 1969–70 being the only post-war financial year before 1987–8 with an overall government surplus. But it did mean that the fillip of which we were in desperate need had eluded us.

Whether I could have improved the reception is another matter, to which the answer probably is 'not much', although my ten minutes' telecast was better received. More important, however, was the fact that conceding to Wilson made me foolishly wash my hands of the responsibility for the presentation of the cuts and their relationship to overall government strategy. Having got the package through the Cabinet I handed it over to Wilson like an unwrapped piece of butter thinking that I would supply both the wrapping and the bread in the Budget, which I announced in my speech was being brought forward to 19 March, then a much more unusually early date than it would be today.

Partly through exhaustion at the end of the Cabinet marathon and partly through the division of responsibility, I did not apply myself as seriously as I ought to have done to the question of whether a purely public expenditure exercise would look unbalanced without any restraints on consumption. Such restraints could have been provided in advance of the Budget through the then familiar device of a tightening of hire-purchase credit or by the 'regulator', which was a legacy of Selwyn Lloyd to his successors, and which enabled all indirect taxation to be raised (or lowered) by up to 10 per cent by means of a simple Order in Council. The permanent secretary to the Treasury (Sir William Armstrong) and indeed the Governor of the Bank of England (Sir Leslie O'Brien) did raise the matter with me, but not at all strongly. And Armstrong more than counterbalanced his virtue by effectively killing a very sensible sudden thought (or 'lurch') by which I became very attracted about 5 January. 'Why don't we postpone the public expenditure announcement,' I suggested, 'bring the Budget further forward and do the whole thing in one combined operation in mid-February?' Armstrong's advice was very firmly against. It would mean doing the Budget without the crucial evidence of the short-term economic forecast which was due only at the end of February. Such a course would be irresponsible.

This advice was as wrong as it was well intentioned. When the short-term forecast came, I instinctively felt that it was too optimistic and took very little notice of it in framing the Budget. Respect for this piece of Treasury lore cost us dearly, although not decisively as things turned out. To present one-half of the measures and to threaten a tough Budget in two months' time was not wise, either materially or psychologically. It encouraged a spending spree of anticipatory buying. It also missed the best moment for the bracing imposition of the burdens of austerity in a mood of national self-sacrifice. It probably delayed the improvement in the balance of payments by no more than two or three months, but as we were very close to the rocks of another devaluation when the ship eventually turned this could have been decisive. Happily it was not, but I soon came to reproach myself for these two wasted months, for which the fault, in spite of the above excuses, was essentially mine.

# CHAPTER TWELVE

# *A Budget Born in a Crisis*

As soon as the 'cuts' debate was over we began work on the Budget. The mistaken delay at least meant that we could approach this in a measured way. I did not start with any firm figure for additional revenue, but my working assumption was that I ought to raise taxes by at least £500 million, which was then unprecedented.

It was still the heroic, post-Gladstonian period of Budget secrecy. Only a couple of dozen senior officials and their secretaries were 'Budget-cleared'. No one else could take part in the discussions. There was even a secure zone in the Treasury marked by white tape, within which alone Budget papers could circulate freely. I responded by developing a slight neurosis, but not allowing it to affect my convenience. I used occasionally to dream that I had left the whole Budget on a train, but this did not prevent my constantly taking the accumulating papers between Paddington and Didcot. Nor could I ever persuade myself to lock it in a safe, the combination of which always defeated me, at East Hendred at night. I preferred a hidden cupboard above the entrance to the wine cellar. I did however keep all Budget papers that I took out of the Treasury in a special small red box. At first I used the 'Gladstone box', then just over a hundred years old, which most Chancellors of this century have traditionally exhibited on Budget Day. After a short time it occurred to me that if I persisted in this the tradition was likely to be brought to an abrupt end by the collapse of the already battered box. Accordingly I had a replica made (which turned out to be about as much like the original as the Birmingham Town Hall is like the Parthenon), with which I travelled up alone on the 8.40 from Didcot on five or six dark Monday mornings (summer time in winter thanks to another of my Home Office changes), as good a target for a bag-snatcher as there can ever have been.

Outside the Treasury I consulted three ministers and the Governor

231

of the Bank of England. I had four evenly spaced meetings with the Prime Minister, each lasting about three-quarters of an hour, at which I told him exactly how my mind was moving. He made no difficulties on any point of significance. I also had three substantial talks with Crosland, putting him completely in the picture and receiving from him the strong advice to raise Selective Employment Tax (a Callaghan innovation, discriminating against service-sector employment), which I received reluctantly but eventually accepted. The Healeys came to stay at East Hendred for the weekend of 10–11 February (an indication of the importance I attached to his position in the Government, for, despite (now) over fifty years of close acquaintanceship this was, and remains, a unique occasion). Denis fully accepted my general schema and the particular proposals I had arrived at by that time.

With the Governor of the Bank I also had two or three talks. He was modestly reticent about advocating specific courses, although he expressed a general preference for a big Budget (that is, a lot of additional taxation) and for indirect as opposed to direct taxation. I found him a useful sounding board for how badly my Special Charge (or non-recurring mini capital levy) would be received in the City and was given a reasonably reassuring answer.

My initial position was that I wished to avoid any increase in income tax or in surtax upon earned income, and that I was antipathetic to Selective Employment Tax, which I regarded as a symbol of Callaghan's Treasury. The first repugnance I managed to sustain, but the second fell a victim to my determination not to undershoot. At an early stage I decided to increase almost every indirect tax within sight: purchase tax, the vehicle licence fee, the betting tax, the petrol tax, the tobacco duty, the wine and spirit, although not the beer, duty, because it bore heavily on the cost of living index about which I was getting worried. By the beginning of March I cracked on SET and agreed to increase it by 30 per cent. I raised £100 million from the so-called Special Charge, which was calculated from investment incomes, and as it went just over the 100 per cent rate at the top was clearly a modest impost upon capital, but one which I made clear I had no intention of repeating in future years; nor has any other Chancellor since done so. To the surprise of nearly all commentators I decided not to tighten hire-purchase restrictions. There were a variety of reasons for this, but the principal one was that I wanted to keep at least one shot in the locker for the autumn in case, against our hopes, a further turn of the screw proved necessary.

On the Friday eleven days before the Budget I was therefore in a position of having nearly everything settled, but still in my view not having quite enough revenue. At a meeting of the Budget Committee that afternoon I was urged to go for one of three possible further imposts which we identified as realistic options. The first was to double the increase in petrol duty; the second was to increase SET by 50 per cent rather than the 30 per cent already agreed; and the third was to bring pet foods, crisps and biscuits within the scope of purchase tax. I said that I would decide between them over the weekend and announce which it was to be at a resumed meeting on the Monday morning.

I went to East Hendred later that Friday afternoon, played a lot of tennis with the Bonham Carters, whom we had staying, but spent nearly all the rest of the weekend, apart from meals, rewriting or writing afresh the Budget speech. I had a draft but I was engaged in substantially recasting nearly the whole of it into my own language. I also wrote in a lot of explanation of why I was choosing one tax change rather than another, thereby arguing for and not merely announcing each proposal. This was not in accordance with the Treasury tradition, and there were therefore no drafts for this. This innovation made what was already a long speech longer still, but I think that it gave it a greater coherence and conviction. It eventually came out at two hours and twenty-eight minutes, which was the longest since the war, but it was also much the biggest Budget.

On the Sunday evening I made the decision between the three possible courses. I decided to choose two of them rather than one and hope to be on the safe side. David Dowler and John Harris had been strong advocates of this course. I opted for petrol and SET, leaving pet foods, crisps and biscuits immune. There was no objection in equity to this last one but I thought it might cause more trouble, in Parliament and outside, than it was worth, and might also fasten a silly label on the Budget as a whole. I did not want it to be called the Pedigree Chum or even the potato-crisp Budget. At the meeting on the Monday morning I announced these choices, which were well received by practically everybody there, and closed the books on all the main decisions. The total increase in revenue was estimated at £923 million. I brought the meeting to an end with a sense of fatalistic relief. God knows how it was going to be received, but there was no point in worrying further about the shape of the Budget. I went off to a relaxed lunch in 11 Downing Street with Irwin Ross, an old New York journalist friend. I could not discuss with him the things which were uppermost in my mind, but at least he was less curious about them than an English journalist would have been.

After textual changes to accommodate these decisions the Budget speech was in nearly final shape by Wednesday, 13 March. This state of advanced preparation was as well, for the most nerve-racking and time-consuming crisis blew up on the Thursday and continued to the eve of the Budget. Sterling had held up during the first three weeks of February, but on Friday the 23rd it took a sudden plunge. The rate fell by half a cent, which brought it close to $2.38, below which it could not fall under the Bretton Woods rules without a formal devaluation. This was in spite of the expenditure of the Bank of England of about $100 million of our remaining $2000 million of reserves on its support. A week later the Friday pressure repeated itself, except that the loss on this occasion was $250 million, and again on Friday, 8 March. The underlying cause of these upheavals was the beginning of the end of the role of the dollar, battered by the improvident financing of the Vietnam War, as the effortless sun of the Bretton Woods solar system. For the first time since 1945 the dollar was not seen to be as good as gold. There was a widespread expectation that the fixed parity of $35 an ounce could not hold (as the dollar/gold rate went, temporarily, to over $800 an ounce within a few years this expectation proved well founded) and those who could were moving out of dollars into gold. But even faster did they move out of sterling into dollars in order to buy gold. As was invariably the case in the 1960s, whatever currency the gale was directed against the side-winds were devastating for sterling.

On Sunday, 10 March, the central-bank governors had their normal monthly meeting in Basle. The Americans built it up into a crisis occasion by announcing that the chairman of the Federal Reserve, then William McChesney Martin, was exceptionally coming over, clearly with the object of getting a joint statement of support for the existing gold price and thus steadying the market. When nothing of any significance emerged the market held its breath for thirty-six hours and then went into a renewed frenzy. Wednesday, 13 March, was very bad both for us and for the Americans. Thursday morning was even worse in London, and when I came out of Cabinet at lunchtime I was informed both of further appalling losses and of the fact that Martin had telephoned Leslie O'Brien at about 4.30 a.m. US time (which did not point to a calm state of mind in Washington) to say that the Americans were going to take some drastic action during the day, but that he could not yet tell us what it would be. He would inform us as soon as possible.

This left us both mystified and apprehensive. The only action I could think of to fill in the time of waiting was to set up a joint Treasury/Bank of England working group to guess at the possible American action and make contingency plans. At 4.15 p.m. Sam Goldman (then a third or deputy secretary in the Treasury) came out of this meeting, which was continuing under William Armstrong's chairmanship, to report to me. He said that it was the unanimous view of those present that any American action would create shock waves which could submerge us within twenty-four hours. Sterling had become so exposed and our reserves so nearly exhausted that we were almost bound to be driven off the $2.40 rate.

I then summoned the whole group to join me and with waning scepticism took them through the whole dismal scenario. At 6.00 p.m. I decided to go across to 10 Downing Street and warn Wilson of how near to the brink we were. He already had a good idea of the hazard, and accepted my intelligence with fatalistic calm. I then returned to the Armstrong/O'Brien group in my room in the Treasury and continued a desultory discussion with them (which was more time-killing than constructive) until 8.45. We could still get no sense out of Washington. Fowler (Secretary of the Treasury) and Martin were first closeted with the Congress, from which they succeeded in getting freedom to suspend the gold cover for the currency, and then in a long White House conference with Johnson.

At 9.00 I took William Armstrong, Harold Lever, Robert Armstrong and John Harris to a scratch dinner upstairs in 11 Downing Street. At 9.30 Wilson asked me to go and see him again, but neither of us had anything new to say to the other, except for his casually informing me, which became of interest later, that he had been trying unsuccessfully to get in touch with George Brown (then Foreign Secretary and always second man in the Government). I returned quickly to the gloomy No. 11 dinner, which was more of a vigil than a party.

At 10.40 p.m. Fowler eventually telephoned. It was of course only 5.40 in the afternoon in Washington and he had had a busy day. But he had kept us on tenterhooks for an appallingly long time. His specific request was that we should close the London gold market, the principal market through which dollars were being traded for bullion, for the following day. His tactic, just agreed with the President, was to summon a conference of ministers and governors to meet in Washington on Sunday, 17 March, at which he would propose a dual price for gold: $35 to remain the price for official transactions, but the pressure to be relieved by unofficial transactions being allowed to find their own level.

My specific request to him (as always until 1969) was that they should give us a large stand-by credit to tide us over the dangerous cross-currents arising from their action. He was non-committal, even unforthcoming. The whole conversation was unsatisfactory. He was an amiable rather limited man, whom I then hardly knew, who was not a master of lucidity even at the best of times, and who that evening was as strained as I was myself.

As soon as that conversation was over, Siegmund Warburg arrived in response to my invitation. I had thought during the evening that if we were going to plunge over the precipice to perdition I might at least satisfy myself that there was no non-Treasury, non-Bank of England advice which might avoid this fate. Harold Lever suggested that Warburg was the best man to plug the gap. Not only did he respond to the summons discreetly and uncomplainingly, he also provided clear and succinct advice. We should accede to the American request to close the gold market and use it as a smokescreen to close the foreign exchange market as well. We should proclaim a Bank Holiday, keep it going for at least four days, and in the meantime try to block the sterling balances. He confirmed the official view that we were on the very brink of another devaluation.

Warburg was in and out within a quarter of an hour, which was as well because by then the senior ranks of the Treasury and the Bank of England had reassembled downstairs. The Governor had talked to Martin and had got rather more clarity out of him than I had achieved from Fowler. They were unanimous that we should accede to the American request and use it as a golden (literally and figuratively) opportunity to close the foreign exchange market as well as the gold market. Saturday, it was thought, could look after itself as both London and New York were habitually closed for foreign exchange transactions and we did not worry about Tokyo or Hong Kong (except the latter as a major owner of sterling balances) in those Atlantic-centred days. No one noticed the lacuna that if banks were open for normal domestic transactions on the Saturday this would enable capital to flood out of London to the rest of the sterling area. This error had to be corrected by a one-day extension on the Friday so that the Bank Holiday covered Saturday too.

I then went through to No. 10 for the third time that evening to tell Wilson of our recommendations. He accepted them without demur, subject only to the very sensible point that if we did what the Americans wanted on the gold market the Fed must support sterling in New York on the Friday, when their foreign exchange market would be open (they claimed they had no federal power to close it) and prevent it going through the floor of $2.38 on which it was already lying. O'Brien immediately arranged this by telephone with Martin, although the undertaking was not in fact fully implemented.

Meanwhile arrangements had been made to have a post-midnight Privy Council (the first in the early hours since the Accession Council following the death of King George VI in 1952) which was necessary to make the Order in Council proclaiming the Bank Holiday. For this we needed three ministers who, with the Queen's private secretary (Sir Michael Adeane) would make up the quorum of four. Wilson reiterated that he had failed to trace George Brown, but added that he had fortunately got Peter Shore, who was Secretary of State for the emasculated DEA, but widely then regarded as the Prime Minister's office boy, to stand by. This was in fact singularly unfortunate as it was an exacerbating factor in the subsequent George Brown eruption.

Shore's presence was interpreted by Brown as evidence that the whole proceedings were a Wilson ploi, about as dangerous as were Ramsay MacDonald's more diurnal 1931 visits to Buckingham Palace. But as a conspirator Shore was even less informed than was Guy Fawkes when he was brought back from The Netherlands for the Gunpowder Plot in 1605. On the way to the Palace Shore rode with me, Wilson's car being encumbered with private secretary and detective as well as driver. As we swept through the Horse Guards arch I suddenly realised that Shore had not the slightest idea why we were going. It might have been to devalue, or to declare war on France (which would probably have aroused his enthusiasm), or almost anything else one could think of. He had in the most literal sense come along for the ride.

At the Palace Wilson went in first and had a short private audience with the Queen. Shore and Adeane and I were then summoned. I am afraid that I instinctively moved to go in first, but an equerry intervened. 'Mr Shore goes in first,' he firmly said, 'for he is a Secretary of State.' Thus, crisis or no crisis, night or day, was the Chancellor reminded of his lowly Court status as Her Majesty's Under-Treasurer and of the fact that the Cabinet precedence is not Palace precedence.

I half expected to find the Queen looking pale and dishevelled, if not exactly in her night-shift at least a little like Queen Victoria in 1837, and certainly bad-tempered. On the contrary she was *tirée à quatre épingles*, a great deal more cheerful than the rest of us, and almost excessively chatty for the circumstances. We were there about ten minutes. When we came out on to the steps on the north side of the courtyard, Wilson's principal secretary (Michael Halls) greeted us with the news that he had at last been in touch with Brown, had given him a brief outline of what was happening and had received the truculent response that he deeply disagreed with and disapproved of what we were doing.

With these encouraging words ringing in my ears I drove to the House of Commons (which was sitting all night with a three-line whip on both sides to push through highly controversial guillotine motions on the Transport Bill) to see Edward Heath. I had asked him to my room for 1.00 a.m. in order that I might explain to him, as leader of the opposition, that we were responding to an American request. He took my briefing without excitement, grimly, gravely, flatly, not particularly hostilely. He probed about possible damage to the future of the London gold market, but he did not seize on our vulnerable point, which was why were we closing the foreign exchange market as well as the gold market, and did this not mean that sterling was in grave danger.

I then returned to 11 Downing Street where senior officials of both the Treasury and the Bank were sitting around rather aimlessly, like wartime fighter-pilots between sorties. Before I had time to stand them down I was once more summoned to No. 10 – for my fourth visit that night. On this occasion Wilson was in Marcia Williams's little office off the Cabinet room, with one or two other members of his 'kitchen cabinet', and was for the first time highly agitated. He had just had George Brown on the telephone in a state of hysteria, he said, although not drunk. A moment or two later George came through again, saying that he had assembled a meeting of more than half the Cabinet in his room in the House of Commons (it was a great misfortune that they were all locked together by the all-night sitting) and summoning Wilson to come and explain himself to them. Wilson, quite properly, said that he was not going to be summoned before any irregular meeting by Brown, but that the ministers could come over to No. 10 if they wished, and that he and I would see them in the Cabinet room. Patrick Gordon Walker then came on the line (I spoke to him) and stressed that, apart from Brown's hysteria, there was widespread disquiet.

About ten minutes later they all trooped into No. 10. Crosland, I remember, looked particularly glowering. Wilson then asked me to explain what we had done and why. This I did as briefly and coherently as I could. It was not difficult, for the case for seizing the American life-line was overwhelming. No one in his right mind could have refused it when there was no price to pay and the alternative was to be drowned within twenty-four hours. This was quickly accepted by nearly all of those present. Gordon Walker, George Thomson, Ray Gunter and Dick Marsh were particularly gracious and expressed themselves wholly satisfied. Crosland and Michael Stewart continued with rather sour complaints about lack of consultation. Brown did a good deal of incoherent shouting. He soon diverted from the merits of the issue into a rather obscure quarrel with Wilson about his style of government. Eventually Brown got to his feet, very red in the face, and attempted to denounce the Prime Minister like a puritan preacher, which did not suit his style. 'You know you've done wrong,' he said, and departed with a great slamming of the door. He never appeared in the Cabinet room again.

This in my view was a grave misfortune for the Government as well as for George Brown. I could not however blame myself, even though I was clearly the catalyst of his going. First, I was too occupied with the swirl of the crisis and the shadow of the impending Budget to have any time for guilt; and second, it was obvious that he was really resigning because he had passed the point at which he wanted to go on working with Wilson. The events of that night were merely a pretext, and it was indeed pleasantly noticeable that Brown, for all his explosive temperament, never subsequently reproached me for his downfall.

As soon as the Brown storm subsided (or rather departed, for it was like a hurricane moving away on an unpredictable course) a fresh gale blew up. Crossman came through on the telephone to say that the House of Commons was now in a great state. The news of the early-morning Privy Council and the proclamation of a Bank Holiday had come through on the tape, no one could understand what it meant, but everyone talked of it and of nothing else. The chamber was packed, there were constant demands for a statement and no possibility of getting the business through without one.

I was horrified by the prospect. Nothing is more likely to go wrong, even at the best of times, than a statement on international monetary questions. Half of our trouble of the previous twenty-four hours had stemmed from the reserve losses following Callaghan's statement on the Thursday before devaluation. I would naturally have had to make a statement on the Friday morning following our midnight perambulations although in the immediate excitements this had hardly crossed my mind. But to add to the normal hazard the prospect of doing it in the feverish atmosphere (to put it at its most polite) which always prevails in a packed House in the middle of the night was to enter the realms of a Castle of Otranto horror story. My reluctance was fully supported by the assembled ministers. It required about three calls from Crossman, backed by the chief whip (Silkin), to make me change my mind. Eventually Crossman's mounting hysteria, no doubt reflecting that of the House, made me accept the inevitable. He was told he could promise a statement for soon after 3.00 a.m., and at about 2.45 I went back to No. 11 to prepare it.

Officials had already produced a draft, which at least had the advantage of brevity. It was on a single sheet of quarto paper. I fiddled about with it sufficiently to make my reading page almost illegible. But it was not the delivery of the statement but the subsequent half-hour of question and dangerous answer that I was fearing. Jack Diamond, Chief Secretary to the Treasury, kindly came over from the House to give me moral support, but brought with him the news that both sides were in a state of high excitement and that he believed it would be very difficult indeed. At 3.15 we drove out of Downing Street and swept down a deserted Whitehall. At 3.19 Wilson and I walked together into a chamber that seemed to be in complete uproar. At 3.20 I got up and the House became quieter and calmer than I had expected. The questions were mostly responsible and the answers seemed to go well. The Speaker wisely stopped it after twenty minutes. I went back to No. 11, feeling not merely relieved that it was over but positively glad that I had made the statement and lanced the boil. I at last stood down the officials and went to bed at 4.15, exactly twelve hours after Goldman had brought me the dread appraisal from the working group. We were still alive, but not sufficiently securely so for me to do other than sleep badly.

The Cabinet met at ten the next morning and I opened with a statement of what we had done the night before, which was unanimously approved, George Brown having stayed away. The end of the morning was occupied with seeing William Armstrong off to Washington. The Governor was already on his way, and at the last moment I decided to strengthen the representation by adding Harold Lever, who was eager to be at the scene of action. There was unfortunately a division between the Bank and the Treasury about increasing the official price of gold. The Bank was in favour. We were against, on the economic ground that it would be inflationary and the political ground that the undeserving beneficiaries would be South Africa, the Soviet Union and France, which had just vetoed our second application to join the European Community and which was generally unhelpful on international currency problems. It was partly because of this that I sent Lever. It also led me to ask David Bruce, the wise and influential American ambassador, to come and see me that afternoon and to tell him (for transmission) that whatever the US Administration might hear to the contrary the policy of Her Majesty's Government was firmly against a change in the official price. This, and an associated point which arose during that same Friday, was the only significant hiccup that ever occurred in my relations with the Governor.

The Bruce message delivered, I was driven to East Hendred in the early evening. There I had a relatively calm thirty-six hours, although the Friday evening was marred by one piece of unwelcome news. The Prime Minister himself telephoned after dinner to say that Brown's resignation was definite. I asked him whom he intended to make Foreign Secretary in his stead. He said he thought of sending Stewart back to the Foreign Office. I said that this would be a mistake and that he would do much better to appoint Healey. I was anxious to argue the case, but as soon as it became clear to him that I was disagreeing his one desire was to get off the telephone. The reason for this became clearer fifteen minutes later when I turned on the television and learned that Stewart had already been appointed. I had mistaken a polite advance warning for consultation.

On the Saturday morning we had a posse of photographers for the traditional pre-Budget 'relaxing weekend' pictures, but I managed to keep most of the day free for speech titivation until dinnertime, when the crisis atmosphere was stoked up again by messages from William Armstrong in Washington. He feared we were not going to get nearly as big a stand-by credit as the $6 billion which we had agreed on Thursday was necessary for it to be safe to reopen the foreign exchange market. Accordingly, he recommended that we should proclaim Monday a further Bank Holiday, and Tuesday as well unless we could bring the Budget forward to Monday afternoon. This last point was a wholly impractical suggestion of Leslie O'Brien's – but it was not his business to understand the workings of Parliament or even the inflexibility of the stately Treasury, Cabinet, Palace and broadcasting procession towards a Budget. Armstrong, however, ought to have known better.

Whatever their wisdom, the messages were sufficient to shatter any prospect of a continuing pre-Budget lull, and I decided that I must go to London on the Sunday morning, decide on my policy at a noon Treasury meeting and consequently have a clear course to advocate to Wilson and to any other ministers he thought it necessary to consult – his fingers somewhat burned by the Brown incident. This Treasury meeting, under a constriction of time, for we had to give transatlantic instructions to William Armstrong at 1.30, and with our minds no doubt concentrated by the imminence of disaster, was one of the most mind-clearing and constructive that I ever had in Great George Street. There was a small Bank team under the Deputy Governor; and the Treasury was reinforced by the brief reappearance from an extended Irish holiday before his retirement on 1 April of Denis Rickett, the urbane and experienced second secretary in charge of overseas finance, as well as by the more strenuous overnight return from Washington of Michael Posner, who could inform us of the possibilities there. But the star of the meeting was Sam Goldman, who eliminated false options and advocated the least bad in a range of unattractive choices with a clarity and incisiveness his possession of which I had not previously fully appreciated.

We established (1) that without a substantial credit from Washington we could not hold the rate and (2) that the easy idea that we would then have a choice between blocking the sterling balances and floating the pound was an illusion. They were not alternatives but were symbiotically linked. If we floated we would have to block. If we blocked we would need to float. Neither was desirable. But we were unlikely to avoid them by keeping markets closed. If we could not open on Monday morning there was very little reason to think that we would be able to do so on Wednesday morning. The only difference was that by then a weak opening for the pound would be the equivalent of a market vote of no confidence in the Budget. The effect of £923 million of additional taxation would have been washed away by a technical misjudgement.

Accordingly we decided to get Armstrong on the telephone as quickly as possible and tell him, and through him O'Brien, that we were unattracted by further Bank Holidays, that the Budget would be on Tuesday afternoon as announced, that he was to do his best to get $5 billion, and that on the basis of that, or somewhere near, we would open on Monday morning. Armstrong accepted the decisions, conveyed first by Rickett and then by me, as reasonable.

I then prepared to go over to 10 Downing Street and report to Wilson. I asked Rickett if he wished to be part of the small group of officials I was taking with me. He behaved with an imperturbable detachment which has always made me treasure his official memory (he is still alive) as the last of the old-style Treasury mandarins. He declined, saying that if I would excuse him he would prefer to get off to lunch, and implying that he had seen more than enough of No. 10 throughout his long career. However, as I was about to be driven away from under the Great George Street arch he came loping along the corridor to the entrance. I felt a stab of disappointment: Rickett had weakened. Happily I had underestimated my man. He tapped on the window, which I wound down. 'Chancellor,' he said, 'I wonder if your car could take me on to Pall Mall when it's dropped you in Downing Street. They are awfully awkward these days about serving lunch late at my club.'

Wilson was calm, helpful and acquiescent, although Thomas Balogh was hanging around muttering. The Prime Minister said that he had summoned a meeting of Stewart, Crosland and Shore (and of course him and me) for 3.30 p.m. I filled in the intervening seventy-five minutes by taking Harris and Dowler to lunch at No. 11. At this afternoon meeting, which lasted two hours and was also attended by officials, Shore was mildly tiresome, Crosland sceptical and Balogh very tiresome. By this I mean that he was critical of everything we had decided, and of the motives of everyone who had advised the decisions, without propounding any practical alternative course. As however the Prime Minister declined to be enticed along his branch lines without destinations he failed to achieve the leverage necessary to do much harm.

When this meeting was over I went back through the connecting doors to the downstairs study in No. 11, and remember being suddenly suffused with a wave of total exhaustion. I lay down on a sofa for an hour or so, too tired to sleep, or read, or even to think coherently. I then went across to the Treasury to take a 7.15 telephone call from Armstrong reporting on his morning's work. For the first time he sounded reasonably encouraging. I relayed this to Wilson and went back to No. 11 to receive William Rees-Mogg, then editor of *The Times*, who had suggested the visit with a view to a helpful leader for the following morning. As we faced a hazardous opening of the London foreign exchange market at 10.00 a.m., this could be of importance and value.

With faint recollections flickering through my mind of the controversies about who had seen whom before both the 1916 *Times* leader which was a considerable factor in the fall of Asquith and the 1938 one which presaged the dismemberment of Czechoslovakia, I thought that Rees-Mogg's visit should be kept secret (although I had covered a flank by telling Wilson that he was coming). I therefore made elaborate arrangements for him to be let in through the garden gate by Jennifer and taken upstairs. This turned into farce. He arrived at the front door, passed through the waiting throng of journalists and television crews like Moses separating the waters of the Red Sea, and was ushered into my downstairs waiting room, which was full of Treasury and Bank of England officials. One of these – I think Jeremy Morse – poked his head round the door of my study and said, 'A gentleman who looks remarkably like Mr Rees-Mogg has just arrived.' William assured me that our attempt at secrecy was unnecessary as it was unsuccessful. The press, he said, always preserved its own confidentiality. He was certainly right to the extent that not a word about his visit appeared in any newspaper.

At 10.30 that night I got the news from Armstrong that his final result was a line of credit of $4050 million. It was only two-thirds of the amount we had decided was necessary sixty hours before. But it was a great deal better than nothing. I again went through and told Wilson, and we together took the final decision to open the next morning. In his 1971 account of *The Labour Government, 1964–70* Wilson records that when this was done I paid him a 'most moving' tribute. I do not precisely recollect this, but as he says that it was so, I have no doubt that I did. It was a moment of temporary relief, and he had been very steady throughout the seventy-two hours of crisis. I thankfully went to bed at 11.30 knowing that Monday and Tuesday were not going to be exactly rest days after this particular battle.

On the Monday morning we had the Budget Cabinet, the first half-hour of which was occupied by my explaining where we had got to on the gold crisis. There was no trouble about this. Then I outlined the Budget proposals for thirty-five minutes. These also had a remarkably smooth passage. I think everyone was feeling queasy after the buffetings of the previous four days. The discussion lasted well under an hour, and at least half of it was devoted to a wonderfully minor point – the effect of the SET increase on rural hotels, on which Cledwyn Hughes, supported by two or three others, led off, and on which I was able to make a mollifying concession. The lesson I learned was that it is always useful to have one or two small concessions up one's sleeve for a Budget Cabinet, and to pray to be able to divert the discussion on to one of them.

In the afternoon I made another statement on the gold crisis to the House of Commons and sustained a longer period of questions than on the previous Thursday/Friday night. I then settled the details of the SET hotels concession before going to Buckingham Palace for my Budget audience with the Queen at 6.30. This lasted a full hour. I opened for about ten minutes and for the rest she asked questions, partly about the proposals and partly about loosely related background issues and other countries. I found her informed and interested.

I got back to 11 Downing Street in time to watch the BBC *Panorama* profile of me, which they had been preparing over the previous couple of months and which filled the whole programme. I then had a quiet evening working mainly on the script for my post-Budget broadcast, drafted by David Dowler but undergoing considerable modification from me.

The next morning I was cocooned in an even stronger envelope of artificially induced calm. I felt like a boxer told to relax before a prize fight on the result of which all the trainers and seconds had invested more money than they could afford. From 9.30 until noon I sat uninterrupted by bell or person in the downstairs study of No. 11, going through my speech for the last time and rather randomly underlining sentences in red in the hope of inducing an undulation of emphasis when I came to declaim it in the afternoon. Any sense of being tuned to the pink of condition was marred by my having woken with a small dagger-like headache going down into one eyeball. It persisted all day, but did not seem to affect my performance, only my comfort.

At noon I discovered that, for all the careful checking, one sentence contained a redundant word which seemed to me to make nonsense of a stage in the argument. I telephoned Robert Armstrong and told him it had to come out. He was horrified, and said that 300 copies, of which 200 were already sealed in envelopes, would have to be changed. Nonetheless he accomplished the maddening task. At 12.15, John Harris came over and we paced up and down the garden (which is at the back of No. 11 but belongs to No. 10) for half an hour. The fresh air failed to improve my headache.

Tom Bradley joined us towards the end and we then went upstairs and lunched in a sextet which was completed by Jennifer, Robert Armstrong and David Dowler. Although I was determined to get through the afternoon's performance without the bogus prop of some specially prepared alcoholic concoction on the despatch box, I drank a fair amount at lunch. The wine seemed to do my headache more good than the fresh air had done. Nevertheless the waiting time until 3.20, when we were due to go over to the House, felt almost endless.

When we at last departed there was a large crowd of photographers and even an adequate sprinkling of the public (allowed into Downing Street in those days). At the Houses of Parliament I sat in my room until summoned by a whip, then went into the House, unlocked the Gladstone box which Tom Bradley had traditionally carried from No. 11 and started on the sacred text by 3.45. I ploughed through it in a packed but attentive House until nearly 6.15. I remember thinking that swimming the Channel must create a similar sensation. I soon lost sight of the Dover of the beginning without seeing the Calais of the end, and went into a limbo between giant but gentle waves. There was only one interruption, typically from Sir Gerald Nabarro. When I eventually sank back into my seat there was to my amazement and great relief a demonstration of unusual support from the Government benches. Nearly everyone stood up and waved their order papers.

Heath followed for twenty minutes, and was peculiarly ungracious, as was then his wont. It was usual to congratulate a Chancellor on his stamina and sometimes his lucidity, if on nothing else. But Heath (as was much commented on) refrained from doing even the former and merely said it was 'a hard, cold Budget, without any glimmer of warmth'. As soon as he finished I was able to escape to my room, where I sat at my desk, physically upright but mentally collapsed, and had two large whiskies with the private secretaries as well as receiving nice messages from a few people who looked in. After about half an hour I had to pull myself together, go back to No. 11, and begin serious work on the television broadcast. We did not like the first 'take' and only finished the second one at 8.45, which meant that we had no choice between accepting that one and risking doing it live at 9.05. We decided it would do, and with that the strain of the Budget was effectively over.

As this first Budget was a major (although perhaps somewhat illusory) success in my life it may be permissible – exceptionally – to cite contemporary views upon it. Harold Wilson, who it must be remembered was a remarkably kind chronicler of those who served with him, wrote, 'It was widely acclaimed as a speech of surpassing quality and elegance and, despite its contents, Roy Jenkins received a great ovation and well-merited compliments from both sides of the House.'[1]

The 'Labour diarists' were mixed. Barbara Castle, although in general more astringent, was on this occasion as generous as Wilson.

His unveiling of the proposals was absolutely masterly. . . . The sheer daring of it took everyone's breath away, won the reluctant admiration of the Tories opposite, and brought our people to their feet waving their order papers at the end. It certainly was an impressive performance, but more important still it depended for its effect entirely on intellectual content and marshalling. Its brilliance is proved by the fact that the most swingeing Budget in history left our people positively exultant.[2]

Crossman preserved a better sense of proportion (or at least of repose). 'The Chief Whip was away,' he wrote for that day,

so I was able to sit in his corner, which is much more comfortable and where unfortunately one can lean one's head. I must have closed my eyes and slept a good deal at the beginning, but I heard with the closest attention all the end of the speech and I watched its effect on both sides of the House. I noticed how nearly Roy lost the House when he said something, expected a laugh, and waited too long for it, and I didn't find the actual delivery very good. It was the content and construction which impressed me. . . . It was a tremendous performance and for once deserved the back-benchers rising behind him and waving their order papers.[3]

Tony Benn was at least equally detached. On the Monday he described my Cabinet presentation as 'a clever Budget from Roy's point of view', but on the Tuesday he confined his afternoon entry to 'John Wren-Lewis, the industrialist and writer on theology, came and had a sandwich lunch with me in the office.'[4] I deduce that, in spite of the austerity of the fare, the vigour of the post-prandial conversation kept him away from the House.

From the other side, Iain Macleod, whose past and reputation I admired but whom I found difficult to get on with as shadow Treasury spokesman, was more gracious on the following day than Heath had been on the Tuesday, and said that there was 'a lucid elegance about the phraseology which remind me of Mr Harold Macmillan's Budget speech in 1956'. He added, with a typical twist of the knife into relations within the opposing party, that Macmillan had had time to introduce only one Budget before he became Prime Minister. Two weeks later, in the *Spectator*, of which he had only recently ceased to be editor, he wrote: 'Mr Jenkins is the vogue. If he had stood up on Budget day and recited the list of trains arriving at Victoria the trendier commentators would have been breathless with admiration.'[5]

The 1968 Budget could therefore be counted a great and surprising short-term success with the political classes. It did not however have the same effect upon the electorate. The Labour Party lost every possible parliamentary bye-election and local election in its wake – although we had been doing almost equally badly before. Nor did the economic indices respond as enthusiastically as did the Labour back-benchers and the political commentators. In the long run that Budget of 1968, with a couple of reinforcing turns of the screw, worked completely, although the long run was a long time coming and in the interim there were many moments of disappointment and dismay following that high peak of 19 March 1968. But that it was a high peak is I think a matter of surprising but objective reality.

# CHAPTER THIRTEEN

# *Rough Times with Sterling and with Wilson*

After the Budget of 1968 the sad fact was that relations between the Prime Minister and me deteriorated much faster than the balance of payments improved. Looking back, the fault may have been mine at least as much as Wilson's, but I did not feel this at the time. It required the acute sterling crisis of November 1968 to bring us at all close together again, and in retrospect I see a pattern of, when things were going well, suspicion arising in his mind, and perhaps ambition in mine, to an extent which neither of us could sustain when we were again being dashed against the rocks.

The first trouble arose over Cabinet dispositions. I suppose, looking back, that I felt in a position half comparable with Lloyd George's vis-à-vis Asquith in November/early December 1916. Being told by most of the press, and quite a lot of the parliamentary Labour Party, that I ought to be Prime Minister rather than Wilson, I was graciously prepared to let him have the position provided he let me have a good deal of the power. I was nearly, but not quite, strong enough for this. Therefore there was an uneasy balance, with the frequent frontier incidents inherent in such instability.

At the time of the Budget I was mildly irritated by Wilson's appointment of Stewart rather than Healey to the Foreign Office. Not only was it against my view but it seemed likely to perpetuate both the greyness and the stubborn traditionalism of the Government. But I could not claim that by any stretch of the imagination the question of who was Foreign Secretary was a direct interest of mine unless I was claiming to be a co-Prime Minister. What came up consequentially was of much more direct impact. Michael Stewart's transfer had left vacant the first-secretaryship (an office created in 1964 for George Brown and therefore already essentially otiose). In addition, Peter Shore by an unfortunate performance during the Budget debate had made it clear that he did not have the guns to carry through the

248

House of Commons the new Prices and Incomes legislation which I had announced.

Wilson was eager to appoint Barbara Castle as First Secretary and Minister of Economic Affairs. I could not possibly accept that. I admired many aspects of Barbara, although I was occasionally put off by her obsessiveness, but there could be no question of my allowing such a strong minister to reactivate the Department of Economic Affairs. A large part of the troubles of the first three years of the Government had arisen from the split of economic responsibility between Callaghan and Brown, with issues constantly decided either by the arbitration of Wilson or not resolved at all. After four months, aided by the weakness of Shore, I had just about succeeded in reknitting together the power of the Chancellor within the Government. For that to have been pulled apart would have been a resigning matter for me.

I told Wilson this on 2 April, although not needing to make the threat explicit, and he accepted it, obviously without much pleasure. Barbara Castle, he said, could instead be given the title of First Secretary as head of a Ministry of Labour dressed up in the new name of Department of Employment and Productivity. Thus was begun the train of events which led fifteen months later to the *In Place of Strife* débâcle.

I was due to go to America at noon the next day, but I decided that before I did so I must tell Barbara Castle what I had done and why. She was certain to hear it from others, and I thought that the only hope of preserving decent relations, to which I attached importance, was to try to get in first. She came to 11 Downing Street at 9.30 the next morning. I was not much looking forward to the occasion, but it appears from her diaries that she accepted remarkably well my refusal to have her at the DEA, the reasons for which I naturally but truthfully put in flattering terms. She asked for my support for the setting up of an effective inner Cabinet, to which I readily agreed and advocated to Wilson half an hour later. It was then his turn to react, and when Mrs Castle was summoned to see him before lunch he was, she recorded, 'stumping around tight-lipped. "I've just sent the Chancellor off with a flea in his ear. He was trying to tell me how to run my own Cabinet. I told him he had better remember who was Prime Minister." '[1]

Of course he had done no such thing. He never spoke like that in direct confrontation. But no doubt he wished he had done so, and paid me back quickly by retreating from his absolute promise to put Jack Diamond (who had been Chief Secretary to the Treasury since 1964) into the Cabinet in this reshuffle. In Boston two days later I received from the Prime Minister a splendidly inconsequential telegram. He was convinced in principle, it said, that Diamond should enter the Cabinet *immediately*, but there were difficulties which meant that this had to be postponed. It was postponed for six months, until October, when Wilson also brought in Judith Hart and thus ensured that there was no tilting of the balance away from 'his friends' as opposed to those who might be mine, with which balance, as Mrs Castle also made clear in her 3 April entry, he had become preoccupied. It was not an elevating issue compared with some of those we had faced together, but it had the effects of sending me off to New York with a great desire to get away (for the moment) from Downing Street, and it started a fraying of our relationship which gathered momentum as the summer wore on.

The planned purpose of my American visit was to strengthen my relations with the twin heads of the official financial establishment, Secretary of the Treasury Fowler and Chairman of the Federal Reserve System Martin, to call on the President, and to blow a post-Budget British bugle by speaking at a Pilgrims' dinner in New York and a Chamber of Commerce luncheon in Boston, as well as doing *Meet the Press*, a major television programme. All of these went reasonably well, except perhaps for my White House call. It was four days after Lyndon Johnson had announced that he would not be a candidate for re-election in November, and this decision no doubt accentuated the mood of truculent but sentimental self-righteousness in an isolated bunker which characterised the last sombre phase of his presidency.

It was the first time that I had visited a President since my private call on Kennedy (in the same room) in January 1963. The contrast between the two visits could hardly have been greater. Kennedy saw me alone, talked for an hour on subjects of close mutual interest and, despite the fact that I was merely a back-bench member of Parliament of no great significance, showed himself closely informed about my background and interests. Johnson saw me with several aides (and our ambassador) and filled up any vacant space with a posse of photographers (none of whose pictures appeared) and a bar-tender who asked me to make a written choice between root beer, Coca-Cola, milk or Seven-Up, and then twice reappeared to bring and remove the glasses.

The President placed himself on a high rocking chair, with me on a low sofa beside him, and leaned over throughout the conversation so that he was constantly gripping my knee, seizing my arm and almost digging me in the ribs. He began by pulling out what seemed to be a well-thumbed piece of paper from which he read a two- or three-minute entirely non-spontaneous encomium of my Budget. Then he spoke about his new grandchild which he threatened to have summoned down for inspection (my grandfatherly instincts were then less strong than today) and passed from that to his cattle herd in Texas. Neither subject prospered, and I was relieved when the interview subsided to a conclusion after about twenty-five minutes. There was, as I am well aware, a great deal more to L.B.J. than this, and I was no doubt too susceptible to the contrasting easy flattery of Kennedy's tailor-made conversation, but as a meeting of minds this particular White House encounter could hardly have been less of a success.

Fortunately I had a successful lunch in the Treasury with Joe Fowler (whom I had got to know at an IMF Group of Ten meeting in Stockholm a week before), and a long talk with Martin at the end of a British Embassy dinner that evening, achieving an approach to intimacy with that taciturn tennis-playing central banker who presided over the Federal Reserve System with steady sense from 1951 to 1970.

Late that afternoon Martin Luther King was assassinated in Memphis. We got the news at about 7.15 p.m., and were almost immediately aware that this was a traumatic event for a United States which was already deeply divided by the Vietnam War. We were protected that night by the seclusion of the Lutyens compound on Massachusetts Avenue from seeing the blazing pyres of more easterly parts of Washington, but when we flew out to Boston early the next morning there was a sense of escaping from a city which lay sacked and riot-bound under menacing palls of smoke.

I had the weekend off in New York, and suddenly realised in the course of it that Saturday, 6 April, was the first day without at least four or five hours of work relentlessly imposing themselves that I had had since before becoming Chancellor. In the course of it I decided that I would go to King's funeral in Atlanta on the Tuesday. Quite why I am not in retrospect sure. I suppose that it was a mixture of curiosity and of desire to express respect from my Home Office race-relations experience to the American black community at a moment of crisis. The ambassador in Washington (Sir Patrick Dean), when informed of my intention, was distinctly unenthusiastic, mainly I think because it meant that he felt he had to go too.

The journey was easy for I managed to get a lift each way in Governor Nelson Rockefeller's private plane. But the day was long and the Atlanta arrangements from arrival to departure almost totally chaotic. The occasion was however unforgettable. It was a mixture of black revivalist bewailing and national political *passeo*. In the morning the former was predominant, when I succeeded in getting, with McGeorge Bundy, only into the standing area of Ebenezer Baptist church. Then the latter took over as we set off for a constantly held-up four-hour (although only four-mile) march under an unrelenting even if vernal sun to the Morehouse College stadium on the other side of the city. At times I walked with a liberal Republican group of governors and senators and congressmen loosely headed by my transport-provider Nelson Rockefeller. They made some attempt to turn the shambling mass into a march. They held their heads up, linked arms and burst into 'We Shall Overcome' whenever the opportunity presented itself.

I preserved my foreigner's lack of political affiliation by at times joining Robert Kennedy. Walking with him was quite different. He did not link arms or sing or even hold his head up. When we could advance he walked with a slovenly speed, rather like a boy kicking a tin can along a gutter, and subsequently reminding me of the well-known photograph with his dog taken at Oregon Airport a few days before his assassination in Los Angeles. His only attempt at introducing order was occasionally to look back a few rows to his wife and call out in his clipped Massachusetts voice, 'Can't you keep up, Ethel?'

As we came into downtown Atlanta through an area that looked both a security man's nightmare and an uncanny replica of the infamous Dallas scene of four and a half years earlier he turned to me and said: 'You know why L.B.J. is not here, don't you? Just frightened of being shot.' It may have been a prejudiced and foolish remark, but it was said without bravado. I think he was aware of his own degree of exposure, but pushed it away from him. It occurred to me only subsequently that as at that moment we did a left wheel, leaving me involuntarily guarding his right flank which faced the depository-like buildings, it must have been one of my more dangerous moments. I never saw him again after that day. He was shot eight weeks later.

I flew home the next day and went to East Hendred for a week's Easter holiday. With the Budget out of the way there was a more relaxed rhythm. The next excitement was the Cecil King affair in the second week of May. It is difficult today to explain or recreate the 1960s importance of the King/Cudlipp *Daily Mirror* and its Sunday stablemate. It combined radical chic with immense popular success. It was also a genuinely responsible newspaper, on big issues at least, nearly as much interested in broadening the minds and elevating the tastes of its readers as in retaining their loyalty. This was largely because Hugh Cudlipp, as well as being a popular editor of genius, was a responsible and civilised man. Yet King's share in the partnership should not be underestimated. Before he succumbed to his hereditary megalomania (he was Northcliffe's nephew) he was the most interesting newspaper tycoon since the early days of Beaverbrook, and a great deal more sensible in the causes he embraced. After Cudlipp was forced to dismiss King as his chairman, an act of necessary patricide from which he has never wholly recovered, he kept the spirit of the enterprise alive for five years until 1973. But the greatest days were when King and Cudlipp worked together in spontaneous harmony.

The importance attached by the Labour leadership to this newspaper empire was understandably great. The *Mirror* Group was not slavishly wedded to the party in the way that the old *Daily Herald* had been (it could hardly have been so successful had it been so), but it was broadly sympathetic and ultimately dependable at general elections. For me it was even more of a sustenance than for Wilson. The King/Cudlipp line was essentially one of the radical centre, liberal and internationalist, although believing in the smack of firm government, particularly in the management of the economy. I accordingly cultivated my *Mirror* relations carefully. I note from my engagement diary that on the day I took office as Chancellor (that is, the day after Wilson had sent for me) I lunched with Sydney Jacobson, the Group's political editor, and entertained Cudlipp to a brief Brooks's dinner. Both engagements had been arranged well beforehand of course, but the interesting thing was that I did not cancel either of them.

I was also punctilious in accepting King's invitations to eat rather bad food but drink Château Latour in his Queen Anne-style panelled suite with its coal fire ventilated by a specially built chimney at the top of the International Publishing Corporation's modern block in Holborn Circus. After each luncheon he recorded what his guest had said and published it embarrassingly soon in 1972. Fortunately he alerted me on an occasion early on, when I queried some opinion he attributed to Iain Macleod. He immediately rang a bell and commanded a secretary to bring in the transcript of the last lunch with Macleod. Thereafter I let King do most of the talking. This had a doubly happy result. I escaped relatively unscathed from the publication of the King diaries, and I think King enjoyed the occasions more.

Wilson was equally attentive to the *Mirror* Group. He ended up, with a profligacy which had been rivalled only by the Younger Pitt, having created three direct *Daily Mirror* peerages (Cudlipp, Jacobson and Ardwick) and another three (Ted Castle, Ryder and Birk) which were effectively from the same stable. Only Baring Brothers as a private institution has ever, before or since, so enriched the House of Lords. However, King himself was not amongst these creations. He was said to have wanted an earldom, no doubt wishing retrospectively to outrank both his uncle Northcliffe and his uncle Rothermere. Quite rightly this was not forthcoming. Instead Wilson put him on both the National Coal Board and the Court of the Bank of England. The first exposed him to the centrist influence of Alf Robens and the second led to his finding a natural affinity with Maurice Parsons, the sour and unbalanced deputy Governor and, seizing upon the traditional *nettoyage* of the gold and dollar reserve figures (the rules were that dollars were swapped for sterling on the eve of each month so as to show a more favourable position, but that the trend must not be misstated), King decided that he was Savonarola denouncing the improvident sins of the Florentines. On 7 May he called with a sceptical Cudlipp on Mountbatten, who luckily had Solly Zuckerman robustly present, and tried to organise a *coup d'état*. On 9 May he wrote me a letter of some import. On 30 May he was sacked by a frightened but brave IPC board.

His letter to me arrived oddly, remained by accident unread for some time, and then led to a good deal of fall-out. I spent the whole night of 8/9 May in a dreary grinding session of the Finance Bill Committee, the first time it had ever been taken 'upstairs' as opposed to on the floor of the House, with much ill-temper from Macleod and little progress. I attended a Cabinet in the morning and then took the 2.15 train to Birmingham, for it was polling day in the municipal elections, and I thought that I should at least show my face at the Labour holocaust for which I could be held to bear a good deal of the responsibility. I got back to Downing Street soon after 9.00 p.m. and saw that there was an unopened, urgently delivered letter from King at the top of my box. It was curious it should have been unopened, for the senior private secretaries were used to dealing with still more confidential material, and I think was only to be explained by the fact that they, as exhausted as I, had gone home early. I decided to have dinner first, and when I read it afterwards was so sleepy that I could hardly take it in. He appeared to wish to resign from the Court of the Bank of England on the ground that he might be engaging in a greater degree of political controversy. It all sounded fairly hypothetical and leisurely, although I ought to have been alerted by the last sentence which desired the resignation to take effect '*forthwith*'. But I was not. I did not react until eight hours later when the newspapers were placed upon my bed and the *Daily Mirror* stood out with its front page entirely occupied with a signed effusion from King.

He pegged this on the local government election disasters, which were also that morning's news, saw them as the culmination of Wilson's disastrous leadership, brought in the cosmetic treatment of the gold figures for good measure and demanded an immediate change of Prime Minister. As soon as I had taken this in (and had reread King's letter with more attention than the night before), I had a very excited Barbara Castle on the telephone. She had obviously been in touch with an equally agitated Wilson and announced that the only thing which could hold the Government together was that I should issue an immediate statement denouncing King and expressing my total confidence in Wilson. Believing profoundly that such statements are nearly always a mistake, because they look as contrived as is their origin, I nonetheless said that I would consider the matter, and did in fact spend quite a lot of time on a draft for a public letter to my constituency party. This is a device to which politicians sometimes resort (cf. Michael Heseltine in early November 1990) when they feel they ought to say something but are hesitant over exactly what result they want to achieve. The more I tried the less convincing I thought the result, and my temper was not improved by a message every hour on behalf of the Prime Minister, who was in Bristol, asking when a statement was coming. I was also asked why I had not reacted to King's letter the night before, and Wilson and his entourage were not I think entirely convinced by the reply that I had been too sleepy to take it in.

Eventually I decided that the best thing was to send a very cool dismissive acknowledgement to King, and to speak about him in equally laconic terms when I had to deal with the matter in the House. Having got the reply off, I put on my Chancellor's robes for almost the only time, and went off to the Goldsmiths' Hall for the archaic ceremony of the Trial of the Pyx, at which the integrity of the currency is pronounced upon by a jury of the livery. It was I suppose as well that Mr King was not part of the panel.

Thereafter the incident and the fame of King (effectively punctured by the IPC board) subsided. He did some damage to sterling (it was a poor gesture which could not manage that), but none to Wilson, behind whom in the short run at least he produced a closing of ranks. In reality, therefore, the whole incident was indirectly more damaging to me than it was to the Prime Minister, but I do not suppose that it was seen that way in 10 Downing Street.

During that summer of 1968, which like 1965 was one of peculiarly dismal weather, I lived on a see-saw so far as both the monthly trade figures and my relations with the Prime Minister were concerned. But the two did not rise or fall in unison, which made the movements still more unsettling. April and May produced bad trade figures, sterling was still very weak and the effect of the Budget seemed appallingly slow in working its way through. By midsummer our Treasury mood was that, if the June figures (due in early July) were as bad as we pessimistically expected them to be, they would unleash a July flurry (it was the traditional month for sterling crises) which we could not sustain on present policies. We would be driven to staunch the haemorrhage not by increasing exports but by retreating from the free-world trading system and blocking with or without agreement (that is, defaulting on) the sterling balances.

The June days therefore went by not only under leaden skies but on leaden wings. But for once July brought a clearance. The trade figures, which came on 5 July, were much better, and on 8 July I was also able to announce that the Governor of the Bank and Harold Lever had between them put together a brilliant deal with the other countries which participated in the Basle meetings of central bankers by which they provided a $2 billion credit under cover of which we could set in train the overdue dissolution of the sterling area. It was a good deal from the point of view of the other countries as well as from ours for the top-heavy and constantly capsizing sterling area had become a menace to world currency navigation. But it is not always easy to get others to see where their enlightened self-interest lies, and it required the unique combination of O'Brien's respected integrity and Lever's quicksilver ingenuity to achieve it.

There remained the task of getting the sterling area countries to agree to the orderly dismantling, which presented considerable problems, particularly with Australia. These obtruded on to my summer holiday in Cyprus (the location a final obeisance to the too long a'dying sterling area) in the form of unwelcome visits to the High Commission in Nicosia for semi-secure, inconclusive and doubtfully comprehensible telephone conversations with William McMahon, later Prime Minister but then Commonwealth Treasurer. Eventually they had to be resolved by sending Leslie O'Brien on a secret early-September mission to Canberra, which amazingly he accomplished in total anonymity.

The July trade figures were almost as disappointing as the June ones had been good, but we had taken in some money and were in a better position to withstand them; and by the time the holidays were over they had been overtaken by the very good August ones, which were published on 12 September. We then enjoyed the calmest few weeks I had known as Chancellor. The relaxation of exchange market pressures was such that we were even able to reduce Bank Rate by half a point, and a down-turn in unemployment (from 561,000 to 547,000) produced an almost equally welcome diminution of tension on my Labour Party flank.

Summer politics had not however been calm. In late June the most explosive face-to-face row that I ever had with Wilson blew up. The background to it was that there was still a great deal of discontent with Wilson's leadership, not only in the press, but in the Cabinet and the parliamentary Labour Party. In the former Ray Gunter was a particular focus of discontent. He hated his new job as Minister of Power, to which he had been transferred to make room for Barbara Castle at the Ministry of Labour, and, although we were far from natural soul-mates, he came to see me on several occasions to complain about life in general and the Prime Minister in particular. Healey was also a truculent critic of Wilson's, as most certainly was Callaghan, although during this period the latter was sufficiently discredited not to be a major force and in no way a possible alternative Prime Minister.

Paradoxically this was Wilson's strength during that summer, at once flat and febrile, of 1968. In contrast with the following year, when Callaghan had recovered his buoyancy, ambition and reputation, and when Healey became a third man between the two of us, more acceptable to the 'Callaghanites' than me, and more acceptable to my supporters than was Callaghan, there was no alternative to Wilson in 1968 except for me. This rather put the rest of them off, maybe on merits, but certainly on grounds of age. I was the youngest and therefore the most sealing off of the ambitions of others. I would sum up the Cabinet mood as one of fretful discontent with Wilson, reluctant respect for me as Chancellor, but without any approach to a settled desire to make me Prime Minister.

The parliamentary party position was different. There was a dedicated group of commandos, waiting as it were with their faces blackened for the opportunity to launch a Dieppe raid against the forces of opportunism. Christopher Mayhew, Austen Albu, Patrick Gordon Walker (removed from the Government in the spring reshuffle) were platoon commanders or higher. They accumulated surprisingly large lists of those who were prepared to act. I was both sceptical and nervous. I believed parliamentary plots rarely came to anything. I knew that the economy was so fragile that a change could not be carried through against a fighting Wilson without the likelihood of a general collapse – certainly of the Government and maybe of the economy too. I was therefore basically a cautious power sitting on Wilson's right flank – much more so than Callaghan was when he came to share this position with me in the following year. This caution was balanced by the fact that I did not wish to lose control of the right-wing Labour cohorts and did not therefore preclude an occasional harrying incident, rather as, at the height of the Cold War between the Russians and the West, the absence of desire for a major blow-up over Berlin did not preclude tiresomeness along the corridor. And there was also the danger of nuclear war breaking out by accident. So it nearly did on the occasion of the June row.

On Saturday, 15 June, I was due to speak at an afternoon gala in Tony Greenwood's Lancashire constituency of Rossendale. In the train to Manchester that morning I was flailing around for something to speak about. The economy seemed temporarily unpromising as a subject. John Harris, who was with me, suggested a warning to the Lords, where the Conservative leadership was reported to be on the threshold of rejecting a Rhodesian Sanctions Order. He wrote out a rather provocative passage, threatening that this might mean the end of the all-party talks on Lords reform. With considerable hesitation, but perhaps attracted by 1909–11 thoughts that an aggressive role towards the Lords was suitable for a Chancellor of the Exchequer, I decided to use it.

Like a lot of statements which subsequently reverberate, it went down flatly in a wind-swept Lancashire recreation ground. But it was the lead story in most Sunday newspapers the next morning. Crossman reported to me on the Monday evening that Wilson was furious about this. In his diary he described the Prime Minister as 'suffused with a jealousy which shocked me'.[2] On the Wednesday morning, the Lords having duly but narrowly defeated the Government on the Tuesday evening, I went to see Wilson at my request and asked him what were now his intentions about the Lords. He answered me a little coolly but thoroughly informatively and, typically, without mentioning the speech at Rossendale to which he objected so strongly. He intended, he said, to introduce legislation further curbing the powers of the Lords and to give this priority over the projected reform of their composition – the classical radical position at least since the days of Campbell-Bannerman.

By the weekend this statement of intent was comprehensively leaked to the newspapers in a form which Wilson regarded as damaging. At the Cabinet on Tuesday, 25 June, he launched into one of his great attacks on Cabinet leaking. This was routine. We were all used to and bored by it. It provoked Crosland on one occasion about this time to become a temporary Cabinet hero by saying: 'Prime Minister, I wish you could spare us this waste of time, particularly as we all know that the majority of the leaks come from the 10 Downing Street leak machine.'

What was unusual about this Tuesday, however, was the violence with which Wilson expressed himself and his ending up by saying: 'I know where a great part of the leaking and backbiting comes from. It arises from the ambitions of one member of this Cabinet to sit in my place. But I can tell him this: if he ever does sit in my place he will find that the difficulties which have been created by the present atmosphere in the Cabinet are such that life will be as intolerable for him as it is for me.' As a statement it had a certain affronted dignity which Wilson's words normally lacked, but it also happened to be based on an entirely false premise and was therefore unfair. There was no doubt to whom he was referring, but on the principle of not showing that caps fitted by wearing them, I ingested my anger and merely passed him a note saying that I must see him as soon as the Cabinet was over.

I waited behind for this. I think he was reluctant for he disappeared for some time into Marcia Williams's room, but eventually came back. I said that what he had said was insufferable. I was not responsible for the leak, but even had I been he ought to have charged me with it directly and not done this elliptical smear in open Cabinet. In my view personal relations had become intolerable because of his method of conducting business, and I had pretty well had enough of it. As usual, when confronted directly, he attempted to be conciliatory, but did say, bitterly but honestly and therefore impressively: 'Well, you may find this an intolerable Cabinet to sit in, but I can tell you that you cannot be any more miserable about it, or find it any more intolerable, than I do to preside over it.' He then said that he accepted my assurances, but did I know who was responsible for the leak? I said yes, but he had better find out for himself. In any event I proposed to see him the following evening (Wednesday) when we could discuss the form of his retraction for Thursday morning's Cabinet. Otherwise it was the end.

The reason I was so completely confident was that I knew exactly what had happened. Wilson had told only two Cabinet members – Crossman and me – of his intentions. Crossman had perfectly reasonably told Carrington, with whom he was locked in negotiations over the House of Lords reform bill. Carrington had equally reasonably told the shadow Cabinet. One or more of them had told the press, being under not the slightest obligation to preserve Government secrets.

When I next saw Wilson on the Wednesday evening he had discovered all this. He apologised profusely, exonerated me entirely and said he would make whatever statement I wished in Cabinet the next morning. I said I would leave the form of it to him. We then went on to more general talk. He said that the Cabinet worked well when relations between us were good and badly when they were not. The last month had been bad, and we must try to improve them. I acceded gladly to this. He then for the first time raised the question of the succession. He said that it would obviously be mine, and that he did not intend to stay too long as Prime Minister. We cemented the better atmosphere with about twenty minutes' conversation on nineteenth-century railways, and then concluded the meeting, which had lasted an hour and a half.

His retraction the following morning was not quite as handsome as I had been led to expect. But it was adequate, the previous evening had lanced the boil and there began a very much better chapter of relations which lasted for several months. This was as well (at least for the stability of the Government) because three days later there was a new crisis.

On the Sunday morning (30 June) when it was exceptionally hot for that summer and I was playing croquet alone at East Hendred I heard the telephone faintly ringing. I reluctantly went in and just caught it on the twentieth ring. Jennifer was in America and there was no one else in the house. It was Wilson. He opened cautiously. 'Have you heard of our latest trouble?' he said. I had not, but it took me a little time to get the information out of him, in spite of his having originated the call and initiated the subject. Gunter had resigned, delivering an offensive letter the previous day. His name does not now have much resonance, but he had a considerable public following at the time, and the ground on which he went – distaste for Wilson's style of government – echoed the reason given by George Brown three months before and was potentially very damaging. Wilson's main purpose was to know whether I was privy to Gunter's decision or not, and whether it was the beginning of a plot or an isolated act of pique. Hence his short delay before telling me, in order to have a better opportunity of judging how genuinely mystified I was.

He should have been reassured, for I knew absolutely nothing, and had in any event made my peace with Wilson three days before. But had Gunter resigned while my quarrel with the Prime Minister was unresolved, or had Wilson declined to apologise and withdraw, the resignation might have lit a fuse leading to a more explosive powder-keg. The margin by which it did not was narrow, but it was probably desirable that it existed. Looking back, however, I think that those troubled summer days of 1968 were for me, in a small way, the equivalent of the same season of 1953 for Rab Butler. Having faltered for want of single-minded ruthlessness when there was no alternative to himself, he then settled down to a career punctuated by increasingly wide misses of the premiership. People who effectively seize the prime ministership – Lloyd George, Macmillan, Mrs Thatcher – do not let such moments slip.

## CHAPTER FOURTEEN

# *Confusion in Bonn and Gloom in the Pennines*

The September calm in the economy did not last long. By mid-October the consumption trend began to look too high. I decided over the weekend of 19–20 October that exactly the circumstances for which I had kept a tightening of hire-purchase controls in reserve had arisen, and that they should be activated forthwith. For almost the only time as Chancellor I then was mildly frustrated by colleagues. Hire purchase was nominally a Board of Trade matter, although clearly a weapon of macro-economic management. But this meant that the decision fell to be made by the little economic strategy committee known as Misc. 205.

It was a classic example of the disadvantage of split control and fully justified my refusal to allow a revival of the DEA which would have made dyarchy endemic. At the Misc. 205 meetings Wilson was firm and Shore tolerable, but Barbara Castle sceptical and Crosland (crucial, because as President of the Board of Trade he had to make the announcement) half in favour, half against, but always opposed to an immediate decision on any particular course. His view (very typically) was that we ought to do something different from the proposition currently under discussion, maybe more drastic, maybe less, but certainly much later. As a result the action came ten days after it ought to have done, and he and Barbara both got their fingers burned, she because of an apparent denial of any impending action at an eve-of-poll meeting in a Bassetlaw bye-election, and he both because her alleged chicanery put him hopelessly on to the defensive in the House of Commons and because his statement had been so long trailed that it became a mouse out of a mountain.

More important however was the fact that the delayed tightening of the screw had no time to take effect before it was submerged in bad October trade figures (September like August had been good) which left us naked and exposed before the storm of a new international

261

currency upheaval which broke in mid-November. The trade figures were published on 13 November (although I had known them since 7 November) and on Friday the 15th we had one of those days when the Bank had to spend more than $250 million (about one-eighth of what we had left) to keep the pound from going through its floor. The cause of the trouble this time was a threatened French devaluation, provoked essentially by their inability to hold the parity with the D-mark. The central weakness of our position in the fraught days which followed was that sterling was also overvalued against the D-mark, although probably not by as much as the French franc, but we were resolved for political reasons not to correct this by a second devaluation within a year. We therefore wanted it done by a German revaluation, which the Germans, partly because of internal tensions within their 'Grand Coalition' Government, were determined to resist. The Americans (now a lame-duck administration, for Nixon had been elected on 5 November) also wanted a German revaluation, but not at the price of upsetting their most important European ally. They were more concerned at preventing the French devaluation being too big, and were slow to see that the best way of achieving this was to get the Germans to do half of the necessary bilateral adjustment.

On Sunday, 9 November, I had entertained Joe Fowler to a farewell dinner at 11 Downing Street, and in the course of associated talks something of these discrepancies emerged, although we were able to agree that as soon as we got wind of a French move (which Fowler did not regard as imminent) a conference of Finance Ministers should be assembled, preferably in Washington rather than in Bonn, for neither of us relished the prospect of the chairmanship of Karl Schiller, the German Economics Minister.

Six days later O'Brien reported from Basle that the Governor of the Bank of France had just told his fellow central bankers that his government was determined to move the following weekend. Blessing (President of the Bundesbank) had indicated a willingness to split a 15 per cent adjustment with the French. This sounded reasonable from our point of view, although our Treasury judgement was that the cross-currents even from this satisfactory adjustment would require a further battening down of our hatches. In any event we had become convinced, following the mishandling of the hire-purchase move, that a further fiscal package was necessary. At a Treasury meeting on the Monday morning we determined on a policy of using the regulator to increase indirect taxes by 10 per cent and imposing a 2 per cent lower ceiling on bank lending. We considered the introduction of import deposits (regarded internationally as much the least objectionable form of import restraint) by which importers had to pay for their foreign currency early, thereby making an involuntary loan to the

Government, temporarily reducing their own liquidity and increasing that of the Exchequer, as well as having a marginally discouraging effect on the total volume of imports. Official opinion was against, and I did not press at this stage. In the early evening I got preliminary approval for the plan from Misc. 205 without promising any action on imports.

It was however clear to me that the other members would be much happier and regard the package as better balanced if a measure against imports were included. That evening Jennifer and I had a dinner party for, amongst others, Geoffroy de Courcel (French ambassador). He left me in no doubt that the French were determined to devalue and not to take much notice of what anyone else said. Overnight I became convinced that it was a mistake to hold out against import deposits. They would greatly ease the passage of the package through both the Cabinet and the parliamentary Labour Party. They would not be politically controversial, for both Macleod and Maudling had advocated them. The French would not have hesitated to use them. They might even do some good, and could not possibly do any great harm.

I therefore announced to officials at the beginning of my Treasury meeting the next morning that on reflection I had decided to add them to the rest of their desired package which I was securely delivering. This was then accepted without demur, as I have always found that high-quality civil servants will accept a clear decision provided they think that the contrary arguments have been properly considered. I have also always found it better, on a second round, to announce a decision and not to relock the horns of argument. An hour later I moved across to 10 Downing Street to re-engage with Misc. 205 and got the amended package through on what Asquith would have called 'oiled castors'.

It was certainly as well that I had got this, as it were, under my belt, for within a few hours there was a simultaneous speeding up of the pace of action and deterioration of the prospects. I spoke to Fowler later that morning. He had got to Bonn on his farewell tour, which effectively scuppered the possibility of having a conference anywhere else. I strongly urged however that it should take place, with markets closed, before the Germans or the French announced their decision. He was sympathetically disposed, although we were still divided over whether the primary pressure should be on the French or the Germans.

Then at 8.00 p.m. we were told that the Germans had issued a statement offering a 4 per cent border tax adjustment, which should produce a medium-term worsening of their too strong balance of payments, but which was useless in the short run, and firmly excluding revaluation. A catastrophic view of this was taken by O'Brien and by Sir Frank Figgures, who had replaced Rickett as the Treasury second secretary in charge of overseas finance. They argued strongly that a conference *after* a firm German decision would be not only pointless but disastrous. Without a significant result, that is a German revaluation, we would never be able to reopen our markets at the existing sterling parity.

I therefore spoke to Fowler and told him that in the new circumstances I thought a conference was a mistake. He failed to understand how much circumstances had been changed for us by the German statement and thought I was running out on the course I had urged upon him that morning. Leslie O'Brien then came on the line and put my point even more strongly. The Bank at this stage were urging me to decline either to attend or to close markets. This was not sensible. We needed help too much to sulk, and to insist on unilaterally keeping open a foreign exchange market through which we were rapidly bleeding to death would have been perverse, to say the least. If we were putting our head on the block either way, which seemed to be the encouraging choice before us, it was surely better to do so amongst friends rather than in surly isolation. And the snarl-up with Fowler had already gone quite far enough. I therefore agreed that I would come to Bonn the next morning and close our market provided he closed New York. He agreed that he would join me for lunch at the British Embassy. I do not think I left him in any doubt that we were going to put all possible pressure on the Germans in the meantime.

At about 10.00 p.m. we adjourned upstairs for a late dinner, leaving Figgures and Jeremy Morse to prepare draft messages for Wilson to send to President Johnson (urging his intervention with the Germans) and Chancellor Kiesinger. While we were still in the dining room Wilson arrived unexpectedly with Burke Trend and two private secretaries. He had been addressing an Export Council dinner. He seemed over-ebullient for the circumstances, at once elated and relaxed by his dinner and speech. He approved the two drafts and then proposed that the German ambassador, Herbert Blankenhorn, be immediately summoned for the receipt of the message to Kiesinger. I opposed the idea. I thought Wilson was too excited. Let us see what you think in the morning, I said. Wilson appeared to accept this but then David Dowler came round the table and whispered that Douglas Allen and the other Treasury officials present thought I was being too cautious and that pressure exerted that night might make all the difference between survival and disaster. I weakened, for I too was nervous of crashing through inactivity, and therefore told Wilson that this was the official Treasury view. He seized on the life-line and Blankenhorn was summoned. Before he arrived, Michael Palliser, who was then the Foreign Office private secretary in No. 10, told Wilson with great firmness that (1) he must work out what he was going to say and (2) Michael Stewart, as Foreign Secretary, must be informed and given the opportunity to be present. The advice was brave but ineffective. Wilson still spoke off the top of his head, and Stewart, although arriving quickly, contributed little.

Blankenhorn presented himself at about 12.30 a.m. There was no question of his arriving dishevelled from bed as was subsequently reported. He was bland, alert and in a dinner jacket. Uncharacteristically, I like to think, I was not aware of what a distinguished German he was. He had been an important member of the anti-Hitler group within the German Foreign Ministry in 1943–5 (see the *Berlin Diary* of 'Missy' Vassiltchikov) and he had also played a key role in the setting up of the Christian Democratic Party at the end of the 1940s. He smiled, nodded, said the message would go at once to both Kiesinger and Brandt, and was no doubt deeply resentful. He had some reason to be, for Wilson spoke very roughly to him. He said that the attitude of the German Government was 'irresponsible' and 'intolerable'. He did not, however, as was also subsequently reported, directly say, 'Revalue or we will withdraw our troops.' The line as spelt out by me, intervening to support Wilson, was: 'If your refusal to revalue forces us to let the pound float down, as it may well do, we could not in these circumstances afford anything like the present level of military expenditure in Germany.'

After twenty-five minutes he escaped, no doubt thankfully. Wilson was put into a euphoric mood by the encounter. ' "Irresponsible and intolerable", that's what I told him,' he gleefully repeated, walking up and down the private secretaries' room. And encouraged by this combative self-satisfaction he sent off a second and stronger message to Johnson, the text of which I did not see until the morning. I was less happy. I had agreed to the diplomatic *démarche* and took some part in it, but when I went to bed at 2.15 I feared we might have done a bad night's work with Blankenhorn, and indeed with Johnson.

The next morning we flew to Bonn in an RAF Comet. It was a gloomy journey. We were promised breakfast, but it was slow in coming and I got bad-tempered. David Dowler was soothing. Douglas Allen read his brief. The Governor read the *Tatler* and seemed the calmest. We got to the Embassy soon after noon. The weather was misty, but cold and invigorating in place of normal Bonn mugginess, and so persisted for the next forty-eight hours. It was the only good thing about the conference.

At 1.15 the Americans (Fowler, Martin, Demming the Treasury under-secretary, and Cabot Lodge the ambassador) arrived. They looked more like a Soviet delegation at a bad time in the Cold War. When I asked Fowler how he was, he said: 'Not at all well. I slept

very badly. I was wakened in the middle of the night to be told of
your Government's message to the President. I did not like that at all.'
Most strenuous efforts over lunch got him and the others to thaw. We
agreed to use all our joint pressure for a fifty/fifty split between the
Germans and the French. He stuck to this and, having worked off his
initial grumpiness, was personally forthcoming throughout.

At 3.15 I went to see Schiller. He also opened frostily, but this
was soon drowned in his usual flood of words. The verbal diarrhoea
of Professor Schiller was indeed the most constant and maddening
feature of the conference. He must have talked from the chair for
a good twelve of the fifty hours we were in Bonn. It was simply
impossible to get him to listen. The flood just swept on. At this first
meeting we were joined after a time by Franz-Josef Strauss, with whom
Schiller, across parties, rather uneasily shared financial responsibility
in Germany. (Strauss was Minister of Finance; Schiller was Minister
of Economics, and therefore, under the unusual German arrangement,
primarily responsible for exchange rate policy.) However, the presence
of that redoubtable Bavarian did nothing to staunch Schiller's flow.

At 4.30 we moved into the plenary session. Schiller opened for
an hour or so, stressing the finality of the German decision against
revaluation. Fowler and I, supported with varying degrees of force by
the Canadians, Swedes, Belgians and Dutch, but not by the Italians
or the Swiss, put the contrary case.

Having thus reached an impasse we adjourned for an early dinner.
In fact the adjournment lasted for five hours, for 'the Six' (really five
as the Luxemburgeois were represented by the Belgians) decided to
have a long caucus meeting. This was a favourite trick of theirs at all
the Group of Ten conferences I attended. It was an experience which
fortified my conviction that Britain should be part of the European
Community. The five G-10 non-EEC members were left hanging
about for hours. The British mostly talked to the Americans. Whether
the Swedes and the Swiss talked to the Canadians I do not know. What
I do know is that the Americans were much more relaxed in these
time-killing chats than were we. They could mostly live with whatever
came out of the Six and negotiate with the co-ordinated position on a
basis of equality. We, on the other hand, were desperately vulnerable
to the decisions of the Six, but unable to participate in their making.

From this long adjournment I retain two particular memories. The
first was that during the buffet dinner, when I was helping myself
from a well-laden sideboard, Strauss came up to me and said with a
slightly menacing humour: 'Make a good meal, Chancellor. You need
plenty of sustenance before a session with Herr Professor Schiller in
the chair.' The second was my first encounter with François-Xavier
Ortoli, then briefly French Finance Minister and later to be both my

predecessor and senior deputy as President of the European Commission. The French asked urgently for an entirely private bilateral meeting with me, without even an interpreter present, which meant that we both had to subject ourselves to the limitations of my pre-1976 French, for there was then no question of Ortoli speaking English. When he came in he looked tired, with bloodshot eyes, friendly, slightly furtive, rather like an escaped prisoner on the run. Curiously, as he had asked for the meeting, he took no initiative in providing information, but he would answer questions, as though he were in a witness box. 'Are you going to devalue?' 'Yes.' 'When?' 'Not certain.' 'Saturday?' 'Probably.' 'By how much?' 'Not fixed.' 'Ten per cent?' 'More.' 'Fifteen per cent?' 'Perhaps.'

His real purpose, I think, was to discover whether there was any chance of our covering French devaluation with a small British fig-leaf, in other words a little voluntary devaluation of our own. I had to tell him firmly no, which he accepted with disappointment and never raised again, although I had to repeat our refusal even more firmly to a restricted meeting of the ten ministers later that night.

This restricted meeting was the best moment of the conference. There was a concerted and fairly rough line-up against the Germans, and I, with others, had a strong impression that, with their post-war tradition of international conciliation, they would take the issue away and concede on the next day (the Thursday). I was wrong. I did not allow for the extent to which the German renunciation of chauvinism then excluded the management of the currency.

At 1.30 a.m. I returned to the Embassy full of temporary optimism. We did not even mind the demonstrators – by then fairly sleepy – who thronged the approaches to the conference venue with placards bearing such legends as 'Wilson – hands off our D-mark.' The spontaneity of their protest was somewhat thrown into question by their being frequently invited into the Economics Ministry for sausages and beer. And there was even a suggestion, probably only from David Dowler, that they were assistant principals in the Department.

I returned to the conference at 10.00 the next morning, having slept solidly and feeling surprisingly well physically. I had sent Harold Lever back to London early to report to Wilson before the Cabinet meeting that morning at which the 'regulator package' had to be approved in my absence. In Bonn we had a long semi-restricted morning session, with I think three from each country present. The German position seemed to have hardened not softened overnight. Strauss defended it in his only semi-public intervention of the conference with much more force than Schiller could muster. Then I had lunch alone with Fowler in his room. The Six were meeting again and were at it for hours. Fowler and I gossiped until the autumn dusk began to fall. We had

long since exhausted the tiresomeness of Schiller and Strauss and all
the possibilities of further pressure. He produced many reminiscences
of the Roosevelt and Truman years, interlaced with leisurely stories
from Virginian folklore. He was a soothing rather than a scintillating
companion for a nerve-racking wait of indeterminate length.

Eventually we were summoned back in the very late afternoon for
another semi-plenary session. The German Cabinet was meeting, and
Strauss was absent for this reason. Schiller felt that he had to stick to
the conference. The last hope was that Kiesinger and Brandt on wider
defence and foreign policy grounds would persuade Strauss to come
back and announce a concession. At first I felt this was sustained by
Schiller appearing to filibuster until Strauss returned. Then Strauss
came in. There was no change, and Schiller had clearly expected none.
He had not been filibustering, merely behaving normally.

Hope of a German move having finally disappeared, there was little
more left to discuss except the size of the French devaluation, and this
we almost unbelievably did from 7.00 p.m. until 3.30 a.m., with only
two short adjournments, one for dinner and the other for Ortoli to
telephone Paris. It was a dreary pointless session. Ortoli wanted a 15
per cent devaluation. The Americans countered by trying to restrict
it to 5 per cent. Schiller then produced with great portentousness
an almost completely nonsensical statement. 'Speaking as a modern
economist', he said, he had worked out exactly what the French
needed and were entitled to do, and it came to some such figure
as 8.725 per cent! But so far from Schiller being accepted as God
everyone was pretty fed up with the Germans by this time, and the
argument resumed. The parameters were that if the French accepted
an agreed figure they would get a line of credit of $2.6 billion with
it. Our Bank and Treasury judgement was that, if we could sustain
anything without a German move, we could stand 12.5 per cent, maybe
even 15 per cent. But 20 per cent would almost certainly knock us
off our perch. I was therefore in favour of giving the French a fair
amount of rope in order to avoid their cutting loose and doing a
unilateral 20 per cent. Eventually a rather ingenious suggestion of
Pierre-Paul Schweitzer's (the French Managing Director of the IMF)
was more or less agreed, with Ortoli reserving his position overnight.
The magic figure was to be 11.11 per cent, based on a change in the
franc price of gold from 160 to 180 per ounce. It was as arbitrary as
the Schiller formula, but at least it was presented as a device and not
as a revelation.

In the course of the evening we had heard from Wilson that
the package had gone through the Cabinet, although only with
considerable difficulty, and I had settled with him an awkward (but
familiar) point about who should make the statement to the House

of Commons. I said it must be on the Friday. He offered to make it as I might have difficulty in getting back. The Governor in particular was insistent that this would be disastrous. Wilson gave way, provided I was back to speak by 4.00 p.m.

When I returned to the Embassy at 4.00 a.m. that still seemed a long way off. I got up early and worked on the House of Commons statement, which I had hardly considered before, for two hours. I then went to see Schiller before the conference reconvened to make some attempt to repair relations and to tell him of our intended measures. I am not sure that he noticed the need for the former or took in the latter. The words just continued to pour out. As soon as the plenary session opened Ortoli made the most extraordinary statement. The French, he said, accepted the 11.11 per cent (and the $2.6 billion which went with it), but did so under protest, and as they were not allowed to devalue by more they might do so by less, or indeed not at all.

While they were all picking themselves up after this bombshell, I slipped off for the airport, leaving Douglas Allen and Leslie O'Brien to deal with the communiqué. I had David Dowler, John Harris and Sam Goldman with me. In the Comet we worked furiously at the statement, which was after all a mini-budget. I was writing, Goldman and Harris were checking, Dowler was dictating to a girl who was putting it straight on to a typewriter. As we taxied to a standstill at London Airport at 2.55, her last sheet came off the machine. We were met by Jennifer and Tom Bradley, Frank Figgures and David Hancock (second private secretary), who had all, I think, come out more for moral support than for anything they could do on the way back, although I did go through the statement with Figgures as we swayed and lurched towards Westminster. Under motorcycle escort we did the journey in seventeen minutes. It was the finest and nearly the last hour of my Treasury driver, Michael Rees.

Thanks to this feat of roadmanship I was able to have ten minutes' exchange of briefing with Wilson before going into the chamber and getting straight on my feet at 3.45 p.m. There was a House of only about 150, which was large for a Friday afternoon but small for a Budget. That was perhaps as well, as was the fact that Macleod was away and Maudling led (moderately as usual) for the opposition. I answered questions until 4.30.

I then went to 11 Downing Street and worked hard for three hours or more on a totally unprepared script for a straight-to-camera telecast that evening. When the broadcast was done I went through and saw Wilson for another ten minutes (adversity had brought us back on to good terms) before departing for East Hendred. So ended one of the more testing eighty hours even of the hard and for long unrewarding slog of my first twenty-two months at the Treasury, and so ended too one of the most chaotic and ill-organised monetary conferences ever to have plagued the Western world. There was however one last scene in that particular farce to be played out. On the following (Saturday) evening General de Gaulle swept poor Ortoli into a corner and announced that he had decided to demonstrate the power of France by maintaining the parity of the French franc. And it was maintained for another nine months, until after de Gaulle had ceased to be President of the Republic.

Thereafter conditions appeared to settle for ten days or so. There were no substantial foreign exchange losses, although the gilt-edged market (on which we were only beginning to focus with adequate attention) continued very weak. The next eruption of crisis came on Friday, 5 December. I took the 2.00 p.m. train from King's Cross to Newcastle-on-Tyne. Everything was calm when I left, except for considerable apprehension in the private office about the November trade figures, of which we were due to receive advance warning that evening. I had no one with me, for it was a purely political expedition, and I was not therefore strictly entitled to take anyone who was on the public payroll; and I was of course in my usual detectiveless state as Chancellor. (I remember subsequently telling Wilson that whatever the rules said, I was not again going away in that isolated and exposed state and that either John Harris or a private secretary was always going to be taken.) Nevertheless I had an agreeable enough late luncheon on the train and arrived in the sombre splendour of Newcastle Station in as good a mood as I ever am preceding an evening speaking engagement.

I was much surprised to be greeted by a pack of photographers and a few 'stringers' for national newspapers, who asked whether I had any statement to make (I had no idea about what), although a *Daily Express* girl seemed convinced that I had resigned. I disentangled myself with difficulty and was driven to Sunderland where I was due to address a Fabian dinner. As soon as I got to the hotel there I telephoned David Dowler and was given two pieces of news. The first was that in the early afternoon the City had been convulsed with rumours that I, and then Wilson, had resigned. One or other of these events was apparently thought bad for sterling, the market had gone into a plunging panic and we had lost over $100 million. The gilt-edged market had also gone through the floor.

The second piece of news was that the November trade figures were remarkably good. I thought the package of information by no means intolerable. However, an imbalance was created by the bad news but not the good news being known to both press and public. As a result the following morning's newspapers were very alarmist (the fact that we had not resigned seemed in no way to restore the status quo), and the weekend was passed in an atmosphere of dark and menacing crisis. I stayed the Friday night with Ernest Armstrong MP at Bishop Auckland (a locality which, having had Hugh Dalton as its MP for twenty-four years, ought to have been used to beleaguered Labour Chancellors), and on the Saturday had my first experience of a North of England December morning under my innovating Home Office legacy of summer time in winter. It was almost pitch dark at 9.00 as I read the panicky headlines of the newspapers, and never seemed to achieve more than a reluctant half-light all day, during which I was driven by James Tinn, then MP for Cleveland, first to open a Labour Club near Middlesbrough, then via Consett across the Pennines to Carlisle. I was much pursued by the press at every point. In Carlisle I tried to encourage a Labour Party 'social' and then took the sleeper back to London. The Sunday newspapers at Euston were even worse than the Saturday ones had been at Bishop Auckland.

On the Monday sterling was weak but not disastrously so. On the Tuesday morning it was still weaker and very near to disaster. A message was brought in to me in Cabinet saying that we had lost over $100 million in about forty minutes. I departed to see Douglas Allen and the Governor in the Treasury. By then the loss was over $200 million and we had practically nothing left. The question was whether we should bring forward the publication of the trade figures which were due (and of course known to be due) only on the Thursday. Holding our breath we decided against. It would look desperate and might easily therefore result in throwing away the one ace we had up our sleeve. Furthermore, it would vitiate everything for the future. The day of publication would be speculated on almost as much as the result.

Wilson, however, without consultation, did well in getting the best of both worlds during his House of Commons question time that afternoon. Without actually saying anything he managed to leave the distinct impression that there was good news in the pipeline. The market in some mysterious way had steadied while I was apprehensively lunching in the City. In mid-afternoon it turned dramatically up. Both the rate and the atmosphere improved abruptly. By 4.30, when I went to Westminster Hospital to see Crosland, who had slipped on ice and most painfully broken his arm outside his house in Lansdowne Road, the mood was transformed. I was a very cheerful sick visitor. The next day the Bank even managed to bring off an effective 'bear squeeze', a form of animal endearment after which they were constantly hankering, but which had eluded them for some time past. They took in $100 million. When the scheduled publication of the good trade figures took place on the Thursday they reinforced the upturn.

The markets then remained calm until Christmas. We feared that they would turn sour again with the early January dyspepsia. But they did not. Indeed we never again experienced quite the combination of irrational flurry and rational apprehension which had been the keynote both of Bonn and of that dark northern weekend. I felt deep rational dismay in May 1969, but we were not then quite so near to the end of our resources; and we were buffeted by dangerous irrational squalls as late as August and September of that year, but by then our underlying position had decisively improved and it was merely a question (quite important in itself) of making sure that we were not killed by the last shots of a war that we had already won. My stygian Pennine excursion was a classic example of the darkest hour being the one before the dawn.

# CHAPTER FIFTEEN

# *The Sun Climbs Slow, How Slowly*

Nineteen sixty-nine was the year of the long-awaited turn-round in the balance of payments and of Barbara Castle's brave but mishandled attempt to reform the trade unions. The first appeared the greatest (although was not the most lasting) of any achievements I ever had in government. It was the sweeter for having been so long postponed. The second was not an issue on which I covered myself with glory.

The balance of payments did not turn until the summer. The January trade figures were good, but the February and March ones were thoroughly bad. These at least had the advantage of reinforcing my conviction that there was no alternative to giving a further substantial turn to the screw in the 1969 Budget (which came on 15 April). This was in many ways the most difficult, and certainly the worst received, of my three Budgets. The main reason was that it was a moderate (and therefore rather boring) additional dose of the same medicine imposed on an increasingly sceptical patient. March 1968 increased taxation by £923 million, over twice the increase of any previous Budget, including the wartime ones. The post-Bonn mini-Budget then added a further £250 million, and April 1969 a further £340 million, still sticking almost entirely to indirect taxes.

This Budget got a much worse press than that of 1968. The *Financial Times*, following my most careful discussion of the issues with Gordon Newton, its quiet but formative editor, was helpful, but *The Times*, then in general an ally of mine, was disenchanted and denounced it as inadequate and uninspiring. And most Fleet Street, City and international banking opinion on this issue followed *The Times* rather than the *FT*. It was an occasion when I might have paraphrased a famous remark of King George V and said, 'I may be uninspiring but I'll be damned if I am inadequate.'* Such a reply would have

---

* In 1915 H. G. Wells spoke of 'an alien and uninspiring Court'. The King said: 'I may be uninspiring but I'll be damned if I'm an alien.'[1]

273

been wholly justified, but I was becoming too downhearted to make it. Nobody criticised the 1968 Budget for being inadequate, based as it was on the principle of always going for the higher rather than the lower number. But inadequate it nevertheless turned out to be, as was demonstrated by its having to be reinforced both in November and the following year. The Budget of 1969, *per contra*, led on to the only excess of revenue over total Government expenditure between 1936–7 and 1987–8, a massive turn-round in the balance of payments and a vast consequent replenishment of our gold and dollar reserves and overseas borrowing capacity. It classically illustrated the force of Iain Macleod's dictum that the immediate judgement on a Budget is almost invariably wrong. (I may add that this did not prevent Macleod from joining with peculiar ferocity, being increasingly bad-tempered with me, in the short-term wrong-headedness of 1969.)

What was worse was that there was no early sign of improvement after the Budget, that I felt for the first time that I had used up all the shots in my locker, and that from the beginning of May onwards the medium-term menace was supplemented by a return to the day-to-day market plunges which had punctuated 1968. In addition we had to engage in a sticky negotiation with the IMF for a further stand-by credit from the end of June. It was a rolling over rather than additional money, but some new regulations for the surveillance of those in our position had been agreed during the previous summer without our greatly noticing. As a result we could get the necessary money only by agreeing to quarterly visits of inspection and trigger clauses based on tight targets for the growth of the money supply. No major country (New Zealand was the nearest relevant approach to one) had hitherto accepted such a degree of surveillance, although France was to do so within a few months, and the issue became a political hot potato at home, provoking a number of tricky private notice questions in the House of Commons.

At the end of April I went to America, nominally to establish relations with the new Administration, but at least equally importantly to make a largely unavailing attempt to get Pierre-Paul Schweitzer to soften the IMF terms. Retrospectively I half sympathise with him. My appeal was essentially based on bogus dignity. 'We will in fact obey the rules,' I said in effect, 'but, please, don't make them nominally apply to us because we are such an important country.' At the time, however, being an unsuccessful suppliant was both frustrating and depressing.

The bilateral aspects of the visit were more satisfactory. The Nixon Administration was fresh in office, and although I was far from being an admirer of that flawed President who nonetheless showed streaks of imaginative boldness before subsiding into tragedy, I was curious to inspect the new regime at home. I had already seen Nixon in operation

Hugh Gaitskell, with Harold Wilson, George Brown and Sir Leonard Williams, party secretary, behind, at his last Labour Party conference. Brighton, October 1962.

'Mine eyes dazzle': with François Mitterrand, *circa* 1962, at a Labour Committee for Europe luncheon in London.

'Roy Jenkins's Nightmare' (Cummings). *Daily Express*, 1962.

*Above*: Caroline Gilmour before
the Washington Memorial on our
Kennedy election American visit,
October 1960.

*Above right*: Ian Gilmour and me
with the New York skyline.

*Right*: (*left to right*) Ann
Fleming, Mark and Leslie
Bonham Carter at Covent
Garden, September 1966.

Jacques and Marie-Alice de
Beaumarchais in Berlin a short
time before we first met them.
He looks more like Bogart than a
future *ambassadeur de France*.

In office for the first time (as Minister of Aviation) and celebrating by looking ministerially patronising to the distinguished Air Marshal, Sir Patrick Dunn.

The young Home Secretary: in charge of the uniforms or nervous of being handcuffed?

Budget Day 1968 in Downing Street. Tom Bradley (*behind*) had the 'Gladstone box' – and the Budget speech.

At an OECD meeting in Paris, February 1969. David Dowler (behind me at the right) makes a typically sceptical joke about the proceedings to Sir Douglas Allen, the permanent secretary to the Treasury, now Lord Croham. John Harris, now Lord Harris of Greenwich, takes matters more seriously.

'Heel' (Mahood). *The Times*, March 1968.

'We thought it had gone out'
(Garland). *Daily Telegraph*, 5 November 1969.

Pre-Budget weekend at East Hendred, 1969, with Jennifer, Cynthia, aged seventeen, and Edward, aged fourteen.

Charles Jenkins, not overdressed for his brother's wedding.

Spring-time in the White House Rose Garden. Secretary of the Treasury David Kennedy
on my right, British Ambassador John Freeman on President Nixon's left, Henry
Kissinger, apparently as note-taker, on the far right.

during a bizarre day in London in late February. It was bizarre because
it had exhibited a bewildering variety of Nixon's facets. It had begun
with a scheduled two-hour Cabinet-room discussion between the
President with a small entourage on one side and three or four senior
members of the British Government on the other. Nixon opened with
a half-hour informal exposé and did it brilliantly. Then coffee was
brought in, and mixed up with putting or not putting sugar and milk
in his cup the President mysteriously succeeded in picking up a crystal
inkwell and pouring its contents over his hands, his papers and some
part of the table.

Consternation broke out, particularly on the British side. It was
like a Bateman cartoon, with extremes of surprise, horror and
sympathy being registered. Sir Burke Trend even poured cream
over his own trousers, although it was not clear whether this was
because he was so shocked or because he thought the President
would feel less embarrassed if carelessness verging on slapstick
appeared to be a Downing Street habit. Blotting paper, napkins
and towels were rushed in, and eventually Nixon was taken out
to nailbrushes and pumice stones. They were unavailing. After a
long interval he came back with his hands still stained. It was a
real Lady Macbeth scene, and it completely ruined his concentration.
He could do nothing but look at them for the rest of the morning.
His brilliance was all gone. The discussion never regained any verve
and was adjourned early. He somewhat recovered his composure
over lunch.

Before his next appearance with us the resources of the travelling
field laundry or whatever accompanies the President had proved adequate for at dinner he was spotless and once again on very good form.
He made an excellent speech partly welcoming ex-left-wing-weekly
editor John Freeman, whom Wilson had just appointed to Washington
after four years as High Commissioner in Delhi, and suggesting that as
Freeman became the old diplomat he (Nixon) would endeavour to be
'the new statesman'.

The festivities were rounded off by a little post-prandial charade
which Wilson had organised in the Cabinet room. All members, those
who had not been at dinner as well as those who had, were required to
be present and perform for the benefit of the visitors, as though they
were taking part in a real Cabinet. Some of us, notably Crosland and
I, were I am afraid a little sullen or shy about doing our pirouettes, but
we were more than made up for by Crossman and Benn, who put on
bravura performances. Crossman at least struck some rather mordant
political paradoxes while Benn trilled away about sputniks and Bible
readings. The President took up what was perhaps the only possible
polite position, looked amazed that 'two little heads could know so

much', and expressed suitable admiration to the Prime Minister about the brilliance of his Cabinet.

Meanwhile, as I discovered when I got back to No. 11, Jennifer had had the British Special Branch and the American Secret Service streaming through her drawing room because our son Edward (aged fourteen) had decided to make an expedition across the roofs of No. 11 and No. 10 Downing Street and had created a security panic. It was all that was needed to complete the gaiety of the day.

Two months later, on my post-Budget American visit, I delivered a successful address to a 2000-strong audience of the Economic Club of New York (it is curious how persuasive orations explaining failure can sometimes be); I had a long *al fresco* meeting in the White House rose garden with the President; and I established a good relationship with David Kennedy, the nice but naïve Secretary of the Treasury. He took me to Camp David for twenty-four hours. While we were there we received the news of de Gaulle's unexpected defeat in his minor constitutional referendum and his consequent resignation.

For a day or so sterling held up against this (which aroused new fears of a French devaluation) better than we had expected. The fears were then reinforced by rumours of an impending German revaluation, and while the reality of this had been regarded as essential for the survival of sterling in November, the threat of it was damaging in May. It was one more proof of the fact that once a currency has been knocked down into the gutter almost any subsequent event is another vehicle which swishes by and prevents it rising to its feet. In any event, Friday, 2 May, was a bad day and Friday, 9 May, a very bad one, with a loss of over $200 million. But it was a week later, Friday, 16 May, that is imprinted on my memory as the nadir day of my whole Treasury experience. The crisis was private and not public, and arose, not from the violence of the storm, for I had seen worse, but from my new inability, already mentioned, to see any way out of it.

The external events of the day were almost a caricature of routineness. At 10.00 I attended a little regular hebdomadal 10 Downing Street meeting jocularly known as 'prayers', at which the Prime Minister, the Foreign Secretary, the leader of the House of Commons, the chief whip and I endeavoured to foresee the pitfalls of the following parliamentary week. At 10.30 I received the Governor of the Bank of England for his regular Friday call. While he certainly brought no great message of cheer, I do not think that on this particular occasion he had any fresh horrors to impart. Later I took the 1.15 train from Euston to Birmingham. At 3.00 I opened a so-called international week – a good multiracial venture – in Sparkbrook. Then I adjourned to the Grand Hotel (unusual, for the Midland Hotel was my habitual Central Birmingham base) and saw first Denis Howell MP, who brought a canon of the cathedral, and then Sir Frank Price, a former Labour Lord Mayor and chairman of numerous Midlands and national public bodies. From 6.30 to 7.30 I did my monthly advice bureau at the East Birmingham Trades and Labour Club. Accompanied to the train, as was his supportive habit, by George Canning, my agent and later chairman and later still Lord Mayor of Birmingham, I caught the 7.55 from New Street Station to Didcot. It was not a great train, looking more like a bus, but it had a little empty first-class section in the front, and in this as soon as I had pulled up the window from talking to George Canning I settled down, by prior arrangement with myself, to a hundred minutes of intensive ratiocination.

I fairly quickly came to certain broad conclusions. The first was that unless the trade figures for May and June showed a decisive improvement the strategy which we had pursued since devaluation would have failed, both in reality and in appearance. New policies would be inevitable, and these would involve a pound floating heavily down, blocking measures against the sterling balances and indeed against the convertibility into dollars of all foreign holdings of sterling, a severe restriction of imports and a further assault on consumption (in order to push resources into exports), this time involving a substantial reduction and not merely a holding of the standard of living. It would also, I decided, require a new Chancellor of the Exchequer. Having set my hand for eighteen months to a strategy which had not worked, I did not see how I could create or deserve the authority to impose a new one on the country. All the analyses and predictions I had made in the preceding eighteen months would undermine the force of any fresh leadership which I endeavoured to give.

I was also doubtful whether the Government as a whole, however reconstituted, could do it. We had been massively behind in the polls for a year or more. We lost every bye-election in sight. We had just been slaughtered in the local elections. The authority of the Prime Minister was at a peculiarly low ebb. And yet the fragility of the Government was such that I did not feel he could be replaced without the upheaval proving fatal. If a new strategy were attempted the opposition would say that the need for further sacrifices arose, not from the inherent difficulties of the position, but from the ineffectiveness of the Government. Most of the country would believe them, and where would our moral authority then come from? There are times when a government needs more than a majority in the House of Commons, and it seemed to me that such a conjuncture might be fast approaching.

I also had a sneaking fear that one part at least of the opposition case might, almost by accident, have validity. It was not that their economic criticisms had coherence or constructiveness. They did not. But if our post-devaluation policy, like our pre-devaluation policy, ended in near disaster, it might well be that the country could escape with less hardship under a new government. If we had to float, confidence as much as reality would determine the point to which we floated down. I could therefore see looming up the dilemma which, at least since 1931, every non-doctrinaire Labour politician had probably most dreaded: a clear short-term conflict between the interests of the country and those of the party. To go in one direction might mean unnecessary national hardship, to go in the other might involve the near destruction for a generation of the Labour Party, in which I still had great faith, as an instrument of government. I then had no desire to participate in a coalition, which many people were advocating. It was merely that I could begin to see, as an added complication in a web of gloom, the emergence of a case for it.

However, I decided that these musings, and in particular the thought that, by July, I might have become a used-up Chancellor, were no more than indulgent self-dramatisation unless I set down some hard criteria by which the outcome was to be judged. For May and June, I said, we must achieve current account balance. A good deal more would be most welcome, and was long overdue. But that was the minimum. But how was current account balance to be measured? The outturn for invisibles, which was then always favourable, would not be known until September. I must make some allowance for it, but not too much: £35 million a month was a likely hypothesis, although I decided that this should be adjusted up or down according to what was the actual result for the first quarter, which would be known in June. The likely assumption would allow a visible deficit for the two months combined of £70 million. Up to that figure was just permissible. Above it, the signs of failure must be recognised as unmistakable.

I wrote these simple figures down on a piece of paper which I still have, and having done so felt rather easier in my mind, as perhaps do those who have just completed writing a suicide note. The criteria I was setting seemed at the time to be strict, although by no means impossible. The average trade deficit for most recent pairs of months was about £110 million. I therefore pinned my fate to an improvement of £40 million over the two months. However, having done so, I got out of the train at Didcot with perhaps a touch of Sydney Carton's scaffold hubris in *A Tale of Two Cities*, but also with more buoyancy than I had got into it at Birmingham.

This new fatalistic mood enabled me to cease fretting about the balance of payments and to pay some belated attention to Barbara Castle's industrial relations activities. It also produced a dramatic change in the run of the cards. All the ill luck began to correct itself, as surely but belatedly as does a period of exceptional weather. The first turn came on the evening of Thursday, 29 May, in the Whitsun holiday, when David Dowler rang me at East Hendred to announce that a combination of Customs and Excise and the Board of Trade statisticians had just reported the uncovering of an underestimate of exports, going back over several years, but building up and amounting recently to between £16 million and £20 million a month. It was dramatic news. Monthly trade figures improved by this amount would have transformed our lives during the previous year.

In consultation with Wilson and Crosland it was decided to play the revelation fairly coolly. Crosland, I think wisely, was particularly in favour of this playing down, which became easier to embrace when we knew that the trade figures for May, even on the old basis, were very good. We published our discovery as little more than a quiet footnote to them. Even so, it rightly attracted a moderate amount of attention, which was increased, as was the favourable confidence reaction, when I underlined the significance in a speech (distributed well in advance to the Sunday newspapers) delivered in the rather surprising ambience of a Labour open-air fête, presided over by Angus Wilson (later to be my predecessor as President of the Royal Society of Literature), at Bury St Edmunds on Saturday, 23 June. The issue resurfaced briefly in early November, when Anthony Barber, supported by Heath and Macleod with the almost incredible unwisdom which sometimes afflicts frustrated oppositions, decided to accuse us of falsifying the defalsification. The result was the nearest I ever got from the Government bench to a repeat of the Blake debate of 1966 (but still some way off it) and a Garland Guy Fawkes Day cartoon which I still treasure (and which is reproduced following page 274).

The visible deficit for May was only £13 million. The invisible surplus for the first quarter was at the rate of £50 million a month against the £35 million I had been expecting. With the publication of these two figures and the uncovering of the error the Bank of England began to take in foreign exchange quite heavily. The replenishment of the appalling losses of the previous two years seriously began. The June trade figures were almost as good as the May ones, with a deficit of no more than £20 million. As against the overall bare balance which I had stipulated for May and June the outcome was therefore a surplus of £67 million. The improvement of £40 million for which I had looked on my Birmingham/Didcot train journey had become one of £107 million.

The suicide note could therefore be withdrawn without weakening. Indeed, so far from having to arrange resignation in mid-July, I was able to announce on the 18th of that month that we had improved our foreign exchange reserves by a net figure of almost exactly $1 billion since the beginning of the year. There was still a nasty engagement to come, but it was much more comparable with the 1944 Battle of the Bulge than with March 1918, when the Allied line was hurled back to the threshold of Paris.

The Germans, as on both these occasions, were once again expected to be the cause of the trouble even if in a more peaceful and beneficent way. Their federal elections were due on 28 September, and the uncertainty associated with them was thought likely to upset our poor nervous sterling. However, they were pre-empted by the French, who had learned from their November experience not to hawk their devaluation around from conference to conference (to paraphrase Ernest Bevin) and who acted without any notice to anybody on Friday, 8 August, thereby turning what was expected to be a seven-day period of currency excitement into a seven-week one.

I was on holiday in the Var, where we had taken an attachment to the house of Freddie and Dee Ayer, near Le Beausset. Although this might have been thought to put me near to the scene of action, it in fact made me one of the last people in Europe with any financial responsibility to hear about it. When French devaluation was announced at 8.00 p.m. we were on our way to dinner in a remote restaurant which appeared to have neither telephone nor wireless. When we got back at 11.00 there were messages in French English from a neighbour awaiting us. One said, 'We, the French, have devalued our franc.' The other said that M. Giscard d'Estaing (who had replaced Couve de Murville, who had replaced Ortoli, as Finance Minister) and Mr Dowler had telephoned. Dowler, not unnaturally, was more persistent than a preoccupied Giscard, who had done his duty by one attempt to reach me. David and I agreed that all we could do was to make it clear that there was no question of a move on our part and hope for the best when markets opened on Monday morning. Unfortunately, as nearly always when we least needed them, we had mildly disappointing (July) trade figures in the pipeline for publication in the following week. By the standards of a year before, they were rather good – a deficit of £37 million, which with invisibles was equivalent to a small overall surplus – but they were worse than those for May or June.

To understand the next few days it has to be appreciated what a different telephone age it was before direct international dialling came in. One began by getting the exchange at Le Castellet, which then tried, via Toulon, to get London, which then dialled Whitehall 1234 for the Treasury. This often involved a delay of an hour or more, at the end of which one mostly could not hear very well and was liable to be cut off at any moment. From the other end it was somewhat better but not much.

On the Monday the market was weak, but not dramatically so. On the Tuesday it was worse, and the Bank at upper-middle level (the

Governor was away, like me) made an extraordinary decision to let the rate rather than the reserves take the strain. As a result it dipped below what we regarded as the conventional floor of $2.38.25 and closed at $2.38.17. This I had never allowed to happen in London (there had been one or two such slippages in New York) and was furious, both because I thought the Bank had acted (or not acted) without adequate consultation with the official Treasury and because I feared it might be taken as a sign that we were no longer determined to maintain the central rate of $2.40 (with 1 per cent margins either way).

This fear was misplaced. The market interpretation was the opposite, but it led, in combination with my attempt at remote steering, to almost equally unfortunate results. It was assumed that the Bank knew of very good trade figures and in its infinite subtlety was enticing market operators into one of its famous but rarely achieved bear squeezes. When the trade figures were announced at noon on the Wednesday they were received with incredulity. In combination with my instruction that the rate was to be put back to the mystical $2.38.25 they produced a haemorrhage worthy of the great days of 1968. By lunchtime I decided that my attempt to drive from the back seat, which in this case meant on a bad telephone line from the South of France, was not a success and that the power of decision, provided they kept in close touch with Frank Figgures (who was in charge in the Treasury) and did not go near to $2.38, should be restored to the Bank. We ended the day at $2.38.11 and minus $247 million.

For some reason or other all our nerves were bad during this August flurry. Mine were especially agitated by my being stuck away. I longed to go back to London, but could not do so without the near certainty that the news of my return would provoke another wave of panic selling of sterling. I occasionally bounced down the ten kilometres or so to the little *calanque* where we used to swim, but more to kill time before the next telephone call than to enjoy myself. However, I was far from being alone in my edginess. There were plenty of other frayed tempers and judgements in the Bank and the Treasury. This was not wholly rational, both because there was substantial evidence that the balance of payments really had turned, and because following the stabilisation of the sterling balances we had worked out a convincing equation which showed that we now had more resources available than there was free money which could move out of sterling. But these considerations were outweighed by our nerves having become like those of many people in London during the flying-bomb raids of the summer of 1944 – a number of military similes seemed apposite in 1969. The real Blitz of 1940–1 had been much worse, but that had been expected. The V-1s were rattling because they came when victory was thought almost to have arrived. It was much the same in that August of 1969. In June and July we had got used to taking in money and believing that the worst was well behind us. We were distinctly unamused by paying it out again and facing the possibility, if not of defeat, at least of further privations and casualties.

On the Friday we decided that if I could not go back to London David Dowler had better come out and see me. He said that there was a special factor of which he wished to inform me and which he did not think he could easily express either in writing or in an open telephone call, even though, under the stresses of the previous few days, we had shouted some pretty sensitive secrets over the extremely weak line between London and Le Beausset. He got to Marseille early on the Saturday evening and the whole Jenkins family plus the William Rodgerses who were staying in the neighbourhood went in and dined with him at a restaurant on the Vieux Port. But before the restaurant he and I had an intensive hour in a dark corner of a bar alongside the old Hôtel Beauvau, where he was staying.

The import of the special message was that he was worried by an unexpected onset of Treasury defeatism. If French devaluation caused this degree of turbulence, they were doubtful whether we should hold the rate through what was expected to be the much worse storm of a hesitant German shuffle towards revaluation. It might be better to float than to incur further heavy liabilities to get through this period. I, as he rightly divined, was violently opposed to this approach. It might have been better to have floated in November 1967. It might have been necessary but unpleasant to have floated if the balance of payments had failed to come right in mid-summer 1969. But to float (and float down) in the autumn of 1969, when we had at last got our surplus as a result of vast efforts, and thus to throw away victory just when we were achieving it, seemed to me the height of perversity. So long as we had resources left, and there was every indication that we now had enough, I was resolved to defend a rate which had shown itself to be defensible by its results. And I was fortified by the experience of the summer having shown that money so expended came back quickly enough when the storm was weathered.

This information made me more eager than ever to get back to London. Fortunately Wilson, who in those days much preferred activity to holidays, provided me with the perfect excuse. He called a Cabinet for Tuesday afternoon, 19 August, to consider the new wave of trouble in Northern Ireland. From that meeting there stemmed more than twenty years of military commitment, which should perhaps be set rather heavily in the balance against the value of a temporary smokescreen for me. But for the moment I was more concerned with the latter. I got to London on the Monday evening and had Douglas Allen to a long dinner at Boodle's club. It was for both of us an improbable locale and arose only because Brooks's was closed and I therefore had temporary rights of use. But it was a very valuable dinner. He fortified me by expounding in detail the theory that we now had more resources than there could be strains put upon them, and I had no difficulty in getting his assurance that he accepted my determination to use them to defend the rate.

I had meetings with Jack Diamond, with the Governor of the Bank and with Frank Figgures the following day, as well as attending the fateful Cabinet in a somewhat preoccupied mood, and was ready by the Wednesday morning to go back to France for another week. I flew to Paris and took a fine train called *Le Mistral* from the Gare de Lyon to Toulon. The French countryside smiled under the late-summer sunshine, *wagon restaurant* food was still good and I congratulated myself on having seen that the best way to rejuvenate a stressful holiday was to break it.

Back in London before the end of the month, I found the mood still nervous if no longer panicky. On 2 September Cecil King resurfaced with a long jeremiad in *The Times* saying that the universal feeling in the City was that on present policies and under the present Government there was now no prospect of ever getting the balance of payments right. But by then King's sense of timing had become almost infallibly wrong: 2 September was the exact day when hesitant balance turned into headlong surplus. I was at East Hendred when David Hancock telephoned me with the news that the August export figures had shown a sensational jump. On top of a good July performance they were up by another £70 million. The import figures, available six days later, also behaved loyally. We had a visible trade surplus of £40 million, certainly the first I had ever announced and almost the first (admittedly only on a one-month basis) since some time in the 1870s or 1880s. With invisibles this gave a current account surplus at an annual rate of over £1000 million.

However, such was the degree of apprehension about the German hippopotamus getting into the water that it did no more than steady the market. On the following Saturday I had Allen and Figgures to East Hendred to help entertain Paul Volcker, later to bestride the Federal Reserve System like a colossus from 1979 to 1987 and at the time under-secretary of the US Treasury. He was duly impressed by our trade figures, but nonetheless thought that sterling (and the dollar) would have the most appalling time at the end of the month. I was oppressed by his pessimism and retaliated by taking him for a walk on the sodden Downs. I did not realise that he had no possibility of changing his rather thin shoes before going that evening to Covent Garden. For the moment he became a colossus with very damp feet. Surprisingly, this formidable but modest man has ever since treated me with the greatest possible consideration.

On 22 September I departed on a ten-day transatlantic visit. I had a Commonwealth Finance Ministers' conference in Barbados as well as the annual Bank/Fund meeting in Washington to attend. But before either of these I had a preliminary Washington visit to assemble support from the American Government and the IMF against the rough weather at the end of the month. Oddly, as it seemed, they were both at least as eager to provide the money as we were to have it available. Schweitzer was enthusiastic about putting together a package, and David Kennedy at the end of a very long and ill-organised meeting which meandered on for nearly five hours, including a desultory dinner, made it clear that plenty of US money would be available. All this should have made me realise that the fears for the end of the month were exaggerated, for it is almost as invariable a rule of international as of personal finance that money is easy to get when you do not need it and difficult when you do.

Nevertheless the prophets of doom, American just as much as British, were so insistent that they had to be taken seriously. On the day we were due to go to Barbados (Wednesday, 24 September) the Germans suspended foreign exchange dealings in Frankfurt. Was this to be the signal for the unleashing of the storm? If so, ought we to be marooned in a Caribbean resort? We got the consul-general in New York to arrange a special conference/telephoning/information room at Kennedy Airport, through which we had to pass. When we got there the European markets had closed calmly and New York was following suit. Had I turned up late or not at all for the Commonwealth Finance Ministers I would have looked incredibly foolish. As it was we were able to spend a not very exciting three days in Barbados. But when we returned to Washington on the Saturday night we were still only on the eve of the German elections. Were they going to ignite the fuse, or had it gone happily damp?

We never knew, for the fuse was pulled out before the match was put to it. Old Karl Blessing, the President of the Bundesbank, whose international monetary experience went back to the setting up of the Bank of International Settlement at Basle in 1931, volunteered to call on me in the British Embassy at 3.30 on the Sunday afternoon. It was a real mission of mercy. Accompanied by Leslie O'Brien, I saw him in the library at the top of the stairs. If the receipt of the August trade figures marked the victory of substance, this represented the news that the armistice was signed and that the war really was over. (It had not of course been in any way a war against the Germans, who, the Bonn conference apart, had been one of our more helpful partners, but against our own weakness.)

What Blessing came to say was that he saw a long interregnum ahead in which he would have no political masters. He did not wish speculation in favour of the D-mark to disfigure the international monetary scene during this period. He had seen too much currency trouble in his time to wish to add to it. He therefore proposed, on his own responsibility, to let the D-mark float up until there was a new German government. It could then be pegged at a higher level. This would remove both the point and the damage of speculative flows into Frankfurt. I was grateful, both for the advantages of an independent central bank (without wishing too many ideas to be put into Leslie O'Brien's mind) and for the sensitivity which had made Blessing come and tell me this.

That evening I had a happy Embassy dinner party. John and Catherine Freeman were at the peak of their considerable Washington success, and *inter alia* they procured for me Dean and Alice Acheson, Joe and Susan-Mary Alsop, Katharine Graham, Polly Kraft and Alice Longworth, Theodore Roosevelt's still coruscating daughter. The next day was routine. On the Tuesday I made a much more successful IMF plenary session speech than at the previous year's meeting, and became only temporarily intimidated when I got on the plane to London at Dulles Airport and suddenly realised that in less than twelve hours I was due to be on my feet at the Labour Party conference in Brighton to reply to a debate which would start at 4.30 a.m. Washington time, and that I had nothing approaching a complete speech for this important occasion. By dint of working throughout the short night John Harris and I got it into shape, and I had a better reception than the previous year. Even in the sometimes perverse Labour Party, there was nothing which succeeded like success. By 12.50 p.m., or 7.50 a.m. Washington time, it was over and I was in the bar of the Grand Hotel, Brighton, savouring a well-deserved dry martini and one of the best moments of my chancellorship.

On the balance of payments front nothing went wrong for the remainder of 1969. The September trade figures were almost as good as the August ones and we ended the year in massive surplus. Money began to pour back in and we more than repaid all the debts which had been incurred.

In spite of this dramatic turn-round, which meant that the limited but central purpose of my Treasury regime had been achieved, 1969 ended sadly. David Dowler left on 13 November, having been with me, in three departments, for nearly five years. It was well up to the maximum for which a civil servant of the highest quality should ever serve one master if he is not going to become too much his creature to be good for anything else.

This was a point which Hayden Phillips was to put to me with irrefutable force in Brussels in 1978. He was with me for exactly the same length of time as Dowler. Although there are great differences of appearance and personality, Phillips came a decade later to occupy a position similar enough to Dowler's in my pantheon that I now sometimes take a moment to recall which unravelled which impossible knot or relieved which moment of gloom with which joke.

Dowler went back to the Home Office, promoted at the age of thirty-nine to be the youngest under-secretary in Whitehall, and was replaced by the admirable (Sir) William Ryrie, who stayed until the end of my time as Chancellor and is now head of the World Bank's International Finance Corporation subsidiary.

The sadness of Dowler's departure lay in much more than the inconvenience of losing a private secretary on whom I had grown to depend heavily. Within two weeks of taking up his new job he became ill. It began as an unspecified viral infection. A week after that I went to see him in hospital and was deeply disturbed by his condition and by an uneasy feeling that neither great skill nor great urgency was being applied to his treatment. The day after that I began to develop pneumonia. It was the only time that I was significantly ill during the six years of that Government, and it abstracted my mind for the next week or so. I have always feared that this may have made a difference to Dowler's fate. By the time I had recovered he had been properly diagnosed and transferred to highly specialised care at the Hammersmith Hospital. But a vital ten days had been lost. He was suffering from a general septicaemia (which may have originated from a lacerating encounter with the lock of one of my 'boxes' in America) which had affected the heart valves and which could be countered only by a dangerous operation, from which he never recovered consciousness and died after sixteen days on 8 January.

By then I was in the United States to which I had arranged a celebratory and British trumpet-blowing visit to mark the turn-round in the balance of payments. Having gone there so often in supplicatory and almost desperate circumstances it seemed reasonable to go for once when conditions were almost unprecedentedly favourable. Accompanied by Douglas Allen, and also by Harris and Ryrie, I made speeches in San Francisco, Chicago and New York, as well as doing the major Sunday political television programme. The celebratory aspects of the visit were hopelessly marred by the tragedy of David Dowler, the poignancy increased by the fact that he had frequently participated in and indeed organised visits over similar terrain. He had been a remarkable private secretary, critical in judgement and mordant in phrase, yet devotedly loyal, and willing, despite the speed at which he transacted business, to work immensely long hours. He was very good at seeing the dangers around the next corner, or even the next corner but one. He was probably not easy to work under, for his standards were high and his patience not notable, but he worked up superbly. I owe to him a great part of such success as I was able to achieve as a minister in that first Wilson Government. Shortly before he went under the anaesthetic for his fatal operation (and being fully aware of the risks) he went out of his way to tell me that whatever the outcome he would not have wished to spend the past five years in any other way.

The problem which became acute over the turn of the year 1969–70 was that of wage inflation. The form which it took was to a considerable extent a result of the sad failure of Mrs Castle's trade union policy. She had produced her bold scheme at the beginning of 1969. I had attended a special meeting of a small group of ministers on 2 January, which had been followed by an all-day Cabinet on 3 January. I strongly supported her proposals, but from these early meetings onwards argued that the very leisurely timetable advocated by both her and Wilson was a mistake. The plan was to publish only a discussion document in the current session and not to legislate until 1969–70. I thought that this was presentationally bad. If the matter was as vital as she argued, then it must also be urgent. Still more strongly, however, I thought that it was a dangerous approach. Trade union reform, particularly for a Labour government, was so sensitive that it could be carried through only on the run. Delay would almost certainly provide an opportunity for the rats to get at the package. I got some Cabinet sympathy for this view, but not nearly enough to overcome the different view of the responsible Secretary of State backed by the Prime Minister.

At the end of March Mrs Castle changed her mind, and between us we persuaded the Prime Minister to do the same. I think that first she and then he were swayed by the increasingly open challenge which a rejuvenated James Callaghan was mounting against the whole enterprise. On 26 March Callaghan had carried a critical resolution through the National Executive Committee of the Labour Party. The prospect of his building up from this to and through the Trades Union Congress in September and the Labour Party Conference in October, with the issue still unresolved, was hardly an encouraging one.

Wilson was in Nigeria until 2 April, but within twenty-four hours of his return Mrs Castle and I had three meetings with him. During them it was agreed that I would announce in my Budget speech (due on 15 April) that an interim Industrial Relations Bill would be pushed through in the current parliamentary session. In return for this I agreed also to announce that the full rigour of the Prices and Incomes legislation would not be renewed in the autumn. I thought, mistakenly, that this was a good bargain.

The last of our triad of Wilson/Castle/Jenkins meetings was held immediately before the temporarily famous Maundy Thursday Cabinet of that year. The Prime Minister told us several times before this how roughly he was going to denounce Callaghan in front of his colleagues for his gross disloyalty. In fact he completely failed to do so, but compensated by assembling a meeting of parliamentary lobby correspondents immediately afterwards and telling them, who told the nation, that he had, with the result that his private failure became an apparent public success. But Callaghan, it remains imprinted on my mind, excoriated minister although he was portrayed as being, was televised that evening walking through the crowds at Victoria Station to his Sussex train with a defiant dignity which made me realise how formidable a politician, freed of the incubus of the Exchequer, he had become.

The memorable events of that pre-Budget Easter holiday were continued on the following Tuesday with a tripartite early evening and dinner conclave at East Hendred when Mrs Castle was so shocked by both Jennifer's 'old skirt and plimsolls' and 'domesticated' (sic) fare[2] in what Richard Crossman regarded as 'a rather ramshackle old vicarage'.[3] However, despite these deprivations they stuck to the arrangements and the Budget Cabinet on 14 April approved my announcement of early legislation with only the odd combination of Callaghan and Richard Marsh (who now seems a surprising defender of unfettered trade union rights) dissenting.

For the next four weeks, as I explained at the beginning of this chapter, I was too preoccupied with my own troubles to have much time for Mrs Castle's. By mid-May however two developments had taken place. First, Wilson's leadership had come under even more criticism than in the previous year, and this time there was no Cecil King in a position to throw him an unintended lifeline. This had the result of putting me under great pressure to abandon Mrs Castle's bill. The right of the party was mostly more opposed to Wilson's leadership than it was in favour of *In Place of Strife*. Tom Bradley told me several times that the bill was the only thing standing between me and the premiership. The party, he said, desperately wanted a change of leader, but it did not want either the Industrial Relations Bill or Callaghan. Others, however, indicated that Callaghan was gaining ground, partly through his opposition to the bill, and I could no longer assume that I was the favourite son of the anti-Wilsonites.

Nevertheless I was not tempted to renege on the bill in order to replace Wilson. Apart from anything else, this would be fatal for the future. The real count against Wilsonism was that it was opportunistic and provided leadership by manoeuvre and not by direction. To replace him by outdoing his own deficiencies would make a discreditable nonsense of the whole enterprise.

The second development was that Wilson and Mrs Castle had got themselves deeply involved in a series of negotiations of almost Byzantine complication with a variety of trade union leaders. The issues became so convoluted that I ceased to follow them, and was dismayed when an attempt was made to draw me into the centre of the web. Wilson had arranged a semi-secret Chequers dinner with Vic Feather, Jack Jones and Hugh Scanlon for Sunday, 1 June. Mrs Castle was due to be in Italy, where she and Crossman with their families had planned a Whitsun holiday on a yacht. Wilson, who was always good about other people's holidays – and she desperately needed one – urged her to stick to her plans, saying that he would ask me to the dinner in her stead and as a sort of guardian of her intransigence. I reluctantly agreed, but to my relief she changed her mind and flew back to be present herself.

Even this truncated holiday was a disaster for the bill. It put her on to thoroughly bad terms with Crossman ('I knew he was an intellectual bully, but I did not know before that he was a social one as well,' she wrote),[4] whose support was crucially necessary, and led to a damaging loss of momentum at home. The papers were full of negotiations, but without guidance as to what concessions had to be made by the TUC. The expectation of a settlement became almost universal, and nearly everybody lost their stomach for a fight. This might not have mattered if the TUC had been moving towards substantial concessions. But they were not. They decided they had the interior lines of communication, dug in and waited for the investing forces to disintegrate.

On Thursday, 5 June, when we dined at the Christopher Mayhews with the Gordon Walkers and Marquands (as dedicated a band of desperados from the right of the Labour Party as one could hope to assemble) I said that I thought the moment when we could have won the *In Place of Strife* battle was past. Delay had allowed too great a wave of desertions to build up. There was dismay but no real dissent around the table.

The collapse, however, did not come until twelve days later. The Cabinet met all morning, during which every erstwhile supporter of the Castle/Wilson line, except for Jack Diamond and me, fell away. It then adjourned until 4.30 p.m. I had Ronald McIntosh, a very old friend who was then one of the deputy secretaries to the Cabinet, to lunch in 11 Downing Street. He knew that I had lost my faith in the ability of the Government to put the legislation through, and upbraided me for having remained so silent during the morning. I owed it to the Cabinet, he over-flatteringly said, to tell them what I thought.

What I thought was that dilatory tactics had predictably produced a build-up of opposition which now meant that there was more chance of the Government breaking up on the issue than of getting the legislation through. I did not want a Government smash and I therefore thought that we had no alternative but to retreat, no doubt pretending that the retreat was a compromise. But Wilson and Mrs Castle, badly though they had mishandled the tactics, were now showing signs of desperate courage, and it was humiliating to desert them.

Partly to salve my conscience I decided to have another of my face-to-face encounters with Mrs Castle. We met at 4.00 and I told her that I could not repeat my silence of the morning, of the meaning of which she must have been aware. She indicated that she was so aware, did not recriminate, but accepted the news like St Sebastian receiving another arrow.

At the resumed Cabinet Wilson behaved with a touch of King Lear-like nobility. He sounded fairly unhinged at times and there was a wild outpouring of words. But he did not hedge and he did not whine. He left us in uncertainty about what he was going to do the next day, with resignation accompanied by denunciation of everybody, the TUC, the Cabinet and the parliamentary Labour Party, sounding a real possibility. Yet we could not quite believe it, and we proved to be right. The next day he patched up the 'solemn and binding' cosmetic deal with the TUC and presented it to the Cabinet and the country as a tolerable outcome. But he, and even more Mrs Castle, knew that it was not. It was a sad story from which he and Barbara Castle emerged with more credit than the rest of us.

# CHAPTER SIXTEEN

# *Defeat Out of the Jaws of Victory*

Back in London from America in mid-January 1970 I got down to the usual three months of Budget preparation. Even before Christmas it had become apparent to me that the 1970 Budget was in its way going to be just as difficult as the two preceding ones. There was no problem this time of having to search around for new net increases in taxation. Government accounts and the balance of payments were both in substantial surplus. But there was a great problem of the disappointment of high expectations. The 'two years' hard slog', the need for which I had proclaimed in 1968, was successfully over, and even had it not been an election year (which it almost certainly was, although the spring of 1971 was a technical possibility) there were many people, both inside and outside the House of Commons, who would have looked for a bonanza. With an election pending, they regarded it as a certainty.

Yet there was not much room for this. The economy looked in reasonable balance without a stimulus, and one (although in an undesirable form) was in any event being provided by the more rapid rate of wage increase which had started with a dustmen's settlement in October and gathered momentum with nurses, teachers and gas workers over the turn of the year. Furthermore I had sweated much too hard to turn the balance of payments (and it had happened only just before the resources ran out) to be willing to put it all at risk by a give-away Budget, which in any event I regarded as a vulgar piece of economic management below the level of political sophistication of the British electorate.

The official Treasury took this view 'with knobs on'. They became in my view somewhat obsessed by 1964 guilt. Douglas Allen took the opportunity of a long plane journey in America to pour this into John Harris's ear, obviously for transmission to me. He felt that William Armstrong had behaved weakly in his restraint of Maudling in the spring and summer of that pre-election splurge and balance of payments disaster, and he was determined not to repeat this fault in his 1970 dealings with me.

Up to a point this was reasonable, but the danger was that it would lead him into the opposite fault of giving such austere advice that it would be counter-productive, particularly if he accompanied it with an unwonted self-righteousness which made him treat all politicians (but I was in practice the only one with whom he had to deal) as profligate pariahs. This surfaced only briefly and produced the single real hiccup in my relations with the outstanding Allen during the two and a quarter years of great external strain which we spent together as Chancellor and permanent secretary. At a Treasury strategy meeting on 15 January he assumed a gruff and growling manner which made me feel that I was a flighty young minister being reproved by Sir John Anderson, except that Douglas did not look much like 'Jehovah', as that eminence was known in Whitehall.

I was not having this from Douglas, of whom apart from anything else I was much too fond for this sort of arm's-length stuff, and sent him a message by Ryrie saying that I resented this hostility and that if he thought this was the way to influence me he was making a grave mistake. As a result he came at his request to see me alone a few days later, half apologised, and thereafter behaved with perfect good feeling. It was accepted between us that I was going to be a little, but not much, more generous than he wanted, but that, provided we did not diverge too far, neither of us was going to get too upset at a constant friendly tug-of-war.

In fact the 1970 Budget as it eventually emerged was more restrictive than perfect economic foresight would have made it. Had I still been Chancellor, I would have thought it right to do some loosening in the autumn. But, contrary to popular myth, it caught the political mood better than a more generous Budget would have done, and I therefore did not (and do not) feel that Treasury caution was in any way responsible for the Labour defeat in the 1970 election.

On 30 January at the annual dinner of the Leeds Chamber of Commerce I attempted a deliberate dampening down of expectations. A Chancellor, I said, ought to be judged not by what he did on one day in April but by his general control of the economy over the year as a whole. This was a pretty good indication that I did not expect many popular plaudits for the Budget and it was treated as such in the substantial newspaper reports the next morning, which led to a wholly desirable change in the climate of expectation. Typically, the large, prosperous but adequately responsive audience appeared to miss the import of this passage and were more attentive to some general bits of economic guff.

The January trade figures (published in mid-February) worked against this new mood of realism. With a £39 million surplus on visible trade alone, they were dangerously good. Such are the gusts of short-term fashion that nearly all commentators, including those who had been hopelessly defeatist six months before, spent the early spring treating the balance of payments problems as solved for the foreseeable future. (This did not prevent their swinging back to treat the chance deterioration which came in May as a major threat.) Naturally this mood spilled over into the Cabinet. Crosland led the view that I ought to control the surplus, and Callaghan on one occasion suggested that I announce I was going to hold it at £100 million a year, despite the years of deficit which needed to be balanced. Fortunately these unrealistic views never got off the ground. They were unrealistic because the idea that one could measure out the surplus like a grocer with a cheese wire was ludicrous; and they were largely prevented from getting off the ground by the fact that the Prime Minister's arithmetical and non-ideological mind liked having the surplus as big as possible for electoral and debating reasons.

Nevertheless, for the first and only time in my chancellorship, I was genuinely relieved when the February trade figures showed a worse result. 'Thank God, they will help preserve a bit of realism,' I instinctively said to myself. On 8 March the whole Cabinet came together for a Chequers Sunday. The morning was devoted to a general political discussion, but after lunch there was a budgetary discussion, which I welcomed, although Wilson carefully reserved my position, saying that I should not open it and need not wind up unless I wished to do so (which I did).

As I thought might be the case, the Cabinet were all over the place, which made it easier for me to make my own decisions. Only Barbara Castle advocated a sweeping give-away Budget, although it has subsequently become clear from the Crossman *Diaries*, which also indicated the excitable pre-election political atmosphere of the time, that he too wanted this.*

I took Crosland back from the Chequers meeting and expounded

* He had written for 1 March: 'I talked to Harold on the telephone about Roy. . . . The P.M. was extremely alarmed by the posture Roy was adopting. Harold said, "Remember his attitude at that meeting of S[trategic] E[conomic] P[olicy] and how he turned down the suggestion that he might do a Maudling." I talked to Nicky Kaldor too, as we have all been constantly talking to each other, because of course Roy is omnipotent now. Harold can only pressure him. I believe the only sensible thing to do is for Harold to say to Roy, "Look, if you give me the right budget I will make you Foreign Secretary." Would that be practicable? I shall certainly put it to Harold when Barbara and I see him next week because the whole future of the Government depends on Roy. The Chancellor is inscrutable and remote. He knows very well what everybody is thinking but he is in two minds. He is certainly under pressure from the Treasury this way and that way but so far he has avoided any possible decision.'[1]

to him on the way my detailed Budget thoughts. Later, apart from
my regular pre-Budget fortnightly meetings with Wilson, I consulted
Healey and Barbara Castle as in previous years. This year I added
Willie Ross, the Secretary of State for Scotland, and at a very late
stage (9 April) Tony Benn, who, apart from Mrs Castle, Crosland
and myself, was the other principal economic minister. My object
was to involve a representative cross-section of the Cabinet, and thus
to minimise the risk of any dangerous build-up of opposition at the
meeting on the day before the Budget.

These 'consultations' proved a success, particularly with the new-
comers to the list, Ross and Benn. Such was the traditional aura of
Budget secrecy that the flattery of being bilaterally told produced
statements of agreement and assurances of support. The Prime Minister also accepted perfectly well that I was not going to 'give away'
more than about £150 million. Equally the Treasury had moved from
their early growling in favour of nothing at all to accepting that this
was a reasonable interpretation of iron chancellordom. I remember
that about mid-February Michael Posner, who was a very effective
Treasury economist (and personality), released a number of tensions
by returning to the Budget strategy group after a couple of weeks away
and suddenly saying something like: 'Well, of course, when one talks
about a neutral Budget, £100 million or so between friends is nothing
much to worry about.' There was a moment of mandarin consternation
followed by a general realisation that a happy phrase had resolved the
dispute between the official Treasury and me. By such methods of
scientific precision are Budget judgements arrived at.

Budget day was Tuesday, 14 April. The Budget Cabinet on the
Monday had gone smoothly in spite of the Castle/Crossman rumblings
in early March. Much of the discussion focused (adversely) on my
proposal to abolish the expensive-to-collect stamp duty on cheques.
It was a 1970 equivalent of the 1968 additional SET on rural hotels,
except that I did not make a concession. But it was of such little
importance that it provided an excellent safety valve.

The speech was the only one of my three which lasted under two
hours, but by a small margin. Again like 1968 it was delivered with
an uncrippling but nasty headache, although headaches were rare
occurrences with me. The early part, describing the improvements of
the past year, was received with great enthusiasm on the Government
benches, the latter part, outlining the proposals, with a good deal
less. I ended to only subdued cheers. As usual I sat in my House
of Commons room with John Harris and the private secretaries for
a half-hour drink afterwards, towards the end of which Tom Bradley
came in and said that he had been round the tearoom where the general
feeling was one of disappointment. This was discouraging, but there

was not much that I could do about it, so I took myself back to 11 Downing Street and got down to work on the television recording for that evening. Soon after dinner we received the first editions of the two newspapers, the *Daily Telegraph* and the *Daily Mirror*, which were always delivered to us at night. In their differing styles and from their differing points of view they were both favourable, more so than I had expected after Tom's gloomy report. So was the rest of the press the next morning. And so in a quiet way was the meeting of the parliamentary Labour Party in mid-morning. It was placid, and the general atmosphere here, and elsewhere as the week wore on, was one of anticlimax. I said to John Harris that there did not seem to be much force in the Tory attack. 'No,' he said with frankness rather than (for once) encouragement, 'there does not need to be because they are not frightened of the Budget.'

I hesitated over whether to go to Birmingham on the Friday evening for my monthly advice bureau. In Budget week it would have been reasonable to have cancelled. But I eventually decided that this was burying my head in the sand, and that I had better go. I was encouraged by the atmosphere in the East Birmingham Trades and Labour Club, as I was by a few stray comments during the East Hendred weekend. I began to feel that the Budget might have been better received by the public than by the vote-hungry parliamentary Labour Party.

On the Monday (20 April) I made a 3.30 statement on the future of the sixpence coin under decimalisation (which grave matter had been occupying the public mind at least as much as the Budget), and wound up the Budget debate at 9.30. On the Tuesday, after answering my monthly ration of parliamentary questions, I departed with Jennifer for a week's holiday in Ireland. I woke up the next morning in the Shelburne Hotel, Dublin, to be greeted by a satisfactorily early delivery of the London newspapers and the most extraordinary and encouraging news. The Harris Poll (not conducted by John) showed the Government ahead of the opposition (by two points) for the first time in over three years, with a substantial part of the change attributed to the Budget. In the *Daily Telegraph* Gallup still showed us a little behind, but having moved into a challenging position, and contained still more satisfactory indications of reactions to the Budget. Sixty-six per cent of those polled considered it fair, which was the highest rating since Gallup first began to ask the question in 1955. And the question whether or not I was doing a good job as Chancellor produced a result which had only once been surpassed (by Rab Butler in 1953) and once equalled (soberingly by Callaghan in 1966) since the question had first been asked in the early 1950s.

That sent me off in high morale on a tour of the sites, Dublin Castle,

Phoenix Park, Kilmainham Gaol, the General Post Office and the Curragh on which, in the political lifetime of my main biographical subject, Asquith, the hopes of an Anglo-Irish 'union of hearts' had died. After lunch by a peat fire in County Kildare we drove under an appropriate downpour via Tipperary to Cork. There we learned, without it detracting from my new-found enthusiasm for my Budget, that my Irish opposite number, Charles Haughey, who had very kindly said that he would come and greet me at the airport the day before, but had had to cancel because he had fallen off his horse, had been placed under arrest for gun-running, and superseded for the delivery of his Budget that afternoon by the Taoiseach, Jack Lynch. By comparison my relations with Harold Wilson seemed satisfactorily steady. We proceeded to an hotel at Ballylicky, where I was kept in touch by telephone and the English newspapers with the mounting mood of election fever which had seized Whitehall and Westminster following the publication of the two public opinion polls.

The morning after I returned to London (29 April) there was a meeting of the inner Cabinet (then called the Management Committee and about eleven-strong) at which Wilson opened a discussion, which he insisted was to be in no way conclusive, of an early election. He asked my opinion, which I declined to give, saying that I had been away for a week, but that I would reflect on it and give a considered view the following Monday. I must have sounded like Crosland. I then said that, having consulted Douglas Allen, I thought economic factors were neutral as between June and October; I would however be strongly against going on to the spring of 1971, not because I thought the economic indicators would go wrong, but because I thought a year's run-up would be bad for Government decision-making. Politically, I could see arguments both ways between June and October and thought we should at least wait and see the outcome of the 7 May local elections. So it was left.

Two days later, however, still before these elections, Wilson asked me to go and see him at short notice and began talking in a way that made clear to me, as indeed I pointed out to him, that he had gone over some sort of emotional divide. He was firmly off down the runway towards an early election and it would have required some dreadful news to get him to reverse engines. On that occasion, my recollection is, I neither encouraged nor discouraged him. However, a few hours in Birmingham on the following day, where I discovered enthusiasm and expectation, accompanied by very good local election results that night, were enough to infect me with Wilson's fever. I had another meeting with him on the Friday morning, by when it had become an accepted assumption between us that the election was to be in June.

If so, 18 June had long been the accepted day of the month. Wilson indeed claimed to have pencilled it in to a future diary as long ago as 1966. John Harris, however, had been strenuously urging upon me the claims of 11 June, so much so that I eventually sent him to see Wilson and argue his case direct. His main reason was what turned out to be the false one of fear of the Government being damaged by left-wing rioting at the Lords Test match against the South Africans. But this, he said, was buttressed by a sneaking fear that, after such a good run, the May trade figures, due to be published on 15 June, might be bad. Had he carried his point, who can tell what changes in the pattern of British politics over the years which have since gone by might not have followed?

As it was he was listened to but not heeded (by me as little as by Wilson), and when I next saw the Prime Minister, for a long post-dinner conversation on Wednesday, 13 May, 18 June was accepted as settled, with an announcement to be made on Monday, 18 May. This conversation was interesting not for anything bearing on the election but for an over-confident excursion into post-election dispositions. Wilson wholly confirmed his desire and intention (expressed already several times and well before Crossman thought of it as such a brilliant bribe) that I should go to the Foreign Office. We also discussed other dispositions: Denis Healey to replace me at the Treasury; Fred Peart to replace him at Defence, which department he said had experienced a strong minister for sufficiently long that it could do with a weak one who would please the generals; Michael Stewart to become leader of the House of Commons; and Richard Marsh, sacked in the autumn of 1969, to be brought back in some unspecified position.

He also went out of his way, without any prompting from me, to repeat what he had glancingly expressed to me on four or five previous occasions, that although he would still be well short of sixty, he was determined to hand over the premiership in the course of the next Parliament. On these previous occasions I had not known whether to believe it or not. On the one hand it seemed so contrary to the natural likelihood of events and indeed to his own predilections that it was difficult to countenance. On the other hand he had gratuitously repeated it to me in so many different circumstances – when he was weak, and when he was strong, late at night and early in the day, when he was distinctly ebullient, and when he was bleakly sober – that it was impossible to see any motive other than telling the truth. On this occasion moreover he added conviction by adding precision. He said there were two possible dates: the one was at the Labour Party Conference in October 1972; and the other, which might attract him for reasons which I, particularly, would easily understand, would be just before midsummer 1973. This assumption of my understanding left me mystified. My slowness at picking up his jocular hints eventually exasperated him. Finally the penny dropped: 14 June 1973 would be the date on which he would have been in office for a day longer than Asquith and therefore, in that pre-Thatcherite era, the longest-serving Prime Minister of the century.

On the following morning the election date was taken first to the Management Committee and then to the Cabinet as a whole. The former was allowed some discussion, the latter was accorded not much more than advance information. Both seemed content with what had been decided. In the Management Committee the least enthusiastic was Crosland, who said that he thought people would have experienced a more sustained rise in living standards by the autumn, and that it might be better to wait for this. But he did not press his dissent.

The next eighteen days were passed in a 'night before the battle' atmosphere: agreeable enough on the whole because optimistic, but shot through with enough caution to make me aware that I might be discharging ministerial tasks for the last time. On that same Thursday I gave a dinner at 11 Downing Street for Pierre-Paul Schweitzer, half to thank him for having lent us so much money and half to demonstrate that having paid off all his beastly debts I could give him with a thoroughly easy conscience particularly good wine, pretty good food and what I regarded as amusing company. On Monday, 18 May, I had Emilio Colombo, the Italian Finance Minister, for a return visit to London following mine to Rome in the dark days of November 1968, and ended a day of talks with an Anglo-Italian Lancaster House banquet. On the Wednesday I went to Paris for a two-day OECD meeting and at meals with Valéry Giscard in his Second Empire Finance Ministry (now taken over by the Louvre) and Christopher Soames in the Embassy found them assuming (perhaps out of politeness) a Labour victory. Nevertheless, on the way back, I recalled to Harris and Ryrie that in writing about a November 1916 visit to Paris by Asquith I had deflated a description of his enthusiastic reception by British soldiers on the quayside at Boulogne by concluding a chapter with the minatory words: 'He never went abroad again as a minister.'

The campaign proper began on a First of June of glorious weather, and began for me about as badly as it could have done. In the morning I recorded a major interview for that evening's *Panorama* programme on the state of the economy. My interview was neither very good nor very bad, and Macleod's balancing one was about the same. The net effect of the programme was however damaging, for Cromer, ex-Governor of the Bank, spoke sceptically, partisanly and in my view dishonestly about the reality of our balance of payments turn-round, and was in no way balanced by Kearton, who was supposed to be his left-of-centre counter-part.

After that unsatisfactory morning things proceeded to get much worse. I took John Harris to lunch at Brooks's. On arrival he went into a telephone box to get from Ryrie the May export figure, which was due in at noon. As soon as he came back into the hall I could tell from his face that something was seriously wrong. Exports were down by £45 million on the previous month. As we knew that there had to be absorbed into the import figure the big lumps of two Jumbo jets which had arrived for British Airways in May, the outlook for the trade figures, due out three days before polling day, was bleak. I proceeded gloomily to Preston, where I had my opening meeting of the campaign and delivered a desultory speech to an audience of 400 in a hall for 1200.

On the Tuesday I came back to London and had a good evening meeting in the Chiswick Town Hall. Then I opened a box when I got back to Downing Street and incredulously discovered that the export figure had been corrected, but corrected downwards, so that it was now £58 million worse than in April. With the wretched Jumbos there seemed a real possibility of a May trade deficit of £70–80 million. At the nomination ceremony in the Birmingham Council House on the next morning, when all the candidates for the thirteen constituencies of the city milled around for an hour with civic dignitaries and press, I was embarrassed by the balance of payments congratulations I received, and found it difficult to decide what expression which suitably blended confidence and caution I should adopt. It was a problem which was to remain with me for the next twelve days.

That evening I presided over a large, would-be enthusiastic Birmingham meeting for Wilson, at which he made a soporific speech. Afterwards I dined with him in the Albany Hotel and we discussed whether there was anything we should do about the trade figures. There were two points for consideration. First, could we treat the Jumbo jets in a special way? They were the first to be delivered and were lumps on a bigger scale than anything previously known. And there was the precedent of the treatment of US military aircraft purchases, which we had inherited from the previous Government and which spread the impact over the period of payment rather than of delivery. Wilson and I were both attracted by this course, which a Board of Trade note accompanying the figures had advised against, but almost equivocally. I was clear, however, that it was worth doing this only if we could carry civil servants and expert advisers along with us. It was not a question of morals but of sense. A new methodology, introduced during an election campaign, would be worse than useless if muttered against in Whitehall. Professor Claus Moser, then head of

the Government Statistical Service, was opposed. That was it as far
as I was concerned. The Prime Minister did not take a significantly
different view.

The second point was whether, knowing that we had this time-bomb
ticking away for explosion on the Monday before polling day, we ought
to switch our tactics from concentration on the strength of the economy
and the balance of payments in particular. We decided against on three
grounds. We were as sure as we could be that the bad figures were an
aberration which would be more than balanced by the results of the
following months (which proved abundantly so). We remembered old
adages about not changing horses in mid-stream. And we comforted
ourselves with the hope that nothing which happened as late as the
last Monday of a campaign would make much difference to how
people voted on the Thursday. It was like being told halfway across
the Atlantic on a smooth flight that you were going to have appallingly
bad weather conditions for the arrival in New York. I still wanted to
arrive and believed that the chances were substantially in favour of
getting safely on to the runway. But it was difficult to take one's mind
off the horrors of the approach.

I went to Plymouth for the following evening (to help David Owen)
and then to Exeter on the Friday morning. There I had a swirling but
satisfying meeting with a large, casual, standing audience of about 1500
in a hall abutting on one of the busiest streets. As soon as it was over
I rushed to the Royal Clarence Hotel in the Cathedral Close where I
was awaited by Bill Ryrie with the other side of the trade figures. The
deficit was £31 million, much better than I had feared but, of course,
much worse than anything we had experienced for nine months past.
With mild relief I proceeded to Bristol, Swindon and eventually home
to East Hendred through a most perfect June twilight.

The second week of the campaign produced equally beautiful
weather, mixed meetings and a slight suspicion on my part that,
as Rab Butler had memorably said about the 1964 election, this one
might be slipping away from us. On the Wednesday evening I had a
dismal meeting in Manchester (always a bad place for meetings in my
experience) and not much better ones in Bradford and Halifax on the
Thursday. The Friday I spent in London, devoting five hours at Lime
Grove to trying to get my ten-minute straight-to-camera telecast right.
In the evening I went to suburban Essex, and came back to the news
that the following morning's NOP would give the Government a 12.3
points lead over the Conservatives. It ran somewhat counter to my
instincts, but nonetheless seemed to indicate a nationally impregnable
position.

On the Sunday I went to Glasgow for the afternoon and Edinburgh
for the evening. The meetings were not great. At the Edinburgh one

the news came through that England had been defeated in the World Cup. I remembered that I had heard Wilson propound a theory of almost mystical symbiosis between the fortunes of the Labour Party and the English football eleven. But presumably that did not much apply in 'Auld Reekie'. However, I remember walking with John Harris down the Royal Mile from the Castle in a near-midnight twilight without much enthusiasm for the last week with its hidden trap.

I got back to Birmingham for a home-based final three days at noon the next day, just as the trade figures were being released by the Board of Trade. The rest of that day I spent trying to give reassuring interviews which would limit the damage. It is difficult to look self-confident when running round trying to plug holes in a dyke. Perhaps as a result (although Wilson thought it was also due to the interviewer and the lighting) the BBC one came out badly, although the ITN one was satisfactory. We also thought that the BBC's own early-evening coverage of the figures lacked proportion and balance. As a result, following some instigation from 10 Downing Street, I telephoned the Director-General (Charles Curran) and complained. It was a thing I had never done before and have never done since. It produced some small improvement for the nine o'clock news, but I disliked giving such a sign of being in a neurotic and defensive mood.

Despite these vicissitudes I did not seriously think that we had lost. I had three lunchtimes of very enthusiastic factory-gate meetings. I did a lot of shopping-centre expeditions and found the atmosphere on the whole good, although (perhaps only in retrospect) I thought I could detect a certain detachment on the part of too many women under fifty. The Thursday was as perfect a day as could be imagined for a summer election. There was not a cloud in the Birmingham sky from early morning to sunset. If there was any validity in the old myth about the Labour Party doing well when the sun shone and Tory voters being more willing to go out in the rain, we ought to have won by a landslide.

A little before the close of the poll (which Wilson had determinedly moved back to 10.00 p.m.) Jennifer and I retreated to the house of Mrs Hitchman, where I always stayed when in Stechford and where all our three children (then aged twenty-one, eighteen and fifteen) joined us for supper. At about 11.00 we all crammed into a small car and I drove the four miles into the centre of the city. On the way, partly to calm my nerves, although it was an extraordinarily fate-tempting subject to choose, and one which has ever since provoked great family hilarity, I discussed what it would be like being Foreign Secretary and whether we would spend weekends at East Hendred or Dorneywood (which was then a perquisite of the Foreign Secretary) or a mixture of both.

Our Stechford count was as usual in a remote and inconvenient room which was part of the adjacent Art Gallery rather than of the Council House. On arrival we were greeted with news of the Guildford result, which with its 5.7 per cent swing to the Conservatives was really all that one needed to know. But for some reason or other I did not take it too seriously, and applied myself to what was coming out of the Stechford boxes, which did not seem to show anything sensational one way or the other. Jennifer went through to the Council Chamber where she could watch television, and ten minutes later, at about 11.50, I joined her. As I came in, she said, 'We've lost, you know.' I absorbed one or two further results and had no alternative but to agree. We then went back through to the Art Gallery and sat on a bench beneath a not particularly notable tondo and outside the Stechford count. There we assimilated what had happened and what it would immediately mean. We decided that we must get back to London early the next morning, order a removal van and do everything we could to get out of 11 Downing Street in the course of the day.

The Stechford result came out at about 1.30 a.m. It was not at all good, but not all that important either in the circumstances. The majority was 6700, and the swing 7.1 per cent, which meant that I had lost most but not all of my great surge in 1966. I got through my little speech without difficulty, went to the rather gloomy party in the Birmingham Co-op Rooms, heard sadly of particular casualties such as George Brown and Jack Diamond, and eventually went to bed in the Hitchman house at 3.30.

I slept hardly at all, which was perhaps as well for it would have been difficult to have awakened from a heavy sleep at 7.00. Instead I lay on my back and thought, not altogether dismally. I had no great difficulty in reconciling myself to the position. My belief in a Labour victory had been firm, but skin-deep, for I had not believed in it for long. I had been more pessimistic than most of my colleagues, at least until the morning when I read the polls in the Shelburne Hotel, Dublin. My new belief had had no time to settle and harden and was therefore easily broken through. I was surprised but in no way incredulous about the result.

Furthermore, I had always taken the view that being out of office offered many compensations. After five and a half strenuous but on the whole lucky years I felt there was quite a lot to be said for a change of pace. At forty-nine, I do not think it occurred to me that most of my ministerial career was over or that I had suffered what was in any way a decisive setback. I also felt some sense of relief not to be going to the Foreign Office. Almost subconsciously I had developed a slight unease that I was making a mistake by exchanging the central power of the Treasury and my acquired authority over it for the more peripheral and, for me, more hazardous glamour of the Foreign Office. None of this meant that I did not regret the defeat. I did, very much. Apart from anything else I thought that we deserved to win, which has by no means been my view at all elections. And there was also an inevitable sense of personal humiliation associated with being prominent in the defeat. It was broadly my policies on which Wilson had chosen to fight and on which we had lost. Nevertheless, while disappointed, I was not shattered by what had occurred.

I recall that the sense of humiliation came to the surface as – on yet another hot summer morning – I walked carrying a heavy suitcase down the long slope to the platform crowded with businessmen at Hampton-in-Arden Station, to which we had been driven for the 8.26 train. Both the suitcase, off which I had hurriedly torn a 'Chancellor of the Exchequer' label, and the mild sense of exposed shame were quickly removed from me by the stationmaster, who behaved to us with great kindness and respect and shepherded us to a comfortable breakfast car table. It was the last occasion for some time on which I was met by a stationmaster.

Bill Ryrie was at Euston, looking sympathetic and depressed, and we then went to 11 Downing Street, where I had a long talk with Douglas Allen, who also seemed sad at the result. I then suddenly thought of Wilson next door, thought of him almost as a corpse, or at least as someone who had suffered a most dreadful bereavement. It seemed callous to stay without contact, so I sent a message asking whether he would like me to go and see him. This he accepted with alacrity, and I went through at about 11.30 and talked to him for twenty minutes. He was looking appallingly battered, but he was wholly calm and unrecriminating, said, 'Well, there it is,' and displayed his great resilience almost ludicrously by rehearsing to me the speech he proposed to make in the debate on the Address, pinning Heath's promises upon him. He was altogether rather impressive, and the occasion moving.

Meanwhile Jennifer was desperately packing up. We had the Michael Barneses (he had done remarkably well to hold Brentford and Chiswick, defending a majority of only 600) to lunch in a half-dismantled house. In the afternoon I had a series of Treasury farewells and then returned to Downing Street for a meeting of the old Inner Cabinet which Wilson had called for 4.00 p.m. On the way back my admirable government driver asked whether there would be anything more. I said, 'Probably not, but wait if you will until about 5.30.' He said, 'Well, if you don't mind, sir, the garage is already agitating to have the car back for reallocation.' I said, 'No, I don't mind in the least,' and shook his hand warmly. So quickly did some of the trappings of power shake themselves off.

Wilson was less good at this four o'clock meeting than he had been in the morning. He had sagged, and seemed to have no idea why he had called it or what he wanted it to do. There were only about seven present, Callaghan, Crossman and Barbara Castle being still away. Benn managed to bring things to a climax of embarrassed bathos at the end by producing his camera and asking if he could take a photograph of Wilson sitting in his Prime Minister's chair for the last time. Healey and I both thought this was a bit much and left in a hurry for a drink in No. 11. I then completed my Treasury farewells, Jennifer completed her packing, the removal van drove off and we left together in our own small car, which the children had driven down from Birmingham, from the garden gate at 5.55 p.m., eighteen hours after we had made our dispositions on the bench in the Birmingham Art Gallery.

We went to Ladbroke Square, did a little regrouping there, and then drove to East Hendred, dining briefly near Henley on the way. So ended the first Wilson Government and my main experience of British office.

# PART THREE

# 1970–1976

# CHAPTER SEVENTEEN

## *European Unity and Labour Party Schism*

For the remainder of the London summer of 1970 I felt neither dismayed nor desolated, but disorientated. To an extent that I have never subsequently experienced, even when in 1981 I shed all the Brussels appurtenances and came back to England, I had some sense of what it must be like to emerge from a long prison sentence, to stand at the gate of the gaol almost blinking at the light, free but feeling it was a strange world which had moved on since I had last experienced it, and that the freedom was balanced by a lack of familiar props of support.

The loss of 11 Downing Street was a minor matter. I had throughout been used to spending a lot of time in our own house at East Hendred so that the sight and feel of official furniture had never become addictive; Ladbroke Square, although it had recently been mistakenly let to the Nicaraguan ambassador,* was available, much preferred by Jennifer, and equally satisfactory to me. Transport was more serious. I was not only without a driver but effectively without a car. Until the end of July we had only a battered Morris of Jennifer's which was mostly kept at East Hendred. I took to taxis and, then, to occasional and reluctant forays on public transport. It was 16 July before I self-mockingly noted in my diary that I had penetrated into the tube for the first time for seven years.

Much more important, however, was the collapse of any supporting staff. I had been used to a powerful private office, particularly at the Treasury. Not only was this inevitably withdrawn overnight, but my personal secretary, Bess Church, who to my great benefit had been with me since the mid-1950s and was to stay until 1980, remained true

---

* Mistakenly because he never paid the rent, eventually dying rather than discharging even the fifty/fifty settlement we had been advised to agree to by the permanent under-secretary of the Foreign Office.

to her one disadvantage of going on holiday at the most inconvenient times, and disappeared for three weeks. For most of July, when I was trying to put together a new pattern of life, I had nobody working for me. Then Bess returned, she and I eventually engaged an assistant typist as well, and I arranged that John Harris would provide press and general political advice on a part-time basis as well as working for the *Economist*.

Financially the putting together of a new pattern presented few difficulties. Although Edward Heath had just fought a successful election campaign against the ravages of inflation the value of money still remained qualitatively different from that to which subsequent governments have since reduced it. Cabinet ministers were more or less content with a salary of £8500 and members of Parliament had to make do with £3250. When, therefore, I was able that July to assemble from my publishers, for whom I envisaged a series of 'back-to-back' studies of American Presidents and British Prime Ministers, and from *The Times*, for which William Rees-Mogg commissioned a series of long biographical essays which subsequently grew into a book entitled *Nine Men of Power*, a package which gave the prospect of a writing income of about £20,000, I had no need either to bemoan the material privation of opposition or to seek the sustenance of the City.

It was however noticeable that the City did not seek me. Before I had made my writing arrangements I dropped one or two hints through friends who were leaders of the financial establishment that I might be interested in suitable part-time employment. The response was singularly unforthcoming. About eighteen months later I received a solitary small offer, conveyed through the Governor of the Bank of England, which I declined. As it happened, my attention quickly shifted in literary directions and I had no feeling of deprivation. But it could not fail to cross my mind that as an ex-Chancellor who had, maybe by luck, acquired some reputation for stringent management of the economy and for success in turning round the balance of payments, I was being treated utterly differently from the way that an analogous Conservative politician would have been.

Perhaps this was the result not of prejudice but of prescience. In 1981-2, after my return from Brussels, I did briefly become a part-time banker, but found that the occupation did not arouse my interest, and that in consequence I was not much good. My boredom was greater than my greed. I therefore made an escape after eighteen months when I was elected leader of the SDP, which turned out to be a lucky exit as a few years later Morgan Grenfell, the merchant bank concerned, suffered considerable vicissitudes which I am sure I would not have been able to foresee or circumnavigate. No subsequent offers were made to me by commerce or industry. I have not even been asked to join any of the numerous international advisory councils through which great banks or businesses on both sides of the Atlantic provide sustenance for former political leaders in return for advice of doubtful value for themselves.

To add to the puzzle I have frequently been asked to address such bodies, in other words to advise the advisers. This is perhaps the best of both worlds, particularly as on one occasion I discovered that I was being paid twice as much for a single appearance as they were for a whole year's admittedly intermittent advice. Nonetheless the fact remains that I have never been regarded as a desirable commodity on anybody's paid board or council (unpaid ones are different; there the invitations have flocked in, even for ones of high prestige). I have not the slightest reason to complain, for this involuntary abstinence from the temptations of mammon has given more time for writing and speaking, which I enjoy more and which have turned out to be adequately lucrative.

Much of this was far ahead in late June 1970. What was immediately pressing was an election for the deputy leadership of the Labour Party. George Brown, although out of the Government since March 1968, had continued to hold this post without it meaning much in terms of the hierarchy of power within the party. But his ceasing to be an MP necessarily created a vacancy. A new freshly elected figure in the job might have a political significance which Brown's erratic although occasionally memorable continuance had not possessed. So at any rate Bill Rodgers argued with his usual persuasive loyalty when we dined with him and his wife Silvia on Monday, 22 June, our first day back in London after the post-election East Hendred weekend. I am not sure that I needed much persuasion to consider myself a candidate, but if encouragement were necessary he provided it. The reverse was the case when I had a drink with Tony Crosland the following evening. We had enjoyed a new surge of friendliness over the election, but when on the way out of his house I mentioned the matter with false casualness he made it clear that I could not count on his support. He would have to think long and carefully, he said, between giving his vote to Callaghan or to me. I remember remarking afterwards that, had I been engaged in a constituency canvass, I would by all the rules have marked him down as 'against'.

The next day I received an offer of support from what ought by the tests of the past to have been a more surprising quarter. Harold Wilson, showing his first sign of life since the day after the defeat, asked me to go and see him urgently in the House of Commons. There he seemed to have commandeered nearly all the available opposition accommodation for himself, and was sitting in it surrounded by vast piles of packing cases full of papers which he had taken from

10 Downing Street. He offered to make one small room available to me (he eventually made two), but not he implied to anyone else. This, it elliptically emerged, was a sort of grudging mating offering, for it appeared to carry with it his support for the deputy leadership. This offer, if not the small box-room, was generous.

On the evening of the day after that I attended a meeting of about twelve MPs in Dick Taverne's flat in South Kensington, out of which there emerged the nucleus of a campaign organisation and indeed of the continuing focus of the committed pro-Europeans in the parliamentary Labour Party. This group became the 'Walston group', so called because of occasional meetings for buffet luncheons in the Albany apartment of Lord Walston, which continued at least until the leadership election of March 1976, and even a few times thereafter. When the new House of Commons assembled on Monday, 29 June, the deputy leadership election and associated ones for the shadow Cabinet became the dominant recovery therapy for the defeat-shocked Labour Party.

Crosland was freed from having to ratiocinate between James Callaghan and me. Callaghan took a shrewder view than I did about the limitations of the office of deputy leader. While Attlee had succeeded from it to the leadership when Lansbury unexpectedly resigned in 1935, there was already in 1970 the much longer list of Arthur Greenwood, Herbert Morrison, James Griffiths, Aneurin Bevan and George Brown who had been deputy without proceeding further, and they were subsequently to be reinforced by myself, Edward Short, Denis Healey and Roy Hattersley. Only Michael Foot was to move from deputy to leader, and he without happy consequences.

Callaghan therefore did not enter the contest, but lurked like a big pike in the shadows, powerful, perhaps menacing, but restrained. I was left to engage with lesser fish, Michael Foot and Fred Peart. Foot was the hero of the left, but inhibited in the then governing-party-minded Labour Party by never having held office. Fred Peart had been Minister of Agriculture and then leader of the House of Commons, and was thought to be a solid centre-right figure with no enemies. This inspired David Wood, the political editor of *The Times*, to announce on 2 July under the headline 'Hopes fading for Jenkins as No. 2' that Peart was set to run me close on the first ballot and probably to win on the second.

This was not in accordance with our informal canvassing, but it did not make enjoyable reading, the more so because such prophecies can have a self-fulfilling quality. It was, however, more than made up for by the painless way in which I heard the actual result. The first ballot had closed at noon on 8 July. We were not expecting the result until the evening, but the tellers decided to be both quick and informative. I was driving myself to lunch at the Reform Club where Roy Hattersley had assembled a group of supporters. As I came through Admiralty Arch and swung into Cockspur Street the one o'clock news which I had turned on without tension, expecting nothing, began with the succinct announcement that 'Mr Jenkins has been elected deputy leader of the Labour Party on the first ballot.' I had 133 votes, Foot 67 and Peart 48. It was much better than I had expected.

For the rest I had an easy summer. I made one speech of substance in the House of Commons, during the economic day of the debate on the Address, which was notable for it being the last appearance by my successor at the Treasury, Iain Macleod. During the wind-up speeches (we had both spoken in the afternoon) he sent me a note saying that he had to go into hospital that night, to be operated upon the next day, and expected to be away for several weeks. He survived his hospital visit, but died on 20 July, collapsing in the 11 Downing Street bedroom in which I had slept most of the nights of the preceding two and a half years. It was a horrible irony that the job which he had coveted was snatched so soon out of his hands and placed into the much feebler ones of Anthony Barber. It was also a great blow to the balance and force of the Heath Government. 'We have lost our trumpeter,' someone said, and that Government was short on trumpeters. But Macleod was more than that. He was a politician of insight and insolence, which latter quality put him in a tradition of Canning and Disraeli, Joseph Chamberlain and F. E. Smith. In spite of his resentment of me as Chancellor, I greatly regretted his disappearance from the scene. He might have made a significant difference to the evolution of politics over the next twenty years.

On 29 July we left for Italy, where we had taken a house between Pisa and Livorno, and did not return until 4 September. I worked a fair amount, as I like doing on holiday, mainly on the memoir raw material which has provided the basis for the preceding Treasury chapters in this book, but it was the longest break that I have ever had, and it was an unagitated one. I remember being interrupted by only one 'political' telephone call from London, which posed the untesting question of whether I could be announced as reading the second lesson in the church service during the Labour Party conference at Blackpool in October.

This did not unduly ruffle the Tuscan peace, with which my own mind was reasonably in tune. I felt no reason to be dissatisfied with what had gone before or with the prospect. Over the previous five and a half years I had made an unexpected breakthrough from being a back-bencher with a certain outside reputation but with no real political achievement or position in the party, to having presided over two out of the three great departments of state and become the second man, both in power and familiarity to the public, in the Government. Admittedly that Government had been swept away, but I believed that alternating governments were good both for the political health of the country and for the balance of politicians' lives, and I accepted the prospect of a few years in opposition with contentment. As a moment for pause 1970 seemed well timed from my point of view, and was neatly symbolised by the satisfactory outcome of the deputy leadership contest. It was the first Labour Party position of any significance to which I was ever elected. I had never stood for the National Executive and my two or three attempts to get on to the shadow Cabinet in the early 1960s had not been successful. It seemed the equivalent of cashing in one's winnings after an exhausting period of intensive and high-risk play at the tables.

The day after my return to England from Italy a less expected risk erupted. I was driving my daughter Cynthia on an unnecessary expedition from East Hendred to Wantage when, two miles from home, a horse ridden by a small girl leaped over a ditch out of a field and then attempted a second leap over my car. Unfortunately this feat was beyond its capacity and it landed on the front of the roof and the top of the windscreen. The car was a write-off. Cynthia and I were luckier, thanks mainly to the then recent innovation of seat-belts. But we had to be removed by ambulance to the Radcliffe Infirmary in Oxford. I with concussion was detained for only a few hours, she with lacerations overnight.

It was a bizarre and nineteenth-century-like accident to have occurred. Through my concussed confusion I remembered wondering, as the soft underbelly of the wretched animal came down upon the car, why the world had gone mad and a cavalry charge had been launched against us. No permanent damage was done: even the horse survived, and the girl merely described a parabola in the air before landing safely on her hard hat. (Next year she wrote to ask me if I would sponsor her ride to the same gymkhana, but I thought that was beyond the call of duty.)

Nevertheless it took me over a month to recover from the elongated jet-lag effects of the accident, and this may have had something to do with the fact that I found my eight days of Labour Party conference, longer than I had ever spent at such a gathering before, peculiarly lowering. Blackpool weather excelled itself, with an unrelenting muggy wind whipping up the rain-laden clouds and the coffee-coloured Irish Sea. My principal speech went reasonably well (not more), but I chafed at my obligation to fulfil an endless round of semi-social, semi-political engagements, and was also dissatisfied with my performance when I got to these gatherings. I even managed to read the wrong lesson in church, despite the seven weeks of advance warning. That week in the Fylde took some of the edge off my zest for the politics of opposition.

During October I revived and wrote on Ernest Bevin the first of my *Times* essays (it was actually published second with 'Robert Kennedy' coming before). I also did a long comparison for the *Sunday Times* of the respective outlooks and methods of operation of the Home Office and the Treasury. At the end of the month the House of Commons resumed and Barber immediately produced one of his numerous mini-budgets. In the debate on this on 4 November I made one of the best speeches I made in that Parliament, and then followed it up two weeks later by getting badly carved up by Heath at Prime Minister's question time. Wilson was away and I was in charge for the opposition. I therefore intervened two or three times, each intervention being still less successful than the previous one. Heath did it very well, and I was not on good form. But beyond this I suddenly realised, as I had not previously done, what an enormous built-in advantage lies with the responder rather than the questioner in such exchanges. In cricketing terms the questioner always has to try to force and score a boundary off every ball, whereas the minister replying can choose his time, play a defensive shot when he wishes, and then punish any loose ball which comes along; and once he is on top it is almost impossible to seize the initiative from him.

The press made a fair amount of Heath's triumph and my humiliation the next morning, and for two or three days I slunk around in an exaggerated state of gloom, although I tried to restore proportion by reminding myself of a wartime anecdote about Austin Robinson, the Cambridge economist. After some faulty argument of his had been crushingly refuted in the *Economic Journal* he was found sitting in his War Cabinet office at the weekend having for once not gone to Cambridge. 'It was out of the question,' he said. 'Even the porters at the railway station would have laughed at me.'

I recovered, and at the end of the month went to America for eight days where I made an economic speech to a business audience in New York; stayed part of the time in Gracie Mansion with Mayor Lindsay, an old marching companion from the Martin Luther King funeral who had subsequently become a possible Democratic candidate for 1972; made a particularly enjoyable expedition with Arthur Schlesinger to the Roosevelt house at Hyde Park, where for some inexplicable reason we walked round like Siamese twins, linked by a machine which emitted a commentary, which Arthur could probably have done better himself, and which must have been cheaper if hired in this dual form; and then went on to Washington, where John and Catherine Freeman were winding up their ambassadorship (and, as it transpired, their marriage) before handing over to Lord Cromer, against whose performance in the June *Panorama* programme I continued to bear a perhaps excessive grudge, which meant that this was the last time I went to that Embassy until 1975.

In Washington I met the other three seriously discussed Democratic candidates, George McGovern, Teddy Kennedy and Ed Muskie. The Muskie encounter was the most memorable event of the whole visit, although it did not take a form flattering to that amiable Senator from Maine. It was also the last occasion on which I saw Dean Acheson, who died ten months later. Acheson I had known fairly well throughout the 1960s (he had dined once or twice at Ladbroke Square) and I respected his record as a great Secretary of State to Truman as well as enjoying his coruscating conversation. By this stage, however, he had come to embrace, at least for the purposes of provocation, some eccentric and even reactionary views. This was particularly so on this (for me) last evening with him at the house of Douglass Cater, an American academic and writer whom I had known well since 1953, and who was to become deputy chairman of the (London) *Observer* during the period of Atlantic Richfield's ownership at the end of the 1970s.

Before dinner Acheson stood in front of the fire looking purple, with his veins and eyes standing out alarmingly, and announced to me that Brandt was a dangerous semi-Communist and that one of the best regimes in the world was that in Rhodesia. He did it as always with lucidity and indeed brilliance, and did not intend to be taken wholly seriously. It was indeed fatal to do so, and this was Muskie's trouble after dinner, when the men were seated semi-circularly in a smoking room. Muskie and Acheson had never previously met (amazingly to anyone used to the tight political world of London – at least until John Major came along), addressed each other formally as 'Senator' and 'Mr Secretary', and were influenced in their relations by the fact that Muskie much hoped to get Acheson's support for his presidential candidature. When therefore Acheson delivered a fifteen-minute *tour d'horizon* which was as sparkling as it was outrageous, Muskie listened with attention.

'Well, Senator, what do you think of that?' Acheson concluded. 'Well, Mr Secretary,' Muskie fatally responded, 'I reckon I could go along with about 90 per cent of it' (which no sane man could have done) and then took another slow and rambling twenty minutes, in sharp contrast with Acheson's taut epigrammatic phrases, to explain that his 10 per cent reservation related to the need for more democratic consultation in foreign policy formulation. When he had finished this unimpressive performance Acheson closed on him like a matador about to finish off an old bull, and said: 'Do you mean to tell me, Senator, that it is your view that United States foreign policy ought to be made at a series of little town meetings in the state of Maine? Don't ask them, Senator, tell them. When I believe you will do that, I will support you. Until then, not.' He then turned away, dismissing Muskie from the conversation. It was a devastatingly cruel performance. Acheson was not easy to deal with, but the incident left me with a strong feeling that someone who aspired to be President of the United States ought to be able to do it better than that.

The Christmas recess was largely occupied with writing my 'Robert Kennedy' essay for *The Times* and peering somewhat apprehensively ahead at the forthcoming European dispute within the Labour Party, for which 1971 was clearly going to be the year of crunch. The Heath Government was vigorously pursuing the negotiations for British entry, which the Wilson Government had initiated and of which George Thomson as a minister within the Foreign Office but also in the Cabinet and I as Foreign Secretary would have been in charge had the result of the election been different.

Nevertheless, when 1971 came, the European strife within the Labour Party built up only gradually. This was partly because the issue did not become politically dominant until about May, and partly because the leading figures in the party, Wilson, Callaghan, Healey, Benn, and Crosland, who remained more equivocal, only gradually shifted away from the support they had all given to Britain's third application to join in 1969.

In the third week of January, for instance, when there was a two-day Europe debate, there was no attempt in the shadow Cabinet to prevent my opening on the second day and no complaint from Wilson or anyone else that I did so with a more hard-line pro-European speech than was forthcoming at this stage from three of the four ministerial speakers. (Heath was obviously the exception.) Nor did it ever occur to me that this might be a rash issue on which to be reported on in the early-evening news bulletins of a day on which, almost as soon as I had spoken in the House of Commons, I left for Birmingham to attend a reselection meeting in Stechford. This had been made necessary by some minor readjustment of constituency boundaries, was I think arranged specially early by the sympathetic foresight of the Labour Party regional office, but involved what struck me in those easy-going days as the rigid procedure of a paper ballot during which I had to leave the room. The result was unanimous and, as opinion developed in Stechford, would probably not have been any different a year later, but I nonetheless think it interesting in view of subsequent national Labour Party feeling that it simply did not cross my mind at that stage that the conjuncture of Commons speech and Stechford vote could be awkward.

Equally in February I went to Bonn in double harness with Denis

Healey to attend a meeting of the Jean Monnet-led Action Committee
for a United States of Europe. The party leadership had had some
difficulty about getting the National Executive of the Labour Party
to agree to affiliation to this body. It required the combined efforts
of Wilson, Callaghan, Healey and me to secure a wafer-thin majority
for affiliation. Then we were defeated on the next proposition – that
we should pay our subscription. Perhaps Callaghan, as Treasurer,
defected between the two votes. In any event we participated from
the somewhat undignified posture of a non-paying member, but the
indignity was not compounded by any disarray between Healey and
myself. We were as well adjusted as were the two Conservative
representatives, Alec Home and Reggie Maudling, and we called
together on Willy Brandt (then Federal Chancellor) for an hour's
serious discussion of the prospects for British entry without any
embarrassment at doing it in each other's presence.

Nevertheless, I regarded these winter months as being the calm
before the inevitable Labour Party storm. From late January onwards
I made frequent attempts to have a serious bilateral discussion with
Harold Wilson about the difficulties which the European issue was
inevitably going to pose for the Labour Party in opposition, and how
we could best hope jointly to handle them. He procrastinated hard.
This procrastination gave no impression of being due to hostility,
but rather to his natural instinct never to have a possibly unpleasant
meeting about an issue which had not become immediately difficult. It
was ludicrous that weeks slipped by without our finding an opportunity
to talk alone, for at that time we saw each other almost every parliamentary day. Mondays to Thursdays we had a quarter-hour meeting
at 3.00 with the chief whip (Robert Mellish) and the chairman of the
parliamentary party (Douglas Houghton), as well as a weekly shadow
Cabinet and frequent cheek-by-jowl encounters on the front bench.

When I eventually succeeded in capturing him for a brief direct
exchange it was I who was apprehensive about the prospect ahead
and he who was blandly optimistic. I recorded the following exchange
(tiresomely and unusually without a date, although it seems likely
to have been late February). I said: 'I think that there will be a
great upheaval in the party if and when the Government succeeds in
negotiating terms of entry. I am sure you understand that I am fully
committed to going into Europe, and will, if the terms are anything
like reasonable, be determined to support them. But I think you will
find that the party in opposition is not prepared to go along with this.
I therefore believe that the only way out will be a free vote without
recrimination.' To this Wilson replied: 'I am more optimistic than that.
I hope that we may be able to get the party officially to vote in favour,
but at the worst, the very worst, we can fall back on a free vote.'

By 19 April, however, the date of the return from the Easter parliamentary recess, there was a unanimous feeling amongst the Labour Europeans that the ground was beginning to slip away from us, and that the party, leadership and local activists alike, were gearing up for one of the bouts of old-fashioned British nationalistic fever to which both the old-fashioned British parties have been intermittently susceptible for the past forty years and more. The best attempt at a prophylactic of which we could think was to prepare a statement of European welcome signed by about a dozen continental socialist leaders, responded to by as many Labour MPs as we could muster, and published as a manifesto advertisement in what we regarded as the three key newspapers. The confirmation that our fears of the fever were not imaginary came with a speech of Wilson's on 26 April. This was not by subsequent standards a hard-line anti-European speech, although it raised one or two issues in a tentative but prejudicial way and contained one phrase about the possibility of an invasion of 'Italian black-leg labour' which was at once ludicrous and offensive.

The other odd thing about this speech was that he had chosen to make it in Birmingham, to a so-called Socialist Businessmen's Luncheon Club which existed throughout the 1960s and some part of the 1970s and was composed in large part of supporters of mine. Wilson, as soon as he had delivered this speech, disappeared to America for a week. This left me to discharge the routine fixtures of the leader of the opposition, presiding over the shadow Cabinet on the Wednesday and taking Prime Minister's question time as well as the meeting with the lobby correspondents on the Thursday. At the lobby meeting I tried to deal lightheartedly with the Birmingham effusions. I had no alternative unless I was to endorse or denounce them, neither of which I regarded as desirable.

When Wilson returned from the United States he was conciliatory. He accepted my complaints about the Italian black-legs phrase with guilt rather than truculence, and raised no objection when I told him about our plans for a manifesto/advertisement. This appeared in the *Guardian* alone on 11 May. We had dropped our plans for taking space in *The Times* and the *Daily Mirror* as well, partly because we did not wish to look too well heeled (the Labour European cause was nervous of the false charge that our coffers were lined with Brussels gold), and partly because we judged rightly that in the circumstances a single announcement would reverberate throughout the rest of the press. With difficulty at the margin we managed to get to our goal of a hundred signatories (out of a total of 287 Labour MPs). Eighty-five to ninety of these signed with spontaneous enthusiasm. These included five members of the shadow Cabinet, George Thomson, Shirley Williams, Harold Lever, Douglas Houghton and myself. The last ten to fifteen of our hundred required varying degrees of persuasion, but all eventually decided that, the project having been launched, they would rather be on than off the list. This last batch would have preferred not to have to make the choice. This group included three other members of the shadow Cabinet, Healey, Crosland and Edward Short.

Healey's position was in many ways the most interesting. On 26 May he had chosen to write a *Daily Mirror* article which proclaimed a strong pro-European line. It was dramatically entitled, 'Why I Changed My Mind', which might well have been the choice of the editor and not of himself, but which turned out to be singularly unfortunate as he was to change it again within a few weeks. However, when we had a joint meeting of the shadow Cabinet and the National Executive Committee at the Great Western Hotel, Paddington, on Sunday, 16 May, he was still on our side, as was Crosland. Crosland indeed opened the debate on Europe with a speech which was cool but firm and effective. But when he and I drove home together it became clear that he was less firm than he had sounded in semi-public. He began to develop what subsequently became his familiar line that the European issue was a minor one: he was in favour of entry but not at the price of diverting attention from the major issues of domestic politics.

This attitude and the beginnings of Healey's second switch reflected themselves a week or so later when we had a meeting of the shadow Cabinet members who had signed the *Guardian* advertisement. Crosland and Healey both came, but only to make it clear how uncomfortable they were with the association. Thereafter we gave up trying to keep them in the group. By July Healey was stridently back into the other camp. Crosland maintained more consistency accompanied by his own peculiar sense of proportion.

Well before that, however, a bigger fish than either had flipped with a loud splash. On 25 May I was in Birmingham to attend a Lord Mayor's dinner and go the next morning to a bye-election at Bromsgrove. In the course of a telephone conversation about the detailed arrangements for the latter, I discovered that the candidate (who it must be said won the seat) would rather I did not come. This was a shock to me, for my presence at elections had been urgently sought for at least the preceding four or five years. It was the first real indication that the European issue was becoming a deeply divisive one and that much of the party on the ground was moving away from the position it had accepted in government. With uncanny sensitivity Jim Callaghan chose that exact moment to launch himself into mid-stream under brand-new anti-European colours. The papers that same morning were full of a speech he had made at Southampton, which subsequently became known, a little mockingly, as the 'language of Chaucer' speech. He had in no way confined himself to attacking the likely terms, but had launched a wider-ranging onslaught on the idea of a European commitment which would involve sacrificing the heritage of Chaucer's English. French, he implied, would become a language of government, rather as after the Norman Conquest. It was not much worse, I suppose, than the 'thousand years of history' argument of my hero Hugh Gaitskell in 1962, but it filled me with a mixture of gloom and disapproval as, repulsed by Bromsgrove, I travelled back to London that morning.

What was of more significance was that it filled Harold Wilson with fear. Tony Benn, a diarist writing from a very different point of view from mine, has testified that Wilson became 'obsessed' that summer with the survival of his leadership and that what most frightened him was being outflanked on Europe by Callaghan and then squeezed by a pincer movement from an infamous alliance between him and the left.[1] This may have had some influence on the fact that Wilson at last agreed to have the serious talk which I had been seeking for several months. I saw him for an hour on the morning of Wednesday, 9 June. His opening remark as we started the central topic indicated that while he may have procrastinated he was now prepared to open up the heart of the matter for discussion. (I give the conversation in direct speech, as I subsequently recorded it, but it should be understood that his words were filtered through my memory and that mine may owe something to *l'esprit de l'escalier*.)

'You may think this is a difficult issue for you,' Wilson began, 'but let me assure you it is a more difficult one for me. You are in a much happier position than I am because you have no choice. I have a choice, and it is always much more difficult to have one than to have one's line of conduct clearly laid down, as is the case with you.' This interesting and up to a point endearing opening led to the conversation proceeding with amity and frankness. I was determined, although without great hope of success, to make a direct appeal to him and to put it in terms which were daring enough to move his mind without being offensive enough to alienate. To the best of my recollection I spoke as follows:

'I know it is a difficult issue for you. I know you have great problems with the party, which I in no way underestimate. I know you are genuinely much less committed on the issue than I am, and it would be silly to criticise you for that. But what you should be equally aware of is that what is most damaging to your reputation and position in the country is that you are believed, perhaps wrongly, to be devious, tricky, opportunistic. If you stick to the pro-European position which you took up in government, difficult though it will be with the party, you will kill that damaging reputation. If on a major issue of this sort you take the hard, difficult, consistent, unpopular line, it will do your long-term reputation an immense amount of good. You may be defeated at the party conference, although that is by no means certain, but if you swing your whole influence pro-Europe it will only at worst be a narrow defeat, and you could sustain that at least as easily as Gaitskell sustained his 1960 defeat. I therefore beg you, not so much in the interest of the committed Europeans, but in your own interest and that of the party as a whole, as well as that of the country, to take this line.'

I added, switching from the high to the low note, that if he did this there could be no question of the Labour Europeans joining in any intrigue with Callaghan or anyone else to embarrass him, still less to endeavour to replace him. He did not have to rely on our goodwill; we would be locked into this position. He received all this with perfect good temper and even seriously, half giving me the impression that he was still genuinely undecided. Yet when I left the room I had little doubt that, courteously though he had listened and even if his mind was not formally made up, he was slipping, gradually, inevitably, irrevocably (for a few years at any rate), and perhaps more under the influence of his own personal staff than of his own volition, into the anti-European camp. But I felt that I had at least tried, with all the arguments at my disposal, and that I had also secured a licence, almost a blessing, for the course that I intended to pursue, without any complaints against the propriety of my behaviour as deputy leader being raised.

This mood of mutual tolerance persisted for another six weeks, until in the second half of July, the traditional season for political tension, it broke in bitterness. Wilson and I had jointly but unsuccessfully resisted the summoning of a special Labour conference on the issue, which took place in London on Saturday, 17 July. Our resistance had been defeated by one vote on the National Executive owing to the sudden 'democratic' defection of Shirley Williams, who of course remained passionately sound on the substance of the argument. The conference did not in fact do much harm, except for requiring a speech from Wilson which, while pedestrian, took him quietly almost out of intellectual hailing distance with us. It was like watching someone being sold down the river into slavery, drifting away, depressed but unprotesting. There was no vote, and we thought (as no doubt we would) that we won the argument. John Mackintosh, MP for East Lothian and Edinburgh politics professor until his early death in 1978, made the outstanding speech.

If Wilson was forced to make an indentured speech, I was prevented from making one of any sort. My views prevented my making one on behalf of the Executive Committee, my position from making one against it. I therefore spent the day in a state of frustration. My irritation may have been aggravated by hubris following an experience with the Stechford Management Committee thirty-six hours before. I thought it sensible to go and set out both my arguments for British entry and my determination to go through with my support for it. I did not expect trouble, but nor did I expect the response which I got, which was the support of about 90 per cent of those present on the merits, with unanimous support for my acting in accordance with my convictions. One of the most left-wing members there helpfully attempted to move a resolution instructing me to vote *for* British entry. I was attracted by the prospect of this being carried unanimously and available for use as a good card in London politics, but the chairman, wiser than I, resisted it on the ground that the GMC had refrained from any attempt to instruct me when I had been clearly at variance with them on German rearmament in 1954, or when there had been a more confused position in the great Gaitskell/unilateralist dispute of 1960, and that to set a precedent now would be undesirable.

It was a remarkable example of how well the Stechford Labour Party consistently treated me and how small was the contribution of local problems to my subsequent disenchantment with two-party politics. It also made less deserved any reputation for political courage I acquired as the Common Market battle unfolded itself. It is easier to be steadfast under fire if there is none forthcoming from a potentially dangerous sector. The experience of most of the other Labour Europeans was markedly worse in this respect. Dick Taverne was the extreme example, but there were a lot of others who were under a pressure nearly as disagreeable. George Thomson was so struck by my lucky immunity that he developed a theory (only about two-thirds as a joke) that Stechford, which unlike Dundee or Lincoln carried no geographical identity in its name, did not really exist. It was a fictitious pocket borough which I had made up long before, and for which by a superb confidence trick I had succeeded in sitting unchallenged in the House of Commons for many years.

The immediate effect of the combination of Thursday's hubris and Saturday's frustration was a subsequent week of frenzied political activity, such as I have hardly before or since achieved, which greatly sharpened the conflict on Europe and shattered the amicable mutual respect with which Wilson and I had hitherto padded the issue. While this mêlée was going on on one side of the stage I was also endeavouring in my capacity as shadow Chancellor to engage in an economic duet on the other. On the Monday afternoon (19 July) Anthony Barber introduced one of the three or four mini-Budgets with which he celebrated the first year of his unfortunate chancellorship, by far the biggest liability of the Heath Government. He did so in a half-hour statement to which I had to make a six- or seven-minute immediate response preparatory to a full debate on the Tuesday.

My more important engagement for that day was to address a meeting of the parliamentary Labour Party on Europe at 6.30. After a series of meetings from which the shadow Cabinet had stood back – just listening to opinions from the floor, a typical Wilsonian ploy – it had been agreed that we should round off the series with two setpiece debates, at the first of which Barbara Castle and I would speak, with George Thomson and Willie Ross following on the next day.

The meeting was in a big committee room and was packed with about 250 MPs. Mrs Castle had made an issue out of her desire to speak second, but I had been determined not to concede what we both regarded as the more favourable position, to which I was formally entitled as deputy leader, and I thought morally entitled as the one who was swimming against the tide. Furthermore, she had at the time, unlike other periods before and since, no reserves of goodwill with me, for I considered that she had just been making a most appalling ass of herself, and of the Labour Party, by frenziedly opposing the Government's Industrial Relations Bill as a monstrous piece of class oppression, despite the fact that it owed about 80 per cent of its inspiration to her own *In Place of Strife*.

This contretemps over speaking position may have put her in a bad temper. In any event she made a speech which was at once sour and surprisingly ineffective. It lasted over forty minutes and involved the reading out of a lot of very complicated arguments of detail which sounded as though they had been prepared for her by someone else. It was an uncharacteristic performance and completely failed to engage with the meeting.

I then spoke for a little more than twenty minutes. I did not have to read my speech, although it was a carefully prepared statement. Most of Sunday had been devoted to it, both because I thought it likely to be a key stage in the dispute within the party and because I knew that when a major news story was likely to emerge from a nominally private meeting (that is, without reporters actually present) it was essential to have an authentic text for hand-out rather than to allow it to be transmitted through the inevitably distorted leaks of others. It was, I suppose, an uncompromising, even an inflammatory speech, making no attempt to paper over cracks. This was despite the fact that I had been reluctantly persuaded to take out an anti-Callaghan passage (earned by tergiversations on the issue culminating in his Southampton speech), which I thought was in the form of a rather good joke. I recalled an engine-driver who became a folk legend for careless derailments in early American railroad history and who was known as 'off-again, on-again, go-again Flanagan'. My intention was to pause heavily at this stage, and then to add: 'I said *Flan*agan.' John Harris vetoed it.

Even without this prop, the speech, which read in retrospect does not strike me as all that good, was a riotous success. I suppose because it released some pent-up feelings against the sophistry of the party's change of line, it produced more violent applause than any other speech which I have ever delivered. It came from about half the audience, punctuated every few sentences, and at the end continued for several minutes as a major demonstration. I remember in particular George Lawson, MP for Motherwell and a dour if right-wing Scottish ex-whip, far from a member of the metropolitan liberal establishment, achieving almost a Khrushchev-like UN effect by banging the table in front of him with his feet.

Tony Benn's diaries refer to 'Roy's great speech' while describing the adverse effect which it had both upon the left of the party, whom it made angry, and upon Wilson, whom it made nervous. Of the former I had direct evidence later that evening when I was walking out of the members' dining room after dinner and passed by a table at which Barbara Castle was sitting with Dick Crossman and others: 'Roy,' she said in a voice of controlled hysteria, 'I used to respect you a great deal, but I will never do so again as long as I live.' I hoped that this owed more to the frustrations of the evening than to settled judgement and passed on. For signs of Wilson's reaction I had to wait another twenty-four hours, but it then came in double-barrel form. During that interval I had to digest the following morning's newspapers, in which my speech at the party meeting made almost as big a story as Barber's mini-Budget, as well as prepare and deliver my speech for the economic debate on the Tuesday afternoon and also do the script for a straight-to-camera reply to Barber's ministerial telecast of the previous evening. For once I had to sacrifice my lunch, noting in my diary the rare and dismal experience of 'sandwich in the office'.

My speech in the House would have been one of my most pedestrian efforts had it not been for a mystifying piece of luck. The Prime Minister chose to sit in a rather thin House throughout my speech and towards the end to engage in a long joust about the state in which I had left the economy in 1970 and whether or not the dire predictions he had made on the basis of the May trade figures were justified. It was extraordinarily ill-chosen ground for Heath. He intervened three or four times. It was the mirror image of his put-down of me the previous November. This time I could hardly fail to win. It saved my speech, both in the next morning's press and with the Labour back-benchers.

What was so odd about his behaviour was that I was becoming his crucial potential ally on the issue about which he cared most.

To want to pick *and win* a quarrel with me at that stage was crazy. Had he been of a devious cast of mind, more like Harold Macmillan than himself, it might have made sense to pick *and lose* one. But such Machiavellianism is unimaginable in his case. It must just have been good curmudgeonly Heathian honesty of which I was the beneficiary.

Two hours later I saw a different form of prime ministerial perversity in operation. At 6.30 the second parliamentary Labour Party meeting of the week assembled to hear the continuation of the debate. It was a smaller meeting, but Willie Ross made a more effective anti-European speech than Barbara Castle had done, marred however by an obscure and vicious personal attack upon Robert Maclennan, then a junior Scottish MP. It was a symptom of mounting bitterness. Preceding it, Wilson had intervened to make an almost incomprehensible statement: it was half defensive, half threatening, and unclear in both purpose and argument. It left most people uneasily bewildered.

Perhaps fortunately I had to escape from that atmosphere of 'fog and filthy air' to go to Lime Grove for my telecast and from there back to Ladbroke Square where, at his insistent request, I awaited Crossman at 10.30 p.m. He had implied that he was coming as an emissary of Wilson, although it transpired that he was there more in his temporary capacity as editor of the *New Statesman* and in his permanent capacity of stirrer of troubled pots. He had however had a substantial talk with Wilson the night before and pronounced him as being appallingly upset, 'broken' was I think the word that he used, by my speech to the parliamentary party, and even more by the reaction of the meeting to it. But he had no message from him.

Speaking for himself, however, he said that I ought to resign as deputy leader. This was not, he insisted, because he thought my conduct had been improper. He was looking more to the future than the past, and he thought that I would be more at ease without this office. I was not in any event, he added agreeably, one of nature's deputy leaders. Then he fortified his argument by saying: 'Of course, the trouble with you is that you think you are a Gaitskell and you are nothing of the sort. You are much more a Bevan than you are a Gaitskell. You have all the Welsh capacity for wrecking. But maddeningly for the rest of us you are a Bevan with the big difference that you have the press and the establishment on your side.' This was said with perfect good humour, and was so received by me, although mine evaporated a little when I found that several of the remarks I made to him in confidence appeared in the following week's *New Statesman*.

The evening then degenerated into a mixture of high farce and minor tragedy. After about three-quarters of an hour of Crossman I decided that, with the pressures of the week, I must either go to bed or get on with preparing the next speech. I therefore suggested getting a taxi for him, and with his words about 'press and establishment' ringing in my ears picked up a telephone and dialled what I thought was a taxi number. A moment later a fruity voice said: 'William Rees-Mogg here.' I was quite incapable of concealing from Crossman whom I had by accident got on the other end of the telephone. At the time he treated it with appropriate hilarity, but I am sure that to the end of his life he remained convinced that what I had done was not to confuse numbers in the house telephone book but to pick up by mistake my own private line through to the editor of *The Times*.

I was sufficiently thrown by this to abandon the attempt to get a taxi by telephone and to say that I would drive Crossman until we found one in the street. When I returned I left my car unlocked, as a result of which the radio was wrenched out of it during the night for the second time within a few months.* It completed the pressures and confusion of the week.

Wednesday was a day of remission. I had no significant obligations except to listen to the opening of a four-day European debate and to attend an edgy two-hour meeting of the shadow Cabinet. On the Thursday I had to speak yet again. The opposition was still operating on the basis of no collective front-bench line on Europe, which meant that I could continue to say what I wanted from the despatch box. I was due to open at 3.30 p.m. on this second day of the debate, and despite a feeling of anticlimax after the excitements of Monday and Tuesday I attached importance to the speech because nearly all the other Labour front-bench speakers were growling away in increasing hostility, and I thought the Government case was presented with force by nobody except Heath, and without persuasiveness (for Labour supporters at any rate) even by him.

My trouble was that I was lacking in both time and energy to prepare yet another speech and that my one of Monday was unsuitable for repetition by virtue both of its reliance on internal Labour Party polemics and of the wide reporting which it had already received. Most exceptionally for me I was forced into dictating large chunks of the speech in my House of Commons office during the morning, and then went back to Ladbroke Square where I presided over a lunch party before appearing in the House with my unchecked text just before the appointed time. Looking back, I am surprised by both my stamina and my calm. I think repeated exposure had dulled my nerves, rather in the way that in a series of surgical operations fatalism

---

* Since when the trouble did not recur for eighteen years, after which, with shattered windows but no wrenching thanks to the advance of technology, it again happened twice within six weeks in the streets of Notting Hill.

replaces apprehension. Also I was carried along by some temporary release of daemonic energy which stemmed partly from an unusual sense of self-righteousness and partly from the fact that, although we were losing control of the party, we were having all the exhilaration of a war of movement while the others lumbered gloomily behind in ineffective pursuit.

At any rate I survived that exceptional political week. It marked the effective end of summer campaigning on the European front. The House went on until 5 August, but nothing much happened during these two weeks. Relations between Wilson and me, and within the shadow Cabinet generally, were half patched up, but underlying wariness and even distrust persisted. We all knew that the bombardment would begin again and with increased ferocity in the autumn.

Jennifer and I went to the Lebanon as the guests of their ambassador in London for a week on 9 August (I remember several politicians in that now desperate country expressing surprise that we could not handle communal relations in Northern Ireland as well as they did the balance of 6:5 between Christians and Muslims), and then Jennifer went to Greece and I to Italy, where I bounced up and down the peninsula like a yo-yo, staying with the William Rogerses on Lake Bracciano (where Hattersley also was and kept us even more full of political gossip than we would otherwise have been), with the Bonham Carters in the far south, then driving up to Modena and Mantova before returning to Florence by train to stay in a great house rented by Ronnie and Marietta Tree which overhung the city like a box looking down on the stage of an opera house. For two days at the end I went for the first time to Isaiah and Aline Berlin's house near Portofino where one looked down at about the same angle to the sea instead of the Duomo.

On the day I passed through Rome going to the south President Nixon brought the Bretton Woods system to a premature death at the age of twenty-seven, thereby producing the immediate effect of closed banks and cashless foreigners, and the longer-term effect of a decade and more of violently fluctuating currencies, from which Europe did worse than America or Japan because the consequences for us were internal whereas for our trade rivals they were only external and transoceanic.

# CHAPTER EIGHTEEN

# *The Road to Resignation*

I came back to London on 2 September 1971 and began an eight-week run-up to the crucial House of Commons vote on accepting the terms of entry. Our objectives for this long period of nerve-testing waiting were: first, to keep our numbers high and steady, so that the most convincing possible majority for entry should be obtained. A good majority we regarded as necessary to provide a momentum for the difficult further stages on the road to entry, as well as to send a message of the seriousness of Britain's purpose to the Europe of the Six. We also wanted to encourage Ireland, Denmark and Norway to accept the terms which they had negotiated for themselves. (We were successful only with the first two of these countries.)

Second, we wanted to build up support in the country for the Labour European case. And, third, we wanted to get through with as little damage as possible to the Labour Party and to our own position within it. We did not see ourselves as Peelites or Liberal Unionists preparing to move across the political spectrum. We regarded the issue as of such importance that there could be no question of our using it as a stick with which to break the back of the Heath Government. But we did not support that Government on other issues. As soon as it had got us into Europe we wanted it out of office.

The difficult defile through which we had to pass on our way to these objectives was the party conference, due in Brighton in the first week of October. Unlike Blackpool the year before the weather was superb. It was the beginning of a golden month, punctuated by East Hendred weekends of tennis and meals in the garden, with the Rodgerses coming down from the cottage they then had eight miles above us in the Downs to confer and report on who was sound and who was wobbly. Bill even wrote the opening lines of an elegiac poem beginning:

> They are mixing dry martinis at East Hendred.
> The croquet balls are clinking on the grass.

327

We at least kept our beleaguered garrison well provendered and in good heart, but Brighton and its sequence was more strain than this sounds. I had several encounters with Wilson, whose mood varied from the suspicious to the frosty, although I had known it worse, most notably in the same place five years before (see Chapter 9). His main complaint to me was about Bill Rodgers's activities as an unofficial but extremely effective whip for the 'Europeans'. It was one of Harold's weaknesses that his complaints were almost always vicarious. I said that with nearly all the official whips working the other way there was no question of my trying to call Rodgers off.

As in London in July, I was not allowed to speak in the conference itself on Europe. I nonetheless got maximum exposure for my face even if not for my arguments. Television and press judged that I had a 'silenced man' news value, and I was constantly televised or photographed when entering or leaving the hall or just sitting on the platform. I decided, particularly during the Europe debate on the Tuesday, of which the result was a predictably massive majority against entry on the terms negotiated, that the best course was to try to cultivate a persistent impassivity. This camera attention communicated itself to the public who, in the fine weather, thronged the route from the Grand Hotel to the conference hall and applauded loudly whenever I came through. At first I thought this pointed to strong Euro-enthusiasm on the part of the Brighton crowds, but I soon decided it signified little more than a higher than usual recognition factor.

I was unmuzzled on the Wednesday morning to wind up the economic debate, and made a speech which was both better in quality and better received than the one at Blackpool the year before. However, I apparently (and inadvertently) offended Wilson with a passage which I thought did no more than state the obvious to the effect that the 1945 Government had effected more long-term change than did the 1964 one. I also spoke at the crowded European rally which we held in the basement of the Metropole Hotel, but I did not succeed in arousing the enthusiasm of that gathering to quite the extent that I ought to have done. My most bizarre fringe engagement of the week, arranged long before, was to speak at a meeting of the Labour Parliamentary Association under the chairmanship of Tony Benn, who had in the meantime swung into an extreme anti-European position. He recorded in his diaries that he was 'friendly' and that I was 'amusing'.[1] It seemed the best thing to be in the circumstances.

Parliament resumed on 12 October. There was no business of any significance until the beginning on 21 October of the six-day European debate, which was no longer a dummy run but was on this occasion to culminate in the decisive vote. The intervening days were largely taken up with interviews with MPs, either because Bill Rodgers urged me to see them for stiffening purposes, or because they came to try to persuade me to abstain rather than to vote for the Government. I remember Fred Mulley (a committed European but a cautious man) and George Thomas (not a European but a great believer in all-round emollience) arguing particularly strongly for abstention. I also received a petition to this effect signed by about a hundred Labour MPs. I did not find this unsettling because I was convinced that it was one of the decisive votes of the century, and had no intention of spending the rest of my life answering the question of what did I do in the great division by saying 'I abstained.' I saw it in the context of the first Reform Bill, the repeal of the Corn Laws, Gladstone's Home Rule Bills, the Lloyd George Budget and the Parliament Bill, the Munich Agreement and the May 1940 votes and was consequently fortified by my amateur historical interest.

This 'settled mind because of historical destiny' approach was probably infuriating to others with a different view, but it was comforting to me and its settled-mind aspect was shared by a large number of others who harped less on history. There was remarkably little wobbling during this period of final waiting. The other issue which then occupied us was what whip was to be applied to Labour MPs. Harold Wilson, it will be recalled, had told me in February that there would be a free vote 'at the very worst'. Bob Mellish, the chief whip, had told both Rodgers and Taverne that an anti-European three-line whip would be applied only 'over his dead body'. Nevertheless, as soon as the party conference had pronounced, they were both determined to apply the full rigour of three lines. Nor were they deflected when Ted Heath announced on 18 October, admittedly as a bold and skilful tactical ploy, for he had more to gain from us than to lose from his own side, that there would be a free vote on the Government benches. All Wilson and Mellish did was to call a shadow Cabinet at such short notice that I could not get to it, and there to decide that this made no difference. This disgraceful decision was then endorsed, although by a narrow majority, at a meeting of the parliamentary party the following morning. In practice it did not matter for we were indifferent to the whip whatever it said, but it was the only time in the long-drawn-out battle that I thought Wilson and his adjutants behaved not merely with mistaken judgement but without decent friendliness. By this stage, however, they no doubt thought themselves much provoked by us.

The debate itself, as opposed to the vote at the end of it, seemed to me an anticlimax. This, I suppose, was partly for the good self-centred reason that I was not allowed to speak. After the party conference the agreement to differ of the summer was suppressed. Equally silenced were George Thomson, Shirley Williams, Harold Lever and Douglas Houghton. It was a striking example of the distorting effect which parties and the attempts at discipline which go with them can have upon the House of Commons as a representative forum. This was supposed to be the key debate of the decade (at least) and we were the leaders of the one-eighth of the House of Commons which, with the exception of the Prime Minister and those immediately around him, were most interested in the outcome and, because we were the hinge, were going to make the biggest difference to it. Yet of the more than one hundred speeches which filled the six days we were not allowed to contribute one. We could, of course, have gained our freedom of voice as well as of vote by resigning from the shadow Cabinet, but that would have meant prejudging the future shape of the Labour Party, and was a course that practically no one, inside or outside our group, urged upon us.

We had plenty of surrogate spokesmen. Apart from those who were actively and organisationally involved like Rodgers and Taverne, Marquand, Maclennan and Owen, there were a number of ex-ministers, such as Michael Stewart, Patrick Gordon Walker and Roy Mason, who remained staunchly on the side of the European commitment which had been entered into by the Wilson Government. For morale reasons I sat in for most of these Labour European speeches, but I felt no obligation to listen to my front-bench colleagues explaining with varying degrees of conviction why what had been white in government had become black in opposition. There were no new arguments which anyone could deploy. We had all become expert exponents of our own arguments and impervious to those of the other side. We could play with the speed of a chess master who simultaneously took on twenty opponents and moved around the room shifting his pieces on each board with hardly a glance or a thought.

On the final day (Thursday, 28 October) I lunched with John Harris and Roy Hattersley at Brooks's and was amazed to discover that the latter was agitated by the prospect of strong-arm tactics being used against me before or after the division by some of the more aggressive members of the Labour left, and was therefore organising a bodyguard to escort me out of the House and into a car for which he had rehearsed a quick get-away. It all seemed ludicrous to me, and although I was touched by his considerateness I also thought that it pointed to too much taste for drama accompanied by inflamed nerves.

That evening Jennifer and I dined early with George and Grace Thomson at Lockett's, a Westminster restaurant. Dick Taverne came and joined us late from one of his discouraging expeditions to Lincoln where he had been subjected to all sorts of threats and pressures

(Hattersley's vigilantes might have been more valuable there than in the House of Commons), which, however, had the effect of making him more determined than ever to vote. We then went back to the House and listened to the wind-up speeches, Callaghan for the Labour Party and Heath for the Government. I sat beside Wilson on the front bench and we exchanged one or two deflating jokes about their respective oratorical styles. Relations were not bad in the circumstances. As soon as the division was called Douglas Houghton and I went into the Government lobby and walked through together. When we came out there was a sort of corner gang of Labour members who seemed to have assembled to watch us perform the symbolic act of apostasy of bobbing our heads to the tellers. This group at least gave some verisimilitude to Hattersley's fears, but they neither did nor said anything that I can recall.

The only person who said anything coherently insulting to me that night was Reg Freeson, former middle-rank minister and MP for Willesden (later Brent), where ironically he was subsequently jettisoned by the left in favour of Ken Livingstone. Perhaps fortunately I cannot now remember exactly what he said, but it was loud, repeated several times and I think drew on his study of the habits of rodents. It came just after the announcement of the result of the division, which was better than we had expected: a majority of 112, to which we had contributed 69 positive votes and 20 abstentions. Had we all followed the whip, and had the Tory anti-Europeans all continued to rebel (perhaps an unlikely conjuncture) the terms of entry would have been rejected by a majority of thirty-six.

It was remarkable to hold sixty-nine Labour members against the pressures from constituencies, trade unions, whips and the leadership, which all exploited the simple atavistic appeal to party loyalty and solidarity. We could even have been a few more, for there were one or two whom we persuaded *not* to vote with us because they were in deadly constituency danger and lacked Dick Taverne's reckless buoyancy. It was a tribute both to the man-management quality of Bill Rodgers and to the attachment of at least a third of Labour MPs to the politics of principle as opposed to those of place. By this I do not mean that the other two-thirds were unprincipled. There was a sizeable group amongst them whose hostility to the European Community was just as strong and genuine as was our attachment to it. The difference was that at this stage in the tangled politics of Britain's relations with the Continent the issue was in party terms an easy one for them and a difficult one for us.

The difficulty for us was compounded by the fact that this was not a clean-cut, 'once and for all' vote such as, for example, that which brought down the Chamberlain Government and created the Churchill coalition in its place in May 1940. The decision of principle would be a nullity unless the Government were able to carry, in the new session which began on 2 November, a bill to give it legal form. On the face of it this was simple enough. Surely no one could will the end without willing the means. The continuing majority must be abundantly there.

This was precisely what it was not. As 28 October had shown, there was no majority without the Labour Europeans. And the Labour Europeans had signed up not for the duration but for one quick engagement. Our position was at once totally illogical and wholly comprehensible. We judged we could make a dash for Europe without endangering our long-term relations with the Labour Party. But to vote with the Government throughout the long stages of a bitterly fought piece of legislation was a different matter. We would be moving towards the position in which the Liberal Unionists had found themselves when they had to sustain the second Salisbury Government on the Irish Crimes Bill in the 1887 session of Parliament. I remember William Rees-Mogg urging this and the Peelite parallel upon me at some stage during that coming winter. 'I think you would be freer and more powerful,' he said, 'if you became an entirely separate group of sixty or seventy members with your own whips and no obligations to the Labour Party.' From the point of view of a Tory commentator this made perfectly good sense. From my point of view it did not. Apart from anything else, I could not have carried a quarter of that number with me. We were miles from such a move.

Indeed the majority of our group positively wanted to go back to voting with the Labour Party on the legislation. On the morning after the big vote even such a staunch figure as Douglas Houghton told me it was his position, and when Jean Monnet came to see me an hour later with profuse congratulations I thought it necessary to warn him that we might not be quite so forthright in the future. He reacted with sympathy and understanding. Joel Barnett, in whose constituency near Manchester I addressed a dinner that evening, was of the same view as Houghton. So was Hattersley, who indeed pre-empted the issue the following week by publicly promising his constituency management committee that he would vote with the Labour Party on all subsequent divisions. They rationalised their position by saying that it was the duty of a government to provide its own majority on all routine divisions and that they must get through by disciplining their own rebels.

This was not exactly my position. I knew that I was going to be miserable voting against the legislation, and I knew too that if by chance we defeated the Government on any aspect of the issue we would have made absolute asses of ourselves. On the other hand I accepted the strategy overwhelmingly urged by my closest associates, which was that we should endeavour to hold all our positions in the hierarchy of the party, and that in particular I should stand again for the deputy leadership in the election immediately due. Only one of my intimates dissented. He was Bob Maclennan. He argued strongly that it was a mistake to try to cling on to this uncomfortable position. What I should do was to challenge Wilson for the leadership. I would lose but I would get a lot of votes, probably well over a hundred, and this would strengthen my position for the future much more than would another unhappy year as second-in-command. In retrospect I think he was right.

However, he got little support at the time, and I proceeded to my second deputy-leadership election, anxious to get as close as possible to the resounding victory of the previous year. This desire to have the best of both worlds – or the thirty pieces of silver *and* the crown of thorns as Aneurin Bevan once put it in a different context – proved a recipe for a mounting unease which eventually culminated in my resignation five months later.

The anti-European creator of a particularly uncomfortable trap into which I obligingly fell is now, by an irony at least as great as Reg Freeson's deselection by the Brent left, a member of the European Commission. Bruce Millan in 1971 was an unflamboyant chartered accountant who was MP for the Craigton division of Glasgow. He had been a Scottish Office junior minister. I thought him nice but pedestrian, which shows the danger of taking patronising views. At a parliamentary Labour Party meeting on 3 November, he got up unexpectedly and asked me to declare my intentions about future voting on the European issue. It was ruled from the chair that an impromptu reply would be inappropriate, that I should be given until the regular weekly meeting to prepare a reply, and that, to preserve symmetry and fairness, the other two candidates (Foot again, and Benn as a new contestant) should also be invited to make statements. Thus was the perhaps casual question elevated into a major exchange.

Foot and Benn had no difficulty in giving the most categorical assurances. They did not even have to apostasise themselves on the issue (although over the years Foot's record had been immensely less 'loyal' than my own), for Foot was a consistent anti-European and Benn had recently switched to being a still more passionate one. I sounded sophistical. I said that I did not expect that there would be difficulty about voting with the party in subsequent divisions provided that I was not called upon to undo my vote of 28 October; and that if, unexpectedly, I found it necessary again not to vote with the party I would resign.

What I ought to have said was that the party knew what I had done, knew my record, knew my continuing beliefs and could vote for me or not as they liked. However, we were too eager to get the few extra votes which might once again see me clear on the first ballot. Millan's own vote was certainly at stake, and we knew of at least two others (those of John Golding, the West Midland whip, and of Terry Davis, the victor of Bromsgrove and subsequently my successor in Stechford). I do not think I got any of them. I had merely erected a spike on which to impale myself.

The first result, on 20 November, vindicated the view that marginal votes were important. I got 140, seven votes up on the previous year, Foot got 96 and Benn 46. The poll was higher, but I had failed by two to get an absolute majority. Had I just scraped by the result would have been hailed as a triumph and the combined total of Foot and Benn submerged by their weak individual showings. As it was I had to go on to an anticlimactic second ballot. I thought at first that Foot would concede, as Maudling had done in the Tory leadership contest of 1965, but I underestimated both the persistence of the left and the real value from their point of view of proceeding to a further round of which the result was only a rather unconvincing 140 for me to 126 for Foot.

At first I was amazed that my vote had stuck so adhesively at 140. We were sure we had some second preferences amongst the nearly fifty Benn supporters. Then the truth dawned. The two 140s were coincidental. Their composition changed marginally but significantly between the two ballots. I got quite a few Benn votes and lost a number of right-wing anti-European votes, I think including Callaghan and his close associates, and maybe even Crosland. Their behaviour was wholly rational. They did not want a deputy leader of the left, but nor did they want me boosted by superfluous votes. Once they regarded the actual outcome as beyond doubt they comfortably abstained. Their number certainly did not include Wilson, who defensively insisted on showing me his ballot paper with his cross against my name.

Douglas Houghton was also re-elected chairman of the parliamentary party, although with a margin even narrower than my own, and Shirley Williams, George Thomson and Harold Lever were satisfactorily returned to the shadow Cabinet. Edward Short, who had abstained on 28 October, moved into first place, and Denis Healey crashed down from second to twelfth place, which seemed a just reward for his two shifts of position in the summer.

I went to America on 3 December, spent part of the first weekend with the reunited and newly married Averell and Pamela Harriman, occupied the inside of the week with a mixture of New York enjoyment and delivering three Henry L. Stimson Memorial lectures at Yale, which I subsequently turned into a little book entitled *Afternoon on the Potomac?*, and wound up the visit with a Washington whirl for the second weekend. Over the Christmas holidays I wrote the third of my *Times* essays, this one on Maynard Keynes, and on 15 January set off for a two and a half week visit to Iran (the Shah and Isfahan), Singapore (a lot of Lee Kuan Yew), Calcutta (for a harrowing visit to a disease-ridden refugee camp and a brief excursion to the newly independent Bangladesh), Delhi (Mrs Gandhi) and Bombay (my cousin Pita Karaka and her Parsee and weekly-magazine-editor husband).

The visit to the refugee camp had its elements of macabre farce as well as of horror. It was about forty miles from Calcutta and had a population the size of the city of Nottingham. I drove out early one afternoon with an accompanying car-load of British journalists including a *Daily Mirror* photographer. I am afraid I may have gone there partly because in the immediate aftermath of the Indo-Pakistan war it was a trendy place for politicians to visit and in which to be photographed. Ted Kennedy had been there the previous week. To that extent I deserved all the menaces of the afternoon. I knew there was a lot of cholera in the camp, but there was worse to come. As soon as we got there I was taken into an administrative hut which for some reason or other had no glass in the windows. Through each of these vacant spaces there peered a small sea of agitated and hostile faces. A figure who appeared to be in charge greeted me but said that I had chosen a bad day for the visit. I asked him if he were the camp commandant. 'No,' he said, 'the deputy commandant. The commandant was murdered last night. There is a very bad and dangerous atmosphere in the camp. In addition, which is not yet known, we had eleven cases of smallpox diagnosed yesterday and another twenty this morning.' He then asked what I would like to see, suggesting some of the tented 'lines' in which families lived and at least one of the hospitals. I had no alternative but to agree, although by this time I was beginning to count the minutes until I could decently leave. As we walked down the lines camp officials pulled up the flaps of occasional tents and encouraged one to peer in at appalling scenes of misery and squalor, with many of the inhabitants looking as though they were already far advanced into one or other of the dread diseases.

Then we got to the Caritas hospital and were met by a young doctor, with whom I had almost a repeat of the conversation in the commandant's office. 'Are you the medical superintendent?' I asked. 'No,' he said, 'I am his deputy. He is sick. He is in that tent over there, where he has particularly asked that you should visit him before you go.' 'What's wrong with him?' I asked. 'Chicken-pox, we hope,' was the encouraging response. The medical deputy then asked what wards I would like to see, indicating the ones for infectious diseases, for malnutrition, for undiagnosed admissions. I searched desperately for what might be the safest and eventually suggested the gynaecological one. I wound up, as required, with a visit to the medical superintendent, who was in a solitary brown sheeted bed in the middle of a vast brown tent. He was an intelligent man who I greatly hope recovered from his chicken-pox.

I then regained my car and set off back to Calcutta. At that stage in my life I was devoted to medium-sized Havana cigars. I had a case with me and have never more wanted to smoke one and hope thereby to calm my nerves. But I was too frightened to do so for my method was to nip off the end with my thumb-nail, and this, with my medical illiteracy, I thought might increase the risk of infection. Back at the consul-general's house I threw my clothes off and plunged into a disinfected bath, which was probably an equally ineffective prophylactic.

Then I recovered my sense of proportion (or of false equanimity) until I got back to London and went to my Viennese doctor. When I told him the story he treated me with distinct apprehension, inquired anxiously exactly when I had been to the camp, pronounced that the incubation period was not fully over, and seemed eager to get me out of his consulting room as soon as possible. Later he told me that the reason for his neurosis was that his father had died of smallpox as a government medical inspector on the frontiers of the Austro-Hungarian Empire. (As he had previously told me that his father had been Freud's doctor, this seemed a demotion.) I hope that an additional reason was not that the vaccine with which he had injected me a few months before had been weakened for economy reasons. The whole episode was a just retribution for politicians' conceit that they serve some purpose by being present at scenes of action or tragedy.

During the winter and early spring months of 1971–2 the prospect that I would one day be Prime Minister, which for three or four years until then had seemed more likely than not, was quietly but ineluctably slipping away from me, but its disappearance (of which in any event I was not really aware) was lubricated by a good deal of worldwide public recognition and private flattery. There is no doubt that standing out against the apparent chauvinism of one's own party is a good recipe for attracting international acclaim. The cause of European integration seemed suddenly to have become as popular in India and New England as it was in Bonn and Rome. In January I was offered a Harvard degree (to be conferred at Cambridge, Massachusetts, in June) and in February the Charlemagne Prize (to be conferred at Aachen on Ascension Day in May). Amongst British politicians since the war, only Home had previously received a Harvard degree and only Churchill and Heath the Karlspreis. I was naturally pleased.

I find it understandable in retrospect that Harold Wilson (his language no doubt made untypically coarse by the strength of his feeling) complained at about this time that he spent his time wading in shit to hold the Labour Party together while I went around the world with a halo on my head. But my sympathy is tempered by my conviction that if he had taken the advice I gave him on 9 June 1971 he could have avoided most of the shit, at least shared the halo and come back more and not less convincingly as Prime Minister in 1974 or 1975.

Nevertheless I was far from basking in satisfaction during these months. I dreaded the arrival before the House of Commons of the European Communities Bill. By 1 February, the date of my return from India, I had succumbed to a cataclysmic mood about the prospects of going through with the commitments into which I had entered in my reply to Bruce Millan. This feeling had been exacerbated by a long luncheon with Michael Foot in Brooks's just before my departure for the East. I had arranged it partly as a general goodwill exercise and partly to try to make him see why I could not allow the Government to be defeated on the bill. The first part seemed to me a splendid success, the second a ghastly failure. We gossiped easily for an hour on books and history. Then I tried to make him see that his hope of defeating Heath on the legislation rested on the intolerable premise that Enoch Powell (about whom he was nearly as starry-eyed as he had been about Beaverbrook) and the other Tory rebels were men of honour who would stick to their beliefs in contrast with the Labour Europeans who would show themselves men of straw. He could not see the point at all. 'But surely you must regard the opportunity to defeat the most reactionary government for a hundred years as more important than a particular piece of legislation' was the unyielding essence of his position.

Such partisan hyperbole about what even Foot would now regard as one of the more moderate of Conservative administrations, delivered without any hint of self-mockery by that normally deflatingly witty man, stuck in my mind for eight years until it resurfaced as one of the sub-themes of my 1979 Dimbleby lecture. The more immediate impact of the conversation was that it destroyed any hope that the majority of the Labour Party would accept that there was no mileage for it in the deeply divisive European issue, and that the only sensible course for the party was to play it as quietly and tolerantly as possible. It is a curious feature of the tribal culture of political parties that they cannot leave internally divisive subjects alone. This wound-picking habit has by no means been confined to the Labour Party. For twenty-eight years from 1903 to 1931 the Conservative Party whenever in trouble always made things worse by rushing into a new bout of protection/tariff-reform/Empire-free-trade fever. David Owen, when he decided in 1986 that nuclear weaponry was the most divisive issue for the Alliance, could talk about little else for two years. And it has recently looked possible that the Conservative Party in the 1990s could be equally split and equally obsessive about national sovereignty versus European unity as was the Labour Party in the 1970s.

Second reading of the European Communities Bill came on 17 February. Together with most of my closest parliamentary associates I voted against the bill. I remember it as a day of misery. Shamefacedly slinking through the 'no' lobby made a pathetic contrast with striding through the 'aye' lobby on 28 October. The Government had a majority of eight. This was a sad decline from the 112, but it was not that which primarily worried us or them. We were no longer concerned with sounding a great blast on the trumpet. What we were desperately concerned about was avoiding a single defeat in any one of the ninety-two divisions on the bill which were to follow until, on 13 July, third reading was secured by a majority of seventeen. Had any single one of them gone wrong we would have been confronted with the most stark alternatives. Either we could have let the adverse vote stand, in which case we would have destroyed our vote of 28 October, for the legislation was so drafted that it had to be carried unamended for Britain to be able to enter the Community. Or some of us would have to switch our vote, in the most exposed position and under the most powerful searchlight, when the issue was brought back before the House and when there could be no doubt that we had the fate of the Government in our hands.

In a sense our position was even worse than this. One factor in the Government's majority of eight was a small Labour abstention. This, with the numbers and individuals varying somewhat, was to be a constant feature of the divisions on the bill. The abstainers were made up in almost equal proportions of old men who had decided their political fate no longer mattered and young men with the gallantry of 1916 subalterns. Typical of the former group was George Russell Strauss, left-wing rebel and 'angel' of *Tribune* in the 1930s, who by his seventies had become a firm European. Typical of the latter was Michael Barnes, the thirty-nine-year-old MP for Brentford and Chiswick. They at once provided us with an essential little shield behind which to shelter and made our political calculations rather tawdry. It is never comfortable to be dependent on men braver than oneself.

I therefore passed the six weeks between 17 February and the run-up to the Easter holidays in a state of mounting discontent, both with myself and with the Labour Party. A lot of the seeds of my disenchantment with party politics were planted during that period. Its rules and conventions made monkeys out of everyone: first Wilson, not to mention Healey, Callaghan, Crosland, and then me. The artificiality of the game and my relations with Wilson at that time are well summed up by a vignette that I retain for 7 March, the day my award of the Charlemagne Prize had been announced. As Wilson and I came out of the House of Commons chamber together after questions, he took me aside with some display of embarrassment. 'I imagine this prize means a good deal to you,' he said rather as Queen Victoria might have spoken to David Livingstone about some hottentot bauble which he had collected, 'and that being so I would like to say that I am very glad you have got it; and if any newspaper or anyone else asks you whether I have congratulated you, I hope you will answer "yes", as of course my press office will do if the query comes to them.'

I had a two-day burst of 'resignationitis' following a particularly dreadful three-hour shadow Cabinet on 23 February, but was persuaded out of this without too much difficulty. On Saturday, 11 March, I went to John Roper's constituency at Farnworth in Lancashire and addressed a Labour Party tea. The speech was carefully prepared and put out to the press well in advance. It was the first of a series of seven which, with the help of a group of supporters of whom David and Judith Marquand were the most intellectually fertile, I was planning to deliver over the next six months and then to publish as a paperback book. The intention was to set out an across-the-board range of policies which would strike a more serious and a more principled note than the short-term party manoeuvring which, in contrast with his performance in 1963–4, had by this time become the stock-in-trade of Harold Wilson's leadership. They would also show that I had not become obsessed with Europe to the exclusion of all else.

Yet such was the uneasy ambiguity of my position at the time that, when the press interpreted the purpose of the Farnworth speech as exactly this, I recoiled in apprehension. When I got to Paddington late that evening on my way from Lancashire to East Hendred I bought the following morning's newspapers. The *Sunday Times* and the *Observer* both gave prominence to the speech and in particular to one of its concluding sentences: 'In place of the politics of envy, we must put the politics of compassion; in place of the politics of cupidity, the politics of justice; in place of the politics of opportunism, the politics of principle.'* The news angle was that this last contrast was aimed directly and damagingly at Wilson. I should have been pleased at the notice given to the speech (that, after all, was the purpose of

---

* Thanks to the hand of David Marquand the peroration also contained a quotation from Andrew Marvell, 'Casting the kingdoms old into another mould', which foreshadowed part of the message of the SDP.

preparing it so carefully) and for the rest should just have shrugged and said to myself, 'If the cap fits, let him wear it.'

Instead I had a rather uneasy journey to Didcot, fearing that I was opening up too wide an anti-Wilson front for the breach ever to be healed, the unease made worse by the fact that the train managed to break down and take two and a half hours. And next morning, much influenced by telephone advice from Roy Hattersley, who had been deputed by John Harris, absent for several months in America, to act as my tactical guide, I went into Oxford and redid a BBC *World This Weekend* interview, which I had recorded the previous morning, so as to make it more emollient. How much better I would have done to follow Joseph Chamberlain's axiom of 'never withdraw, never explain'. There was too much willingness to wound accompanied by fear to strike about my attitude.

However that may be, of these two conflicting fixed points, 23 February shows that the possibility of resignation was by then already buzzing round in my mind, while 11 March shows that I was by no means moving steadily towards it. As late as Tuesday, 28 March, two days before the beginning of the Easter holidays, the prospect seemed no worse (although no better either) than at most times in the past few months, and my assumption was that I would stagger on uncomfortably as deputy leader through the summer and perhaps to re-election in the autumn. Late that afternoon I gave a quasi-historical foreign policy lecture to the British Academy, had an inspiriting talk afterwards with Isaiah Berlin, who had presided, and returned to the House of Commons in a calm and even cheerful mood.

Then, over the next twenty-four hours, three unexpected blows fell one after the other. At 7.30 on that same evening George Thomson came to see me at his urgent request. A few weeks before he had told me of the likelihood of his being offered one of the two European Commissionships to which Britain would become entitled the following January. As he added that he had decided to refuse I dismissed the matter from my mind. Now he came to say that the offer had been made firm, and that after a week's hard thought he had changed his mind. It offered him the best prospect of useful service over the next four years, and would also be a release from an increasingly uncomfortable relationship (over Europe) with his Dundee Labour Party.

In view of the similar change of mind I was to undergo in four years' time, it would have been intolerable had I reproached him. And, luckily, I (just) did not. But it was a bitter blow. Thomson was then the most valuable of all my allies. He had weight as well as charm and steadfastness, and he came from a helpfully different background and part of the country. Furthermore, the fact that Dundee pressure was a contributory factor sounded a knell of doom which might presage many other future erosions of our forces. The good morale with which I came back from the British Academy had completely gone by dinnertime.

The next day brought two more vicissitudes. In the morning the National Executive of the Labour Party met to elect a new general secretary. The candidate of the right was Gwyn Morgan, assistant general secretary and a staunch European (indeed he subsequently went to Brussels, first as George Thomson's *chef de cabinet* and then as a member of the *services* of the Commission), and the candidate of the left was Ron Hayward, national agent of the party. But there were complications. Morgan was supported by some non-Europeans such as Callaghan and a few trade union members. Hayward was himself not so much left-wing as without intellectual ballast and incapable of seeing beyond the narrowest confines of party politics. He was supported by Wilson, who had switched to him a few weeks before, probably out of fear that Morgan would be too much my man, or Callaghan's man, or both (a difficult feat).

Nevertheless Morgan was the favourite, overwhelmingly so before Wilson's defection, and by a few votes even after it. This was not how it worked out. After two or three hours of procedural wrangle and bitter semi-farce, Hayward was eventually elected on the casting vote of the chairman, Tony Benn. It was a serious defeat because it both symbolised and reinforced a significant leftward shift in the control of the party machine. It also gave notice that Europeanism was becoming a bar to preferment. Morgan was much the abler man. A year before he would have romped to victory. His supporters left the meeting angry, deflated and fearful for the future.

One or two of us (I think in fact only Shirley Williams and I, for there was surprisingly small overlapping membership between the two bodies) having been sand-bagged in the morning, then proceeded to be garotted in the afternoon. Two weeks before, the shadow Cabinet had rejected by a majority of eight to four a proposal of Benn that we should support an amendment to the European Communities Bill which demanded a referendum before Britain could sign the treaty. I and my associates were strongly opposed to the proposal on at least three grounds. First, it would throw the whole issue into doubt, and might therefore result in nullifying our vote of 28 September, which was throughout our proclaimed sticking-point. Second, we were resistant on principle to the importation of the then novel device of the referendum into our constitutional arrangements. (Shirley Williams was more open-minded on this point than were the rest of us.) We saw its extensive use as being the likely enemy of many progressive causes from the abolition of capital punishment to race relations legislation to effective land-use planning controls. Third, we feared that a referendum campaign, fought, as it would have to be if the result were to have any democratic validity, with most of the intensity of a general election, would sunder the Labour Party, effectively drive us out of it and cripple the remainder as a party of government.*

This new instrument of dissension had completely seized Benn's imagination and he had been working hard at its promotion for several months. Nor had he been without success. Before Christmas he had brought it before the National Executive Committee and had seen it rejected without a single vote, save only his own, in its favour. But on 22 March he had succeeded in getting the same body to carry by thirteen votes to eleven a mildly worded resolution asking the shadow Cabinet to give further consideration to the advantages of voting for the referendum in the House of Commons. I had been absent from this meeting (unavoidably, as I had to take a full meeting of the parliamentary party on the Budget), and so had both Wilson and Callaghan. It was this thirteen-to-eleven vote which nominally brought the issue back to the shadow Cabinet so soon after it had been rejected.

We were not unduly apprehensive for we assumed on the basis of the experience of a fortnight previously that we had the votes. The dislike of the referendum extended well beyond the ranks of the Europeans. Both Healey and Willie Ross had spoken strongly against it on that previous occasion. Wilson had not spoken clearly, but he had seemed content with the adverse decision. By 29 March he had done a major tactical switch and become a firm advocate of our voting for the Tory back-bench amendment for the referendum, which was due to come before the House almost immediately after Easter, and which, with Labour support, was only too likely to be carried. Indeed he followed what had been his old Cabinet practice when he was resolved to influence a decision, and came in at an early stage in the discussion, speaking after only Foot and I had done so. In addition, I believe that he persuaded Ross to stay away from the meeting. That curmudgeonly Scot was the most regular of attenders and was known to be about the House. He hated the referendum because he saw it

---

* After the second Wilson Government had survived its split approach to the 1975 referendum campaign these fears came to seem over-dramatic to nearly everybody, including myself. Now I am not so sure. In the first place there was greater tolerance in 1975 than there would have been in 1972 (mainly because by then it was the left and not the right who were the minority). Even with this greater tolerance, however, many of the seeds which sprouted into the weeds which destroyed the Labour Party as a governing party for a decade and more were sowed during that 1975 referendum campaign. Certainly the handling of the European question by the leadership throughout the 1970s did more to cause the party's disasters of the 1980s than did any other issue.

as a potentially dangerous weapon for the Scottish Nationalists and he was not prepared to perjure himself in its favour. But he hated the Common Market even more, and he was also a very dependable ally of Wilson's. So he agreed not to vote against it.

That left us two down on our previous vote, for Healey was also absent, but at a somewhat greater distance. We were at this stage reduced to our hard-core European five plus Crosland, who spoke crisply against the referendum, although inevitably adding that he did not think it very important. The other side had Foot, Shore, Benn, Peart – and Wilson. Then Mellish, the chief whip, spoke, and gave what in view of subsequent events I would judge to be one of the worst pieces of advice ever given by a whip to a shadow Cabinet. He said he was sure the party would be happy to vote for the amendment if it embarrassed the Government. That made it six all.

We still thought that we had Ted Short, who had been an abstainer on 28 September, and whom Shirley Williams had canvassed and thought 'all right' on the issue, and were half hopeful of Callaghan, who was not a natural supporter of Bennite gimmicks. However, Callaghan produced a masterly piece of tactical exegesis in which he reserved his position on the referendum but said that he was in favour of voting for the amendment because in present circumstances we ought all to support the leader. We ought still to have been seven all, but to our total dismay and amazement Ted Short, who had come in late to the meeting after I had spoken, announced that he was on balance in favour of voting for the amendment. The significance of his lateness was that he subsequently said that had he appreciated how strongly I felt about the issue he would not have voted as he did. But whatever were people's varying motives the indisputable outcome was that our previous victory of eight to four, without Wilson declaring his hand, had turned itself within two weeks into defeat by eight to six, with him leading the pack.

The only thing I could think of to do was to ask for the right to speak and vote against the majority shadow Cabinet decision at the parliamentary party meeting after Easter. There was the precedent of the party-meeting debates in July 1971. But Wilson ruled sharply against this. In retrospect this made me think that he must have fixed upon a strategy of forcing us into submission or resignation, probably the latter, because he normally so hated taking a difficult and divisive decision that it would have been natural for him to grasp at subsequent emollience.

The meeting then broke up in mild disorder, and the European group, less Douglas Houghton, who was engaged elsewhere, retreated to my room to lick our wounds. We were stunned, but the determination not to accept this sudden lurch in the party's position was strong. Harold Lever was the most resolute, but George Thomson was as firm as I was. Shirley Williams was torn between disapproval of the tactical cynicism of the reversal of the previous decision and her democratic populist feeling that it was difficult to oppose a referendum. Douglas Houghton, as I discovered in long subsequent telephone conversations, was as opposed to the new decision as was Lever, but suffered from what I regarded as the illusion that it could be overturned at the meeting of the parliamentary party. We adjourned in suitably cataclysmic mood to a wake for Gwyn Morgan's hopes of the general-secretaryship of the Labour Party.

The next day being Maundy Thursday I drove down to East Hendred, accompanied by David Owen for some reason which is not now clear to me, except that we were in general then close. We lunched on our way out of London at a pub in Hammersmith. I think that it was there that he formed the view that resignation from the deputy leadership, while unwise, had become psychologically necessary to me. That being so, and in the circumstances of the time, he loyally supported it, although he put in a paper arguing against.

I had ten days of 'holiday' in which to make up my mind. The only politician I saw over the first weekend was Bill Rodgers. He was determined not to push me in the direction of resignation, partly because he had been falsely accused of doing this when the second-reading vote in February had made me flicker in that direction, and partly because he strongly believed it should be my untrammelled decision. He merely reported his considered view that a party meeting on the referendum issue, without the spur and excitement of a resignation, was likely to produce an attendance of no more than eighty to a hundred, and would probably split sixty-to-thirty against us. I believe this was an accurate assessment.

Easter Monday I spent drafting a resignation letter. I thought it would clarify my mind and would be useful to have in my knapsack. The danger of this was that, given my slow drafting and consequent 'tablets of stone' approach to the painfully produced result, the exercise tended to pre-empt the decision. Over the next few days the eight hundred words of that letter received an excessive amount of attention. It was read over the telephone to both George Thomson and Douglas Houghton. It was shown to one or two others who came to East Hendred or with whom we went to lunch, and it was frequently titivated by me. The disappointing (but perhaps in the circumstances not surprising) fact is that, when for the purposes of writing this chapter I came to reread it for the first time for seventeen years, I found it singularly lacking in pith or sparkle.

Despite this lack of inspiration in the basic text my mood moved increasingly towards resignation over the middle of that week (for the whole of which I stayed firmly at East Hendred), and by the Friday had become more or less settled. To the best of my retrospective belief my motivation was as follows. I was convinced after the previous week's shadow Cabinet meeting that Foot, Shore, and Benn in particular, were resolved to go on and on raising any issue they could think of which would embarrass the Labour Europeans, and no doubt the Government too. There was no question of their using their majority with restraint so as to contain the fissure within the party. And with Wilson apparently having committed himself to go along with them, their majority was not in doubt. The prospect for me for the summer was that of being made to jump through a series of humiliating hoops, with the inevitable erosion of any position I had in the country, and a consequent increasing difficulty of ever again being able to find any firm ground on which to stand.

Nor was it just a matter of personal humiliation. If I went along, they would sooner or later find an amendment, maybe the referendum, maybe something else, on which the Government would be defeated and the whole European argosy would be shipwrecked. I could hardly strut around Europe (I was due for example to receive the Karlspreis in Aachen on 11 May) making sonorous European pronouncements while quietly allowing the European cause to be defeated in Britain.

Then suddenly over the Friday night I became filled with doubt and got up on Saturday morning in a sea of confusion. With a difficult decision and conflicting advice from trusted friends and collaborators such an occasional swing of mood is probably inevitable. We had Robert McNamara as well as Catherine Freeman and the David Owens coming to lunch, and the disparate nature of the party (and also my desire to preserve secrecy; we were mercifully free of press speculation) clearly precluded agonising in the dining room. Jennifer and I therefore decided that we would endeavour to put the obsessing issue out of mind for the Saturday and make a definite decision on the Sunday, when the George Thomsons and the Tom Bradleys were summoned for a more serious lunch.

This had the perverse result that, having as it were instructed my mind to concern itself with other things, it settled itself easily and almost subconsciously back into its pro-resignation groove. When I said goodbye to David Owen I left him in no doubt that resignation was settled. In spite of his paper, he accepted the decision without complaint, almost enthusiastically.

I then started to track down John Harris, who was still in America. I much wanted him back, both for his advice and for his help in dealing with the mountain of press attention which would be inevitable from Monday onwards. Ironically it was Hattersley who was the agent of our making contact. Hattersley was strongly against resignation and was keeping careful track of Harris's movements in the hope that he might be wheeled in as a powerful ally against my being headstrong. He was therefore able to get Harris on the telephone to me from Chicago by 7.30 p.m. (British time). Harris, however, was strongly in favour of my decision. Moreover he said that he would gladly change his plans and come back, and did so with such determination that his taxi drove into the yard at East Hendred at 11.15 the next morning, just under sixteen hours after I had alerted him. He was therefore present at the Thomson/Bradley lunch and was subsequently with me throughout.

At this Sunday gathering the Thomsons were both strongly in favour of resignation and the Bradleys were rather silent, although dismayed and depressed at the prospect, not for themselves but for me. Knowing this was likely (and that I would therefore have to test the validity of my arguments) in combination with the vast regard I had for Tom Bradley and the importance which I consequently attached to keeping him with me was indeed the main reason for the shape of the gathering on this crucial day. In the course of the afternoon he rallied and argued strongly against doing anything until after the party meeting on Wednesday. I was convinced that once Parliament was back the secret of my intentions could not be kept and that this would mean 'hawking one's conscience' around the House of Commons for three days. Furthermore there was no way in which I could convey the seriousness with which I viewed the issue to the party meeting without putting a pistol to their heads, and this I thought undesirable. Resignation should never be threatened; it should either be done or not.

By the end of the afternoon I think that Tom Bradley had accepted this particular argument of timing, although probably not the general case for resignation. The Bradleys and the Thomsons went at about six. As I saw George off in the yard, I said, 'Well, that's it then. The decision is finally taken,' and as he was resigning with me that made it irrevocable.

Jennifer and I and John Harris then walked two miles to West Hendred and back before I got down to some necessary telephoning. I spoke to Harold Lever, who had typically just got back from Deauville, where the issue did not seem to have much occupied his mind, but who greeted the news with a simple 'Thank God,' and unhesitatingly said that he would come too. That was inspiriting.

Bill Rodgers and Dick Taverne were also pleased with the decision. My constituency chairman and secretary in Birmingham accepted the news without either surprise or remonstrance. Hattersley accepted it with regret, but without complaint. Shirley Williams, who had been incommunicado the previous week, I had difficulty in finding. When I eventually got her she was friendly and sympathetic, although inevitably in a somewhat different position from me because of an instinctive sympathy for the idea of a referendum. Nonetheless she thought she would probably come with us.

The next morning (Monday, 10 April) I drove Jennifer and John Harris to London in unrelenting rain. As soon as I got to Ladbroke Square I sent a message to Wilson saying that I must see him urgently at 12.45. In the meantime I had a meeting with Thomson, Lever and Shirley Williams. When I got to Wilson's room he opened blandly by asking whether I had had a good Easter. 'Not very,' I said, and plunged in. I do not think he was surprised. He expressed what can best be described as calm dismay, and made a somewhat more than nominal attempt to dissuade me. I got him off that and on to modalities. 'I find it difficult to start making the funeral arrangements before I am absolutely convinced of the death,' he felicitously said. However, I eventually got him to contemplate the baked meats and told him that Thomson and Lever were coming with me, but probably not Shirley. So far as those who held junior spokesmanships (that is, were on the front bench but not members of the shadow Cabinet) were concerned, I was advising them not to resign, although a few seemed determined to do so.* He would get my letter immediately after lunch (it was still being typed) and it would not be released for two hours after that, so that he could issue a reply at the same time if he wished (he did). I would then hold a lobby at which I proposed to say that I had no intention of being a candidate for any office in the parliamentary Labour Party that autumn; in other words I would not run against him. He showed too much pleasure at this, but otherwise he put on a good avuncular act, reminiscing sympathetically about the difficulties of resignation as he had found them in 1951, and, true to his practice of never blaming the principal if he was present, expressed the hope that I had not been pushed by others.

In the afternoon as the news naturally began to leak all over the House of Commons, I went to ground in my room there. I did the lobby at six, and then went home feeling exhausted. The next day began better than it continued. The press was on the whole favourable, as I suppose was sufficiently predictable not to be interesting. But by the afternoon it seemed clear that the reaction amongst Labour MPs was not good. Too many of them thought we had been self-indulgent. George Thomson and John Harris and I subsequently agreed that this was our most depressed moment during the entire enterprise.

Fortunately it was an island of low pressure and not a decline into a whole season of depressions. At the meeting of the parliamentary

* Eventually Bill Rodgers, Dick Taverne, Dickson Mabon (who wrote a particularly good letter to Wilson) and David Owen did, while Roy Hattersley, Denis Howell and Ivor Richard did not.

party the following (Wednesday) morning the sun came out strongly. A bewildering but beneficent change of mood seemed to have set in overnight, and our speeches went as well as those of our opponents went badly. Lever was particularly effective, while Shore opened with a hyperbolic speech composed in about equal parts of intolerance towards us and 'this England set in a silver sea' rhetoric, while Foot at the end was flailing and tub-thumping.

Still more significant was the vote. We got ninety-six, which far exceeded our expectations, and were beaten only by a margin of thirty-three. This meant that, so far from the party being 'happy' to vote for the referendum, the turns and twists of the leadership had split it into two nearly equal parts on the issue. This clever weapon had become a fine instrument of self-destruction but useless against the Government. When the vote was taken on the floor of the House in the following week, about a fifth of Labour MPs either abstained or did not bother to turn up, and the amendment was defeated by forty-nine. Not only did this dispose of the threat of the referendum, it also took the stuffing out of the attempt to undermine the 28 September vote by carrying an amendment to the European Communities Bill. The resignation may not have been tactically wise, but it was not in vain.

Some of my supporters who had been most opposed to resignation (notably Charles Pannell) were inclined to argue that this result showed that had I held my hand we could have defeated the forces of unrighteousness in the parliamentary meeting and rendered resignation unnecessary. I did not believe that at the time, and I do not do so now. Imprisoned by continuing membership of the shadow Cabinet we would have been mute at the meeting, and without the drama of resignation we would have had an attendance of 100 and not of 220 and would probably have lost by two to one. Nothing that happened subsequently invalidated Bill Rodgers's estimate of 2 April.

On the Thursday and Friday I was inundated by letters of reaction. The mail was large by my standards, but not vast by the quantities that others report. I had about 400 letters by the Friday morning, which broke 79 per cent favourable to 21 per cent unfavourable. Encouragingly the overwhelming majority of the favourable ones were from Labour supporters or floating voters. On the Friday afternoon we went to Sandwich Bay to a vast old seaside villa, redolent of a mixture of Nantucket sailing ships, Shavian Fabianism and the arts and crafts movement, which a kind friend had lent us, rightly guessing that with the attention we were attracting East Hendred would be too exposed. There I read the letters, digested the weekly and the Sunday press, and reflected on the dramas of the past two and a half weeks. I felt shell-shocked, but not desolated. I recorded five weeks after my resignation that only once in thirty-five mornings did I wake with a gloomy conviction that I had made a mistake. That exception was eight days after the event, on the Tuesday morning immediately following our return from Sandwich. In the circumstances an adverse score of one out of thirty-five was not bad.

The question which continues mildly to intrigue me is whether or not Harold Wilson wanted my resignation. My view a short time after the event, from which I still see no reason to deviate, is that my speech at Worsley on 11 March had a disproportionate effect upon him. He became needlessly worried about a challenge from me to his leadership in the following autumn. It was needless because I probably would not have had the deadliness to stand, and would not in any event have won, although I might have done damagingly well. His reaction to Worsley may well have been a decisive factor in swinging him against Gwyn Morgan and in favour of the referendum. In the week before Easter he pursued a relatively settled course of endeavouring to provoke my resignation. He set up the 29 March meeting of the shadow Cabinet with that in mind.

Over the Easter holidays, being both a nice and a conciliating man, he probably weakened. I cannot decide whether he was pleased or not on that Monday morning (10 April). His stratagem, no doubt suggested by some over-partisan member of his staff (as I write this it occurs to me that I am doing exactly that of which I accused Wilson a few pages back), had worked. But was it really what he wanted? He was essentially a weak leader of a broad party. To become a ruthless leader of a narrow party was not at all his style. However, he was good at putting an optimistic face on affairs. Later that evening, so the then Speaker, Selwyn Lloyd, subsequently told me, he (Lloyd) ran into Wilson, who said: 'It has worked out for the best. Roy will go off and write books, which is what he most likes doing, and we will all have a more comfortable life.'

# CHAPTER NINETEEN

# *A More Comfortable Life?*

Although the office of deputy leader of the Labour Party trailed no great clouds of prestige or perquisites my renunciation of it had one considerable consequence. For the previous four years I had held the lead position on the inside track for the succession to Harold Wilson. This did not go *ex officio* with the deputy leadership. But given my age (fifty-one when I resigned), offices held and degree of support, it was undoubtedly so. The length of my lead had fluctuated during these four years, and there had been times when I could hear the breathing of Jim Callaghan or of Denis Healey uncomfortably close behind me, but it had never disappeared.

Moreover the succession to Harold Wilson mostly appeared, not as a remote eventuality providing political columnists with intellectual exercise during flat periods, but as something which could easily be round the next corner. I think none of us fully appreciated (although I had the guidance of our May 1970 conversation) how firmly his mind was set on a voluntary early retirement. This apart, however, his style of leadership, put in circus terms, was so much more like that of the acrobat skilfully riding a bicycle on the tightrope than of the ringmaster imperiously cracking the whip that a fall seemed constantly possible, and he was open to the additional hazard that there were always a few willing to give him a push. Except for the first three and a half years of his fourteen-year spell he never looked wholly secure. And this was peculiarly so in 1971–2 when his leadership seemed not only to others but to himself also to be going through a trough of despond and danger.

The inside track in that race for the future premiership was therefore of more than contingent importance. I was never to hold it again. I had lost the inertial loyalist vote, that quite significant body of MPs which set more store by the party than by any question of issue or ideology. They did not become violently hostile to me; they merely thought that

350

I had behaved undependably and maybe self-indulgently. I was more or less aware of this, and not unduly dismayed. It was an inevitable price for escape from the intolerable position into which I had got as a result of my 'Millan commitment' combined with the mounting determination of the Labour anti-marketeers, sweeping Wilson along with them, to risk breaking the party in the hope of breaking the Heath Government and its European policy first.

Nor did the fact that I had lost the inside track mean that I was out of the race. It merely meant that I had to be running faster and do an overtaking swoop if I was to win when the time came. When I settled down to a new, relatively liberated regime after my shock-absorbing Sandwich weekend, that seemed by no means impossible. I had struck a note of resonant protest against what appeared to many inside and outside the Labour Party to be Harold Wilson's uninspiring, constantly manoeuvring and doubtfully successful leadership. The Labour Party was beginning its period of secular decline. Third-party politics was rearing its head, bye-election results varied between the indifferent and the bad, and the public opinion polls failed to put the party into the high forties which had been the almost automatic lot of previous oppositions in mid-term. To have exchanged as it were the position of a semi-inhibited vice-president for that of a well-known and free senator therefore had some advantages of position as well as many of convenience.

Yet the analogy was a dangerous one for it ignored the vastly greater rigidity of the British two-party system compared with the American one. As a result, and so long as I was still competing for the top place, I had merely escaped from one contradiction into another. In order to maintain my Labour Party credentials I had to become, if anything, a more vigorous party campaigner than I had been as deputy leader. My post-resignation engagement diary fully reflects this. Within two weeks of my resignation, although not speaking, I was in Birmingham for the May Day march. I was meticulous in the next year in my attendance at local elections there, and more importantly at bye-elections up and down the country. The problem was that I did not have my heart in the cause for which I was campaigning. My interest was much better served by defeat than by victory. Every bad bye-election result strengthened my position, every good one weakened it.

This is not an unfamiliar position for any 'loyal' rebel. It was almost exactly that occupied by Michael Heseltine in 1986–90. Equally Edward Heath was an indefatigable but hardly single-minded campaigner in many of the bye-elections (including my own) of the first Thatcher years. But even if by no means a unique position it is not a comfortable one. In a most extreme form this contradiction expressed itself in the Lincoln bye-election on 1 March 1973. Dick Taverne, goaded by the banderillas of the Lincoln Labour Party, decided to break free, resign, and fight the seat again at a bye-election. I was opposed to his doing so, perhaps because it made things awkward for me. I could not go and speak for him without burning my Labour Party boats. Probably I ought to have done so, even though all my most loyal supporters (except for Taverne himself, and he never emitted a hint of reproach) were against.

Great pressure was put on me to speak against him. I never contemplated this, although Crosland and Healey (whose parliamentary private secretary he had been) did so with apparent appetite. When the result came out, which was a triumph for Dick and a humiliation for the Labour candidate, I was delighted. But I had to go to ground like a skulking fox. Even resignation without permanent renunciation brought no freedom from the humiliations of trying to play a two-party political game for which, as far as I was concerned, the times were becoming out of joint.

With the benefit of hindsight I can see that after my resignation four requirements had to be fulfilled to give me a chance of succeeding to Wilson as leader. I doubt however whether they were schematically clear to me at the time. First, I had to keep my reputation with the general public, and particularly with floating voters, which was currently higher than that of most of my rivals or contemporaries. Second, I had to preserve enough of a Labour Party base to be electable as a leader of the Labour Party, not perhaps because I was the favourite son but because I might be the best vote-puller. Third, and crucially, Labour under Wilson had to lose the next election, which in 1972–3 it looked well set to do. And fourth, I had to avoid supersession by an alternative potential leader on the reformist/internationalist wing of the Labour Party emerging as a result of my temporary withdrawal from the central councils.

This last consideration no doubt played some part in prompting me and those closely associated with me to vote for Ted Short rather than Tony Crosland in the election for my successor as deputy leader. I did not have to force them in this direction. They were spontaneously and almost unanimously in favour of so doing. Our motives were not just to block Crosland. We genuinely thought that Short had behaved better than had he. On the referendum issue Short had voted the wrong way without appreciating the seriousness of the issue, and had subsequently apologised. Crosland understood all the implications and had voted right, but then absolutely declined to take the matter seriously. When I endeavoured to enlist his support over Easter he shrugged his shoulders and said he was off to Japan to study urban planning, which was much more important. If Short had been a little uncomprehending, Crosland had been the pharisee.

The result was that on the first ballot Short more or less tied with Foot and led Crosland by fifty votes. On the second ballot Short sailed to victory. In spite of our old friendship Crosland had in no way behaved well or friendlily to me in the previous few weeks, and it would have been ironic and perverse had my resignation, from which he had walked away, led to a great leap forward for him. Yet I feel uneasy about that election. There was the consideration that Crosland was a potential leader and that Short was not.

Ted Short did not succeed to the whole of my previous front-bench responsibilities. Healey became shadow Chancellor and Callaghan succeeded him as shadow Foreign Secretary. Short became shadow leader of the House of Commons. Thus was the pattern for the allocation of the main offices in the 1974 Government firmly set in the immediate aftermath of my resignation. And it was set in a pattern that was much to my disadvantage. I could hardly complain about that. Nor did I much worry about it. Apart from anything else I was sceptical (like many others) whether 1974 (or 1975) was going to bring another Labour Government.

I was more concerned with organising my new non-official back-bench life. I was not like one of those politicians – Rab Butler or Denis Healey for example – who continuously sat on one or other front bench for three decades. It was barely eight years since I had last spoken from a back bench, but that period embraced by far the greater part of my impact as a parliamentary speaker, and I had grown used to a despatch box in front of me, the advantage of which is that it gives the opportunity to make carefully prepared speeches which, with a little artifice, do not give the impression of being read.

A despatch box is also curiously helpful to standing undismayed by noise. Noise was not however much of a problem of mine during that Parliament. The Tories were not disposed to shout at me, and while one or two Labour members might have been, this was much disapproved of by the others, including many who were hostile to my position. Nevertheless I do not think that I succeeded in making a single notable speech during that eighteen months' back-bench interlude. Five or six were competent and even mildly interesting, and that was that. I spoke mainly on broad Treasury or Home Office questions with an occasional foray into foreign affairs.

My speeches outside had more impact. I continued with the series of seven which I had somewhat explosively begun at Worsley in March and which were published as a paperback entitled *What Matters Now* in time for that year's Labour Party conference. The general theme in my words of the time was 'the stubborn persistence of avoidable deprivation and injustice, and the need for a radical and coherent strategy to combat them'. There were speeches on the problems of the regions and of the developing countries, on the poverty trap, on Europe's role in the world (the Aachen Karlspreis speech), on inequality at work (between men and women and between manual and non-manual employees, to take two examples), and on the problem of the cities, which I saw as transport, planning, land use and housing, with race and decay at the centre seeping in as imports from America supplemented with the vulnerability of the countryside to suburban sprawl as a more indigenous menace. In a concluding essay which had not been delivered as a speech, I tried to stress the importance for the Labour Party of getting a radical cutting edge on 'new' issues, while avoiding the three dangers of a narrow class appeal, of equivocation about upholding the rule of law, and of insularity.

I also spoke at a good number of Labour Party meetings in the country, not only at bye-elections but on more routine occasions, as well as at trade union conferences, to which I got two or three eagerly accepted invitations a year. My Gaitskellite training made me respectful of the political influence and prestige of moderate trade union leaders, and I set up an institutional framework of contact with them. Sir Fred Hayday, a former chairman of the TUC who had long headed its international committee, and Alf Allen, general secretary of the Shopworkers and a future chairman of the TUC and life peer, were both immensely helpful. During 1973 they organised a regular dining group in the Charing Cross Hotel which met on seven occasions and to which nine or ten leading figures typically came to meet me. Not the least striking indication of their commitment was that they and not I paid for the dinners. I also maintained close social contact with a range of Labour MPs and with the leading editors and political journalists. My diaries for 1972 and 1973 are heavily studded with luncheon and dinner engagements of this sort, in both London and East Hendred.

Altogether Wilson's view, comfortably expressed to Selwyn Lloyd, that I would retire to the country and write books proved wide of the mark. He would have been right of course, as events turned out, not to have been frightened of my activities, but that is different from believing that they would not take place. There were too many people determined to keep me as it were in training for the big fight for indolence to take over. Nor have I ever found it easy to be anything approaching a full-time writer, except for occasional bursts of up to a month, and in addition I did not at that time have any particularly engrossing writing commitments.

I was proceeding with my biographical essays for *The Times* and published Keynes, Adlai Stevenson and Cripps in 1972 and Halifax, Gaitskell and Léon Blum in 1973, but this was no more than in accordance with a rhythm I had established when still deputy leader. I was getting behindhand with my projected tome on American Presidents and British Prime Ministers, but not sufficiently so to begin to cause panic. I had done a complete fifty-thousand-word essay on Baldwin in 1971–2, which was subsequently lengthened and somewhat remodelled into my 1987 book, and although I was thrashing about between the two Roosevelts and Eisenhower as a possible subject for my first attempt at an American President (I did not settle on Truman until 1982), the fact that I was failing to settle was the reverse of an incentive to concentrate on writing. In principle I was endeavouring to spend Fridays and Mondays up to the early evening writing at East Hendred, but the principle was breached about as often as it was honoured.

This resignation, as opposed to the involuntary one of 1970, did not make much difference to me so far as back-up services were concerned. I kept my two secretaries and, thanks to the Rowntree Trust's scheme for helping leading opposition politicians, gained an outstanding assistant in Matthew Oakeshott, then a twenty-five-year-old Oxford graduate student and city councillor, who stayed with me until 1976 and remained a close friend and associate throughout the SDP days. John Harris continued to give overall advice and an immense amount of voluntary service. There was no car or driver to lose, so that position remained constant. There was however a problem about House of Commons accommodation, for I lost my small suite and failed to persuade the Serjeant-at-Arms that as the leader of a group which amounted to one-tenth of the House of Commons I was entitled to good rooms independently of any shadow Cabinet allocation. Eventually I settled down in a small eyrie above my old suite supplemented by the use of a splendid but even more remote room which belonged to Harold Lever as the chairman of the Public Accounts Committee, but which he never used because he found his own flat in Eaton Square little further away and better furnished.

During these eighteen months of relative freedom I travelled less than might have been expected, particularly in Europe, which was after all the reason for my being off the front bench. I gave a Churchill lecture in Zurich, attended one European Movement Conference in Amsterdam, visited the European Parliament in Strasbourg for a day, and spent a week's holiday in Italy. But I did not go once to Paris or to Brussels, the embryonic capital of the Community. Germany seized me a little more, and I went there on three occasions, partly to receive my Charlemagne and Schuman prizes, and partly to pay long calls on Brandt and Schmidt. I also saw both of them whenever they came to London. William Rees-Mogg wrote a striking *Times* leader a little later saying that, with Britain's membership settled, our politics should settle into a European pattern, with Brandt the natural leader of the left, as Pompidou was of the right. I think that I spontaneously accepted this even before I had read it, and liked to keep in close touch with the leaders of the German Government much as, say, Sir Robert Menzies had done twenty years before with Churchill.

About distant travel I was more adventurous. I went to the United States four times, including visits for Harvard and University of Pennsylvania degrees and a month's sojourn in August 1972 at that great intellectual ghetto of Aspen, Colorado. Unfortunately that did not really work. I liked the company, which comprised a remarkable roll-call of 'the wise men' and/or 'the brightest and the best' to use the titles of two subsequent books about American public servants who were neither exactly politicians nor bureaucrats. At Aspen we lived amongst Robert McNamara, John McCloy, McGeorge Bundy, Eugene Macarthy, Arthur Schlesinger, Katherine Graham, Marietta Tree and Douglass Cater. On one occasion we dined with the Caters and experienced almost as memorable a conversation as that between Acheson and Muskie at their Washington house twenty months before. There were present, apart from us, four couples who had in common that the husbands had all worked for Lyndon B. Johnson in the White House and the wives had all experienced a good deal of tactile dancing with him. (They were the Caters themselves, the Harry Macphersons, the Walter Jenkinses and the Bill Moyers.) Then, three and a half years after the end of his presidency and five months before his death, they made me appreciate, as I have never done before or since, the animal magnetism of his presence. The Caters the least, they were all one-third repelled, two-thirds fascinated, and wholly obsessed by his personality.

Unfortunately the physical conditions at Aspen were not up to the cast. The weather was unstable in a way that the Americans who had come from a hot summer in Washington or New York liked, but which I found a disappointing reward for a five-thousand-mile journey. It rained every afternoon. What was worse was the effect of the altitude. It was about 10,500 feet, which meant that I could not write with any degree of sustained concentration, that the aerodynamics even of specially heavy tennis balls totally defeated me, and that I could not absorb my normal quantity of alcohol without awakening being accompanied not only by a sense of cosmic doom but also by a nasty hangover. It is apparently a well-known syndrome. I could confidently expect to grow out of it after about three and a half weeks. As we were only due to stay there for four weeks this was not much comfort. I could improve my morale only by plunging down 5000 feet to the doubtful comforts of Salt Lake City (no wine or whisky except in speakeasy conditions) or the gorges of the Colorado River. After this parole we returned to Aspen for another week, but eventually left early to drive to San Francisco. It was an interesting but unproductive summer. The words would not flow and any telephone call (particularly from England) which might involve my making the smallest decision reduced me to a state of nervous prostration. I have never since been back to Aspen, nor have I ever again been tempted to stay anywhere else above 10,000 feet.

The gaps in my knowledge of the world lay heavily in the poor parts of it, and particularly in Africa. I had never been anywhere in the 'dark continent' except for the totally untypical Cairo and Marrakesh. I decided that the time had come to reduce this deficiency, and in January 1973 Jennifer and I, accompanied by Matthew Oakeshott, who had managed very young to become something of an old East African hand, set off on a two-and-a-half week tour of Nigeria, Kenya, Ethiopia, Zambia and Tanzania. We also passed through the then distinctly unwelcoming Uganda. I quite enjoyed myself, improved my knowledge and deepened my sympathy, but I did not fall under any African spell.

In September of that year we went on a still more substantial eastern trip. I had agreed to make my second visit to Australia (the first having been in 1965 when I was agitatedly waiting to become Home Secretary) to deliver a Melbourne lecture sponsored by the Australian Broadcasting Commission and one or two leading businesses. The subject was to be Anglo-Australian relations in the context of Europe, and the organisers regarded it as major enough for them to offer two first-class tickets plus all other expenses and a moderate honorarium. One of the reasons that they felt able to be so generous was that one of the sponsoring companies was Qantas, but I did not apprehend this until I had already arranged to fit in on the way out a substantial visit to China, to which Qantas did not fly. However, they took this on the chin, and on 30 August, propelled by Air France but paid for (partly at least) by Qantas, Jennifer and I departed from Paris for Shanghai.

China was much less open then than it was in the ten years up to June 1989, or even than it has remained since Tianamen Square. There was however a brief unlatching of a small window for a few years between the Nixon visit in 1972 and the clampdown by the Gang of Four in 1974. The Chinese Government was pursuing a foreign policy which in theory was hostile to dominant leadership being in the hands of one or both of the superpowers, but which in practice was half shamefacedly well disposed towards any country or organisation which provided countervailing power to the Soviet Union. Thus they were ambiguous about NATO and cautiously moving towards better relations with the United States. The European Community, on the other hand, qualified satisfactorily both in theory and in practice, and a doctrine was evolving by which any strong supporter of European unity was 'a friend of China'.

They were therefore willing to welcome us following some hints dropped to the Chinese ambassador in London by the most appropriate of intermediaries in the circumstances, our close old friend Jacques de Beaumarchais, who had come as French ambassador to London in 1972. (Beaumarchais when Directeur Politique at the Quai d'Orsay had worked closely with the Chinese on an early accord, one of the small fruits of which was Air France's advance position as the only European airline with direct flights into China.) Having got ourselves there, the Chinese entertained us internally for a fortnight. They treated us lavishly (good interpreter, high-level Foreign Ministry guide and so on) and were semi-amenable about what we wanted to do, subject to one major issue of itinerary dispute. After the obvious five days in Peking we wanted to go to Chungking in Szechuan and then down through the Yangste Gorges to Wuhan. They wanted to confine us to the coastal strip 'milk-run' which was then habitual for visitors. But they were loath to pronounce a direct refusal of our more ambitious plans. So there was a good deal of fencing. Eventually they announced that we could go to Chungking and the Gorges, but only if we would stay a month instead of two weeks. The airline schedules and other logistic difficulties did not permit a shorter tour. The validity of this was doubtful, but not within our capacity to refute.

It was a splendid 'Merchant of Venice' verdict. There was no way in which we could so extend our Chinese sojourn without missing the Melbourne lecture and thus undermining the whole financial base of our journey. Had the Chinese bothered to find this out? In other words, did they know they were safe, or would they genuinely have allowed us to do this then unusual journey had we been more flexible? I have remained mildly intrigued by this question. In any event, honour and courtesy were maintained intact. We were not refused, they were not inconvenienced. And we proceeded along the routine path to Nanking, Wushi, Shanghai, Canton and out to Hong Kong.

Apart from many obvious observations and reflections, I retain vividly two quirkish memories and one more serious one from the fourteen days. The first was that it hardly ever stopped raining. Martial music and compulsory calisthenics (not for us fortunately) in sodden dawns remain imprinted on my mind. The second was that we must have confused ideological categories in the eyes of our immediate hosts. David Bruce, who was from 1961 to 1969 one of the most distinguished of all American ambassadors to London (as well as previously to Paris and Bonn) had recently come to Peking to open up the first US mission to China for twenty-five years. He had been summoned back to see Nixon over the period of our visit, but Evangeline Bruce was there, installed in a residence which was hardly grand by the standards of Wingfield House or the Avenue d'Iéna but which had nonetheless to be approached with difficulty through a guard of honour of packing cases reminiscent of the avenue of animals which leads to the Ming tombs. As she was a close friend and alone there, we went to see her whenever we could. We managed four meals together in the five days. What the Chinese made of this I cannot think. We were there as European challengers of American hegemony. But whenever we had a free moment we rushed off to the local arch-priestess of dollar imperialism. Jennifer's presence made a romantic interpretation improbable. We explained about old personal friendship transcending frontiers and politics, and they looked impassively uncomprehending. Did they think we had cheated them and were really in the pay of the CIA? Or were they just not very interested?

The third and more serious memory is of an unexpected meeting with Deng Xiaoping (or Teng Hsaio-ping, as I then spelt it), who was just emerging from his first disgrace and had apparently not been allowed to see foreigners for some years past. We reacted to the meeting with only modified enthusiasm. As I wrote in my record of the visit:

At 7.30 p.m. we were taken to the Great Hall of the People to see Teng Hsaio-ping, Vice-Premier and Secretary of the Communist Party until after the beginning of the Cultural Revolution, when he fell into disfavour for being too much on the Liu line, and was rehabilitated only this spring. Until 6.30 they would not tell us what they were arranging, and the information when it came was a slight disappointment, as it was accompanied by many apologies that owing to the immediate aftermath of the Tenth Party Congress we could not see Chou En-lai, as we had hoped. However Teng, we were assured not only by the Chinese but also by the British ambassador (then Sir John Addis, a distinguished sinologist, perhaps more interested in art than politics) whom I telephoned to ask about him, was a very interesting man to meet. He proved moderately so. The meeting lasted from 7.30 to 9.10 and was then brought to an end by me as we seemed to have covered most of the ground and he was making no move. It took place with about sixteen present (but no one but me, Teng and the interpreter speaking) in a huge room at the south end of the building. Curiously it was the only place in Peking where I saw a fly, which buzzed round my head fairly continuously. Lord Attlee's famous 1954 dictum ['There are no flies in China'] was not quite right; it should be rewritten as 'The only flies in China are in the Great Hall of the People.'

As a comment on an unexpected opportunity to meet a man who within five years became one of the half dozen most powerful men in the world, this seems rather blasé. When I next met him, in 1979, on an official visit as President of the European Commission I was more impressed by the aroma of power.[1] But perhaps now my earlier scepticism looks more percipient.

On the substance of the conversation I recorded that he said that if a full-scale Soviet attack came against China 'they could withstand it and survive. . . . The devastating effects of nuclear warfare were exaggerated. They had dug a lot of tunnels and stored a lot of grain. They would be all right. . . .' I asked him if he saw any chance of an improvement in relations with Russia. He said, 'Maybe, although this depended on a Soviet change of attitude. . . . But the ideological break was irreparable and could never be bridged.' He talked a good deal of nonsense about 'social imperialism', which was a paper tiger like the atom bomb, but paper tigers 'could turn into real tigers' (so where was one, I said to myself, except watching tigers, real or imaginary, chasing their own tails?), but he then followed with a rather good quotation from Mao, which he used about the Russians, although Mao had used it against the Kuomintang: 'You must despise your enemy strategically, but respect him tactically.'

Although I retained adequate scepticism China made a deep impact on me. After it Hong Kong seemed brash and Australia provincial. The Cultural Revolution (which had already clearly wrecked Peking University) did not impress me, but the mystique of the Middle Kingdom did.

Back in England on 24 September 1973 I found that a new political situation had quietly evolved. The 'more comfortable life', insofar as it had ever existed, was drawing to an end. In the autumn of 1972 I had had no difficulty in deciding to stand back from all the parliamentary Labour Party elections. Apart from anything else I could be held to be committed for that year by my statement at the time of resignation, although there was ambiguity over whether the term 'office' embraced membership of the shadow Cabinet. Harold Lever decided that, the European Communities Bill being through, his resignation had served its purpose and he could honourably return. He was comfortably elected in the lower half of the list. I in no way disapproved of his decision, but had not felt tempted to follow it.

Nineteen-seventy-three was different. I had to do something if I was to remain a major player in the political game. The issue on which I had resigned was temporarily resolved and in a way which meant that I had achieved my objective. Britain was in the Community. I could not sit on the sidelines indefinitely. Excluding the possibility of forming an independent party, which at that stage neither I nor my supporters were remotely prepared for, there were two things that I could do. The first was to stand against Wilson for the leadership. The second, much less dramatic course was to stand for re-election to the shadow Cabinet. Over the parliamentary year of 1972–3 there were a lot of advocates of the bolder course, not only amongst those who were working most closely with me, but also such disparate figures as Willie Hamilton, the stridently republican but otherwise moderate MP for Fife, Christopher Mayhew, Tam Dalyell and Arthur Palmer, a senior Bristol MP.

I always felt a little sceptical about the feasibility when it came to the point of this 'big challenge', but it was nonetheless discussed as a realistic option up to and over the time when we dispersed for that summer recess. By the end of the Labour Party conference of 1973, which followed within a week of my return from China and Australia, it had ceased to be so. An election, although expected in the autumn rather than the winter of 1974, began to loom and brought with it an inevitable ranks-closing mood. As we dispersed from the pleasures of Blackpool we were agreed with hardly any dissent that it was not the year for a challenge. The moment had slipped by. Wilson's satisfaction when I told him that I would not be a candidate in 1972 was better founded than I realised. I had given him immunity not just for a year but for the rest of his leadership.

The onset of this pre-election atmosphere also increased the pressure on me to return to the shadow Cabinet. My close MP associates, almost without exception, were in favour of this. So, strongly, were the moderate trade union leaders when I dined with them on 8 October. So was Willy Brandt when I saw him in Bonn on 16 October. There was thus a clear line-up amongst those connected with the Labour movement at home or abroad. Those outside it took a different view. David Steel, when I had lunched with him in July, urged me strongly not to go back. So did Nicko Henderson, a close friend whom I saw frequently in England and in Bonn, where he was ambassador. He thought it much more sensible for me to keep my distance from Wilson.

However, I was still too much of a Labour politician to rate these outside voices higher than the internal ones, and on 24 October, in a Birmingham television interview, I announced that I would stand. The result was satisfactory without being outstandingly good. I got 143 votes and came fifth. The top votes were very closely bunched, so that another seven would have made me top, which in the circumstances would have been sensational. However, I did not get them and came after Callaghan, Foot, Prentice and Crosland. I think that Wilson was pleased at my return, because his desire to win the 1974 election was much stronger than his objection to me, which through all the fluctuating and often provoking circumstances of the previous decade had remained, in my retrospective view, remarkably restrained. His leadership was not admirable, but it was nearly always friendly and tolerant. His problem was which spokesmanship to give me, for the obvious one without upsetting his new balance with Callaghan and Healey was the shadow home secretaryship. But this involved demoting Shirley Williams, who was currently occupying it and who had just suffered an uncharacteristic setback of dropping from equal first to eighth place in the shadow Cabinet elections. I was loath to be the cause of her being pushed to a less welcome role. Wilson at first dealt with the problem by procrastination. Three weeks after the result he had neither had a bilateral talk with me nor announced any other dispositions. When we eventually met I rather grandly offered to do nothing, that is just to be available at large, like himself. Not altogether surprisingly, he refused this, and we eventually settled on the Home Office job, because there was not really any alternative. Shirley accepted the outcome with a good grace.

I felt I had to pay the price of passing over to her a visit to New York where I was about to earn substantially the largest fee that I had then ever been offered for a speech. It clashed with a race relations debate in the House of Commons, to which subject I returned after a gap and with a smug sense of putting duty before gallivanting. My dutiful behaviour over this debate also had the effect of making it possible for me to take part in a more significant one on 19 December. This was on the second of two days on the economic policy of the Government and of the Chancellor in particular. At the relevant meeting of the shadow Cabinet there was a pause when we came to the question of who should wind up before the vote. Wilson did not want to do it, for he thought he should follow Heath on the first day, but he did not want me to do so either. Nor did Healey, who was to open on the second day. Our second Treasury spokesman was suggested. I swallowed twice and said that I thought I, as the last Labour Chancellor and Barber's almost immediate predecessor, had better do it. There was an awkward silence, but as no one could think of any effective counter-argument my nomination of myself was reluctantly accepted. It was the only time in a Cabinet or shadow Cabinet that I can remember making such a suggestion against the grain, and it would have been impossible had I blown in after a week in the United States as a result of which I had missed the first debate within the field of my renewed Home Office responsibilities.

This piece of self-promotion not unnaturally produced a fine state of nervous tension as first the day and then the hour of the speech approached. I was due to speak from 9.00 p.m. to 9.30. I did not attempt to dine, but I can remember sitting and fortifying myself in the smoking room with Bob Maclennan and one or two others until about 8.15, when I returned to the chamber, in as great a state of neurosis intermingled with terror as I have ever managed to produce before a speech.

The House filled up rapidly just before nine, and when I got up it was already packed, a big contrast with debate attendances in the 1980s. In reality it was an easy wicket, except only for having Wilson and Healey, cast for the moment in ugly-sister roles, as my immediate flanking neighbours. But as they are both of generous temperament they were full of praise when I sat down. The Tories were on the defensive and listened in uneasy silence, aware that Barber and his whole economic record were deeply vulnerable. In any event the result was the best (and the best-received) winding-up speech that I had made since the censure motion following George Blake's escape in 1966. *The Times*, for instance, gave me exactly the sort of comment that I most wanted at that stage, and was not untypical of the rest of the press. 'Mr Roy Jenkins came back with a thunderclap into the front rank of the Labour leadership tonight,' it began, '. . . with a shattering denunciation of the Chancellor's energy measures. . . . Where Mr Healey earlier in the day had uttered mainly party political bombast and Mr Wilson, opening the first day of the debate, had been full of recrimination and bickering, here was the voice of authority that the Labour Party had so sadly lacked in the long months since Mr Jenkins retired to the back benches on the European issue.'

Altogether, it was a lucky speech to have made, particularly as, which I did not expect, it turned out to be the last of any substance that I made in that Parliament. But it also turned out, less desirably, to be something more than that. It was the last major gladiatorial triumph, with blood on the floor and cheering cohorts behind, that I was ever to achieve in the House of Commons. But I did not know that and 19 December sent me away in high morale for the Christmas holidays.

# CHAPTER TWENTY

# *Unwillingly Back to Office*

Nineteen seventy-four, according to my strategy, was the year in which temporising Labour Party leadership was due to receive its just reward in the shape of a lost general election. The electorate perversely declined, for the second time running, to fit in with my strategy. In 1970 I wanted Labour to win and thought it deserved to do so. In 1974 I took a different view on both points. Whatever may have been the position about deserts, there was no doubt about the outcomes. To paraphrase Wilde, getting one election result wrong might have been excused as a misfortune, but to make a mistake about two pointed to carelessness.

The first 1974 election was far from being a triumph for the Labour Party. The result gave the party only 37 per cent of the votes cast (as opposed to 43 per cent in 1970 and 48 per cent in 1966) and can be seen in retrospect as a station on its road to the deep trough of the 1980s. We were even 1 per cent behind the aggregate vote of the Conservatives. But the outcome was to put Harold Wilson back into Downing Street and for the purposes of immediate political developments that was what counted.

In mitigation of my misappraisal, no one could have been expected to foresee how much help Edward Heath would give to Harold Wilson's return to Downing Street. No shoe-horn could have more eased the reinsertion. In its last months the Heath Government was severely blasted by the first oil crisis, for which it bore no responsibility. But it had made itself unnecessarily exposed by the improvidence of the Barber boom, and it responded to the storm with measures which were surprisingly trivial and hesitant for such an experienced rough-weather sailor as Edward Heath. On top of that he misjudged the date of the election. Under the British system almost all elections lost by Prime Ministers are *ex hypothesi* thought to have been held on the wrong date. The only immunity from retrospective blame on this account is enjoyed by Alec Home for 1964, and this is because he waited until so close to the statutory date as to turn it into a fixed-term election, and had passed no earlier date when there was a flicker of belief that he might have done better.

Heath's choice of date was doubly flawed. It would probably have been better to have held on for nine months or a year until the shock of the energy crisis and the industrial shut-down to which it led were semi-forgotten. But if an early election was held to be the right strategy, the right tactics were undoubtedly to take it as quickly as possible. It ought to have been called in January for early February and not on 7 February for 28 February, which was the worst of both worlds. It was also a miscalculation that a one-issue campaign (even when the issue was the superficially very attractive one of 'who governs Britain: the elected Prime Minister or the National Union of Mineworkers?') could be sustained for several weeks. The Prime Minister did not have the authority which Gladstone had possessed in Midlothian ninety-four years before of fixing the country with his eye and forcing it to talk about what he wanted it to talk about. And Heath was dogged throughout by reports or pronouncements from semi-official bodies which seemed to undermine a large part of the Government's case against the miners.

Nevertheless, my expectation during the campaign, and that of nearly everybody else too, including Harold Wilson, was that Heath would win a lacklustre victory. My last encounter with Wilson before polling day was on the final Sunday afternoon when we spoke at a big Birmingham Town Hall meeting and talked for some time afterwards, although we also did a brief London Tuesday press conference together. He seemed tired, depressed and expecting defeat, keeping going with some difficulty and gallantry until by the Thursday night he would have completed his final throw in politics. We were both wrong.

The campaign was not as flat as this sounds. I was less central to it than to the balance-of-payments-obsessed election of 1970. But not all that much. Wilson was insistent, against some opposition, that I should have the whole of one of the five party political telecasts, and I spent as much time outside Birmingham, ranging from Caithness and Sutherland to Devon, as I had in 1970. If anything, I had better meetings than in 1970, the outstanding ones being in Plymouth, Bury, Oxford, Warley (in the Black Country) and the Birmingham Town Hall, and, paradoxically in view of my detachment and low morale, spoke better at them.

The Stechford campaign was easy enough, but faintly disappointing. We had few meetings, for I decided that Stechford with its scattered suburban housing estates was not made for them. The conventional wisdom is that the main result of election meetings is not the swaying of marginal votes but the inspiring of the faithful. I came to the view that their essential purpose may be the even narrower one of bolstering the ego of the candidate. Without them electioneering is flat low-pressure work. I had the compensation of plenty of excursions away from Birmingham, but when I was in Stechford I devoted myself to visits to clubs and to forays into any cluster which could begin to pass for a shopping centre. The object was to shake as many hands and engage in a snatch of direct conversation with as many people as possible. As previously, I used my clicking counting machine and managed to tick up a Stechford score of almost exactly 2000. I did not do any house-to-house canvassing, because this would have meant a substantial fall in output per hour, although this had to be balanced against the inconsiderate tendency of inhabitants of big cities (it applied even more strongly in Glasgow ten years later) to do even their suburban shopping across constituency boundaries.

From these encounters a number of reflections emerged. First, the persistence of our weakness amongst fairly young women, which I had noticed in 1970. They seemed noticeably less pro-Labour than their husbands or their mothers or even their older sisters. Second, there was much more of a party response to me than I expected and hoped for. My recognition factor in Stechford was high (as it ought to have been after twenty-four years there), but it was not vastly higher than it had shown itself in, say, the Accrington covered market or on the Plymouth waterfront, and it was not universal. There were a good 10 per cent of the burghers of Stechford who looked at me with incomprehension. Of the rest, a lot had an appreciation of my broad political position, and were either pro or anti me as a result. But they were reluctant to let this influence their votes. For every one who said that he would vote Labour because I was the candidate, I must have met two who said that they disagreed with me on the argument within the Labour Party but that they would nonetheless vote the ticket out of party loyalty.

This at least held out the promise of undeserved support, and what was more depressing was the substantial number who claimed that they would have voted Labour had I been leader of the party, but who nonetheless would vote Tory or Liberal even in Stechford. 'But how can you possibly say that you would support me for Prime Minister and are yet not willing to give me your vote as your MP?' I exasperatedly argued. 'Cannot you see that massive local support would help to make me leader?' 'But you are not leader,' they doggedly replied. 'Mr Wilson is.' We would then part in mutual misunderstanding. Perhaps some of them were more determined Tories than they admitted, and would never have voted for the Labour Party whoever was its leader, although I do not think this was true of most of them.

This experience left me feeling that, in the West Midlands at any rate, the British party system was so rigid as to make it almost impossible to build up a cross-party constituency base, such as any well-known American senator easily achieves. These impressions were well borne out by my result. Superficially it looked good. My majority went back up to over 10,000 from the 6000 to which it had fallen in 1970, with a swing which was above average for the country. But it was slightly below average for Birmingham and the West Midlands. This was a logical outcome, for the big pro-Labour swing in the region was generally attributed to the antics of Enoch Powell, who declined to fight his Conservative seat in Wolverhampton and urged a Labour vote. As the reason for his switch was anti-Europeanism and much of the reason for his resonance in the region was his 'rivers of blood' attitude to race relations, it was natural that less of his blessing should rub off on me than on most others. What I resented was the fact that 6000 voted Liberal in Stechford. I already regarded myself as such a closet Liberal that I naïvely thought they ought nearly all to have come to me.

Of more import was the overall result. I had sensed some strengthening of the Labour position in the last few days, but I nonetheless went into the Birmingham Council House for the count in the reverse of my 1970 mood. I thought that a Tory majority of forty to sixty seats was the most likely outcome. It was more difficult to get a quick overall impression than in 1970. The results fluctuated, with Labour doing better in the north than the south and best of all in the West Midlands. I remember asking Matthew Oakeshott, a considerable amateur psephologist and with me for the count, for reassurance that we had not really won. After several minutes with his slide-rule, he declined to provide it. By 3.00 a.m. when I went to bed it looked as though Labour would have a modest overall majority, but this faded away with the later results and we ended up with 301 seats, compared with 297 for the Tories and only 14 for the Liberals, despite their strikingly good 19 per cent popular vote.

On the Friday morning I motored to London with Jennifer and John Harris and attended a long and rambling shadow Cabinet which Wilson had summoned for 2.30 p.m. at Transport House (then still Labour Party headquarters). There was no mood of euphoria, and the only excitement that afternoon was provided by the arrival of the news that Heath was not resigning immediately but was endeavouring to stitch together a majority with the Liberals. Wilson got agitated at this and talked about issuing a denunciation of constitutional impropriety. Callaghan and I were both strongly against his doing so. It was better

to lie back and let Heath play his hand. This would give Wilson a
weekend in which to recover from his tiredness and think ahead,
and would enable him to come in, if he was to come in, in a calmer
and less exhausted state. Furthermore it would have the longer-term
advantage that Heath would have shot his bolt for the Parliament.
This would both put Wilson in a stronger moral position and give him
an unquestionable right to a dissolution at any moment he judged
favourable. If, on the other hand, Heath had not tried there would be
a respectable constitutional argument for saying that if Wilson could
not live with the Parliament he should resign rather than dissolve after
a few months, and let Heath see what he could make of it.

The counter-argument was the danger that Heath might succeed in
making his Conservative/Liberal coalition. In turn the reply to this was
first that it was unlikely (as was borne out by events), and second that
if the confluence was attainable it could equally well be achieved in a
fortnight's time to defeat Wilson on the Address. In a hung Parliament
there is a lot to be said for getting your opponent to use up his room
for manoeuvre first. Eventually these arguments seemed to prevail,
although it required a telephone call on the Saturday morning to make
sure that Wilson was accepting them.

By that time I had gone to East Hendred and was wrestling with what
turned out to be a false dilemma. I was dismayed rather than excited
at the prospect of going back into office. To return as Home Secretary
at the age of fifty-three in a government for whose general policy (on
trade unions, or Europe, or the management of the economy) I felt
little sympathy, was very different from going to the Home Office
for the first time at forty-five with a much stronger sense of political
conviction. It was not a prospect to set the blood racing.

There was another possibility, but that in a different way I found
even less rationally desirable, although more exciting. As long ago
as the previous 25 July, when our group had all lunched at Dickson
Mabon's house in Highgate, there had been unanimous pressure upon
me to insist that, if a Labour government were to come in, I should
again be Chancellor. That would be the price that I should extract
from Wilson for returning to the shadow Cabinet. I had more than
enough strength to do it, they said. That could have been right,
but I nonetheless said firmly that I would do no such thing. In the
circumstances produced by a combination of Barber and OPEC being
Chancellor would be as thankless a task as in 1967–70. I would have
to tell the Labour Party for the second time running that the golden
coach of pet projects which, encouraged by Denis Healey's promise
to provoke 'howls of anguish' from the rich, they had been quietly
furbishing for the previous two years must be quickly transformed back
into a pumpkin. No one could begin to command the authority to do

this unless he was given the appointment freely, as in 1967. To force myself into the Treasury over the reluctance of my colleagues, and to believe that I could then command their loyal acceptance of what I laid down was a non-starter. That remained as much my position in early March 1974 as it had been in the previous July.

Over that Friday/Saturday however a different possibility began to develop, which was that, in the menacing circumstances, I would be offered the Exchequer by Wilson without any question of pressure from me. A lot of people were canvassing for this, but what was more to the point was that strong hints were beginning to come out of the Wilson camp, via Marcia Williams and Terry Lancaster, political correspondent of the *Mirror* Group, that this was Wilson's own unforced desire. His manner to me both on Friday afternoon and in our Saturday telephone call was also wholly compatible with such a disposition.

I still did not want to do it. The Treasury is a very wearing and mostly thankless job. I had been lucky to get away with it once, and I was chary of risking a repeat performance. The only offices which positively enticed me were those I had not held. However, Callaghan was sitting firmly in the doorway of the Foreign Office, and the result of the election precluded a quick change at the top. Yet just to say 'As I can't be Prime Minister it's the Foreign Office or nothing' was clearly not an attractive posture. And there seemed no sense in offending my supporters by trying to hold out against an offer of the Treasury, which was in the circumstances the more challenging prospect. I remember David Watt, then the much respected political editor of the *Financial Times* but always a man of somewhat down-beat temperament whose rare positive words therefore commanded the more notice, telephoning to say that it was essential I did this.

I therefore reluctantly decided on the Saturday evening that I was probably going to be Chancellor again by the Monday or Tuesday, and, rather ludicrously as things turned out, set about trying to whip some zest into myself. I even spent the Sunday morning drafting an initial memorandum of policy, for circulation to both the official Treasury and the Cabinet. We lunched with the Owens at Buttermere, where I not only tried out the memorandum on David, about which he was enthusiastic, but also consulted him on whether some latent health problem, which had been mildly worrying me since January, was likely to give trouble under the pressures of the Exchequer. About this he was dismissive. It was some time later that I came to realise that his opinion on the first point was more valuable than that on the second.

In fact, however, his or anyone else's opinion on either point was unnecessary, for the whole bubble collapsed on Monday. Bernard (now Lord) Donoughue, Herbert Morrison's biographer, who had become a senior Wilson aide during the campaign, telephoned me as soon as I got to London to say that he had to see me at the beginning of the afternoon to deliver a most important message. When I asked him what it was he said that he could not tell me for the very good reason that he did not know. When I got to the House of Commons just before the 2.30 shadow Cabinet meeting he was better informed but seemed more agitated. He said that Wilson had instructed him to tell me that to his regret he had been unable to break the Healey/Callaghan matrix and that it was therefore the Home Office rather than the Treasury which he would wish me to take. I felt no major stab of disappointment, although there was inevitably a sense of anticlimax after my gearing up of the previous forty hours. Six and a half years earlier Wilson had taken a late lurch towards making me Chancellor. This time he had taken a late lurch against doing so. I had no reason for complaint, particularly as I had wanted the job much more in 1967 than I did in 1974.

Untypically, however, I think he must have omitted to give Healey the good news, even though he had (indirectly) given me the bad news, for the Chancellor-to-be put up an unusually jumpy performance at that afternoon's shadow Cabinet, proclaiming his wares with more agitation than confidence. No doubt a little more thrown than I was prepared to admit, I launched into a somewhat doom-laden analysis of the prospect facing us which ended by saying that for the purposes of our survival as a government the two most vital countries were the United States and Germany. Denis immediately assured us that his two closest friends in the world were Henry Kissinger and Helmut Schmidt. How lucky we would be to have the advantage of a Chancellor who enjoyed such intimacy with these statesmen.

The meeting over I saw Shirley Williams in my attic room. She was unhappy and talked in terms of our all standing out from the Government. I was unconvinced that this was right, but may well have been influenced by her mood when the wretched Donoughue next turned up like a bad penny. He said he had another message from Wilson. Would *I* let *him* know when I wanted to see him. My temper snapped on this. 'Go and tell him, Bernard,' I said, 'that if he sends for me in the normal way I will come and see him at once, but that if he goes on messing about like this I won't be in his bloody Government at all, on which I am not in any event very keen.' Donoughue asked how much I wanted the message toned down in transmission. 'Not at all,' I said and stumped back up to my attic.

Within a very few minutes the telephone rang with Wilson himself on the other end. He announced that he was immediately coming up to see me. And within another few minutes he arrived, having apparently got lost once, puffing his pipe and panting for breath after the unwonted exercise of the stairs. I had certainly succeeded in getting Mahomet to the hill, but, as subsequently occurred to me, Mahomet having made this small gesture then proceeded to get almost everything that he wanted and to give little away in exchange.

He began with a long explanation of why he had retreated from his weekend plan of making me Chancellor. He had hoped to get Callaghan to take overall charge of industrial relations, to switch Healey from the Treasury to the Foreign Office and thus to make the vacancy for me. But Callaghan had absolutely declined. He was determined to be Foreign Secretary. All that he (Wilson) could offer me at this stage was therefore the Home Office, which pill he strangely offered to sweeten by reuniting it with the Northern Ireland Office, at least at Secretary of State level. He was sure I could carry the two quite easily. With singular lack of prescience he added that I need hardly go to Northern Ireland, where I could have a resident Minister of State.

I at least had the good sense to turn that down immediately, but I did not show much other sense. I indicated that I would probably accept the Home Office, although I would not give him a definite answer until I had thought about it overnight. A vital condition for me was that Shirley Williams should be satisfactorily placed. I also asked about the general shape of the Government, to which he responded by giving me a frank outline of his main intentions. But I did not, as I ought to have done, lay down clearly that my coming in depended on satisfactory opportunities for all those who had resigned with or after me. There must either be complete reunion or no reunion at all. This was a tiresome error. I let slip my period of maximum strength (as was indicated by his supplicatory presence) and had to try in three meetings with him during the remainder of that week to catch back some of the ground for which I had not fought on the Monday evening.

As soon as he could get away from these awkward questions of personnel, Wilson turned to more general conciliatory points. He said that now that we were in government again he had reverted to his 1960s belief that I would be his natural successor. And he reiterated his intention not to stay for very long. He then ended with one of the oddest remarks that a Prime Minister can ever have made to a colleague in a new Cabinet. Maybe the Home Office was the best solution after all, he suggested. If, as was perhaps inevitable for a time, I wanted to be a semi-detached member of the Government, it was the most suitable department from which to play such a stand-off role.

I had an hour to spare before a previously arranged dinner with my group in Harry Walston's apartment. I went to Brooks's and silently and gloomily communed with my thoughts. When I got to Albany I met a wall of disappointment and dismay. They were upset that I was not to be Chancellor ('We can't mount a political campaign on the basis of penal reform,' Bill Rodgers memorably said), but there was also disappointment about their own prospects in the Government. I recorded that Bob Maclennan, Dick Mabon and Cledwyn Hughes showed the greatest indifference to their own positions, or at least the greatest generosity of expression towards me. It was not an inspiriting evening. It served me right for my lack of foresight and considerateness, but it was hardly a platform of encouragement from which to return to office.

The next morning I went to see Wilson at 10.30, formally accepted, and began my wearisome and wrong-footed negotiations about the positions of others. Then I went over to the House of Commons and did some desultory work with my long-standing secretary, Bess Church. Suddenly, towards 12.30 it occurred to me that, if I were Home Secretary, I ought perhaps to go to the Home Office. So I said that I would call for a short time before lunch, prior to engaging more seriously after I had been sworn in during the afternoon. There could hardly have been a greater contrast than between this flatness of mood and the way in which I had previously approached the Home Office in 1965, or for that matter the Ministry of Aviation in 1964 and the Treasury in 1967.

# CHAPTER TWENTY-ONE

# *A Recidivist Home Secretary*

I was the first Home Secretary to go back for a second term since Sir John Simon, who had presided over the Home Department in 1915–16 and 1935–7. He did not provide an inspiring precedent. The only other twentieth-century recidivist was Herbert Samuel, who served for a couple of almost derisorily short terms in 1916 and 1931–2. The nineteenth century had contributed a quartet: Liverpool (called Hawkesbury at the time), George Grey, Spencer Walpole and R. A. Cross.

William Rees-Mogg provided a more relevant and (in some ways) comforting comparison in the following week. 'You will just have to sit and wait for a bit,' he said, 'but no doubt in the course of doing so you will be a Home Secretary rather like Rab Butler was, one who without too much effort instinctively and easily avoids the well-known pitfalls of the office.' I complacently accepted the compliment, for such any comparison with Butler from Rees-Mogg most certainly was, but began by signally failing to live up to it. In 1965–7, in addition to making a lot of running at the Home Office, I believe that I was fairly adept at avoiding the traps which had so engulfed Henry Brooke and Frank Soskice. In my first months of return in 1974, when I had far more time on my hands, I showed no such skill, and completely mishandled the first two issues of public impact with which I had to deal. They were both concerned with immigration. I had inherited with enthusiasm from Shirley Williams's period as shadow Home Secretary a commitment to three measures of administrative liberalisation. The first was a residual problem from the 1972 wave of Ugandan Asians and enabled about 300 split families to be reunited. This I did quickly and without much controversy. The second related to those illegal immigrants who were at risk because of the retrospective provisions of the 1971 Act. Not many of them were caught but they lived in a constant state of uncertainty which had wider repercussions because they were the cause of fairly frequent police trawls through immigrant neighbourhoods. We were committed to give an amnesty to those who had been here before 1971. The third issue was the right of women settled here, whether of British birth or recent immigrants, to bring in their husbands. They had lost this right in 1969, and, as men retained it, were subject to an obvious sex discrimination. The trouble was that this was the only one of the three which was likely to be significant from a numbers point of view. The Home Office estimate was that, because of a combination of arranged marriages and the pressure of young males from the Indian sub-continent, about five thousand a year might be involved.

I therefore decided to go slow on this change, and to balance it by conceding the amnesty point. This was a dangerous equation, for the cause of the women was popular and that of the illegal immigrants was not. To make matters worse I set out my position on the husbands clangingly rather than persuasively on 28 March, and then made the announcement on illegal immigrants in the House of Commons on the morning of Maundy Thursday, 6 April, with few people there and no newspapers the next day. It was not a deliberate subterfuge. It was just unthinking, and I was genuinely surprised when even such a liberal vis-à-vis as James Prior blew up and created a nasty scene which dominated much of that morning sitting. I performed like some allegedly considerable tennis player putting ball after ball straight back into the net.

My only good move in the five pre-Easter weeks at the beginning of that Government was to propose to the Cabinet that the Speaker's Conference on matters relating to the shape of the House of Commons should be invited to consider electoral reform. The Liberals, having just won fourteen seats (instead of their proportional entitlement of 125) for 19 per cent of the vote, were bound to request this. It was much better that the Government should take the initiative. Barbara Castle in her diary entry for this day (4 April) expressed appropriate disapproval at the 'very interesting revelation of Roy Jenkins's mind'. After describing the shocked opposition of Wilson, Foot, Mellish and Willie Ross, she concluded: 'So we sent Roy away with a flea in his coalition ear.'[1] I was to find this entry and the facts which it recorded very useful in the politics of the 1980s.

I went away for Easter, partly to East Hendred and partly to the Beaumarchais' house in the south-west of France, in low morale. My immigration ineptitude had two effects, one desirable, the other less so. First, it taught me that it was rash to attempt to ride a bicycle with no hands. Second, it made me nervous about riding the bicycle at all. I entered a period in which I became loath to take decisions, and it lasted for a month or so. Two things brought it to an end. One was the arrival in the Home Office of Anthony Lester as a special adviser to me, and the other was the emergence of a typical Home Office issue, news-dominating at the time but easily forgotten when it was over, with which I had to deal on a peculiarly unguided basis, carrying the Department with me but making the policy rather than following advice, and even conducting the negotiations myself.

Lester, now perhaps the most eminent human-rights QC, was then a thirty-seven-year-old junior barrister who was a prominent Fabian and had been a dedicated Gaitskellite. In 1967 he had edited a volume of my occasional writings entitled *Essays and Speeches*. In 1974, soon after the Government was formed, he offered to come and work for me on a four-days-a-week basis. There was no difficulty about his importation into the Home Office. The climate over Whitehall as a whole had substantially changed since 1965. Ministers in the second Wilson Administration were positively encouraged to bring in outside advisers. Within the Home Office it had changed even more markedly. Sir Arthur Peterson, who had succeeded Sir Philip Allen as permanent under-secretary in 1972, ran a very laid-back regime, far different from Sir Charles Cunningham's centralised martinetdom, but different also from Allen's positive social reformism. Peterson was shrewd and amenable, but sceptical and easy-going. His attitude suited me well enough at the time, but we did not form a constructive reformist partnership, such as Allen and I had achieved in 1966 and 1967.

Lester came in May, and helped to fill several gaps. John Harris was not lost to the Home Office, but he had been half lost to me on the formation of the Government. Harold Wilson, at a time when he was being rather sticky about adequate appointments for most friends of mine, decided to up-end the cornucopia on to John. He offered him a peerage and direct promotion to be one of the two Home Office Ministers of State. It was an offer that neither he nor I could refuse, although whether intentionally or not it exacerbated discontent amongst some members of our European group, which was however quickly dispelled by the quality of Harris's House of Lords performance. This necessarily meant that, while I had an excellent deputy on about a third of Home Office business, I could not habitually use him on the old basis for the other two-thirds. I was also in a transitional stage so far as private secretaries were concerned. When I arrived there was an able assistant secretary in place as head of the private office, but he was not in my view a natural private secretary. However his number two was, and with a little (but not much) difficulty I got him promoted to the number-one position and so propelled Hayden Phillips on the first stage of his rapid ascent, as well as starting an exceptionally enjoyable five-year relationship, in London and Brussels, for myself. But this took until October to effect.

Lester found me in a half-bereft state, rather as I had been in my first few weeks in the Treasury. His main medium-term role was to encourage and give direction to my human rights commitment, particularly the preparation of anti-discrimination legislation, both sexual and racial. Odd as it may seem to those who regard me as a frenzied promoter of liberal laws in the 1960s, by the 1970s these instincts required a little stimulation. In the first period I saw my primary task as Home Secretary as the opening of windows of freedom and innovation into the fusty and restrictive atmosphere of the Home Office. This was not incompatible with some hard anti-crime measures, such as majority verdicts and the reorganisation and re-equipment of the police. But there was no doubt where my emphasis lay. In my second term, on the other hand, I saw my primary task as the maintenance of the proper authority of the state, first against the threat of terrorism, which became acute in the autumn of 1974 and persisted throughout my period of office, but also against a view which I saw as dangerously prevalent within the Cabinet. What the Trades Union Congress wanted was becoming more important than upholding the rule of law. My hostility to this was in no way incompatible with important legislation on the rights of individuals. But, given the change in my order of priorities, it was both desirable and necessary to have Lester there to keep me up to the mark.

Together we had produced by the end of that summer of 1974 a Sex Discrimination White Paper, which was both a sensible and a popular addition to the Government's manifesto for the October election, and which was turned into legislation in the 1974–5 session. 'Together' was the right word, for although Lester wrote the White Paper almost single-handed he required a good deal of Secretary of State support, for there was more departmental opposition at upper-middle level than I had ever previously encountered. Shirley Summerskill, who was the parliamentary under-secretary concerned with this side of Home Office business, and had a hereditary commitment to women's rights, although to my mind exceeding in both sense and charm her redoubtable mother Edith Summerskill, was a pillar of support. That same summer we also published a scheme for the independent review of complaints against the police (it is amazing that there was no such provision until the mid-1970s), and in the parliamentary session of 1975–6, my last as a minister, we carried another Race Relations Bill, which strengthened the 1969 legislation.

Despite the fact that it was these longer-term purposes which were the reason for Lester being recruited, it was on a short-term Home Office crisis that he first made an impact and through our joint handling of which I recovered my morale and again became a fully engaged

Home Secretary. In November 1973, Dolours and Marion Price, then aged twenty-two and nineteen, had been convicted of causing the Old Bailey and Army Central Recruiting Depot explosions (both with major casualties) and sentenced to long terms of imprisonment. They were in Brixton Prison because they had from the beginning refused to take food by normal means, although they allowed themselves to be artificially fed. At least the nominal reason for their action was their demand to be sent back to serve their sentences in Northern Ireland.

This not totally unreasonable claim (except that it was of course rendered so by the duress under which they sought to place the authorities) was advanced on a mixture of mystical homeland and practical compassionate grounds. One difficulty was that the British public was not at the time disposed to feel much compassion towards this pair of dedicated terrorists. I was struck by the force of feeling against them in Birmingham, one Catholic lady with Irish connections who was amongst my closest supporters having expressed herself with peculiar vehemence. Another difficulty was that the relevant Home Office officials advised against a transfer on security grounds.

My instinct was that they should go back. This was partly because I always believed in keeping as much as possible of the contagion of Northern Ireland terrorism out of Great Britain. I thought we had responsibilities in Northern Ireland, both to uphold security and to assuage the conflict, but I did not think they extended to absorbing any more than we had to of the results of many generations of mutual intolerance of a degree which was inconceivable even in the most sectarian cities on this side of St George's Channel. This not very 'unionist' attitude resurfaced when we came to the Prevention of Terrorism Bill in the autumn of 1974. But in the early spring I allowed myself to be steered away from an early transfer, although I always had it in mind to effect one at a suitable time.

Events, however, did not wait for such a suitable time. In mid-May the Price sisters decided to resist artificial feeding. When it was attempted one of them nearly died of a choking fit. The prison medical officers consequently made a clinical judgement (that is, one which neither the Secretary of State nor anyone else could overrule without running dangerously up against the prerogatives of the medical profession) that they would not continue with the artificial process. This transformed a continuing irritation into an imminent threat. The likelihood was that one of the girls would die within a few weeks. News of these developments came through on the afternoon of Tuesday, 21 May, and began a two-and-a-half-week crisis.

The Price sisters were supported in word and deed by two prisoners, Kelly and Feeney, who had been convicted with them, and were respectively at Gartree and Wormwood Scrubs. There were two more peripheral figures, Gaughan and Stagg, who were also in an advanced stage of hunger strike. We therefore had six Irish prisoners who were on the threshold of death in English prisons. But Dolours and Marion Price were the *fons et origo* of the problem. They were the stuff of which Irish martyrs could be made: two young, slim, dark girls, devout yet dedicated to terrorism. I thought of the violent repercussions when Thomas Macswiney, Lord Mayor of Cork, starved himself to death in Brixton Gaol in 1920, and decided that if an alderman, even though also a scholar/poet, could produce such a wave of retaliation, the consequences of the death of these charismatic colleens was incalculable. No one, in Home Office, police or Cabinet, was inclined to dispute these forebodings of menace.* The Provisional IRA issued appropriate threats.

I therefore gave serious thought to seeking to protect the country from this threat of violence by giving a date by which the sisters would be moved to a prison in Northern Ireland. I worried over it during the long spring bank-holiday weekend at East Hendred. On the Tuesday evening my friend Jack Donaldson, who had become Northern Ireland Office Minister in charge of prisons, came to dinner and said that there would be no difficulty from his point of view about a transfer. On the Wednesday I went to London and persuaded Home Office officials, who were a little guilty about having been too short-sighted and intransigent when I had raised the matter in March, that this was a reasonable way to proceed. John Harris, over lunch, was a harder nut to crack. But he eventually came loyally along.

I then returned to East Hendred with the intention of devoting the next morning to an uninterrupted drafting of the most persuasive case for the course I intended to pursue. I realised that the task was both important and intractable enough for it to be worth doing myself. It was a classic example of the value of a minister sometimes subjecting himself to this discipline. The words simply failed to come. The essential problem was that to be respectable I had to pretend I was not acting under duress. But as that was in fact what I was doing I could find no convincing words to act as a cloak. The awkward corners always showed through.

Anthony Lester and his wife came to lunch. He said he was not surprised that I could not draft a good statement because he was unhappy about what I was trying to do. He argued with force and cogency that the correct thing was to make it absolutely clear that I was not moving under threat and that if the sisters were determined to

---

* Barbara Castle gave direct expression to this by writing in her diary (after the crisis was over): 'If the Price sisters had died I have no doubt that the women members of the Cabinet would have been at serious risk.'[2]

kill themselves we must allow events to take their course. There was no need to bang doors on the future, or to decide against action which I would have taken without the hunger strike, but if they wanted to go to Northern Ireland the girls must save their own lives and hope for the best. At the end of half an hour I said: 'I'm persuaded. I have been havering long enough about this. I will take a decision now for the firmer line and see if I can draft it better this afternoon.'

In the afternoon Jennifer went to London, the Lesters went for a long walk and I wrote in a garden chair for two hours. It went much better than in the morning for the good reason that the new statement had a logical coherence and even a moral force which the previous one had completely failed to achieve. The next day I took it to London, explained it to the Home Office, titivated it a little but not much and took it over to show to Wilson at 5.15 (he was not back from the Scillies until then). I think he would have preferred a softer line, but he accepted my now firm view satisfactorily, making only one drafting suggestion, and that a sensible one. I then saw David Astor, still the editor of the *Observer*, because Nora Beloff had been telephoning to say that opinion on the paper was moving towards a soft line, and as the *Sunday Mirror* had already taken that view the week before, it was desirable not to lose the whole of the left-of-centre Sunday press. The *Observer* under Astor's leadership I in any event regarded as the paper with which I felt most affinity. Astor appeared impressed by the statement, and it pulled the paper back into a position of benevolent neutrality that weekend, and into something much better after that.

Wilson and Astor between them had made me miss my train to Norfolk for Solly Zuckerman's seventieth birthday dinner, but I eventually got the 7.30 from Liverpool Street and arrived at Burnham Thorpe by 10.30, in time for a little more than the debris of the dinner and a good deal more than the dregs of the superb wine. We stayed until the Monday morning and that weekend remains imprinted on my mind by a combination of the weight of the foreboding and the solace of the hospitality. My statement was not released until the Saturday morning, and press reaction to it had to wait until the Sunday papers, which were then on the whole strongly favourable. The statement had however dominated the news bulletins throughout the Saturday. Dora Gaitskell rang up with an exceptionally warm message of support, which gave me as much pleasure and reassurance as almost any telephone call has ever done.

We were under tight security, with a double ration of my Metropolitan Police detectives as well as some reinforcements from the Norfolk constabulary. Early on the Sunday evening Jennifer and I and Joan Zuckerman went for a walk in the great park of Holkham, and I was vividly reminded, not by an immediate fear in the stomach but more by an immanence of doom, of the fatal walk of Lord Frederick Cavendish and his permanent under-secretary, Thomas Burke, in Phoenix Park, Dublin, ninety-two years before. I did not expect an assassin to leap out from behind any or every tree, but as I glanced back at the heavy police protection splayed out behind me even in this epitome of the agricultural stability of eighteenth-century England, the sad thought arose that if those damned girls stuck to their perverse intention I might never again be able to walk in freedom and security down a street in Boston or New York or Chicago.

The security oppression reached its depths the next morning when I arrived back at Liverpool Street and was met by an armoured-car contraption of the Metropolitan Police which combined the worst features of a biscuit box and a goldfish bowl as well as weighing about two tons. After being submerged in it for the two-mile journey to Westminster I announced that amidst all the uncertainties one thing was certain, and that was that I was never entering it again. If I did, suicide would become a much greater risk than assassination. This was accepted, but the monstrous vehicle remained in attendance, like a clumsy destroyer accompanying a merchant ship, and passed and repassed my own car whenever we went anywhere during the next week.

That evening we went to Oxford, for a long previously arranged dinner to me as President of the University Labour Club since 1967. Whenever we went under a bridge the armoured car drew alongside us and we both proceeded at 100 m.p.h. in line abreast for a few hundred yards. (There was fortunately less traffic on the motorways in those days.) When we got to Oxford my detective informed me that he had just had news that Gaughan – one of the peripheral two – had died in Parkhurst. When we got back to Ladbroke Square at about midnight we were greeted by a modest-sized and apparently entirely non-violent demonstration. The perverse irrationality of their slogans, however, was provoking. As I went into the house they asked, almost conversationally, 'How does it feel to be a murderer, Mr Jenkins?', and kept this up for some time afterwards. In view of the people the hunger strikers had blown up and mutilated, it was, as one might say, a bit rich. The demonstrators dispersed at about 1.30 a.m. with a goodnight cry of 'Enjoy your breakfast tomorrow morning, Mr Jenkins. Remember *they* won't be having any.' As we would happily have provided 'them' with anything from bacon and eggs to devilled kidneys or indeed caviar, if only they had been disposed to eat it, this also struck me as a convoluted piece of logic in relation to the deprivations of those in whose favour the demonstration was taking place.

Despite these trials to the nerves, I was on a hesitantly mounting curve of optimism during the middle days of that week. A number of people were trying to act as intermediaries. Lord Longford offered his services in a House of Lords speech. Jock Stallard, the Irish-orientated Labour MP for St Pancras North, did so more discreetly. So did Paddy Devlin, the former SDLP member of the dissolved Northern Ireland Executive. Fenner Brockway was also indefatigable and claimed to have some special, almost spiritual, ability to communicate with the sisters. He also had a special and apparently irresistible capacity to communicate with the *Daily Mail*, almost on an hour-to-hour basis. The Cardinal Archbishop of Westminster (Heenan) also approached me, via Shirley Williams, and sent a nun as an emissary to the two girls.

I did not regard these interventions as busy-bodying, although they varied in their effectiveness. (Stallard and maybe the Archbishop's nun were in my view the best.) I felt that I had the firm ground of my weekend statement from which I was not going to move, but that this did not preclude those who might have influence with the girls telling them that if they came off hunger strike there was every likelihood of their being transferred to Northern Ireland, as they would have been within a year had they been anonymous long-term prisoners. I also thought it desirable that they should have plenty of contact with the outside world, should as it were be kept talking, and not allowed to sink into a bunker of martyrdom. On one occasion I instigated Shirley Summerskill to go and see them from the Home Office.

I was, however, resolved to protect my flanks from two directions. First, there must be no hole-and-corner negotiations, no whispered and very likely misunderstood politicians' exchanges in the corridors of the House of Commons. When I had a key meeting with Stallard, Brockway and Devlin, I insisted that it should be in the Home Office, and asked the permanent under-secretary to be present. He said he would be at the Derby, but I got the head of the Prison Department in his place. Second, as a general election was likely to take place in the autumn, it occurred to me that I had to be careful when making assumptions about Home Office policy beyond then. Accordingly, on the morning of Wednesday, 6 June, I went to see Heath in a great solarium of a flat near Vauxhall Bridge where he was temporarily installed. I told him exactly what I proposed to say to the intermediaries, explained why I thought this the proper course and said that I hoped any Conservative Home Secretary who came in before the transfer to Northern Ireland had taken place, would act as I was proposing to do. He was wholly forthcoming, said 'We would not go back on that policy,' and volunteered to speak to Prior and to Joseph (between whom a shadow switch was about to take place) and ensure that they were fully aware of the position and that there was no official Conservative criticism of what I was doing, which he regarded as right.

I went down to East Hendred again on the Thursday evening (there was no House of Commons that week), and during the Friday the whole storm blew itself out as completely as in the last part of the William Tell overture. The main decision I had to take that morning was whether to let the sisters talk on the telephone to Feeney and Kelly and thus co-ordinate the end of their hunger strike. This was hardly in accordance with the rules of prison discipline, but it seemed to me that if Paris was worth a mass the end of this menace was worth two STD calls. By that evening they were all eating as normally as is possible after a sustained period with no food and the crisis was effectively over.

Probably most of the public breathed nearly as big a sigh of relief as I did, for the apprehension of danger was considerable. This did not of course preclude the possibility of press and popular accusations of a climb-down and a sell-out. There is nothing like a disappearance of danger to make people brave. But there was not much of a backlash. I received a handful of outraged letters and the *Sunday Express* and the *Daily Express* denounced my pusillanimity, while the *Daily Telegraph* teetered on the brink of doing so too. So did a few back-bench Tories. But that was it.

The Price sisters were transferred to the women's wing at Durham within a few weeks, and then quietly to Northern Ireland in March 1975. They were subsequently exemplary prisoners, were released on medical grounds in the early 1980s and now seem to be living quiet lives, Dolours married and in England. I take no credit for their subsequent renunciation of violence. My intense desire to prevent their dying was based on no starry-eyed view of their reformability but simply on a part-selfish and part-unselfish wish to avoid the massive retaliatory violence which, rightly or wrongly, everyone assumed would follow. It was unselfish in that I did not want innocent people to die or be maimed (I had not so far had to witness any of the results of this, but I was to see plenty of it in hospitals from London to Guildford to Birmingham in the course of the next six months). It was selfish insofar as I did not want to have to deal with the consequences.

There was little respite following the lifting of the Price sisters' threat. There was a combustible 'law and order' event during each of the two following weekends, with private notice questions in an excitable House of Commons on each of the Mondays. But my morale was vastly different from what it had been before the hunger-strike threat. I had recovered my nerve from its Easter and subsequent sag, and I had engaged with the peculiar balance-striking challenges of being Home Secretary in a way that I had not done since 1967. I remained detached from the Government, but not from my office.

One effect of this detachment from the Government was that it gave me a different psychological relationship with the Security Service than that which I had in 1965–7. Then, although on the whole a self-confident and even a successful Home Secretary, I was a relatively junior one. I was beholden to the Prime Minister for my appointment and, although this never looked likely, would have been dismayed had he shown any desire to sack or demote me. As the ministerial responsibility for MI5 is unsatisfactorily divided between the Prime Minister and the Home Secretary, a fact which is symbolised by the Cabinet Secretary, who is certainly not the servant of the Home Secretary, being the principal official involved, this balance of power was significant.

Furthermore, Wilson, particularly in the first half of his first premiership, showed signs of fascination with the cabalistic glamour of the Security Service. His June 1966 denunciation of a 'tightly knit group of politically motivated men' in the Seamen's Union was provoked by MI5 evidence. And from October 1964 until 1967 he employed the half-comic, half-sinister George Wigg nominally as Paymaster-General, but in fact as a licensed rifler in Whitehall dustbins and interferer in security matters. Wigg as an unofficial emissary of the Prime Minister used to pay me occasional Home Office visits during which he delivered cryptic messages. As they increasingly came to refer back to previous ones which had passed over my head the crypticism became compounded. Out of a rash mixture of boredom and supineness (for I did not wish to embroil with Wilson over him) I decided to roll with his punch, particularly as nothing ever seemed to follow from what he said. 'You know that matter I talked to you about last time,' a typical conversation would begin. 'It hasn't moved much, but I'll keep watching it.' If one nodded sagely he went quickly away, apparently satisfied, and no harm (or good either) ever seemed to result. But his activities hardly conduced to a coherent control of security policy. I think he fairly soon lost some of Wilson's confidence, and when hints were dropped to me that he would like to retire from the Government and become chairman of the Horserace Levy Board I was delighted to facilitate the change. Colonel Wigg knew a lot about racing and I thought he would be safer out of Downing Street.

His earlier role, combined with that of the utterly different Sir Burke Trend as Cabinet Secretary, did however symbolise the inability of a Home Secretary with normal ambitions to stay or rise in the Government, and under a vigorous Prime Minister, to exercise the disentangled control over the Security Service that he did over the prison or fire services or even the police. This ambiguity, combined with the arcaneness of their operations, greatly strengthened the independent power of MI5.

In 1974–6 several circumstances were more favourable to the power of the Home Secretary. First, there was my indifference to office. Wilson wanted me to be in the Government more than I wanted to be part of it. This necessarily changed the balance of power between us. Furthermore, he had become much less vigorously interfering, and any glamour which the Security Service had possessed for him had long previously disappeared. This was fortified by there being considerable mutual suspicion between him and them. In the mid-1960s I sensed that they thought of him as certainly a more powerful and maybe a wiser man than was I with my rash reforming zeal and possible iconoclasm. By the mid-1970s they had moved to regarding me as a more reliable defender of authority, and one or two hints were dropped that they would rather confide in me than in him.

This was the nearest that I ever got to seeing a shred of evidence for the subsequently widely spread allegations that MI5, or some significant part of it, regarded Wilson as a security risk and even planned operations to 'destabilise his Government'. When, soon after he left office, Wilson himself gave credence to these allegations and demanded an investigation I frankly regarded them with deep scepticism and as a product of his sometimes fevered imagination. But by 1986, after the publication of Peter Wright's tawdry book which nonetheless chimed in with a chorus of other allegations, I came to believe that, while the allegations against Wilson remained ridiculous, the feverishness may have lain elsewhere, and that the Prime Minister (Mrs Thatcher) should have set up a full inquiry, particularly as it was then asked for by Callaghan and had been previously demanded by Wilson, her two relevant predecessors. On 3 December of that year I said in the House of Commons:

Then we have Mr Wright's allegations that a surveillance operation was mounted against Lord Wilson when he was Prime Minister in the mid-1970s. Mr Wright, as I understand it, says that he was attracted by such an operation but resiled from it. That hardly enhances his reputation. During most of the period at issue I was Home Secretary. I need hardly say that I know nothing of any such operation. If it took place it was therefore wholly illegal. I would add that it could only have been conceived and mounted (if it was) by people with dangerously unbalanced minds. There are many criticisms which can be made of Lord Wilson's stewardship. . . . But the view that he, with his too persistent commitment to Britain's imperial role, with his over-loyal lieutenancy to Lyndon Johnson, his fervent royalism, his light ideological baggage, was an actual or even a likely Communist agent could only be entertained by somebody with a mind which was either diseased by partisanship or unhinged by living so long in an *Alice Through the Looking-Glass* world where falsehood had become truth, fact had become fiction and fantasy had become reality.

Even at the time, in spite of their somewhat greater propensity to me than to Wilson, I had considerable reservations about the intelligence services. I thought that the division between MI5 (responsible to the Home Secretary) and MI6 (responsible to the Foreign Secretary) led to another lacuna which was the enemy of effective ministerial control. Both agencies did some of the very limited telephone tapping which occurred within the United Kingdom. But neither Secretary of State knew what the other was authorising. As a result there was no minister who could see the overall picture. I decided to go on strike and say that I would sign no further MI5 warrants until I knew the MI6 picture as well. This led to enough consternation to suggest strongly that the ministerial warrant procedure was not camouflage but effective, and eventually to the production of the combined list, although only after a great deal of flapping of easily outraged feathers. (I was also persuaded that this procedure was not a deception by the tremendous trouble which would sometimes be undertaken in order to get a quick signature. My second private secretary was once despatched to the northern edges of Dartmoor to get a Saturday evening as opposed to a Monday morning signature. This could be regarded as the ultimate charade, but such elaborate cynicism was not, I think, likely.)

Nevertheless I experienced an inherent lack of frankness, an ingrowing mono-culture and a confidence-destroying tendency to engage in the most devastating internal feuds. This has been very damaging to an organisation eager to maintain an enamel front not only to the public but to ministers as well. Two of the four chapters of MI5's work have become in my view invalidated. The political-surveillance role, involving a fine and cool judgement between what is subversion and what is legitimate dissent, is inherently unsuited to be performed by an organisation of those who live in the distorting world of espionage and counter-espionage.

The associated political-intelligence role is doubtfully worthwhile. The object of this is presumably that of helping ministers with useful information. But in my experience the Security Service wastes far more of ministers' time in dealing with its own peccadilloes than any possible benefit which it provides. I spent many hours listening to representations for and against the guilt of Sir Roger Hollis, the former head of the service who had died in 1973. I have little doubt that he was innocent, but it was as difficult to prove as innocence always is, and there was an obsessive faction the other way.

I would therefore pull MI5 out of these two roles. There would remain the anti-terrorist and the spy-catching functions but whether the former requires an organisation totally separate from the Special Branch, and not always wholly co-operative with it either, is not self-evident. Counter-espionage does I think require some continuing specialised agency, although I would not regard it as of the very highest national priority. It should be subject to more effective political control first by clearing up the lacunae between the Prime Minister and the Home Secretary on the one hand and between the Home and Foreign Secretaries on the other, and probably by moving somewhat outside the executive and by associating senior MPs of other parties with the supervision.

The two weekend incidents to which I referred before this Security Service digression were first the Gaughan funeral in Kilburn on 10 June when eight pall-bearers marched in the highly provocative uniform of black spectacles, black berets and black clothes, which was probably the most offensive street display in Britain since Mosley's East End marches in 1936; and second the Red Lion Square riot of 17 June when clashes between National Front and far-out left demonstrators led to the death of one left-wing student and (after a delay) one police inspector. There was then a gap of nearly five weeks before the next significant incident, which was a terrorist attack at the Tower of London. The victims were mainly foreign tourists. I visited some of them in St Bartholomew's Hospital, where several were in an appallingly mutilated condition.

During that summer I settled two or three Home Office issues as well as making more forays into the general politics of the Government than I had done since the February election. At the end of June I lanced the boil of the inability of British women to bring in their husbands. I had always intended to make the change at some stage, and decided that there was no point in piling up odium through delay. In mid-July, following on the Price sisters' experience, I announced the virtual end of forced feeding in prisons. It was to be made clear to prisoners who went on hunger strike that, while food would always be available to them if they changed their minds, if they did not the natural consequences would be allowed to follow.

At the end of the month I announced the details of our police-complaints scheme, which was mainly the result of skilled work by John Harris, and because of his persuasive consultation of the various police bodies was reasonably well received by them as well as by the press. Later, however, the scheme ran into more police trouble, mainly because Robert Mark, the otherwise admirable Commissioner of the Metropolitan Police, saw the issue out of proportion and eventually resigned over it. This did not prevent the scheme becoming law in mid-1976.

On 22 July Denis Healey introduced a mildly reflationary mini-Budget which endeavoured to take a couple of points off the retail price index by cutting VAT and introducing some food and local rates subsidies. With inflation running at 16.5 per cent and other economic menaces looming this seemed to me a frivolous way of proceeding, even if an election was only two months away. It was like throwing stones at a potential avalanche, a dangerous pursuit. Callaghan and (more surprisingly) Peter Shore were also critical. Wilson was strongly in favour of the Chancellor's measures.

Still less satisfactory was the hardening of the Labour Party position towards a European referendum. At the February election the manifesto had said that an attempt would be made to renegotiate the terms of entry, and that the British people would be consulted about the results either by a referendum or at a general election. The renegotiation seemed to be proceeding satisfactorily, by which I do not mean that many hard changes were being achieved, for in fact the whole exercise had more of cosmetics than of reality about it, but that 'the European education of Mr Callaghan' (as I described it at the time) was proceeding apace and that the Prime Minister, back in office, was reverting to his natural position as a joiner and not a leaver of international organisations. But the likelihood of the manifesto for an October election containing an unqualified commitment to a referendum was also gathering momentum.

On 11 July I went separately to see both Callaghan and Wilson to say that if this were so it would prevent my playing a central part in the election campaign. They both affected to take this seriously, Callaghan if anything more so than Wilson. Looking back I find it surprising that they were not more tempted to shrug their shoulders and say 'Too bad', or even 'Good, then there will be more time for us on the television programmes.' The explanation I think is that the Labour Party of those days, in sharp contrast with the position in the first half of the 1980s, was dedicated to winning elections. And these two at least fairly consistently believed that, even if the thought was sometimes unwelcome, the prominent support of my social democratic wing was essential for that purpose.

Wilson used the opportunity of the meeting to have a much longer and intentionally more friendly talk than for some time past. In the course of it he urged me to make a general speech with impact. His particular interest was that I should scotch the idea of coalition, which was gaining ground in the press. I said that I was prepared to express general scepticism about this, but that if I did so I would have to range over a lot of other points too. He said: 'Such as what?' I said: 'That a Labour government must show an absolute respect for the rule of law, must explicitly accept the mixed economy, with enthusiasm and not merely toleration for the private sector, and must accept with equal enthusiasm our full membership of the Atlantic community, which had implications for economic policy (no siege economy) as well as for foreign and defence policy.' He said, 'Very good.' It could

I suppose be argued that I was merely pontificating platitudes, but at a time when Benn was threatening most of industry, when Foot was running before the trade unions as well as bringing unilateralism into the heart of the Government, when half the Cabinet was in favour of coming out of Europe, and when even Crosland was putting the Clay Cross councillors above the law, they were not so platitudinous.

The ironical result of the conversation was that Wilson knew at least two weeks before it was made the main lines of the speech which I proceeded to deliver at Haverfordwest on Friday, 26 July, and which was treated as one of the most explicit and critical speeches that I had ever made about the Labour Party's drift to the left. I stayed the night of the speech in the Dragon Hotel, Swansea, and took an early train back to Reading for East Hendred. The speech dominated the newspapers. As I unfolded them one after the other over breakfast through the decaying industrial landscape of the eastern exit from Swansea, I took in with a mixture of excitement and trepidation that I had certainly achieved the 'impact' for which Wilson had asked. And, almost inevitably, a lot of presentation was in terms of 'Jenkins warns Wilson'.

The result was a Labour Party furore. A lot of moderate MPs, including some surprises, expressed satisfaction that I had made the speech. 'About time that it was said' was a widespread response. On the other hand the hard-line Tribunites, led by Ian Mikardo, bitterly denounced the speech, and a few members of the Cabinet, including Crosland, did lobby briefing about how singularly ill-timed it was. In addition I had a lot of letters about the speech, more than at any time other than when I resigned the deputy leadership. They were 90 per cent favourable, and made it clear that I had struck a chord which a lot of people in and on the edge of the Labour Party had been waiting to hear.

A week after my Pembrokeshire expedition I retreated first to East Hendred and then to Italy until nearly the end of August. While I was away I wrote about the events of the spring and summer in a way that showed I regretted neither the content nor the timing of the Haverfordwest speech. If anything, I thought I had delayed too long. I also noted that it had made me much more engaged with politics than had been the case a few months earlier, although I saw the outlook as 'shrouded in darkness, danger and confusion'. What is also the case, although I did not write it, is that on that Italian holiday I began for the first time to contemplate the possibility that the only way through this miasma might be outside the mould of traditional two-party politics. I had disagreed too deeply on too many issues over too long a period with too many people in my own party. I did not reach any clear conclusions, but I felt that the divide was becoming unsustainable and the shape of British politics increasingly ill-fitting.

Almost as soon as we were back the election campaign began to dominate. I found it the dullest election since 1955. My main contribution to the early stages was to publish the popular Sex Discrimination White Paper on 6 September. On 16 September we had a day-long Cabinet/National Executive Committee meeting on the manifesto. I argued strongly against the absolute commitment to the referendum and got a surprising amount of support, but not quite enough. The concession Wilson and co. made to me was to use the phrase 'consult the British people through the ballot box' rather than to flaunt the red cloth of 'the referendum' in my face. But it was a distinction without a difference. I therefore said that I would not do any early national press conferences, although I could do one or two at the end when the issue had died down. It was not a question of pique but of the fact that they could lead to nothing but embarrassment, even more for the party than for me. Wilson had the sense to accept this quietly, but the egregious Hayward blustered to me on the telephone saying that Shirley Williams was making no difficulty at all about appearing.

The difficulty she made was not about appearing but, with her spontaneous honesty, what she said when she got there. Three days later, sharing the platform with Wilson, she suddenly blurted out (the right phrase according to those present) that if the referendum produced a negative result she would resign from the Government, resign from Parliament and retire from politics. This was the major headline of the day, which displeased Wilson far more than my non-appearance. The spotlight then turned on to me. Would I stay if Mrs Williams went? I was never much in favour of hypothetical commitments, but the issue having been raised I could not dodge it. When I went to Birmingham for nomination the next morning I therefore issued the following statement: 'My conviction that it would be a major mistake to come out of Europe is just as strong as Mrs Williams's. I hope and believe the negotiations can succeed, but naturally I would not stay in a Cabinet which had to carry through such a withdrawal, damaging for the world and doubly so for the country in its likely economic circumstances.'

This inevitably kept the story running for another twenty-four hours or so, but it was better than being pursued by it for the rest of the campaign, in which, having been dealt with, it played little part. I did another straight-to-camera party political telecast, following the usual dispute between Wilson, who was insistent that I should do it, and the party apparatchiks, who would rather it had been done by, say, Mikardo. The drama of the campaign was concentrated for me on the last weekend. On the Friday evening I spoke in King's Lynn and then went to the Zuckermans' at Burnham Thorpe for thirty-six hours off. It did not prove a restful respite for I was oppressed during most of the Saturday by the difficulty of putting together an appropriate and original speech for my Sunday afternoon meeting with Wilson in the Birmingham Town Hall. Six months before in exactly the same circumstances I had enjoyed a minor home-ground triumph. And nothing is more difficult to repeat than a triumph where the circumstances are the same but the content must be different.

Late on the Saturday evening this oppression faded into insignificance when I received news of major terrorist attacks in Guildford. Two pubs, much frequented by army personnel, had been blown up. There were five dead and a lot of other casualties. Apart from its other horrors this presented me with an acute problem of what to do on the next day. Should I go to Guildford and give up Birmingham, for me the major meeting of the campaign? Or should I ignore Guildford and go to Birmingham in the normal way, no doubt to be accused of politicking while turning my back on carnage? Or should I attempt to do both, probably ending up by doing neither satisfactorily? My office (Hayden Phillips was not yet in charge) proved singularly ineffective at making a plan and organising aircraft. At 10.00 a.m. I was still in Norfolk, undecided between Guildford and Birmingham. I had to fall back on telephoning Wilson and mobilising his private office. He was at his prime ministerial best, calm, decisive and unselfish. I should go to Guildford and then come on to Birmingham and speak after him. His office (in the efficient shape of Lord Bridges, son of a Secretary of the Cabinet as well as grandson of a poet, and himself a future ambassador to Rome) would organise an aircraft to make this possible.

At Guildford I saw the surviving victims, the scenes of the outrages, the police and other services and got to Birmingham in time to make a *deus ex machina* entry into the Town Hall which solved most of the problems of my speech. Harold Wilson had disadvantages as Prime Minister, but trying to upstage his ministers at times of national tragedy was not one of them.

The result of that election was better in Stechford than I had expected – the majority went up to nearly 12,000, but I achieved no swing significantly better than the Birmingham average – and indeed did slightly worse than the result in the country as a whole. Labour got forty-three seats more than the Conservatives but its overall majority was only four. The weather had been exceptionally dismal throughout the campaign. I once saw a patch of sunshine over the kingdom of Fife while flying south from Wick to Edinburgh in a small plane, but that was unique. I drove back to East Hendred from Birmingham on a raw and dirty Friday morning after the count without any sense of a new chapter beginning. It never occurred to me that I would be moved from the Home Office, and there was indeed no post-election reshuffle.

Wilson was beginning to coast towards his retirement, the date of which (although few suspected it at the time) he no doubt had firmly in his mind. So far as stimulation from the centre was concerned it was a very different government from that of 1964–70. In some ways but not in all this was a good thing. There were fewer gimmicks and greater calm. But there was also a sense of purposelessness. After the 1970 shock Wilson desperately wanted to have his 'tit-for-tat with Teddy Heath', but once he had had it and walked back through the front door of 10 Downing Street in March 1974, there was little that he wanted to do inside. He liked re-exercising his 1966 skill in the choice of date for a follow-up election and achieving the remarkable feat of winning four times out of five. And I think he always wanted to announce that the European renegotiation had been a success and to win the referendum for staying in. He saw this both as nationally desirable and as a rectification of the adverse personal balance with which he had come out of the events of 1971–2, and which had inflicted a deep trauma on him. But there were very few policies that he wished to impose. He left me remarkably free. In making Home Office decisions I hardly thought of 10 Downing Street as a factor.

That autumn there were two Home Office issues of major political import, and one general one with which I was much concerned. It was only in the last, that of how the referendum was to be handled, that the Prime Minister's attitude was a crucial factor. The first Home Office issue concerned two (originally three) building-worker pickets, Warren and Tomlinson, who became known as the Shrewsbury Two. In December 1973 they had been sentenced to three and two years of imprisonment respectively for their roles in nasty picketing riots on a number of building sites about a year before that. A third man, Jones, received a much shorter sentence, but he was released and out of the way soon after I became Home Secretary. Warren and Tomlinson were rough thugs, who in my view deserved their sentences. But the TUC, following rather than resisting a Communist- and Trotskyist-inspired campaign, decided to turn them into trade union martyrs. This was at any rate their view until they themselves experienced some of their thuggery. Tomlinson got out under the normal working of remission arrangements in the summer of 1975 and proceeded to make a determined attempt to break up the Trades Union Congress of that year. Thereafter there was a noticeable diminution in the fervour of the General Council's demands upon me.

The cases were not handled helpfully by the judiciary. In June (1974) the Court of Appeal decided to let the men out on bail pending its slow resolution of the appeals. This naturally created an expectation that it

was going to quash or reduce the sentences. In October it decided to
do neither. This meant that the two men had to go back inside with
a lot of their sentences still to serve. In the week after the election,
the Lord Chancellor (Elwyn-Jones) came to see me almost literally
wringing his hands. The Lord Chief Justice (Widgery) had warned
him before the delivery of the judgement. 'Dreadful news, dreadful
news,' he began in his beautiful voice. He expressed great sympathy
for me. 'Of course, for the sake of the rule of law you will have to
uphold what they say, but it will be difficult, very difficult.' I think he
was surprised at the alacrity with which I assured him I would do this. It
was absolutely clear to me that, while there was room for doubt about
the tactical wisdom of the Court of Appeal's handling of the matter, I
could not go round the country fulminating about the rule of law and
even contemplate taking a purely political decision to commute these
sentences.

Elwyn-Jones was however right in expecting a lot of trouble. I think
I had to see five TUC deputations. I remember one in particular when
so many members of the General Council came that they had to sit
round my big table in rows, looking more as though they were at the
cinema than part of a deputation. Jack Jones took the lead, but most
of the right-wing leaders came too, although one or two of them a little
sheepishly. I had the impression that the bulk of the deputation was
not so much angry as amazed that I would not accede. The climate of
the time was that of ministers finding out what the TUC wanted and
giving it to them. Michael Foot, with whom as Employment Secretary
they dealt most frequently, was totally of this disposition, but he was
not alone. Jones was never abusive, but he was not friendly either. I
remember at the end of one long meeting suggesting that we had a
drink, at which several faces lit up, for the TUC like a little liquid
refreshment. But Jones gave a firm collective refusal and shepherded
them all out.

Nor was the trouble only with the TUC. For nearly a year each of
the monthly days when I was first for House of Commons questions
was half dominated by a cluster of demands for the release of the
convicted pickets, accompanied by complaints about their treatment
in prison. In addition there were two meetings of the parliamentary
Labour Party devoted to the issue. At one of them Cledwyn Hughes
as chairman horrified me by saying that he proposed to have a vote. I
thought it was rash. I would have felt I had to resign had it gone wrong.
But he knew his parliamentary Labour Party better than I did. We had
a substantial majority.

There were also sporadic small demonstrations during my political
official visits around the country. And the *Morning Star* devoted its
main headline about one day in four to the plight of the Two. I did

not find any of this formidable, for I had a settled mind on the issue, and I never had any trouble with the Cabinet. I think many of them would have behaved differently themselves but they were happy to leave the matter (as it should have been left) for unilateral decision by the Home Secretary.

The second Home Office issue was the devastating terrorist attack in Birmingham on the evening of 21 November and the subsequent decision to take the Prevention of Terrorism (Temporary Provisions) Bill through Parliament in a rush. During late October and early November there had been a number of minor but potentially nasty bomb incidents. One was in the dining room of Brooks's and when I went late at night to inspect the damage a chunk of the ceiling fell on to the nape of my neck and almost knocked me over. The bruises persisted for a few weeks, but as that was the nearest to damage I ever came I reckoned I had escaped lightly.

This wave of incidents was mostly in Birmingham. At first it produced very few casualties, but there was always a threat and a danger, and indeed the wife of Denis Howell, MP for Small Heath and an old friend, although escaping unhurt, might easily have been killed by a bomb placed under her car. On 1 November I made a special non-constituency visit to Birmingham to discuss security with the police and other services. And in London the normal Armistice Day service on 10 November, which produced a more concentrated target of royal family, Cabinet and other political leaders inside and outside the Home Office than any other annual event, also caused very special precautions in 1974, and intense relief in the Home Office when it was over without incident. But none of this prepared us for the Birmingham horror. Two pubs in the centre of the city, packed mainly with young people, were the scene of twenty-four deaths and nearly 200 injuries, many of them severe. It was a different order of casualties from anything we had previously known.

The news reached me when I was dining in that same Westminster restaurant, Lockett's, where I had prepared for the key European division in 1971. I immediately went back to the Home Office, where John Harris came in and joined me within the half-hour. We spontaneously and jointly agreed that an emergency bill would now be both necessary and acceptable. This might I suppose be regarded as legislation by rush of blood to the head (to quote the phrase which I have used about George Brown's Concorde antics of ten years before), but it was not as much so as might seem to be the case for we had carefully prepared contingency plans. These were made up of one measure which was for show and three which were of real practical importance. The first related to making the IRA an illegal organisation in Great Britain. When I came back into office I inherited from the outgoing Conservative Administration the view that this would be a mixture of the fruitless and the harmful. This view was lukewarmly supported by the police, who thought that driving the IRA underground might make it more difficult to penetrate. On that fraught November evening, however, I decided that the IRA's continued legal existence and ability to march as at the Gaughan funeral had become an intolerable affront to the British people, that there was not much in the contrary arguments, and that the public should be given the satisfaction of seeing the organisation made illegal. The police were willing to change their minds.

Much more important, however, were the provisions of practical impact. The first empowered the police to detain terrorist suspects without having to formulate charges for forty-eight hours on their own authority, and then for another five days, provided they sought authority from a minister of the Crown in each case. The second introduced much tighter physical controls at the points of entry into Great Britain from both the north and the south parts of Ireland. The third, which was the most controversial, enabled the Home Secretary to exclude from Great Britain citizens of the Republic of Ireland or those originating in Northern Ireland where it appeared to him, on advice, that they were involved or likely to be involved in acts of terrorism. This was drastic, particularly in relation to those from Northern Ireland, who of course held United Kingdom passports. To banish someone from a part of the territory of the polity of which he is a citizen is not something which could or should be proposed in normal circumstances.

It was modified in two ways which were sufficiently limited as almost to underline the toughness of the measure. Those of Northern Ireland origin who had been continuously settled in Great Britain for at least twenty years could not be excluded. And, while there was to be no formal mechanism of appeal from my essentially executive decisions, I proposed to appoint two independent advisers to whom representations could be made by or on behalf of those on whom exclusion orders were served, and whose advice was clearly likely to be decisive. My first two advisers were Lord Alport, a notably liberal former Tory minister, and Ronald Waterhouse QC (now Mr Justice Waterhouse), who had been a parliamentary Labour candidate. The relatively smooth working in its early stages of this difficult piece of legislation owed a great deal to the fairness and diligence of their work.

These were the main original provisions of the Prevention of Terrorism (Temporary Provisions) Bill, which became an act 180 hours later, and which, despite the parenthetical part of its name, circumstances have regrettably made it necessary to keep on the statute book. Within a few minutes of my deciding that the time had come to introduce this legislation, influenced alike by the desire to give reassurance to the country and by the belief that its provisions, which had now become acceptable although they would not hitherto have been so, would be of considerable and practical anti-terrorist utility, Wilson came through to me on the telephone. He did not ask me to go to 10 Downing Street, because as he thoughtfully said I was no doubt very occupied. As was frequently the case at a time of crisis, he was at his best and most helpful. He did not have anything of his own to propose, but he immediately accepted my view that emergency legislation had become necessary and said that he would back it to the full in Cabinet.

The next morning I saw Heath and Keith Joseph, who had become shadow Home Secretary, in Heath's room in the House of Commons and told them of my intentions. They did not demur. I then made a statement to the House, which presaged legislation without specifying its provisions, and left to go to Birmingham by train. I was in the city for four hours. It seemed an eternity and was one of the most difficult, draining and unpleasant visits that I have ever paid. It was a dry, still, misty, rather cold day, one of the very few of that exceptionally wet and windy autumn, and the atmosphere in the unusually deserted centre of the city hung heavy with some not wholly definable but unforgettable and oppressive ingredients. Others felt it as strongly and physically as I did. Partly no doubt it was the lingering scent of the explosions, but there was also a stench of death and carnage and fear. Maybe this was all in the imagination, but what was certainly physically present was a pervading atmosphere of stricken, hostile resentment such as I had never previously encountered anywhere in the world.

The two blasted pubs were almost adjacent to New Street Station and I went first to look at their ghastly wreckage. Then I went to the local police station, then to the Council House to pay a call of formal sympathy to the city on the Lord Mayor, and then to Archbishop's House where I paid a less formal because less obvious call on Monsignor Dwyer, the Roman Catholic prelate. I was deeply worried (and not without reason) about a dangerous schism developing between the large Irish community and the more indigenous population of Birmingham, and I thought in an inchoate way that this might make a small contribution to preventing it.

At that stage I was supposed to do a press conference at police headquarters, but that had to be put off because the building was evacuated following a new bomb warning, which everyone took very seriously in the circumstances. So I began the most searing part of the day, which were the visits to the mutilated, divided between the General and the Accident Hospitals. Between the two hospital visits I did my postponed press conference, and also made some brief television statements coming out of the Accident Hospital. I am afraid they did not come over as confidence-giving. I looked too dismayed and shattered for that. After these interviews I escaped and was driven to East Hendred in a fair state of prostration. There had been some but not a vast amount of shouting and demonstration. Predictably there were cries of 'bring back hanging' and even some for the mass expulsion of the Irish population. Behind the shouts the silence was heavy and ugly, and understandably so. It was four months before I again felt at ease in Birmingham.

On the Sunday Home Office officials came to East Hendred with the text of the bill, on which they and parliamentary draftsmen had done a remarkable rushed job. On the Monday morning I took it to a special Cabinet. Wilson was as good as his word but I nonetheless had considerable difficulty. Merlyn Rees as Northern Ireland Secretary did not like the exclusion order provisions. Nor would I have done in his circumstances. It was shovelling back the terrorists on to his plate. But that was from where they came, both in origin and in motive, and it was hard-headed sense to try to protect the trunk against the gangrene in one limb. Being an unobsessive and wide-sighted man he did not press his objection, but Callaghan was inclined to do so on his behalf. Foot and Benn joined in with different motives. Healey and Crosland were coolly unhelpful. After a nerve-testing hour and a half I got exclusion orders through only by making it clear that if this part of the bill were cut out the announced statement from me in the House that afternoon would not take place, with all the consequences which would follow from that. It was the balanced package or nothing.

The disputed parliamentary statement then went smoothly enough. What was probably more important was the straight-to-camera ministerial broadcast that I did that evening. Despite the fact that we arrived in Broadcasting House with most of the script still to be written, and had to go through to the third take (generally a bad sign) before feeling it was remotely right, it was an important turning point. It apparently corrected any impression of defeat which I had given in Birmingham on the Friday.

We took the bill through all its stages in an eighteen-hour marathon on the Thursday night/Friday morning. I moved the second reading in the afternoon and then had to make twelve or fifteen mostly short interventions during the all-night committee stage. We made a few concessions when convinced by the arguments, but the framework survived intact, although not without considerable pressure at some points. This was by no means all from a civil-liberties direction. There was a lot of fulmination against the BBC, with demands that I should take powers to tell them how to handle terrorist activities and Northern Ireland affairs. This I firmly refused to do.

The Lords sat specially early on the Friday morning and took the bill almost automatically. It was law by 9.30. John Harris, Hayden Phillips (well blooded by Birmingham and this House of Commons marathon into his role as principal private secretary) and I went to Brooks's – a suitable locale after a strenuous anti-terrorist night – and had a large, late breakfast. The sheer exhaustion and sense of having come temporarily into a harbour after eight days of buffeting storm inevitably created a sense of accomplishment. Was it justified? I think that the Terrorism Act helped both to steady opinion and to provide some additional protection. I do not regret having introduced it. But I would have been horrified to have been told at the time that it would still be law nearly two decades later. It is a classic example of the truth of the adage that it is only the provisional which lasts. It should teach one to be careful about justifying something on the ground that it is only for a short time.

I wonder also whether I was influenced in the speed and determination with which I pushed through the legislation by the fact that I was a Birmingham member of Parliament. I do not think so. I took the decision (although this is not of course fully refuting evidence) before my visit to the city on 22 November, which certainly had a searing effect on me, and I was subsequently uninfluenced by the wave of pro-hanging feeling which inevitably swept Birmingham in the aftermath. It was the only occasion in twenty-seven years there when I had piles of bitter mail from Stechford.

There appeared at first to be a great defection of anti-death penalty MPs, mostly Tory, but some Labour as well. Our assumption for a week or so was that we would be swept away as by an avalanche. The only tactic I could think of was to avoid the issue coming before the House of Commons until after the Christmas recess. Bob Mellish, the chief whip, was on this occasion wiser than I. He said that it was better to get it out of the way. He told me on 5 December that there had been a steadying of opinion amongst Labour members, and that we would certainly have a majority, although he could not be sure how big. We decided to take the debate on 11 December, and in the outcome secured the massive majority of 152.

This was largely due to the splendid courage of Willie Whitelaw. Joseph, the shadow Home Secretary, had defected into a position at once tortured and nonsensical. He was still an abolitionist, but thought an exception should be made for terrorists. After the fears aroused by the prospective deaths of the Price sisters (how much worse it would have been had one of their victims died and they had been about to hang on a British gallows) this seemed to me nearly insane. It did not seem much better to Whitelaw, although he had been in favour of the death penalty until he had gone to Northern Ireland as Secretary of State. Joseph held the right of speaking for the opposition which Whitelaw did not feel he could usurp. However, he agreed that he would intervene in my speech, express his own continuing conviction that the death penalty for terrorism would greatly increase the danger to the security forces in Northern Ireland, and say that he was speaking on behalf of Heath as well as himself. It was a remarkable display of courage on both their parts, particularly with Heath's leadership coming under heavy challenge and Whitelaw a possible contender for the succession. They could so easily have stood back. I was not only greatly relieved but much moved by the attitude they took. They ensured that 1974, which was the most testing year on the terrorist front, ended better than had seemed likely at several times in its dark and fluctuating course. As it happened, Whitelaw was also to play a considerable role in a quite different facet of my life which was to dominate 1975.

# CHAPTER TWENTY-TWO

# *The European Referendum*

It is a perverse but indisputable fact that the event I most enjoyed during 1974–6, my second and last period in a British government, was the one which I had striven most officiously, even to the point of a resignation which may have cost me the prime ministership, to prevent taking place.

By December 1974 it had become obvious that I had finally lost my battle against a European referendum and that one was inevitably going to take place in the late spring or summer of 1975. But it also seemed that it would do so in circumstances much more favourable, so far as the attitude of the Labour leadership was concerned, than had appeared possible in 1972 or likely in early 1974. By December I was not in serious doubt that Wilson would recommend a 'yes' vote and that Callaghan as Foreign Secretary would do the same. I did not therefore feel that there was any need for me to contemplate a second resignation, or indeed any basis other than a very sterile attachment to form as opposed to substance on which I could have justified it.

Chancellor Schmidt of Germany had played a key role in the evolution of Wilson's position. During a visit to England in the last days of November he had performed three crucial services. First, he had made a brilliantly successful speech at a postponed and shortened (because of the election) Labour Party conference in the Central Hall, Westminster. It was during the only session I had been able to attend because of the preoccupations of the Prevention of Terrorism Bill, and I there experienced a splendidly contradictory morning. An hysterical debate on the Shrewsbury pickets had preceded Helmut Schmidt's virtuoso performance. It was the greater tribute to him that he had been able to lift the audience out of a mood of truculent leftism. Wilson, I believe, was much impressed not only by what Schmidt said but by the way the conference responded to it. Second, Schmidt had successful talks with Wilson at Chequers. Third, he had the excellent idea of acting as an intermediary to arrange a bilateral dinner in Paris between Wilson and Valéry Giscard d'Estaing, who had been elected President of the Republic in May. These conversations seemed to arouse Wilson's interest in the grand league of foreign-policy involvement in a way that had not been so since his relationship with Lyndon Johnson in the late 1960s. But there was a big difference. He could play a more or less equal hand with Schmidt and Giscard, whereas he had been very much a junior partner of L.B.J.'s.

All this paved the way for a meeting which I had with Wilson, Callaghan and Short on the Friday morning before Christmas. It was to decide what could or should be done about the legislation necessary to make possible a referendum. Obviously such a bill could not be introduced by the Government without the Home Secretary having his name on it. (It would indeed have been normal for the Home Secretary himself to take charge of such legislation, but I managed to devolve this on to Short, as leader of the House of Commons and Lord President, who, as he was dealing with the plans for Scottish and Welsh devolution, could be held to have some constitutional role.) No one knew until this occasion whether I was going to accept the bill or not. I said that I would, provided it was not introduced until the negotiations were complete and the Cabinet had decided its recommendation and announced it to the House of Commons. If this were negative, I would leave the Government, to which course I was indeed committed by my statement following Shirley Williams's election press conference, and fight the referendum campaign from outside. I would not avail myself of the almost unprecedented 'agreement to differ' with which Wilson was already playing. But if there were a positive recommendation I would stay in the Government in spite of the referendum. I added a reserve that if the economic roof collapsed in the meantime, as was not improbable, I thought we ought to cancel or at least postpone the referendum. This reluctant acquiescence was greeted with relief by Wilson, and as far as I could tell by the others. They accepted my argument that such a course would not much delay the Referendum Bill, for if accompanied by a positive Government recommendation the opposition would let it through on oiled castors, and if not, not.

This meeting had a fall-out which both provided an interesting vignette of life in that Government and was probably a factor in a new deterioration of relations with Wilson which set in during February (1975) and persisted until our official relations tailed away. During the Christmas recess *The Times* carried a report on the Government's strategy for dealing with the Referendum Bill which suggested that the writer was privy to most of the decisions of this 20 December meeting. He probably got his information indirectly from me. Having decided to swallow the referendum, I thought that I was fully entitled to an *explication de vote* in the serious press. Wilson, who may or may not have thought that the culprit was me, decided to mount an old 1960s hobby-horse and initiated a leak inquiry. A questionnaire was sent round on the private-secretary net to all relevant ministers asking them whether they knew the journalist in question, when they had last seen him, and so on. Influenced no doubt by a mixture of impatience and guilt, I decided I was too old for this sort of game. I told Hayden Phillips to write back in the following terms: 'Throughout a political career almost as long as the Prime Minister's, the Home Secretary has always declined to fill in questionnaires. He feels that he must maintain this practice, however elevated may be the source from which they come.' It was insolent insubordination, and Hayden properly checked that I was sure I wanted it to go before he despatched it to Robert Armstrong. With a little trepidation we waited for the counterblast. But none came. It was the last we heard of the issue.

During February John Harris brought to me the proposition that in the referendum campaign I should be head of the 'umbrella' organisation which was being set up on a cross-party basis to campaign for a 'yes' vote. He and Bill Rodgers had been meeting for some weeks with a number of Tories – Douglas Hurd, Anthony Royle, Michael Fraser and Geoffrey Tucker – as well as David Steel for the Liberals and Con O'Neill (former ambassador to the European Community) as a non-party figure to create the skeleton of an effective organisation. Our attitude to the referendum had become that of the 1878 music-hall song: 'We don't want to fight, but by jingo if we do . . .'.

I was determined that, in the Government or out of it, I should play an uninhibited part in the referendum campaign. I was not going to swallow both the unwanted referendum itself and any attempt to restrict my role in fighting it. Apart from anything else, we were in total doubt at that stage about what the outcome would be. A referendum was uncharted ground (no one had the slightest idea what the percentage turn-out would be), and the polls suggested that public opinion had recently hovered between the apathetic and the hostile. I was therefore greatly attracted by the opportunity offered by John Harris's proposal, and was not prepared to give Wilson the right of veto over whether or not I accepted it. On the other hand I did not want to do or say anything which might upset Wilson before he had committed himself on the outcome of the Dublin European Council (10–11 March), which was to conclude the 'renegotiation', had got his recommendation through the Cabinet and indeed had announced it in the House of Commons.

A few weeks of finessing was therefore necessary. First, I had to ascertain that the Tories really were of a settled disposition to offer me the presidency. They were in a delicate condition. On 4 February

Heath had been toppled from the leadership. On 11 February Mrs
Thatcher's breakthrough was confirmed. She had pushed out the
great European but she had inherited a party which was then deeply
committed to Britain's position in Europe and strongly opposed to
Labour Party shilly-shallying on the issue. She therefore had to throw
the weight of the Conservative Party machine behind a 'yes' vote. But
her future aloofness from Europe presaged itself by her decision to
support from the sidelines but not herself actively to participate in
the campaign. The suggested arrangement by which I was to take
the lead therefore probably suited her well enough. At one stage
her chief whip (Humphrey Atkins) sent back a counter-proposition
for a troika of presidents: Mrs Thatcher, Jeremy Thorpe (as leader
of the Liberal Party) and myself. I turned that down, both because it
would be markedly exclusive of Wilson and because such a dispersal
of authority would make the presidents figureheads whereas a single
one could be a leader. Mrs Thatcher then intervened to say that
the original proposition was acceptable and that she intended to
nominate Whitelaw and Maudling as vice-presidents, perhaps with
Carrington as a third. I would have been glad to have all three,
although Carrington eventually stood down for Heath, who, rather
to my surprise and much to my pleasure, made it clear that he would
like to be a vice-president.

I cannot imagine how all this coming and going (conducted throughout by intermediaries) took place without news of it getting back to
Wilson, whose political intelligence was normally plentiful if sometimes fantastical as well. Perhaps he was always informed and merely
waited with superior calm for me to come and tell him. But, from the
form our conversation then took, I do not think so.

During the weekend between the Dublin summit and the British
Cabinet's consideration of its results Jennifer and I stayed in the
Bonn Embassy for the twenty-fifth Königswinter Conference. It
was a memorable visit for a variety of reasons, a great gathering
of the pro-European clans, combining something of the atmosphere of the Duchess of Richmond's pre-Waterloo ball with that
of Wellington's battle-planning headquarters. Heath was also staying
at the Embassy, and I happily surrendered the ministerial suite to
him, thinking he needed a poultice, that the gesture might help
to lubricate the ball-bearings of the Britain in Europe campaign,
and that in any event those rooms were so suffused for me with
memories of the ghastly November 1968 monetary conference that
I was glad to be out of them. The Hendersons had just received
news that, with their successful Bonn tour drawing to a close,
they were to go next to Paris, and were in buoyant form. On
the Saturday night they gave an exceptionally enjoyable informal

dance at which I remember Bill Rodgers performing with particular verve.

The twenty-fifth birthday of Königswinter and its parent the Deutsche–Englische Gesellschäft, both so devotedly and rewardingly nurtured by Lilo Milchsäck, was also well worth celebrating, and it gave me pleasure to make the British commemorative speech on the first morning. I announced that, as the referendum loomed, I was beginning 'to savour the scent of battle in my nostrils', and this phrase attracted a lot of attention in the press. I was planning as well as savouring. Jo Grimond and Shirley Williams were also staying at the Embassy (the Hendersons seem to have been widely hospitable as well as ebullient), and I devoted two long meetings with each alone to persuading them – they were both reticent for differing reasons – to become vice-presidents. However, they eventually agreed, and we later completed the list with Cledwyn Hughes, Jeremy Thorpe, Vic Feather (recently retired as general secretary of the TUC) and Henry Plumb of the National Farmers' Union, for whom it was the beginning of a road which he travelled so faithfully that it led to the presidency of the European Parliament.

The two 'Dublin' Cabinets took place on the following Monday and Tuesday mornings. It was typical of Wilson's methods to have these two bites, but on this occasion it worked well and he got a satisfactory result from his (and my) point of view at the end of the Tuesday morning. What was less sensible was to have a parliamentary Labour Party meeting on the Monday evening between the two, to which he gave no clear lead and as a result got a more equivocal response (there was no vote) than he could have achieved.

Much of Monday's Cabinet was taken up by Callaghan giving a detailed, rather good and not over-neutral description of what had occurred at Dublin. Even Tuesday's began early with an hour and a half of abstract discussion on some tangential paper produced by Edward Short. Again it was Wilson's technique of never going straight at the difficult issue, but always taking the edge off people's energies first.

He even had a short adjournment for coffee after Short's paper had been disposed of. But when he could postpone matters no longer he handled them well. He began with a crisp little speech which ended by saying that his recommendation was firmly in favour of staying in the Community. We then went round the table for two hours, but as everyone spoke this did not mean that the speeches were long. Healey spoke early and made the most effective case for staying in. I hung back until nearly the end. I did not feel that there was anyone I could convert and that I might indeed alienate weak or hesitating supporters. Of the sixteen who voted 'yes', Merlyn Rees and John Morris, the

Secretaries of State for Northern Ireland and Wales, were the most equivocal. Short, about whom I was also uncertain, put on a splendid caricature of his schoolmasterly self. First, he announced that he was going to give marks out of ten on each of the points, then went through them scoring austerely, I thought, then said his vote was firmly 'yes', so much so indeed that if the decision were unfavourable he would wish to record his dissent and be free to campaign for Britain in Europe. He then left to attend a meeting of the Privy Council.

Of the seven 'antis' Eric Varley sounded doubtful and miserable, and was reported to have said a few hours later that he thought he had voted wrongly. Willie Ross was as growling as usual in manner, but in matter detached from the extreme 'antis'. John Silkin was the reverse: suavely moderate in form but unyieldingly hostile in substance. That left the fearsome four, Foot, Benn, Castle and Shore, intransigent and irreconcilable, resolved not merely to record their dissent but to campaign for a 'no' vote with every resource at their disposal. Even from them, however, this was not a Cabinet of fireworks. It produced a majority which was two bigger than I expected, but it did it flatly.

Equally flat was Wilson's delivery of his statement in the House of Commons that afternoon. So keen was he to sound balanced that he lacked zest or verve, conviction or leadership. But an important stage had been passed and I had become free to tell him my plans, which indeed I needed to do urgently as we were running close up against the date for the Britain in Europe launch. I tried to see him that evening, but was warned off by Robert Armstrong, always helpful to me although thoroughly loyal to Wilson as principal private secretary, who said that I might find him tired and bad-tempered and have an unpleasant interview.

A meeting was therefore fixed for the next afternoon, Wednesday, 19 March. The postponement was insufficient to avoid the unpleasantness. We did not have a row, as on a few occasions in the past, but this meant there was no catharsis with the difficulty then cleared away. Throughout he was edgy, most unusually bitchy, and gave the impression of being thoroughly displeased with himself. Even more surprising, he insisted on having Callaghan present. Never over the past ten years had there been any question of our conducting our business, whether easy or difficult, friendly or confrontational, other than face to face and alone. To point the matter up Callaghan was appreciably late, so that I made two attempts to get the serious discussion started. 'No, no,' Wilson said, 'we must wait for Jim.' Two days later I teasingly congratulated Callaghan on having become so indispensable that he could keep us all waiting. 'Oh, Harold will see nobody without me at present,' he said, with a mixture of satisfaction and amusement.

The Foreign Secretary having at last arrived, I announced that I proposed to be president of the 'umbrella' organisation. Wilson, to whom that bare statement was obviously not a shock, said he regretted this. He asked whether there might not be a conflict between the role and the electoral-law aspect of my responsibilities as Home Secretary. I said I didn't believe that for a moment. Home Secretaries had never been inhibited from taking a full part in election campaigns. Furthermore I proposed to appoint Sir Philip Allen (ex-permanent under-secretary) as 'the great returning officer' for the referendum and completely devolve all this part of my duties to him. In any event, it was not reasonable for the Prime Minister, having procured a referendum greatly against my wishes, then to try to prevent my taking a full part in it.

Callaghan, who I think was intended to perform a heavy-uncle role, then put on a rather light avuncular act. It would probably be better I did not do it, but he could understand that I might want to, although I must take into account that it would undoubtedly do me harm in the Labour Party. 'For a long time, Jim,' I said, 'you and I have taken different views both about how important the party is and about what does one harm in it, so I don't think we will gain anything by arguing that at this stage.'

Wilson then tried to get alternative birds to fly. He would prefer a titular head, 'someone like Jebb'. Callaghan, I regret to say, failed to show a proper respect for one of his Department's most distinguished former ambassadors and snorted his disapproval. So Gladwyn fell before he had even got on the wing. 'What about Cledwyn?' Wilson next said, perhaps influenced by word shapes. There were no Callaghan snorts at that, but I said that I did not think the Tories would accept him as sole president. They would probably revert to the troika arrangement of Mrs Thatcher, Thorpe and me, which they had raised a few weeks before. This was a most lucky intervention, for insofar as anything convinced Wilson (and maybe Callaghan too) that he had no alternative but to accept what I had proposed it was raising the spectre of this, for him, still less desirable solution.

He then asked about vice-presidents, consistently assuming that they would be less senior than had been arranged, and accepting the corrections gloomily. 'Tories like Rippon and John Davies?' he suggested. 'No, Whitelaw, Maudling and probably Heath,' I said. 'Pardoe from the Liberals?' he tried again. 'No, Grimond.' But at least the fact that he was asking for these snippets of information meant that the crunch was over.

However, the interview was not. Most unusually for him Wilson was out to make himself unpleasant. I think this was part of the reason for having Callaghan there, as his natural friendliness made him find this so difficult in a vis-à-vis situation. He began by asking why I did not make more party speeches. I said I had made a great number during both the 1974 elections. 'That doesn't count,' he said. I said I thought it was exactly the time when it did count. Anyway the country had had more than enough of partisan speeches. I was intentionally off them. And when you do make speeches, he rather contradictorily added, they are often not helpful – such as Haverfordwest. I said I thought we had discussed that several times before.

He then said he had a lot of complaints to make about John Harris, whom I must discipline. This was despite the fact that he had praised him almost extravagantly to me at Chequers two months before. He had discovered that Harris was responsible for spreading a lot of disobliging comments about him. I asked what were they. He said he could not disclose them. I was getting exasperated by this time, and even Callaghan was looking like an ace police chief who had been called in to bust a major crime ring and found himself booking motorists for parking offences. But it was nothing compared with what came next. Wilson announced that there was one thing he was now definitely in a position to prove. I waited for the great revelation. When it came I could hardly believe my ears. It was that Harris had been responsible for leaking *in 1965* the news of the Harold Davies peace mission to North Vietnam. This had been one of Wilson's more foolish early gimmicks: an attempt to square the circle of propitiating the left and being a faithful servitor of Lyndon B. Johnson by sending a wild and whirling Labour MP to see Ho Chi Minh. It came to nothing, but, whether the mission was foolish or otherwise, the thought that the Prime Minister of Britain, on the day after he had steered the Cabinet to a major decision for the country's future orientation and when we were discussing dispositions for a crucial and hazardous referendum, should be preoccupied with wastepaper-basket investigations of Foreign Office news releases (Harris was then working for Michael Stewart) of ten years before was almost incredible. There must have been some inner discontent which was dragging him down so far below the level of events, for he then proceeded to make uncharacteristically sour remarks about almost everybody and everything in and out of sight. The meeting trailed off rather than came to a conclusion. When I left (to receive yet another TUC deputation on the Shrewsbury pickets) I felt that it had been unpleasant but not too disadvantageous.

The only point left unsettled were the so-called 'rules of conduct' for the Cabinet during the referendum, which I think the Prime Minister had drafted himself and which he had presented but not discussed at the end of Tuesday morning. Most of them were innocuous, but there was one which forbade appearance on a public platform with an MP of another party and would have been destructive of the campaign we intended to wage. I therefore told him it was unacceptable to me. He said I would have to argue the case in Cabinet the following morning. Callaghan fortunately sided with me and advised Wilson not to stick to it. Probably as a result, the Prime Minister postponed the issue the next morning and absented himself from the following Cabinet, when it was excised under Short's chairmanship.

This was as well for I was then within twenty-four hours of the announced press launch of the Britain in Europe campaign, which I did in the St Ermin's Hotel on the Wednesday before Easter, flanked by Willie Whitelaw, Reggie Maudling, Cledwyn Hughes and Jo Grimond. We got good press photographs out of that occasion. To see politicians of different parties sitting and working together was a pleasant shock for most of the public. Also, as I mockingly said to the celebratory dinner two weeks after the campaign was over and won, we looked like good solid men who had been well fed by the Common Agricultural Policy.

It was then ten weeks before Referendum Day, and I decided that for this period the bulk of my time must be devoted to the campaign. I summoned Sir Arthur Peterson and said that if, as I assumed, he wanted the 'yes' cause to win, he must be prepared to protect me as much as possible from Home Office business. It was probably the most political point I ever put to a permanent secretary, and I suppose that I felt able to do so because it was not party political. My assumption was however safe. Peterson expressed enthusiastic commitment and kept my departmental business to a minimum. By a miracle, for this was wholly outside his control, no significant Home Office crisis erupted during that spring.

Peterson's attitude was not surprising, for there was a great weight of establishment opinion in favour of Britain's staying in the Community. This was due not to a conspiracy, but to the fact that for once the establishment was spontaneously on the more sensible side. Nevertheless I have no doubt that it made the 'no' campaigners feel that they were underdogs unfairly discriminated against. This was accentuated by the fact that we had little difficulty in raising money and that they had a lot. It was the only campaign I ever fought with business mostly on my side. To revert to the 'jingo' analogy, we had the men, we did not need the ships, and we certainly had the money too. The question was whether we had the votes, and that remained doubtful for some time, although we never had the depressing sense of an adverse flow.

My first duty I regarded as being that of bringing the various strands of the campaign together into an unfamiliar harmony. It would not be much good having an umbrella organisation if the spokes stuck out all over the place. Thus, during the Easter week, I had Ted Heath to dinner at East Hendred, and went to North Wales to stay for three nights with David Harlech, who as well as being a friend was the chairman of the European Movement, which was an important tributary to the mainstream of Britain in Europe. While I was there I rewrote the text of the 'yes' manifesto, which was to be officially distributed, together with a 'no' one and a less partisan statement by the Government, to every elector, and had to be ready ridiculously early.

Back in London the following week I attended the press launch of the Labour Campaign for Europe (LCE) on the Monday afternoon, held a planning dinner on the Tuesday with Charles Guggenheim, an American political film-maker whom we had hired to assist us with our five 'party political' broadcasts, and presided on the Wednesday over the first meeting of the executive committee of Britain in Europe in the Old Park Lane headquarters building, with a good location and address but run-down accommodation, which we had rented very cheaply. All three of these occasions started trails of activity which ran throughout the campaign.

The Labour Campaign for Europe (there were also Conservative and Liberal ones, but they did not much impinge on me) was an attempt to provide a halfway house for those who were pro-Europe but for whom inter-party co-operation was still strong meat. Shirley Williams was its president, and she concentrated upon this activity, not playing much part in the umbrella organisation beyond giving her name as a vice-president. Others, like Crosland, Hattersley and some trade union leaders, confined their appearance to LCE platforms. But others again, like Prentice, Feather, Dickson Mabon, Denis Howell and Bill Rodgers, were equally happy to appear under either LCE or Britain in Europe auspices. It was thus a room in the mansion of the father, but one to the exclusiveness of which some of its inhabitants attached considerable importance. However, this semi-sectarianism sat ill with the spirit of the referendum weeks, and I never felt that the LCE wholly took off. I addressed five LCE meetings, in London, Oxford, Derby, Newcastle and Birmingham. None of them was bad and the Oxford one almost good, but the audiences – between 150 and 400 – were small compared with Britain in Europe attendances, and less stimulating too.

Guggenheim's speciality was the making of rapid-paced, confront-ation-situation, attention-gripping (it was hoped) short programmes. His work had acquired a high reputation in America. It was the opposite of the straight-to-camera pieces to which I was used, and I took to Guggenheim's methods with some reluctance. He organised a lot of anti-European Stechford constituents to hurl hostile questions at me. The result was said to be good fast film which brought out the combative side of me in a way that was never normally seen on television. But as I had never much encouraged my constituents to argue, let alone hurl hostile questions, I remained doubtful about the performance. We also had Vic Feather shouting through the clanging clamour of a steel mill and Willie Whitelaw expatiating on the beauties of the Cumbrian landscape while he drove a Land-Rover with more speed than attention. However, he brought it safely home, just as, with a splendid logical leap, he announced that the quality of the English countryside proved that we would be safe in Europe. I think that the programmes, a little modified from Guggenheim's original ideas, were probably persuasive and successful. They certainly broke new ground.

The executive committee, loosely put together, was a body of about twenty-five, including the senior staff of our *ad hoc* organisation. Willie Whitelaw was my most important collaborator, although I also remember David Steel, Michael Fraser of the Conservative Research Department, Douglas Hurd, Bill Rodgers and John Harris playing considerable parts. Whitelaw and I were both anxious (but not competitively) to perform Eisenhower-like roles – no quarrels between allies – and almost invariably supported each other against any critical juniors from either side. The body met for about two hours each Wednesday for five weeks. Then, on 13 May, it removed itself to the Waldorf Hotel, where it began to meet more briefly four or five times a week before the regular morning press conferences which we held for the last three weeks of the campaign. These meetings became smaller, for the politicians were increasingly out of London for at least half the time.

Our national campaign was based on these press conferences, on poster advertising, on the Guggenheim television programmes, on major public meetings in the big cities, at which all three parties were always represented, and, towards the end, on a heavy concentration of sometimes over-elaborate television magazine programmes on the issue. These last were of course not under our control but under that of the producing companies.

The allocation of broadcasting time was strictly equal. This was partly due to defensive generosity on my part. Six weeks earlier the chairman of the BBC (Michael Swann) and his director-general (Charles Curran) had come to see me (as Home Secretary) and suggested that they should divide time on the basis of the relative sizes of the pro and anti votes in the House of Commons. I had advised against, saying that it would provoke great resentment, and that it would be much better, not least from the point of view of the validity of the result, to strike an even balance. This made a substantial difference for the vote in the House gave a favourable majority of 396 to 170.

The effect of my advice was that in the first half of May those like Heath and Whitelaw who were used to having their speeches well covered found that they were less reported than usual, while obscure people on the other side were suddenly given prominence. I was deputed to complain to Swann about our lack of attention. I decided that in the circumstances it would be wrong to summon him to the Home Office. But nor should I wait upon him in Broadcasting House, for I was still Home Secretary. So I asked him to meet me on the neutral ground of Claridge's Hotel on a day (13 May) when I had been lunching there with Averell Harriman. We were both amused by the irony of the situation. He said that he thought my 'heavyweights' would be more satisfied when the BBC stepped up their overall coverage of the campaign in about a week's time, and this proved to be so.

The Britain in Europe meetings were exciting. I did nine of them, the opening one in the Free Trade Hall in Manchester with Whitelaw and Thorpe, two in London, and one each in Edinburgh, Tees-side, Aberdeen, Liverpool, Plymouth and Norwich. The most crowded and enthusiastic were in the Central Hall, Westminster, with Heath and Thorpe, at Norwich with Whitelaw and Steel, and in Liverpool with Maudling and Thorpe. The Liverpool success surprised me. I had decided to go there as a presidential penance, thinking it would be our most difficult city. But the result was a packed Philharmonic Hall and a swinging, cheerful meeting with just the right handful of hecklers. I also enjoyed the Edinburgh meeting with Carrington and Steel, although the Usher Hall there was more friendly than crowded.

Two days stand out for me from the campaign: first, Tuesday, 27 May, when I behaved most rashly; and second, Monday, 2 June, which was one of the most testing days I have ever spent. On 27 May I began by denouncing Benn at the morning press conference to an extent that produced sharp protests from Wilson; and went on to libel Hugh Scanlon, the leader of the Engineering Union, at an afternoon meeting at Birmingham University, to an extent that produced a writ within three days.

The Benn attack was deliberate, which the Scanlon one was not. Benn had been making a lot of running. He had emerged as the dominant figure on the anti side, fluent and persuasive, even if also arousing a lot of mistrust and dislike. He had well outpaced Foot or Shore or Mrs Castle or Enoch Powell as a standard-bearer. His methods were to my mind illegitimate in that he never replied to any argument, but merely moved on to a still more extravagant statement when the previous one was challenged. Nevertheless his position as Secretary of State for Industry gave a spurious credence to his economic claims. His reiterated statement that entry into Europe had cost half a million jobs was becoming damaging. Healey (in I think his only intervention in the campaign) had refuted it strongly on the merits, but without stopping it in its tracks. I decided that it was necessary and right to attack Benn's credibility, so I simply said that I found it increasingly difficult to take him seriously as an economic minister. I had thought of the phrase about a quarter of an hour before the press conference, and it was probably near enough to the bone to be effective. It certainly attracted a lot of publicity.

Wilson was furious. I suppose, looking back, he had some right on his side. I had arguably transgressed the Cabinet campaign rules against personal attacks, although I had been dismissive rather than abusive, and I had done so in a way which caught not merely Benn himself but the Prime Minister as well for keeping such a frivolous fellow in his Government. The fact that at this time the Prime Minister's favourite 'hair-down' conversation was to say how much he would like to get rid of Benn was hardly a possible public defence.

I received an unusually sharp minute of rebuke from Wilson, to which I replied in a tone which I hoped was at once emollient and firm. He came back with another to which it subsequently emerged that he was annoyed I did not reply. There seemed no point in continuing a sterile exchange. Also, I thought that he had more time than I had, for during the first part of the campaign he largely sat on his hands. This turned out to be unfair for he was later effective, but for the moment I felt like General Patton receiving a signal from (very) rear headquarters saying that he was advancing too successfully.

I had fitted in the afternoon visit to the Birmingham Students' Union at a late stage, the President having enticed me with the promise of a big attendance and a pro-European student body. He was as good as his word and produced an enthusiastic audience of 800, with a recalcitrant minority of about thirty who shouted from the back without much support. During the question period one of these asked me why as Home Secretary I was presiding over the destruction of democratic rights in Britain, as exemplified by my refusal to let the Shrewsbury pickets out of gaol. I began an answer which not unnaturally rejected this extravagant claim and was engulfed in further noise. 'What democratic rights do you think there would be,' I said in exasperation, pointing to the hard-line group, 'if that lot were in charge?' 'You wouldn't be allowed here for a start,' they conveniently responded. 'No, indeed,' I said, 'nor would anyone of independent mind. If you were running this Union you would be rigging the ballots like Hughie Scanlon.'

Mr Scanlon was currently and prominently accused of allowing the manipulation of the votes in his union elections, but the moment I said it I knew that I ought not to have done so. I returned to London praying, but not confidently, that press and radio would miss it. The Birmingham papers did, and so did Radio Birmingham, although they covered the speech, but that great news portmanteau of the *Daily Telegraph* did not omit to have it in a four-line item on its front page. LBC news was, I believe, equally diligent.

The writ from Lord Scanlon (as he now is) was quickly followed by an offer of legal assistance from Lord Goodman. He was calmly reassuring and kicked the ball into touch until well beyond the duration of the campaign. In the autumn we settled by giving an apology which was accepted but which was so circumscribed that Hugh Scanlon decided not to publish it. I withdrew any suggestion of personal falsification, but maintained my objection to the undemocratic voting system over which he presided.

Nevertheless that Tuesday could not be counted as a sagaciously handled day. I do not know why my normal verbal caution deserted me. I do not think it was overstrain, for this campaign did not exhaust me, and if there was any day when the pressures began to tell it was not that day but the second of the two days of particular note, Monday, 2 June. I began with a three-and-a-quarter-hour recording of a too long and too complicated Granada television programme for showing that evening. There were six of us from either side seated in a mock version of a House of Commons committee room. On our side were Heath, Maudling, John Davies, David Steel, Roy Hattersley and myself. The antis had been intended to be Benn, Shore, Enoch Powell and three others whom I have forgotten. But Benn had spent the Sunday making the most ridiculous fuss about the seating arrangements. Granada, reasonably, wanted the pro-Europeans to sit on one side and the antis on the other. Benn insisted that the members of the Government must sit together and all the members of the opposition parties, whether pro or anti, be opposite. It was another surfacing of the old paradox that those who had done most to bring about a referendum, Benn and to a lesser extent Wilson, were most denunciatory of one of its natural consequences, which was the encouragement of a coalition of mood if not of form.

Benn was isolated on this point. We refused to give way, and after hours of argument he withdrew from the programme and was replaced by Judith Hart. Peter Shore moved up into the lead position and put on a formidable oratorical performance in his winding-up speech which was immediately before mine. I feared that he would sweep the audience along with him, but I gathered later that his dramatic rhetoric had been more impressive in the flesh than when transmitted to a million firesides – or to however many gluttons for punishment were still awake after two and a half hours. Indeed, as the programme wound its weary way through its second and third hours I began to think that Benn might have been wisely reserving himself for his more important *Panorama* encounter with me which was due to be recorded that afternoon.

The estimated audience for this was nine million. It was to last the full forty-five minutes of the programme with only David Dimbleby as an unobtrusive moderator between us. It was unprecedented for two members of a Cabinet to indulge in such a vastly exposed debate, and the tension was heightened by my flick at Benn the previous week. Moreover, with only sixty hours to go before polling day there would be no time for the repairing of any serious damage which was inflicted. As I tried to recrank myself up during that lunchtime I felt like Admiral Jellicoe in command of the Grand Fleet in 1916: I was the only man who could lose the war in the course of an afternoon.

I therefore decided that it would be rash to attempt a knock-out victory over Benn and possibly fall flat on my face in the attempt. What was called for from me was not heroics but the more self-abnegatory course of making sure that I was still on my feet after fifteen rounds. We were winning the campaign. I had not so much to win the debate as to make sure that I did not start a reverse trend. I also decided that, particularly after the previous week, I should be very courteous to him, as he was likely to be with me. There were only two occasions in the long exchanges when either of us came near to slipping from these standards. The first was about halfway through when I thought I had him up against the ropes on the contradiction in the 'no' position between their commitment to coming out of Europe in order to run a protected economy, which they believed would safeguard jobs and living standards, and their 'best of both worlds' solution which was to be part of a free-trade penumbra around the Community; this made him irritable. The second was in the last few minutes when Dimbleby asked him why he had changed his mind on Europe over the past four years. I knew that he had a good and persuasive answer to this, and that he was preparing to coast out on it. I therefore had to jerk the final exchange on to a different track, and did so roughly.

When I came out from the studio Jennifer, who had been watching on a monitor, thought that I had let Benn get away with too much, and that, with his typical combination of good-mannered style and demagogic substance, he had landed some effective slogans. Others were more encouraging, or sycophantic, and I think the general view was that I had certainly done nothing to upset our lead, and might even have won on points. But whether the afternoon went well or ill there was no time to think about it for in just over two hours I had to be at Central Hall, Westminster, for our last London meeting. We had an audience of about two thousand, which was made more testing by containing the highest proportion of personal friends of any public meeting that I have ever addressed. I persuaded Heath to speak first, not out of gamesmanship but because otherwise I and not he would have led the BBC nine o'clock news, much of the audience for which would just have been watching me with Benn and would be bored with a second helping. Thorpe then made one of the best speeches I ever heard from him, and I wound up the meeting, having the great gift of a single, foolish, non-stentorian heckler. Later that evening, at supper in Ladbroke Square with Jacques and Marie-Alice de Beaumarchais (she had been at the meeting but he had observed diplomatic discretion) and Mark and Leslie Bonham Carter, I felt that I was over the hump. And so indeed I was, in spite of the stimulus of the splendid Norwich meeting on the following evening.

On the morning of Referendum Day I woke to pouring rain in the Midland Hotel, Birmingham. The weather throughout the campaign had been almost as filthy as during the previous October's general election. There was even a light covering of snow on 2 June. I visited a polling station in Stechford and was photographed talking to a few determined voters in a sodden school playground. Then I went to London and was photographed with Jennifer voting in the Portobello Road. Notting Hill, from posters in windows and friendly crowds at that polling station, gave every impression of voting heavily and enthusiastically 'yes'. Then I went to lunch in an enclosed South Kensington restaurant. When I re-emerged a miraculous weather transformation had taken place. The sun had come out, and it continued to shine from an almost cloudless sky for the next five weeks, and then, following a little break, for twelve weeks after that. England had one of its few sun-baked summers since 1911, when the Parliament Bill had passed in a temperature of 97 degrees. God at least, I blasphemously said, seemed pleased with the way the referendum was going.

That evening the rudimentary exit polls of those days, reported on the ten o'clock news, seemed to put the issue beyond all doubt. The turn-out had been nearly as high as at a general election and the 'yes' majority was clearly decisive. That was the moment when, in company with Bill and Silvia Rodgers, John and Pat Harris and Anthony Lester, who all dined at Ladbroke Square, I apprehended victory. It had been a long and often hazardous road since 1971.

The next day we had, as it were, to ratify the victory. I spent five hours of half celebratory party/half rolling press conference in the Waldorf Hotel, as well as watching the individual county results come in. The spread of support was remarkably wide. The only two county units we lost were the Western Isles of Scotland and Shetland, both with tiny electorates. Our worst result in England and Wales was Mid-Glamorgan, largely made up of the Rhondda and Aberdare valleys, but even there we got a 58.5 per cent positive vote, which would have been thought inconceivable a year before.

At 5.15 I decided to go ahead with the culminating press conference, even though the Greater London result tantalisingly refused to emerge. But even that great wen, had it voted perversely (which it did not), could not have upset the overall result. I was supported at the conference by Willie Whitelaw, Jo Grimond (who dealt elegantly with his Shetland hiccup) and Vic Feather. I said that the result far exceeded our expectations, referred to a 'day of jubilation' and recalled that it was the thirty-first anniversary of D-Day, 6 June 1944, when we had to fight a much more painful campaign to end our exclusion from Europe. That evening I went to East Hendred, satisfied, a little exhausted and more than a little uncertain about the future.

A short time later I wrote down my impressions of the individuals I had worked with during the campaign. On the Labour side I was enthusiastic about Shirley Williams, Bill Rodgers, John Harris, Dick Mabon and Cledwyn Hughes. Cledwyn had worked very successfully to produce the remarkable result of a 72 per cent 'yes' vote in Gwynedd, the more rural half of North Wales. I also noted that Reg Prentice had been eagerly helpful despite having been an anti-European in 1971, that Edward Short had made several strong and effective interventions and that Sam Silkin had been very determined. Of the union leaders Feather had been a pillar of strength, and Roy Grantham and Tom Jackson, although I saw less of them, had also been good.

Jim Callaghan, I thought, misjudged his campaign. He had been anxious for some time to get a positive result, but was equally anxious to stand aside from what he regarded as our excessively partisan organisation. What I think he hoped to do was to come in at a late stage of the campaign and make some widely reported statements with all the authority of a Foreign Secretary and the greater persuasiveness because he could point to what a sceptic he had been. Yet it misfired, and he made little impact. Operating on his own, he apparently got poor audiences, and not much in the way of press reports. Then, at almost the last moment, he said he would like to appear in one of our 'party politicals', providing he could have such a *cordon sanitaire* erected around him that no one could think he was in full communion with us. We accepted his conditions, but were afterwards doubtful whether it had been worthwhile. He was good, but not quite good enough for the trouble.

Harold Wilson was more effective. He held his hand for some time, but then made three or four major speeches, hardly inspiring but with some prime ministerial weight, always choosing his own ground with small hand-picked audiences, but getting a good deal of television and press coverage, putting the case firmly, and undoubtedly swaying a lot of Labour voters.

The principal Tory with whom I worked was Willie Whitelaw. He was deputed to do this job and did it with vigour and determination. He was not only a fine ally with whom to work, he was also a pleasure to be with. I formed the view, well before his anchor role in Mrs Thatcher's Government, that he was one of nature's great second-in-commands, loyal, resourceful, comforting. He did not exactly inspire crowds, but people liked seeing him, thought they were listening to an honest man whom they could respect and went away feeling better about the campaign and themselves. He epitomised the feeling that the 'yes' side was the side of sense, substance and public spirit, which was our greatest single asset.

Heath was different. He was passionately committed on the merits of the issue. He waged an extremely effective campaign, and my respect for him, already considerable at the beginning, went steadily up as it progressed. Yet he was always a difficult morsel to digest. He never tried to be awkward, but there was a certain inherent awkwardness about his character and indeed his physique. He stood resolutely there, as impervious to the waves and as reliable in his beam as a great lighthouse, but sometimes blocking the way. But he was never negligible. Not unnaturally, as an ex-Prime Minister who had not been asked to be president, he played little part in organisational meetings, and turned up only when he was due for a performance. Then he was dependable and powerful.

One rare feature of the campaign was that it gave me occasional glimpses into the hitherto shielded intimate life of the Conservative Party machine. I had the impression of greater smoothness and discipline than in the Labour Party. At the Manchester meeting, for example, the regional organiser, who had worked well to produce a good share of the audience, behaved towards Whitelaw with an almost military obedience. Yet I did not carry away the memory of an organisation so formidable as to be a major factor in the political balance.

The Liberal Party machine I found unpredictable to deal with, and there were also elements of this in their leader, although compensated for by his wit and capacity for bravura performances. And I found even more compensation in the future leader. 'A most admirable Liberal was David Steel,' I wrote at the time. 'Of all the people I dealt with during the campaign he was one of the best. A man of great sensitivity, reliability, imagination, somebody certainly well worth a major Cabinet place if he belonged to a major party.'

Was our campaign necessary? In other words, if we had played it as quietly as Wilson and Callaghan wished us to do, would we have coasted safely to an equally decisive victory? The question is not susceptible to a provable answer. My guess is that the poll would have been lower, maybe substantially so. And my certainty is that in the absence of a committed campaign pro-European morale would have sagged. In early May we were deliberately slower to get going than were the anti-Europeans, and this provoked complaints both within our own organisation and from the public. Had we allowed arguments to go unanswered through late May and into June it is difficult to believe that this would not have been damaging. As it was, we had a well-timed campaign with a crescendo in the last days of May and a climax on Monday and Tuesday, 1 and 2 June, which were the crucial days on which to maintain our ascendancy.

Of course we were always winning, which is a great deal better than always to be losing, but it is not necessarily the most secure position either. There was always the danger of a revolt of the underdogs against a complacent establishment. We had to ensure that we played the card of inspiring confidence in rational internationalism in such a way that it beat the sometimes stronger appeals of chauvinism, populism and the desire to cock a snook. On the whole we succeeded.

Both sides were sometimes accused of fighting low-level campaigns with sterile arguments about the price of butter, claims and counter-claims about levels of unemployment, and the frequent bandying of meaningless statistics. In general such a criticism was not justified against the 'yes' campaign. At one press conference we did produce a lady whom we had sent to Norway (outside the Community) and who had come back with an incredibly expensive shopping basket. But we did not pretend that it was anything other than a spoiling riposte. Mrs Castle had been to Brussels two days before and had produced a fairly expensive one. We went to the much vaunted EFTA and did still better or worse. All that we claimed was that one was as peripheral to the argument as was the other.

More to the point was that, when the campaign was over, Heath and I, who had probably addressed the most large meetings, agreed that it was always the high arguments, the broad discussion of the country's future orientation in both foreign-policy and economic terms, which most captured the attention and fired the imagination of audiences. Nor did either of us attempt to play down the importance of the issues or to suggest that all that was at stake was a narrow trade-policy decision. It was political Europe in which we were interested. A common market, which existed and of which we were part, was a vital step on the road but it was not the ultimate goal or the primary purpose. The Wilson/Callaghan line was more cautious, but so far as the leaders of the 'yes' campaign were concerned there was no question of our trying to persuade the electorate that Europe was an affair of packages and of nothing else.

Several on the other side of the argument found and responded to the same current of interest in direction as opposed to detail. As a result the nation debated its future in a way that it had not done for a long time past, at least since the 1945 election. To that extent the 1975 referendum, bitterly and maybe mistakenly though I had opposed it, was a good thing. It should also have settled for a generation the vexed question of Britain's membership of the Community. But it was allowed to do no such thing. Within two years Tony Benn was campaigning for a reversal of the verdict of the oracle of direct democracy, about which he had spoken so sacerdotally before it had given him the wrong answer; and within six years he had got the whole of the Labour Party committed in this direction.

If my argument against the principle of the referendum had been exaggerated or even wrong, my warning of 1972 that it would have a loosening effect upon the tribal loyalties of British party politics was abundantly right. Things were never quite the same for the Labour Party after June 1975. Before that, peacetime cross-party co-operation could never be discussed without raising the spectre of Ramsay MacDonald. After then it called up for about a third of the party the much more benevolent image of referendum success.

# CHAPTER TWENTY-THREE

## *Goodbye to Whitehall*

With the referendum campaign successfully concluded I hoped for a period when I could bask quietly in a glow of achievement. This was not forthcoming. In a general sense it was frustrated by the economic situation, which was heavily menacing, with largely wage-induced inflation spiralling up to 30 per cent, the worst level ever attained in Britain, and the Government dealing with the trade unions about as effectively as a rabbit with a snake. I had no direct responsibility for economic policy, but as a senior member of the Cabinet who was also an ex-Chancellor I could hardly ignore it. As I thought that the Prime Minister and the current Chancellor did not take the threat seriously enough these developments had the effect of further alienating me from the core of the Government.

Of more immediate impact was the unexpected and bitter quarrel I had with Wilson on the Monday night immediately following the referendum. It was probably the nastiest of all the disputes between us. The only thing to be said for it was that it was also the last.

It was all to do with Reg Prentice. Prentice was a man of flat-footed courage who had emerged in the previous two years out of the rather stolid centre of the Labour Party into a determined right-winger. He had been a Transport and General Workers' Union official who had become the most forthright challenger of trade union presumption. He was MP for the East London constituency of Newham North-east, where he was under considerable threat from a militant local party, and since 1974 he had been Secretary of State for Education, having been Minister of Overseas Development in 1967–9. He was never an intimate of mine, but by 1975 he had become my most unhesitating ally in the Cabinet, although Shirley Williams and Harold Lever were also staunch. No one had any idea at that stage that his hostility to the left was going to become that of a Conservative and not of a Social Democrat. He had the best 'core of the party' qualifications of any of

419

us. I remember a time when Tony Crosland (whose Minister of State he had been in 1965–6) erected him into a kind of proletarian oracle whose views, when they could be ascertained, should be treated as socialist gospel. He had been amongst neither the sixty-nine positive voters nor the twenty abstainers in the great Common Market division of October 1971, and, perhaps as a reward, topped the poll in the shadow Cabinet elections of 1972 and 1973.

Prentice also had a taste, like me, for making occasional general political speeches, and we had both delivered anti-inflationary ones on Friday, 28 February 1975. Mine was more extreme in substance, for I said that inflation was becoming 'the greatest threat to Britain since Hitler', but his was perhaps sharper in tone. At any rate it was against him that Wilson chose to rail, both in public and still more in private, to such an extent that I thought I should send a message to the Prime Minister, which I did through Robert Armstrong in a deliberately low-pressure way, saying that I could not stay in a government from which Prentice was sacked. I had indeed offered Prentice this guarantee a few months before, and he had gratefully accepted it. Like most international guarantees it was given more out of enlightened self-interest than generosity.

This early-March row died down, but on 10 April when I lunched with Harold Lever he strongly pressed me to speak to Wilson before we all separated for the referendum campaign and reiterate that I would not accept Prentice's demotion or dismissal from the Cabinet. This was based on Lever's shrewd view that as soon as the referendum was won Wilson would wish both to propitiate the left and to remove Benn from the Department of Industry. The way in which he might seek to reconcile these objectives was to move also against Prentice, the most vulnerable right-wing member of the Cabinet. I saw the force of this, but treated it without urgency and spoke to Wilson only on 19 May. I did not regard it as an easy point to make, for it involved both a threat and a restriction of the Prime Minister's authority. I did it as part of a meeting with a wider agenda, and I remember saying that I had several easy points to raise and then a difficult one. There was no need for worry or for circumlocution. Wilson was full of reassurance. He had no thought of a move for Prentice in June, still less of dismissal. He might do a bigger reshuffle in the autumn, and that might involve a sideways move for him. The tone of the conversation is indicated by the fact that he then invited me to discuss various autumn possibilities for Prentice, and that my mention of Defence or Northern Ireland was well received. The assurance for June was absolute.

The only further development on this front was that one evening towards the end of the campaign, when John Harris, as he sometimes did, had dropped in at Downing Street for a talk with Marcia Williams

and they were later joined by Wilson himself,* a half-threat to Prentice
had been delivered in the course of a generally gossipy conversation.
Prentice had made a speech at Leeds, sharing a platform with Heath,
which had apparently aroused Wilson's ire, so that he had said
something to the effect of: 'That young man should not feel too safe
or chance his arm too freely.' This was mildly disturbing, although not
excessively so, for I could not regard such vague threats delivered
late at night and through an intermediary not charged to pass it on,
as beginning to amount to a cancellation of the clear and specific
undertaking given to me on 19 May. Nevertheless when I learned
that Prentice was departing on the Monday (9 June) for a not very
important education conference in Stockholm I felt a stab of unease.
Vulnerable ministers should never be abroad at times of reshuffle.

I hesitated over whether to advise Prentice not to go, but decided
that he was probably irrevocably committed and that there was no
point in unsettling his mind. That evening I dined in an old 'Fitzrovia'
restaurant (the White Tower) which has now been familiar to me for
nearly fifty years. Fortunately I fixed it early – at 7.45 – for I was
intending to vote in the House of Commons at 10.00. Otherwise I
would have got no dinner at all. As it was, I got little. At 8.35 Prentice
came through to the restaurant from Stockholm to say that Wilson
had offered him the Ministry of Overseas Development *outside* the
Cabinet, and was pressing for an answer that night.

My first reaction was a curious amalgam of boredom and dismay.
Theories of deterrence are all very well provided they do not have
to be put into operation. However, it was obvious to me within ten
seconds of hearing Prentice's intelligence that I had no option but to
go down the line of the guarantee. I told him to give no answer until
he heard from me, and got Hayden Phillips to demand an immediate
meeting between Wilson and me. I saw the Prime Minister at 9.10 in
his room in the House of Commons for about twenty-five minutes. I
left him in no doubt that if Prentice went from the Cabinet I would
go too.

It was a lowering occasion. Wilson sat with his head down and
poured out a stream of petty venom. There were all the old complaints
(we even had the Harold Davies mission again) and some new ones
against Prentice and me as well. His main complaint against my Benn
statement was that it had stolen the publicity from a carefully prepared speech of his own. He defended his retreat from his promise of
19 May on the ground that his chance remark to Harris gave me perfectly adequate notice of his change of mind. I am afraid that, under

---

* Strangely it might be thought in view of Wilson's strictures on Harris, which
he had delivered to me only two months before.

the provocation of all this, I said some ultimately unforgivable things about the general triviality of his mind and his incapacity to rise to the level of events. We moved towards no solution and parted with distaste.

I went upstairs to my room and summoned Shirley Williams and Harold Lever. I already had Bob Mellish coming by appointment about another matter, and saw no reason to put him off. It would all be public soon enough and the sundering of the Government was very much chief whip's business. Furthermore he had been friendly to us during the referendum campaign, as he was on this occasion. Shirley was shocked at my news, and appeared ready to do whatever I did. Lever, I am afraid, did not want to resign on this occasion, despite his instigation of me on 10 April. He had I think already been informed of the plans and regarded Benn's removal from Industry (even if not from the Cabinet) as such a prize that he was prepared to swallow Prentice's demotion. He was however good enough subsequently to say that he would in fact have resigned, not for Prentice but because he would not have wished to remain in a Cabinet in which I would not serve.

At this stage it never occurred to me that anything else could happen. The end of my interview with Wilson left no room for manoeuvre. To my great surprise I was then resummoned. I found him calmer and somewhat, but not vastly, more agreeable. He wished for an assurance that I had not previously been threatening him. A little mystified but willing to play a game with words, I said that there was no need to interpret it as a threat but merely as the pointing out of certain inevitable consequences. He seized on this, and said, provided we were dealing with a statement of consequences and not a threat, he was prepared to relent and keep Prentice in the Cabinet, although he still wished him to be Minister of Overseas Development. I said that if that were acceptable to Prentice it would have to be acceptable to me, for although I believed it was a mistake moving him, I thought the actual disposition of offices as opposed to the balance of the Cabinet must be the prerogative of the Prime Minister.

He then attempted to make the deal dependent on its receiving no press publicity, although how the time mechanics of this could have worked I cannot imagine. I said I could not possibly guarantee this. I had talked to three other ministers and it must be obvious to a great many people that there had been a lot of scurrying between rooms – Foot, for instance, had been lobbying on Benn's behalf. This point therefore died, although there were in fact remarkably few leaks. Wilson and I parted without the catharsis of rapidly clearing skies after the storm.

Ironically in view of the state of agitation he had provoked, Prentice was unobtainable that night. With singular phlegm he had simply closed down and gone to sleep in his Stockholm hotel. In the morning he said that he would accept the new Wilson deal. He reminded me that he had resigned from the Government in 1969 in protest against being moved *from* the ODM job. He could hardly do so again in 1975 in protest against being moved *to* it! Six months later, however, we both agreed that we would have done better to hold out for his not being moved at all. Wilson would probably have given way on that too, and the ill-feeling could not have been worse.

The heart of the matter was that relations between Wilson and me had gone over the watershed between constructive tension and debilitating irritation. It was like the stage in a marriage going wrong (not that our political relationship was ever as close as that) when the quarrels become more trouble than they are worth. Perhaps not altogether untypically this occurred at a time when (compared with 1968 and 1969) the disputes were not stirring great interests on either side and were over an issue about which neither of us cared desperately. In 1968–9, and again in 1971–2, Wilson was dedicated to preserving his own leadership, and I was full of ambition to succeed him, although not necessarily so soon as to create a conflict. By 1975 he was preparing for withdrawal from the political scene, and I had lost much hope of leading the Labour Party. Equally Prentice was a temporary ally of mine, and I do not suppose that Wilson really cared much whether or not he had him in the Cabinet for the last nine months of his premiership. But my respect for the Prime Minister was finally eroded, and his tolerance of me, which looking back I find had lasted remarkably long, was at last exhausted. All in all I am not surprised that when it came to the choice of his successor in 1976, he preferred Callaghan to me, inconceivable though this would have seemed to him seven years before.

What were the sins for which he would privately have blamed me, apart from the general one of being a turbulent minister commanding a phalanx of parliamentary and public support? I dismiss this, both because Wilson, to his credit, rather liked turbulent ministers, and because the previous objection to the phalanx was that I might be a threat to him, and this had ceased to matter. No one was going to push him out of the Labour leadership in 1975 faster than he wanted to go.

I suppose therefore that his main objection and fear had become that I might be instrumental in forming a coalition. His fears here would have been increased by the form of the referendum campaign, and surfaced in the fact that although its outcome must have been what he wanted he clearly took no pleasure in it. It is also perhaps significant that the fault of Prentice's provoking Leeds speech was that it seemed to be raising a coalition thought. I do not think that Wilson would have morally disapproved of a coalition. Indeed, less than three years later when he came to see me in Brussels he was advocating such a course and urging me to play a part in it.* But in 1975 it would have meant an ignominious end to his second Government, for there would have been little tendency to ask him to serve in, still less to lead, such a grouping. So he could have discerned a rational threat, even if not in the old form.

To what extent was he justified in seeing me as a possible agent of coalition? 'Up to a point, Lord Copper' must be the answer. I thought that the Government was working badly, and that there was a real danger of inflationary take-off which would have destructive consequences going beyond economics and into the whole fabric of society. Party governments seemed incapable of dealing with the trade unions. The Heath Government had been inept with the miners. The second Wilson Government was supine before both wage claims and demands for legal privileges. Were two governments to founder on the rock of union intransigence it would be an appalling recognition of union omnipotence and invitation for it to be exercised still more arrogantly in the future. The thought that a broader-based government might succeed where both Conservative and Labour ones had failed certainly crossed my mind.

Furthermore I had found the referendum campaign a considerable liberation of the spirit. My heart had been much more in those large Britain in Europe meetings than in any Labour Party gathering for some time past. And, admittedly only on one issue, but a big and wide-ranging one, I had felt more spontaneous agreement with platform-sharers at them than with Benn or Foot or Wilson. I had begun to feel that British politics was like a river with several arms all of which were rigidly channelled within high and artificial banks from which they were increasingly pressing to escape into a different shape of delta. As I said to our celebratory Britain in Europe dinner on 19 June, we had all had an excursion away from our domestic hearths and our humdrum lives were never going to be quite the same again.

However, all these vague yearnings were very different from actually

* The entry in my *European Diary* for 6 April 1978 included the following sentences: 'However, he [Wilson] was at pains to urge me not to cut myself off from British politics now. I might well be needed in the future, he said. Callaghan was too old, Owen was too young. The whole outlook was very bad. He was filled with dismay. He did not think that there was much future for the Government, or indeed the Labour Party. A coalition government would almost certainly be necessary; he would bless it from the outside, but not serve. I, however, would undoubtedly be needed. Taking all this with several pinches of salt, I kept the conversation going. . . .'[1]

plotting to bring about a reshuffling of the political pack. I am sure that Wilson thought I was doing far more than I was. I did not contemplate an induced cataclysm. But I thought one might be spontaneously generated by inflationary collapse. I arranged with Willie Whitelaw that he and I would keep in touch, partly just to reminisce about the great days of the campaign, but partly also to look at political events and to complain about our colleagues. Thus the Whitelaws dined with us alone at Ladbroke Square on 29 July, and we dined with them on 15 December.

More significant, perhaps, was the fact that on 20 June, after doing my Stechford advice bureau, I had a long talk with my outspoken constituency chairman, George Canning, and warned him that I saw a possibility of the Government failing to survive on the existing basis. In that case some political realignment might be necessary. He was shocked by this, and urged caution upon me. But with typical loyalty he added that if I judged it necessary in the interests of the country he would support me. He thought that some others would in the Stechford party, although probably not a majority. He did not doubt that a majority of the electorate would be strongly in favour.

I suppose that all this, plus the fact that I was undoubtedly more solicitous at this period of my non-party than of my party constituency, does add up to some basis for what I assume to be Wilson's suspicions of the time. But it was far from meaning that a political coup which would have brought about the downfall of his Government was imminent. I would not have moved far ahead of Bill Rodgers and Shirley Williams, and they were certainly not then ready for a move which was not forced by dire national emergency. Furthermore there was the built-in tribal loyalty of the Conservative Party, which in the mid-1970s I thought was less devoted to putting party before country than was the Labour Party. In the early and mid-1980s I discovered that I was mistaken. Conservatives who believed that Mrs Thatcher was doing the most profound harm to the country nonetheless preferred to accept this than to risk an organisational break with party orthodoxy.

Looking back, I think that I should have been more and not less 'disloyal' in 1975. The country could not long sustain a continuance of gross inflation and subservience to the unions. Some force was going to jerk it away from these tram tracks. A coalition of the right of the Labour Party and the left of the Conservative Party might have done it with much greater precision than the bombastic manichaean Thatcherite revolution. There need have been none of the monetarist obsession of the early years ('the indefinable in pursuit of the unattainable') with its heavy price in unemployment and excessive reduction in industrial capacity, none of the narrow chauvinism which became the hallmark of Downing Street in the later years of

Mrs Thatcher, and above all none of the destruction of public services, and, perhaps even more damagingly, of the spirit of public service, which disfigured the whole 1980s.

One powerful argument against a grand coalition is that if things go wrong it leaves no alternative. But it was the unique result of Thatcherism that it long produced neither consensus nor alternative. By the same token the Labour Party as a progressive force would have lost little by the formation of a 1975 coalition. The years 1976–9 contributed practically nothing to the achievements of Labour as a party of government, and for a decade after that it excluded itself from power (and even influence) far more completely than a political realignment would have done. All in all I look back on 1975 as a great missed opportunity for Heath and Whitelaw and a whole regiment of discarded Conservative 'wets' as much as for Shirley Williams and Steel and me. They and we could have had much more the sort of government we broadly wanted than anything which was in office in the 1980s, and the country would in my view have greatly benefited. It is a hidden 'might have been', for it was much less discussed, either in public or in private, than, say, a possible breakthrough of the Alliance in 1981–7.

The second half of 1975 was anticlimactic. The Government was pushed by foreign exchange pressures into a weak incomes policy at the beginning of July which just kept disaster at bay, although it did not avoid the IMF crises of 1976. There were occasional terrorist explosions and shootings, as well as the two dramatic 'sieges' at the Spaghetti House, Knightsbridge, and in Balcombe Street, Marylebone,* but nothing comparable to the horrors of the same period in 1974. Home Office legislation progressed satisfactorily. We got the Sex Discrimination Act on to the statute book by the end of the 1974–5 session, and the third Race Relations Bill was ready for the session of 1975–6. I succeeded in moving to a disused airfield near

---

* In the first case, a gang of armed criminals with no political motivation were cornered by the police but held hostage a group of Italian waiters in a small Knightsbridge restaurant. In the second case four IRA terrorists after shooting up Scott's Restaurant in Mount Street were followed by the police to a flat in Balcombe Street, where they held an elderly couple under threat of death. In both cases a mixture of patience, ingenious surveillance of what was happening inside the premises and the assembling against eventuality of a skilled and powerful force produced satisfactory outcomes. There were no serious injuries and the criminals were caught, convicted and severely sentenced. It was noticeable that the psychological moment when it proved in both cases possible to get the hostage-holders to surrender occurred at very nearly the same time – about a hundred hours – after the siege had begun. (Sir) Peter Imbert, later Commissioner of Police, then a young Special Branch detective superintendent, showed particular skill at Balcombe Street.

Faringdon a mass pop festival which had been building up for a number of years into an annual semi-riot in Windsor Great Park and causing Prince Philip near apoplexy. Watchfield, the new site, was in the same county and district as East Hendred, and our local authorities got very agitated, as did a lot of local inhabitants. One of the few who did not seem to mind was my dear friend Ann Fleming, who lived only about a mile away from Watchfield. However, all passed off calmly. The disused airfield appeared to bore the pop fans and that festival was never heard of again.

Non-Home Office affairs went less well. Foot's plans for trade union legislation continued as an overhanging menace. Earlier in that Government I had got him in bilateral discussions to retreat from his worst proposals which would have given strike pickets the same authority as the police, and one possessed by no one else, to stop vehicles on the highway. The responsibility for the police gave me the *locus* to do this bilaterally, which was crucial, for in the Cabinet on these sort of issues we were mostly a beleaguered minority of four: Shirley Williams, Lever, Prentice and myself. Occasionally one or two others, most often Elwyn-Jones, the Lord Chancellor, might express misgivings, but not reliably so. (This was a reason why it was so vital to keep Prentice in the Cabinet.) This depressing line-up repeated itself in the autumn of 1975 when Foot brought forward closed-shop provisions which were dangerously inimical to press freedom. His own editorial background seemed to count for nothing compared with his union worship. In his pantheon the dead Lord Beaverbrook had been superseded by the living Jack Jones. We fought very hard on this (Shirley playing the most effective role) but when a little succour came it was more through Lord Goodman's influence on the Prime Minister than because we had been able to move minds in that curiously Bourbon-like Cabinet.

The last scene of 'Labourism', for such it was much more than socialism or radicalism, was played out by one of the most experienced and intelligent Cabinets of recent British history (Wilson, Callaghan, Healey, Crosland, Castle) with an amazing lack of imagination combined with a dogged but unconvinced determination. It almost beggars belief with hindsight that, in that same autumn of roaring inflation and sterling collapse, legislation (not Foot's responsibility this time) for the nationalisation of the ports and the aerospace industry should have been brought forward. It was not that the leaders of the Government retained a passionate or dogmatic faith in the virtues of nationalisation, or even (Foot apart) a great love for union leaders (how could Wilson have done after his experiences in 1969?). It was more that they regarded themselves as living on the lower slopes of a mountain which nurtured higher up a number of dangerous wild beasts. The

bigger ones were known as union leaders and the smaller ones as
constituency parties, and in both cases it was hoped without much
faith that they would spend as much time as possible in the upper
fastnesses. But when they did come down they must on no account
be enraged – this was another of Wilson's lessons of 1969, particularly
when he remembered what a dangerous Trojan horse (if they and wild
mountain beasts can live together in the same metaphor) Callaghan,
now his principal colleague, had then been.

Perhaps happily in these circumstances there was no attempt over
the summer of 1975 to draw me close into the economic or other
general problems of the Government. At a Chequers Cabinet day
on the Friday after the Prentice row Wilson made an attempt to
be friendly, to which I responded fully. 'Well, we got through the
week better than looked likely on Monday night,' he said with a
truly panglossian benignity. I assumed from this that he wished, as
on previous occasions, to let bygones be bygones, and to show that
he was such a complete politician that exchanges of views, however
offensive, at moments of political tension, had no effect upon his
personal feelings. But I was wrong. The fissure was too deep. I
never saw him again alone that summer. He continued absolutely to
respect my Home Office prerogatives, but we sometimes had irritable
exchanges in Cabinet when I intervened on wider matters. On broad
policy we effectively lost contact with each other.

My most exciting (and most publicised) event of that six months was
again Prentice-instigated. That bravely accident-prone politician had
no sooner been saved from Wilson than he was seriously set upon
by his far-left constituency party. It was an early case of threatened
deselection. We regarded this as raising the serious constitutional issue
of the right of a small, unrepresentative caucus to get rid of a conscien-
tious constituency member who, on all the available evidence, was far
more in touch with the electorate at large than they were. We decided
we must rally to Prentice's support and did so in one of the few ways
which politicians know, which was to organise a meeting. Accordingly,
on a rainy mid-September evening we proceeded, Shirley Williams,
Tom Jackson (the moustachioed and moderate Post Office Workers'
leader who subsequently got fed up with unions and with politics and
retired to run a second-hand bookshop in Ilkley), Prentice himself and
I, to the old East Ham Town Hall in the Mile End Road.

I think we must have been expecting a little trouble, or at least
some fun, for Jennifer came too and so did Bill and Silvia Rodgers,
as well as the less political Noel and Gabriele Annan, with whom we
had been dining the night before. There were a lot of policemen in
attendance, but I gave strict orders that on no account were they to
interfere with the opposition in the audience. One thing that a Home

Secretary cannot do is to appear at a meeting in favour of democratic rights and have his own police discipline the crowd.

What we had not bargained for was cross-fire. At the back there was a large group of Militants or Trotskyists or Workers' Revolutionaries or whatever they currently called themselves in Newham who made a lot of noise and from time to time advanced menacingly down almost to the front of the right aisle, where Silvia Rodgers counter-attacked with a knitting needle. But they never actually threw anything except abuse. On the left at the front was a wedge of National Front supporters who had come specifically to demonstrate against me because of the imminent Race Relations Bill. They gave the other speakers relative immunity but, as soon as I started, a few strident ladies let go with flour bags. One hit me hard on the chest. It did not hurt much, but slightly winded me and turned me into a temporary snowman. The unhelpful picture of Rab Butler standing forlorn and suffering with eggs dripping down his face and gown during his 1958 Glasgow rectorial address flashed through my mind and I brushed furiously.

This was too late, for a picture of me at the moment of impact appeared the following morning on the front page of every London newspaper save only the *Morning Star*. At least the bursting of the bag and my expression of shock gave a more dynamic impression than Butler's photograph had done. After this alarum I managed to get through the text of my speech with more speed than authority. Whether the meeting did any local good for Prentice I doubt. But it benefited me nationally. The public combines liking to see politicians suffer with an instinctive sympathy for those under attack from extremists.

That autumn, when I was almost flaking away from the Labour Party to the centre, was curiously and rather helpfully marked by a number of demonstrations against me from the extreme right. Two weeks after Newham I went at the invitation of the Dean to give a Third World address in Chichester cathedral. Hugh Cudlipp, who had recently become a local resident, was in the chair, if that is the appropriate phrase for such august surroundings. The nave was half filled with several charabanc-loads of National Front supporters who had come over from Brighton. No doubt some of them had enjoyed themselves at Newham, although on this occasion they looked more as though they might be stormtroopers in jackboots and less like ladies with rolling pins. They managed to create a vicious little riot. While I am happy to say there was no murder in the cathedral, a riot in a cathedral is an almost equally rare event.

In general, however, those last months of 1975 were flatter than these happenings make them sound. I was politically becalmed. The Home Office, when not erupting, did not stretch me. At the end of November I renewed the Prevention of Terrorism Bill for a second

year, and in early December a move for the reintroduction of the death
penalty was again defeated by a convincing majority. There were no
other parliamentary excitements. Jennifer and I began a programme
of taking our old friends the French ambassador and Marie-Alice de
Beaumarchais on a series of two- to three-day excursions to various
parts of Britain. Within seven months we went to North Wales,
to the West Country, to Norfolk, and to Yorkshire, Durham and
Northumberland. It could I suppose be regarded as a form of official
visitation (although not on an official expense account) extended into
a European dimension, and it was certainly both enjoyable and
topographically educative (mostly re-educative in our case), but it
hardly pointed to an intense preoccupation with official business.

For Christmas I managed to spend a full two and a half weeks at East
Hendred, a record for any year in or out of office. On Boxing Day we
lunched with Ann Fleming at Sevenhampton, which had survived the
depredations of the Watchfield pop festival. In the midst of a large
party, including Isaiah Berlin and Peter Quennell, Arnold Goodman
took me aside and said, 'I think you ought to know that Harold Wilson
is resolved to resign in March, probably on his sixtieth birthday. It is, of
course, a great secret, but I decided that I ought to tell you, because I
would much prefer that you rather than anyone else succeeded him.'

This information, for which I was grateful and which I accepted as
90 per cent authentic (there can always be slips between cups and lips)
ought to have destroyed at a leap my political lethargy. It gave eleven
weeks' notice – no more – of the moment for which in a sense I had been
waiting for eight years. As events turned out after that interval a swing
of fifteen votes from Callaghan to me would have made me and not him
Prime Minister. If I could have swung an average of one and a quarter
MPs a week it would just have done the trick! It ought to have galva-
nised me into the most intensive politicising of my life.

Yet, somehow, it did not. For the last week of January and
fluctuatingly throughout February I had a debilitating low flu. But
this was not the fundamental cause. I had done nothing to win votes
in the month before this set in, and indeed I think it as likely as not that
the flu was a psychosomatic response to my reluctance to be assiduous
in the tearoom, rather than the other way round. What I had done in
January was to go to North Wales and deliver my most provocative
speech (the referendum apart) since Haverfordwest. Cledwyn Hughes
had pressed me to visit Anglesey, and we arranged that on Friday,
23 January, after opening a police headquarters at Mold, near Chester,
in the afternoon, I should go on to Llangefni, the little county town
in the middle of the island and address a Labour meeting there. My
chosen theme was that, if freedom in a pluralistic democracy was to
be preserved, there were limits both to the proportion of an economy

which could be state-controlled and to the proportion of the national income which could be spent collectively; and that these limits were fast being approached.

It was a thesis of truth and relevance at the time, and it did not appear to cause offence to the Anglesey audience, or indeed to Cledwyn Hughes (although he bore no part of the responsibility), but it was a crazy sermon to deliver to the Labour Party in view of Lord Goodman's tip-off. If it had any effect at all on votes it was likely to be alienating, as indeed was exemplified by Roy Hattersley using it as his explicit reason for switching to Callaghan. Why I was impelled to do it is not in retrospect clear to me. I think the reason was something to do with my disapproval of much of the policy and outlook of the Government being such that I could bear to remain part of it only if I released my frustration in occasional outbursts.

I observed the courtesies by sending a copy of the speech over to Denis Healey's office in the Treasury that morning. Hayden Phillips, who was with me in North Wales, received various messages of protest during the day, but under instructions ignored them. He was more disturbed by the journey back (we had stayed the night with Cledwyn), when he claimed that as the car switch-backed over the hills of Wales I smoked three large cigars during the morning while working steadily through two Home Office boxes. He enjoyed lunch near Hay-on-Wye less than I did.

On the day before this Anglesey expedition I had a meeting with Wilson which was more low pressure and friendly than either of the two I have recently described, but which turned out, although this was not at first apparent, to be much more decisive for the future course of my life. I went to see him in the early evening of 22 January 1976 for an hour's routine ramble around the ramparts of Home Office and other government business of mutual interest. In the course of it he raised the future presidency of the European Commission, in which a change was due at the beginning of 1977. He said that there was a feeling that, all the original Six save Luxembourg with its population of less than half a million having provided one president, the next choice ought to come from one of the 1973 new members. Britain was much the biggest of these. There was therefore a predisposition in favour of a British candidate, but it was not so strong that the British Government could nominate whomever they liked. Wilson would have been content to put forward Christopher Soames, who was just beginning his fourth year as a very successful vice-president. But Giscard d'Estaing did not want him, and as was so often the case Schmidt and he kept in step. What it came down to, I gathered, was that the British Government could confidently put forward Heath or me, but no one else. Whether he consulted Heath I do not know. In any event he offered the job to

me, saying that I ought to have the first refusal, although he expected
that I would not want to go; and he was polite enough to add that he
hoped this would be so.

I reacted at the time as he expected. As I put it in the introduction
to *European Diary*:

I thanked him, but reached for an old gramophone record and said that I
was resolved to remain in British politics. Over the next few days I became
increasingly doubtful of the wisdom of this reply. Brussels would certainly
be an escape from the nutshell of British politics. It would be an opportunity
to do something quite new for me and in which I believed much more than
in the economic policy of Mr Healey, the trade union policy of Mr Foot or
even the foreign policy of Mr Callaghan. There might also be the chance to
help Europe regain the momentum which it had so signally lost since the oil
shock at the end of 1973.[2]

As I left the next morning for my North Wales visit it might be
thought that this offer provided the basis for my Anglesey rashness.
It was more complicated than that. The Llangefni speech was written
well before the Thursday meeting with Wilson. Moreover the offer,
while firm at the time, had been refused, and could not be resurrected
with certainty from a Wilson whom I had yet again affronted, except
on the basis that he would be glad to see the back of me. But even
this did not make sense, for he was going even earlier himself. Getting
me to Brussels would serve no malevolent purpose for him. What was
the case was that Healey's protests against the speech made me still
more semi-detached from the Government and therefore more open
to the offer, and that its existence introduced a note of ambiguity into
my approach to the leadership contest. It was not that I wanted to
be President of the European Commission more than Prime Minister
of Great Britain. The reverse was true, as it would have been,
*mutatis mutandis*, for every politician in all the major countries of
the Community, and for many in the minor ones too. But it made
me more inclined to seek the leadership only on my own terms, and
perhaps also to accept too easily that the time for victory was probably
four years past.

In any event, at some stage over that weekend I decided to withdraw
my refusal, and wrote to Wilson to that effect on the Monday
afternoon. I could not substitute a positive acceptance because of
his pending resignation. The added complication was that this was not
open to discussion between us. He did not take me into his confidence,
and I was bound by Goodman's request for secrecy. However, I knew
that there could be no question of my slipping off to Brussels before
the contest. I still had a lot of troops behind me who had long been

in training for the contest. Probably they as much as I had come to realise that the time for victory was past. But they nevertheless wished to fight. To have left them without a figurehead on the eve of the battle would have been intolerable.

I therefore had to procrastinate. Quite how I managed this I cannot remember. It never seemed to become an issue. Probably Wilson realised what I was up to, and as nearly always when his own security was not directly threatened behaved considerately. More difficulty arose in Paris four weeks later. I had gone there for forty-eight hours, nominally to pay a bilateral visit to my opposite number, Michel Poniatowski, then Minister of the Interior, and always, in or out of office, the devoted adjutant of Valéry Giscard d'Estaing. In fact the visit was at the express wish of Giscard himself. Its centrepiece was an hour's meeting with him alone at the Elysée. I had known Giscard quite well when we were both Finance Ministers, but had not had much contact with him since. His purpose was to urge upon me, saying that he spoke on behalf of Schmidt as well, the presidency of the Commission. I was not only flattered but attached great practical importance to being the candidate of this most powerful European axis. Not only did it free me from obligation to Wilson; it would also strengthen my hand if I did the job. But what was I to say to him? I muttered that there was an election I had to get out of the way first. He thought for a moment I was telling him of an imminent British general election, but I quickly corrected this. I could not plant such a false rumour in the French Government. Apart from anything else, Jacques de Beaumarchais would probably be blamed for his poor intelligence. Giscard then allowed the nature of 'the election' to drop, and did not press for an immediate decision from me. One advantage of Wilson's apparent but false dedication to office was that, even with a hint, no one could conceive of his voluntary withdrawal.

The next day I went to Montfort l'Amoury, thirty miles west of Paris, to lunch with the then eighty-seven-year-old Jean Monnet. He too pressed me to accept the Commission presidency. To quote again the Introduction to *European Diary*: 'Insofar as I was still doubtful, the net could be perceived as closing in oppressively. Insofar as I was increasingly tempted, I was exhilarated by being blessed by the spiritual as well as the temporal authorities of Europe.'[3]

Throughout this period Harold Wilson's imminent resignation remained a closely kept secret. I did not feel at liberty to talk about it to even such a close ally as Bill Rodgers. Given the number of people involved in my Paris discussions, it was not surprising that news of my possible departure for Brussels began to seep around more widely than news of Wilson's (allegedly) certain departure from office. Then his sixtieth birthday (11 March) came and went without anything happening. Maybe the well-kept secret was just a false rumour. It was only a temporary hiccup. The Government had been defeated in the House of Commons the night before, and Wilson did not feel that he could announce his withdrawal until he had reversed that vote. That was done on the Monday, and the resignation was announced at the Cabinet on the morning of Tuesday, 16 March.

Callaghan had been informed beforehand, but I had not, which was a clear indication of the way that Wilson's preference had shifted. It was not exactly like 'the blubbering Cabinet' in Gladstone's famous and dismissive description of the proceedings in 1894, when he had been forced to resign and when Sir William Harcourt pulled out of his pocket a crumpled manuscript from which he proceeded to read an embarrassing tribute. Callaghan did avail himself of his prior notice to the extent of having a prepared little encomium ready, but unlike Harcourt he had chosen the words well. Most people were I think genuinely moved. It came as a shock and marked the end of an era, and the combination of these feelings naturally releases human emotion. Also, almost all of us had received more kindnesses than tiresomenesses from Wilson. There were one or two cloying statements round the table, which Wilson rather elegantly brought to an end by withdrawing to prepare some necessary statements. I confined myself to trying to draft the little declaration of regret and appreciation which the Cabinet proposed to issue.

Although he was no longer party leader Wilson remained Prime Minister for two weeks, as there was no one to take his place until an exhaustive ballot of the parliamentary Labour Party was complete. I was only directly concerned with the first round of this, which produced a result after nine days. These nine days were a curious mixture of campaigning and non-campaigning. Immediately after the resignation Cabinet I had a fortuitously arranged lunch of the Walston group in Albany. They were all in good morale, and we arranged to fight as hard as we could. The general mood was that the odds had moved against us, but that victory remained a possibility.

I did not canvass, which would have been crude and likely to be counter-productive, but those doing so on my behalf let it be known that I would be happy to see anyone who wanted to talk in my room. A number did. Thus my diary for Thursday, 18 March, contained the cryptic entry 'Interviews: 4.30 to 11.00 p.m.' These had mixed results, although none of them was remotely unpleasant. But they were no substitute for the quiet, undemanding fostering of relations to which I ought to have devoted January and February. About half my meals were 'plotting' occasions in the House of Commons or at Brooks's (or perhaps more accurately by this stage morale-boosting ones for me) with Bill Rodgers, Ian Wrigglesworth, John Harris, Dick Mabon and so on. On the Friday I spent eight hours in Birmingham, found a lot of warming but misplaced optimism in Stechford, and was heavily photographed. Equally on the Saturday we had the Sunday papers' photographers to East Hendred for an hour, and dutifully played tennis for them. But on the Sunday our luncheon guests were only the Beaumarchais and Ann Fleming, none of whom commanded many battalions of votes, and which did not therefore suggest an obsessive campaign.

On the Monday all six candidates did substantial interviews for an extended edition of *Panorama*. Mine was apparently judged to be best in the House of Commons members' television room, where about a third of the electorate were assembled, but I should think not enough so to affect votes. But by that time even an unproductive boost to morale was welcome, for we were running up against a disappointing wall, not of hostility, but of cautious regret. It was best expressed by Ernest Armstrong, MP for North-west Durham and my host during that dark Pennine weekend seven years before, whom I regarded as both representative and influential. He told Bill Rodgers that he had long looked forward to supporting me for the leadership, but that he had now decided with regret that the party was in such a fragile state that it needed Callaghan's more mollifying bedside manner. Typically Armstrong also came and straightforwardly expressed his intention and sadness to me. The news of his decision left me without much doubt about the outcome.

I had the support of most of the press, but I knew that, with that electorate, *The Times* and the *Daily Mirror* and the *Observer* were no match for Ernest Armstrong. Perhaps the best newspaper comment on the campaign was a Garland cartoon in the *Daily Telegraph*, which showed me as a small cavalier boy surrounded by a lot of roundhead dignitaries saying accusingly, 'When did you last see the TUC?' Parallel with these skirmishes for the future the obsequies of the Wilson leadership were taking place. On the Monday there was a Cabinet dinner, at which some good speeches were made, sitting down as I recall. On the Tuesday there was a more formal dinner to which the Queen came, a rare Downing Street event.

Two days after this there was the first result. My mood that day was best summed up by the fact that I had Michael Palliser, the permanent under-secretary of the Foreign Office, to lunch at Ladbroke Square in order that we might discuss some of the detailed provisions for the Brussels job. Bill Rodgers, probably unaware of this, was anxious that the result, to be announced at a party meeting at 6.00, should not come as a shock to me, and solicitously warned me during the afternoon that Callaghan was decisively ahead of me. The figures were: Foot 90,

Callaghan 84, me 56, Benn 37, Healey 30 and Crosland 17. Foot's lead was not of primary importance. He could be comfortably overhauled, even with the transfer to him of most of Benn's vote, by whichever of Callaghan or me got into the position for a run-off. It was the relative positions of Callaghan and me which were therefore the news headline. And Callaghan's lead while not overwhelming was nonetheless enough to settle the issue. The country, I thought, needed a new Prime Minister quickly, and not the long-drawn-out agony of a third, or even a fourth, slow round, and from fifty-six votes that Prime Minister was not going to be me.

I therefore immediately decided to withdraw. Benn did the same. Crosland was compulsorily eliminated. Healey, with characteristic pugnacity, decided to fight on, but that in no way unsettled my mind. As soon as the party meeting was over those who had been working closely with me assembled in my room. There were only two who were opposed to my decision. I drafted a short statement of withdrawal, in effect releasing my votes to Callaghan. Although I had substantially differed from him on a number of issues, believing him to have been wrong on devaluation, East of Suez, immigration policy, most libertarian issues at the Home Office, trade union reform and Europe, I nonetheless greatly preferred the prospect of him as Prime Minister to that of Michael Foot, the only practical alternative. Foot, although a man of charm and honour, would have been a hopeless head of a government, as indeed he proved to be a leader of the opposition in 1980–3. Callaghan at least was sound on the Atlantic Alliance, was no dogmatic supporter of nationalisation and had a built-in respect for the rule of law. He also had the capacity, both in public impact and in substance, to be a more effective Prime Minister than Wilson had been in his latter days.

Dickson Mabon, who had been a determined and helpful supporter, volunteered to go and take the good news to Callaghan's room, where I hope that he was gratefully received. He has recently reminded me, which I had forgotten, that in announcing my decision to withdraw to the assembled roomful I quoted (or more probably misquoted) Robert E. Lee's message to the Confederate army after Appomattox Court House:

After four years of arduous service, marked by unsurpassed courage and fortitude, the Army of Northern Virginia has been compelled to yield to overwhelming numbers and resources. I need not tell the brave survivors of so many hard-fought battles, who have remained steadfast to the last, that I have consented to this result from no distrust of them. . . . By terms of the agreement officers and men can return to their homes and remain until exchanged. . . . With an increasing admiration of your courtesy and devotion to your country and a grateful remembrance of your kind and generous consideration for myself, I bid you all an affectionate farewell.

I went off to dine with the Other Club, where I received a lot of commiserations, which I did not greatly need for I was neither shocked nor shattered, just disappointed that I had got about ten votes less than I had realistically hoped for. It was the end of a phase, which had begun about eight years before and during which it had mostly seemed more likely than not that I would one day be Prime Minister. But even that had probably been something of a complacent illusion, for it is hardly ever more likely than not that any one person, certainly one who is not leader of the opposition, will be Prime Minister. The most I should have assumed is that I looked more likely than anyone else. But even that had now disappeared, never to return except for one rather wild flicker at the beginning of 1982. I turned my thoughts to Brussels, where perhaps too many of them had already been during the preceding two months.

# PART FOUR

# 1976–1990

# CHAPTER TWENTY-FOUR

# *Cross-Channel Packet*

My political view of the new Prime Minister I have described. More personally my views were equally mixed. Although he had a number of more amiable characteristics, I regarded Jim Callaghan as a bit of a bully. That I did not greatly mind for I thought that after the very easy-going regime of Wilson's final days a bit of bullying might do the Government no harm. Moreover I did not expect the bullying to be exercised against me. I assumed that, both on grounds of seniority and out of gratitude for the early release to him of my fifty-six votes, he would offer me the reversion to the foreign secretaryship which his elevation had left vacant, or that, if I preferred it, he would without question maintain the European offer which Wilson had made to me, and where the matter had in any event been somewhat taken out of the hands of the British Government by the patronage of Giscard and Schmidt.

The latter assumption proved correct, but not the former. I saw Callaghan for the first time as Prime Minister on the morning of 6 April, the day after his election. He was eager to tell me that he was dropping Barbara Castle, Edward Short, Willie Ross and Robert Mellish, and forthcoming about wanting me to stay in the Government, but imprecise about exactly what position he was offering. It appeared that the Home Office continued to be available to me, that he was prepared to hold out a prospect of the Exchequer in the autumn, but that the Foreign Office was not on offer. This had the perverse temporary effect of shaking the order of preference which I thought I had settled upon after my conversation with Giscard in Paris at the end of February. The first place in that order was as obviously occupied by the prime ministership as the possibility of it had been eliminated by the time of the 6 April meeting. My second preference was to be President of the Commission. My third was to be Foreign Secretary, and my fourth, a long way behind, for I had been it long enough, was to remain as Home Secretary.

441

Callaghan's resistance infused the Foreign Office, the only one of the three great departments of state over which I had not presided, with a new and foolish glamour of the unattainable. It was compounded by the fact that Callaghan would not say why not. In his autobiography, published eleven years later, he put the reason with convincing frankness. The events of 1971–2 had tarred me with too European a brush: 'every action he [I] would have taken as Foreign Secretary would have been regarded with deep suspicion by the anti-marketeers on our benches. . . .'[1] It might have been better had he said this at the time.

My reaction was foolish because I really wanted more to be President of the Commission than to occupy any subordinate position in a British government, and because it was in any event time for me to be off from that particular Labour Government with which, whether under Wilson or Callaghan, I had grown too out of sympathy to be a good or patient member, except on a narrowly departmental basis. Furthermore, old friendship for Anthony Crosland and a memory of the cruel events for him of 1967 should have made me glad that Callaghan's determination not to have me as Foreign Secretary gave him the opportunity to occupy that office for the last ten months of his life. But neither at my 6 April meeting with Callaghan, nor at a subsequent one the following day, did I know that Crosland was his alternative candidate, and still less that he (Crosland) would die in 1977. At least I was undiverted by any vague promise of becoming Chancellor in six months' time. That was a bird in the bush if ever there was one, and I had in any event been there before.

Having been adamant about the Foreign Office, Callaghan then proceeded to show great consideration about everything to do with the Brussels appointment. I do not think this was simply due to a desire to be rid of a troublesome colleague, for both in April and again in July he tried hard to persuade me of the advantages of staying in British politics: he stressed that it would be difficult to get back into a Labour seat after Brussels, and that the succession to himself, who would not remain long in the leadership, was open. The interest of the July conversation was that it provoked me into saying that I did not want a future in British politics in their existing shape. I only envisaged returning to a reshuffled pack, in which circumstances the anti-European prejudices of the Labour Party would be irrelevant. Callaghan looked surprised and pensive rather than hostile.

He encouraged me to stay on in the Government as long as was mutually convenient. I thought that July would be the right time to go, but he preferred September. He gave me complete freedom of choice over the second British Commissioner, accepting my surprising but, as it turned out, sensible suggestion of Christopher Tugendhat,

The Labour Cabinet, summer 1969.
Front row (*left to right*): Shore, Healey, Mrs Castle, Gardiner, Stewart, Wilson, Jenkins, Crossman, Callaghan, Peart, Crosland. Back row (*left to right*): Mrs Hart, George Thomas, Cledwyn Hughes, Marsh, Short, Ross, Thomson, Benn, Greenwood, Shackleton, Mason, Diamond, Burke Trend (Cabinet Secretary).

At a Birmingham factory gate, May 1970. This was used for a national election poster with the caption 'Together we have made Britain strong', but the appeal was not strong enough to win.

Prime Minister and Chancellor at a 1970 election press conference in Birmingham.

The Economist

13-19 June 1970 UK 3s/USA 75c (West Coast $1)
FF 2.80/DM 2.50/Lit 400/Fl 11.85/BF 28/Dkr 5/Nkr 4/Skr 3.25/ASch 18/PtS 2.50/Pts 40

In Harold Wilson's Britain

'In Harold Wilson's Britain'.
*The Economist* cover for 13 June 1970. The next week it was Ted Heath's Britain.

'The days when smoking was still permitted'. In my Ladbroke Square study, *circa* 1972.

With James Callaghan and Denis Healey, Labour Party conference, Brighton, 1971.

Bill Rodgers: 'The Organiser of Victory
for the Labour Europeans'.

With Anthony Crosland at the 1973 Labour Party
conference. More old friends than current allies.

Jakie Astor plays serious croquet with me.
Hatley, July 1970.

Receiving the Robert Schuman Prize in Bonn,
November 1972. With Nicko Henderson, then
British ambassador in Bonn and friend for over
fifty years.

'The Devils' (Cummings). *Daily Mail*, 1971.

'When did you last see the T.U.C.?' (Garland). *Daily Telegraph*, March 1976.

'To see politicians in different parties sitting and working together was a pleasant shock for most of the public.' With Jo Grimond, Cledwyn Hughes, Willie Whitelaw, Reginald Maudling and Con O'Neill at the launch of the Britain in Europe campaign, April 1975.

Twenty-five years as Member for Stechford. *Left to right*: Sir Frank Price, former Lord Mayor, Denis Howell, MP for Small Heath, unknown, me, Jennifer, Clive Wilkinson, leader of the City Council, Mrs Elsie Smith, Roy Hattersley, MP for Sparkbrook, George Canning, previously my agent, then my chairman and soon to be Lord Mayor, Brian Walden, MP for Ladywood, and Julius Silverman, MP for Aston. Birmingham, 1975.

Guildford bombing, the
morning after. October 1974.

Attacked from Left and Right:
flour bombs at the East Ham
Town Hall, September 1975.

then the young (thirty-eight-year-old) Conservative MP for the Cities of London and Westminster, with a mixture of acquiescence and enthusiasm, and was undismayed by the fact that this meant offending Mrs Thatcher.

On the other hand I also had an early experience of Callaghan's rough side. He was determined to get rid of Alex Lyon, MP for York and one of my two Ministers of State. I was not resistant to this for Lyon had proved himself a disappointment as a junior minister, mainly because he entrenched himself with his private secretary (Clare Short, now MP, whom he subsequently married) in a bunker of suspicion against almost everybody else, myself, his fellow Minister of State, the permanent secretary and nearly all other officials. This dismissal obviously involved a replacement, and Callaghan telephoned me a day or so later to suggest (as I thought) Brynmor John, a South Wales solicitor and something of a crony of his. I said I hardly knew him but would happily look him over and let the Prime Minister know what I thought within twenty-four hours. Callaghan in effect said, 'You've got him now,' and I realised that the era of Wilsonite consideration was over. Harold Wilson, it may be recalled, had in fact done something similar to me in 1964 when I was a new minister in a junior department, but he would not have dreamed of behaving so abruptly at any time in the previous ten years. John in fact turned out to be a good if reserved (from me) middle-rank minister. The incident nonetheless left a mark upon my mind, and I felt glad that I was leaving the Government within a few months. The reverse side of this coin of prime ministerial discourtesy was however the fact that the Cabinet became more tautly and efficiently run.

There was another hiccup that spring. At the end of April Giscard indicated that he was against any early announcement of my presidency of the Commission. His mind was firm on the substance, he insisted, but there should be no premature publicity, for this might prejudice the position of François-Xavier Ortoli, the incumbent French President who still had eight months of his term to run. This was strange, in view both of Giscard's own urgent pressure of February and of the fact that he had never previously shown much consideration for Ortoli – and nor did he do so subsequently. It was balanced however by enthusiastic support given publicly by the Italian Government and more privately by the German Chancellor, Helmut Schmidt, who did not however wish to announce himself as being out of step with his friend and partner in the leadership of Europe, Valéry Giscard. Thus I had an early taste of a pattern of European attitudes which was to become only too familiar to me over the next few years.

The explanation of Giscard's wobble, I retrospectively decided, was that my candidature, launched by him and Schmidt, was being too enthusiastically received by the small countries of the Community. This was not particularly a personal tribute. They wanted a politician and not a bureaucrat – 'someone who might have been Prime Minister of his own country', as Schmidt once put it – and found a Briton who had European conviction such an unusual combination as to be almost heady. When I visited three or four countries that spring I was already treated as a president-elect who might infuse some new life into the then somewhat low-burning embers of European unity. Giscard's response, which well represented his ambiguity in office between the cause of European integration and the dignity and power of the French state, was not to change his mind, but to try to demonstrate that I was becoming president not by the acclaim of the little ones but by the favour of a much greater president, that of the Fifth Republic.

The issue was however safely out of the way by soon after midsummer when the European council, meeting in Luxembourg, conveyed to me a public and unanimous invitation to assume the presidency at the beginning of January 1977. Thereafter the majority of my time and the overwhelming part of my interest was applied to the affairs of Europe. I remained Home Secretary for another ten weeks, but that was only because it suited the Prime Minister, and more than half of this twilight period was taken up by parliamentary and governmental holidays.

I was in a higher state of morale that summer than at any time since 1970–1, if not earlier. Once the decision to go to Brussels had been finally made, I felt both liberated and exhilarated. I realised retrospectively how ill the shoe of British politics had been fitting me. I had been neither at ease in, nor derived pride from, my membership of that Government of 1974, and I ought to have got out of it before. My exasperated instruction to Bernard Donoughue in March 1974, that he was to tell Wilson I did not much want to be 'in his bloody government at all' contained too much of the continuing truth for comfort. It was quite different from my attitude to the Government of 1964–70, of which, despite its mistakes and tensions, I was throughout a fully committed member.

By 1976 I had come to believe that Britain was one of the worst-governed countries in Western Europe, and I was too starry-eyed about the economic and social achievement of the other Community countries. Like Sterne 200 years before I tended to believe that they ordered these matters better in France, and not only in France but also at other points to the south and east of it. Although this was an exaggerated view it was not an unhealthy one with which to start my new assignment. I was in fact riddled with subconscious prejudices in favour of British methods of administration, British presentation of an argument and British jokes. If I was to have any hope of melding together a nine-nation Commission and, still more difficult, getting some control of a Brussels bureaucracy which had over twenty years settled into a largely French or at least Gallo-German tradition, it was essential that I should compensate with a superficial counter-flow of contrary esteem.

This starry-eyed approach was buttressed by the fact that, over that summer, encouraged by the enthusiasm with which they had greeted my appointment, I exaggerated the extent to which I could persuade the governments of Europe to do what I wanted. In my excitement in finding myself on a much wider stage after the confines of the Home Office in a government with neither the economic nor the foreign policy of which I was prepared to identify, I ignored the extent to which the width of the stage was balanced by the uncertainties of both the position and the power of the President of the Commission upon it. For a minister in a British or any other national government there are levers of executive power which, if pulled, lead to more or less predictable results. In Brussels, outside a narrow field of coal and steel and agricultural decisions, which were not of primary interest to me, nothing much happened unless the majority of member governments could be persuaded to join in leaning upon the lever. Fluctuating influence was the most to be hoped for.

It was not however a bad thing that these harsh realities were concealed from my temporarily euphoric mind over the summer of 1976. Occasional bursts of optimism, even if misplaced, are a desirable source of energy. And I much enjoyed myself for four months. In July I had the existing Commissioners who were candidates for staying on over to London to see me. I also began a series of visits to the governments of the member states, partly to discuss new Commissioners and partly for familiarisation; by mid-November I had made twenty such journeys to capitals. I assembled my own staff. I took a four-week holiday, the longest since 1970, partly in Italy and partly in France, and liked the illusion of visiting the provinces of my future domain. I worked hard during this holiday as I did at home, particularly after leaving the Government, both at improving my French and at learning about the detailed history of the Community and the working of the Commission. Both were necessary. My French was based on School Certificate in 1935, two months in Paris in the summers of 1938 and 1939, and some intermittent reading and restaurant practice. My fluency was not great and my vocabulary was not wide. Unless I was going to be as linguistically ill-equipped as George I was when he arrived in England in 1714 I had to do something about it quick. I succeeded in doing a good deal about both the vocabulary and the fluency, and came rather to enjoy chattering in French but not doing serious business in it. My grammar remained uncertain and my accent insular.

My lack of detailed knowledge about the Community was even more serious. As I put it in the Introduction to *European Diary*:

My conviction was complete, but my experience was negligible. The only ministerial portfolio that I held after Britain's entry in 1973 was that of the Home Department, which as its name implied, and its ethos confirmed, was about as far removed from the business of the Community as any within the compass of the British Government. I participated in no Councils of Ministers. I liked to say, only half as a joke, that I kept my European faith burning bright by never visiting Brussels. And this was almost startlingly true. France, Italy, Germany I knew fairly well. But the embryonic capital of Europe I visited on only four occasions between 1945 and the date of my appointment as head of its administration. I was an enthusiast for the *grandes lignes* of Europe but an amateur within the complexities of its signalling system.[2]

I worked hard at those complexities, both on paper and in discussion.

Probably the most important of these preliminary activities was the assembling of my own *cabinet* or personal staff. I was determined to take Hayden Phillips to Brussels. He had been an exceptional private secretary since my reluctant return to the Home Office. He was attracted by the thought of an excursion away from Whitehall confines, and it was settled early on that he should come as deputy head of my office. It was thought that, aged only thirty-three, he ought to be supplemented with a more senior and diplomatically trained *chef de cabinet*. The Foreign Office was eager to provide a candidate, and as an admirer of the foreign service I was happy to fall in with this suggestion. They offered two principal candidates, Crispin Tickell and Ewen Fergusson, and I also played with the idea of Antony Acland. As, within ten years, these three were respectively permanent representative to the United Nations, ambassador to Paris, and ambassador to Washington after already having been permanent under-secretary, it could not plausibly be claimed that I was being fobbed off with second-rate material.

Acland was bespoken, but Fergusson was a most powerful candidate. However, I gave the edge to Tickell, and never subsequently regretted his appointment. He had recently returned from a sabbatical year at Harvard, where with a mixture of luck and judgement he had surprised everybody by devoting his time to writing a thesis not on arms control or European integration but on climatology. It was one of the best intellectual investments ever made, the equivalent of buying a penny stock in a company which quickly grew into a great profit-spinning multi-national. As a result Crispin Tickell, before retiring to become Warden of Green College, Oxford, spent his last period as a diplomat, not only an outstandingly resourceful ambassador in New York, but also a guru of the Western world on anything to do with ecology, pollution and the future of the planet.

Of more immediate concern to me in 1976 was whether he was going to be a good *chef de cabinet* and hunting companion in the European jungle. I thought of this jungle as essentially benign, and our role as much more that of trapping butterflies than of shooting tigers or strangling cobras, but I nonetheless wanted someone who was sure-footed and had some knowledge of the paths. This Tickell had acquired as private secretary to Geoffrey Rippon during the Heath Government's negotiations for British entry into the Community. More important, his inherent qualities turned out to be even better than I expected. He had a cool muscular intelligence, good judgement, occasionally better on issues than on people, and great self-discipline and application. In addition he never flickered in his determination to see the job through. He had voluntarily signed on for the four-year voyage, and even at the most dismal periods he never gave the slightest hint that he might be happier as an ambassador.

He and I, although different in many ways, also got on well together. Like all the best civil servants he would always accept a decision once the arguments had been considered and it had been clearly given. We had some, not many, disagreements, but not I think a single quarrel during the four years. This was in spite of the fact that he had to overcome the same problem which had confronted Robert Armstrong in 1968. Hayden Phillips, at any rate to begin with, knew me much better, and also rather liked an occasional teasing of Crispin. Tickell's countervailing strength was that he knew Europe – and French, the language of the Berlaymont – much better than did Hayden.

To the core of these two we added (Crispin doing much of the recruitment) Michael Emerson and Graham Avery, both of them Balliol economists as it happened, although I do not think I was aware of their provenance at the time, the former a monetary, the latter an agricultural expert. Emerson left my *cabinet* on promotion fairly soon, and was replaced by an excellent Belgian, Michel Vanden Abele, but continued to play a key role in the creation of the European Monetary System. In addition we took on two more junior members, Klaus Ebermann, a German, and Etienne Reuter, a Luxembourgeois. Laura Grenfell, Leslie Bonham Carter's daughter by a first marriage who subsequently herself married Hayden Phillips, came as a general and parliamentary assistant, and Michael Jenkins, who became ambassador to The Hague in 1989 and had been George Thomson's *chef de cabinet*, remained for six months or so as a crucial transitional aide. Bernard Ingham, I discovered many years later, had made a tentative approach to John Harris, suggesting he might come to Brussels as my spokesman, but was told that the post was already filled with Roger Beetham of the Foreign Office.

We inherited profitably from both the Thomson and the Soames establishments. My two secretaries, Celia Beale and Susan Besford, came one from each. Of my two drivers, one, the inimitable Ron Argent, who had been expatriate for many years but carried a distinct whiff of an early exponent of the South London enterprise culture at the time when there were post-war austerities to be got round, was from the Soames stable. So also was his Spanish wife, José, who had the great laundering and ironing skill of the Iberian peninsula. A still more special Soames legacy was their Belgian cook, Marie-Jeanne Belsack, who had received a lot of direct training from Christopher and who, once we had lowered the richness of the sauces by a few notches, was a great asset for the whole four years.

The other chauffeur, Peter Halsey, had first driven me at the Home Office in 1965–7 and remained with me until 1983, which was when I was last able to enjoy the luxury of a driver. He came from the Metropolitan Police, not the Government car pool, was used to working with my detectives, and in my view protected me, as well as seeing to my convenience, more effectively than did the various Commission and Belgian security guards who were mobilised when assassination threats developed in 1979. Alas, he died young in 1988.

We also needed a house. The presidency of the Commission is unique amongst the major international jobs of the world in that it carries with it no official residence. This in itself neither Jennifer nor I regarded as a deprivation. I (and particularly she) had been less than enchanted with our only previous experience of one at 11 Downing Street in 1968–70. But it did mean both that a fair amount of effort had to be put into finding a house to rent, and that my apparently high pay (by the standards of the 1970s, although not of today, and with which the British press was obsessed) was much reduced by the expenses of running it. The Secretary-General of NATO, in our day Josef Luns, later Peter Carrington, who was the other head of an international organisation resident in Brussels, was provided free with a substantial villa and a lavish domestic staff. We settled on a small *art nouveau* town house, which had a certain turn-of-the-century charm but whose only pretension to grandeur was a *porte-cochère*. It could sleep no more than five, and it was difficult to exceed ten for lunch or dinner. Nonetheless it was a rare week in which we did not entertain thirty or forty people, visiting ministers, ambassadors, other Commissioners, staff and friends, to one or other of these meals. As Jennifer, who from 1975 to 1985 was chairman of the Historic Buildings Council for England, had considerable commitments in London, and was on average only in Brussels for about ten days a month, the small staff was clearly necessary to provide these. The total costs of the house came to about £25,000 a year, as compared with my salary of about £50,000 (subject to Community tax at 32 per cent) supplemented by allowances of £15,000 to £20,000. The position was obviously more than tolerable, but hardly the Croesus-like existence which was constantly presented – always to the amazement of the continentals – to the British public. I stopped overspending, which the low ministerial salaries of the mid-1970s had made inevitable since my return to office in 1974, but I do not think that I saved anything during my four Brussels years.

My first sight in mid-November of this house, which had been settled on by Jennifer two weeks before, coincided precisely but accidentally with the end of my four months of euphoria. It was the only time that I went to Brussels over the nine months when I was president in waiting. This was deliberate. I decided that if I was to make any impact both upon the bureaucracy (which I thought of as being dedicated but rigid) and upon the tone of Europe, I must arrive only with full powers and not become a familiar figure hanging about the corridors in the preceding months. This may or may not have given drama to my eventual arrival, but it certainly had the effect of making the ambience of the Berlaymont, the ways of those who lived in and around it, and indeed the whole atmosphere of Brussels seem almost gothically strange to me. The impact of this was to be at much its most powerful when I was plunged semi-permanently into the gloom of a Brabant January, but the gloom of a Brabant November put on a fairly good dress rehearsal on the morning of that first visit to the house in the Rue de Praetère. Half-furnished, which was how we took it, it lacked the modestly eccentric attraction that it eventually turned out to have. But that was not the cause of my dramatic change of mood. That stemmed from overnight reflection upon an hour's meeting with Helmut Schmidt, which I had had in Bonn the previous evening.

It was ironical that my first significant setback in Europe should have been at the hands of the German Government and of Schmidt in particular. It must be seen against the background of my very high expectations of them both. I regarded Schmidt (as indeed I still do) as the most constructive statesman of that period, and the one with whom I had the easiest personal relations. I regarded the SPD/FDP government as a model of centre–left internationalist good sense, and likely to be my strongest champions in any battles which lay ahead. But it was they who tripped me up in my strategy of assembling a very strong Commission which, by virtue of the sum of the individual prestige of its members, would necessarily carry a great deal of weight with the member governments. Moreover the Germans did so in a way which, while not remotely malevolent, still less aggressively nationalistic, was symptomatic of an unwillingness adequately to sustain the Community institutions which has been the one weak aspect of the otherwise impeccable European record of the Federal Republic.

In 1975 the Tindemans Report on the future of the Community (so called because it had been drawn up by the then Belgian Prime Minister at the request of the other governments) had recommended that an incoming president should have a substantial voice in the choice of his fellow Commissioners, even though the formal right of nomination remained with the individual governments. I attempted to implement this recommendation, achieving only limited success, but gaining useful experience by practice in the art of arguing with the different governments. I think that I intervened more actively in the process of selection than have either of my successors, Gaston Thorn and Jacques Delors, notably strong a president though the latter has been. Perhaps they learned from my mistakes.

There were two members of the previous Commission I was determined to keep – Claude Cheysson, the French career diplomat and then recent socialist convert, who had built up a semi-imperial role for himself as the distributor of Community beneficence throughout Africa and the other Lomé Convention developing countries; and Finn-Olav Gundelach, the Danish official, who had a lot of international experience in the GATT (General Agreement on Tariffs and Trade) and elsewhere, and whom I saw as the best candidate for the difficult but crucial Agriculture portfolio. I would also have been glad to have Christopher Soames stay,* but he would only have been attracted by doing so if he could keep his External Relations job, which he had done with great success. But I did not see that Britain could both occupy the presidency and be in charge of Directorate-General I without upsetting the national balance. Indeed I had a firm view that a German ought to have DG-I.

There was no problem with the Danish Government. They were as keen to keep on Gundelach as was I. The French Government, with whom I had complicated discussions at Giscard level, were cool about Cheysson but enthusiastic about keeping the Development Aid portfolio in French hands. That was my bargaining card with them. They would have preferred to keep on Ortoli, my predecessor as president, and switch him to that portfolio. I was not sure that I wanted my predecessor in my Commission. Conventional wisdom advised against, and Ortoli, a nice and sensitive man, saw my

---

* On personal grounds I would also have been delighted to see George Thomson continue, but he was excluded on grounds of political balance. There could not be two members of the Labour Party from Britain without destroying the bipartisanship which Heath had established in 1972 and to which I was firmly attached.

dilemma. He was uncertain himself. But we both believed that, if he did stay on, he should have Economic and Monetary Affairs (DG-II). Eventually, after Giscard had demonstrated his consideration by insisting that he would not impose Ortoli on me against my will, but had nonetheless endeavoured to concentrate my mind on Ortoli by suggesting one or two unsuitable but high-ranking candidates, and I had hinted that without Cheysson the French would not keep the portfolio they wanted, we settled on Ortoli and Cheysson.

The Dutch and the Irish, both of them supposed to be highly *communautaire* governments, produced after discussion candidates who they knew were not in accordance with my views. Both Governments did it for internal political reasons. Neither nominee was a success in the Commission, although this was nothing to do with their not being my choice. I came rather to like both of them.

The Italian Government played an elegant hand. They wanted two new Commissioners as did I, and they wanted them to strike a political balance, one Christian Democrat and one Socialist, and therefore steered me gently away from one or two non-politicians, such as Guido Carli, former Governor of the Bank of Italy, whom I had in mind. Eventually in Lorenzo Natali and Antonio Giolitti they appointed the two they had wanted from the beginning, but not before they had brought me also to feel that they were the best choices. And in the course of this they gave me a fine familiarisation course in Italian politics, encouraging me to discussions with all parties, Communists included.

That left the Federal Republic of Germany, the 'middle kingdom' of the Community and indeed of Europe as a whole, which had long been a massive, crucial and generous supporter of the European ideal, and indeed of the policies necessary to achieve it, but which had nonetheless been reluctant to play a part in the European institutions commensurate with its economic strength, leaving the leadership very much to France. The paradox of post-war Europe has been that Britain and France, each in differing ways, have tried to puff themselves up to exercise more political muscle than their economic strength has justified, while Germany, by contrast, has tried to push power away. The future may be different, although current fears of a German juggernaut are in my view misplaced.

One facet of this German reticence has been a reluctance to appoint first-rate people to Brussels. Since the end of Walter Hallstein's 1958–67 reign as President this has broadly applied both to Commissioners and to permanent representatives. As a result Germany has exercised an intellectual weight in Brussels which has been not only much inferior to that of France, but also below that of Britain or Italy.

I was anxious that the appointment of the new Commission should make a break from this shoulder-shrugging tradition. Although I had not at that stage worked out that the monetary route was the essential axis of advance for Europe, I nevertheless saw that German support was crucial to any move forward, and therefore attached particular importance to having German Commissioners who would carry influence with the Federal Government. As late as a Bonn visit on 2 November I was encouraged by Helmut Schmidt to seek two new ones. It was not that I disliked the two existing German Commissioners, both of whom were anxious to stay on, but that I thought the one lacked application, the other lacked weight, and that neither was taken very seriously by Schmidt. I should, however, have noticed that a much more reserved attitude towards replacement was taken during this visit by other German ministers, most notably by Hans-Dietrich Genscher, Foreign Minister and leader of the Free Democrats.

I overestimated the power of the Chancellor. At our 15 November meeting he told me that he could not make the changes. The political pressures were too great. The FDP insisted on the renomination of their existing Commissioner, and the trade unions were equally adamant about the continuance of the long-serving SDP one from their ranks. It was a classic example of getting the worst of two worlds. The German Commissioners knew that I had tried to replace them and had failed. Furthermore it presented me with a severe practical problem about the allocation of the major portfolios. My negotiations with Giscard had brought me to an acceptance (even with some enthusiasm) of the continuance of Ortoli in the new Commission. That being so, he had in my view to be given Economic and Monetary Affairs (DG-II). Nothing else, except External Relations (DG-I), would be compatible with his dignity as an ex-president and would therefore start our relationship off on a good basis. But a Frenchman in DG-I did not offer the best prospect of conducting relations with the Americans and the Japanese on the liberal basis that I desired. So it had to be DG-II. That meant prising Willi Haferkamp, the senior German Commissioner, out of the squatter's rights he there exercised. And that could not be done without giving him DG-I. An attempt to persuade this former trade unionist of the glories of the Social Affairs portfolio (DG-V), accompanied by relations with the 'Social Partners', foundered just as ignominiously as had Wilson's attempt at the beginning of the 1974 Government to get Callaghan to take overall responsibility for industrial relations and to leave the Foreign Office to Healey and, in consequence, the Exchequer to me.

The Germans were also clearly entitled to a big portfolio, and although Schmidt had half invited me to work off my and his irritation by not giving them one, I judged that this would be a foolishly short-term reaction. However, the other part of the German Government in the shape of Hans-Dietrich Genscher at the Auswärtiges Amt, which did care about German portfolios, wanted Guido Brunner and not Haferkamp to have External Relations. So it was a real dog's breakfast, particularly as I did not feel I could settle finally on the next rank of portfolios, which were Gundelach for Agriculture, Davignon for Industry and Cheysson for Development Aid, until I had untied the DG-I/DG-II knot. This I did not finally do until the new Commission was in office at the beginning of January, when I put Haferkamp into DG-I, hoping that his genial good sense on big issues would compensate for his lack of application to small ones, and rode out Brunner's shrill protests, hoping, correctly, that they would not be given resonance by sustained support from Bonn.

Apart from creating these practical portfolio problems, the German reversal had a disproportionate effect upon my morale. I think I was poised for a change of mood in any event. The euphoria of the summer and early autumn had been too great, and was bound to be corrected as the happy prospect of preparing for an exciting new job gave way to the harsh reality of having within a few weeks to plunge into the complexities of actually doing it. Probably therefore the German experience did little more than tear along a perforation which was already there. But that it certainly did. Four days before the Bonn setback, on my fifty-sixth birthday as it happened, I remember walking through the division lobby with the Prime Minister, who lightly inquired whether I was still available to be Chancellor of the Exchequer. Sterling was crashing, the Government's economic policy was in disarray, and there was press and parliamentary speculation that Denis Healey's days were numbered. I would at least have been buying at the bottom of the market. However, my mind was enthusiastically fixed on Brussels, and I took Callaghan's suggestion even less seriously than he made it. The following week I might have been more unsettled by this tentative inquiry.

In reality, of course, I could not possibly have changed direction at this stage. The juddering would have been appalling: my assembled *cabinet* to be stood down, the Brussels house to be unrented, my constituency farewells to be unsaid, as well as confirming every suspicion of the governments of Europe about the insularity of the British. So I settled down to the last stages of preparation. But it was 'never glad confident morning again'.

On the contrary, and in sharp contrast with the preceding months, I remember that December as being spent under a thickening cloud of apprehension. My preliminary visits to member states were over, for my fellow Commissioners had all been appointed, but I did go to America for five days in mid-month. There I delivered a lecture (on the future of the European Community) in a grand bicentennial series at the Massachusetts Institute of Technology, paid a call on a defeated President Ford in the White House, and met Mondale (Vice-President), Vance (Secretary of State) and Blumenthal (Treasury), but not Carter himself, from the Administration in waiting. High up in the Boston Ritz on the night after the MIT lecture my new *Angst* rose to a peak. Unusually for me, I could not sleep, and the blizzard which swirled round my tower seemed to symbolise the only half-understood European problems and the potentially menacing old Brussels hands which surrounded me.

At home there was a variegated round of send-off banquets which kind friends and well-wishers had organised for me – the French ambassador, the German ambassador, the Labour Committee for Europe, George Weidenfeld, forty MPs brought together by Bill Rodgers, the Stechford Labour Party, a group of a dozen friends assembled by Victor Rothschild and Jakie Astor, even the CBI, all organised dinners. But they became more like desperate attempts at cheerfulness before setting off on a hazardous 'last sight of England' voyage than joyous festivities.

On 21 December, after voting at 10.00 p.m., I left the House of Commons for what I thought would probably be the last time in my life. As this was after twenty-nine years of continuous membership it did seem a wrench, even though the choice had been entirely mine. David Owen walked with me down the back stairs into Speaker's Court, where I got into my car and was driven off in a 'parting is such sweet sorrow' mood.

On 22–23 December I assembled the new Commission, with wives, for twenty-four hours of discussion and communal (but not simple) living at Ditchley Park in North Oxfordshire. This Foreign Office-sponsored but largely Wills-family-financed establishment, mainly used for Anglo-American conferences, had been built in the 1720s and achieved fame two hundred years later when, under the ownership of Ronald Tree (Marshall Field heir, MP for Market Harborough, convenor of the pre-war Edenites group of Conservatives in the House of Commons and latterly husband of my great New York friend Marietta Tree) and on weekends of the full moon, Churchill and his entourage had used it as an alternative to Chequers at a time when they were making desperate decisions. It is a nearly perfect medium-sized eighteenth-century house.

Despite these recommendations, I am not sure that the excursion was a success. It was inconveniently close to Christmas – because there was no other time we could find. It was a summoning of the metropolitan Europeans almost to the periphery of the domain, which perhaps symbolised too brutally to the men of the core, who had run

Europe since the days of Schuman, Adenauer and De Gasperi, that an outsider was taking over in Brussels. The weather was raw and misty, and some of the wives were more struck by the coldness of the bathrooms than by the glories of Ditchley. Some progress was made with the allocation of portfolios, but the most memorable outcome was a *Financial Times* fantasy by David Watt with an Orient Express-style murder mystery. All the other twelve Commissioners had separate but convergent motives for committing the crime. The apparent victim was obviously me. The encouraging aspect was that I was only the *apparent* victim. I had duped them into thinking that there was a corpse, but eventually turned up safe and well having gained most valuable insights into their motives and relationships.

This happy outcome was not sufficient to give me a Christmas holiday of satisfied relaxation. Each morning when I awoke my first thought was that 4 January, the day of departure for Brussels, and 6 January, the day of my installation as president, were drawing inexorably nearer. I had previously believed that a measured and leisurely introduction to office, as in the American system, was a more rational and desirable arrangement than the British practice by which a new Prime Minister starts in the exhausted aftermath of an election campaign, while the old one is unceremoniously bundled out of Downing Street. After my 1976–7 experience I am not so sure. There is much to be said for plunging into office on the run, as I had done in a small way in 1964, and learning to act quickly and decisively because the momentum of events leaves one with no alternative, rather than having too long to hover apprehensively on the brink.

# CHAPTER TWENTY-FIVE

## *Monetary Union Reproclaimed*

My first six months in Brussels were not a success. I regarded them as depressing at the time, and I see no reason in retrospect to change my view. This does not mean that there were not minor achievements and periods of temporary uplift. But they were outweighed by more frequent days of frustration and a vague but overhanging apprehensiveness. I felt I had no clear objective, and feared that even if I had one I would not be particularly well qualified to achieve it. This made me uneasy during much of January/July 1977. At the end of that year I wrote: 'Certainly my mood for the greater part [of 1977] . . . was such that I would not have made the decision to go to Brussels had I been able to see things in advance. The job is more difficult to get hold of and less rewarding than I thought. Also in many ways I am not particularly well suited to do it, lacking patience, perhaps at times resilience, certainly linguistic facility. . . .' However, I added that 'The year has been sharply divided into two parts. . . . Since 5 September, the date of return from the holidays, although there have been setbacks, my sense of direction (provided by Economic and Monetary Union) and morale have improved greatly.'[1]

The first month I look back on as a numb period, comparable with my first weeks in the army on the frozen parade grounds or in the fuggy Nissen huts surrounding the pinnacled extravagance of Alton Towers. My reactions were not peculiarly slow or my performance unusually wooden during these early Brussels weeks. I worked hard and quickly, I delivered some adequate speeches in my normal style, and made a lot of downbeat jokes to those closely around me. But I find it difficult to relate what happened then to my normal scale of experience. On our second Saturday Jennifer and I drove off for the first time alone, without driver or staff, went to Namur, walked around the Vaubon citadel above the junction of the Sambre and the Meuse in the late morning, and lunched in a good bourgeois restaurant on the

456

*quai*. It could hardly have been a more normal weekend expedition. It is fixed in my memory, however, like some other events of the period, as outside any habitual scale of measurement, in limbo, as though I had made an expedition to some castle on the moon, or experienced it in a dream.

February brought two misfortunes, the one personal and the other political. The first and much heavier one was the death of Anthony Crosland. For the first five weeks of my presidency he had been an active Foreign Secretary of the country which held the presidency of the Council of Ministers. As a result our paths crossed several times, in Strasbourg, Brussels and London, and happily without friction. Then, on Sunday, 13 February, he was suddenly struck down. He never regained consciousness and died six days later. Denis Healey was paying a Berlaymont call on me when we heard the first news on the Monday morning, without then appreciating the full devastation of the attack. On the Wednesday David Owen, Crosland's deputy but not expecting the succession, was also in Brussels. He left no room for doubt. 'He said he regarded Tony as morally and mentally dead; it was settled; there was no question; he would probably live only about forty-eight hours; he might live longer but there could be no possibility of recovery.'[2]

Nevertheless when the final news arrived its impact was not diminished, the more so because of a strange coincidence which I recorded at the time. I was by then in Rome, on my inaugural visit to Italy:

I awoke about 6.30, having had a vivid dream about Tony being present and his saying in an absolutely unmistakable, clear, rather calm voice, 'No, I am perfectly all right. I am going to die, but I'm perfectly all right.' Then, at about 8 o'clock we had a telephone call from the BBC saying that he had died that morning, curiously enough at almost exactly the same moment that I awoke from my dream about him.[3]

Having done a brief BBC tribute I had to leave for L'Aquila, and made myself write a *Sunday Times* obituary during the drive. Writing about him brought 'the immense closeness of our earlier relationship flooding back into my mind',[4] and the day in the Abruzzi and indeed the whole Italian visit passed under a heavy shadow. Although there had been many contretemps and mutual irritations in our political relationship of the previous ten years, he remained, as I described him in Chapter 2, the most exciting friend of my life, and I have missed him greatly in the subsequent years.

A week later a tiresome and in some ways ludicrous dispute blew up with Valéry Giscard d'Estaing, who, it will be recalled, was the first sponsor of my presidency. This issue came to dominate that spring, and continued to let off diminishing reverberations throughout my four

years of office. Fifteen months earlier Giscard had inaugurated a series
of 'intimate' meetings between the leaders of the Western world. He
had brought together at Rambouillet the heads of government of the
United States, Germany, Britain and Japan, with Italy added reluctantly at the last moment. In June 1976, President Ford had responded
almost too quickly by organising a second meeting in Puerto Rico,
to which Canada had been added at the request of the Americans.
There had also been a move away from the informal country-house
gathering, which Giscard (perhaps I did the same at Ditchley) had
sought to contrive at Rambouillet, towards the international circus
trappings of more recent Western Economic Summits.

There had been considerable feeling amongst the little five of the
European Community that Ortoli, my predecessor as president, ought
to have been present in Puerto Rico. The gatherings were specifically
'economic' and not political or military in their intent. The countries
of Western Europe had charged the Community with much of the
responsibility for conducting and co-ordinating their economic policies,
particularly but not only in the field of trade relations. It was thus
perverse and divisive for four of them to go off and try to settle matters
with the Americans and the Japanese, leaving the co-ordinating body in
the dark and five of the member states unrepresented. There had been
some suggestion that Ortoli ought simply to have packed his suitcase
and arrived forcefully, even if uninvited, at the Summit. However,
no invitation was forthcoming, and Ortoli, wisely, did not attempt
to gate-crash. The issue left a scar, but also a settled determination
on the part of the little five, who were supported by Italy and less
wholeheartedly by Germany, that there should be no repetition of
the crime.

A repetition of the Summit itself was inevitable, and by the time I
took office one had been firmly arranged for May 1977, in London.
What had not been settled was whether I would be present. Ortoli's
absence had unfairly been seen as a blow to his prestige and to that
of the Commission. Part of the role I was expected to perform was
to restore that prestige. My credibility as an effective new president
was therefore at stake. But there was more to the issue than pride
or position. The little five regarded my determination to get there
as an essential test of whether I was to be a true spokesman of the
Community as a whole or a lackey to the big countries, from one of
which I came and by another of which (France) my appointment had
been initiated.

Almost independently of my own views, I therefore had no choice
but to fight for a place at the London meeting. And when Giscard,
at the conclusion of my first Elysée call upon him as President of the
Commission on 28 February, announced with a silken politeness that

he was equally resolved the other way a battle between us became inevitable. It lasted for a month and consumed a good deal of time and even more emotional energy. The outcome was a partial victory for me (I was allowed to attend half the London meeting), which almost inevitably led on to a full subsequent victory, for there was no argument about my attending all of the Bonn Summit in the following year, and the position of the President of the Commission has never since been challenged.

My partial 1977 victory was based on solid support from Italy and the little five (but none from the British Government) aided towards the end by the German Chancellor's willingness to persuade Giscard to accept a compromise. Schmidt's motives for wearily doing this were probably a mixture of desire to help me, to maintain his European credentials with my six supporting countries, and not to run into trouble with the Bundestag, where there was a cross-party desire for Community representation. The battle, like most, was won only at a price. It used up some, but not much, of my capital with Schmidt. More seriously it produced a long-term deterioration in the relationship between Giscard and me (interrupted by a brief and cautious EMS-occasioned second honeymoon in the summer of 1978), which mattered more to me than it did to him.

Yet with the benefit of hindsight, I cannot see that I could or should have accepted defeat on the issue. What I can see is a little more merit in Giscard's position. At the time I could see none. Now I can understand his wanting to defend the semi-spontaneous intimacy of the new forum for Western leaders which he had successfully launched. It was a formula which he and his friend Schmidt particularly liked, because they were the best at it. Already he had been forced to admit first Italy and then Canada. Now there was me. Furthermore, the Americans, with their need for back-up, were already making the meetings more bureaucratic, and the Commission was famous for bureaucracy. Where was it to stop? The Australians were already knocking at the door. The Spaniards might soon do so too. And was the Prime Minister of one of the little five, when his country held the presidency of the European Council, also to be admitted?

If Giscard had taken the issue in these quantitative and practical terms he might have got more support, certainly from Schmidt and maybe from Jimmy Carter, who in the battle as fought was a staunch ally of mine, and would also have removed some of the personal and ideological heat. However, his status-conscious and schematic mind did not see things in these terms. Instead he propounded theory in a condescending way. His central syllogism was that the Summit was a meeting of sovereign governments, the Commission was not a sovereign government, and therefore manifestly could not participate.

This, apart from being nonsense, as subsequent events have shown, struck deep at the heart of Community doctrine, and indeed sits ill with the advanced European position which Giscard has taken up since leaving office. In the Elysée, while he had a subtle and sometimes constructive mind, he was almost as reluctant to surrender national powers to European authority as were the British governments of James Callaghan and Margaret Thatcher. He was however more skilful at not allowing France to be consistently isolated, and he had the great advantage of his friendship with Helmut Schmidt. At that time the effects of this could be observed spreading downwards like water seeping from the surface to the roots of a plant, and thereby being institutionalised into a continuing Franco-German partnership.

The pattern of European Councils, at which Schmidt changed seats with his Foreign Minister so that he and Giscard could always be next to each other, like two 'best friends' who insisted on sharing the same double school desk, was not repeated at lesser Councils of Ministers or meetings of officials. It nevertheless became true at all these meetings that both the French and the Germans would go to great lengths to avoid contradicting each other in semi-public. Their natural approaches were often different, on any protectionist/free-trade issue for example, but they would try hard to reconcile their differences bilaterally and *pas devant les petits pays* (a category in which Britain and Italy, for differing reasons, were in danger of being included). As time went on I increasingly found that the best way to avoid one of these two leaders of Europe holding up a consensus (there was no majority voting in those days) on some medium-grade or lesser issue was not to appeal to them across the Council table but to go to the other partner (more frequently the Germans for the French were the more obstructive) and get them privately to persuade their friends to come off it.

Not unnaturally no surge of morale followed from my partial Summit victory. Extracting an invitation by stubborn complaint is rarely a recipe for enjoying the party. And as that uncertain spring of 1977 led into a still more dismal summer my spirits went to the lowest point of my presidency, and to one of the lowest of my life so far. It was a horrible contrast with my enthusiastic anticipation of a year before. Pathetic fallacy played a full role. I have always been too weather-influenced, but never more so than in my first Berlaymont summer. One of the few advantages of working in that architectural monstrosity was that if one was lucky enough to have a large room on the thirteenth floor its windows commanded a great deal of sky. The trouble in 1977, in contrast with the great drought year of 1976, was that the Brussels sky was hardly ever even partially blue. There were seventeen consecutive days in June on which the sun never once appeared, which I believe must be a record for the midsummer month in any normal climate. The Belgian weather is by no means uniformly awful. Two of the four autumns were long and spectacular, and I preferred the rather colder winters with more persistent snow than in London, but the summers were all a notch worse than the English ones, with 1977 in a class by itself and greatly contributing to my general gloom.

The nadir was a little later than the June cloud-tent, on Saturday, 16 July, to be exact. I recorded it in an entry which did not survive into the published *European Diary* in the following terms:

I awoke feeling already late Julyish.* . . . After a very desultory morning's work Jennifer and I went to picnic in the Forêt de Soignes near Groenendaal. A nice place to picnic, but slightly too many people and dogs about; weather not very good, just tolerable. However, the expedition was rather spoilt by buying the *Economist* on the way and reading a particularly disobliging article (it was not malevolent, which made it worse, just deeply discouraging) about my first six months.

I record this dismayed and certainly not glorious day for three reasons. First, because of the vividness with which it remains in my mind. Second, because of the reflections it provokes on why some press criticism bites and some does not. It is in my view a function of whether the criticism is near the bone, of what is the repute and audience of the paper in which it appears, and of whether one reads it at approximately the same time that others of importance in one's life may be doing so too. Thus a blunderbuss attack which is miles wide of the mark can usually be taken with equanimity – Crossbencher in the old *Sunday Express* used to specialise in this sort of noisy but harmless bombardment. Its attacks were extreme but delivered with a sort of cheerful irrelevance which made them almost unobjectionable. An attack which coincides with one's own doubts is much more disturbing. But even in these circumstances the audience remains important. I have never cared much what the *Sun* said about me, except perhaps when I was fighting an election, for the non-heroic reason that the feedback to me from its readers has been negligible. The *Economist* is obviously a different proposition from the *Sun*. As it happens I am not a dedicated reader of the *Economist*, despite the narrow margin by which I missed becoming its editor in 1963, regarding it as essentially a journal for foreigners. But it was precisely this direction of its beam which made me peculiarly depressed by its view in July 1977. For

* A well-known British political condition which, aided by sterling and other crises, has produced some notable misjudgements and famous last rows of summer.

anglophone Europeans in Brussels (and maybe in the Elysée and the Bundeskanzlei as well) the British press *was* the *Economist*. Most of my Commissioners and all the permanent representatives would read this British appraisal of my first six months.

This leads me on to another aspect of politicians' vanity vis-à-vis the press. It makes a vast difference whether you are reading something disagreeable at approximately the same time that others are doing so too. If, after say a month's absence abroad, your attention is drawn to an old attack, its effect is small. You know that nobody else is reading it at the same time. It is over. It has no more vitality than a few curled leaves in a gutter. But read on or close to the day of publication its capacity to depress is infinitely greater. Press criticism is more effective in causing private pain in politicians than in influencing public perception of them. This does not mean that it should not be made. What it does mean is that kind friends should refrain from drawing the attention of the subject to disagreeable articles which he has been lucky enough to miss. There is nothing to be done about them, and therefore no point. 'Save me, oh, save me, from the candid friend', one of the quartet of adages which Canning put into the English language (a remarkable score), is not only the most heartfelt but also the most sagacious of the four.

The third reason is that the day of the Forêt de Soignes picnic and the *Economist* effusion was another classic example (see Chapter 14) of the darkest hour being that before the dawn. After moaning under the beech trees I was given a great talking to by Jennifer, and began to feel that if I wanted to escape from these doldrums rather than wallowing in self-pity I had better strike out with some major new initiative. The Europe of the Community was bogged down at that stage. The March European Council in Rome had been dominated by the peripheral issue of my presence at the Western Economic Summit. The late-June one in London was even less inspiring. It was the most negative of all the twelve that I attended. Giscard and Schmidt, who supported each other on every point which came up, were firmly in control of Europe, but for the moment they had no direction in which they wished to take it. They were rather hostile to Callaghan, whom they saw as off-shore from Europe, too attached to the unesteemed President Carter, and running an ineffective economy to boot. They thought he was dragging his feet on the British legislation for direct elections to the European Parliament and they were disinclined to help him to get the JET nuclear-fusion project for the United Kingdom or to be sympathetic to British complaints about the UK's budgetary contribution, an issue which was just beginning to raise its head. They thought that Britain was always wanting to renegotiate something.

Towards Italy and the little five they were also sullen. Nor were they helpful towards the Commission. Giscard was irritated at the outcome of his joust with me over the Summit, and Schmidt was always potentially critical of it as an institution. He had a prejudice against Ortoli, who as my senior colleague accompanied me to European Councils, and at this one was more prominent than usual because our main proposition was a new Community loan fund which, when we eventually got it into place after a subsequent Council, rightly became known as the 'Ortoli facility'. In London however it received a negative response from both the big two, in spite or because of support from the other seven. The Franco-German axis was working smoothly internally, but temporarily it was doing no good for Europe.

A new initiative was therefore manifestly necessary. But what direction should it take? I was much influenced by the advice of Jean Monnet, given both publicly and privately. On at least two occasions his ideas had been spectacularly successful in gaining the initiative, and in the second case he had done so by rebounding from setback and switching from one blocked avenue to another which was more open. The successful inauguration of the Coal and Steel Community in 1951 had been followed by the crashing halt to the plan for a European Defence Community in 1954. By the following year the Messina Conference was meeting to plan the Economic Community, and by 1957 the Treaty of Rome was signed. The lesson he taught me was always to advance along the line of least resistance provided that it led in the right general direction.

It was against this background, in the last two weeks of July, that I came firmly to the conclusion that the most open axis of advance for the Community in the circumstances of 1977 lay in reproclaiming the goal of monetary union. This was a bold but not an original step. There was advantage in both attributes. The boldness meant that it was not reactive but an unmistakable attempt to break out and mount an offensive. The lack of originality meant that I had some Community mythology on my side and was not, as a brash newcomer from a new member state, offering a journey in a direction the old Six had never contemplated. At least since the 1970 Werner Report (named after the then Prime Minister of Luxembourg) 'economic and monetary union' had been a proclaimed early objective of the Community. But no obvious progress had been made towards it, and in a curious way the Janus-like title had the effect of making rapid advance less likely. If economic convergence and monetary integration were never to move more than a short step ahead of each other there was no place for three-league boots.

I decided that there was a better chance of advance by qualitative leap than by cautious shuffle. And such a leap was desirable both to get the blood of the Community coursing again after the relative stagnation of the mid-1970s and on its merits – because it could move Europe to a more favourable bank of the stream. The era of violent currency fluctuations, which had set in with the end of the Bretton Woods system in 1971, had coincided with the worsening of Europe's relative economic performance. In the 1960s, with fixed exchange rates, the Europe of the Six had performed excellently, at least as well as America or Japan. In the mid-1970s, with oscillating rates, it had performed dismally. Nor was this surprising. For the other two main economies the fluctuations had been external, affecting only relationships across oceans. For the Community they had been viscerally internal, with the French franc and the D-mark diverging from each other as much as either had done from the dollar or the yen.

Some time in that last half of July, not a normally favourable time of the year for forward decision-taking, I settled on the desirability of announcing a monetary initiative in the autumn. I cannot remember a particular moment when my mind became so set. But by the time I got to 2 August, when I assembled my *cabinet* plus a few other advisers at East Hendred for a 'beginning of the holidays' day-long strategy meeting, I was more anxious to rally them for a battle on which I had already decided than to have an uncommitted discussion about whether it should be fought at all. Fortunately, Michael Emerson, who was our monetary expert, was just as committed as I had become, and his knowledge and intellectual quality plus my *ex officio* authority had no difficulty in carrying the day. The old sweats of previous campaigns, notably Renato Ruggiero (later Italian Minister of Foreign Trade), who had become my spokesman and head of information services after being George Thomson's director-general in charge of regional policy, were amused by our presumptuous boldness, but not hostile.

The next significant dates were 17–18 September, when I balanced the East Hendred 'beginning of the holidays' meeting of my *cabinet* with a 'new term' forty-eight hours at a hotel in the Ardennes for the whole Commission. This Commission weekend proved a considerable success and was repeated in each of the three subsequent autumns. Getting Commissioners together away from Brussels made possible about fifteen hours of serious discussion, without the interruption of messages from *cabinets* which were a constant feature of our Wednesday Berlaymont meetings, and was also on balance good for improving the social cohesion of our multi-national (and multi-lingual) Commission.

On this first occasion my main interest was to get the endorsement by the Commission of a monetary union paper which I had written a few days beforehand. We spent Saturday on a number of other subjects principally related to the applications to join of the three recently liberated Mediterranean former dictatorships, Spain, Portugal and Greece, and did not come to monetary union until the Sunday morning. Ortoli was the vital passenger to get on board. There were three reasons for this. He was a naturally cautious person, my initiative meant an invasion by me of the area covered by his portfolio, and he had a vested interest in defending the old gradualist approach, which had been that consistently pursued, even if without any obvious success, by the previous Commission under his presidency.

At the beginning of the Sunday-morning session Ortoli was noticeably jumpy. So was I. He opened defensively. As the morning wore on, his essential niceness and loyalty made him wish to see the best in my scheme, and he advanced sufficiently to give it a sceptical blessing. That left only two in opposition: Haferkamp, who as the holder of the Economic and Monetary portfolio in the previous Commission was also wedded to the old approach; and Burke, the Irish Commissioner, who launched into a principled defence of monetary sovereignty which was worthy of Mrs Thatcher's best rearguard defences. There was a double irony in his position. First, it expressed a yearning rather than a defence of what existed, for the Irish between the proclamation of the Free State in 1922 and 1977 had never enjoyed monetary sovereignty. They had always been tin cans on the tail of the Bank of England. Second, the move which he resisted, when it led on to the European Monetary System, gave the Irish Central Bank its first opportunity to escape from the tutelage of Threadneedle Street. When Britain decided to stay out, Ireland decided to come in, and the punt had the first freedom to diverge from the pound for several centuries.

These two apart, and with Ortoli trying to make loyalty triumph over scepticism, the Commission was strongly favourable. Davignon, Gundelach, Natali, Vredeling, Tugendhat, Giolitti and even the previously disaffected Brunner spoke with enthusiasm. They wanted an initiative, and this, they thought, was the best they were likely to get. This corner was therefore satisfactorily turned, although there was some internal Commission difficulty later that autumn.

The next steps were to prepare the ground amongst governments and publicly to launch the initiative. The first I did both in a series of bilateral contacts and at the Foreign Ministers' regular six-monthly informal weekend on 8–9 October, again in the Ardennes. There, under the helpful chairmanship of Henri Simonet, who had succeeded to his country's Foreign Ministry about the time that Belgium had succeeded Britain in the presidency of the Council of Ministers (which led immediately to the Commission operating in a more encouraging atmosphere), I did a twenty-minute exposition of my ideas on monetary union. 'This was not at all badly received round the table,' I wrote at the time, 'notably (as one would expect) by Ireland, Italy, Belgium, Luxembourg, but also by Denmark, Holland

and even Genscher for Germany. David Owen* was sceptical, but not particularly hostile or indeed particularly informed.'[5]

The reasons for noting with faintly surprised pleasure the attitudes of Denmark, Holland and above all Germany were that Denmark was traditionally cautious of anything beyond a 'Europe of packages' in which they could freely sell cheese;† that The Netherlands while a high priest of the European creed was also a jealous guardian of the strength of its currency; and that Germany was the key to the success of any monetary advance, while Schmidt, as I have noted, had been in a negative mood during the summer and was preoccupied for much of the autumn by the threat (and reality) of terrorism within the Federal Republic. The dog that did not bark (one way or the other) was France, but the British Government was always willing to play a surrogate Gaullist role. Hence my lack of surprise that David Owen, my acolyte in the Labour Party European battles of the early 1970s, should be cool.

The public launching took place in Florence on 27 October. I was engaged to deliver at the European University Institute the first in a yearly series of Jean Monnet lectures, and this seemed from a variety of points of view an eminently suitable occasion for my purpose. The lecture had the right name and came at the right time in the right place. Britain or France would have been wrong as geographical locations. But a big country was probably better than a small one. And a famous non-capital city with a banking history had much to commend it. The alternative would have been to go straight to the heart of the citadel at Frankfurt. I judged this as over-bold to the extent of being counter-productive. An investing move was necessary rather than a direct assault on such a fortress. And the Italian Government could be counted upon to provide a supporting base on the way. '*Certamente,*' Giulio Andreotti said in Rome the next day when I asked him whether I could count on the support of his government for my Florence ideas. It was better than the *Economist*, which under the heading 'A Bridge Too Far' dismissed them as utopian. This was irritatingly patronising as their complaint of the summer had been that I was not providing enough direction for the future. However, I had no reason to complain at the outcome. Their July article had been a factor in stimulating me to action, or at any rate to words. And these October words in Florence, while they proclaimed the desirability of a grand suspension bridge

---

* He had received the great promotion to Foreign Secretary following Crosland's death in February 1977.

† There was an old Brussels jibe at the time of Denmark's (and Britain's) first application that 'Mr Krag (then Danish Prime Minister) does not want to join Europe. What he wants is to sell cheese.'

which has only recently become a practical probability for the 1990s, led on directly to a serviceable and durable little temporary job being thrown across the river within eighteen months. This was almost a record for words becoming action through the slow-moving machinery of the European Community.

Such speed of response looked unlikely during the remainder of 1977. There was an immediate small dividend in the shape of a noticeable improvement in my standing amongst the committed European *militants*. The next week when I gave a brief address to a European Federalists' Conference in Brussels I noted that the enthusiasm of my reception was markedly different from what I would have expected a few weeks earlier and that this could be attributed only to the Florence initiative. But there was no echoing applause from the Elysée or the Bundeskanzlei, let alone Downing Street. Cheysson reported on 4 November that Giscard had said to him: 'Jenkins has put forward his monetary-union hobby horse. I agree in theory, I am not sure it is practical, but it is a good thing he should have said it.'[6] That was better than it might have been.

Schmidt, whom I went to see in Bonn on 10 November, was full of Teutonic gloom, occasioned by a Lufthansa hijacking and the kidnapping and murder of the prominent industrialist, Hans-Martin Schleyer, but spilling over into wider issues. He was proud of having kept the German garden tidy (these terrorist incidents apart) but it was becoming a walled garden and so maybe was the whole of Western Europe. It needed a lead, as did the whole world, but he insisted that a German Chancellor could not give it. Germany was at once too big and too small, at any rate too much resented because of its past. (The implied criticism here was of Carter on the one hand for not leading with the inherent strength of the United States and of the Benelux countries for lecturing Schmidt for lack of adequate European fervour from their little pulpits.) I urged him at least not to throw cold water on monetary union when he could not see an alternative way forward himself. He half agreed that he would not. He was in favour of monetary union in principle, he said, but not if it meant German inflation going to 8 per cent. I did not dissent from that. It was a long and friendly talk, but I had to be content with this distinctly less than ringing endorsement.

I then became locked into an internal Commission dispute with Ortoli. As is often the case with disputes it was nominally about form, but the formal argument cloaked a difference of substance. We needed to submit a Commission paper on monetary union for the European Council which was fixed for early December in Brussels. Ortoli wanted it to be in the traditional Commission form, outlining a centipede's advance towards EMU, which, *mutatis mutandis*, had been submitted many times before. I wanted it to be short and sharp (which would offer the prospect that some heads of government might read it themselves) and manifestly breaking new ground in accordance with my Florence speech. We had an inconclusive discussion about this on 8 November, which resulted in our respective *cabinets* being deputed to meet together and see if they could square the circle. Not unnaturally they failed, and when I returned to Brussels on the evening of Sunday, 13 November, from a three-day 'opening of negotiations' visit to Portugal I was met at the airport by Michael Emerson, who reported impasse and was in a cataclysmic mood.

I saw Ortoli alone for one and a half hours the next morning and for another hour at six in the evening without making much progress. The morning meeting I described in my diary as *pénible*. At the evening one I said that if you wanted to move people's minds it was better to shock them than to bore them (with the unspoken implication that Ortoli preferred to do the reverse), while he said that he was not prepared to play Martha to my Mary (which was an odd way of putting it, for precisely what I was urging him to do was to give up being such an obsessively tidy Martha). In spite of these pleasantries we parted on good terms, although without a solution, which was more of a problem for me than for him, because I was trying to make a new move, and he was not.

My position was superficially strong. I could easily vote Ortoli down in the Commission meeting on the paper, which, it being a Parliament week, was due to take place at Strasbourg on the Wednesday. Both the La Roche-en-Ardennes meeting in September and subsequent soundings left me in no doubt that this was so. But the price of doing it would be heavy, even if questions of personal relations were left aside. It would be difficult in any event to persuade enough governments to support an initiative. If it were presented (as the paper would have to be) to the Economic and Financial Council by a bruised and disaffected Ortoli, and then brought before the European Council by me with a glowering Ortoli sitting alongside and the knowledge of a split Commission in everybody's mind, the chances of success would be negligible. After a talk with Davignon, who favoured compromise, I took the problem home with me and half played with it during a typical Rue de Praetère dinner party and overnight.

I had to decide before flying to Strasbourg at 9.00 the next morning. I therefore had a meeting of the core of my *cabinet* at the airport, and resolved in favour of compromise. Crispin Tickell and Michael Emerson went back to the Berlaymont to get the best compromise they could. Hayden Phillips and I went to Strasbourg, bumping through that curiously and almost constantly agitated slice of airspace over the European centres of Brussels, Luxembourg and Strasbourg in the low spirits associated with having chosen anticlimax rather than conflict. The Commission on the following day accentuated this mood. They had turned up expecting to see a cock-fight – Cheysson in particular, who for once would have broken the French front and voted with me – and when the cocks would not fight went away disappointed and muttering. It was the one low point of my monetary union campaign of that autumn, but I nonetheless think that I was right not to force the issue with Ortoli. Commission papers did not much matter, particularly if they were kept so dull that they were read only at adviser level. A major Commission split would have mattered. And, however muted because jumbled the paper was, all the players in the European game knew that I was banging the monetary drum.

The European Council, for which all this was a preparation, when it met on 5–6 December, was neither a disaster nor a success. I opened with a thirty-minute presentation. The Prime Ministers of Italy, Belgium, Holland, Ireland and Denmark (the last an unexpected bonus) responded enthusiastically. That left three major countries to pronounce. Oddly, Callaghan was the most friendly. He was warmly complimentary to me in private and nicely so around the table. I am not sure he was much engaged. He looked at the debate from outside. It was like a farmer judging a pig show rather than a statesman settling the future of his country. Giscard was cool. He specifically said that he 'accepted' the Commission paper, but whether this meant anything more than Carlyle's interlocutor accepting the universe I was not sure. Schmidt was more reserved. He was rambling and seemed to be struggling with himself to keep his November promise to me and not be as sceptical as his instinct prompted him to be.

At this European Council we got through our Community loans scheme, which had been frustrated in June, renewed and fixed the size of the Regional Fund for the next three years and settled one or two long-running semi-technical disputes. The mood was better than six months before, and while my monetary union initiative had not been offered anything like a safe passage it had not been shot down in flames. Enough support had been given for my continuing campaign to be taken seriously and not written off as an unrealistic flailing of the arms. On this basis I went to Bonn in the week following the European Council and addressed a meeting of about 350 organised by the German Institute of Foreign Affairs. A range of politicians from Richard von Weizsäcker, the future President of the Bundesrepublik, to Horst Ehmke, a policy guru of the SPD (who was the most critical), were present. After my speech there was close questioning for an hour. This was testing, particularly as Bonn was the place which counted for this enterprise and in which I could not afford to be unconvincing. At least interest was shown.

In London two weeks later I proselytised an array of gryfons of British industry, including the heads of Unilever, Shell, Dunlop, ICI and Imperial Tobacco, with whom Edwin Plowden, then himself the chairman of Tube Investments, had kept me in touch since my days as Chancellor. They were all in favour of monetary union but did not believe that politicians would ever promote anything so sensible. I half agreed with them. At the end of 1977, five months after the choice of route and two months after the Florence lecture, I thought that the reproclamation of monetary union had done well in providing me with a message, but I was far from confident that it was going to provide Europe with a monetary advance.

For the first two months of 1978 there was no significant development. I harangued the Parliament on my favourite subject and also visited the heads of government of France, Denmark, Belgium and Ireland. Then, on 28 February, I motored to Bonn for a routine meeting with Schmidt. I did not attach particular importance to the occasion, as is indicated by the fact that I did not take Crispin Tickell with me. He and I gave a farewell luncheon for the Chinese ambassador *comme chez soi* (it is curious how in those days we thought of the Chinese as much more friendly, civilised and liberal than were the Russians). Crispin then went to his office to get on with the serious work of preparing the agenda for the next day's Commission, while I tore down the autobahn, accompanied only by his young Luxembourgeois assistant, to be in time for my 5.30 appointment with Schmidt. He, for once, was almost on time, and we talked alone for two hours. He bounded into the subject most on my mind. In my diary I recorded him as saying:

You may be shocked, you may be surprised at what I intend to do, but as soon as the French [Assemblée Nationale] elections are over [12 March for the first round, 26 March for the second], probably at Copenhagen [where a European Council was due on 7–8 April] – assuming that the elections go all right and there aren't any Communists in the French Government – then I shall propose, in response to the dollar problem, a major step towards monetary union; to mobilize and put all our currency reserves into a common pool, if other people will agree to do the same, and to form a European monetary bloc. There will be great risk . . . if it all goes wrong, then maybe the Community will fall apart. Do you think it is worthwhile?[7]

The last question was like asking the Pope, or, as that is perhaps too grand a self-designation, the Cardinal Secretary of the Holy Office, whether he was in favour of Catholicism. I shall never forget how my heart leaped during that exposition. It was one of the few occasions in my life when that cliché could justifiably be used. It transformed the prospect. What had been launched in October with at best a 20 per cent chance of success suddenly zoomed in February to having a 70 per cent chance. Germany was the key country on any monetary question. Schmidt, with his powerful, mercurial personality, could be both a considerable wet blanket and one of the most inspiring allies I have ever known. His announcement of his conversion transformed my physical as well as my intellectual morale. In principle at that time I jogged for twenty minutes each morning. I had not done so for ten days owing to ankle trouble. The next morning, despite a late return to Brussels followed by a midnight supper with Crispin and Laura Grenfell, to whom I poured out the news of the extraordinary turn-up for the book, I was up and on the piste. Schmidt's stimulus was powerful enough for me rashly to set aside my tendon weakness – rashly because it made it much worse. There was no symbolism in this for monetary advance thereafter went from strength to strength.

What had moved Schmidt from his reluctantly benign scepticism of December to his almost rash enthusiasm of late February? It will require a sharply self-analytical autobiography or a detailed and closely informed biography of Schmidt to provide an authoritative answer. My guess, only of limited value, is as follows. First, Schmidt was a lurcher. By this I mean that he could go through negative periods and then suddenly be brought out of them by an idea and pursue it with the utmost verve. Of this I rather approved, being (*pace* Crosland) something of a lurcher myself, although I did not have Schmidt's capacity either for Teutonic gloom or for moving mountains once his mind had become engaged.

Second, he had come out of a long autumn of inward-looking preoccupation with German terrorism. The incidents were severe, although less so than those which Northern Ireland has inflicted upon Britain or perhaps even than the French and the Americans have intermittently suffered. But the Federal Republic, no doubt as a desirable reaction to the horrors which took place within its borders and those of East Germany a generation before, had become preternaturally sensitive to any form of violence. When the wave subsided, Schmidt may have thought that he had overreacted, as I felt I had done to the prison escapes of 1966 and perhaps even to the Irish bombings of 1974. The natural corrective was to take an international initiative.

The third factor was the decline of the dollar. It was not vast. Between my Florence speech and this crucial Schmidt encounter it had declined from 2.30 to 2.02 D-marks, a devaluation of 12 per cent, less than either that which almost destroyed the Wilson Government in 1967 (and made me Chancellor of the Exchequer), or than that which took place under the Thatcher Government in 1984–5. The dollar was subsequently to decline much further. By September 1978 it was down to 1.76 D-marks, another 12 per cent. But already by February 1978 the fall was enough to provoke

Schmidt to add monetary slovenliness to the long list of sins by which he saw Carter devaluing his great *ex officio* position as captain of the West.

The trouble with Schmidt's attitude to America was that it was essentially romantic. He admired Roosevelt's grand suppleness and Truman's cocky firmness, the latter displayed at a time when Schmidt briefly drove a taxi cab in Boston and learned his excellent English. He had become a national politician during Eisenhower's confident if easy-going leadership of the Atlantic Alliance. Compared with me he had been less dazzled by Kennedy, but he was also less critical of Lyndon Johnson and less prejudiced against the foreign-policy achievements of Richard Nixon by the awfulness of his early campaigns. Gerald Ford he regarded as a respectable and steady figure. But Jimmy Carter he could not abide.

Exactly why I could never understand. Carter and Schmidt were rather like each other, at any rate a good deal more so than either was like Giscard, with whom Schmidt was locked not only in partnership but in friendship, and who in turn seemed to feel no antipathy for Carter beyond a certain inherited Elysée disdain for things American. Schmidt had a harder and sharper intellect than Carter and was a more critical, sometimes more cynical judge of men and events. However, Carter's weakness did not lie in his brain, which was quick, orderly and fact-absorbing. His faults, such as they were, were mainly ones of style. But Schmidt, unlike Giscard, did not care a great deal about style. He and Carter both cared much more about the substance of things than about their form. Their social origins were similar, as were their indifference to fashionable life and their broad positions in the political spectrum. But all this counted for nothing with Schmidt compared with his conviction that Carter was an inadequate leader of the Alliance, and that presiding over a degraded currency was an important symptom of his weakness.

It was one of Schmidt's most basic convictions as Chancellor that Germany, because of its past, could not provide military or political leadership. There could therefore be no question of his trying to fill the gap left vacant by Carter. Monetary matters were different. Although in the 1960s there had been cautious German resistance to the Deutschmark becoming a reserve currency (in contrast with the 'imperial' attitude of successive British govern-ments to sterling) that battle had been decisively lost and the currency had become the symbol of Germany's post-war success. The Bundesbank had replaced the Wehrmacht as the country's most famous and powerful institution, which has been a highly desirable development for the rest of the world, and indeed for

Germany. Monetary action therefore offered Schmidt the possibility of some escape from his frustration at knowing better how to run the world than did Carter or Brezhnev or Callaghan, but mostly feeling himself inhibited by his country's past from trying to do so.

# CHAPTER TWENTY-SIX

# *The Creation of the EMS*

There were five and a half weeks between my Bonn meeting with Schmidt and the European Council in Copenhagen, at which heads of government were to be informed of the monetary plans. Perhaps fortunately I was away from Brussels for an exceptionally high proportion of the interval. On 2 March I left for an Edinburgh and North-east of England visit, followed by an East Hendred weekend broken by a long monetary union interview with Brian Walden for *Weekend World*. Then I went direct from London on a five-day official visit to Canada with a New York weekend as a bonus at the end. I came back via Paris and a Parliament session in Strasbourg. The return journey was memorable for it being my first Concorde trip, and for the great bird whose neck I had come so near to wringing in 1964–5 showing one surprising attribute. It was not that it avoided jet-lag. On this occasion it proved less than averagely effective in doing this. But the 10.30 a.m. Air France from Kennedy had on board the first edition of *France-Soir*, the Paris *evening* paper which had come out with the morning eleven o'clock service from Paris, on almost the only day in my life when I wanted to spend several hours reading that unimpressive journal.

This was because it contained the detailed results of the previous day's first round of the French legislative elections, and my concern with French politics was then such that I studied them obsessively for the three-and-a-quarter-hour journey. It did not, however, require this degree of application to take in that, against the expectations a short time before, the left had not won, that Giscard would not have to share power with Mitterrand as Prime Minister, that there would be no question of Communists being in the government. Schmidt's first, somewhat uncomradely stipulation for proceeding to the creation of a European monetary bloc had therefore been met.

After barely a week back in Brussels, during which I did proselytising visits to the Prime Ministers of The Netherlands and Luxembourg and spent much of the rest of my time writing a 1500-word pre-European Council letter to them and the other heads of government (which was a way of trying to leapfrog the opaque jargon of Commission papers), I went to East Hendred for a ten-day Easter holiday and returned to Brussels only a few days before Copenhagen. The reason it was a good thing to be away so much was that Schmidt wished his grand design to be kept secret at least until Copenhagen, and that this was easier to do the less I saw of my Commission colleagues and others deep in the workings of Europe and the more I saw of those who were not so closely interested in them – Trudeau in Canada was ideal from this point of view.

The question of confidentiality was a teasing element throughout the incubation of the EMS. Schmidt was a naturally indiscreet head of government. But this did not mean that he liked other people betraying his confidences before – or sometimes even after – he had done so himself. At this stage I appeared to be almost uniquely in his confidence. Normally he first talked his European moves over with 'my friend Valéry', but in February and the first half of March Giscard was too preoccupied with his own elections to be adequately available. Schmidt therefore elevated me to be his chief foreign interlocutor, and told me in February that this uniqueness was diluted only by two or three in Germany. This was up to a point flattering but also meant that I carried a heavy responsibility if leaks occurred.

I had to steer a delicate course. I knew what a big fish I had on my monetary union line and certainly did not wish to run any risk of shaking it off with talkative clumsiness. I had the advantage of a reliably discreet *cabinet* (mostly trained in Whitehall when there was much less leaking both at ministerial and official level than is the case today), but the disadvantage of having to keep in some sort of array both the traditionally sieve-like Commissioners and the six remaining governments of the Community (beyond the French, whom Schmidt was eager to consult as soon as Giscard ceased to be preoccupied by elections, and the British, whom he was willing fully to inform as long as he thought there was a chance of Callaghan participating). But a *European* Monetary System obviously could not be made without Italy and the little five. I therefore felt a certain responsibility for keeping these governments, if not fully informed, at least somewhere in the picture. Frequently and reasonably, however, they saw no reason why they should respect secrets of which their big brothers had not bothered to inform them directly. Difficult choices about whether to inform X of what Y had said about Z consequently constituted a sometimes comical sub-plot throughout 1978.

On Friday, 7 April, I went to Copenhagen in a state of high expectation mingled with apprehension that everything might go wrong. Ortoli and I went together from Brussels in the same small plane. It was typical of the secrecy entanglements that Schmidt had been particularly importunate that I should not tell Ortoli. This was for the understandable reason that he thought Ortoli would send the news back to Paris and that it would therefore reach Giscard indirectly, whereas he attached great importance to disclosing his mind to Giscard in full and face to face, as he had done with me. But although understandable it was awkward to be asked to treat Ortoli in this way, and I compromised by giving him some broad hints of how the wind was blowing, particularly after the crucial Schmidt/Giscard encounter had taken place at Rambouillet.

In Copenhagen we went on with this cat-and-mouse game, aided by our being provided by the Danes with a considerable selection of castles around which to play it. We began with a royal lunch at the Amelienborg Castle and then moved to the Christianborg Castle for the formal opening of the European Council. It was then suggested that we ought immediately to go into a highly restricted session of heads of government and me, and for this it was ordained for no very clear reason that we should scamper off to the Marienborg Castle, twenty miles away. I assumed from this that Schmidt had decided to lead with a full presentation, and had asked for the small meeting and for the leaving of Foreign Ministers and advisers behind in the city-centre Christianborg. But no, he told me as soon as we arrived, he intended to hold his hand even in this restricted gathering until after a tripartite breakfast with Giscard and Callaghan which he had arranged for the following morning. Accordingly we went into a somewhat artificial discussion, which I opened by in effect arguing the case for the Schmidt monetary-bloc scheme but without being able to refer to it as such. Giscard then did much the same, although standing back a little more, and clearing the ground rather than starting to erect the building. He gave a very well-presented analysis of the disadvantages suffered by multi-currency Europe, compared with either America or Japan, as exchange rate fluctuations became more violent. Schmidt went into a long soliloquy, mainly about the problems of a provident Germany in an improvident world, but disclosed nothing. Even though we had not taken in Elsinore Castle, it was Hamlet without the Prince of Denmark.

Then, when we reassembled after a dinner of desultory general conversation, Schmidt suddenly and mystifyingly changed his tactics and proceeded to spill the whole beans. Perhaps he had just got bored with circumlocution. What he said was closely in line with what he had told me in Bonn in February. As I recorded it at the time:

He deployed his plans for dissolving the Snake [which linked the Benelux, Swedish and Norwegian currencies to the D-mark] in the new arrangement, using the European unit of account [the term écu had not then been invented] far more extensively, both for transactions between the member governments [and] for joint intervention against the dollar and third currencies, and possibly indeed for providing a full parallel currency, which could deal in stocks of raw materials and in which OPEC money might be encouraged to invest.[1]

The only point on which he made a small retreat from Bonn was that the proposal for the participating countries to commit *all* reserves to a common pool became one to commit *a significant proportion* of each country's dollar reserves. But he had more than made up for this by having got Giscard to be both a committed supporter and a powerfully lucid advocate of the scheme.

Callaghan was taken aback by Schmidt's presentation, although he ought not to have been, because he had been given a full rehearsal of it on a visit to Bonn two weeks before. But on this occasion, I believe, he and Schmidt had passed like two friendly ships in the night, close but not seeing or at least not listening to each other. Callaghan was intent on a pound/dollar initiative within the framework of the IMF, of which he wished to give Schmidt notice before trying it on Carter, whom he was to visit in the following week. As a result he was as inattentive to Schmidt's own scheme as Schmidt was to Callaghan's. It was a typical difference of direction in gaze between British and German leaders. There was moreover another difference, which was that Callaghan's scheme came to nothing, whereas it is difficult to exaggerate what has flowed and what continues to flow from Schmidt's scheme.

Given this unnecessary lack of preparedness, however, Callaghan handled the situation with aplomb. He expressed interest, was politely non-committal, but did not turn things down out of hand or deliver himself of any hostages to fortune. The main fear that he expressed, again a typically British reaction, was that what was proposed might appear as hostile to the dollar and thus be divisive for the Atlantic alliance. I believed that this was in reality the opposite of the truth and that few things were then more helpful to the Americans than to have some of the weight taken off the dollar, which since 1968 had staggered under the burden of being the sole lynchpin of the international monetary system. But it was understandable that Callaghan should take the point, for Schmidt in his introduction had made several side-swipes against Carter and the mismanagement of the dollar.

When we broke up at 11.30 p.m. Callaghan asked me to go back to the hotel where the British were installed and check his debriefing of his officials on exactly what Schmidt had said. It was unnecessary as his own notes were wholly accurate, but it enabled me to witness an encapsulation of British attitudes towards European initiatives. 'But it is very bold, Prime Minister,' the senior and somewhat insular Treasury official there present kept saying. 'It leaves the dollar on one side. I do not know what the Americans will say about it. It is very bold.'

So concluded the first round of the European Council's approach to the EMS. Schmidt had committed himself, and been fully supported by Giscard. Italy and the little five had been delighted. Tindemans of Belgium withdrew the proposals that he had announced he would table, saying that the Schmidt ones were better. Callaghan had kept his options open but left Schmidt with the impression that there was a real possibility, although not perhaps a probability, that he might come in. I, knowing my British, was a little more sceptical, but not much. It was agreed that further intensive work should be done before the next European Council in early July, but with a great attempt to keep it secret. Why there was this addiction to secrecy I find difficult to explain, unless it was not to embarrass Callaghan, whom Schmidt greatly wanted to bring in, although Giscard was indifferent.

At the huge press conference of about 600 journalists which followed and which was taken, in accordance with custom, by the head of government of the presiding country (Anker Jørgensen) and me, I was reported as looking extremely pleased without saying much. That, for once, meant that I had given exactly the impression I intended.

The next major staging post on the road to the EMS was the Germans succeeding the Danes in the presidency and the assembly of the European Council within a week of that event. This was a happy conjuncture. In general a big country finds it easier to achieve a constructive presidency than does a small one, both because of its greater inherent authority and because of its greater resources of official back-up. In addition Schmidt might be expected to be a more forceful chairman than the occasionally *farouche* and not fluently anglophone Jørgensen. And there was much to be said for thus enabling Schmidt to marry his commitment to his own scheme with the opportunity to drive it through.

He decided to hold this Council in Bremen, which choice no doubt expressed his preference for the more northern and outward-looking parts of Germany without appearing unduly to favour his own Hamburg, with the governing mayor of which city he was not in any event on good terms. Bremen's great sixteenth-century Rathaus provided us with the most satisfactorily intimate small room in which I ever saw the European Council meet, although the city somewhat balanced this by welcoming us with unrelenting downpours of tropical intensity.

Bremen turned out on balance and after a nasty hiccup in the middle a major success. The trouble was with the British. Callaghan was unhappy about either coming in or staying out, and his failure to see any satisfactory course made him surly. When I saw him in Downing Street on 3 July, although personally amiable, he was complaining unreasonably that Schmidt and Giscard had been doing things behind his back. They had admittedly had a bilateral meeting and their officials had produced a joint Franco-German paper (which became known as the Schulmann/Clappier paper), but he had been sent a copy of this, which was more than the little five had received, and he could hardly expect to be in the drafting seat for ordering the advance when he had not accepted the principle of a move forward. Nonetheless he was distinctly miffed and responded by refusing to come to the opening luncheon in the Bremen Rathaus. The excuse was that he had to preside over the Cabinet that morning, but it was assumed that had the wish been there this could have been more flexibly arranged. When the British did arrive they marched in in single file like a jungle expedition into hostile territory, first Callaghan, then Owen, then six or seven senior officials, then about fifteen bearers carrying twice that number of red despatch boxes, which must I felt have been more for show than use during a twenty-four-hour stay.

The afternoon session was concerned with matters other than the EMS. Then after a short adjournment the heads of government and I were reconvened, but it was not clear whether for a restricted session or for an early dinner. For some time neither could take place because Schmidt, Giscard and Callaghan did not turn up. The two good companions had been having a private go at Callaghan, but without success. Schmidt arrived with a look of doom on his face, came up to me and said, 'Things have gone very badly.' Giscard came in ten minutes later and gave the same report in substance, but in a more disengaged way and differently expressed. 'It seems,' he said, 'that Callaghan wishes to stand aside; nothing more can be done with him.'

Callaghan's mood when eventually he returned was more like Schmidt's than Giscard's. At dinner he sat at the end of the table, looking at once aloof and dejected. Indeed the whole company was thoroughly subdued, so that for the only time at a European Council dinner in my experience conversation died of its own inertia. There was neither a transaction of business nor an exchange of gossip.

After this dismal preparation our long post-prandial session (9.30 p.m. to nearly 2.00 a.m. including the final drafting) went miraculously better than there was any reason to expect. Giscard did a good opening exposition, but Callaghan remained sullen for some time and this, fortified by Schmidt's depression, had a lowering general effect. The atmosphere changed when I recited a bit of doggerel to Callaghan. It was a classic example of how small and doubtfully relevant things can affect the course of great events, made the more remarkable by the fact that what I said was at first incomprehensible to most of those present. Callaghan asked Giscard whether it was not essential that economic convergence and monetary integration did not get out of step with each other. We ought surely not to advance one without the other. It was a point of some importance for it revived the old Janus-like approach which had been such a recipe for stagnation in the Community of the mid-1970s. If I had one insight of significance it was that this was a fundamentally hobbling doctrine. If a breakthrough was to be made a monetary leap had to occur on its own, in the hope that economic convergence would thereby be assisted and would follow, but certainly not making it a prior condition.

Giscard said I had better answer Callaghan's question. Strongly though I felt on the issue, I could easily see myself getting involved in convoluted arguments which would be unpersuasive with Callaghan. Suddenly the old satirical quatrain about the Walcheren campaign of 1809 came into my mind:

> Great Chatham with his sabre drawn
> Stood waiting for Sir Richard Strachan,
> Sir Richard, longing to be at 'em,
> Stood waiting for the Earl of Chatham.

In other words, waiting for everything to advance together was a recipe for never advancing at all. Callaghan half knew the jingle, liked it (probably because of the naval association of Walcheren), desisted from the argument and immediately became in a much better frame of mind. Most of the others – at least the northern Europeans, for it was not Andreotti's style or territory – became intrigued with trying to understand it, and generally perked up. In the latter part of that night session it was possible to make remarkable progress, to draft a highly constructive introduction to the Schulmann/Clappier paper and to agree that the introduction and the paper should be published together; to accept that, while nobody had to make a definite commitment to the scheme at this stage, everybody agreed to work on *this* scheme and not to tour around the intellectual horizon; to fix 31 October as the date by which amendments or refinements should be made, so that definite decisions could be taken at the Brussels European Council in early December. I drafted a form of words which everyone, including Callaghan, accepted as a working hypothesis.

At the plenary meeting the next morning Callaghan somewhat went back on this. There was nothing wrong with having second thoughts overnight. People often do at European Councils, even on much less important matters. What was tiresome was that he challenged the accuracy of the draft, a view which was hotly contested by Giscard and by at least five Prime Ministers. All this led to a long and (for me) nerve-racking meeting. Schmidt got bad-tempered with Callaghan and Giscard became icily unyielding to any cosmetic redrafting to satisfy him, saying that he was not in favour of a papering over of cracks where real differences existed. However, we eventually got a formula which preserved most of the momentum of the night before.

I left Bremen in a high state of morale so far as the prospects for getting a European Monetary System were concerned, but with substantially diminished hope of Britain at last learning its lesson and participating in a European initiative with enthusiasm and from the beginning. Adjusting to reality, my interest became increasingly that of avoiding Britain holding up the advance of others. The achievement of Bremen was the concentration on a single scheme and the acceptance of the timetable, out of which sprang the strongly positive note which both Schmidt and I were able to strike at the press conference which followed the six-hour 'morning' session.

Although the overall pace was incredibly fast by the standards of the dilatory Community of the 1970s, the five months' gap until the next European Council left an uncomfortable amount of time for the rats to get at the scheme. The particular rats (using the word only in relation to their gnawing skill, not their characters) whose nibbling and niggling capacities I feared were Ecofin (the Council of Economic and Finance Ministers) and the central bankers. It was not the British in the shape of Denis Healey and Gordon Richardson who provided my worst worries. Richardson indeed was cautiously favourable to the EMS, and, while Healey was certainly against,* he could be contained provided the other eight remained solid. But would they? This was far from assured, particularly as the most powerful of the central bankers, Otmar Emminger, President of the Bundesbank from 1975 to 1980, had the reverse of enthusiasm for Schmidt's scheme. 'Emminger is, I fear,' I wrote on 16 October, 'anxious if he can to block the EMS and, if he cannot, to be dragged into it only by his hair, screaming and with as puny a scheme as possible.'[3]

This produced considerable hiccups and gave Healey a possible hand to play, which he did with skill. Thus at the September Ecofin there was considerable complaint that a Franco-German bilateral meeting at Aachen had settled all the details over everybody else's head, about which 'Healey made a fairly effective row'.[4] Eventually it emerged

---

* The depth of his hostile scepticism emerges even more clearly from his excellent autobiography than was apparent to me at the time.[2]

however that, whether or not the French and the Germans might have liked to have done this, they had failed to do so. The others cheered up at this and adopted by eight to one (Healey) a Belgian compromise on the main point at issue, which was whether the parity grid system or the 'basket' should be the basis for intervention.

The October meeting was worse. The Germans, led by Emminger, who ought to have been satisfied with the Belgian compromise, which was really a victory for them, tried to move to a still more hard-line position, for which they could carry only the Dutch and the Danes. As a result:

In contrast with the September . . . meeting, when there was a solid front of eight countries, with the British isolated but not too intransigent, at this meeting there were about three floating groups with different positions on a whole range of issues and, if anything, it was the Germans who were becoming isolated. . . .

Healey was [consequently] able to recover a good deal of the initiative, which he exploited skilfully to get support from Pandolfi (Italian Finance Minister) and from Colley (Irish Finance Minister) and also on some issues from Monory (French Finance Minister) and even, occasionally, from the Belgians and the Luxembourgeois.[5]

At the November meeting, however, the British position fell apart, because everybody thought that it was time to know whether they were coming in or were just preaching from outside the tabernacle. Healey, when pressed, failed to give any satisfactory answer. Nevertheless I was glad that this was the last of the series of pre-Brussels European Council Ecofin meetings. I had a sense of the cumulative risk which must have been in the minds of those who flew a series of wartime bombing missions. I had also made a hazardous sortie on 13 November when I visited (by invitation) the central-bank governors at their monthly Basle meeting and engaged with them on what was in every sense their own ground. My apprehension was not diminished by the fact that my Trans European Express broke down between Luxembourg and Metz (they do not always order these matters better in France) and that I arrived for the luncheon discussion at 2.45 instead of one o'clock. My verdict on the meeting was: 'Zylstra, the Dutchman in the chair, was very good I thought. Gordon Richardson was helpful, as one would expect him to be. Clappier said not a word, a useless and ineffective performance for Giscard's vicar at a rather crucial EMS discussion. The sceptics (predictably) were Baffi (Banco d'Italia) and Emminger. The Americans, Volcker and one other, were quite helpful. It was worthwhile and not as technically formidable as I feared it might be.'[6]

Two points of continuing relevance seem to me to emerge from the account of events between Bremen and Brussels. The first is that

Franco-German hegemony, even when as constructively exercised as it was that autumn, breeds a certain impatience and makes other countries flicker their eyes towards the possibility of a British lead, particularly when Britain is represented by as powerful a personality as Denis Healey. But when only negative points are forthcoming the eyes quickly flicker away again. The second is that the Bundesbank although strong is not all-powerful. When there is a dispute on a big issue with the German Government it is the Government which wins. The Bundesbank did not want the EMS in 1978. Schmidt did and got his way. The Bundesbank did not want a quick currency union with East Germany in 1990. Kohl did and got his way. The famous independence can be exaggerated.

Before the too-long-awaited Brussels European Council on 4–5 December, I did an unusually concentrated programme of visits to capitals. I saw the Belgian Prime Minister on 2 December, having been to Bonn the day before, Rome two days before that and Paris the day before Rome. These I judged to be the most necessary governments for last-minute consultation. The Hague and Dublin I had done earlier in the autumn. Copenhagen I felt I could leave as I had been there so much in the previous six months of the Danish presidency, and the Danes were in any event firmly on the German line on currency questions. Luxembourg I was constantly in and out of.

London I had not been to (officially) since 2 November, when I formed the impression that Callaghan was not coming in. But I was not absolutely certain. He seemed genuinely torn in his own mind, and almost plaintively asked why I thought that Giscard, without a very strong economy, did not seem to hesitate over taking the risk. I suppressed the desire to say, 'Because he does not suffer from the British disease of never co-operating fully,' which might have been counter-productive, and replied, 'Because France is much more self-confident than Britain. They believe they can make a success of things, whereas we don't.'[7] Callaghan said perhaps this was right. It was also the occasion, quoted by me in several subsequent speeches, when Callaghan vehemently denied that he was staying out because of political difficulties at home, and insisted that if he was convinced it was right for Britain he would come in whatever the political problems. 'But,' he added, 'I am nervous of being locked in at too high a rate of exchange, which will prevent my dealing with unemployment.' This animadversion was like a scissors-blade, which is of no interest without its pair. This companion was however splendidly provided by Mrs Thatcher six months later when I saw her almost immediately after her election – in the same room to add to the symmetry. She assured me that she was in principle in favour of full participation in the EMS but was 'nervous of being locked in at too low a rate of exchange, which will prevent my dealing with inflation'. In fact under both of them Britain enjoyed for several years a higher rate of unemployment and of inflation than any participating country. But at least we remained bipartisanly faithful to our national habit of never joining any European enterprise until it is too late to influence its shape. Then, when wholly predictably, we are eventually forced to apply for membership, we complain bitterly that the shape suits others better than it suits us.

Britain was not therefore in the central arena of play during this late November round of talks. Giscard was particularly dismissive. 'Not a great deal about the EMS,' I wrote after my Paris meeting with him on 27 November. 'He said it was all satisfactorily fixed: he didn't think the British would come in, but maybe from their point of view they were wise.'[8] Schmidt had more regrets about the British, but his mind too had now switched to the more open question of whether the Italians and the Irish would join. With them we would have a *European* Monetary System. Without them we would merely have an enlarged Snake.

Both these countries had a strong political desire to participate in any European advance. But their governments had convinced themselves and their informed public opinion that they needed significant help from what were curiously called 'concurrent studies' for their economies to stand the strain. Earlier in the autumn the Italians had their mind on a reform of the Common Agricultural Policy so as to make it less favourable to northern products and, maybe, more favourable to Mediterranean ones. By November, however, their attention had shifted to an increase in the Regional Fund and, more importantly, to the provision on a substantial scale of subsidised loans (that is, with interest rates well below market levels), which they wished specifically to apply to infrastructure projects in the Mezzogiorno. These subsidies would have in effect to be provided by the Germans and French with *pro rata* contributions from Benelux and the Danes. The last thing the Irish had ever been interested in was a reform of the CAP, but they were at one with the Italians in wanting the other two forms of aid.

Giscard on 27 November had accepted the idea of subsidised loans without committing himself to an amount (the Italians were asking for 800 million units of account a year in subsidies) but had dismissed by inference a Regional Fund increase. Schmidt on 30 November was more forthcoming. He contemplated an increase of 200 to 250 million units in the Regional Fund and 400 million a year in subsidies for loans. I asked him if he could bring Giscard along on these amounts Schmidt said that he was not sure but he would try, and indeed settled down to telephone him as I left the Bundeskanzlei. With Schmidt and Giscard such determination by one generally meant that the other would come along, and I felt that everything (except for the British) was in good shape for Brussels.

I got nervous in the next three days. On the Saturday I went to see Vanden Boeynants, the street-wise multiple pork butcher who was briefly Belgian Prime Minister between Tindemans and Martens, and found him sound on the main issues but expecting last-minute trouble from the French. The French Government had been defeated in the Assemblée Nationale the night before on a motion to implement the Community's sixth VAT directive. This had been brought about by an unusual alliance of Gaullists and Communists, which Vanden Boeynants shrewdly thought would make Giscard jumpy and mean. Ortoli, on the Sunday evening, was equally but more vaguely prescient. 'Everything is too well set up for the Summit,' he suddenly said. 'It is too well prepared. I think it will go wrong. They generally do in these circumstances.'9

That night I went to bed with a distinct sense of apprehension, which proved well founded. On the first day we spent seven hours of session, finishing only at 2.00 a.m., dealing with the internal mechanics of the EMS. The more difficult points and therefore important issues of the transfer of reserves were left unmentioned until the second day, which I did not think was wise. Nor was anyone asked to make a clear declaration about whether they were coming in or not. Callaghan was allowed to keep his cards close to his chest and to argue as much as anybody else about the niggling detail. Nevertheless I was not unduly dismayed over the short night of Monday/Tuesday.

The next day was much worse. Giscard climbed on Callaghan's back to block effectively and decisively the Regional Fund window. Callaghan, out of whom it had at last been prised that he was not going to participate in the central part of the EMS, the Exchange Rate Mechanism as it has since become known, nevertheless said that Britain would insist on maintaining its 27 per cent share of any increase in the Regional Fund. Giscard then said that if that were so the French, who were taking on the full burdens of the System without asking for anything special for themselves, could not contemplate giving up their quota share of any increase. To bang an extra nail in the coffin he added that if the Regional Fund were going to become more important he would have to ask for a larger French quota than their 18 per cent.

That was that. Two big countries blocking was decisive. That left subsidised loans. Against the Italian bid for 800 million units of account, Schmidt firmly proposed 400 million to be divided between Italy and Ireland, which would have been acceptable, although obviously not greeted with dancing on either the Capitoline Hill or St Stephen's Green. Giscard absolutely refused to go above 200 million. Such an obvious split within the leadership axis was unusual. Giulio Andreotti's head sank even further than usual into his body and Jack Lynch seemed on the verge of tears. Schmidt made a gloomy little speech saying that everything looked hopeless and he was no longer sure that it was worth going ahead with the EMS at all. Germany would in any event be better off without it. I said that, so far from any country being better off without it the whole Community would be in a disastrous position, far worse than if we had never launched the scheme. The sense of dismay, disaffection and falling apart would be overwhelming; we would find everything else from enlargement to the directly elected Parliament (due in six months' time) much more difficult to deal with. Giscard responded coldly that he did not share the dramatic interpretation of the President of the Commission, but I think that most of the others did.

Schmidt then announced a short adjournment, which he ought to have done before, because apart from anything else it was four o'clock and we had had no lunch. During this interval Schmidt told me that he agreed with my cataclysmic statement, but that it was no good his trying to put further pressure on Giscard because his internal position was so difficult. I dissented. Andreotti and Lynch both told me that the expectation of their public opinion was such that they did not think they could come in on the basis of the offer made. I mistakenly told Andreotti that he should see what he could do in a bilateral talk with Giscard. It was mistaken because Giscard merely brushed him off, saying that the Italians might be better advised to stay out like the British. When Andreotti said that his Government might fall whether he came in or stayed out on these terms, Giscard seemed indifferent to what happened in Rome.* It still seems to me impossible to explain what had come over Giscard at this meeting, changing him from the constructive European statesman of Copenhagen and Bremen to the narrow French shekel-counter of Brussels. It cannot surely have all been caused by one adverse vote, not on a matter of confidence, in the French Chamber.

When we reassembled the offer was somewhat improved by being made for five years rather than three, but the Italians and the Irish still went away sorrowing, not because they were rich men but because they saw themselves as the leaders of poor countries (already a bit out of date for Italy) who had been led to expect more help than they were being offered. The attitude of both sides in the dispute was in a sense ridiculous. If the French and the Germans wanted a European Monetary System it was well worth 400 million rather than 200 million to them, as the Germans had the sense to see. On the other hand an

---

* I was not of course present at this bilateral meeting, and my account comes from what Andreotti told me immediately afterwards.

extra 200 million a year shared between two recipient countries was certainly not going to make a decisive practical difference to their ability to survive in the System. It was merely going to convince their parliaments and newspapers that a successful deal had been achieved.

It had to be determined how the sharing was to be done, to which issue no attention had been paid. Schmidt asked me for a suggestion and after a brief pause I proposed a basis of two for Italy to one for Ireland. This was arbitrary but surprisingly was accepted by the Italians without protest, although their population was over ten times the size of Ireland's. But the whole amount was so small that the Irish share would have been totally derisory if split in accordance with population. As the departing position of both the Italian and Irish Prime Ministers remained that of being unable to join on the basis offered they did not perhaps take too seriously the division of the subsidies they were not going to accept.

There were two further bizarre developments before the dismal conclusion of the European Council at 9.30 p.m. Both of them emanated from Giscard and concerned the écu or European Currency Unit, which was just about to be born. The Commission had put forward what we regarded as a largely technical proposal for introducing the écu into agricultural pricing. Giscard would not agree without getting into the communiqué a declaration that no new Monetary Compensatory Amounts – the device by which member countries were allowed to vary their exchange rates for agricultural products from those which prevailed for other transactions – should be created and that those which existed should be dismantled quickly. At first I could not see what he was up to. Then I feared that this was a device for giving French farmers a big price increase by the back door, that is to say by devaluing the green franc so as to bring it nearer to the ordinary franc. As a counter-ploy I succeeded in getting into the communiqué a semi-counteracting device. It was all most convoluted stuff which left most of the tired heads of government bemused. I thought that Giscard must be trying to get in a paving text which could be used for some manoeuvre in the Agricultural Council. What I still did not realise was that it was in fact a paving move for holding up the coming into operation of the EMS on 1 January 1979.

In view of this, Giscard's second late intervention was even more mystifying. As we went round the table for concluding speeches, Schmidt tired and depressed, but not quite as depressed as I was, the Italians and the Irish sad, the British trying hard not to gloat at the prospect of things falling apart, Giscard suddenly assumed the air of a visiting dignitary at a school prize-giving and announced that as the écu had played a splendid role in French history and was now a symbol of European unity he was going to have some specially minted in gold and silver (gold for the Prime Ministers, silver for the Foreign Ministers) for presentation to members of the Council. This fell like a soggy suet pudding on the already heavy atmosphere.

After this dismal anticlimax of a European Council (how right Ortoli had been) the affairs of Europe retreated behind an opaque screen in a way that I have never known them do before or since. The key and highly disadvantageous development was the new and growing sullenness on the part of the French Government. This was increased but not created by a row over the Community's budget which blew up while I was on a mid-December five-day visit to America. Almost as a last fling the old indirectly elected Parliament passed the budget in a form which had not been agreed with the Council of Ministers and which at least three member states (France, Britain and Denmark) therefore regarded as illegal. Emilio Colombo, the Italian President of the Parliament, nonetheless certified it as valid, which was within his constitutional rights. The Commission therefore accepted the budget as a fact. We would endeavour to effect a reconciliation between Council and Parliament, but in the meantime we would implement the disputed budget. There had been some irregularities in the Parliament's conduct, but we were going to compound them by rejecting Colombo's certificate and piling one irregularity upon another.

This drove the French Government into a state of affronted hysteria. After a meeting which I had on 19 December with Jean François-Poncet, the usually good-mannered and Euro-enthusiastic French Foreign Minister, whom I found 'in a highly excitable state about the budget and everything else', I wrote in my diary in more irritated terms about the French Government than I used on any other occasion about them or any other Community government:

The French do get into an enormously excited state and find it difficult to believe that there can be different interpretations of things and that people who don't agree with them are not necessarily knaves or fools. They treat people as craven, threaten them too much [Poncet had talked about calling off direct elections and my Commission finding itself in the same position as Hallstein's had been in vis-à-vis de Gaulle], and believe that they will succumb to a 'thunderbolts of Zeus' treatment. I think that it stems from the fact that the French Government is too hierarchical and authoritarian, and that they are all terrified if they can't bring home to Giscard exactly what he wants. This corrupts people like François-Poncet, who is in general a decent, sensible, intelligent man. The whole interview left a disagreeable taste in my mouth.[10]

More important than the taste in my mouth, however, was the fact that this mood of the French Government led them over the Christmas holiday to decide to hold up the coming into operation of the EMS on 1 January. They did not peg this to the budget dispute, which would have seemed a ludicrous act of petulance. Instead they tied it to their dissatisfaction with the working of Monetary Compensatory Amounts and said that this had first to be resolved. But the excuse did not hold water, as will soon be seen.

There were some compensating improvements during that December. Schmidt came back to Brussels two days after the Council, and showed that he had become more worried about his failure to put successful pressure on Giscard. He was keen to do more for the Italians and the Irish, but suffered from the illusion that I might be able to persuade Barre (French Prime Minister) to persuade Giscard to reopen the Regional Fund window. However, that proved unnecessary. On 12 December the Italian Government announced with great courage that they would take the plunge and participate fully in the EMS even on the present unsatisfactory terms. Thus, by the narrowest of margins, there was avoided a damaging north/south split with the inevitable consequence of a two-speed Europe. For Italy the decision has had the effect of successfully tying their economy, or at least the northern and central parts of it, far more firmly into the Franco-German core of Europe than would otherwise have been the case. Ireland followed suit a few days later.

These decisions repaired the direct damage of Brussels, but they were not sufficient to avoid my feeling at the end of the Christmas holidays that the EMS, and with it Europe, might be falling apart. I was particularly depressed by the newspapers on the morning of 5 January, when I was in London. I was due to go on a week's visit to West Africa two days later, but I thought I must find out what the French Government was up to, and try to unravel the knot, if I possibly could, before I went. The best prospect, it seemed to me, was to go and see Barre, who was steadier than François-Poncet, and whose friendly if occasionally pedagogic lucidity was likely to make him more informative than Giscard, whose moodiness could sometimes make him opaque. I therefore arranged a Sunday-morning meeting with Barre before taking the lunchtime Air France Concorde to Dakar, and on the Saturday evening I first dined alone with the British Ambassador, Nicko Henderson, with whom I was on much more than normal diplomatic terms, and then paid a long late-night call on Ortoli in his apartment in the Rue de Bourgogne. The curious thing was that none of the three (that is, including Barre) could satisfactorily explain to me what was happening. Nicko was frankly baffled. Ortoli was deeply apprehensive and Barre was fluently obfuscating. But no one could produce a convincing explanation of why Giscard, having spent much of the previous year promoting the EMS, had suddenly prevented its being born *en beauté*. Barre resolutely denied that there was any French cooling towards the System as such. MCAs, however, were of great importance to them. They unbalanced the market between France and Germany. But, as I pointed out, this was not new. They had been present for years past. Why had they suddenly assumed such compelling importance between 7 and 31 December? To this even that master of conducting politics by the expository lecture had no approach to a convincing answer. So I left as mystified as I had been when I arrived, but nonetheless a little reassured, for Barre has almost as much of the bedside manner of a physician to the famous as of the lecturing skill of a professor of economics and I felt that the prognosis for the EMS was good.

So indeed it proved to be, which was the final act in the mystery. In early March, the MCA issue having been in no way resolved, the French quietly moved aside their objection and the EMS was born, two months late. But no flags were flown. That was the price which was paid for the French hold-up. What interest the French Government, of whose rational if often self-interested diplomacy I was in general a considerable admirer, thought they were serving by this ploy I have never fathomed. However, the EMS has more than made up for its awkward birth by its successful performance and by the fact that it has been the central channel from which most subsequent European advance has flowed.

We were remarkably lucky in the unfavourable climate of the late 1970s to have achieved it at all, and particularly so fast, even with the last two months of delay. We were lucky that the dollar dipped almost to order, thereby securing such a powerful and far-sighted animator as Helmut Schmidt. We were lucky in having the European Council, which in spite of its Brussels failure was a far less inspissated institution than the Council of Ministers had then become, to drive it forward. And we were lucky that the British, while showing that they had learned nothing from their previous mistakes, at least had the restraint and decency not to try to prevent what others wished to do without them.

# CHAPTER TWENTY-SEVEN

# *Bloody British Question*

Just as the creation of the EMS was the dominant issue of the first half of my Brussels presidency, so the BBQ was the dominant one of the second half. 'BBQ' originally stood for British Budgetary Question, not in the sense of the Chancellor of the Exchequer's annual pronouncements, but in that of the balance between Britain's payments to and receipts from the Community. But when in 1980 the issue became for a time all-dominating the initials came increasingly to stand in my mind for Bloody British Question.

It was inevitably a less satisfactory because a less constructive issue than the creation of the EMS. It was also for me a more difficult one because of my British provenance. On the EMS I was obviously floating high and free of any national partiality. British governments would rather the EMS had never been thought of, for they wanted to be neither in nor out. But my enthusiasm for creating something for the rest of Europe was tinged only with disappointment and not with hesitation when it became clear that my efforts were going to result in a product which was not for home consumption. On the BBQ, on the other hand, I was endeavouring to promote a solution of which Britain would be the substantial and sole beneficiary. I was nonetheless almost as determined to get the second as the first, both because I thought the British claim had justice on its side, and because I became convinced that the issue, unless satisfactorily settled, would alienate any British government from the Community. I had not devoted all those years of effort to get Britain into Europe to see it all undone, under my presidency of the Commission moreover, by failure to resolve a fairly marginal budgetary problem. I also believed that the issue had considerable capacity to damage the whole European enterprise, as indeed proved to be the case in the early 1980s, when the revived dispute dominated European Council after European Council to the effective exclusion of any other serious business.

491

Nevertheless it became the case at the end of 1979 and in 1980 that, as opposed to the other three years of my presidency, I could be accused of playing a British hand and putting my full force and attention behind it. I believed that this was in the general European interest, but I doubt if this view of my motives was taken in Paris, and perhaps not in some other capitals either. I noticed a strain in my relations with even the Belgian Government, and with some Commission colleagues too.

The essence of the problem was that the Community received its resources from a mixture of a fixed percentage of the VAT levied in the member states and the customs duties and import levies which were charged on goods and produce coming in through the common external tariff, and then proceeded to spend about 70 per cent of these resources on agricultural support. The VAT provision operated neutrally as between Britain and the rest of the Community, but because Britain brought in from outside the Community a higher proportion of its imports than did the other eight it paid more than average in import levies and customs duties, and because it had only a small agriculture it made relatively few demands on Community outgoings. The result was that, although Britain had become one of the poorer countries in the Community, its net budgetary contribution was the largest with the exception of that of Germany, the richest country.

This problem was perceived during the Heath Government's negotiations for entry in 1970–1 and was one of the main subjects of the Wilson Government's 'renegotiation' of 1974–5. That renegotiation was a largely cosmetic enterprise, producing the maximum of ill-will in Europe and the minimum of result (except for a smokescreen under which both Wilson and Callaghan could make their second switch of position on Europe within five years). It created a device known as the 'financial mechanism', which by the late 1970s was capable of dealing with about one-fifth of the problem. To add to the complication the problem itself had disappeared underground in 1976–7. By an odd combination of circumstances Britain had virtually no grievance during those years. But in 1978 the problem resurfaced like the Loch Ness monster, except that no one was in serious doubt that its subsequent normal position, unlike that of the monster, was going to be above and not below the water. The first reference to the issue in my *European Diary* was on 2 November 1978, when Callaghan was recorded as expressing considerable concern.[1] It was also much on his mind when I saw him for the last time in Downing Street on 8 March 1979 and at his last European Council in Paris four days later. Two weeks after that he was defeated on a major vote in the House of Commons and the general election of 3 May was set in train.

During that election I was about as near to neutral as it is possible to be. I had some but not much residual loyalty to the Labour Party. I had no personal animosity towards Callaghan, with whom I had enjoyed easy Prime Minister/President of the Commission relations for the previous two years, and I thought that, for the cautious leader of an insular party, his instincts towards Europe were at least as good as Mrs Thatcher's, who had not given an impression of either comprehension or enthusiasm when she had visited Brussels at the end of 1977. On the other hand the Conservative Party of those days still wore with some pride the European mantle which Edward Heath had thrust upon it (and many of those who did not feel the pride at least regarded Brussels as a shield against the insular socialism which they then regarded as a serious threat), and both the would-be Foreign Secretaries, Peter Carrington and Francis Pym, had expressed their determination to open a new chapter of British Europeanism. I did not vote, half erecting a bogus theory that it would be improper in my position, but in reality because I did not wish to do so. Jennifer voted Liberal for the first time in her life. When the result came I had mixed feelings. My rational thought (over-optimistic as the eleven and a half subsequent years turned out) was that a Conservative government would be better for Britain's relations with Europe, which was obviously the political issue of most concern to me, but my emotions were against a Tory victory and a Labour defeat.

When Mrs Thatcher emerged from the sea of electoral hazard, perhaps looking more like Boadicea than like Botticelli's Venus, it was natural that she should quickly seize the BBQ as her main point of engagement with Europe. Carrington, who had won the struggle with Pym to become Foreign Secretary, was left to make (effectively) the noises of greater British commitment while she limbered up for the best fight that she could see on the horizon. There was nothing wrong with choosing this encounter. Callaghan, indeed, would have had to do the same had he won the election. His tactics would have been different, in some ways better and in some ways worse, but he would have fought the same campaign.

When I saw Mrs Thatcher for the first time in Downing Street, a couple of weeks after the election, she was already snorting in anticipation of this battle. This created no difficulty between us, for I was in favour of the engagement, although I came deeply to disagree with her tactics at later stages. During the twenty months of overlap between her prime ministership and my presidency, I in general enjoyed my relationship with her. I found her friendly and unpompous to deal with, although often far from logical in her approach to the deployment of an argument or the structure of a meeting, undismayed by disagreement, and in no way resenting my not acting as an agent of Whitehall. In her early days of international statesmanship at the Strasbourg European

Council of midsummer 1979, or the Tokyo Economic Summit which followed a week later, she gave the impression of being glad to have a fellow British face at these high tables.

At Strasbourg she was very oddly treated by Giscard, who was presiding because the European Council was in his own country and during the French presidency. At neither of the small but elaborately contrived banquets did he have her to sit next to him. It was an extraordinary performance for the would-be Sun King of Europe. Merely as a new Prime Minister from one of the four major countries she would have been an obvious choice. As the first woman ever to appear at a European Council the obviousness was at least quadrupled. Yet I do not believe that Giscard did it out of simple anglophobia. He was in any event semi-anglophil, although not with a discriminating knowledge of English life. It was more a certain clumsiness of manners in Giscard which sat ill with his intelligent, condescending sophistication, but which nonetheless undoubtedly existed.

Whatever his motive, Mrs Thatcher had every reason to feel offended, far more than Callaghan had before the Bremen meeting a year before. To her considerable credit, she showed no sign of reacting to the slight. What she did complain about was that he cheated her over the agenda. She told me at the luncheon that she had made an arrangement to have the BBQ taken first. I told her this was a mistake. It would be a pity for her to have to open cold on such a difficult and vital subject. Typically she could not see the force of this slightly nuancé point. However, whether with malice or generosity, Giscard did not allow her to open, but began with a report on the working of the EMS over the first three months. Then, at what was in fact the best time to take the difficult issue of substance, he got me to open the convergence/budgetary discussion, which I did in a way as helpful as possible to the British, and which gave Mrs Thatcher the opportunity to come in next and deploy her full case. She nevertheless persisted in the view, which may have been formally true, that Giscard had reneged on an agenda undertaking.

Her presentation of her own case, in contrast with her few previous interventions which had been crisp, was ill-judged. What she needed at this stage was to get support for our proposition that a problem existed and that the Commission should be charged with bringing forward proposals to deal with it for the next European Council. Instead she spoke shrilly and too frequently, and succeeded in embroiling not only with Giscard (which maybe was unavoidable) but also in turn with van Agt (Netherlands), Jørgensen (Denmark) and Lynch (Ireland). Then, worst of all, she got into an altercation with Schmidt, whose support was crucial to her getting the outcome she wanted from the meeting. Furthermore she had distributed round the table without any notice to the Commission or anybody else a paper which looked as though it came from us because it was essentially a list of figures prominently attributed to Commission sources. These figures were no doubt accurate enough, but I was loath to be cross-examined on them without preparation, which Schmidt immediately tried to do. Mrs Thatcher had thus performed the considerable feat of unnecessarily irritating two big countries, three small ones and the Commission within her opening hour of performance at a European Council. She did, however, sense that she was not achieving great success and allowed me to suppress her attempted third intervention by (just) getting through the proposition that the Commission should bring proposals before the next meeting. She even thanked me quite graciously afterwards.

The next European Council was not due until late November in Dublin, but the commitment that it should be primarily a BBQ occasion cast long shadows before it. As early as 11 September, for instance, when I visited in Rome the new Italian Prime Minister (now President of the Republic Cossiga), I was primarily concerned to point out that although the Italians thought they had a similar budgetary problem it had in fact corrected itself and that it would be a mistake if they used some retrospective grievance about this as an excuse for not assisting a solution to the more deep-seated British problem. (Eventually the Italians played a crucial and helpful role in finding the solution the following spring.) And on 18 September Klaus von Dohnanyi, the German minister for European affairs, who was also to be central to this solution, tried hard to get me to put an 'order of magnitude' figure on the amount by which the British deficit would have to be reduced in order to make a settlement possible. There was an extraordinary prudery prevalent which made the mentioning of such a crude figure indelicate. Even in my detached position I hesitated before saying to Dohnanyi with more than appropriate hedging, 'Maybe around one thousand million units of account.' Schmidt complained to me on 7 November that Mrs Thatcher would not think in such arithmetical terms, and as late as 5 February 1980, well into the next phase of the battle, I had exactly the same difficulty in getting Peter Carrington to pronounce the dread words of a figure which Dohnanyi had had with me. Eventually I persuaded him, like an abbot passing on the secret, at once sacred and profane, of a liqueur-manufacturing process, to let the words pass his lips. 'Perhaps,' he said, 'somewhere around a thousand million units of account might be not totally unreasonable.'

On 22 October I had what I described as 'a wild and whirling interview with Mrs Thatcher, lasting no less than an hour and fifty minutes'. This occasion led me to the view that her reputation for having a well-ordered mind was ill-founded, and led Crispin Tickell, whose duty it was after such meetings to produce a well-structured 1500-word résumé, to say that of all the numerous bilateral meetings we had all over the world, and only a minority of which were conducted without any language complication, the ones with Mrs Thatcher were the most difficult to reduce to such a coherent form.

It was also the occasion when I was most struck by her lack of pomposity. She launched into an anti-European diatribe: 'They are all a rotten lot. Schmidt [a fine accolade in view of her anti-Germanism] and the Americans and we are the only people who would do any standing up and fighting if necessary.' She then suddenly swept into a fantasy about taking the Crown jewels with her on a forthcoming visit to Paris and using them to soften Giscard, who was temporarily immersed in the Bokassa diamonds scandal. It was a good bad-taste joke, but as with many people who have made one she immediately began to backtrack. 'I think that had better not be recorded,' she said. 'Maybe indeed the whole discussion had better not be recorded.' I had a rush of frivolity to the head and said: 'Oh, don't you know, Prime Minister, that it is an absolute rule of the Community that when the President of the Commission has meetings of this sort a verbatim account has to be on the desks of all the other heads of government the next morning?'

'It is not really so, is it?' she said, half-believing, two-thirds apprehensive, and looking more like a Garland cartoon portrayal of her as a bewildered schoolgirl than I have ever seen her, before or since. 'No,' I said, 'it is not true, just a joke.' While I am not sure that Mrs Thatcher found this hilarious, she took it without apparent resentment, which is more than most of her predecessors would have done. It remains one of my best early memories of her as Prime Minister.

My objective during those months before Dublin was threefold. First, to get a helpful paper through a united Commission; a seven-to-six or even a nine-to-four majority would not have been much use. Second, to avoid this taking the form of the Commission laying down a single recommended solution, with a specific figure for the amount of money which was to be transferred to the United Kingdom from the other eight countries. This may sound a rather supine ambition, but it was in fact essential to the success of the enterprise. It was necessary both to get a united Commission and to keep the Commission in a key position in relation to the inter-governmental bargaining. Our job, as I saw it, was to explain why there was a real problem and to expose its size, then to provide a methodology by which it might be solved, and finally to assist in finding a figure which the eight governments would pay and Britain would accept. And third, with this end in view, to proselytise, as with the Italians in early September, as many of the eight as I thought I could have some influence upon.

All this may sound straightforward but it nonetheless raised several points of delicacy. The essential difficulty was that everything was seen in 10 Downing Street (and to some extent throughout Whitehall) in such utterly different terms from those in which matters were seen in the other eight capitals. Mrs Thatcher thought she had an inalienable moral and legal right 'to get her money back'. The others thought that Britain had twice (once in 1971 and once after the referendum in 1975) put its signature to acceptance of the arrangements to which she now objected. If the contract had produced a bad bargain for Britain the other eight were prepared, with varying degrees of reluctance, to do something to ease it, but they were damned if they were going to be lectured for moral obloquy as well. I tried to get them to accept that Britain's high contribution to Community resources because of large transoceanic imports and low claim upon those resources because of a small agriculture were not due to Anglo-Saxon perversity but arose out of historical trading patterns and socio-economic structures. This was not assisted by Downing Street filling in any interval with denunciations of the CAP and of the generally inward-looking behaviour of the other eight.

Indeed my first attempt in September to get a paper through the Commission led me temporarily to retreat with burned fingers. Ortoli, Gundelach, Davignon and Natali, my four most powerful colleagues, were all awkward in somewhat differing ways, although with the common ground that not enough obeisance had been made in the paper to Community mythology. By dint of 'mythological' redrafting and of careful massage of these colleagues this setback was reversed in early November, but the path remained strewn with egg-shells.

The proselytising of governments proceeded with only moderate success. I did not believe I could have much effect on the French, and that indeed proved to be the case when I went to see Giscard on 23 November. He was prepared to do something, but not much, and gave notice that he would be in a detached but awkward mood in Dublin. With Schmidt I had a more constructive dialogue, mainly by telephone, for he liked long (up to an hour) prearranged conversations of this sort, and was much better at them than I was. He was prepared to do a good deal, provided Mrs Thatcher became less hectoring.

My best achievement was with the Dutch. I went to The Hague on 19 November and lunched with the Prime Minister and about eight other members of the Cabinet. I spent nearly the whole meal expatiating on the problem, why it was acute, why it was not the fault of the British, and why it was in the interest of Europe as a whole to find a solution. For some reason or other it went peculiarly well, the words and the arguments for once came to me exactly right, and both van Agt and van der Klaauw (the Foreign Minister) said that I had considerably moved their minds. Back in Brussels, I dined that evening with the Irish (Foreign Minister, permanent secretary and ambassador) and tried to do a repeat performance. It did not come off. In spite of the practice in The Hague, I did not do it nearly as well, and they were not as receptive. I suppose one could not hope to overcome 300 years of history between the fish and the pudding. Nonetheless Jack Lynch, the Taoiseach (not present on this occasion), was a conspicuously fair chairman when we got to Dublin.

The Dublin European Council was the occasion for Europe's first head-on encounter with Mrs Thatcher in full flood. The circumstances might have put off a lesser woman or a greater historian. The rest of us were in hotels or embassies but she was installed (or incarcerated) for security reasons in Dublin Castle, the old seat of vice-regal rule. When I went to see her on the second day she was in a room decorated by a plaque saying that it was where 'James Connolly, signatory to the proclamation of the Irish Republic, lay a wounded prisoner prior to his execution by the British military force at Kilmainham Jail . . . 12 May 1916'. This, and the general atmosphere, seemed to oppress her two attendant knights (Robert Armstrong and Michael Palliser) more than it did her.

At the first afternoon session she began well, although she was as usual shrill. Some progress was made, with the Italians and the Irish for instance, both poorer than the British, offering to pay their share of any settlement. Towards the end of that session, however, she crossed the watershed from the forceful to the counter-productive and ensured that she would get no further that afternoon. I then decided she had only one of the three necessary qualities for a great advocate. She had nerve and determination to win in abundance, but she did not begin to understand the case against her and the arguments which she therefore needed to refute. Nor did she begin to appreciate the importance of not boring the judge and jury. However, no great damage was done at that session, for Lynch wisely brought it to an end soon after she had passed over the top.

This was merely a tuning up for the evening's performance. We assembled for the working dinner of heads of government at 9.00. She sailed in last and in full command of herself, although I subsequently discovered that she had just had an explosive row with her senior officials. She kept us sitting over the table for more than four hours, for the greater part of which she talked without pause, but not without repetition. Giscard, who as he had not been in charge of the table plan was next to her, leaned back in contented disengagement. There was not the slightest need for him to intervene. Schmidt got impatiently bored and pretended (but only pretended) to go to sleep. Cossiga, attending his first European Council and knowing that he had to take over the presidency in a month, wrung his hands and proposed a special European Council early in the New Year, no doubt hoping that this might at least bring the evening's embarrassing proceedings to a close. The best thing to be said for Mrs Thatcher's performance was that she always retained her temper, even if not her judgement. But the marathon meal was entirely counter-productive. The other eight were less inclined to let her get her way at the end than they had been at the beginning.

Some time during the short night in the Shelburne Hotel I decided the only thing to do was to go for a postponement of the issue to the next European Council. The alternative was a rupture, because there was no way in which the gap between Mrs Thatcher's demand for total reimbursement and the increasing unwillingness of the bullied other heads of government to be generous under duress could be bridged during the morning session. Postponement for its own sake can obviously be a mistake. But I thought it was better than a rupture, and I also had a sense that the mounting intransigence of the anti-Western forces, from Moscow to Teheran, which was a feature of that winter, might make Europe less willing to split in the spring of 1980 than at the end of November 1979. The possible incident on which I speculated in my diary was an American pre-emptive strike in the south of Iran. These vague forebodings proved more than justified. The abortive American attempt to rescue the hostages from Iran did not take place until 25 April 1980, but it had been preceded by the still more traumatic Soviet invasion of Afghanistan in mid-December 1979.

These events did make it worth waiting until the spring, but this involved obtaining agreement to the postponement on the morning after the midnight feast. Mrs Thatcher was easier to persuade than either Giscard or Schmidt. I went to see her at her request in Dublin Castle at ten o'clock. I had hoped to see Schmidt first but had missed him (there is often an element of blind man's buff at European Councils, with people scattered around different embassies and hotels). Mrs Thatcher unleashed another great harangue upon me, but that was merely a covering bombardment under which she announced she would accept a postponement.

She no doubt thought this was a great concession, but Giscard and Schmidt were loath to accept it. There was no question of their doing so until Mrs Thatcher announced that she would approach a future European Council 'in a spirit of genuine compromise'. It took several hours of plenary session to get this statement out of her. Even then Giscard spoke disdainfully of the danger of pretending that we had a compromise when in fact all that we had was a confusion. He eventually accepted the Commission draft on this and cognate subjects, but not before he had beckoned Ortoli out of the room to complain to him that I was exceeding my powers by putting it forward. We escaped from Dublin in a howling gale. Mrs Thatcher seemed to have created a turbulence which swirled not merely over Dublin Castle but over the whole of Dublin Bay and St George's Channel as well.

I have never been able to decide with certainty whether or not her Dublin eruption served any purpose. Superficially it was not only boring but also alienating. The more difficult question is whether it also made the others realise that they would never have any peace until the BBQ was settled in a way that a more emollient approach would not have done. This view cannot be dismissed, although it would have had more force behind it had Britain been fully participating in all forms of Community activity. Had the Callaghan Government not resiled from the EMS at the Brussels European Council a year before, the others would have been both more generous and more fearful of a rupture and of British *de facto* withdrawal from the Community. As it was, there would have been some willingness, even though with a few shoulder shrugs of regret, to let Britain go. Not only were we always raising special requests, so the argument would have gone, but we were also always asking for special dispensations which allowed us to be half in and half out. Perhaps we were becoming more trouble than we were worth.

It was at once Mrs Thatcher's strength and weakness that she did not appreciate the danger. She could not comprehend that the 'rotten lot' could get on without us. She was like someone riding a bicycle along a narrow cliff path without any awareness of the precipice which lay on one side of her. Provided she did not actually go over this was good for the confidence and verve of the ride. But the risks were considerable; and later the bravura performance went too far, so that it became just a question of show-off without purpose.

Mrs Thatcher's confrontational approach to the limited problem of budget imbalance also carried with it wider penalties. The problem was limited because the total size of the Community's budget has never been more than 2 per cent of the total of member countries' public expenditure and was and remains substantially less than 1 per cent of their national income. The gap around which the argument revolved – approximately 400 million écus a year – was tiny in relation to, say, the size of Britain's defence budget. But it was capable of destroying a large part of the influence which that defence budget was designed to foster. Furthermore, in order to relieve her feelings and justify her position, Mrs Thatcher built up a groundswell of anti-European and particularly anti-French opinion at home. In those days, perhaps more so than now, this was easy to do. But once the genie was encouraged to come out of its bottle it was difficult to get it back in again. In my view the histrionics of Dublin, followed by the cooler misjudgement of

Luxembourg, killed the hope that the new Conservative Government might play some leadership role in Europe, and also implanted the germs which led to the death of the fine legacy of Conservative Europeanism which Macmillan had tentatively revived after Eden had stood back from Messina and Heath had greatly enhanced. It was a heavy price to pay for 400 million écus.

For the first five months of 1980 there was little respite from the BBQ. Very early in the New Year Geoffrey Howe (then Chancellor of the Exchequer) and Ian Gilmour (then second minister at the Foreign Office) were sent on a useless series of missions around the Community capitals. The visits were useless because they had no authority even to explore solutions below the full 1500 million écus a year subvention which was Mrs Thatcher's demand, but which was both unrealistic and incompatible with the 'spirit of genuine compromise' she had reluctantly accepted at Dublin. The Italians complained that this made their presidential task impossible, and indeed Cossiga eventually abandoned his idea of having a special early European Council in February. He could not see the basis for a settlement at that time, and I agreed with him.

The British were nevertheless lucky to have the Italians in the presidency, and to have the Italian Government composed as it was. Ministers in Rome, perhaps a little resentful of too much Franco-German hegemony and provided they were not too frequently abused for Latin turpitude, enjoyed playing an occasional hand in partnership with London. Furthermore Francesco Cossiga had an anglophil mind and method of operation which were more suited to finding a solution to an external arithmetical problem than was the subtle and complicated Giulio Andreotti, who was mostly head of the Italian Government and whose gaze was more cisalpine and Middle Eastern. And Emilio Colombo, when he succeeded the useless Attilio Ruffino as Foreign Minister in April 1980, although a lay monk from Potenza, which made him a long way both geographically and spiritually from Grantham, did more than anyone else to haul Mrs Thatcher back when she finally rode off the edge of the cliff.

Schmidt at the end of January complained that he could establish no rapport with Mrs Thatcher, and made it clear that perhaps as a result he had moved back to a more hard-line position on the BBQ than he had been prepared to take up before being harangued in Dublin. This however was during an even more whirling four-hour conversation with him than the one I had had with Mrs Thatcher in October. In the course of it he divided the leaders of the world into those with whom problems were easier to solve because of the confidence in which he could speak to them and those of whom the reverse was true. The first list comprised Giscard (obviously), then the rather surprising couple of

Honecker of East Germany and Gierek of Poland, and, maybe, Peter Carrington and Cyrus Vance, the latter still but only for another two months US Secretary of State. Those he put on the second list were Carter, Brezhnev and Mrs Thatcher. Out of the difference between the category of Carrington and Mrs Thatcher there arose the suggestion that perhaps the best way to advance a solution to the BBQ would be for him to see Carrington without Mrs Thatcher. This presented difficulties, for a German Chancellor would not be expected to meet a British Foreign Secretary without both Genscher (then and now German Foreign Minister) and Mrs Thatcher being present. I offered to get round the asymmetry by organising a nominally social dinner in our Brussels house. But for some reason or other Schmidt preferred it to be at East Hendred, and there it took place three weeks later. I deliberately left Schmidt and Carrington alone for over an hour after dinner. They both subsequently expressed sufficient enthusiasm about each other for my hope to be that it decisively moved Carrington to the upper tier of Schmidt's world gallery, which cannot have had a bad effect on German generosity.

Cossiga not only abandoned in February his idea of a special early European Council, but in March took the more extreme step of postponing at only a week's notice the regular one which was fixed for 31 March/1 April. He said he still could not see a solution, and because of an Italian Government crisis did not have the time to do enough pre-Council diplomacy. A new fixture for 27–28 April in Luxembourg was then arranged, and in advance of this Cossiga worked hard. Two days before we were due to meet in Luxembourg he turned up in Brussels at nine o'clock in the evening, having breakfasted in Paris with Giscard and lunched in London with Mrs Thatcher, believing that Giscard had a new solution. Cossiga then spent until nearly midnight expounding it to me. A new French idea at this stage seemed more likely to be a last-minute diversion than a constructive solution. But we all quickly became convinced that our suspicions were wrong and that it could be helpful. With modifications it formed the basis of the offer which was put to Britain at Luxembourg.

Mrs Thatcher was much quieter there than she had been in Dublin. Indeed so eager was everyone not to have a repeat of that Hibernian prandial excess that the BBQ was not broached on the first day, neither in the three-hour afternoon session nor at the dinner. This was a mistake. It meant that the offer which emerged at the next day's session had to be accepted or rejected within an hour or so. There might have been advantage in overnight reflection.

The offer, put forward by Schmidt, was that the British deficit for 1980 should not be allowed to grow beyond the average for 1978 and 1979. As the 1978 figure had been low this was a convoluted way of transferring a surprisingly large sum of money. Giscard then capped the offer (illogically but generously) by proposing that the amount paid to the British should be the same in 1981 as in 1980. This held out the prospect of a payment for the two years combined of 2400 million écus, whereas no one was previously contemplating a yearly figure of much above 1000 million, certainly not over 1100 million.

When we adjourned for a typically late lunch at 3.45, the expectation was that Mrs Thatcher, after a suitable interval for reflection and consultation and for not giving the impression of snatching at the offer, would come back and accept. Even such an experienced journalist as Peter Jenkins, when the terms had duly leaked out at about 4.30, decided that the offer was unrefusable and, being almost as serious a gastronome as he was a journalist, set off for an early dinner in some notable Luxembourg country hostelry, thereby missing the last act. Over our more modest high tea at about the same time, Giscard, with his liking for long conversational snooker shots played diagonally down the table, suddenly asked me in the hearing of almost all the Prime Ministers and Foreign Ministers whether I thought the offer was reasonable and should be accepted. 'Yes,' I said, and he looked half pleased that he had got my endorsement and half disappointed that he had not exposed me as a British agent.

Mrs Thatcher meanwhile cogitated in private and decided against. I understood that Peter Carrington and her two senior advisers, Robert Armstrong and Michael Palliser, were in favour of acceptance, and that the only influence the other way, apart from her own bellicose instincts, was Peter Walker, who was attending an Agricultural Council in the same building and, perhaps provoked by his experience in that provoking body, where he had just agreed to an agricultural price increase he ought not to have accepted, was on the side of intransigence on the BBQ.

When we reassembled in the Council chamber at about 5.00 p.m. it was obvious from Mrs Thatcher's face that she was not going to accept. I went round the table to her and said that I thought she was making a great mistake. Perfectly good-temperedly but also impregnably complacently she said, 'Don't try persuading me: you know I always find persuasion very counter-productive.'[2] She then announced her refusal, I announced my disagreement with her, others expressed more amazement than dismay, and the proceedings ground to a stunned end. No one had much idea what was to happen next. The newspapers the next day were full of cataclysmic reports about the future of the Community. I was due to go on an already twice-postponed nine-day official visit to India in thirty-six hours' time and there was some suggestion that the crisis was such that I ought not to go. I decided however that nothing could be done until the dust had been given a few weeks in which to settle, and that in any event, so far as dust was concerned, I greatly needed, after the Luxembourg fiasco, to get that of Europe off my feet for a bit.

I got back to Brussels, via East Hendred, on 12 May. By this time we had decided, paradoxically, that the only thing to be done with the dispute was to refer it downwards. Heads of government had failed. Maybe Foreign Ministers could do better. They at least did not include Mrs Thatcher in their number, although she would obviously be lurking in the background with the right of veto. The next Foreign Affairs Council was due to take place in Brussels on 29 May. That we ordained, mainly because there was nothing else to do, should be the make-or-break jousting ground. The intervening weeks were two of the most disagreeable that I spent as President, at least after I escaped from the 1977 doldrums. The essential trouble was that everybody except Mrs Thatcher had become bored to death with the dispute, and that this ennui expressed itself in personal strains such as I had not previously known. On one occasion I found myself in a minority of two with Tugendhat in the Commission. Over the previous three and a half years I had only been in a minority of any sort on about five occasions (out of perhaps two hundred split Commission decisions) and then never in one of less than five against eight. There are few people I would rather be in an isolated hole with than Christopher Tugendhat, but I nonetheless found it an uncomfortable position in my own Commission, and one which set me to wonder whether Mrs Thatcher had any conception of the extent to which she unnecessarily diminished the European influence of those who were (in my case only temporarily) working with her.

Perhaps more significant than my short-term difficulties with Commissioners was the change of position of the Belgian Government. Independently of personal or political shifts it was a core Community government both ideologically and geographically. With support from the Dutch and the Italians it had been working to promote my re-nomination as President of the Commission beyond the four-year term which had not previously been exceeded since Walter Hallstein's eight years at the beginning. I did not really want to stay on, for, as will be seen in the next chapter, my thoughts were increasingly turning back to British politics. But I was nonetheless pleased with the suggestion, both because of vanity and because of a desire not to become a lame duck too early in my last year.

How it would have worked out had Mrs Thatcher not kept the dispute running into this nerve-fraying last stage I do not know. I cannot believe Giscard would have been enthusiastic and the outcome would no doubt have turned on how Schmidt jumped. Then the issue suddenly became even more academic than my reluctance would have made it. In mid-April I noted that Stevy Davignon, the excellent Belgian Commissioner, had moved from his position of the previous autumn, which was that he would stay on in the next Commission provided that I did so too, to a new one of being willing to stay on in any event. And in mid-May Henri Simonet, a close friend and then Belgian Foreign Minister, made the position more explicit when he told me that his Government had now decided that the gap between Britain and the rest of the Community had become such that they no longer considered that a Briton could be almost permanently President of the Commission, which is what a renewal would amount to. I recorded at the time that, while I was insistent that I did not want to stay on, I did not fail to take in the significance of what he had said, and was not pleased by it. I had liked having the best of both worlds and was irritated when Mrs Thatcher's unnecessary intransigence resulted in one of them being removed.

This did not however weaken my determination to get a solution on 29 May if one was humanly possible. Apart from anything else, it was the only way to get the all-dominating and distractingly boring subject off the agenda. I approached the fateful Council through bramble bushes. 23 May: 'A special Commission meeting, again on BBQ, which went doubtfully well.' 27 May: 'Took a special late Commission meeting from 9.30 to 11.45 [p.m.] trying to get our budget paper into shape. Only moderate success. Late-night meetings are always difficult to move to a decision.' 28 May: 'Saw Cheysson at 10.15, Davignon at 11.15, and then had a Commission meeting, perhaps if anything more difficult than the night before, all on the BBQ. . . . Commission again at 4.00. A bit of progress but not all that much, and then a bilateral meeting with Ortoli, very hard-pounding. . . .' 29 May: 'Meeting with Colombo (President of the Council of Foreign Ministers) in my office from 10.30 to 11.45. Then the Commission again at noon . . . very partial success' – that was the 'minority of two' occasion.[3]

The Council began at 3.30 p.m. and for the first seven hours could hardly have gone worse. Ortoli complained bitterly (but privately) that I presented the Commission paper, arrived at so laboriously, in a biased way, and no significant progress was made in a session which dragged on until 8.30. The essential and considerable difficulty was that those who would have to pay were not prepared to give any more than was on offer at Luxembourg (preferably a little less as penalty money for the extra trouble to which Mrs Thatcher had put us all), and that the British representatives could not hope to get her approval for anything that was not cosmetically better than, or at least different from, that which she had turned down in Luxembourg. As a considerable added complication the eight claimed that the gulf of suspicion had become such that they wanted assurance that the

British would not simply pocket the refunds and prove as awkward as possible on everything else, in particular holding up an agricultural price settlement for 1981. They therefore wanted a 'linkage' formula which made the payments dependent on the British not doing this.

Over the working dinner the atmosphere got worse. Neither the German nor the French Foreign Ministers were present. In the German case this may have been an advantage, for Klaus von Dohnanyi knew the issue better than did Genscher and was prepared to act with all the nerve and authority of a senior minister. (He was a member of the German Cabinet, even though not in charge of a department.) Even in the French case it did not matter much, for Bernard-Reymond, the state secretary deputising for François-Poncet, was in general friendly and well intentioned and seemed under no closer Elysée control than Poncet would have been. He was however awkward at dinner about the timing of future sessions. We were not sufficiently near to agreement for a continuation that night to seem pointful to most of us. But Reymond said he could not stay for the next day (Friday) or come back for the Saturday, while Sunday was unattractive and even Monday was inconvenient, all done without convincing excuses.

This drove Peter Carrington, who may have felt fobbed off by the non-appearance of François-Poncet and Genscher, into a rare state of exasperation, so much so that he nearly broke off the negotiations before they had properly started. He was prevented from doing that by firmness on the part of Ian Gilmour, and then Reymond's inflexibility about times was overcome by Colombo's velvety patience and quiet good judgement. If we could not easily find another time at which to meet, we had better go on while we were together, even though it was by then nearly 11.30 at night. But in order to get away from sterile argument around the table he would proceed by a series of bilateral interviews. It was the technique of the confessional box imported by the lay monk from Basilicata into the less ecclesiastical atmosphere of the Community institutions. But the exclusiveness of the confessional was not maintained. Colombo asked me to sit with him, and he was supplemented by two Italian officials and I by Crispin Tickell. Together, throughout the next seven hours, Colombo and I interrogated every Foreign Minister at least once and some of them several times. The first metaphorical gleam of dawn came when we saw Dohnanyi at about 2.00 a.m. and he advanced a scheme which would give the British almost as much for 1980 and 1981 as the Luxembourg offer, with a more explicit prospect for 1982 than had been mentioned at Luxembourg, and all presented on a sufficiently different basis of calculation that it could be argued to be better, or worse, or about the same, according to which way any party wanted the prism to shine. It was ingenious and generous and came from exactly the right source. Germany was not only the country which would have to pay most of the money itself, but was also the one which could exercise the most influence on the potentially intransigent French. Even so it was 6.30 a.m. before we had a cash offer which was acceptable with varying degrees of enthusiasm all round.

We reassembled in plenary session at 7.15 a.m., eleven hours after we had last been in that forum, and with the issue of 'linkage' still unresolved. A committee of officials under Davignon's chairmanship had been set up to try and produce a modified and acceptable linkage formula. The British officials (Michael Butler and David Hannay) went into it complaining that he would be a partial chairman, but they came out, just before eight o'clock, having accepted a few lapidary words of simple but subtle brilliance which Emile Noël, the Secretary-General of the Commission, had ingeniously produced. As with many of the best inscriptions the words could mean different things to different people, but they served their immediate purpose highly satisfactorily, and, in this respect like many heavily argued-over international formulae, were not I think ever heard of again.

The last stage of the drama was whether these words would be acceptable to the French as well as to the British. At first there was a memorable little scene in the Council room while Reymond and his officials looked sceptical, and Davignon and Noël, inspired by the pride of chairmanship and authorship, argued vehemently with them. Then Reymond asked for a fifteen-minute recess and the French trooped out. The fifteen minutes turned into 105. There was presumably a lot of telephoning to Paris. Waiting for them to return was an agonising process after so many months of apparently interminable effort and frustrated hope. I became more and more convinced that it was going to be a repetition of Luxembourg, with the whole structure collapsing at the end. Then at 9.45 a.m. they trooped back in again, like a jury returning in a capital case, and pronounced the magical words of 'not guilty', couched for this purpose in the form of saying they accepted.

The whole thing was over just after ten o'clock, eighteen and a half hours after we had started the marathon session. Carrington and Gilmour immediately set off for Chequers to try to sell the deal to Mrs Thatcher. Somewhat curiously, it appeared to be *ad referendum* for the British, but not for anybody else. The heroes of the night had been Colombo for his soothing patience, Dohnanyi for his imaginative willingness to ride ahead of his government (he subsequently had some containable trouble with Schmidt), and Noël for his morning shaft of ingenuity.

The Chequers welcome which awaited Carrington and Gilmour,

who had unexpectedly and successfully dug Mrs Thatcher out of
the hole in which she had buried herself at Luxembourg a month
before, was apparently by no means ecstatic. Neither refreshment
nor congratulations were forthcoming for a long time. The former
deficiency was eventually repaired, but not the latter. They departed
after three and a half hours of hostile cross-examination and without
any indication that she would recommend the settlement to the Cabinet on the Monday. In effect she left the issue to be settled by the
British press. The settlement was well received by both the Saturday
and the Sunday newspapers. As a result the Cabinet approved it on the
Monday with neither dissent nor any lead from the Prime Minister.

The load off my mind was enormous, but even in the euphoria of
relief it was not possible to ignore the price which had been paid, not
only in terms of the burden of additional work on Colombo, Dohnanyi,
Carrington, Gilmour and many others, but also in terms of Britain's
future relations with the Community, by Mrs Thatcher's foolish whim
of a month before. That pointless delay over the month of May 1980
cost Britain heavily in terms of Continental sympathy, and made the
disputes of the next decade considerably more difficult to handle.
Nothing worthwhile was gained, but the eight lost their faith in Tory
Europeanism, and Mrs Thatcher became an instinctive Euro-basher.
It would have been an excessive price to pay even for 400 million écus,
which was all that was ever in effective dispute between Britain and the
rest. It was an appalling price to pay for the narrow difference, almost
undiscoverable by the naked eye, between the settlement which was
rejected at the end of April and that which Carrington skilfully but
nervously accepted at the end of May. It was the last major Community
dispute in which I was directly involved. I was vastly engaged from
the points of view of time and energy, but perhaps a little less so
emotionally than I would have been a year earlier. This was because
my mind over the winter of 1979–80 had become half re-engaged with
British politics.

# CHAPTER TWENTY-EIGHT

# The Twitch Upon the Political Thread

During my first two years or so in Brussels I was quiet on any issue of British politics which did not touch directly upon Europe, and most of my interventions even within that area were unpolemical. This was true of the several proselytising speeches for the EMS which I made in England over the summer of 1978, three to bankers, one to the American correspondents in London and one under Rab Butler's chairmanship to a degree-day ceremony of the University of Essex. An exception so far as polemics were concerned was an earlier occasion in July 1977 when I opened the new printing works of my then publishers, William Collins and Sons, near Glasgow, and denounced Tony Benn. This may seem an odd combination of event and person, but he had just exceeded what I regarded as any tolerable bounds of consistency by announcing that the 1975 European referendum, which he had so persistently advocated as the only way to get a decisive answer, had no continuing validity and that he was mounting a new campaign for British withdrawal.

The other exception, not of style but of subject, was an Israel Sieff memorial lecture which I had delivered in the Royal Institution in Albemarle Street in late November 1977 and which trailed a number of the centrist political ideas which were to resurface two years later in the Dimbleby lecture. David Marquand, working close to me in Brussels at the time, had provided much of the text of Sieff; Dimbleby was to be much more my own work. Ironically, for much of the message of Sieff was a revolt against Wilsonite politics, Harold Wilson was sitting in a quiet corner seat at the Royal Institution and came up with unoffended friendliness afterwards. In general, however, this Sieff lecture attracted little attention, and illustrated how much what does or does not make an impact is a matter of time and chance.

My only other British political incident of these first two years was an odd little farce in October 1978 when *Tribune* took up some malicious plant that Jennifer and I had not paid our Labour Party subscriptions. In fact we had, by bankers' order, but our irritation at the false rumour, which ran like an unquenchable forest fire through the incestuous London press (no doubt partly because of the fixation upon my Brussels salary) and produced at least two rather funny cartoons, probably owed something to the fact that, while not true, it was uncomfortably near the bone. We might merely be hanging on to the Labour Party by our eyebrows, but this did not make us willing to be portrayed as leaving in stinginess.

This lack of political activity did not point to a lack of interest in British politics. I was more disenchanted than disengaged. I had little faith in the ability of either of the big political parties to solve Britain's problems, but I continued to watch their claims to be able to do so with a detailed curiosity. I collected three or four London newspapers on my way back from early jogging expeditions to the Bois de la Cambre and gutted them for an hour with more urgent application than I had shown in my last period as minister and MP. I was mostly in England a couple of times a month, as well as for long holidays, and I kept up a range of political contacts, primarily amongst my old Labour European supporters, but also with such friends from other parties as Ian Gilmour and Mark Bonham Carter, as well as with looser (mainly Tory) acquaintances whom I occasionally saw at one of several London dining clubs.

This keeping in touch, however, was done more for interest than for purpose. My working assumption was that I had done with British politics. Yet there are one or two bits of evidence which suggest that while this was my appraisal of the probabilities, I did not rule out the possibility that some twist to the political wheel might open up a new prospect. Thus I twice and without question refused Callaghan's kind suggestions of a peerage. On the occasion of the second exchange, which was on 13 March 1979 and most incongruously took place in a lavatory of the Palais Kléber in Paris, the suggestion was associated with an offer of the governorship of Hong Kong, which I could not take seriously. I recorded myself as saying to him in relation to the end of my Brussels term, 'I want to come back and look around and keep options open.' To this he replied, 'You might find it quite difficult to get back into the House of Commons. And you might not like it when you got there. It has changed. It has deteriorated a lot.' 'Yes, yes,' I rather impatiently concluded, 'all I intend to do is come back and look around at the political landscape, Jim, and certainly not become Governor of Hong Kong.'[1]

I was, however, already clear in my own mind that only a change in the pattern would attract me back into the political arena. When in the summer of 1979 there were Birmingham suggestions that I might consider becoming (on return from Brussels) *Labour* candidate for Northfield, which had just fallen narrowly to the Tories, I was not attracted. Nor had the general election of that spring given me any desire to intervene. On the evening before the poll both Shirley Williams and Bill Rodgers, instigated by 10 Downing Street, had telephoned to say that there was a strong City rumour (the City of London is a great place for false rumours) that I was about to come out with a pro-Tory statement. I assured them that there was not the slightest danger of that; apart from anything else I would not have left it so ineffectually late. The only two speeches which I made in Britain between the dissolution of Parliament and polling day, one to the Birmingham Chamber of Commerce and the other at Strathclyde University in Glasgow, were scrupulously detached, despite my political past in one city and my political future (not then foreseen) in the other.

As soon as the new Conservative Government was in office I nevertheless took an opportunity to deliver to several of its members a singularly unavailing political lecture. One of the thoughts which had become dominant in my mind was that Britain's economic performance, compared with that of Germany or France, had been bedevilled by dogmatic short-lived changes in the framework in which business, and indeed management in the public sector, had to operate. Industries, most notably but not exclusively iron and steel, were shunted back and forth between the private and the public sectors. The previous decade alone had seen three different national pension schemes, each marginally better or marginally worse than its predecessor, but the disadvantage of constant chopping and changing manifestly greater than any margin of advantage between one and another. The Macmillan Government had introduced a body to deal with prices and incomes, which had been wound up and replaced by another by the first Wilson Government, which in turn had been abolished by the Heath Government about two years before it produced its own version under a slightly different name and form. It was adversarial politics at their worst, with each government indulging in a frenzy of ideological legislation not much of which survived the next change of parliamentary majority. Both business and public service suffered from these party games, and the economy languished.

On 16 May, twelve days after the change of government, I had a long-standing engagement to address the Confederation of British Industry annual dinner at Grosvenor House. It was an intimidating audience of about twelve hundred, including exactly a half of the members of the new Cabinet, as well as about a third of the old, and

most of the permanent secretaries, the occasion made more formidable
by the fact that I had been presiding over the Commission in Brussels
until 5.30 that afternoon. I spoke mainly about Europe, but inserted
an admonitory little lecture along the lines of the foregoing thoughts
and begged the new Government, unless they were confident that their
measures would survive the next tilt of the political balance, to spare
us too many 'queasy rides on the ideological big dipper'. It was well
received by the assembled businessmen, but amongst the official guests
it went better with the permanent secretaries than with either the new
ministers or most of the old ones. What I did not foresee was that the
new Government would avoid another tilt of the political balance for
at least twelve years, but that nonetheless nearly all the fine Cabinet
line-up present would survive less long in office than even the most
short-lived of measures. Only Geoffrey Howe amongst them lasted
for long, and even he not indefinitely.

Within a few days of this occasion there came an invitation from
the BBC to deliver the 1979 Dimbleby lecture in the autumn. The
series had been founded in memory of Richard Dimbleby seven years
before, and previous lecturers had included the disparate mix of Noel
Annan, Arnold Goodman, Jack Jones, Victor Rothschild and Quintin
Hailsham. What was on offer was an hour of prime BBC-1 time with
the specific undertaking that I could talk about anything I liked. Even
so, I have no doubt that the assumption was that I would choose a
European theme. But when I announced that my subject would be a
critique of the British party system under the title 'Home Thoughts
from Abroad', there was no demur from the more self-confident
BBC of those days. The combination of the CBI speech and the
Dimbleby invitation therefore made the second half of May 1979 a
decisive couple of weeks for the resurgence of my political sap. For
the first time for three years I felt that I had a general political message
to propound, and that it should be firmly centrist in tone and outside
the framework of traditional party politics.

The message was still in inchoate terms. When I committed myself
to the Dimbleby lecture I was far from having a precise idea of
what I wanted to say. This did not unduly worry me because the
formulation of ideas and the shaping of the sentences in which to
express them have always been yoked processes with me. I have
never been able to think in terms of headings or to prepare a
synopsis. In any event a November commitment was over several
ranges of hills.

On 14 June David Steel came to dinner alone with me at our house
in Brussels. There was no necessary significance to his visit. I think
he had been to see me in Brussels twice before, for he liked keeping
in touch with European developments. But his eagerness to come,

and mine to see him, were undoubtedly enhanced by our desire for a post-election talk. I thought he had fought a good campaign, perhaps the best of the three leaders, and had done well to avoid disaster in the aftermath of the Thorpe débâcle. He thought so too, although he was naturally disappointed to have gone down from the 19.3 per cent of February 1974 and the 18.3 per cent of October 1974 to 13.8 per cent of the votes cast. He had also gone down from fourteen to eleven seats. But given the position he had taken over it was a minor triumph. I recorded him as 'being anxious to tell me that, as a result of [the campaign], he had become a major public figure, possibly the best known after Callaghan, Heath and Mrs Thatcher. In other words he was, I think, underlining in the nicest possible way that in any future political arrangement he wasn't to be treated as an office boy.'[2]

How far was such an arrangement in my mind? I had long been well disposed towards most Liberals. As Asquith's sympathetic biographer I was unlikely to be anything else. It did not occur to me that if we were to launch any effective centre movement we should begin by fighting to the death with the Liberals for the right to be the third party. This I would have regarded as a recipe for disaster. It was going to be difficult enough in any event to land on the enemy coast of the two-party system, heavily fortified as it was by the distortions of the British electoral system. To have engaged in a debilitating preliminary contest with the inhabitants of the offshore islands of the system, who in any event agreed with us on most policy objectives, would have been lunacy. On the other hand my natural and complacent assumption was that any new movement would provide the greater dynamism and the more experienced leadership. Hence David Steel's desire to put down a marker against 'office boy' status. Equally this June 1979 meeting was in no way a plotting one. It was more an occasion to gossip sympathetically about the election campaign and generally to beat the bounds of future possibilities. From both points of view I thought the dinner went well. No undertakings for the future were given or sought for, although we certainly discussed the political scene from the standpoint that we might become allies. David Steel's memoirs[3] give a similar impression of the encounter, although possibly endow it with more significance than I accorded to it at that stage. I was later to have many discussions with David Steel which I regarded as of the utmost significance. But this I would not quite put amongst them, mainly I think because my mind was still at least three-quarters on European affairs. I had, for instance, got back from a day of Paris visits only five minutes before the dinner, and had a special all-day Commission meeting summoned for early the next morning and away from the Berlaymont in order to discuss our relations with the first directly elected European Parliament, which we welcomed but also regarded with suitable apprehension.

David Steel also says that this was the occasion when I explained to him why I did not regard joining the Liberal Party as a satisfactory strategy for changing the pattern of British politics. My records suggest that this was on a later occasion, in January 1980, but it is perfectly possible that the subject came up at both meetings. In any event he gets my essential approach as it developed over this period exactly right. I in no way regarded joining the Liberals as 'fate worse than death'. If I came quietly back from Brussels to a not very political semi-retirement I thought that I would become a nominal Liberal, for that party was now much closer to my outlook than was either the Labour Party or the Conservatives. But if a combination of circumstances and my strength of purpose made it possible for me to mount a major political initiative then I was convinced that it ought to start separate from but in partnership with the Liberals. For I and a few others to join the Liberal Party would be little more of a seismic shock than had been provided by Christopher Mayhew in 1974, although it must be said that his action was quickly followed by a remarkably good Liberal general election result. A substantial social democratic breakaway from the Labour Party, on the other hand, might be a much more repercussive matter.

It would however be a mistake to give too much of an organisational bent to my 'home thoughts' over the summer and autumn of 1979. I was more concerned with what on earth I was going to say in the Dimbleby lecture. The first mention of attempted composition occurred in my diary only on 14 August, when I wrote: 'Spent the morning trying unsuccessfully to start my Dimbleby lecture.'[4] Despite this inauspicious beginning and a busy September I had a text nearly sufficient to fill the forty-eight minutes, which was what a television 'hour' amounted to, and to send to the BBC producer in advance of a call which he paid me in Brussels on 15 October. But it was not the right text. It was far too long and leisurely on historical analysis, and not nearly strong enough on prescription. Had I delivered it in that form (which I had no intention of doing) its impact, so far from launching a new political party, would have been distinctly low key by the standards of the series. Eddie Mirzoeff, the producer, had both the discrimination to see this and the forthrightness to make his view semi-tactfully clear to me. 'He obviously doesn't think a great deal of the incomplete draft, and is probably quite right too, though it mildly depresses me,' I wrote after the October meeting.[5]

On 31 October I went to East Hendred for a four-day half-term weekend. I woke up the next morning thinking that what with Dimbleby and the Dublin European Council, November would be a testing month, and one in which, if I was not careful, I might fall flat on my face in two separate puddles. This pluralism reduced the sense of apprehension, for it is impossible to be obsessed by two equal worries at the same time. But the prospect nonetheless concentrated my mind, and 1 November became one of the most heroic day's desk work that I have ever done. I wrote from 9.15 to 1.00 and then from 3.15 to 8.15 and had at the end of it three thousand additional words for the day and a comprehensive Dimbleby text. The total was about fifteen hundred words too long, but cutting is easier than composition.

Bill and Silvia Rodgers came to dinner that evening. I read them the more controversial new parts at the end of the lecture. I recorded that '[Bill] was sufficiently post-prandial not to be taking it in too meticulously.'[6] He subsequently said that he thought it sounded rather dull on first hearing. The two statements are not incompatible. At least he had been warned of what was coming. On Saturday, 3 November, Ian and Caroline Gilmour came to lunch alone, and Ian was forced to read the whole lecture. He thought much of the end was too right-wing. In particular he objected to the phrase 'the social market economy', saying that he thought that had gone out with Erhard until revived by Keith Joseph. He also thought the concluding Yeats quotation ('The best lack all conviction, while the worst/Are full of passionate intensity. . . . Things fall apart; the centre cannot hold') was too hackneyed.

Six days later I read a tautened and clearly typed version of the whole thing through in the course of a train journey from Liverpool to Euston, and for the first time thought it rather good. However, David Marquand, who was one of the strongest advocates of political action on my part and later one of my most effective allies, came to East Hendred on the following evening and was constructively critical although not noticeably enthusiastic. There was never any danger of my being cosseted in sycophancy in the run-up to Dimbleby. On 12 November I went to a BBC studio accompanied by John Harris and did a full run-through of the text. The BBC was there in strength and I think that they (including Mirzoeff) were more hopeful than he alone had been in October. I then disappeared for a hard ten days in Brussels, during which I continued to titivate the lecture until I had to seal it up for the release of press copies. I did not reappear in London until a few hours before I was due to perform. The preceding twenty-four hours had not been propitious. I had an unusually wearing Commission meeting the day before, lasting no less than seven and a half hours and broken only by a lunch with COREPER (the Committee of Permanent Representatives in Brussels), never my favourite form of half-time refreshment. It was, as always that winter, the BBQ which was causing the trouble, and in particular the need to get a Commission paper agreed for the Dublin summit. Then on the morning of *der Tag* itself (22 November) I had no less than three Brussels speeches followed by a plane which was one and a half hours late and on which there was no food or drink.

However, I eventually arrived more or less in good order at the elegant little lecture theatre of the Royal Society of Arts in the Adelphi where there had been assembled an audience of about 200, which I cautiously described at the time as 'fairly distinguished'. These were in fact composed of a mixture of friends of mine, some politicians and some not (Rodgers, Annans, Donaldsons, Bonham Carters, Ian Wrigglesworth, Caroline Gilmour), journalists and BBC top echelons. The presence of the last group, mostly sitting in the front row with Huw Wheldon taking the chair, meant that they could not easily cut me off when, despite all our careful calculations, I ran three minutes over time.

After the lecture we had a short reception in the building and then went off to a dinner given by Michael Swann as chairman of the BBC. At both events there was a generally friendly, even enthusiastic, atmosphere, and I felt reasonably pleased. Admittedly Ian Waller, the *Sunday Telegraph* political correspondent, was weaving round saying (at large rather than to me) that the lecture was the most absolute nonsense he had ever heard, but this was considerably out-balanced by Bill Rodgers announcing that in the course of it he had a vision of himself sitting in the headquarters of a new party with his sleeves rolled up and actively organising, as he had done so successfully in the Gaitskellite Campaign for Democratic Socialism.

What did the Dimbleby lecture actually say? It began with a substantial historical analysis (although shortened from the original text) designed to show that the British political system had not changed much since 1868, when the two-party system had settled into its classical mould; yet Britain had changed vastly during the 110 intervening years, both internally and in its position in the world, so that the question arose whether the stability which had once been a national asset had not turned into stultifying political rigidity, 'whether the old skin is not now drawn too tight for effective national performance'. Until the second half of the 1950s, when the failure of Britain's last imperial adventure at Suez almost coincided with the formation of the European Community without British participation, the political system of Disraeli and Gladstone both held the loyalties of the British people (to judge by their high and committed participation in elections) and kept us the richest large country in Europe. Over the subsequent twenty years both of these advantages had disappeared. The numbers voting had fallen, the numbers voting for one or other of the two big parties had fallen still more dramatically, and so had the enthusiasm even of those who continued to do this. In 1951 the Labour Party had narrowly *lost* an election while polling 40 per cent of the total electorate, including those who stayed at home. In October 1974 it *won* an election while polling only 28 per cent. Even the substantial Conservative majority of 1979 was secured with only 33 per cent of the total electorate. And Britain had moved during these two decades from being one of the richest to being amongst the poorest of the European countries.

The political cock-fight, however, grew if anything even more vehement. In the eyes of its opponents 'each successive Tory Government became the most reactionary since that of Lord Liverpool or some other hobgoblin figure of the past', and 'each successive Labour Government the most rapacious, doctrinaire and unpatriotic conspiracy to be seen this side of the Iron Curtain'. This excessive partisanship neither convinced nor pleased the electorate but helped to foster precisely the confrontational industrial mood which was 'rapidly turning Britain into a manufacturing desert'. It led to the constant and deleterious imposition upon the statute book of measures which each government knew were almost certain to be repealed by their successors. It also bound politicians in loveless and sterile political marriages. They often agreed with people just over the political fence far more than they did with those of the other wing of their own party. As a result they were held prisoners as would be the separate arms of a river if the banks within a delta were set in concrete. The conventional wisdom was that they could not break out because any party which split was bound to be electorally slaughtered. But was that really true? 'I believe the electorate can tell "a hawk from a handsaw" and that if it saw a new grouping with cohesion and relevant policies it might be more attracted by this new reality than by old labels which had become increasingly irrelevant.'

The British electoral system greatly strengthened these rigid banks. The task of breaking them without proportional representation would be difficult. But it had to be attempted because the alternative was a quiet acceptance of a rotten system. The case for electoral reform was overwhelming. The onus of proof must be upon those who tried to defend the unusual British voting system which virtually disenfranchised up to 25 per cent of the electorate. The usual defence was that 'first past the post' produced strong and consistent government whereas proportional representation meant the weakness and corrupt bargaining of coalitions. But could this be sustained in practice? Did we seriously think we had been more effectively and consistently governed over the past two decades than had the West Germans? And as for coalitions: 'Do we really believe that the last Labour Government was not a coalition, in fact if not in name, and a pretty incompatible one at that? I served in it for half its life, and you could not convince me of anything else.'

In fact all good governments (and a lot of bad ones too) were coalitions, either overt (that is, between parties) or covert (where a single party over-arched a number of different strands). A very good example of the latter was the Roosevelt coalition, contained within the Democratic Party but a great bringing together of different traditions and interests, which provided America with good and effective government for twelve years. The test was whether the coalition was honest, which I defined as being whether those within the coalition agreed more with each other than they did with those outside.

The Labour Party of the late 1970s, with the vast gulf between, say, Benn and Callaghan, failed this test. That was why the constitutional disputes which were currently raging in the party, about who should elect the leader, who should write the manifesto and how easily a small caucus could get rid of an MP, were not minor organisational points but part of a continuing left/right ideological battle which had crossed the divide from constructive tension and made internecine warfare the principal purpose of the party's life.

A further weakness was that the relatively right-wing leadership of the Labour Party could hope to defend itself against the depredations of the constituency militants only by looking to a relieving force from the Trades Union Congress, which was increasingly irritated by the intransigence of the left. But this 'would obviously and inevitably increase the political power of the unions by making the Labour Party more and not less of a trade union party. I do not think that would be good either for British politics or for the unions themselves. . . . The unions have an essential and difficult job to do. . . . But the idea that the British people want a trade-union-dominated and -nominated government on top of the power which the unions today exercise at the work place is far from the truth.'

From here the lecture moved on both to its conclusion and from the framework to the content of politics. It did so in a mixture of third person plural and second person singular exhortatory style, which seemed appropriate to the conversational tone of a talk directed to individuals at their firesides, but which perhaps reads oddly in cold print:

The paradox is that we need more change accompanied by more stability of direction. It is a paradox but not a contradiction. Too often we have superficial and quickly reversed political change without much purpose or underlying effect. This is not the only paradox. We need the innovating stimulus of the free market economy without either the unacceptable brutality of its untrammelled distribution of rewards or its indifference to unemployment. This is by no means an impossible combination. It works well in a number of countries. It means that you accept the broad line of division between the public and private sectors and don't constantly threaten those in the private sector with nationalisation or expropriation.

You encourage them without too much interference to create as much wealth as possible, but use the wealth so created both to give a return for enterprise and to spread the benefits in a way that avoids the disfigurement of poverty, gives a full priority to public education and health services, and encourages co-operation and not conflict in industry and throughout society. You use taxation for this purpose, but not just to lop off rewards. The state must know its place, which must be an important but far from an omnipotent one. You recognise that there are certain major economic objectives, well beyond merely regulatory ones like the control of the money supply, which can only be achieved by public action, often on an international scale. . . . You use market forces to help achieve [your] objectives, but do not for a moment pretend that they, unguided and unaided, can do the whole job.

You also make sure that the state knows its place, not only in relation to the economy, but in relation to the citizen. You are in favour of the right of dissent and the liberty of private conduct. You are against unnecessary centralisation and bureaucracy. You want to devolve decision-making wherever you sensibly can. You want parents in the school system, patients in the health service, residents in the neighbourhood, customers in both nationalised and private industry to have as much say as possible. You want the nation to be self-confident and outward-looking, rather than insular, xenophobic and suspicious. You want the class system to fade without being replaced either by an aggressive and intolerant proletarianism or by the dominance of the brash and selfish values of a 'get rich quick' society. You want the nation, without eschewing necessary controversy, to achieve a renewed sense of cohesion and common purpose.

These are some of the objectives which I believe could be assisted by a strengthening of the radical centre. I believe that such a development could bring into political commitment the energies of many people of talent and goodwill who, although perhaps active in many other voluntary ways, are at present alienated from the business of government, whether national or local, by the sterility and formalism of much of the political game. I am sure this would improve our politics. I think the results might help to improve our national performance. But of that I cannot be certain. I am against too much dogmatism here. We have had more than enough of that.

And so into the quotation from Yeats's 'Second Coming' which, hackneyed or not, survived into the final version.

Despite the journalists who were at the Royal Society of Arts being more sceptical than any other category there present, the press reaction to the lecture was by no means bad. Next morning the coverage was extensive and hardly any of it was 'markedly other than what I would have wanted'. Two days later on the Sunday it was still all right: 'an immensely long but slightly confused leader in *The Observer*,' I recorded; 'a very good leader in the *Sunday Times*' [then under Harold Evans's editorship]; and 'a hostile leader in the [*Sunday*] *Telegraph*, predictably and not woundingly so.'[7]

In the following week more individual reactions came in the form of letters from members of the public. The mail was not enormous – three or four hundred wrote – but I noted them as being 'remarkably favourable and of remarkably high quality'. No doubt I had some tendency to equate the two attributes, but it was more than that. I recorded at the time 'the complete conviction and commitment with which people wrote',[8] and most of them proved this fifteen months later by becoming the core of the new party.

Perhaps desirably, I was far from concentrated upon watching these reactions. On the day after the lecture I went to Brussels in the morning, Paris in the afternoon to call on Giscard (and Marie-Alice de Beaumarchais, whose husband, our dear friend the brilliant ambassador until 1977, had died, unexpectedly and aged only sixty-seven, twelve days before), and back to East Hendred late at night. On the day after that, I had to go full of complaint to London to address the annual meeting of the European Movement. And in the following week I was immersed in the preparations for the Dublin European Council and then in that meeting itself. This pattern illustrated a certain post-Dimbleby ambiguity in my mind. I wanted the initiative to lead to a great deal, but not too quickly. I had just over a year's European commitments to discharge. At times during this interval this led to a conflict between desire to keep the fire smouldering and reluctance to see it fanned into premature flames. 'Oh Lord,' I might have paraphrased St Augustine, 'give me a new party to lead, but not just yet.'

There was no problem, however, of those whose partnership I most cared about wanting me to move faster than I was ready to do. On Saturday, 1 December, both Shirley Williams and Bill Rodgers came to East Hendred. Shirley, no more than Bill, had not been frightened off by Dimbleby, and she, almost but not quite as much as Bill, was prepared in certain circumstances to contemplate a break from the Labour Party. But they both wanted plenty of time in which to convince themselves that those circumstances had arrived.

At this stage they were both far in advance of David Owen. He had not liked the Dimbleby lecture at all. On the evening before it was delivered, having presumably received a copy from a press friend, he had denounced it to Tom Bradley, whom he had encountered at Westminster Underground station. He complained that it was unfair of me to do this 'to those of us who have risked our careers for him'. Bradley, who subsequently and regrettably did sacrifice his career for me, replied robustly, even though he had not been forewarned of the lecture. Owen then dismissed Dimbleby in mildly disagreeable terms in a speech delivered two days later. He warned his allies in the Labour Party not to be tempted away from 'sensible socialism' by 'siren voices from outside', and, bizarrely in view of the subsequent evolution of his thought and priorities, specifically rejected my call for proportional representation.

To put the Dimbleby lecture in its context it is necessary to remember that it was not principally a revolt against the Labour Party's lurch to the left when Tony Benn was riding rampant in the early 1980s. It came before that, although such a development was half foreseen. Insofar as it was against the Labour Party it was against the party at the end of the Wilson/Callaghan era. On 22 November 1979 the Labour Party was still a party of which Callaghan was leader, with Healey his most likely successor. But the lecture was equally against the early excesses of Thatcherism, and against the deleterious working of the two-party duopoly as it had developed in the previous twenty years. 'Bennery', which rode remarkably high even though it never quite made its instigator leader or even deputy leader of the party, was to make it impossible in my view for any self-respecting social democrat to fight the 1983 general election as a Labour candidate except with his head down, his coat collar turned up and in dark spectacles. A few, metaphorically, did precisely that. Others, with less delicate digestions, just brazened it out. It should not be forgotten what was involved in accepting the Labour ticket at that election: withdrawal from Europe, unilateralism, the reduction to a mockery of membership of NATO, massive further nationalisation, the forbidding by law of private education or private health care, the almost total surrender to trade union power.

I was recently reproved for having voted in my last days as a Labour minister for some measures of nationalisation which I certainly regarded as a foolish irrelevance. This reluctant obedience to a party whip, which a member of the Cabinet cannot avoid, was certainly something which left me uncomfortable and mildly ashamed. The half-justified reproof was however delivered by someone who has consistently taken the view that my duty and that of other social democrats was to uphold our corner within the Labour Party and not to withdraw and form a new party. The two complaints are totally incompatible. Under a rigid two-party system fighting from within means the acceptance of whipped votes and election manifestos. The peccadilloes of 1974–6 would have been as nothing compared with the massive hypocrisy of trying to get elected on the 1983 Labour programme. Nevertheless, it must be stated as a matter of historical fact that while the subsequent and already foreseeable excesses of 'Bennery' both justified and made easier our breakaway action they were not the basic cause of the social democratic revolt, which came earlier and went deeper.

It is also necessary to remember that the route between the Dimbleby lecture and the birth of the Social Democratic Party was not only sixteen months long but also bumpy. In retrospect there is a tendency to telescope events and to see Dimbleby as having touched a lucky button of public response after which the great early days of the SDP smoothly and inevitably followed. This was not so. I was pleased with the initial reaction to the lecture, but during the twelve months between January 1980 and January 1981 the outlook was mostly uncertain and my frequent mood was apprehension that I had got myself on to an uncomfortable ledge from which it was going to be difficult to move either up or down.

This apprehension was increased by my feeling distinctly if vaguely unwell from early June to late September 1980. It was the only time during my main political years when I was persistently so handicapped. It added to my fear that, maybe, I had set myself a task which I did not have the energy to perform. It was a little later, but appropriate to the mood of this period, that I recorded a conversation with Harold Lever in the following terms: 'Yes, he would like to have a great political initiative in the direction I want, but he thinks we have not got enough obsessive people. I think that what he really means is what Woodrow [Wyatt] and one or two other people have said, that I have not got the obsessive political interest to be able to stump round the country, fight bye-elections, and create something out of nothing. Alas, he may be right.'9*

Fortunately, this combination of lassitude and apprehension did not make me sit petrified on the ledge. My frequent visits to England became much occupied with trying to recruit fellow rock-climbers for an ascent. In the course of 1980 there were twenty-five strongly political lunch parties at East Hendred, as well as a lot of similar gatherings in London and Brussels. Of the eleven MPs who constituted the original SDP breakaway in early 1981, eight were involved in one or other of these gatherings. In addition there were several meetings with Shirley Williams (not an MP between May 1979 and November 1981), with Dick Taverne, with David Marquand, with three or four peers, and with a number of non-parliamentarians. Of this last group Clive Lindley (a self-made businessman and former Labour candidate of original mind and wise political judgement, settled

---

* The fact that Warrington, Hillhead and many hundreds of SDP meetings up and down the country eventually proved him wrong did not mean that my 1980 hesitation was not genuine. A swimmer eventually getting into a cold pool does not mean that his shivering on the brink had no reality.

outside Monmouth), Colin Phipps (former Labour MP for Dudley and successful oil geologist but always something of a loose cannon), Jim Daly (chairman of the GLC Transport Committee), Matthew Oakeshott (my former research assistant blossomed into a highly talented financier and investment manager) and Roger Liddle (who had worked closely with Oakeshott in Oxford City politics and with Rodgers in the Department of Transport) were the most prominent. All of these, with the possible exception of Liddle, were committed to the idea of a new party from the beginning of 1980, as were Taverne (who had been the first dove out of the ark seven years before), Marquand and the peers, of whom John Harris was the most actively engaged. The back-bench MPs – Tom Bradley, Robert Maclennan, John Roper, Ian Wrigglesworth, John Horam and Neville Sandelson – who had more to lose politically, were naturally more cautious, although probably willing to move if a few others did so too. The two front-benchers, Bill Rodgers and David Owen (with whom in this phase I did not have direct contact until 31 August, although I had known him well from 1970 to 1976) had their membership of the shadow Cabinet to lose as well as the hazard to their position as MPs. Although Rodgers and Owen moved more out of than in step with each other they were both unresolved on a new party for the greater part of 1980.

Shirley Williams was the queen of this chessboard. She no longer had a constituency to lose, but she had her unique popularity with most of the Labour Party and throughout middle England (and Scotland and Wales) except amongst those who could not forgive her for comprehensive schools. In more mundane terms she had her seat on the National Executive Committee of the Labour Party (a position which Tom Bradley also had to renounce). Throughout that year she fulfilled her role as queen with all the dazzling authority of Sarah Bernhardt playing Phèdre. I never came away from an encounter with her without being encouraged, bewitched and inspirited, yet also totally mystified about what she was going to do next.

I did not see Shirley between 1 December 1979 at East Hendred and 19 March 1980 when she came to Brussels, and lunched with me alone at Rue de Praetère, came back to stay the night after addressing a dinner of her own while I was giving another one there for Ortoli, Gundelach and Davignon, talked until four in the morning, and even brightly breakfasted with me before she returned to London and I went to Laeken to have one of my conversations of substance about Europe and life with the King of the Belgians.

I think from the pattern of the visit that it must have been Shirley's suggestion rather than mine, but I was delighted to see her. At lunch she bore me a warm message from Denis Healey, who was confidently expecting to become leader of the Labour Party in the autumn, and who proposed with surprising graciousness that I should come back into the House of Commons on return with a view to becoming Foreign Secretary under his premiership. It was also gracious of Shirley to convey it, for it was a job to which she herself might have had reasonable aspirations. I was unattracted by the offer. I thought that I had burned too many Labour Party boats. Moreover, I did not feel that I could bear dealing with foreign affairs under Healey, which was a subject about which, apart from Europe, he genuinely knew more than I did. As he could never resist lecturing everybody (or at least me) on every subject under the sun, including the few subjects about which he knew less, I thought that the double inferiority would be intolerable.

When I told Shirley this at our second conversation she accepted it with understanding and sympathy, and indeed seemed to go a little off the prospect of a Healey leadership herself. She kept all her options fully open for the autumn, but our marathon conversation was more gossip about the past, including both our relationships with Tony Crosland, than planning or plotting for the future. I enjoyed it immensely but did not feel that her political direction was sufficiently clear for me to be dedicated to preventing her enjoying a few years' excursion away from British politics. A spell as a European Commissioner, or as chairman of the BBC (neither of us then realised that Mrs Thatcher had brought the age of cross-party public appointments effectively to an end), or as a Harvard professor were all possibilities over which we ranged. A day or so later the Brussels correspondent of the *Guardian* displeased both Shirley and me by writing a sour little story saying that she had come to Brussels to give me the 'brush-off' so far as future political collaboration was concerned. In fact I do not think she quite knew what she wanted at that stage, but as I commented at the time 'it was a jolly long brush-off', and as I remember in retrospect it was delivered so engagingly that I was left with no sense of either finality or rejection.

On 9 June I had committed myself to deliver my one major general political speech in London between the Dimbleby lecture and the end of my term as President. It was to the Parliamentary Press Gallery, and although it was only about twenty-five minutes in length I had sweated for many hours over it during the preceding week. On the day before this speech (a Sunday) Shirley, with whom I had not been in touch since the March marathon (but there was nothing odd about this; I had been totally immersed in the two bursts of the BBQ, separated only by my ten days in India), telephoned me in the middle of lunch at East Hendred and asked whether I had just heard her on *The World This Weekend*.

I had not, but despite this and the inconvenient time, we talked for half an hour. We were very friendly, but we nevertheless emulated Schmidt and Callaghan before the Copenhagen European Council and passed like ships in the night. She was concerned to contain or repair any offence that she might have given to me by having just announced that a centre party would have 'no roots, no principles, no philosophy and no values'. I was concerned to secure from her a *nihil obstat* to the speech I had prepared for the following day. As this was still to be made (and was therefore open to minor alteration), whereas her pronouncement was already irreversibly committed to the airwaves, or perhaps merely because I was the more self-centred, I succeeded in concentrating almost the whole conversation upon my proposed words. I very quickly read the whole twenty-five minutes' worth to her, while she never actually got round to telling me what it was she had just said about a centre party, to making the case for which, although not using precisely that term, my speech was directed.

Curiously in the circumstances she raised only one objection. I proposed to conclude with the following passage: 'There was once a book more famous for its title than for its contents called *The Strange Death of Liberal England*.* That death caught people rather unawares. Do not discount the possibility that in a few years' time someone may be able to write at least equally convincingly of the strange and rapid revival of Liberal and Social Democratic Britain.' She asked whether I could not use small letters and leave out the 'and' so that it became 'liberal social democratic Britain' and, I suppose, was thereby given more of an innocuously ideological and less of a committing organisational flavour. 'Thinking that if Paris was worth a Mass [to Henri IV] Shirley was certainly worth an "and" (and a lower case) I decided to do so, after which we rang off on terms of great amity. She said she was sure we would all be together in six months or so.'[10]

The Press Gallery speech also contained a subsequently much quoted passage likening the launch of a new party to an inaugural flight in an experimental plane: 'I do not doubt the difficulty in this as in other fields of human endeavour of doing anything new. The likelihood before the start of most adventures is that of failure. The experimental plane may well finish up a few fields from the end of the runway. If that is so, the voluntary occupants will have only inflicted bruises or worse upon themselves. But the reverse could occur and the experimental plane soar into the sky. If that is so, it could go further and more quickly than few now imagine, for it would carry with it great and now untapped reserves of political energy and commitment.'

* By George Dangerfield, first published in 1923.

Much later I became rather fond of this passage.* But at the time I was dissatisfied with the speech as a whole. Its reception at the crowded lunch had been as good as could be expected with 'an audience of hard-bitten journalists seasoned by a few parliamentary guests like Neil Kinnock',[11] but the press coverage, while very extensive, was by no means universally favourable. The *Financial Times* was good, but the *Guardian* had a discouraging leader. By the middle of the week, back in Brussels, I came to the gloomy and not necessarily accurate conclusion that the Press Gallery follow-up, unlike Dimbleby itself, had been a clumsy enterprise, showing little skill in either timing or phrasing. This led on to several weeks of my deepest trough of dismay between Dimbleby and the launch of the SDP. At one point I discussed with David Marquand, who in general was a most resourceful provider of grappling irons for getting up the cliff, how we might get down from the ledge. Rather in the way that Keynes, after making with college funds as well as his own some rash speculations in wheat futures, was said to have looked across the front court of King's and remarked to Richard Kahn, 'I suppose we could as a last resort turn the chapel into a granary and try to hold out for a bit,' so Marquand and I decided that we might have to join the Liberal Party. For neither of us would this be dreadful in itself. It would just be a disappointing end to a greater vision. We neither of us believed that we were going to change British politics that way.

Nor did David Steel. He never rejected any suggestion of mine that I should become a Liberal. He did not have to. But he had a wider view of his role than that of being a recruiting sergeant. He wanted to be a general, not necessarily a commander-in-chief but one as decisive as, say, Blücher, who turned the course of history. And he pursued this aim with determined nerve, but also with a sensitive consideration for the problems of others, throughout this testing period of waiting. My regard for him, never low, went steadily up. Whereas in June 1979 I had written with gentle amusement of his determination not to be treated as an office boy, in January 1980 I found him 'very agreeable, sensible and curiously mature', in April 'as good and firm and committed as ever', and in June, as he quite accurately portrays in his memoirs, I needed to be reassured by him in my post-Press Gallery gloom. In August 1980, he was recorded as being 'a remarkably buoyant young man'.[12] He was steady under fire from his own party, and he always delivered when he said that

---

* On the morning after the Warrington bye-election (19 July 1981), for example, I remember being asked at a press conference where I thought the flight had got to, and saying happily: 'I think the runway has been left far behind, the seat-belt sign is off and the stewardesses are coming round offering drinks.'

he would. There was no doubt something in the joke that he and I got along well because he was a good social democrat and I was an Asquithian liberal (in other words paradoxically complementary and not instinctive rivals), but there was more to it than that. He showed real political quality, and if one man made the Alliance it was he.

My next contact with Shirley Williams was on 24 July. I wrote about the encounter in baffled but almost lyrical terms. '[She] came to see me for an hour at Kensington Park Gardens on the most lovely evening. She was as engaging but elusive as ever, on the whole taking a pessimistic view, thought the [Labour Party] conference would go wrong, certainly on policy issues, very likely on some of the institutional issues as well, and then most surprisingly, and in contradiction to what she had been telling me in the spring, said she was far from certain that . . . Healey would be elected leader of the party in the autumn. . . . It was nice of her to have come and I wished, as I think she did, that she could have come to our dinner for Crispin [Tickell's] fiftieth birthday which then followed.'[13]

With William Rodgers I had still closer contact over this period on the brink than with Shirley. What has been written about the threshold and the early days of the SDP gives inadequate recognition to the special and close link between Rodgers and me. We had been involved together in almost every political conjuncture of the preceding twenty years and more, since we had gone together on Fabian expeditions in 1957. In 1959 we had jointly tried to promote Labour Party revisionism and bury Clause Four. In 1960–1 (with Bill as the organiser of victory) we had fought together under Gaitskell's banner to reverse unilateralism, and in 1962 we had jointly resigned our commissions when the banner was turned against Europe. In 1969 he had come to the Treasury at my special request. In 1970 he had been the instigator of my becoming deputy leader of the Labour Party. In 1971 he had been the cement which held together the sixty-nine Labour MPs which gave Heath his majority for taking Britain into Europe. In 1972 he and I had both left the opposition front bench. In 1976 he had organised my unsuccessful campaign for the Labour Party leadership, and was the person who naturally took it upon himself to tell me at the end that the result was not going to be good.

My relationship with Bill Rodgers was qualitatively different from that with either David Owen or Shirley Williams. David Owen I had not known at all until 1966 and not well until 1970. From then until 1976 I had been almost as close to him as to Rodgers. He was equally frequently at East Hendred, although his presence commanded less enthusiasm from Jennifer than from me. And he was totally loyal to me up to the end of the leadership election. But once that was over he was at pains to make it clear that a new era had begun, and that the sooner I was off to Brussels the better it would be. Subsequently, in a rare moment of self-criticism, he explained to me that one of the great problems of his life had been getting out of my shadow, although I had not noticed that he suffered unduly from asparagus-like light starvation. When he unexpectedly became Foreign Secretary in 1977 not only I but Jennifer too was delighted. I remember our being told in Rome at an Italian Foreign Ministry banquet and our both exclaiming with pleasure. Despite the good beginning relations between Owen and me did not go altogether smoothly during the two and a quarter years of overlap between his secretaryship of state and my European presidency. I once teased him inexcusably before the other Foreign Ministers (although he had behaved both foolishly and tiresomely) and he sent round a minute reproving the Foreign Office for its growing habit of referring to me as *President* Jenkins. His reaction to the Dimbleby lecture I have already described.

With Shirley Williams I had the background of strong Cabinet alliance between 1974 and 1976 (I never sat in a Cabinet with David) and of my general pleasure in her company. But up to 1980 my relationship with her had been at once less close and less tense than my relationship with Owen. And at that time, although I now like to think that it has since developed into an emotionally loyal partnership, it was not exactly that. Shirley I regarded as a great prize. But to have acted without her would not have left a trauma in a way that acting without each other would, I believe, have affected both Bill Rodgers and me.

Yet, despite this and the fact that he was the only one of the three who had been present and enthusiastic at the Dimbleby lecture, Rodgers was also the one who, over the summer and autumn of 1980, found it most difficult to reconcile himself to leaving the Labour Party. I saw him for substantial discussions on seven occasions during that year. We were never at loggerheads, although there was an August lunch at East Hendred when I felt unusually out of step with him. But personal rapport was totally restored in October. Even as late as 11 December, however, I did not feel that he was of settled mind. I thought he would come, but I wanted him to do so with an enthusiastic heart and not merely out of conscripted loyalty.

Owen's evolution was utterly different. Having disliked my Dimbleby lecture he was more favourable to my inferior Press Gallery speech. The key event which had occurred in the meantime was a special Labour Party conference at Wembley on 31 May. A good indication of how my mind was then operating on alternative tracks is that this event made nil impact on me. It was not even mentioned in my *Diary*. This was because it was the day after the marathon Brussels meeting which settled the British Budgetary Question, and I was enveloped in a mixture of exhaustion, euphoria and temporary fixation with what was happening inside the Conservative Government rather than inside the Labour opposition. Yet that Wembley conference (there was to be another one in January 1981), was of vital significance from the point of view of the other enterprise I was pursuing. Without effective opposition from the 'Labourite right' (Callaghan, Healey, Hattersley, etc.), this conference carried a policy statement which blended unilateralism, protectionism and anti-Europeanism in about equal proportions. This retreat with barely a skirmish broke the authority of ex-Prime Minister Callaghan and his would-be successor, ex-Chancellor Healey, over the social democratic members of the former Cabinet. Thereafter the latter group recognised that they had to fight independently of the leadership, whether inside or outside the Labour Party. This separation which was created by midsummer made the fissure of the New Year much more possible.

There was another more personal impact of Wembley upon one of these former ministers. David Owen's prestige as a former Foreign Secretary did not prevent his being roundly booed when he bravely attempted to deliver a multilateralist speech. This appeared to have a dramatic effect on his view of the Labour Party. It was only a matter of a week or so since he had repudiated suggestions by Bill Rodgers and Shirley Williams that a time limit should be set within which the Labour Party must reform itself. Social democrats must stay and fight patiently, Owen then said, even if the battle took 'ten or twenty years'. But by June he had become much more of a young man in a hurry, much friendlier to those contemplating secession, and even willing, so I was told, to see some virtue in my Press Gallery speech.

This however reached me only indirectly, for it was 31 August before I resumed contact with him. The phrase 'resumed contact' may give too much of an impression of a stately restoration of diplomatic relations after a period when ambassadors had been withdrawn. There had been no rupture. It was perfectly easy to telephone and ask him and Debbie Owen to lunch at East Hendred, as indeed we had done almost exactly a year before, when there was no particular purpose to be served by the occasion. And they had been to us on a couple of other previous occasions since my departure from the House of Commons. But there was no doubt that links were much looser than they had been until then. When we went to Buttermere, the Owens' house twenty-five miles south of us, as significantly we did six weeks after this August 1980 East Hendred lunch, it was the first time we had been there for four years. It was also the case that, when Foreign Secretary, David never came to our house in Brussels, whereas Peter Carrington, his successor, did frequently and almost every other European Foreign

Minister did so occasionally. 'There is undoubtedly a reserve over our relationship,' I wrote after a 1979 visit. 'I think I would find it very difficult ever to be really close to him again. . . .'[14]

In August 1980 I was struck by how dramatically his political position had shifted in the past year: 'He had stiffened and toughened a lot, and also become in my view a great deal more agreeable than he had been since before he became Foreign Secretary.' There was not however on this occasion much firm forward planning: 'Very anxious to keep in touch for the future, and by no means certain what he was going to do if the Labour Party conference went wrong, about which he was definitely pessimistic.'[15]

That late September conference went even worse from the social democratic point of view than expected. There were votes in favour of unilateralism, withdrawal from Europe and the removal from the parliamentary party of the right to elect the leader – and therefore to choose the Prime Minister, if there ever was to be a Labour one again. But, to add the shambolic to the sinister, no majority could be obtained for a new method of election, and the resolution of this had to be postponed to yet another special conference in January. A London evening of television which I saw before going to Madrid for the second half of the week led me to write: 'Benn madder than ever, the conference in an ugly mood, Shirley in great fighting spirit. . . .'[16] When I saw Bill Rodgers, back from the Blackpool front, on Sunday, 3 October, I was still very uncertain what he was going to do, but nevertheless much more optimistic about the general political prospect. 'I now feel much easier about the political situation and whatever it may hold. I do not feel myself boxed in, in the way that I did in June, July and August.'[17]

The next impending event was the last parliamentary party election of a Labour leader, Callaghan having announced his retirement and the conference having voted as it did. The result of the first ballot was due on 4 November, and of the second ballot (the Labour Party believed in inflicting the 'first past the post' system only on the country not upon itself) on 10 November. The conventional wisdom is that Healey's defeat by Foot so dismayed the social democrats as to open the road to the SDP. I am not sure that is correct. What is the case is that it was much easier for us to fight the bye-elections of 1981–2 and the general election of 1983 against Foot rather than Healey as leader, but the truth of the autumn of 1980 was that the social democrats then within the Labour Party had become so disenchanted with Healey that his defeat was rather a relief to them. Foot was still worse on policies of course, but at least his election cleared the mind. From Healey's double change of line on Europe in the spring of 1971, through his contemptuous rejection of my suggestion that we might do something for Prentice in 1975, to his benignly assuring a 1980 delegation of the Manifesto Group (the social democratic right) that their votes were taken for granted by him because they had nowhere else to go, he had ensured with a remarkable determination that he had no dedicated troops. As a leader of the right of the Labour Party I may have cultivated too narrow and dedicated a band, but that was arguably better than having no band at all.

Owen's conversation with me at our second meeting of that autumn, on 19 October, left me in doubt whether he was even going to vote for Healey. He was definitely not going to campaign for him. One of Owen's virtues was that once his black-and-white mind moved he was prepared to act with speed and ruthlessness. Already by that Buttermere occasion he had leapfrogged Rodgers and Williams and seemed to have no emotional hang-ups about leaving the Labour Party. He was however insistent that a new party should be firmly left of centre and, as he rather oddly put it in view of the well-known reluctance of that body to have two parties from one country, 'Socialist International-affiliated'. He was eager to discuss the policy content of a new party, and was full of good ideas. He had also given a lot of thought to how computer technology could be used to run a new party much more efficiently (and centrally) than any old one had ever been.

He did not however absolutely commit himself to move. That he did to me only at our third country meeting – at East Hendred on 29 November. This one lasted a long time, nearly four hours. He said that he was convinced that Shirley would come too, although he was less confident about Bill. Shirley's joining was indeed central to his thought, for part of his mission that day was to tell me firmly that she and not I should be leader of the new party. He advocated this on the ground of her popularity, but also left me in no doubt that he attached importance to it as a symbol that I was joining them (the Gang of Three as they had been known since they had published a joint statement of position in the *Guardian* in the summer) and not *vice versa*. And it was again stressed that this was to be a Socialist International and not a centre party.

All this was presented more agreeably than it may sound, and did not begin to outweigh the great news that we were definitely in serious business. My strategy over the previous year, to the impatience of some of those working with me, had been to wait at least until the end of 1980 for Williams and Rodgers, and now it seemed that, just in the nick of time, I might be getting not only these two (I did not believe that Rodgers would stand aside while the rest of us moved), but Owen as well. The strategy, against the odds though this had frequently looked, had worked with almost copybook precision. I regarded this as much more important than any premature dispositions about the leadership. I was certainly not asking for a guarantee that it should be me, but nor was I accepting Owen's right to proscribe. I merely took note of his view.

I was also sceptical about the practicality of some of his wishes. 'There will now be a real break in the parliamentary party,' I wrote in my diary, 'and I may well get, at the end of the day, much more the sort of party I want than the sort of ex-Labour Party that for the moment he wants.'[18] What I meant by this was that I believed the new party must make a considerable appeal to those who had never been Labour voters (as well as to those who had) and that, while it should be radical, it would not long cling to the imprecise and musty 'socialist' label. This at any rate proved perceptive. By the autumn of 1981 David Owen himself removed the several mentions of 'socialist' from the second edition of his book *Face the Future*, and by the general election of 1987 there was a widespread fear that his leadership was taking the SDP and the Alliance not into the centre but to the right of politics.

What I did not know at that 29 November meeting was how seriously Owen had contemplated trying to exclude me from a Gang of Three socialist-orientated group which he might launch almost exclusively from within the parliamentary Labour Party. Evidence of this emerged both from a position paper which he wrote just about the time of the East Hendred November meeting and which leaked into the press (it however made practically no impact upon me) and from the political memoir which he dictated to Kenneth Harris in 1988. In 1980 he set out, perfectly fairly from his own point of view, the pros and cons of working with me and argued through to the reluctant conclusion that it was better to do so. He decided that too many of the political cadres of the new party were closely associated with me for anything else to be practicable. By the 1988 book he had decided that it was not merely me but Shirley Williams and Bill Rodgers as well that he would have been better without, so this latter effusion should not perhaps be taken too seriously.

Nor should any of this be allowed to detract, like a rewriting of history in the old Soviet Encyclopaedia, from the spurt of satisfaction accompanied by gratitude for his nerve and decisiveness which news of David Owen's adhesion to me (or permission for me to adhere to him if he prefers it) brought forth at the end of 1980. In retrospect I cannot but think that the cause of centre politics over the decade of the 1980s would have been better off without him. Except as a catalyst he was not crucial to the successful launch. There were not many early recruits who joined as Owen men or women. Shirley Williams overwhelmingly, but Bill Rodgers too, brought in more personal adherents. And up to and over the three crucial bye-elections – Warrington, Crosby and Hillhead – he arguably made the least propaganda impact of the four of us. Then, beginning with his 'good Falklands War', from which he emerged as second only to Mrs Thatcher as a trumpet of the nation, he achieved a pithiness of style which both on television and in an increasingly question-time-dominated House of Commons made him superbly suited to the modern political idiom and a great public asset to the SDP and the Alliance.

Unfortunately, as these public gifts developed, so he became more privately divisive. He no longer lacked personal adherents. Many became his devoted followers. But he did not find it easy to work on a basis of equality or semi-equality. It was not only the obvious strains with David Steel and with me. Relations with Rodgers, perhaps never very close, were sundered in 1986 when Owen dismissed the report of the Alliance Defence Commission into which Bill had put a great deal of careful and responsible work, and the saga of Shirley Williams's reluctant alienation from Owen, both personally and politically, was a running feature of the 1983–7 Parliament and the middle years of the SDP. But all this was well in the future in 1980, and can in no way affect the truth that I was keener to have Owen as an ally than he was to have me, and that once that was settled I was able to spend December concentrating on winding up my Brussels term and looking forward to what 1981 might bring with more enthusiasm than at most times in the preceding year.

# CHAPTER TWENTY-NINE

# *The* Annus Mirabilis *of the SDP*

The road from the Dimbleby lecture to the time of my return to British politics had thus been fairly stony for much of its length. Some of these stones, or even small boulders, persisted over the New Year and well into January 1981. The middle week of the month was the most boulder-strewn. During it the 'Gang of Four' met three times. This may not sound surprising, except that we had never previously been all together since before my departure for Brussels, and even then not as a specific quartet. The first two meetings went well, the third created more difficulty, particularly of time and place and avoiding the attentions of the press. The problems stemmed from Shirley Williams and Bill Rodgers still going through decision-making agonies, and David Owen and I, while both then resolved on action, being uneasy partners.

I then left for a five-day belated presidential valedictory visit to America (there had been no time to fit it in during the plethora of Brussels farewells in December), and on the whole I did so with relief. When I got back, on the morning of the special Labour Party conference at Wembley, which was the day before we signed the Limehouse Declaration, I found minds and issues settling into shape. The Declaration itself I had done a draft of before the meeting of the previous weekend, but it had not unnaturally gone through a number of changes during my week's absence, mainly I think at the hand of Shirley Williams. It was further redrafted during the morning meeting on Sunday, 25 January, at David Owen's dockland house. For such a co-operative effort it retained a surprising coherence. It committed us not to form a new party but to set up a Council for Social Democracy. However, the key sentences, which were the first and the last, were adequately committing. The first, which was not mine, said: 'The calamitous outcome of the Labour Party Wembley conference demands a new start in British politics.' The last, which was mine, said: 'But we believe that the need for a realignment of British politics must now be faced.' This gave clear notice that we were moving outside a Labour Party laager. Realignment cannot be a purely internal or unilateral act. There must be somebody with whom to realign. And the most obvious although not necessarily the only people whom this embraced were the Liberals.

It has sometimes been suggested that those who joined the SDP believing they were joining a pure and exclusive party were sold a false prospectus and subsequently hijacked first into alliance and then into amalgamation with the Liberals. In my view this is nonsense. The clearest notice of my intentions was given both in the Dimbleby lecture and in the Press Gallery speech. And this approach was substantially endorsed by the other three when they signed their names immediately after a ringing appeal for 'realignment'. Furthermore an attack on the sterility of exclusive politics, on the view that any party is a sacred tabernacle with those within it anointed and those outside damned, was part of the central message which was hammered home from a thousand SDP platforms right from the inauguration of the party.

This was not of course the same as advocating an immediate merger with the Liberal Party. There would have been no point in starting a new party in order to do that. The case for merger arose only once the partnership had been tried on the ground and found satisfactory in most respects, although considerably burdened by the disadvantages of having two leaders and the travail of allocating seats between two parties and selecting candidates by different methods within a single Alliance. At the beginning, while I was committed in my mind to a close partnership, I had no set view either for or against eventual merger. That evolved, and when it did the concept of merger after six and a half years of working together was in no way nugatory of the purposes of the new party. The Missouri is not a pointless river because, after a fertilising and dramatic course, it eventually unites with the Mississippi.

The essential importance of the Limehouse Declaration was not so much what it said as the fact that after a long period of internal confabulation it took us out into the public domain. Thereafter our course became more the product of the strong currents of public opinion running in the open sea than of over-prolonged harbour conferences. The new mood was perfectly (if not flatteringly, at least so far as my likeness is concerned) caught in a cartoon by Gibberd which appeared in the *Guardian* on 2 February and is reproduced in this book. Messages of support poured in: eight thousand came in the first week, and another fifteen thousand soon thereafter. Many sent money as a token of commitment, although the sums were mostly small and there was never anything worth speaking of from business firms. A temporary headquarters in Queen Anne's Gate was acquired within two weeks of Limehouse, and was manned mainly by volunteers, who were often as distinguished as they were enthusiastic, and in an atmosphere of happy confusion tried to cope with the flood of letters and telephone calls. The belief that 'a new start' would appeal not only to disillusioned Labour activists but also to many of energy and public spirit who had previously been alienated from the political process proved abundantly justified from the beginning.

There was no doubt either that those whose imaginations had been fired by the Limehouse Declaration wanted a new political party and wanted it quickly. They were not interested in the hesitations which had led to the halfway house of a Council for Social Democracy, half in and half out of the Labour Party. In response to this clear mood any vestigial doubts about whether the CSD should lead on to an SDP were swept away from the minds of the founders and there was no resistance to the date of the launch of the new party being brought forward from May or later to 26 March.

This wind of support also had a bracing effect upon relations within the collective leadership, which was the awkward but in the circumstances inevitable formula which we decided to apply within the Gang of Four until such time as we had a party constitution which would enable us to elect officers. The neuroses of January were mostly left behind as soon as we discovered that, whether by accident or design, we had put ourselves at the head of a pulsating popular movement. There were one or two isolated attempts by David Owen to resurrect a 'Gang of Three plus one' approach. One of them, when he proposed that in a division of leadership functions my role should be confined to fund-raising, might be regarded as serious, although he was quickly laughed out of court by Bill Rodgers, and I ended up with policy. The other was ludicrous. He vetoed my suggestion that I should join with the three in giving a wedding present to Alec McGivan, our national agent, on the ground that McGivan had previously worked with the three more closely in the Labour Party than he had with me. This led to McGivan getting two presents instead of one, but I think it was due more to the fact that we quickly fought two bye-elections together that he became a firmer supporter of me than of David.

For the most part, however, Owen was a good partner during 1981 and the early months of 1982, as most certainly were the other two. The period was one of great exhilaration for all of us. It is difficult to recapture its atmosphere, which was a mixture of heady excitement and slight apprehension that we were dicing with the unknown, sailing an uncharted sea, doing things for the first time and improvising as we went along. At first, in order to try to get a structure for the new party, we were too much involved in committee sessions: meetings of the Gang of Four, meetings of the steering committee of about fifteen, which we set up early in February and which met once a week, meetings between the parliamentary group and Shirley Williams and me, because neither of us was then in the House of Commons, *ad hoc* meetings on policy questions, which were supposed to be my special responsibility. This phase culminated in the public launch of the new party, and was redeemed by the fact that every day seemed to bring news of fresh recruits, a trickle of MPs, a larger flow of Labour and independent peers, a lot of journalists, lawyers, academics and former civil servants together with a good proportion of Labour Party stalwarts, often powerfully entrenched in provincial towns and counties. There was a warming impression that the SDP was not only sending a current of interest through middle England but was also bringing together (amongst many others) a lot of the people I most liked and respected.

The launch itself was handled with professional competence by Mike Thomas, MP for Newcastle and a public relations man to his finger-tips. It was just a little too much of a professional show I occasionally thought (as when, after we had all spoken briefly to a vast London press conference in the Connaught Rooms, he tried hard to fly me by special plane to Cardiff for my next leg; I had firmly to insist that the ordinary train from Paddington was much cheaper, as quick and more comfortable). But this was better than it being an amateur shambles, and Thomas deserves full credit for having secured a vast metropolitan impact and then sent the four of us spinning like tops round the main Scottish, Welsh and provincial centres. I did Manchester and Liverpool after Cardiff.

With the launch past we began our public-meeting phase. The SDP was often accused of being a media creation. This was not true. Indeed, as early as 1982–3, many of our by no means neurotic supporters believed we were suffering from media starvation. What we were was a party of public meetings. For a time we restored the public meeting to a position in British political life which it had been steadily losing for the previous thirty years. I estimate that my meeting drawing power as one of the Gang of Four was about four times what it had been as a highly controversial and politically exposed Chancellor of the Exchequer twelve years before. Packed audiences in medium-sized halls became an almost guaranteed feature of life in the early SDP. No doubt curiosity was a part of the motive, but those who came were never hostile, sometimes enthusiastic, sometimes passively attentive. As a result I came to enjoy campaigning in the country, both from the platform and a little later, when bye-elections had become the foci, engaging with casual crowds in the streets, market places and shopping centres more than I would have believed possible in my previous thirty-five years of politics.

In April and May my forays were largely in the south-east of England, although not exclusively so for I went to Edinburgh, Perth and Aberdeen, as well as to Bolton and Birmingham. The occasions I remember most vividly are three. First, an improvised meeting in Wantage, our local town four miles from East Hendred. There was a certain appropriateness about Wantage, for a decade or so before Bernard Levin, more a supporter of the centre left in those days, had written a *Times* column urging me to set up my standard in its market place and assuring me that I would be surprised at how many would rally. This 1981 meeting was not in the market place but in the Civic Hall, arranged at only a few days' notice at the inconvenient time of 7.15 and for only an hour, which was all I could manage. The hall (not large) was crammed, with people not only on the chairs but sitting on every square foot of floor. Every window was open and outside each of them there was a semi-circle of overflow. The audience seemed to be a complete cross-section of this rather prosperous and hitherto quietly Conservative market and commuting town. A posse of nuns from the Anglican convent, who must have arrived early, occupied the front row of seats.

The second was the inaugural meeting of the Association of Social Democratic Lawyers, held in the Old Hall of Lincoln's Inn. Anthony Lester, my former adviser at the Home Office, already well on the way to becoming the leading human-rights QC, had procured my attendance. Robert Maclennan was in the chair. It was the first occasion on which I remember meeting William Goodhart, who with his wife Celia was to play an incomparable role in the history of the SDP. Once again the hall was packed, although it was much larger than the one at Wantage. Lawyers, many of whom must have spent a considerable part of the day 'on their feet', seemed for the moment to have a surprising appetite for listening to more words on their way home. I think I made a better speech than at Wantage. At least the notes for it, undergoing some mutation, formed the basis for many a subsequent one. And a large and active Social Democratic Lawyers' Association was born.

The third occasion was in a location very different from either the downland urbanity of Wantage or the parchment tradition of Lincoln's Inn. It was in the old Ilford Town Hall, deep in East London. The meeting had been going for some time when I arrived and had a swirling quality about it. It was unusual in that there may have been a few interruptions, and there were certainly some semi-hostile questions. But it was boisterously successful and encouraged the establishment of a good area party in that not obviously favourable territory.

There was also a fourth occasion, which illustrated our public-meeting strength, although this comes from a later phase, after the Warrington bye-election. On a Saturday in September I had arranged to do an afternoon's street campaigning in Redhill and Dorking, followed by an evening meeting in the Civic Hall at Guildford. At about six it began to rain torrentially and this continued until we arrived at the hall one and a half hours later. There were 1700 people present, all of whom must have come through the downpour. I have never been more amazed in my life, nor ever before or since been able to attract such an audience in such unfavourable conditions.

News that the first parliamentary bye-election in the life of the SDP was to be in Warrington came in the last week of May, when I was on a week's holiday near Lucca. The sitting Labour member became a circuit judge. I was immediately aware that I might have to fight it. This was odd, for all the accounts of the early days of the SDP refer to the almost universal expectation that Shirley Williams would be the candidate, and it was certainly the case that Warrington with its large (mostly English rather than Irish) Catholic population and its solid Labourite tradition was more suited to her demotic appeal than to mine, such as mine was. Perhaps, although I cannot specifically remember this, I had some private knowledge of the circumstances which made it impossible for her to fight a seat until the autumn, as she subsequently announced. There was no doubt, however, that as a party we had to fight Warrington, unpropitious a prospect though it looked. On some basis of calculation which I suspect produced a bogus precision we had it marked down as 551st in order of hopefulness for us amongst the 635 constituencies of the United Kingdom. But to have let it pass would have been widely taken as an ignominious sign that we were a debating-society party rather than a serious electoral force. We were the more vulnerable on this score because our strong opinion-poll support of April showed some sign of slipping away during May. It was also thought necessary that we should field a national candidate, particularly as we had little in the way of local membership from which to choose.

On 4 June I was engaged to address an international bankers' conference in Switzerland. I persuaded Jennifer to go in the opposite direction to make a private reconnaissance of Warrington. (I could not have gone without attracting a lot of publicity.) So on that night of effective decision I stayed in the Hôtel Beau-Rivage, Lausanne, and looked out from the balcony of my suite across a moonlit Lake of Geneva to the Savoy Alps. She stayed in the Patten Arms Hotel, Warrington, and looked out, without a balcony I think, over the railway station and the soap works which had been a founding pillar of the first Lord Leverhulme's massive combine. We were soon together

again on the neutral ground of the Fir Grove Motel, just beyond the
Manchester Ship Canal and on the southern edge of Warrington,
where we spent nearly the whole of the next five weeks, including
much the longest continuous series of nights in any one place that I
had spent for at least five, maybe ten, years past.

Jennifer's report was not particularly favourable. She said that
Warrington had an attractive cohesiveness and distinct identity, a
fine church and a few good c.1800 buildings, but that it was a
solidly industrial small borough, with a lot of council estates and
not much middle-class population. Furthermore the boundaries of
the borough and of the parliamentary constituency were drawn
so tight that most of that limited middle-class population was
extruded into adjacent constituencies. It looked more interesting
than a slice of anonymous suburb, but it also looked a very hard
nut to crack.

The next few weeks confirmed nearly all these views. Warrington
was very flat topographically, but I never found it so in any
other sense. Geographically it is at the point where the Mersey
becomes tidal, halfway between Manchester and Liverpool, and
was also the southernmost of the chain of Lancashire boroughs,
Warrington, Wigan, Preston, Lancaster, which for centuries ran up
the route to Scotland until 1973 when Peter Walker presumptuously
decided to move Warrington into Cheshire. It had an interesting
late-eighteenth-century history, when it almost became the third
university town of England, although it was barren enough of higher
educational institutions in 1981. It had a large covered market and
a tight little shopping area which made it ideal for the relentless
pressing of the flesh. Apart from soap and detergents it made a
range of somewhat old-fashioned light-engineering products, a brand
of cakes curiously known as Memory Lane, and Vladimir vodka. The
owners of that distillery had shown their wit (or that of their public
relations consultant) by a competition in which the first prize was one
week's holiday in Warrington and the second prize two weeks' holiday
in Warrington. But I amazed myself by the extent to which I enjoyed
my four and a half weeks of non-holiday in Warrington, and I have
long retained an almost physical affection for it. When going through
on the main line from Euston north I have looked out for its landmarks
– the crossing of the Mersey, the elevated station, the soap works, the
Patten Arms (the Fir Tree is not visible), the wire works in the north
of the town – with a nostalgic obsession. This pleasure became heavily
reduced during the break-up of the old SDP in 1987–8 when the taste
of recollection became bitter rather than sweet. Maybe, rather like
the memory of a love affair which went wrong, it is now regaining
its fragrance.

I fear that I have not explained adequately how my decision to fight Warrington ever came to be taken, except to say that Jennifer's report aroused interest rather than provided rational encouragement. Somehow the decision became cumulatively inevitable in my mind, although not in the public expectation, for one significant factor was a column (I have happily forgotten by whom) to the effect that I would never dream of soiling my fingers in such a northern industrial borough. I think the night in the excessive luxury of the Hôtel Beau-Rivage also had something of a topping-off effect. Maybe I required a period if not of penance at least of austerity after the comfort (but not the ease) of Brussels. Needless to say, I have never regretted the decision.

I announced my intention on 8 June, went to Warrington for the first time three days later, was enthusiastically adopted by a meeting of the SDP members in the town heavily fortified by those from the surrounding areas, was accepted at a separate meeting by the even fewer Liberals, and next morning apprehensively put my toe in the waters of contact with the electorate in the covered market. The waters did not seem as cold as they might have been, but the tension of finding out was increased by the fact that, in contrast with my nine quiet Stechford elections, every word exchanged with a voter was done in the presence of about ten press correspondents and television reporters. Five days later we went back and settled in to a campaign with a 16 July polling day.

It was a campaign which went satisfactorily in all respects except one. The exception was that we failed to make any impact on the opinions polls which were conducted locally by the most reputable national organisations. They came out each Monday for four weeks, and made the beginning of the week a dependable day of gloom. We started on 29 per cent with the Labour Party on 60 per cent and we finished on 31 per cent with the Labour Party on 59 per cent. We did not have to win, which indeed we never expected to do, but we had to do a great deal better than that to make the enterprise a success. We thought we detected a number of more favourable signs. There was discontent even in what were nominally the most solid Labour areas. The inhabitants of the council estates felt neglected and taken for granted by the local Labour hierarchy, and were amazed that we took the trouble to canvass them, an experience which they had not had for some time. And that hierarchy itself, quite a lot of whom were Catholic and right-wing, were unhappy with the extremist lurch of the Labour Party. The candidate, Doug Hoyle, a left-wing trade unionist, was then an enthusiastic agent of that lurch, although I believe that he is today a respectable Kinnockite. He did little to provide reassurance to those in this category. I remember vividly my pleasure when the

Labour Mayor, a friendly railwayman, told me that he was going to vote for me and not for Hoyle.

Another hopeful sign was that there seemed at that stage to be no support at all for Mrs Thatcher in the town. The Conservative candidate was a Jewish London busdriver called Stan Sorrell. It was an odd choice, although I suppose was intended to illustrate the classlessness of Mrs Thatcher's party. His background made him no good at holding the 'deference' vote, which small though it was in Warrington might have been steadier than the ideological support. Sorrell was a nice and forthright man, who performed for me the useful service of killing the abortion issue, which there was a considerable attempt to beat up in Catholic Warrington, by announcing that he was just as much in favour of the existing law (introduced by David Steel with heavy support from me in 1967) as were Hoyle and myself. This did me more good than it did Sorrell, who suffered a terrible collapse of his vote, losing over three-quarters of it, polling only 2100 and producing one of the worst results on record for a government candidate. There was also a string of seven fringe candidates, none of whom made much impact upon the result.

The interest therefore lay in seeing by how much I could boost the small Liberal vote of 2800 at the general election and cut the Labour majority of over 10,000. The battle was fought essentially in the streets. Despite our platform success elsewhere and in contrast with Hillhead eight months later, it was not primarily a public-meeting campaign. Warrington was not that sort of town. I had one very successful meeting with Shirley Williams on almost the only hot evening of the summer, and three or four other perfectly adequate ones with David Steel, Bill Rodgers and David Owen. But the emphasis was on less formal contact with the electorate. From the beginning we canvassed the town, almost all made up of small terraced or semi-detached houses and practically no tenements, with the intensity of carpet bombing. Throughout we worked the covered market and the surrounding streets with an unrelenting dedication which must have driven stallholders and frequent shoppers to distraction. Towards the end we came more and more to 'cavalcade' around, with me standing up on the platform of an open truck and trying to get answering waves from passing or shopping or gardening electors, with blasts of music from *Chariots of Fire* or Copland's *The Century of the Common Man* interspersed with Bill Rodgers developing a remarkable and previously undiscovered technique of microphone badinage. This may sound as though it were more an assault upon than a wooing of the public. But it gave us more of an accurate feeling that towards the end we were doing well than did either the polls or canvassing. By the Monday before polling day we began to notice a lot of almost surreptitious waves, often from upstairs windows, and, as it were, around the curtains, on the council estates. By the Wednesday they were more open. On polling day itself we were greeted wherever we went by a chorus of tooting motor horns.

For these varying forms of open-air activity the weather was about as good as it could have been. It was almost continuously dry, cool, cloudy and, of course, light far into the evenings. We deployed nearly all our incoming supporters into these direct-contact efforts. The other members of the four were not encouraged just to do their meetings and go away again. Nor was David Steel, who paid three separate visits, only one of which involved mounting a platform. On the first of them I took him to a fair which was part of the annual Warrington Walks festivities and indeed upon an 'amusement' device which gyrated so violently that he lost his wallet. In the circumstances it was good of him to come back, but important that he did, for the Alliance was made upon the ground at Warrington. The Warrington Liberals could not do much for us except not get in the way. But the Liberals from the North-West Region and beyond did a great deal.

Jo Grimond arrived unannounced one Saturday morning, intending only to cast an eye, half benevolent and half sceptical, over the proceedings, but was sufficiently engaged to stay for most of the day. Laura Grimond was up at 5.00 to deliver leaflets on the morning of polling day. As Mark and Leslie Bonham Carter* were also much in active evidence this may seem to give credence to what was well later said to be a good mordant joke of David Owen's (although it does not sound to me exactly his style). 'Roy claims to love Liberals,' he was reported as saying, 'but he has never actually spoken to one who is not called Grimond or Bonham Carter.'

Warrington made that nearly the opposite of the truth. Cyril Smith, who had at one stage talked about 'strangling the SDP at birth', came across from Rochdale at my direct request and held an effective meeting. The Liverpool Liberals, who had the same connotation for some members of the SDP as marauding bands of football supporters, sent over several coach-loads of skilled and vigorous canvassers, from whom we learned a lot about the techniques of guerrilla politics without the resources of massed battalions and traditional votes. There was no inter-party friction and everybody got along together very well.

In spite of this heart-warming campaign, I remained very uncertain about the outcome. My fears of a humiliating 15 per cent, which I had regarded as perfectly possible in June, had been left behind. But something loosely around 30 per cent seemed likely. I remember

* Laura Grimond is Mark Bonham Carter's sister.

saying at supper between the close of the poll and the count that if I were then offered a devil's pact with a guaranteed 35 per cent in return for the sacrifice of any chance of doing better, I would find it difficult not to accept. An hour later, when we got into the half-completed count, it was at once obvious that we had done much better. A flamboyant Tory councillor and off-licence owner assured me that I had won and offered to bet me a most extravagant bottle of wine that this was so. I was confident that it was not and accepted. (He never paid.)

We got 42.5 per cent and reduced the Labour majority to 1750. It was much better than we had expected, produced headlines of triumph in the next morning's newspapers, and meant that the rest of the evening (if the time from 11.00 p.m. to 3.00 a.m. can be so described) was wildly exhilarating. After the formal declaration Hoyle made a sour and truculent speech, which provoked me to recast what I was going to say at the last moment (something at which I am not normally good), to mock his pretence that he had triumphed when he had achieved the worst Labour result in Warrington for over fifty years, and to announce that, although it was my first election defeat since 1945, it was also 'by far the greatest victory in which I have ever participated'. In other words the SDP was firmly launched as a serious electoral force. This all went out on live television and appeared to create as much impact as the rest of the campaign put together.

The next day, at the inspired suggestion of Jack Diamond, my Chief Secretary at the Treasury a dozen years before,* who had been a devoted and self-effacing supporter throughout the campaign, we toured the town in the battle wagon and to the familiar strains for an hour at the end of the morning. The impression then was that there was not a man or woman in Warrington who had not voted for me the day before. It was sometimes subsequently suggested that had the campaign gone on for a few days longer we would have won. I do not believe that. I think we had wrung out almost every vote that was to be won so long as people did not know how others were

---

* One of my satisfactions from the SDP was the near unanimity with which those who had served in departments with me came over. The Treasury team of 1969–70 did so complete: Diamond, Taverne, Rodgers. So did my PPS, Tom Bradley, and Edward Lyons, who had served the other ministers. The exception from earlier Treasury days was Harold Lever (Lord Lever of Manchester), but he was somewhat incapacitated by this time and always very sympathetic. From the Home Office of 1974–6, John Harris (Lord Harris of Greenwich) joined and worked in Warrington even more of the time than did Jack Diamond. My successive PPSs Gwynoro Jones and Ian Wrigglesworth were most active members, and John Watkinson, who worked with the junior ministers there, became SDP candidate for the Forest of Dean.

voting. In the 'solid' Labour areas there was reluctance to announce this, certainly within streets, perhaps within families. This fitted in with the surreptitious waves.

What I do believe is that had there been a rerun of the election, with the knowledge of the first result in people's minds, we might well have won. That is not as far-fetched an eventuality as it may sound. A candidate who was disqualified because he changed his name to mine and tried to run as a 'Social Democrat' (my designation was 'SDP with Liberal support'), went to the High Court and tried to get an order setting aside the validity of the result. That would have involved a fresh election. My desires were split. I admired the firmness of the returning officer's decision (which his colleague in Hillhead signally failed to imitate in similar circumstances in 1982) and I did not exactly fancy another four weeks in August on the streets even of beloved Warrington. But I think that a different decision by the judge, and that alone, would have given us victory.

I was not disposed to grieve over this 'might have been' as John Harris drove us down from Warrington to Oxfordshire on the Friday afternoon following the triumphal parade. Warrington had succeeded beyond my highest expectations when I had last seen East Hendred four weeks before. It had underpinned the nascent SDP, created an experience and a climate which were highly favourable to the fostering of the Alliance, and increased both my own sense of confidence with the electorate (after nearly five years of separation) and my authority within the party. The fact that I was still not in the House of Commons counted for little compared with this. I wanted to get back only to change the shape of British politics and not for the sake of being an MP again, and towards that end I had contributed much more by the Warrington summer campaign than by winning a quiet bye-election.

The autumn was also very good for the SDP and for the Alliance, which emerged for the first time in September as a name with public impact. Warrington had done much to blend the whisky, but it had not put the label on the bottle. Even before that some important personal links had been formed. At the beginning of the year the three other members of the four did not know David Steel well, although Bill Rodgers had been an intermediary with him at the creation of the Lib–Lab pact in 1977. When I organised a tripartite dinner with Steel and Shirley Williams on 5 March I did so rather in the mood of a nervous duenna who hoped that the young people would get on well together. By April, however, these two together with Bill Rodgers had enjoyed a successful joint expedition to the annual Anglo-German weekend at Königswinter, where they had made at least as much progress towards bringing the SDP and the

Liberals together as to uniting Europe. Then in June Steel and Shirley Williams took the lead in drafting a 'statement of principles' on the basis of which the two parties could work together. When it was issued they were photographed together on a plot of Westminster grass and looking, as one chronicler of the SDP put it, 'like superannuated student lovers'. Rodgers was also a member of a group of nine which was responsible for this document. David Owen and I were not directly involved. I was delighted to be excluded, for I wanted the links between the two parties to become more organic and less dependent upon me as the sole hinge. David Owen may, I suppose, have seen things differently, although he made no complaint at the time, and indeed enthusiastically accepted the constructive idea that the two parties should establish joint commissions on important areas of policy.

The next crucial event was the Liberal Party Assembly at Llandudno in the third week of September. There was some prior fear that the Assembly might rise up in its ancestral pride and reject David Steel's realignment strategy. I was asked to take part in a fringe meeting, which I understood was to be in the form of a brains trust, on the evening before the crucial debate. The other participants were to be Shirley Williams, David Steel and Jo Grimond. I think I envisaged a gathering of a couple of hundred in an ambience rather like that of a BBC *Any Questions* session. I understood that a few introductory remarks might be in order, but that they would be subordinate to essential question-and-answer proceedings. I did not therefore devote much attention to their preparation, contrary to my habit with important speeches. I was in Paris the night before, and merely scribbled out a few sentences in the mid-morning plane from there to Manchester. I then drove to Warrington where I had only once been since the election, and held a reunion lunch of eight or ten of my most active local supporters in the Patten Arms before being driven to Llandudno. I arrived only an hour before the meeting and discovered that it was on a totally different scale from my expectation. There were about two thousand people packed into the Pier Pavilion. Almost inevitably with a gathering of this size the orating took over from the requests for information. David Steel was prepared and spoke authoritatively. Shirley Williams did not need to be prepared and spoke with enveloping persuasiveness. Jo Grimond was less prepared than I was and spoke with that mixture of mocking deflation and fastidious elevation which Liberals, in spite of their alleged inability to raise their sights above the paving stones, have loved for thirty years. My Warrington clouds of glory made up for any inadequacy in my preparation and presentation. Insofar as my speech had a central message it was this:

Is the Alliance creditable? Is it honest? Again I answer unswervingly 'yes'. . . . We can therefore honourably achieve not a marriage of convenience but a partnership of principle. I would go further and say that it can be still more. To use an old Gladstonian phrase, it can be an union of hearts. Of course we can let it all slip. You can fall back on your ancient purity and we can console ourselves with our exciting novelty. But what fools we would be if we did. Mrs Thatcher and Mr Foot would heave sighs of relief. Still more important a great part of public opinion would experience a sense of disappointment and let-down. The duopoly would survive, unloved, uncreative, but almost unscarred. This must not happen. We have jointly made an unprecedented opportunity. Let us seize it together in an Alliance of mutual respect and mutual trust.

By some process of spontaneous combustion the occasion took off and *The Times* led the next morning with a story of 'the rapturous welcome' for Shirley and me in the bosom of Liberalism. It made the following morning's vote almost a formality. The majority for David Steel's strategy was approximately fifteen to one. Bill Rodgers had arrived overnight and Shirley and he and I sat in the gallery and were at once happy observers and centres of media and delegate attention.

David Owen was missing. He was, I believe, still on holiday in America, but it is doubtful if he would have wished to be there even had his vacation been in Colwyn Bay. I am not sure. It may be that his subsequent coolness towards the Alliance stemmed partly from regret that he was not present on 'St Crispin's Day' and that he 'a gentleman then abed in (New) England thought himself accurs'd he was not there'. But he did not express himself in these or similar terms, and it is, I suppose, more likely that his absence was due to his coolness rather than the other way round. Six years later he wrote that he thought Shirley's fringe meeting at Llandudno was going to be 'low key', and that he had no idea that David Steel and I were also going to speak. Otherwise 'permission' might not have been given by the steering committee.[1] What is certain, however, is that Llandudno was crucial to future attitudes towards the Alliance. The three of us who were there henceforth regarded it, even in moments of occasional exasperation, *con amore*, as a union of hearts as well as a partnership of principle. The one who was not there regarded it as a marriage of convenience, necessary and requiring the respectful observance of forms in public, but not to be confused with affection.

This stemmed from a deeper difference of approach, at least between Owen and me, and one which was concerned with our attitude not merely to Liberals but to the whole position of parties in the political process. One of my strongest convictions by 1979–81 was that political parties across the board and independently of their labels had got above themselves, and that their discipline, their exclusiveness, their hubris, their polemicism, were nationally damaging. I thought of the SDP as an anti-party party, which would bring together a swathe of opinion, liberal and internationalist, concerned with conscience and reform, without attempting to reproduce the cells of party fanaticism which showed themselves in Labour selection conferences or Conservative standing ovations for the leader's annual conference speech, and which had done so much to repel many of goodwill and public spirit from the party game. Thus Owen's language about whether 'permission' should or would have been granted to Shirley Williams or to me to speak at Llandudno brought with it a whiff of caucus politics which I found repugnant.

Thus, also, one of our few early open disputes about relations with the Liberals (for the underlying differences rarely surfaced in 1981) was over the question of dual membership. I did not see why Liberals who were enthusiastic about the new party should not if they wished join it without having to renounce their old affiliation. I think I would have taken the same view about former Labour or Conservative supporters who were moving towards us. It would amount to no more than the probably temporary ambiguity of which most of our founders had availed themselves during the Council for Social Democracy phase, and I discounted heavily any practical danger of mass infiltration in order to destroy. Owen, however, easily defeated me on this issue. Unusually, I found myself in a minority on the steering committee.

Owen wanted a tighter and more exclusive party than I did, and one over which, once he had become leader, he could exercise more personal control. I wanted a movement broad enough (and probably necessarily therefore also loose enough) to have a chance of accomplishing the 'one-leap' strategy and breaking through to government, electoral reform and smashing the Labour and Conservative duopoly. He, I think, was always more sceptical about the prospect (rightly as it turned out, although this begs the question of the extent to which his attitude to the Alliance made his scepticism self-fulfilling), and wanted more of a guerrilla band which could alternate between marauding raids and going into winter quarters, always under tight discipline. It was a Tito-like concept of campaigning, whereas mine was more that of Garibaldi, with his loosely disciplined and non-uniformed 'thousand', co-operating freely with disparate figures from Cavour and Mazzini to local figures who joined in on the march.

David Owen has subsequently accused me of seeing the SDP as merely 'a transit camp' on the way to merger with the Liberals. That is not true. From the beginning I had a total conviction that we must not dissipate our energies in fighting the Liberals, but this was balanced by an equal conviction that the creation of a new entity was essential.

My 1981 hope was that we might within a couple of years be able to form a government with the Liberals, and perhaps with some other elements as well. My approach was essentially ecumenical, and I would have been happy to have some cross-benchers or independents and would certainly not have said 'no' to Tory wets or for that matter to a social democrat in the Labour Party who for some reason or other jibbed at changing his label. I assumed that such a government would be more SDP than Liberal dominated, although there would obviously be a major place for David Steel and a near equality in numbers if not seniority of posts for other Liberals. With our ex-Foreign Secretary, ex-Chancellor, five other ex-Cabinet ministers and another half-dozen or more who had held junior posts, this was not an unreasonable assumption. I also naturally hoped that such a government would be enough of a long-lasting success that those in it would not when it was over wish to separate politically. Quite what shape their continued co-operation would take I regarded as a matter for the future. It might be integrated in practice but separate in form as was the relationship of the Liberal Unionists with the Conservatives for some time after the end of their joint Government of 1895–1905. But I must confess that insofar as there was any boa-constrictor work to be done I thought the SDP rather than the Liberal Party would do the swallowing.

Of course I also contemplated the possibility of a 'lower case' outcome, something much more like the actual results of the 1983 and 1987 elections. In these circumstances my view of how the structure of the Alliance should develop was similar to Churchill's hopeful comparison of Anglo-American unity to the course of the Mississippi. 'Let it roll,' he said in August 1940, 'let it roll on in full flood, inexorable, irresistible, benignant, to broader lands and better days.' I believed that no one should seek to set a limit to what grew, naturally and organically, on the ground. Local parties should not be forced together, but nor should they be kept artificially apart. After the 1983 election, but only then, I came to the view that merger would be the most desirable outcome. Even after that, I was still content to wait throughout another Parliament for the concept to gain more general grass-roots acceptance.

Despite these mostly subterranean strains the autumn of 1981 was a golden one. We had our first SDP conference week at the beginning of October. As, until February 1982, we had no constitution, any assembly had no formal validity beyond that of being a gathering of those who wished to come together. We adventurously decided to roll with this punch and not attempt to imitate a Labour or a Conservative conference. Not only did we eschew the Blackpools and the Brightons but we tried to spread our impact by having a touring conference. We started in Perth and after forty-eight hours went by a special train made up of very old LMS first-class restaurant cars (but with no service) to Bradford. After another forty-eight hours the train rolled on to Euston, where we started again the next morning in the Central Hall, Westminster. We repeated this the following year with sojourns in Cardiff, Derby and Great Yarmouth. The train, which seemed to have aged more than a year in the meantime, broke down for several hours in the Fens on the stretch to Yarmouth. So we decided that we had done enough for British Rail and settled down in Salford in 1983 (not a success), Buxton in 1984, Torquay in 1985 and Harrogate in 1986. The last three proved good medium-sized conference centres and I regret that the Liberal Democrats have allowed themselves to be lured to the traditional conference megalopolises.

Perth was a challenging choice of an opening city. It is the centre of the most Conservative region of Scotland, and, while the countryside is smiling as well as beautiful, the burgh, although christened 'fair' like its maid, has a certain closed austerity. I remember going to the City Hall through deserted streets on a rather dreich Sunday morning and once there having to open cold before an audience of perhaps two hundred. Richard Crawshaw, then MP for Toxteth and a former Deputy Speaker, now alas dead, said a few brief words from the chair after which I launched into the first conference oration in the life of the SDP. There was a touch of shouting into the wind about the opening sentences: 'This party is still less than seven months old. Its impact during the 192 days since that wet and hazardous morning of the launch on 26 March has been greater than our highest hopes. We have confounded the sceptics. We have enthused our followers. We have rallied our Liberal allies. . . .'

Things looked up after the cold start. The Perth audience swelled, the Bradford one was substantially bigger, five more Labour MPs, several of the highest quality, announced their adherence while we were there and were hastily transported to join us on the platform during my second speech of the series. They got more applause than even my best rhetoric. Then in London we achieved a really big audience and I made my third full-length speech of the week and endeavoured to put forward a coherent economic programme.

Nevertheless the dominant features of the autumn were not conferences but bye-elections and public opinion polls. Shirley was now eagerly seeking a contest, and would have liked to fight Croydon North-west, where the Conservative member had died in August. This was frustrated by the incumbent Liberal candidate, who had three times fought the constituency with steadily declining success yet insisted on staying put. Quite why the seat was so popular was not obvious, for this candidate had got only 10 per cent of the vote in 1979. Nor was he a conventionally good candidate. But perhaps, by some paradox, a combination of a strongly flowing pro-Alliance national tide and a little man with local roots who was not going to be pushed around by stars from London was a peculiarly effective recipe. At any rate on 22 October Bill Pitt achieved a swing only a wafer less than Warrington, won the seat with a majority nearly as big as his 1979 vote, and became the first MP to be elected under the Alliance label.

Three weeks before that the Conservative MP for Crosby had also died. The Crosby constituency was a group of three towns which lay between Liverpool and Southport, contained a mixture of commuting suburbia, retirement homes among sand-duned golf courses, a flat rural area in which fine church spires rose up across depressing cabbage fields, and the northern fringe of Merseyside dockland. The cocktail had been mixed in such a way as to produce massive Conservative majorities – 19,000 in 1979. Suddenly, at our Bradford conference, Shirley Williams announced that she was going to storm this formidable citadel. There was a slight hiccup to begin with, for hardly anybody, locally or nationally, had been told about this beforehand, but she quickly rallied from this and fought a brilliantly persuasive campaign. She had to circumnavigate the dangerous rocks of independent education (Crosby had a lot of modest fee-paying schools, including one which had educated Archbishop Runcie of Canterbury) and abortion, in which waters the Conservative candidate fished around hard, unlike his opposite number at Warrington. She was much less vulnerable on this latter issue than I was and maintained a close relationship with Archbishop Warlock of Liverpool (this passage is making the bye-election sound very archiepiscopal).

Post-Croydon Shirley had a strong tide flowing behind her but she rode it with as much skill as warmth. The other three of us as well as David Steel went often to Crosby, despite the fact that by then we had a heavy programme of prearranged speaking up and down the country. Between her announcement and her polling day I spoke at SDP meetings in Cleveland, Birmingham, Swansea, Cardiff, Lincoln and Peterborough, as well as at three universities, and to five trade associations or chambers of commerce luncheons or dinners. I nonetheless managed to go to Crosby four times and was there for the final rally, for the poll itself, for the declaration of the result, and for the following morning's celebratory press conference. I defected only to go to Liverpool on the evening of polling day to do a Robin Day *Question Time*. It was the easiest such programme I have ever done. If one wanted an example of rowing with the current that was it. No one seemed to have any doubt that Crosby was in the bag, no answer could go wrong, the audience seemed to have deserted its normal political balance for the pleasure of being on the winning side, and I began to feel almost sorry for Eric Heffer and Jock Bruce-Gardyne, who represented the unloved 'ugly sister' parties.

Back in Crosby the result exceeded expectations. Just as the Tory vote collapsed into my arms in Warrington, so the Labour vote collapsed into Shirley's in Crosby. In addition a lot of Tories stayed at home and some made the direct switch. She had 49 per cent of the vote and a majority of 5000. Thus in three very different seats, united by the fact that in none of them had the Liberal polled more than 10 per cent of the vote in 1979, the Alliance had polled 42 per cent in Warrington, 40 per cent in Croydon and 49 per cent in Crosby. In addition we were quietly winning two-thirds of the contested local authority bye-elections of that autumn. Therefore, when the early December post-Crosby opinions polls put our percentage comfortably into the forties (one gave us 51 per cent) they were not doing a great deal more than reflecting what we had actually achieved. Our average vote in the three parliamentary bye-elections was almost 44 per cent.

Allowing for 'don't knows', our strong position in the forties left only a similar percentage to be divided between the two parties which, save for the small Liberal element in the Churchill coalition, had monopolised the government of the country for half a century. And as Labour and Conservatives divided their combined 40–45 per cent almost equally between themselves, this left them totally exposed to our temporary juggernaut. By an odd paradox, the Alliance, the only political grouping which opposed the 'first past the post' electoral system, would in December 1981 have benefited from it to an extent far in excess even of the unearned bonuses achieved by Labour in 1945 and 1966 or the Tories in 1959 and 1983. These two parties would have been almost annihilated by the vagaries of the system they so stubbornly supported. A mechanistic projection of our best public opinion poll would have given us nearly 600 out of the 635 seats in the House of Commons, while a similar projection of our actual achievement on the ground in Warrington, Croydon and Crosby, although leaving room for more sizeable rumps of Labour and Conservative MPs, would still have given us one of the most crushing majorities of British electoral history.

Of course we did not allow ourselves to inhale these crude statistics. We were more than experienced enough politicians to know that bye-elections were not general elections, that polls at the beginning of a campaign were by no means the same as votes at the end of a campaign, and that in any event a general election was not due.

We more than apprehended the possibility of many slips between the cup and the lip, and I do not even recollect that December as a period of peculiar euphoria. My spirits were less buoyant than they had been over the summer of preparing for Brussels, or in the immediate aftermath of Warrington.

Nevertheless we undoubtedly felt great satisfaction – and indeed wonderment – at the distance we had come in the previous eleven months. We took seriously the prospect of government. And we were eager to keep the avalanche moving. We wanted more bye-elections, and most of all (although almost beyond our dreams) we wanted the destabilisation of the Tory majority and the precipitation of a general election. This, although on the outer rim of possibility, did not seem absolutely beyond it, particularly as we overestimated the fighting spirit of the Tory 'wets'. There was great discontent amongst them at the time, morale in the party was generally low, and Mrs Thatcher was well short of having acquired an election-winning mystique. Norman St John-Stevas had been unceremoniously sacked at the beginning of 1981 – the first of the innocents to be massacred – and the same fate had befallen Ian Gilmour and Christopher Soames in September. They were all dismissed on grounds of ideology or prejudice rather than performance and this naturally created tensions on both front and back benches. It was reinforced by internal distrust of the whole strategy of the Government. I shall never forget the vehemence with which a member of the Cabinet (and one who was to survive for several more years) spoke to me about Geoffrey Howe's Budget as we walked together out of a St Paul's Cathedral memorial service to a previous Chancellor of the Exchequer (Derick Heathcoat Amory) on 10 March 1981.

The question was whether this would lead to a significant break from the Conservative Party towards us. My view is that this was as near as it could be to happening on a small scale, and that, had the small break occurred, the instability of the atmosphere was such that it might well have spread quite wide. However, the more significant fact is that it did not happen. We recruited a significant number of Tories in the country, some of whom had been active in local government or party organisation. But at Westminster we stopped at one MP. Christopher Brocklebank-Fowler, the member for North-west Norfolk, had joined us a few weeks before the launch of the party. It was a courageous act and he played an active role in the first two years, but I fear that he proved a counter-productive recruiting sergeant for the same reasons that I gradually came to find him an unsatisfactory colleague. There were five or six young MPs who hovered on the brink. Two of them came individually to see me and assured me that they were definitely coming. It was only a matter of choosing the time. But the time never quite came. I am sure that they acted throughout in perfect good faith.

There was also the bizarre incident of the then member for Maidstone, John Wells. He had always been a figure of engaging eccentricity, but not, unlike the two mentioned above, of views adjacent to the SDP. However, he suddenly wrote to me and offered to resign his seat if I would agree to contest the bye-election. We followed this up with an hour's late-night meeting on 8 December. The offer was very tempting to me. I was coming to need a seat badly. Otherwise I would be excluded from the SDP leadership contest which must take place some time in 1982. And there was nothing else in prospect. Maidstone would have been a hazard (we lost there by 7000 in 1983 and by 10,000 in 1987), but Croydon and Crosby had made us very confident, and there was the bonus of Wells's apparent support. I was grateful and willing to accept (I remember saying to John Harris that 'Christmas has come early this year'), but Wells drew back. I think his wife had had a few forthright words with him.

There was thus a tendency not to deliver, and even an exceptionally fearless lady who had been a leading Conservative in Heath's day allowed herself to be persuaded not to accept the seat on the steering committee (which became the National Committee when we adopted a constitution in 1982) which we had kept vacant for her. Heath himself, who must have greatly welcomed our success, nevertheless put the telescope to his blind eye, affected not to see us and behaved in form although not in substance as though it was business as usual in party politics. Three months later he came unnecessarily to Glasgow nominally to support my Conservative opponent, proceeded to deliver a slashing attack on Mrs Thatcher's whole policy at a large public meeting, made some amiable remarks about me at a press conference, and departed. It was a mystifying performance, but somewhat typical of the atmosphere of somnambulist fog which enveloped much of politics at the time.

In contrast with these ambiguities there was the behaviour of our ducal recruit. Andrew Devonshire had told me in July how excited he had been by the Warrington campaign. In early November he said he would like to join the SDP. I was pleased but did not press because I thought he ought to have time for second thoughts before causing family and territorial upheaval. I spoke to him by telephone over Christmas and, as he was going to Ireland for a month or so, said, 'Why not think it over there and decide when you come back?' Particularly as we did not then have a good month, I thought that was likely to be the end of it. I was wrong. In February when the Hillhead campaign did not seem to be going at all well and we trudged around the Kelvinside locations of Devonshire Gardens, the Cavendish Hotel and Chatsworth Court I thought that if they were so keen on these names they might respond to a little seigneurial leadership. Jennifer telephoned and asked whether he was still disposed to join. 'Certainly,' he said, 'but it will take me a week to resign from the presidency of the West Derbyshire Conservative Association and to let the *Bakewell Times* break the news locally.' He then delivered absolutely on time.

## CHAPTER THIRTY

# The Path Grows Steeper:
# Hillhead to Ettrick Bridge

The end of the last chapter took me on into 1982 and my second bye-election within eight months. The Hillhead division of Glasgow was a seat on which the SDP, largely on the prompting of Robert Maclennan, who was born and went to school there, had for a few months had its eye. Tam Galbraith, the sitting Conservative member, was the heir to a peerage and his father was ninety. I am afraid that being a party which fed on bye-elections gave us a carrion-like quality. David Owen, in particular, used to specialise in casting a jaundiced medical glance around the House of Commons. Old Lord Strathclyde, safe in the other chamber, proved impervious to this evil eye. He survived until 1985. It was his son who died on 2 January 1982. Tom Bradley, with whom we had lunched two days before and discussed possible seats, rang up on the morning of Sunday, 3 January, got Jennifer, announced cryptically: 'Galbraith is dead,' and rang off. Jennifer came in to see me and said in deep gloom, 'Ken has died,' meaning our great Harvard professorial friend, John Kenneth Galbraith. We then proceeded to hold an informal breakfast wake, discussing when we had last seen him, exactly how old he was, how much we would miss him, for what he would be best remembered, and almost culminating in Jennifer going off to ring up Kitty Galbraith. Fortunately the time was wrong for telephoning America, and even more fortunately J. K. Galbraith shows every sign of surviving at least as long as the first Lord Strathclyde. I proposed the toast at his eightieth birthday party in New York in 1988. However, the ludicrous misunderstanding persisted throughout the day, so that Bradley's efforts to alert me were unavailing, and I then had to make up my mind very quickly whether or not I wanted to go for Hillhead.

There were a number of conflicting considerations. Looked at purely psephologically it had a larger Liberal base than any of the famous three, and most exceptionally the Liberal vote had gone up substantially between 1974 and 1979. This was partly because the Scottish Nationalist vote had gone even more substantially down. On the other hand, again unlike Warrington and Crosby, it had by 1979 become a Tory/Labour marginal. It had in fact always been Tory since its creation in 1918 (represented by another Chancellor of the Exchequer, Robert Horne, for the first twenty years of its life), but the erosion of the Conservative position in Scotland brought Labour to only 2000 votes behind even in the year of Mrs Thatcher's first victory. This carried with it a danger of our being squeezed out of a two-party race. Much more formidable, however, was the thought of crossing the Scottish border. I had practically no Scottish connections. I knew Glasgow better than I knew Warrington, as its fame and size made obligatory for any experienced Sassenach politician. I had been there perhaps ten times before. Nevertheless I do not think that I had ever entered the old Hillhead constituency. I had been to the University, which in 1972 had very kindly (and usefully as it turned out) given me an honorary degree, but in 1982 that Gilmorehill 1870s Gothic eyrie overhung the constituency from the east and was not part of it. English (or in my case Welsh, which was a little better) MPs in Scotland had become much rarer than they were in the days when Asquith sat for East Fife and Augustine Birrell for West Fife. And such few as there were sat upon safe caucus majorities. To challenge at the same time both the national and the party traditions was going to be a rash act.

Yet Hillhead was about the one constituency in Scotland in which it might work. Hillhead comprised most of the West End of Glasgow and with the enlargement of 1983 took in virtually the whole of it. The term West End is much more habitually used in Glasgow than in London, where it has become almost as archaic (except as a traffic sign) as a 'stage-door johnnie', a rather associated term. Glasgow's West End is a residential not an entertainment concept. The only city I can think of where the term has had an equal natural validity is Berlin. This 1983 enlargement paradoxically diluted the exceptionally strong professional-class presence which was a remarkable feature of the old constituency, but made it still more studded with cultural and higher educational institutions of note. After the change had been made the constituency contained, apart from the University, the Glasgow School of Art, the Scottish National Opera and the Scottish National Orchestra, the great Kelvingrove Art Gallery and the Hunterian Collection, three teaching hospitals clustered around the Western Infirmary and three units of the Medical Research Council, Jordanhill College of Education – the largest such establishment in Scotland – and a clutch of schools of note, including the only day school in the United Kingdom to have produced more than one Prime Minister.* Strathclyde University (like Glasgow Academy) was a stone's throw outside, but Hillhead housed a high proportion of its staff and students. After the bye-election, although some said as a direct result of a Conservative bribe offered during it, there came the Scottish Exhibition Centre. With only a little exaggeration it can be said that, with the important exceptions of the Burrell Collection and the Citizens' Theatre, Glasgow's centres of cultural (and intellectual) excellence are in Hillhead.

The enlargement broadly united places of work with places of residence, but it also brought in a large new swathe of riverside Labour voters, who proved my undoing in 1987. But that was three elections away in early 1982, and what for the moment I had to deal with was a compact constituency of only 39,000 electors, which started at the Byres Road (the Boul' Mich of Glasgow) and ran westwards along the Clydeside strip and the hills behind it for two miles. The contrast between the river and the hill was a symbolic one, for the river was mostly inhabited by the skilled but militant manual workers of what had been the most famous heavy engineering area in the world, and the hill was where the Glasgow bourgeoisie had established their encampments. I liked subsequently developing a metaphor (for oratorical use outside as well as inside Glasgow) of how traditional politics had made them like two entrenched armies, who drilled vigorously and shouted fearsome martial slogans at each other but did not in fact much engage, although when they did (at general elections) the Conservatives had always won, for the hill was two-thirds of the constituency and the river only one-third. But we came along and cut through the rigid division, so I rhetorically claimed with at least some basis of truth, gained enough votes from both parts to win, and united the constituency as it had never been before.

What greatly assisted this breakthrough was the exceptional nature of the Hillhead bourgeoisie. Statistically the whole constituency could claim to be the most highly educated in the United Kingdom.† It was very strongly professionally orientated. Almost unbelievably 1300 (or over 3 per cent of the total electorate) were doctors of medicine. There was also a large supplement of doctors of philosophy. The proper doctors amounted to this phenomenal figure because the

---

* Glasgow High School was attended by both Campbell-Bannerman and Bonar Law.

† The only way in which the census showed educational levels on a constituency basis was by measuring the numbers with two or more A-levels in England and Wales and two or more Higher Grades in Scotland. Hillhead's pre-eminence therefore depended on equating the two, which was perhaps marginally unfair on England. Hillhead's Scottish pre-eminence was unchallengeable.

institutions mentioned earlier made this area of Glasgow the greatest medical concentration outside St Marylebone and because a lot of the general practitioners and consultants employed in the rest of the city liked to live in the West End. There were of course some businessmen in Hillhead, but they again were mostly managerial executives of big companies rather than small entrepreneurs. Even with the strong Scottish resistance to Thatcherism I could not have done nearly so well in a constituency of equally sought after residences which was more dependent upon profits and less upon fees, salaries and even royalties.

Before all this could be put to the test I had first to decide that I was prepared to face Hillhead, and second to clear the way with the local Liberals. I was more apprehensive about Hillhead than I had been about Warrington. To begin with I had to win it. Another good second place would be no use to me at all. If I did not win, I would have to give up trying to get into that Parliament, with all that went with that. To fight two bye-elections had elements of valour. To fight three would have been ridiculous. Next, I was nervous of Glasgow, even more as a human organism than as a psephological prospect. On the weekend after I had been adopted we stayed in Scotland but retreated to a country hotel, Gleddoch House, high above the Clyde estuary opposite Dumbarton. On the Sunday morning I went for a walk on the adjacent golf-course, which commanded a fifteen-mile-distant view of the city, with its shipyard cranes, its Victorian spires and turrets, and its 1960s high-rise flats all visible. It had the air of a great city, but also of a place of infinite complication and some menace. Its towers looked as mysterious to me as the minarets of Constantinople must have done to the Russian investing forces in 1878. What insanity has seized me, I thought, to take on this assignment?

I very nearly did not. In the week beginning 4 January difficulties arose with the Liberals, mainly at Scottish headquarters level. On the 5th the Glasgow North SDP invited me to stand. But by the 7th I decided the intra-Alliance difficulties were too great, and more or less wrote off Hillhead in a telephone conversation with David Steel. On Friday the 8th, towards the end of a period of five weeks of unprecedentedly hard early winter, Jennifer and I tried to go to East Hendred. Motoring was too difficult, so we went to Paddington and sat in the five o'clock train. At about 5.15, when the train had not started, a fellow passenger who had come up from Didcot that morning, regaled us with tales of how almost totally immobilising were traffic conditions in the Wantage downland. Suddenly we came to the joint conclusion that it was nonsense to go, jumped out of the train about thirty seconds before it started, and went home to Kensington Park Gardens.

Had we gone we would have been isolated for the whole weekend and would have found difficulty in getting back for several days. In London my appetite for Hillhead sharply revived. That evening we had to dinner Mark Bonham Carter, John Harris and John Lyttle, the SDP press officer who had been with me throughout the Warrington campaign. They were all for resolute action. Bob Maclennan was doing his best to take it on the ground in both Glasgow and Edinburgh (where the Scottish Liberals were meeting). Eventually it was agreed that the adopted Liberal candidate, Chick Brodie, and the Hillhead Liberal chairman, Ken Wardrup, would come down from Glasgow to see me in London on the Sunday evening. It was very good of them to make the journey across four hundred snowbound miles and even better of them to behave as they did when they arrived. Brodie was giving up the real possibility of winning the seat, and getting nothing in return except for the advancement of the cause in which he believed. He was a major artificer of the Alliance. We were closeted for three hours, and then, with the assistance of John Lyttle and Paul Medlicott, the Liberal press officer, produced a statement in which the Liberals endorsed the SDP invitation to me to contest Hillhead. Such a shotgun marriage might have been expected to produce subsequent trouble. On the contrary, however, I always had dedicated support from the Hillhead Liberals throughout my five years there. And such was the interest in the Alliance and in bye-elections at the time that when we went down at 10.30 p.m. and read the statement from the top of the steps of 2 Kensington Park Gardens, there was a cluster of reporters and photographers in the frozen snow of the street.

I went to Hillhead for the adoption meeting on the following Thursday, then commuted for a month, making five separate trips and spending about a third of my time in Glasgow. After that we settled there for five and a half weeks, broken only by one weekend at East Hendred. Stakis's Pond Hotel in the Great Western Road replaced the Fir Grove Motel. It was a substantially longer campaign than the Warrington one. It was also a more morale-testing one. If at Warrington the polls were stubbornly unresponsive they at least never retrogressed. At Hillhead they did precisely that. Already before the adoption meeting we had gone into a harsher political climate than that of the autumn. A temporary hiccup in the negotiations with the Liberals for the allocation of general election seats which Bill Rodgers was conducting for us was blown up in the Sunday newspapers of 3 January. It probably coincided with one of those shake-outs of public opinion which sometimes occur over a holiday period and correct some of the extravagances of a previous bandwagon effect. We were also peculiarly vulnerable to suggestion of internal differences and tough political bargaining. We were supposed to stand for bringing people together and eschewing the squalid wheeler-dealing of old-style politics. In any event about a quarter of our opinion-poll strength disappeared within a few weeks. We were down from the mid-forties to the mid-thirties. But a Hillhead poll taken after Galbraith's death showed that we were still likely to win there.

This favourable prognosis did not persist throughout the long stretches of February and the first half of March. The nadir came on Saturday, 13 March – polling day had been fixed for 25 March. Just before I was about to set out on a hand-pressing, arguing, chatting-up progress along the short half-mile of the Byres Road, escorted by our largest phalanx of helpers from outside and due to last no less than two hours, I was given the results of an *Observer* NOP poll to be published the next morning. It showed the Labour candidate as likely to win with 33 per cent of the vote (he in fact came third with 24 per cent), the Conservative on 30 per cent (he came second with 26 per cent) and me trailing badly with 23 per cent. Not unreasonably, it was accompanied by a story which stated 'Mr Roy Jenkins faces the prospect of a shattering defeat in the Hillhead bye-election.' The Saturday programme, which followed the Byres Road with a long recorded ITN interview with Alistair Burnet, surprisingly an elector in Hillhead but not there in that capacity, and then with an almost equally long walkabout in the Dumbarton Road, the heart of the riverside working-class area, was one which, above any other day, called for buoyancy. It needed a good deal of taking a grip on oneself to achieve it. The *Observer* article probably on balance did good (it drove Shirley Williams, for instance, into a frenzy of dedicated last ten days' activity), particularly as a decisive turn of the tide soon followed, but it was difficult to appreciate its beneficence at the time.

Our Hillhead campaign, totally unlike Warrington, was based on meetings, supplemented by individual calls. At first I concentrated on visits to the head of every significant organisation, from the principals of the two universities and of Jordanhill College to the editors of the newspapers and the managing directors of the radio and television companies. Then I moved into a substantial series of domestic coffee meetings. This was a method of penetrating the gentility of Kelvinside, Dowanhill, Bromhill and Jordanhill and it could have worked only in the relatively large sitting rooms of the hill. These meetings lasted an hour, were typically of about twenty neighbours invited by an obliging supporter, and took the form of my first going round and having a few words with individuals, then delivering a general talk of fifteen minutes or so, then answering questions and then leaving, often for a second such occasion.

Particularly in the third quarter of the long ten weeks I also did a lot of straight door-to-door canvassing. The weather was much less favourable for this than at Warrington. It was dark, wet and windy, although the great cold of the early winter ended on the day after my adoption and never reappeared. Glasgow put on its Gulf Stream weather for us, although I fear the less agreeable aspects of it, until the last few days when it became still, alternatively misty and sunny, and mildly frosty. The earlier rain drove us to canvassing the constituency's ten or twelve tower blocks, which was probably a good thing, for there was a danger of our concentrating on the bourgeoisie. This all had the effect that by the end of the campaign a much higher proportion of the electorate told a MORI poll that they had met me than claimed to have met any of the other three main candidates, all of whom were local. In addition there was the same large 'tail' of fringe candidates as at Warrington, with one of them again changing his name to Roy Jenkins, but this time surviving on to the ballot paper. It took a lot of effort and some money (for leaflets) to prevent his getting more than 282 votes.

The last two and a half weeks of the campaign were dominated by public meetings. Apart from a few all-candidate forums organised by independent and mostly specialised bodies, we arranged what I can best describe as three plus ten meetings. The three were meetings with contrived and small audiences, which we set up before the campaign got fully going and which I used, not to persuade, but to set out in long and fairly boring speeches positions on three issues, two Scottish and one British. The Scottish ones were devolution and education. The former was essential to a north-of-the-border campaign, particularly with a vigorous and attractive Scottish Nationalist candidate in the field. My position, which descended convincingly from a previous speech I had made on the issue in Greenock in March 1976, when, as I was able to point out, the last thing I had on my mind was the possibility of fighting a Scottish seat, was that I was in favour of substantial devolution provided it did not get near to separation, and provided too that there was proportional representation for the Assembly, so that there was no domination by the Strathclyde Labour caucus. Equally I was in favour of as much economic power for the Assembly as was compatible with the preservation of the currency union, the end of which would be a major misfortune for Scotland. On education it was partly a question of getting used to the different Scottish terminology and partly that of some difference in the substance of issues. We were strong on dominies in the Glasgow SDP (even though this had become a rather twee word which I hardly ever heard used) and I received great local help on this second speech. The third speech was an economic programme for reversing the unemployment trend through the United Kingdom, but particularly in Scotland. They were all three of mind-clearing value to me throughout the campaign, rather in the way that essays written at leisure at Oxford enabled one to answer quickly examination questions on proximate subjects.

The ten were full public meetings, all packed. We began seventeen days before the poll when Jo Grimond and I spoke in Scotstoun and advanced until the final Tuesday, putting in additional meetings in response to apparent demand as we went along, when David Steel and I wound up the campaign in the core of Kelvinside. Beyond the Warrington cast, Robert Maclennan, Russell Johnston and Dickson Mabon gave a Scottish flavour. Jo Grimond came back for a second go, and Shirley Williams did a separate series of small schoolroom early-evening meetings on her own. She was worried that I was neglecting the river for the hill.

At the end we calculated that we had addressed indoors the equivalent of 25 per cent of the electorate, which I believed to be an unparalleled number for any bye-election for decades past. I say 'the equivalent', for some gluttons for punishment may have come twice and some keen non-Hillheadians may also have infiltrated. But even with these reservations there was no doubt that our meetings made an exceptional impact. It should be said that such was the nature of Hillhead and the campaign that our opponents had good meetings too, notably the Conservatives for Heath's ambiguous performance and the Labour Party for Tony Benn, his appearances in the constituency at once exciting those present and alienating those not. Our apogee was a week before the poll, when the Gang of Four exceptionally came together on the same platform, and when, the weather having just turned, we proceeded one by one from the overflowing hall of Hyndland Secondary School to address a crowd of almost another thousand, lit only by moonlight, who stood in the frosty playground for nearly two hours.

Looked at in retrospect it was probably at that moment that we began for the first time to get our nose ahead. But elections are not exactly like horse races. At most they are like horse races run on a planet so distant that it takes a long time for the light of what has happened to be carried across outer space. It was only four days later on the last Monday evening/Tuesday morning that I began to feel even cautious optimism. Then I was cast down again by a maverick *Daily Express* poll of which we received news that Tuesday evening. But there was a strong sense of rising confidence on the eve of the poll and polling day itself. At any rate, we did win, and in one sense convincingly. Just over 2000 was a substantial majority in such a small constituency. I was seven percentage points ahead of the Conservatives, who came second, a much bigger lead than any poll had projected. On the other hand I got only 33.5 per cent of the votes cast, nine points below Warrington. It was in one sense the greatest victory of the early SDP, and was hailed as such by the entire press. It was the first time we had won on a slack tide. But, in another sense, it was, if not the beginning of the end, at least the end of the beginning. There were no more ninepins to be easily knocked over, and this was the case even before the invasion of the Falklands, which began only eight days later.

This did not prevent my enjoying a splendid short-term triumph. The day after the poll was one of magical weather, with a March sun emerging from a high-pressure haze for eight hours of unruffled glow, and of accidental and almost excessive Asquith pietism. Having repeated the Warrington victory parade in the morning (with more justification but less bravado) I was driven across central Scotland and the Kingdom of Fife to address the Scottish Liberal conference in St Andrews, the most notable town of his old constituency base of 1886–1918, took in on the way back an SDP dinner in Edinburgh (a city redolent with memories of Gladstone and Rosebery if not of Asquith himself), and finished the evening at another SDP celebration in Paisley, the burgh in which Asquith, by winning a famous 1920 bye-election, had heralded one of the greatest false dawns in twentieth-century politics.

My Hillhead victory heralded not so much a false dawn as an anticlimactic return to Parliament. The House of Commons which I re-entered after an absence of five and a quarter years was one in which Tory morale was low and Labour morale was abysmal, save only for a talented but destructive *fronde* led by Dennis Skinner whose members seemed to be indifferent to the decline of their party's electoral fortunes provided it was accompanied (as it was) by an increase in their own prominence. It ought to have been a scene perfectly constructed for me coming in as an experienced parliamentarian who had just beaten both the other parties. Yet it was one which I completely failed to command.

My success in the House of Commons in 1964–76 had been essentially based on half-hour debating speeches, cumulatively building up a refutation of the opposing case, and delivered from the authority of the despatch box. These speeches also depended on full houses, with enough in front to engage with and enough behind to cheer. In 1982 none of these props or opportunities was available. Jim Callaghan's prophecy to me in Paris in 1979 that I would find the House of Commons much changed for the worse I found abundantly justified. In the first place, although this had nothing to do with the quality of the House, I had no despatch box. That mattered a lot. Furthermore I disliked the position on the front bench below the gangway where the SDP had half established itself a year before. I say 'half' for our rights of occupancy were constantly challenged by Skinner and his collaborators. There was therefore a tedious hassle for seats, which frequently ended up with our sitting scattered and cheek by jowl with our most vociferous opponents.

Even apart from these inconveniences, the position itself was unsatisfactory, at once exposed and uncommanding. It had never occurred to me to claim a seat there in my long years as a back-bencher. Without a despatch box, it is much better to have the back of another bench in front of one's knees. In the Parliament of 1983, indeed, I moved back to the second bench and sat amongst the Liberals. I was happy for there to be ambiguity about whether I had done this as an expression of political solidarity or as a search for a better podium. It must be said, however, that David Owen, whom I think had been responsible for choosing the exposed position, operated from it with aplomb, undismayed by neighbourly interjections, notably but not only during the Falklands imbroglio.

This was partly because he was admirably attuned to a significant change in the style of the House which had taken place in the second half of the 1970s. Except on rare occasions debate had ceased to be central to the parliamentary process. It had been replaced by the quick exchanges of Prime Minister's question time and similar responses to statements by major ministers. There were a variety of contributory causes. One was the personal style of Mrs Thatcher, which led her almost never to make a parliamentary speech and never therefore to deploy a sustained rational argument, but to concentrate on the asseveration, sometimes laced with a ringing populist phrase or a passing slur on the opposition, of the answer to a supplementary question. Another is the change of habits of reporting Parliament. Previously the two 9.00 p.m. to 10.00 p.m. wind-up speeches of a major debate often (as in examples given in the middle pages of this book) dominated the parliamentary coverage. Now their resonance is confined to the relative privacy of Hansard. The sketch-writers have long since written their sketches, the gallery reporters know that modern printing technology cannot be upset by anything so demanding as late news, and television naturally finds gobbets better raw material than continuous prose.

So there developed a parliamentary style with a rhythm like that of a game of snap. Speed of reaction and easily comprehensible points encapsulated in succinct phrases became all-important. It was this at which David Owen was so good (and the same technique served him excellently on television). In my perhaps jaundiced view he could rarely make a satisfying full-length speech, neither in the House of Commons nor, even more noticeably, at a conference, except occasionally when he gave the impression of groping, inelegantly but honestly and impressively, for some new idea. But he was a master of the quick in-and-out intervention, delivered with a darting tongue, which enabled him to hold for a few moments a turbulent House and to be impervious to attempted wrecking asides from Skinner and co.

At all this I was much less good, and as a result floundered in a hostile House. In addition there was the Falklands War, which dominated the parliamentary scene for more than two months after the end of my first week back. It was a war from which I felt far more detached than from the Gulf War of 1991. I had little I wished to say about it. I had no desire to mount a roaring campaign against the Government, which apart from anything else would have split the SDP wide open, but I had no taste either for being a drummer boy to Mrs Thatcher. The snide remark would be to say that I preferred to leave that to David Owen. But that would be neither fair nor accurate. His role was more independent and more skilful than that. He made himself the acceptable in-house critic, and did so essentially I think by assimilating the dimensions which Mrs Thatcher gave to the affair. He often urged a slightly different course upon her, but he never suggested that she was blowing the issue up beyond its due worth. I, on the other hand, was instinctively ill at ease with her sense of proportion. I found bathos in treating it like a latterday recapture of Khartoum by Kitchener, but I did not proclaim this. I just felt detached. Altogether it was a much happier period for Owen than for me.

It was also one in which my relations with him were necessarily obtrusive. After Hillhead there was general acceptance that the date for a leadership election should be brought forward from November to the early summer. There had been a dispute, in which Owen and I were on opposite sides and to which he attached much more importance than I did, about the method by which the leader should be elected. He was wedded to the principle of election by the whole membership. I preferred, but not passionately, that of election by the parliamentary party. (It should be remembered that we were then a parliamentary party of thirty, with the hope of becoming much bigger in the future.) It was the conventional wisdom that election by those who knew the candidates best would produce a more discriminating choice. It subsequently emerged that Owen thought I had betrayed some compact with him by taking this view. This was nonsense. What I had accepted in our conversations of November/December 1980 was that I would expect no automatic reversion of the leadership, which would be determined by election. I have no recollection of discussing the method. However, he subsequently claimed that he felt so strongly on this issue that he would not have stood against me had I been in favour of mass election. I took this with a pinch of salt. It seemed an odd piece of logic to be willing to obviate an election provided one method for it was chosen.

There were several paradoxes involved in the issue. The first was that Bill Rodgers, David Marquand and probably Dick Taverne and Ian Wrigglesworth were more committed to indirect election than was I, but at least partly because they thought it would produce a more secure constituency for me. I therefore felt a considerable return loyalty to them, and continued to support the indirect method well after I could see that it was both difficult to argue and unnecessary in my own interest. This led on to the second paradox, which was that I might well have lost by a whisker in the parliamentary party, whereas I was more secure with the membership as a whole. At any rate a ballot of the membership in May endorsed both a June election (result on 2 July) and a direct franchise, although the latter by no means decisively.

By mid-May Owen had emerged as the sole challenging candidate. Shirley Williams, Owen's and many other people's choice of fifteen or eighteen months before, had been diverted towards the presidency, an office of importance in the party machine, but which was prevented from being a full rival to the leadership by the fact that it could not be held for more than four years. She endorsed Owen's candidature, mainly I think because she believed he would give the party a more left-wing orientation, but she did not campaign for him vigorously or divisively.

Nevertheless the election did prove divisive. In retrospect I think it a great pity that a contest took place. This might be regarded as being in the category of 'he would say that, wouldn't he' remarks. But it was a more obvious contemporary than retrospective thought. At the time I certainly regretted the contest, both because I was suffering from battle fatigue after Warrington and Hillhead and because I had a scare that I was going to lose. In retrospect, however, I might have been expected to be full of bland views that a good clean fight with the right outcome had been a healthy thing for the new party. I was not, for two reasons. First, David Owen hated losing. He had a better campaign than I had, he came nearer to winning than he had been expected to do at the beginning and he had staked out a strong position for the future. He was in a sense the moral victor. But he seemed unable to take any satisfaction in this. He was an unforgiving loser. Second, although this to some extent is a different aspect of the first point, that leadership election created a perforation in the party which subsequently persisted. It was no accident that my 26,300 votes as against Owen's 20,900 represented almost exactly the same split as did the 26,100 votes for merger in 1987 as against the 19,400 who then voted for the convoluted alternative proposition.

Nor did the leadership contest, as some people foolishly believed it would, significantly enhance our public impact. Once Hillhead was over, we had a bleak six months. The Falklands, and the consequent recovery in the Tory position, was no doubt the main factor, but there was an underlying sag of our own as well, which meant that we also weakened considerably vis-à-vis the Labour Party. Thus our last good rating for a long time was in April 1982, when Hillhead had given us a Gallup boost of four points and we stood on 30 as opposed to 22 for the Labour Party and 25 for the Conservatives. By September we were down to 18, with 24 for Labour and 39 for the Conservatives. And this opinion-poll decline was fully reflected in our actual results. The local elections in early May were disappointing. A Beaconsfield bye-election later in the month with a good Liberal candidate was blanketed by a Falklands fog and produced a 'back to normal' result in a constituency which we might easily have won in the previous November. In early June we half lost a seat. Bruce Douglas-Mann, the member for Merton and Morden, who had joined as our thirty-first MP, insisted on resigning and fighting a bye-election. He was roundly defeated by a Tory. In July the first parliamentary vacancy of my leadership was created in Gower, a mixture of Swansea suburb, decaying anthracite mining villages and rural seaside in the peninsula from which the constituency took its name, with a polling day in mid-September. Gwynoro Jones, former MP for Carmarthen and my Home Office parliamentary private secretary in 1974, eagerly became the SDP candidate. This connection and our need for a recovery considerably raised the stakes. I went to Gower once before the holidays and then four times in the first fortnight of September. Bill Rodgers was also very active. It was unavailing. We did somewhat but not much better than at Beaconsfield.

The next six months were on the whole depressing. The publicity of our six days of rolling conference in October put our poll rating temporarily up to 22 per cent, but for every other month from September until March we alternated between 17 and 18 per cent. We fought an unrewarding late-October bye-election in the concrete wastes of Peckham, where even such a strong candidate as Dick Taverne failed to get much response. This was the period when many of our most active members, who had thought that the heady days of 1981 were normal, began to complain about 'media starvation', and we were pushed into some rather squalid rows with the broadcasting authorities over whether they were treating us fairly. The trouble was that we no longer looked a potential government at the next election. This led to some tension within the National and Communications Committees of the party about whether we should allow advertising agents to try to get us out of the slough of disregard by 'shocking' publicity, which I found repugnant. So probably did most of the others, but there was a tendency at this stage for those who had been David Owen's keenest supporters for the leadership to be in favour of anything I was against (and *vice versa*), as well as to make it clear how much better they thought we would be doing if their man had won.

The ebbing of the prospect of government also created problems for intra-Alliance dispositions. In the autumn of 1981 David Steel had been able without bathos to conclude his conference speech with the ringing words 'Go back to your constituencies and prepare for government.' By the autumn of 1982 this would have sounded like foolish bombast, and with the change of mood there came both a need for us to be careful of not puffing ourselves up like the frog that burst, and also a shrinkage of generosity between the two parties of the Alliance. When there was a prospect of winning rewards beyond previous Liberal dreams, a magnanimous disposition of seats and jobs could be more easily accepted than when there was a danger of the Alliance doing no better than the Liberals had done alone in February 1974.

David Steel had agreed in the more euphoric period that if I were elected leader of the SDP he and I should fight the general election as co-equal leaders of our two parties, although with him probably being more active in the campaign because of his safer base in Roxburgh and Selkirk, but that, if we won, I should head the Government and that this should be made clear to the electorate. (There was a hidden contradiction here for, particularly if we were doing well, the press and television were bound to concentrate on the one who might hold the highest office.) As he put it in his 1989 autobiography: 'My motives were both clear and consistent. I took the view that if by some chance we did find ourselves the largest single grouping, then Roy Jenkins was the right person to be Prime Minister.' He then paid some very generous tributes to me before concluding the passage: 'There was absolutely no doubt in my mind that if the unlikely happened, he should lead our Cabinet but with obviously more power for the Deputy Prime Minister as leader of his own party than was possessed by Willie Whitelaw. On this we were agreed.'[1]

This was not just the blowing of bubbles. It was highly desirable that in the difficult job of allocating the most winnable seats between the two parties the issue should not be complicated by treating even a remote chance of the prime ministership as a prize in the lottery of whether we or the Liberals had made the better bargains about constituencies. And it was necessary too that the electorate should know the position. We could not expect to be taken seriously as an equal third force if the Conservatives offered Mrs Thatcher, Labour offered Michael Foot, and we said, 'Vote for the Alliance and you may get Steel or Jenkins according to the internal luck of which party happens to get the more seats.'

Steel did not however wish his self-abnegation to extend to giving himself a subordinate role in the election. This was partly because his party would not have put up with this, and partly because, while he thought I would be a better Prime Minister, at any rate at that stage in our respective careers, he thought he was a better campaigner than I was. This was borne out by the fact that his opinion-poll ratings were consistently much better than mine. My weak showing in this respect was a major disadvantage to me in this phase of relations with both Steel and Owen. I seemed able to do well in actual elections, coming from behind with a powerful finish in both bye-elections and in the leadership contest. Furthermore I had always had good, even very good, personal poll ratings in my prominent Labour Party days. I therefore felt some puzzlement as well as pain at this new weakness. Perhaps it was that Brussels had left too much of a patina of high living. Or perhaps it was the puzzlement which was misplaced and I should have remembered the famous *New Yorker* cartoon of the man who went to see his psychiatrist, asked why he always felt inferior and received the simple but devastating answer that it was because he *was* inferior.

In any event this combination of circumstances led, not to any change in David Steel's view about what should happen in government, but to his being under increasing pressure to maintain his own campaigning position. He therefore both postponed any announcement and pared it down so that it did not relate to the leadership of a fighting Alliance but only to the bestowal of a spoil which we were far from having won. As a result the issuing of the statement, which we had contemplated for at least the previous nine months, dragged itself out until the end of April 1983, and my role inevitably attracted the somewhat Pooh-Bah-like title of 'Prime Minister Designate'. David Steel says that neither he nor I was responsible for the pretentious name, and I do not doubt that he is right. But we ought to have foreseen that it would be hung upon me by others. David Owen regarded the label as a bit of portentous nonsense, and on this occasion he was right.

Nevertheless the autumn and winter of 1982–3 were by no means all setback and dismay. There were some things which went well. Outstanding amongst them was Hillhead. I was often sympathised with for having to take on the burdens of such an inconveniently placed constituency. In fact it was not inconvenient at all. It had over twenty mostly punctually functioning air services a day from London and the journey with experience and nerve could be done door to door in two and a quarter hours. On one ludicrously memorable occasion a year or so later I even succeeded in going there early one morning and getting back to East Hendred for lunch after fulfilling two short engagements. But this quick turn-round was unusual, for in general both Jennifer and I spent a lot of time in Glasgow. By early July 1982 we had acquired a two-roomed flat (or house in Scottish parlance) in one of the two most elegant of the terraces flanking the Great Western Road. The terrace had been designed in 1845 by Charles Wilson and was the most architecturally distinguished façade behind which we have ever lived. There we tried to spend one long weekend a month, as well as a September ten days supplemented by a lot of one-night visits by me alone.

In addition Hillhead was compact, but it was also demanding both because so much went on within its boundaries and because, as the only non-Labour MP for Glasgow, I was asked to speak at a lot of citywide arts, professional and business occasions. But I never resented time spent there – Glasgow retained all the fascination I had felt when gazing upon it from that Clydeside hill in January, while losing most of its menace. I admired its metropolitan quality, its Victorian architecture and its natural site, with the hills rising on either side of the river in just the right places, and beyond that the estuary of the Clyde which, with its associated inlets, islands and mountains, constitutes the most dramatic piece of seascape to be found at the gates of a great city anywhere in the world, with the possible exception of Vancouver Sound. I also much liked my constituents. In a Glasgow lecture which I gave in 1990 I put it in these terms:

There is the well-known warmth of Glasgow, but that is something on which in my view it is possible to talk a good deal of sententious nonsense. Glasgow people are capable of being very friendly, and they are almost invariably polite, but they are also capable, as are all people of discrimination, of being appropriately chilling when they think it is deserved. When in 1982 I first came to know Glasgow well, and in particular its West End, what most struck me was not so much the warmth as the quiet self-confidence. It was not a complacent or narrow or inward-looking self-confidence. It was not based on a desire to keep strangers out, or I would not have been made nearly so welcome. What it was based on was a consciousness of the contribution which this strip of river and hills had made to the advancement of civilisation throughout and beyond Britain, and on a feeling that while it was desirable to go outside the West End from time to time it was as good a place to live in as anywhere in the world.[2]

The only thing that went seriously wrong in Hillhead in this period was that it was redistributed, almost without my noticing because of outside preoccupations, and much to my disadvantage. I lost nothing worth speaking of, but about 18,000 electors were added. That was entirely reasonable on grounds of fair representation. The first scheme would have brought them more from adjacent parts of the hill, but involved the constituency being renamed Kelvin, a change which I disliked. The Labour Party objected, and a second scheme, keeping the name Hillhead but substituting more of the river for more of the hill, was brought forward. I attached too much importance to the label rather than the contents of the bottle, which I did not closely examine, and raised no objection. This made the constituency still more marginal for 1983 and untenable in 1987 when a Labour tide swept through the central belt of Scotland.

In the country generally we continued to have good meetings (although not on the scale of 1981) and I continued to enjoy campaigning. I even enjoyed bye-elections which we lost, notably Gower. Trained as a quintessential staff officer of politics, more at home in Westminster or Whitehall than in the streets or on the platform, I suddenly discovered the joys of regimental soldiering. A large part of the reason was that I had reversed the habit of a lifetime and become better at party meetings or conferences than in the House of Commons. And owing to the complexities of the Alliance and the devolved nature of the Liberal Party, which the SDP half tried to emulate, there were plenty of party conferences to address. Apart from a plethora of constituency meetings, in that autumn and winter I made one speech to the Liberal Assembly, four to our own rolling conferences, one each to the SDP and Liberal Scottish conferences, one to the Yorkshire Liberals, one to the Welsh SDP conference and one to a Relaunch of the Alliance Rally in the Central Hall, Westminster, on 20 January. That was a successful occasion, both as a public meeting for the Alliance and for me personally. It was the nearest approach to a triumph that I had during that difficult winter, and was good for morale. But it was also a striking example of the self-indulgence of oratory. Both I and the audience of party faithful thought that we had accomplished something because I had made a good speech and they had cheered vociferously. But we had only given each other a good evening out. There was no evidence that we had lifted the Alliance off its temporary floor.

That only came five weeks later when Simon Hughes proved a brilliant inner-city Liberal candidate, cracked wide open a rotten old Labour machine and won a landslide victory in Bermondsey. The day after that result we were in St Andrews for the SDP Scottish conference, and the achievement, even if in London and from the other half of the Alliance, sent spirits soaring. This was strengthened by the prospect of the SDP being able to repeat the victory in Darlington a month later. On the Saturday evening we got news of a Darlington poll which showed us poised to win. Alas, this proved the falsest of all the false dawns. Our candidate was a politically inexperienced local TV sports and general reporter who came apart under the cruel searchlight of a key bye-election campaign. We ended up a disappointing third.

Some of the blame for the result naturally washed off on me as leader, and in a sense I deserved that it should do so. This was not because I had selected the candidate, but more because I had failed to do so. I had been sceptical about him from the beginning, whereas others believed that the familiarity of his face with the local public would make him good. I had played with the idea of insisting on putting in a battle-hardened and intellectually resourceful national figure. Dick Taverne, who had not been damaged by Peckham, would probably have been the best, although he would have taken considerable persuading. If we were accused of being a centralised party we might at least have got the benefits of this. But I weakly turned away from the thought. I did not feel strong enough vis-à-vis the still resentful Owen faction on the National Committee, who would undoubtedly have raised the banner of party democracy, and could hardly have failed in the circumstances to get considerable grass-roots response. I ought to have been tougher. Darlington started as an open race and with the best candidate we could have won.

The consequences of not doing so were severe. It was the last bye-election before the 1983 general election. Bermondsey had jerked our poll rating up to 22 per cent for March, but Darlington put it down again to 18 per cent for April, and, whether or not as a follow-through effect, we plunged to 14 per cent in May. The SDP authority within the Alliance was also inevitably weakened by the contrast between Bermondsey and Darlington, although David Steel was peculiarly good at not letting this show in his behaviour.

Mrs Thatcher called the election on Monday, 9 May, for Thursday, 9 June. An early summer election had been assumed, but the actual date was something of a surprise and the notice relatively short. I was in Glasgow, rather ecumenically touring the Govan Shipyard, for there were not many Hillheadians employed there, and Govan was not a constituency we were going to win. I did immediate BBC and ITN statements and then flew down to London for a fifteen-minute *Panorama* interview that evening (Whitelaw and Foot also appeared). There was then a pause for planning over most of the first week, with the campaign proper beginning on Monday 16 May. David Steel and I opened our series of press conferences at the National Liberal Club in the morning, flew to Glasgow, spent much of the day recording a party election broadcast together and jointly launched both the Hillhead and the Scottish campaigns at the Partick Burgh Hall in the evening.

Despite this locally based start I spent only five of the remaining twenty-three days of campaigning in Glasgow, and managed in the rest of the time both to do a lot of London television and press conferences and to make a brief market-square speech in over seventy constituencies, from Glamorgan to Norfolk and from Kent to Northumberland. There were also fifteen full-scale public-hall speeches outside Glasgow. It was a rash strategy to neglect Hillhead to this extent, but I judged both that it was not going to profit me much to dig in there and let the countrywide SDP campaign subside, and that the constituency could sustain a little neglect after being subjected to saturation electioneering little over a year before. So far as the old constituency was concerned this latter assumption proved correct. I think we there registered a significant favourable swing. But in the newly added parts we did badly, so that the majority came down to 1100, and more importantly there began a habit of my not engaging with these new parts in the way that I had with the old.

The campaign on the whole went well. Meetings were full and enthusiastic, the recognition factor was high in the market places, our mostly inexperienced campaign organisers displayed a more than professional competence, and David Steel and I neither contradicted each other in public nor individually committed any major campaign gaffe. I tried to concentrate on the longer television interviews which more easily absorbed my 'ornate gothic constructions' as he later friendlily described them, while leaving him to do the shorter clips at which he was much better than I was.

Judged by its effect on our position, the 1983 Alliance campaign not merely 'on the whole went well', but was a brilliant success. We started with a 14 per cent poll rating and we came out with 25.5 per cent. In 1987 we started with 30 per cent and came out with 22.5 per cent. At the time the 1983 result was nonetheless a disappointment, both in relation to the great hopes of 1981 and to the prospect, which seemed a very real one until the last couple of days of the 1983 campaign, of overtaking the Labour Party. Then the check to our momentum and the steadying of the Labour position became almost as physically discernible as is a change in the pace of two horses in a race, and Labour finished two points ahead of us. Had the dynamics of the previous week continued (I could sense it ceasing more easily than I can explain why it did) and this 2 per cent gap been closed, the repercussions would surely have been dramatic. The effect on Labour Party morale would have been shattering. Beyond that it is difficult to believe that the working of the House of Commons, with the great privileges given to the official opposition, could have survived for a whole Parliament the presence of a third group with only twenty-three seats but more democratic legitimacy. The Labour Party in Parliament would have become a manifest simulacrum. Narrowly this did not happen, although I am convinced that it would have done, with all its consequences, had Darlington gone differently. But that is to move into a 'for the want of a nail the shoe was lost' scenario.

Despite this considerable real success and tantalisingly near great success, I did not enjoy the 1983 campaign. This was because of the so-called Ettrick Bridge Summit and the events leading up to it. Throughout the campaign David Steel registered much better personal poll ratings than I did. He was at the peak of his popularity. One poll two weeks into the campaign suggested that if he were leading the Alliance its position would improve substantially. It was a highly hypothetical proposition on which to place reliance, but a lot of Liberal pressure was put on Steel to try to effect such a change. He telephoned early on the morning of 24 May and spoke with embarrassment and imprecision about the issue. He reverted to the subject at an unfestive breakfast (normally our common meals were enjoyable) which we had together the next morning. I said I would think about it during the day.

I did so as my so-called battle bus toured Kent on one of the prettier days of the campaign. The last thing I wanted was to be an incubus to the Alliance for the sake of clinging to a position which had abruptly ceased to give me any satisfaction. Half seriously I decided that the best solution might be if the bus were to run out of control down one of the steep and narrow Kentish lanes, inflicting preferably only a light but temporarily incapacitating flesh wound. But every political instinct I had told me that short of this it would be a disaster for a party leader to run under fire, or indeed for a serious political grouping to change horses in mid-stream. Every mixed metaphor in the dictionary of clichés rose up in revolt. Whichever way I argued round it in my mind I could not avoid the conclusion that abdication in the circumstances would destroy my position with press and public, not least in Hillhead.

Nor did I believe that it would benefit David Steel, and through him the Alliance as a whole. It is often easier to be admired as number two than as number one, as many political careers have demonstrated. Furthermore, he would be quickly portrayed as having exhibited the alleged treachery of Highlanders (despite being as firmly rooted as possible in the Lowlands of Scotland), and might well find himself dangerously exposed after he had removed the protection of having me as the more vulnerable one of the partnership. I think he came to have more sympathy for vulnerability when he had to live for a time in a more or less similar position in relation to Owen to that which I had occupied in relation to him, with the television programme *Spitting Image* acting as his equivalent of my opinion polls. There are times when things have to be seen through, however disagreeable they may have become.

This at any rate was the conclusion to which I irresistibly came in the interstices between Sittingbourne High Street, the Ashford railways workshops and the Tonbridge shopping enclave. It was reinforced when I got to a Tonbridge hotel for a short pause before my two outer London evening meetings and received a long letter from Jack Diamond, leader in the Lords, who was acting throughout the campaign as anchorman in the Cowley Street office, and whom I had briefly consulted between the breakfast and leaving London. He had spent the morning considering the matter and argued vehemently against the change, which he thought would not only be wrong in itself, but would demoralise the SDP. So I sent a negative message to David Steel, and tried to dismiss the matter from my mind, assuming that it would not surface again, except in my own thoughts.

On the Sunday (29 May) we were due to have an Alliance 'summit' at David Steel's house in the Borders. It was planned partly for serious campaign-discussion purposes, but even more as a good publicity gimmick. About six leading figures from each party were involved, as well as a number of staff. We were all due to converge by helicopter but this did not allow for the dank mist which in my experience the Ettrick Water has a peculiar ability to generate. This did not much inconvenience me, for Jennifer (who was even more against a change than Jack Diamond) and I merely had a dismal drive from Glasgow. The mood stemmed from more than the weather, for Steel had telephoned the night before and conveyed, again without his usual clarity, that he proposed further to raise the leadership issue on the following morning. When we got there we found that he had prepared some sort of draft press statement announcing a change. The London contingent (two of our four plus Jack Diamond and some Liberals) were late, more disorganised by the weather than we had been. When they arrived we sat uneasily round a table and David Steel deployed his case. Shirley Williams killed it dead, I think not only out of loyalty but out of repugnance for the foolishness of the ploy, but in either event with great authority. She was supported by Bill Rodgers and by Jack Diamond. David Owen said nothing.

We then put together an alternative press statement, which reasonably suggested that David Steel would be taking a higher profile for the remaining ten days. He and I then went to a press conference in the village hall. I approached it as one of my less promising press encounters. Fortunately the journalists were kind to us. We could even be regarded as having got useful publicity out of the event, with nothing too damaging even to me. It was more than we deserved.

Diamond returned with us to Glasgow, where I began the last ten days of my campaign with more determination than pleasure. The next morning, when I did some intensive Hillhead canvassing before flying to Liverpool, I struck a peculiarly lucky patch of favourable response, which made me reflect that fate had a certain even-handedness. The others returned from Ettrick Bridge to Edinburgh airport. In the course of the car journey Owen informed Rodgers and Williams that he had for the first time admired Steel that morning.

Later however David Owen seemed surprised and almost resentful that I did not bear more of a continuing grudge against Steel for what, in his 1987 reminiscences, he described as this 'ruthless and savage deed'.[3] Why did I not? I think in the first place Steel's balance in my bank was bigger than Owen could easily imagine. Steel had behaved with great steadiness throughout 1980 and 1981. And not only had he been a dependable ally. He had also been a pleasure to work with, able to laugh at himself, anxious to discuss to an agreement and not to argue to an impasse when there were differences, in general a prop rather than a sour critic. Against this background I attributed Ettrick Bridge to an error of judgement rather than of motive. He was tired and strained, and decided after the election that he had to take three months off. I thought there were people around him who ought to have known better, and that he should have stood up to their amateur machiavellianism. But this was not the basis for permanent resentment. Furthermore, when he and I dined together ten days after the election we had a satisfactory catharsis. I told him that I thought he had uncharacteristically behaved both badly and foolishly. He more or less agreed and apologised. I fully accepted this and said that the event would not affect our future relationship. Soft answers when, as in his case, delivered from a generosity of spirit, can do a great deal to turn away wrath.

Lest I appear as too forgiving a character, however, it should be added that when on the afternoon of Monday, 13 June, four days after the poll, I telephoned Steel and told him that I had resigned the leadership of the SDP and he mildly remonstrated with me both for doing it at all and for not consulting with him beforehand, he got a pretty sharp answer. This resignation was by no means an irrational flounce, although I had sustained myself during the last two difficult weeks with private promises of early freedom. Michael Foot announced his resignation even sooner than I did and this meant that had I continued in office the newest party would have had the inappropriate distinction of the oldest leader – five years more so than Mrs Thatcher.

These considerations would not necessarily have led me to go in June rather than at our party conference in September. For my personal convenience the earlier date was preferable. After four contested elections in twenty-three months I much needed a long holiday. But September would have been less abrupt and probably neater from the party's point of view. The timing was however taken out of my hands. By ten o'clock on the Saturday, our first morning back from our constituencies, David Owen telephoned to say that, unless I resigned forthwith, he would force a leadership ballot in July. I was not unduly thrown by this, given my own wishes, although I found his behaviour somewhat incontinent. I told him that I would summon a small conclave for the Monday at East Hendred, and indicated that he could have his way. Given his hurry, there was no alternative, unless I was prepared to go on for the Parliament. It would have made no sense at all to have fought another divisive contest in July and then to have resigned in September, or indeed at any time in the next few years.

On the Monday morning Shirley Williams, Jack Diamond, John Roper, who had been our chief whip, and Bill Rodgers, as well as David Owen, assembled at East Hendred. Before lunch the first three all strongly resisted my desire to resign. Shirley in particular expressed dismay at the prospect. Rodgers and I had talked things over on the Sunday. Owen kept rather quiet, but I thought I could depend upon him to deal with Shirley and the others when the moment for decision could no longer be postponed. Unwaveringly he made clear his determination to force himself in. Gradually and reluctantly they all then came to accept the logic of my view that his unilateral edict was incontestable. I issued a press statement in good time for the six o'clock news.

Have I subsequently regretted my action? Certainly not from the point of view of my own comfort and convenience. Even had I survived that July election (my fifth in two years) there could have been little but pain and trouble in living with a doubly embittered Owen breathing down my neck. And there would have been no relief that I could work towards, for, Rodgers and Williams having lost their seats, there was no prospect of building up an effective alternative to Owen. Furthermore I am not at all sure that I could have led the SDP to the fine poll ratings which Owen's charisma helped to achieve for the Alliance in 1985 and 1986. Admittedly they were thrown away in the disappointing because (despite Ettrick Bridge) much more split campaign of 1987 and in the awfulness which followed. Yet it is not imaginable that I could have stayed on until then, aged sixty-six, and having been ill, as it turned out, for long periods between 1984 and 1986. Nevertheless I have a sneaking feeling that we all allowed ourselves to be bullied too much on that post-election Monday at East Hendred, and that the result was a redoubling of the perforation created by the leadership contest of July 1982, which led on to schism in the SDP and the consequent near destruction of the Alliance.

# CHAPTER THIRTY-ONE

# *What Went Wrong?*

Following my resignation David Owen was naturally elected leader of the SDP without a contest – there was no rival – and was therefore in place for the opening of Parliament on 22 June and the five weeks of political activity before the holidays. I was not feeling bruised or cast down during this period. I thought that in all the circumstances we had done well to get more than 25 per cent of the vote, and that holding Hillhead as one of our only six seats was a distinct achievement. Of course our thinness in the House of Commons (seventeen Liberals in addition to our six) was a disappointment. But even more was it a disgrace. With a fair electoral system we would have had an Alliance parliamentary party of 160 and the force of our achievement would have been apparent for all to see.

Inevitably, in view of one or two events of the preceding few years, I had some reservations about David Owen. But they did not begin to add up to a desire to prevent his becoming leader. The events stemmed mostly from his resentment at not being leader previously, and I thought that with this grievance out of the way the reservations might disappear. The public endorsement which I gave to his leadership at our conference two months later exactly expressed this mixture of hope and reserve without resentment: 'I assumed and greatly welcomed his uncontested election. I congratulate David and wish him well. A large part of our future is now bound up in him.'

I considered that I had been lucky, in view of how oppressive the leadership had become to me in the middle of the campaign, to get out of it so cleanly. In addition I could see plenty of not too onerous political opportunities for the future. In early July I took on the leadership of an all-party Fair Votes Campaign, with Ian Gilmour and Austin Mitchell, Labour MP for Grimsby, amongst the vice-presidents, the launching of which was an obvious response to the outcome of the election. There was my passion for Hillhead. There was the opportunity to speak in the House of Commons when I wanted to but not when I did not, for David Owen had the delicacy not to suggest that I take on a specific spokesmanship, with the hope (which proved well founded) that my parliamentary form would improve when free of the exposure of leadership. And there was also the self-righteous prospect of being able to exercise an admonitory role as the guardian of the Alliance. It looked well worth guarding. In late July, with a Liberal candidate, we reduced Willie Whitelaw's 15,000 general election majority to 500 in the first bye-election of the new Parliament. I could feel that I had not left the Alliance in a quagmire but put it on a springboard. Altogether I departed for thirty days in France and Italy on 24 July in one of my more contented moods, perhaps a more senescent version of that in which I had gone away in July 1970 after the end of the first Wilson Government.

I came back to the early September conference of the SDP, which we had oddly decided to hold in Salford. As the choice must have been made under my leadership I cannot blame anyone else for it, although I am sure the initiative was not mine. To stop rolling between three places was a good idea. So was the avoidance of Blackpool or Brighton. But to settle down in Salford was to exaggerate our need to demonstrate that we were not a party of the leafy suburbs and the southern counties. Salford University is rather good, but not as a conference centre. I recollect a bleak hall and even bleaker surrounding committee rooms, in which we had several bad-tempered meetings of the National Committee. The conference hotel in the shape of the famous and familiar old Midland in Manchester was at once too grand and too remote, and there was no piazza-like intimacy, which is desirable for a good conference, on the route between there and the hall. The almost continuous rain would have made such encounters difficult in any event.

What I recollect even more than the harshness of the physical surroundings was the harshness of the atmosphere within the leadership. I think David must have spent his holidays deciding that he had to impose the smack of firm discipline on the party. The first time I saw him he was striding into the opening National Committee meeting in a curiously military-looking mackintosh. The curtness of his nod indicated that serious business was afoot, and this took the form of making it clear that he was eager to use his majority to vote down any proposition which presented a 'Jenkinsite' friendliness towards Liberals. In particular he was determined not only to exclude merger but also to use his peak authority as a new leader to exclude for the future the joint selection (by the members of the two parties in the constituency) of Alliance candidates. Still more depressing were the signs that, despite his unanimous election, the keynote was to be not reconciliation across the party but the elevation to authority of those who had been Owen loyalists in the last but one leadership election. I remember saying to Jennifer that the party was slipping into a factionalism only too reminiscent of the Labour Party, and that we must at least resist it in our social habits. Rather against our inclination after these long and uncomradely National Committee sessions, we pursued a determined policy of having 'Owenites' to meals in the hotel.

This atmosphere had not seeped through to most of the delegates, and they were friendly and responsive both to my 'farewell to the leadership' speech on the first day and to my opening of the electoral-reform debate later in the week. By the time of the first speech Owen had already moved and carried a resolution which ruled out merger (although not necessarily for ever, he interestingly said) and countenanced joint selection only in exceptional circumstances. My comments on the Alliance were as follows:

No relationship in human affairs can remain static. That is true between individuals and between institutions. Either relations advance or they recede. We do not want recession. We must therefore be prepared for an advance, and I believe a substantial advance. . . . Of course it would be foolish to seek a premature and therefore disruptive merger. But do not set a limit to the march of the Alliance. Do not try to impose too many rules or bans or prescriptions on local parties from the centre. If the Alliance is to grow closer, which it must, it is best that it should do so organically, on the ground, from the bottom up.

The 'no joint selection save in exceptional cases' rule was to cause endless trouble. The Liberals were almost universally in favour of joint selection, and so were a lot of our SDP local parties, who submitted large numbers of proposals for such arrangements to the National Committee, meetings of which for the next year or so were much occupied with increasingly bad-tempered arguments about whether they should be allowed or not. Broadly speaking David Owen tried to prevent their being endorsed and was mostly supported by a narrow majority of the committee. Sometimes the purity that he was anxious to defend took a very sterile form. In seats which had been allocated to the Liberals they were often anxious that the Social Democrats should participate in the selection process. This, they reasonably thought, would encourage the latter to feel more commitment to the Alliance candidate. And the local SDP members were equally often attracted by the prospect of having a say between different Liberals.

Even these offers of 'something for nothing' had in Owen's view to be rejected because they undermined the principle that each party must have absolute control over its choice of candidates in its own seats. At issue in these cases was what was known as 'joint closed selection'. 'Joint open selection', that is the local members of both parties voting between nominees who were equally unrestricted to one party or the other, raised even more acutely the issue of party sovereignty. Yet in some cases the pressure for it was almost irresistible, for it was the only way in which an allocation deadlock within a county or a borough could be broken. Sometimes, too, the Liberals were willing to open to free selection seats such as Salisbury which had been made by their previous performance into some of the best prospects in the country, and which they would on any other basis have insisted on keeping for themselves.

What was more important than the individual outcomes, however, was the establishment of a rigid pattern of voting which ran accurately down the line of what was to be the 1987 split. It also filled some of us with a distaste for the proceedings of the National Committee, which was a bitter contrast with the mood of 1981–2, and with a determination that we should not again go through the squalid travail of spending months if not years of arguing over seats with an ally with whom we were supposed to be locked in an ever deepening partnership. But this distaste led to no weakening of political commitment. Over the winter six months of 1983–4 I continued to speak almost as intensively at SDP and Alliance conferences, meetings and dinners as I had done during my year as leader. Between the end of January and mid-April my diary shows a total of twenty-seven such engagements from Newton Abbot to Dundee.

On 12 October I had taken the dramatic decision to give up smoking cigars. I had not smoked a cigarette since the early 1960s, and had subsequently fluctuated with cigars, sometimes giving up them too for quite long periods. But from 1975 onwards, encouraged in the centre of the period by the good Brussels supplies, I had become more and more devoted to medium-sized Havanas. In 1983 I decided that I could not afford them, or at least that they were consuming a ridiculous amount of money. So I stopped quite suddenly and have never smoked anything since, which at least shows that my devotion was not an addiction. I regard the deprivation as a diminution of pleasure, but have also become aware of the discomfort I must unthinkingly have inflicted upon others (I once gave the passionately anti-smoking David Owen a lift in a very small private jet from Strasbourg to London and impregnated him with the fumes of consecutive cigars on the way; perhaps all subsequent troubles arose from that journey), and find it occasionally difficult not to let abstention spill over into intolerance of those who have remained unreconstructed.

Whatever this change did for my pocket, it did no good for my health. It became much less good without cigars than it had been with them. In mid-April 1984, I was diagnosed as having a thyroid condition, which had been building up for some time, and which necessitated having six weeks off at East Hendred, although in no great discomfort, and which responded satisfactorily to this rest and to drugs. Half a year later I became more acutely ill with the effects of a neglected and undetected prostate condition, which had become menacing enough that I had to have an operation at three days' notice on 21 December and spend Christmas in hospital. Worse, however, was the fact that this did not clear things up and that I had to play something of a cat-and-mouse game with hospitals and operations for the next eighteen months until, in July 1986, a brilliantly performed feat of delicate rather than dangerous surgery brought this dismal period to an end.

During this two and a half years I was by no means incapacitated. I carried on with my constituency and parliamentary duties and never thought of resigning my seat. And I indulged in almost a frenzy of book output. I wrote the last part of my short life of President Truman and published it in February 1986. I dusted down the biographical essay on Baldwin which I had written in 1972–3, added to it somewhat and turned it into another short book, which came out in March 1987. And by the summer of 1986 I was already deep in the early stages of editing *European Diary* for publication in 1989. I found this very satisfactory hospital work. It kept my attention because it was about my own life, and it was not too intellectually demanding because it merely involved paring down and explaining what already existed. In addition, Clive Lindley, whose contribution to the SDP and the Alliance remained as strong throughout the 1980s as I have described it as being in the first year after the Dimbleby lecture, edited and arranged for the publication of a volume of my speeches of this period, which inevitably involved some work by me. It came out, under the title *Partnership of Principle*, at the time of the Torquay conference of the SDP in September 1985.

Nevertheless I was only functioning at about two-thirds power during these mid-1980s years and could not conceivably have led a party which was struggling hazardously but successfully to maintain its beachhead on the shore of major politics. Attlee had held on to his position in roughly similar circumstances in 1939 and Macmillan might have been wiser to have done so in 1963, but not only were their medical troubles shorter-lived, their parties were also more secure in their political bases. It is therefore academic to discuss whether I ought to have held on as leader in June 1983. Had I put aside Ettrick Bridge and confronted David Owen in a July ballot (which I think would have been a more open contest than he assumed), I would still have had to resign at the beginning of 1985. And Owen would still have become leader. No possible SDP alternative had emerged in the meantime.

The delay of eighteen months in the date of the handover would have made no difference to the conduct of the Alliance in the 1987 election or to the subsequent internecine disaster which befell the two parties.

My immediate post-thyroiditis initiative was a Tawney Society lecture, which I delivered in mid-July 1984 to a fine Alliance audience of two hundred, just about the same size of audience that had listened to Dimbleby, but without, on this occasion, a television audience in the background. The Alliance was externally in good shape at that time, for we had just won a striking bye-election victory in Portsmouth, but there were considerable and cumulative internal strains, arising largely from seat allocation. I therefore took the opportunity to set out how I saw the relationship between the two parties at this stage and also, no doubt, to let off some frustrations accumulated at successive meetings of the National Committee.

First, I have never had the slightest doubt that it was right to set up the SDP as a separate party, although from the beginning envisaging realignment and alliance. We were able as a new body to recruit most valuable people both inside and outside politics for whom the skin of the old Liberal Party would have been too tight. Second, I do not however take the view that there are great ideological differences, still less, as some would have it, almost 'ethnic' differences between the two parties. Others may have sharper nostrils but I cannot instinctively tell a Liberal from a Social Democrat when I meet one in bye-election committee rooms. Certainly the view held at one stage that we would be clearly to the left of a centrist Liberal Party, and would consequently have a greater penetration in Labour seats, while they might be the more effective in Conservative-held ones, is now manifest nonsense. There are of course differences between the two parties. We in the SDP are, I suppose, more naturally geared to government, although . . . we have some way to go before we again enmesh with it. But I honestly believe the Alliance is ideologically about as cohesive as any decent democratic grouping ought ever to be, substantially more so than either the Labour or Conservative parties.

I was then concerned to refute a hardening piece of Owenite orthodoxy, which was that, once proportional representation had been secured, we could revert to electoral competition with the Liberals, although possibly joining with them (or indeed with other parties) in a government. I thought that this was not only counting chickens before they were hatched but was also showing a grave misunderstanding of the whole nature of poultry farming:

Third, I do not believe that there is sense, even if we assumed electoral reform to be in the bag, which would be a very rash assumption, in envisaging a future for four independent mainstream groupings in British politics. We would make a great mistake if we gave the impression that our marriage with the Liberals was one of short-term convenience, and that if we ever felt free and strong enough to do so we would be off on our own. The Alliance in my view is 'for better for worse'. There can be no SDP triumphs or defeats which are not Liberal triumphs or defeats and *vice versa*. Nor can one party effectively immunise itself from weakness or instability in the other. Foolish policies adopted by one are a noose around the neck of the other. This will be even more true if we get to the threshold of winning a general election and have a sharper light of public scrutiny turned upon us. The way to avoid danger here is to work out a sensible joint policy together, and not to believe that one party can deny the sins of the other.

I believe that if this quasi-philosophical point about full commitment to a joint common future is resolved, then a lot of tensions are removed and a lot of problems fall into place. The detailed domestic arrangements can proceed without undue hurry or constitutional complication, and indeed to some extent piecemeal. Where on the ground people in both parties wish to be mingled together, let it happen, where they wish to be somewhat further apart, there can also be local autonomy.

Towards the end of the lecture I made a flick at what I was coming to regard as David Owen's instinctive sympathy for the Thatcherite style and consequent lurch to the right. I put it in the coded form which is so beloved of politicians when they are speaking about differences within their own party:

There have been some ludicrous suggestions in the past few months that the SDP is on its way to becoming a sort of junior Thatcherite party. 'Not while I'm alive it (he) ain't,' as Ernest Bevin said about Aneurin Bevan being his own worst enemy. But happily the silliness of the proposition does not depend upon my prospects of longevity. The whole spirit and outlook of the SDP, its leaders and its members, is and must be profoundly opposed to Thatcherism.

This apparent flirtation with Thatcherism on Owen's part was also damaging his relations with Shirley Williams at this time. She had supported him for the leadership in 1982 on the ground that, although her personal links with me had been closer, she then felt she ought to sustain his neo-socialism rather than my whiggery. The shock of finding him way out to the right, not only of her but of me, was therefore considerable. But I think that the sheer strain of personal relations between a president of the party who specialised in warm goodwill and a leader who believed in cold commands was at least an equal cause of her disenchantment, against which she struggled hard, but which I observed gaining momentum during that summer of 1984.

In June she and I spoke together at the Cambridge Union, and I then stayed the night at her house in north Hertfordshire. Probably for the first time she spoke to me in terms of unhappy complaint against the sheer abrasiveness of David Owen, buttressed by some emerging worry about his policy positions. In early October Shirley and I both addressed a conference in Athens and then went with some of the other participants on a three-day cruise around the islands off the Peloponnese. We there had more relaxed bilateral talk than on any occasion since the long Brussels night four and a half years before, and her June criticisms surfaced still more strongly. I remember with mild guilt that I received them with satisfaction, whereas I suppose in the interests of the future of the party I ought to have received them with dismay. But I think that, in view of David Owen's persistent offensive/defensive attitude to me and of Shirley Williams's position in 1982, I would have needed to be super-human to have done so.

Relations between Owen and me varied between the superficially bonhomous when we met casually in semi-public and a wary mixture of searching to re-establish the old confidence and rough confrontation on the rare occasions when we met in private. The reason for the latter was that I became increasingly aware that he understood only the scorched-earth response to his iron-heel approach. A trivial example that springs to mind was when at the end of 1986 we were discussing the arrangements for another Alliance relaunch and rally in the New Year he suggested that I should speak for five minutes. With anyone else I would have said, 'That is a bit short. Cannot we make it ten?'; that in his case would have produced no result at all. With him I said, 'David, you know perfectly well that is not my length. I will either speak for fifteen minutes or not at all. Take it or leave it.' He took it, because it was the only sort of language he understood. On another occasion when he lunched with me alone, for the only time in that Parliament, he approached intimacy by saying how much his subordination to me had stunted him in the early 1970s, but then retreated into an arm's-length intransigence.

The fault must have been at least partially mine. It always is divided in such circumstances, and no doubt he interpreted my publication at the time of the Torquay conference of 1985 of *Partnership of Principle*, the title, the contents, my introduction and my speech at the launching of which (an occasion which he politely or perversely attended) as being a provocative setting out of my view of the Alliance as opposed to his own. On the other hand he would sometimes during this phase give the impression that the differences between us would all come out in the wash. At the elaborate occasion which was organised in March 1986 to celebrate the fifth anniversary of the SDP he indicated that in due course merger would probably be the natural destiny of ourselves and the Liberal Party. We clutched at these words in a way reminiscent of my cosseting Gaitskell's few pro-EEC phrases in 1961–2.

These tensions were largely below the surface and the Alliance on

With Secretary Kissinger on
the State Department roof,
October 1976. 'Come on, Henry,
don't be such a shrinking violet.'

A floral first meeting with
Jimmy Carter: the White House,
April 1977.

The boyhood of Helmut. Encouraging Chancellor Schmidt to set sail for economic
and monetary union. Bonn, 28 February 1978.

With Crispin Tickell (and Italian protocol accompaniment) in Venice for the
Western Economic Summit, June 1980.

Consternation in Dublin, December 1979. Has Giscard (*back to camera*) stabbed Hercule Poirot (alias Jørgensen, Danish Prime Minister)? Mrs Thatcher averts her eyes from such disorderly Continental behaviour. Peter Carrington (*scratching his nose*) wants to keep out of it. Schmidt and I look sombre but resigned. Gaston Thorn (*arms folded*) appraises whether Giscard has made a clean job of it. Jack Lynch, Irish Taoiseach (*centre*), wishes it had not happened in his hotel.

The Gang of Four in the days of harmony. Limehouse, January 1981.

... which extended to their wives: Jennifer, Silvia Rodgers and Debbie Owen.
Perth, October 1981.

'We haven't even started the motor yet' (Gibberd). *The Guardian*, February 1981.

'What does Mr Jenkins wear under his kilt?' (Garland). *Daily Telegraph*, January 1982.

The beginning of the Warrington Campaign. John Lyttle and I advance cautiously.

With David Steel. 'If one man made the Alliance it was he.'

Spring in the West End of Glasgow. Kirklee Terrace, where we had our flat.

Robed as Chancellor of Oxford, June 1987.

With Isaiah Berlin at All Souls Encaenia luncheon, 1987. We look ornithological as I absorb wisdom.

the whole performed well in the mid-1980s. We had a flat result (20 per cent) in the 1984 Euro-elections, but that apart our electoral performance was mostly in line with our opinion-poll results, which gave us a steady position of approximate equality with the other two parties and sometimes put us first amongst the three. On the same day as the Euro-elections we had an SDP victory in Portsmouth South. The next summer we secured a good win at Brecon and Radnor, coming from third place at the 1983 general election. Triangular politics seemed an established fact. The culmination of this phase was our victory in the Ryedale bye-election in early May 1986 and a very near miss (by a hundred votes) in the West Derbyshire bye-election on the same day. Both candidates were Liberals (as had been the Brecon and Radnor one), but that did not matter if the Alliance was perceived as an organic unity and not as a pantomime horse with built-in rivalry between the two ends.

Was it? Owen and Steel both made considerable efforts to get on well together. They had at once the advantage and the disadvantage of being contemporaries within four months and of looking superficially alike. 'Which twin has the Toni?' became a newspaper joke after they had appeared together in identical yachting sweaters. But some cartoonists as well as *Spitting Image* decided to differentiate by portraying David Steel as about a third of the size of David Owen, despite the fact that there was barely an inch between them. At least Steel and I were incapable of being confused with each other and therefore, in a sense, of being rivals. We would never have appeared together cable-stitched. I would always have been less sportingly dressed, and he would always have had the advantage of looking leaner and keener.

Owen never captured the hearts of the Liberal Party, although he could have done so with only a little stooping to conquer. They reluctantly admired him, and when he made a good speech to them, in his 'groping after truth' style, at their Dundee assembly in September 1985, they responded with hopeful respect. But not more. He essentially regarded the Liberal Party as a disorderly group of bearded vegetarian pacifists, and his treatment of them as such not unnaturally brought out such of these tendencies as existed. I treated them as the statesmanlike heirs of Gladstone and Asquith. The truth was no doubt somewhere between the two, but I am sure that my method pushed them in the right direction from an SDP point of view, and that his pushed them in the wrong direction. At their Bournemouth conference in 1984, where I had gone for a day not necessarily intending to speak, but was pressed into delivering a quarter-hour general greeting, I rather uncharacteristically said that the Alliance ought to be infused, beyond affection and respect, 'even with a little love', and received a rapturous response to this rare excursion into sentiment and/or populism. There was no doubt that, in spite of the 1982 hiccups, I had by that time become the Liberals' favourite Social Democrat, although Shirley was not far behind. However, aided somewhat by my health preoccupations, I kept away from the next two Liberal assemblies, giving David Owen a free run at Dundee in 1985 and not dabbling in the bubbling cauldron of Eastbourne in 1986.

By that latter occasion the Alliance was in serious trouble and there were also great strains within the SDP. The Liberal Party had long contained a sizeable group whose horror at the prospect of nuclear destruction made them attracted by the fallacies of unilateralism. They were normally a minority but in some circumstances they could surge forward to win a snap vote in the assembly. This happened in 1984 when a motion for the removal 'forthwith' of cruise missiles from Britain was carried by a handful of votes. The SDP had virtually no unilateralists within it, although in the early days Polly Toynbee, who subsequently became a hard-line Owenite, had tried to organise a group under some such name as Unilateralists for Social Democracy. It did not prosper, and SDP members were mostly immunised against the seductions of unilateralism by it having been one of the issues central to the setting up of the new party. This near unanimity of the SDP, aided by David Steel's firm multilateralism, meant that there could never be a danger of a merged party becoming unilateralist. There was always likely to be a good three to one majority against, as indeed has proved to be so at Liberal Democrat conferences. Equally, any joint bodies between the two parties within an unmerged Alliance would have a firm multilateralist majority upon it, composed of all the SDP representatives and at least half the Liberals who were likely to be nominated.

Partly with these thoughts in mind the SDP and David Steel were attracted by the setting up of a joint commission to deliberate on Alliance defence policy, and in particular whether the acceptance of Trident as a replacement for Polaris was the only logical alternative to unilateralism. This commission was appointed in July 1984 and worked hard for nearly two years. It was presided over by a retired diplomat who was a specialist in arms-control negotiations, included an intellectual general and Laura Grimond, who was about as sympathetic to unilateralism as her redoubtable mother (Lady Violet Bonham Carter) had been to appeasement, as well as a politically experienced SDP trio: John Roper, who had gone from being our chief whip before 1983 to editing the Chatham House journal, John Cartwright, his successor as whip, who was our defence spokesman and close to Owen, and above all Bill Rodgers. Rodgers had been the constable of Labour anti-unilateralism, in 1960 as the organiser of Gaitskell's fight back, and in 1980 as the last shadow Defence Secretary for nearly a decade who spoke forthrightly for Britain's commitment to NATO. As I wrote in an *Observer* article in June 1986, to accuse him of unilateralism was like accusing General de Gaulle of being a collaborator.

It was the report of this commission, filtered through a series of indiscretions, distortions and overreactions, which set Owen off on a course which led to the destruction of a successful Alliance and of his own political position. Owen was not merely an anti-unilateralist, as were all his co-equals in the Alliance. He was something of a nuclear fetishist. He could talk about missiles with a discriminating enthusiasm which some men reserved for horses or women or wine. He knew the exact angles at which they had to leave silos or the hulls of submarines. He was a master of the techniques of weaponry and would have made a brilliant if somewhat hard-line leader of a Western arms-control negotiating team. He could ruminate without a note on the development and deployment of the weapons of the future. This great knowledge and interest sometimes led to undesirable effects. He was constantly looking for motes of nuclear weakness in the eyes of his colleagues, and he became a supreme example of the rule, which I noted earlier in connection with the Labour European dispute of 1971–3, that most politicians and all political parties cannot leave internally divisive subjects alone. Once he had decided with some justification that nuclear weaponry was the most dangerous subject for the coherence and success of the Alliance, he came increasingly to talk about little else.

Nevertheless I assumed that he would pay due regard to the report of the Defence Commission, with the setting up and membership of which he had been much involved, and would indeed hope that it might provide an acceptable basis for a united Alliance policy. That was the purpose for which it had been established. I was therefore amazed when he rejected it before it had been published. Indeed such was my surprise that at first I hardly took in what he was doing. On 17 May (1986) in accordance with our normal thrice-yearly practice there was a meeting of the five-hundred-strong Council for Social Democracy. It took place in a sodden Southport, the first time I had been in that sea-deserted but flower-bedecked resort since 1928 when I had been taken to a Trades Union Congress there. On that occasion I had been much impressed by the hotel. In 1986 I was less so, but that was not my major Southport worry.

Towards the end of the morning David Owen was delivering a leader's general address and I was sitting on the platform with my thoughts half engaged elsewhere. He plunged into a nuclear passage, which seemed remote from the business before the Council, but I assumed it was just David going on about his favourite subject. 'I must tell you bluntly that I believe we should remain a nuclear-weapon state,' he announced. This did not seem very startling for it had never occurred to me that he believed anything else, and no decision was in any event pending. Then he claimed that any failure to state categorically and at once what would be our late 1990s replacement for Polaris would deserve 'a belly laugh from the British electorate'. Even then I did not take in fully what he was up to, and the majority of the audience was I believe equally in the dark. It required Bill Rodgers, who had been the leading politician on the commission, to walk across the platform to me and point out that it was a pre-emptive strike against the result which two years' work had just produced without even giving the delegates the chance to read what it was that was going to provoke 'a belly laugh' from the electorate.

I then slowly became almost as angry as Bill was himself, and if anything even more depressed, for it is my belief, only dimly seen at the time but subsequently much fortified by the dismal unfolding of a series of causally linked events, that the Alliance began to die on that wet Southport Saturday morning. I was also mystified. I could not see what had sparked Owen off, at a time when the Alliance was doing well (Ryedale and West Derbyshire only a week before) and a general election was beginning to loom, on a gratuitous course which predictably set him at odds, not only with the Liberals, but with all his principal SDP colleagues. Even John Cartwright had signed the commission report, although Owenite loyalty subsequently caused him to retract. Shirley Williams was provoked into making sharper public remarks about Owen than would have been imaginable a short time before: 'It does not follow that what the leader said is the same and identical with the policy of the party. . . . It would be excellent if he [were] prepared to listen to other points of view and possibly even consider whether there is room for some improvement on his part as well as on the part of the rest of us.'

I subsequently learned what was the trigger cause, although this did not seem sufficient to begin to amount to a fundamental explanation. David Steel, who had to face some problem with his own party because the commission report was much nearer to an SDP hard line than to anything which would satisfy the soft half of the Liberal assembly, had spoken rashly but understandably at a lunch with *Scotsman* journalists. He assured them that it was a good report and said accurately that it did not commit the Alliance to advocating a replacement for Polaris. The *Scotsman* interpreted this as meaning that it contained a commitment against, which it did not, and ran a story under the provocative headline: 'Alliance Report Rejects UK Deterrent: Owen's Nuclear Hopes Dashed'.

The newspaper-reading habits of Owen (or of his office) embraced papers published as far away from London or Plymouth as Edinburgh. How much wiser would he have been to have emulated Lord Attlee and read only *The Times* (for deaths and cricket) and the *Daily Herald* for politics, particularly as the *Daily Herald* no longer existed. Instead he calamitously overreacted to the *Scotsman* story, and apparently without consultation outside his *kraal* was on his feet at Southport within twenty-four hours. It was probably caused partly by his thrashing around for something to say, which is the cause of at least half the unfortunate speeches made by politicians. But it was not just that or a sudden impulse for he continued to dig ditches between himself and the rest of us, and in Bonn on 6 June reiterated in still more intransigent terms his Southport views.

I was in Italy (on a holiday) for the last week of May and then went to America and Canada (to launch my Truman book) for the first part of June, but became oppressed enough by news of Alliance disintegration to come back a day or so early. On the afternoon following my overnight return from Montreal I coincided with Owen as we walked out of the House of Commons chamber after question time and led him to the smoking room, where we talked for a full hour. It was perhaps a mistake to risk having such a conversation after a more or less sleepless night (although I was not feeling particularly jet-lagged). I gave him a piece of my mind, of which the burden was that he ought to ask himself why he sooner or later quarrelled with everyone with whom he was politically closely associated. He no doubt thought that he gave me a piece of his mind back. With many people this would have produced a clearing after the storm. But not with him. We parted sullenly.

I have only once since had a significant conversation with David Owen. It may have been a mistake to have spoken so frankly, but there comes a time when thoughts and feelings have to be expressed. In any event, what I reproach myself for in the next two years is not that I spoke too frankly to Owen but that I did not try hard enough to engage with him. Yet it had become an extraordinarily difficult thing to do. If one spoke softly there was only too much evidence to show that he interpreted it as weakness. If one spoke harshly, unless it was on a minor matter where he could accept the quick loss of a trick as in a card game, he took deep umbrage. I have never tried to work closely with anyone with whom it was so difficult to talk things out.

The summer passed uneasily, and the Liberals at their September assembly in Eastbourne proceeded on one thesis to justify Owen's suspicions by carrying an anti-nuclear resolution, this time by a majority of twenty-seven in a vote of 1300. On another thesis, which I prefer, this defeat for David Steel was a direct result of David Owen's 'unilateralism' at Southport. By showing his own lack of consideration for the Alliance he undermined the ability of the Liberal leadership to appeal for responsible loyalty to it at Eastbourne. The difference was worth much more than the fourteen votes which were all that needed to be turned. In any event, Southport and the Liberal assembly between them succeeded in reducing the Alliance Gallup rating from 32.5 per cent in May to 19 per cent in November.

Our poll ratings remained flat throughout the winter, but by April (1987) we came back to 32 per cent. This was largely as a result of the Greenwich and Truro bye-election victories. There was something of a 'chicken and egg' relationship between our poll ratings and the winning of bye-elections. Winning a bye-election sent our rating sharply up. But we needed favourable local terrain and some sense of general uplift to procure the victory which led to the further uplift. This happy combination was present that spring and as a result we entered the campaign for the 1987 general election, which was called on 11 May for an 11 June polling day, on a much higher platform than in 1983. Greenwich was vastly superior as a launch-pad to Darlington.

This advantage concealed a continuing unease within the Alliance. Southport and Eastbourne had left heavy scars, although they did not run straightforwardly between the two parties, for Shirley Williams and Bill Rodgers and I felt more sympathy for David Steel in his defeat at Eastbourne than for David Owen in his pre-emptive strike at Southport. The nuclear difficulty was compounded by a growing difference of political strategy. Owen, perhaps in understandable reaction from the grand hopes of 1983, was against raising the flag of victory. He wanted to campaign for the Alliance holding the balance in a hung Parliament. He could subsequently pray in aid that this was optimistic compared with the outturn. Even so it was not wise politics. First, it was an uninspiring appeal, particularly when delivered from a starting point of 30–32 per cent. It in effect conceded that we were not going to win votes during the campaign. Second, it set an objective which depended as much upon accidents outside our control as upon our own efforts, and was therefore not an effective call to action. To hold the balance we would have to win an adequate though unspecifiable number of seats, but it was equally necessary that the seats won by the other two parties should bear the appropriate relationship to each other, and this we could do nothing about.

Third, to campaign for the balance of power inevitably directs a searchlight on to which way you will tip that balance when you have got it. This is inherently a difficult question for any third party. A clear answer one way or the other would inevitably alienate a lot of votes. This is a good reason for trying to transcend it by campaigning for your own victory and not for the ability to award the prize to one of the other two contestants. Owen's strategy precluded this, and was particularly dangerous because there were conflicting pulls on precisely the issue of which way to go between him and Steel.

Owen was too experienced a politician ever to give a stark direct answer to this difficult question. And it may also be, in view of his subsequent meanderings, that I overestimated the pull of Thatcherism upon him. But there is no doubt that in the 1987 campaign (and in contrast with Steel) he gave the strong impression that we would rather sustain a Conservative government in power than put Labour in. This may have brought certain benefits in the south of England. In Scotland (and probably in the north of England) it was deeply damaging. About the last week in May I began to pick up strong evidence of this in the streets of Hillhead. Both need and opportunity led me to spend much more time there than I had done in the 1983 election. Of the twenty-four days of the campaign proper I devoted fifteen to Hillhead. In my first street encounters after Mrs Thatcher's announcement of the date of the poll I thought the atmosphere seemed good and that I was likely to win. Later I began to meet too many people who said that Owen's 'Thatcherism' made them inclined to switch from me to the Labour candidate. I rather exasperatedly pointed out that his view was not my view and that their best course was to keep me in the House of Commons to counterbalance his tendency. But they stubbornly replied that he and not I was now leader of the SDP. It was somewhat reminiscent of the February 1974 election in Stechford when I was equally exasperated with people who said they would vote for me if I and not Wilson were leader of the Labour Party, but whom as it was I could not persuade to do so.

Owen's 'Thatcherism' was not the cause of the loss of Hillhead. The adverse majority of 3200 was too big for that, and the pattern of increased Labour votes throughout the central belt of Scotland (although not to the north or south of it) in constituencies where the Alliance and consequently Owen counted, as in those where it and he did not, was too strong for that. My failure to get hold of the 'new territories' of Broomielaw, Anderston and Partick East in the way that I had of Kelvinside, Hyndland, Broomhill, Jordanhill and even Whiteinch and Scotstoun was also a considerable factor. Nevertheless I am sure that Owen's conduct of the campaign helped to lose votes in Hillhead just as Steel's conduct of it helped to win them.

There was also the adverse impact, independent of the merits of either approach, of the fact that the two leaders manifestly conducted it differently. It was easy to exploit differences between them. And this strengthened the tendency amongst active Alliance workers, which would have been there even had the leaders marched in perfect harmony, to question the need for two leaders and indeed for two parties. They had this hammered into them on the doorstep, and as a result there was hardly an Alliance committee room, not merely in Scotland but in every constituency in England to which I went, in which post-election merger was not the subject of intensive and mostly favourable discussion.

While I did not feel that the campaign nationally was going well I remained half hopeful of Hillhead until the end. The rational signs were against, but as I had shivered through twice I thought I might do so again. And I had a lot of dedicated and optimistic supporters. Our hopes even survived until well into the count. This, together with those for the other nine Glasgow seats, was in the Kelvin Hall, now the Transport Museum, then as from its beginning a vast exhibition cavern which had survived from the Glasgow Exhibition of 1889. The floor of the hall was divided between the different constituencies rather like the different pens of a livestock market, and had been the scene of some mildly menacing disorder at the 1983 counts.

Partly for this reason I did not go down from Kirklee Terrace until just after midnight. When we arrived the counting clerks were already laying out the separated and counted votes, with our line and that of my Labour opponent, the subsequently notorious George Galloway, of approximately equal length. Rather than watching obsessively while attempting public insouciance, I went off to have a drink with the BBC, who had a pen of their own. After a few minutes Christopher Mason, Glasgow University lecturer, Strathclyde regional councillor and now my successor as candidate for Hillhead, came and told me that it seemed to be going wrong. It looked like a majority of about 500 against us. Then he said it looked more like 1500, and then it was up to 2500 and then it was all over at 3200. Exactly where all those adverse bundles of the last quarter of an hour had been lurking I do not know. There, however, they indisputably were.

It was the first time that I had failed to win a seat since 1945 (Warrington, for reasons explained in Chapter 29, did not count), and the first time ever, with fifteen elections fought, that I had failed to hold one I already had. But it did not greatly hurt, although the thought occurred to me that this might be temporary. The important thing was to get through the public speeches, and the television interviews and then, perhaps more testing, to handle the supporters' celebration, now turned into a wake, which was waiting in the Pond Hotel, where the Glasgow venture had begun.

The next morning, when we packed up (not our flat, which we kept for another four months, but our suitcases) and retreated to East Hendred, proved reassuring so far as the numbness not being only temporary was concerned. The fact was that I did not care about not being a member of Parliament. I had sat there long enough (it was thirty-nine years since I had first been elected) for any good that I was doing (to paraphrase Cromwell). And the more that I contemplated the shape of the new House of Commons the less I wanted to be part of it: another apparently impregnable Thatcherite majority, a Labour Party which had at least maintained its grip on all the perquisites of opposition, and an Alliance which had lost half a million votes and five seats and seemed in danger of being at greater odds within itself.

Why then did I stand, it might be asked? The first reason was that I had no option. To have announced in 1986 or early 1987 that I was not seeking renomination would have been interpreted as a tremendous running away and would have had a bad effect on Alliance morale. Second, there was always a chance that the shape of the new House of Commons would be different and in such a way as to make it well worthwhile being part of it. It was not the possibility of change in politics with which I had grown bored, but with being an MP for the sake of being an MP.

Third, there was Hillhead itself, about which, as opposed to the latterday House of Commons, I cared a great deal. I had grown very fond of it, and insofar as I was wounded at all by the result of the 1987 election it was by the substantial severance of that connection and not by exclusion from the House of Commons. Happily I never felt a twinge of resentment against the constituency for having rejected me. The miracle was that they had accepted me so well for five years. It had been an improbable excursion, and there was no doubt that the sheer bizarreness of being the one non-local and non-Labour member for Britain's most idiosyncratic city added to the attraction which Glasgow's topography, architecture and spirit had for me. It also gave me the unique attribute (although one which I regard as a curiosity rather than a distinction) of being the only person ever to have sat in Parliament for the three biggest cities – London, Birmingham and Glasgow – of post-industrial-revolution Britain.

None of this was contradicted by the speed of my escape to East Hendred when the election was lost. I had not been there for four weeks, and there was a natural desire to recuperate away from the scene of a defeat as well as to confer with others about the post-election prospect. It did not conflict with my being sad that it made no sense to keep Kirklee Terrace after a week's autumn visit. Moreover I had to prepare for my installation as Chancellor of Oxford in twelve days' time (see Chapter 32). The departure combined with this impending event did, however, enable me to be more philosophical about the defeat than were some of those who had worked hardest for me. They had to live much more closely than I did with the change of circumstances which there being no longer an Alliance member for Hillhead produced on the ground.

I had no doubt that, in accordance with the opinions in favour of a single party and against two leaders expressed during the campaign in a thousand Alliance committee rooms and on hundreds of thousands of doorsteps, the time to move towards merger had arrived. I did not have a set view about the exact schedule, except that it should be done soon enough to preclude the need for a repetition of the seat-allocation argument of four years before. But in view of David Owen's pre-emptive strikes in the aftermath of the 1983 election on both the leadership and the joint-selection issues I was determined to resist his foreclosing against merger in 1987. I therefore used a BBC *World This Weekend* radio interview on the Sunday morning (14 June) to state my view in favour of a single party which I knew was also that of three-quarters of the original Gang of Four, as well as, I believed, of a substantial majority of those who had been active workers during the campaign. I wanted to get it firmly but non-provocatively on the record before the Monday afternoon meeting of the SDP National Committee. Owen had already come out the other way at a Friday afternoon press conference.

More impact than came from either of these statements was achieved by David Steel's action on the Sunday afternoon. He drew up a plan for early merger and announced to such part of the world as was interested that he had done so. In my view there was nothing wrong with the substance of his action. The issue had to be faced, and there was a good deal to be said for striking quickly. He knew there was a lot of support for this course within the SDP, and he knew too that Owen would move determinedly to fill any vacuum which was left open. The form of his action was nonetheless unfortunate. He made it look as though he were attempting to bounce Owen and the SDP as a whole. And to compound the error he appeared to be using a barrage of newspaper and television publicity for the attack. Owen received more explicit notice of what was happening from the Press Association than from Steel himself, and the television cameras were called in to Ettrick Bridge to watch the composition of the final paragraphs of the Steel memorandum. It made the exercise look more like a media stunt than the advancement of a serious proposition between allies. As a result it offended a lot of people within the SDP who were not opposed to merger, and who indeed eventually supported it, although more reluctantly than they would have done without that Sunday afternoon's activity.

Mockingly though I have written of alleged 'ethnic' differences between the Liberals and the SDP, I think this mistake did stem from a divergence of attitude to the press between the leading figures of the two parties. SDP ex-ministers had been used to being pursued by the press. They often kept journalists at arm's length and did not fear lack of attention as a result. Liberals, on the other hand, felt much more the need themselves to pursue the press, were consequently less discreet, and veered towards believing that even bad publicity was better than no publicity. I had been dimly aware of this difference for some time. Ettrick Bridge II brought it to the surface.

David Steel, I discover from his memoirs,[1] had telephoned David Owen between 3.00 and 5.00 a.m. on the Friday morning (not as uncivilised as it sounds for the election results were still coming through) and had announced his desire for early merger. Then on the Sunday afternoon he had sought to give him an hour's notice of his memorandum exercise, but had discovered that Owen was 'out for a long walk with Robert Maclennan'. Like mobilisation in 1914 the trains could then no longer be stopped, and when Owen and Maclennan got back from their walk they were greeted with a vague private message from Steel and a more precise public announcement from the Press Association. I do not think that this unfortunate sequence of events made any difference to Owen's attitude, but I would guess that it was a considerable contributory cause of Maclennan being unamenable that summer and taking until August to accept the case for merger. And Maclennan represented an important swathe of SDP opinion.

Matters did not therefore get off to a happy start. And they certainly did not subsequently pursue a happy course. There were three horrible meetings of the SDP National Committee that summer. A combination of those who agreed with him on the demerits of Liberals and those whose loyalty his leadership commanded gave Owen a narrow but dependable majority on the committee. The most crucial vote (on whether the committee should recommend the membership to oppose merger) he won by eighteen to thirteen. What was horrible, however, was not so much being in a minority (although what appeared to me the irrational destructiveness of the case for SDP isolation made such a position exasperating) as the bitterness and poison which quickly came to flow along the divide. It was a classic example of civil wars being the most vicious.

At the first meeting Shirley Williams's proposal that the annual conference (long since fixed for the end of August so that Mrs Thatcher could not kill it by an early October election; we would have been lucky if she had) should be asked to approve an autumn ballot on merger was buried by the Owenites in the unpropitious atmosphere following the Steel pronouncement. But by the next meeting, two weeks later, there had been a reversal of positions and the Owenites imposed upon us the most rushed ballot possible, with a July campaign and a result on 6 August. I think that Owen's authoritative and impatient temperament must have suddenly seized him with an *il faut en finir* determination.

He carried enough people with him for his majority to remain solid during the squalid quarrels over how the rival propositions to be put to the membership should be worded. The Owenites wanted the proposal against merger to be presented as though it were for a strengthening of the Alliance and that for merger as though it were not a marriage of equals but a Liberal takeover. Rarely, even in the voluminous history of family feuds, can there have been such unrelenting argument over the details of a will while the whole inheritance was manifestly being allowed to slip down the drain. I also became depressingly aware that a few of the people I most liked in the SDP saw things very differently from the way I did. The large majority of those I was closest to, Shirley Williams and Bill Rodgers obviously; Dick Taverne, David Marquand and John Roper; Celia and William Goodhart; John Harris, Anthony Lester, Matthew Oakeshott, Caroline Thomson (and her husband Roger Liddle), which last group had all worked for me; the party officials Alec McGivan and Richard Newby; as well as nearly all my Glasgow activists, were for merger. But at first all the surviving MPs appeared to be against, as did the majority of SDP peers.

It was the one time when I regretted being out of that Parliament, believing, maybe mistakenly, that I might have exercised some counter pull – I could at least have contested the lunacy (particularly as even the Owenites claimed they were advocating closer co-operation short of merger) of breaking off joint spokesmanship arrangements in the Commons within a fortnight of the election. Gradually the MPs and ex-MPs began to move. The Scots led the way. Dickson Mabon, who because of his Greenock experience had more reason to complain about Liberals than all the Owenites put together, nonetheless had the judgement and generosity to see what was the right course for the party. Charles Kennedy, still only twenty-seven despite having been MP for nearly a third of Scotland throughout the previous Parliament, made the most dramatic move. Unexpectedly to both sides he suddenly renounced Owenism at the end of a long meeting of the National Committee. Ian Wrigglesworth also moved, in his case to a position of benevolent neutrality in the ballot, but then to full acceptance of its result.

There were less gratifying encounters. I shall never forget my failure (temporarily in one case and permanently in the other) to move either Bob Maclennan or Jack Diamond, both of whom had been closely associated with me for long before the birth of the SDP. The Maclennans came specially to a Sunday evening dinner at East Hendred, arranged for argument not pleasure. He had been the one man whose tactical advice to me had been both bold and right in

1971 and he would unhesitatingly have backed his judgement with his political career. We did not quarrel but nor did we synthesise. Jack Diamond, the leader in the Lords, I harangued on the telephone for nearly an hour one fine Saturday morning. He had not only been a vital prop at Warrington, Hillhead and Ettrick Bridge, but a decade and a half earlier had been my Chief Secretary at the Treasury, had come into the Cabinet at my instigation and had then been such a loyal supporter that the only times we differed were when I changed line and forgot to tell him beforehand. Yet my telephone barrage failed to move him.

I remain convinced that in both exchanges I was right and they were wrong. Had they and others been able freely and from the beginning to embrace union, so that the Owenite heresy had no soil from which to sprout even a three-year life, the old Alliance and the present-day Liberal Democrats would have avoided the most terrible vicissitudes. Yet I also fear that I should have taken more notice of the flashing warning signs which came from the Diamond and Maclennan signal posts. If they were both red there must be dangers ahead. It is however easier to say that than to know exactly what alternative course I ought to have pursued. To slow down might be regarded as the obvious response to warning lights. That however I and others offered to do. Over the weekend following the decision to hold the early ballot David Sainsbury, a trustee and major benefactor of the SDP, as well as a dedicated Owenite, became worried about the divisive effect which the precipitate ballot was having upon the party. He asked whether, if others would do so too, I would agree to the pause for reflection which a postponement until the autumn would involve. A little cautiously and over several telephone calls, I agreed. I did not suspect a trick, for that would not have been in Sainsbury's nature, but I did suspect that Owen might somehow portray our acceptance as a sign that we knew we were losing.

However, I decided that it was worth the risk and told Sainsbury so in the early evening. He expressed gratification, said that he would get a decision out of Owen, who was coming back from Stockholm that night, and then rather defensively warned me that, if Owen turned the postponement down, this would not affect his allegiance to him on the substantive issue. I was surprised because I assumed he would have cleared the matter with Owen before making so many telephone calls to me and others. On return Owen, who loved the smack of firm intransigence, turned the proposal down flat, as Sainsbury had embarrassedly to explain to me later that night.

This is a watertight legal alibi against the widely held view that we were the swine who rushed towards the cliff edge and Owen a model of sagacious caution. But legal alibis are not everything, and I have a nagging feeling that I ought to have done more to transcend the mood of destructive bitterness which seized the party. The obstacles were first that the early ballot having been forced upon us, and attempts at postponement rejected, we had no alternative but to try to win it. To have lost, given the anti-Liberal tone which infused Owenite campaigning, would have meant the sundering of the Alliance and also the disappearance of any non-Owenite influence within the SDP. We could not sound an uncertain note on the trumpet in the middle of the battle. Secondly, there was the awful boulder in the path of the impossibility of talking things through to a synthesis with David Owen. But I ought to have done something, although exactly what it was I still do not know.

The ballot, on as high a poll as in the leadership contest of five years before (which was remarkable given the disillusionment which internecine quarrelling was already spreading in the party), came out at 57.5 per cent for merger and 42.5 per cent against, although the latter were nominally for a closer Alliance. David Owen immediately abandoned the leadership, although not the struggle. Bob Maclennan was drafted in his place. The only possible alternative was Charles Kennedy, and it seemed to him and to most of the rest of us that his youth needed protection as a growth asset for the future.

Immediately after the holidays we had to survive – we could not be expected to do more in the circumstances – our annual conference. Not only had it been fixed early so as to give it immunity against an October election, it had also been located in Portsmouth so as to help Mike Hancock, the winner of the 1984 bye-election, to hold his seat in that city. Alas, he had already lost it by the time we got there. This was typical of the way in which the sacred sites and the early battle honours began to turn sour at this time. It was the period when I temporarily disliked going through Warrington by train. However, Portsmouth might have been worse. Despite strenuous attempts to create an impasse we got through the vote, which threatened to make a nullity of the ballot result, and were enabled to proceed to negotiate with the Liberals on the modalities of merger. John Cartwright and I, winding up the key debate for the two sides, both tried to avoid digging deeper the ditch of bitterness. (Owen was beginning to withdraw into a position which became still more marked at our next and final conference in Sheffield in January from which he could only act and issue pronouncements through intermediaries.)

The autumn and first weeks of January were occupied with a tedious but successful negotiation with the Liberals (in which fortunately I was not involved), interspersed with three or four final loveless meetings of the National Committee of the SDP, in which I was. Although loveless, they were not as bad as the summer ones. Passion was spent, and there were only spurts of bad temper as we prepared to separate. In the more constructive discussions with the Liberals two mistakes were made, although I do not think that the responsibility for either lay exclusively with one side. The name 'Alliance' was abandoned in spite of the emotional capital which had been invested in it. We ought to have called ourselves 'The Alliance of Liberal and Social Democratic Parties', or 'The Alliance' for short. This would have linked us in to the substantial reservoirs of goodwill which survived from past campaigns, as well as making it much more difficult for the rump Owenite party to confuse legitimacy by appropriating the SDP name to themselves. Instead we called ourselves the Social and Liberal Democrats (SLD) and spent eighteen months of identity crisis compounded by trying to escape from the herbivorous and unrespectful sobriquet of 'Salads'.

Then there was an unfortunate attempt to try to confound or reassure the Owenites, who were not much interested in either process, by writing too much policy commitment, some of it ill thought out, into the aims or constitution of the new party. This led to the fiasco of the 'dead parrot' manifesto, which is now best left shrouded in fading memories, and produced some last-minute fears about a revolt against merger at a special Liberal assembly which had been summoned to Blackpool for the penultimate weekend in January. I had been in the United States for a longer period than for fifteen years and had happily escaped the birth and death of the parrot, but was urgently pressed to come back and address a large fringe meeting with Jo Grimond and David Steel (shades of Llandudno in 1981) on the eve of the decisive vote. I was irrevocably committed to address an Oxford dinner in Houston, Texas, on the evening before that, but by an odd quirk of airline schedules it was possible to combine the two.

Houston is the one city in the US from which you can fly to Europe after a dinner speech. There was an Air France plane to Paris at midnight. From there I progressed via Heathrow and Manchester Airport to arrive in a Blackpool which was most unusually snowbound and be on my feet seventeen hours after I had sat down in Houston. (Fortunately I do not suffer much from jet-lag.) I do not think that my journey was really necessary. The majority the next morning was nearly six to one. But I made it in the spirit which prompted Ludovic Kennedy to ask what anyone thought he was doing in that 'watering hole' at that season of the year if he did not care deeply about merger.

The next weekend we went to Sheffield for the final meeting of the Council for Social Democracy. There the majority was in reality about two to one, although it was made nominally bigger by a tactical Owenite abstention. The atmosphere was unfortunately worse. When

I spoke shortly before the vote on the Sunday morning, there was some heckling (inconceivable at a speech of mine during any previous SDP conference) and even a few boos. It seemed ironically sad that the history of the SDP as such should in one sense have begun with David Owen being booed at a Labour Party conference in 1980 and ended with my being booed (even if rather faintly and while winning an important vote with a big majority) at an SDP conference in 1988.

We had achieved the nautical manoeuvre of bringing the two ships alongside each other without either going down, but I am afraid that the SDP one had lost a fair segment of its crew, and that it was some time before we were ready again to set out on a major voyage. The rump SDP (spuriously claiming the name as we thought) achieved a half-life of two and a half years. It was rather mule-like, both in its stubbornness (which can of course seem splendid if seen from the other side of the hill) and in lack of pride of ancestry, for the rump was not the party of Warrington or Crosby, or hope of posterity, for the exercise always lacked constructive purpose: it could (and did) hobble the Liberal Democrats, but it could never realistically hope to achieve anything for itself. The remarkable thing was that while this confusion persisted in the centre of politics the numbers eager to vote for a third-party candidate remained as high as they did. Poll ratings were never exciting, but we continued to do well in council bye-elections, and it seems strongly likely that, without a split vote with the so-called SDP, we would have won both the Epping Forest and Richmond (Yorkshire) bye-elections in the winter of 1988–9 as convincingly as we won the Eastbourne and Ribble Valley ones in 1990–1. We led the SDP rump at Epping, but they led us at Richmond, which was a considerable humiliation for us and only a delusion for them, as they never did well again and within fifteen months had wound themselves up.

During this period when we were battling with the new SDP (almost exactly the same position, incidentally, in which the anti-Liberal fringe of the old SDP would have liked us to place ourselves vis-à-vis the Liberals in the hazardous launch year of 1981) almost the only good political news was the excellent performance of Paddy Ashdown as the new and first leader of the Liberal Democrats. When David Steel decided that he had had enough of leadership, Ashdown was the unanimous choice of Shirley Williams, Bill Rodgers and me, and was strongly supported by most other former Social Democrats and a lot of Liberals too. We did not then know him well, and he was politically inexperienced to be a leader. So it was not a choice without risks. Fortunately we turned out to be right on this. Ashdown has led with steadiness, grace and mounting authority. It is a great satisfaction that he is now getting the better results that he deserves.

The adversity which persisted for more than two years did not, in my view, stem from any foolishness within the new party. After the two initial errors it hardly put a foot wrong. The Owenite argument that an amalgamated party would expose the SDP to the dangers of a wild conference proved wholly unfounded. The successive autumn conferences have been responsible in decision, almost too sober in appearance and impressive in debate. But this was slow to counteract the harm we did ourselves by indulging in an internecine quarrel. Because we had stood for avoiding the sterile old partisanship and for bringing people together across a wide political spectrum we were peculiarly vulnerable when we failed to work amicably with each other. It was the especial misfortune of the Alliance to be a political grouping which stood for consensus but which contained one of the two most abrasive figures in British politics.

How do I see the whole chapter of the 1980s from the still short perspective of today? I do not in the least regret the adventure of the SDP and the Alliance. There were three levels of success which, together with abject failure, I regarded as within the bounds of possibility when we set off in the experimental plane. The first was a complete breakthrough to a recasting of the political system with the Alliance becoming a party of government. This I regarded in 1979–80 as only at the extreme upper end of the bracket of possibility, with at most a 10 per cent chance of occurring. But in 1981–2 we came within a hair's breadth of achieving it. It cannot be wrong to attempt something which so nearly resulted in such spectacular success.

The second band of possibility was that, without displacing either of the two major parties, we would nonetheless give a firmly triangular shape to politics with the electorate offered an effective non-vote-wasting choice outside the duopoly. That would have been achieved with vaulting ease under any electoral system which exists in the rest of the European Community. Even with the handicap of the British device to give majority powers to a minority of the voters we effectively created such a pattern in 1981–7 for every aspect of politics except for the rigged one of membership of the House of Commons. Then there were two years when, because of our self-inflicted wounds, it looked as though we might be driven back on to only the third level of achievement. Since 1990, however, thanks to a mixture of the quality of Ashdown's leadership and the desire of large sections of the public to escape from the Labour/Conservative strait-jacket, we are almost back to the second band.

The third and lower-case possibility was that, without achieving any rewards for ourselves, we would drag the Labour Party back from the wilder shores of lunacy and arrogance which made it for nearly a decade as unelectable as it would have been dangerous had by chance the safety catch failed and the impossible occurred. Without the harsh reality of our nearly overhauling them in 1983 and beating them into second or more often third place in bye-election after bye-election before and after that general election, they would not have begun to reform themselves on the whole range of issues on which they were eager to lead the country into a dogmatic and sullen isolationism which, had it prevailed, would have left us today more isolated from the Western mainstream than Poland or Hungary or Czechoslovakia have since become. So, while I greatly regret that so much should have been thrown away in 1987, I do not at all regret the course on which we set out in 1981. Better to have tried and partially succeeded than never to have tried at all.

# CHAPTER THIRTY-TWO

# *Establishment Whig or Persistent Radical?*

For a few years from 1987 nearly everything except politics went well for me. The splitting up of the SDP constituted a horrible blot on the landscape, but provided I looked in other directions, which there was an increasing temptation to do, the prospect was fair. It reminded me of a grand hotel in Palermo in which I had stayed on a presidential visit to Sicily in 1979. Three-quarters of its view commanded a rocky headland and a fine seascape. In the other quarter were the cranes and industrial grime of the Palermo shipyards. In theory one could sit at an angle and gaze only at unspoilt beauty. In practice one's eyes kept flickering towards the unwelcome sight.

In the centre of the fair segment of my post-1987 view were the dreaming spires of the University of Oxford. The chancellorship of Oxford had begun in 1224 with Robert Grosseteste, a scholar of humble origin (although later Bishop of Lincoln), and for the next three hundred years was mostly held for short periods, sometimes repeated after an interval, by clerkly figures resident in Oxford who nonetheless exercised great arbitrary powers over both city and University. In the late sixteenth century the grandees began to take over. Since Cromwell and his son no one who was not an hereditary peer, except for Sheldon who was an archbishop, held the office until Harold Macmillan was elected in 1960, and he became an earl for his final years. The period of office went up with the rank, and life became the invariable term from the Glorious Revolution onwards. As a result, while there had been over fifty Chancellors in the fourteenth century, five sufficed for the eighteenth century and four for the nineteenth. The twentieth century so far seems to have contradicted the advance of medical science by needing eight, although Macmillan and his predecessor, Edward Halifax, between them covered fifty-four years.

605

As the occupants of the office became grander so the powers they exercised became less. In the 1840s the Duke of Wellington controversially imposed his nominee as Vice-Chancellor upon the University, but in the twentieth century Curzon was alone in moving into Oxford for a season, presiding over the Hebdomadal Council, and trying to exercise an executive authority. As with his viceroyalty, this attempt produced a mixture of achievement and chagrin. Macmillan summed up the more normal modern pattern of power by saying that the reason Oxford needed a Chancellor was that, without one, there could not be a Vice-Chancellor, and without a Vice-Chancellor there would be no one to run the University.

Despite this divestment of power, the absence of a stipend, a residence, or even an office, and the obligation in a traditional and very devolved university of thirty-six separate colleges (the last one added only in 1990) and many other institutions to fulfil a lot of ceremonial, representational and commemorative engagements, the office had nonetheless been a sought-after one amongst Oxonian politicians. The list of those who had held it guaranteed this, although in this century it could be argued that the distinction of the defeated candidates exceeded that of those who were elected. In 1907 Rosebery failed against Curzon, and in 1925, much more scandalously, Asquith was overwhelmingly defeated by Cave, one of the least distinguished of Lord Chancellors. The reason for these results was political affiliation. The electorate is the MAs of the University, although to make their membership of it effective they have to come to Oxford and vote in person. Up to the first part of this century a lot of these were country parsons, the majority of whom as of most other occupations represented were almost automatically Tories. In consequence there was only one Chancellor (Edward Grey) elected between 1834 and 1987 who had not been a member of a Conservative government. Whatever the results Oxford at least remained unfrightened by contested elections. Cambridge, perhaps intimidated when Baldwin died in 1947 by the threat of a Smuts/Nehru contest which might have been more divisive for the Commonwealth than comfortable for the University, took refuge from 1950 in Marshal of the Royal Air Force Lord Tedder, and has since stuck to politically non-controversial Chancellors, culminating in the Duke of Edinburgh.

Thoughts of an Oxford election began to surface in the mid-1970s when Harold Macmillan reached his eightieth birthday. This was at a time when my connections with the University had become closer than in my first twenty-five years after leaving it. In 1969 I had been made an honorary fellow of Balliol, in 1973 I was given an honorary DCL (fairly rare for a non-Prime Minister politician) and I was President of the University Labour Club (having beaten Wilson in a contest of which neither of us was aware). There were enough hints that I might be a possible candidate for the chancellorship to make the issue cross my mind, but I think I probably saw myself more as a left-of-centre candidate willing to lose than as a likely winner. Quintin Hailsham, then under seventy, seemed the most likely candidate of the right and, although the University had changed, I doubted if it had changed enough to upset the pattern of results established by Curzon/Rosebery, Cave/Asquith, or indeed Macmillan himself against Oliver Franks in 1960.

All such thoughts proved irrelevant. Macmillan passed not merely his eightieth birthday but his whole ninth decade with hardly a tremor. He was a splendid Chancellor for ceremonial and for oratory which mingled wit and sentiment in such perfect proportion that the mixture could be imbibed many times over without cloying. And if anything he became better as his venerability made the shuffling gait, the hooded eyes and the theatrical pauses still more appropriate. Even his nineti-eth birthday came and went. On a visit soon after it he began a speech by saying, 'This is a sad occasion for me, Mr Vice-Chancellor. It is the last time that you and I will perform this ceremony together.' Then, after an even longer pause than usual, he continued, 'For by next year *your* term of office will have come to an end.' The quality of such jokes and the continuing stylishness of the performance obviated any question of impatience, and in any event the contract was for life.

Eventually he did die, at the age of ninety-two and in the last days of 1986. In January a poll for a successor was arranged (in accordance with statute) for the two separated days of Thursday, 12 March, and Saturday, 14 March. The Conservative candidates soon emerged as Edward Heath and Robert Blake. There were two because Heath made it clear from the beginning that he had an immovable determination to stand while commanding neither the enthusiasm of the Prime Minister and Government nor the confidence of the Oxford right-wing establishment that he could win. He was in fact supported by the left, particularly by development economists, inspired by his Brandt Commission commitment, as much as by the right. Blake was a strong and well-liked internal candidate. He was about to retire as Provost of the Queen's College having previously been a history don at Christ Church for many years, and was particularly well backed in these two colleges. He had the support of those who had been most active on the Prime Minister's side in the 1985 battle over her honorary degree, and was thought to have received early Downing Street encouragement. Although a peer he would have broken the strong 250-year-old tradition that Oxford elected only those who had held major offices of state. But traditions are rarely sacrosanct and were certainly not so in the 1980s Conservative Party.

My offers of support were also solid from the beginning. The architects of my victory, as it turned out to be, were Anthony Kenny (then Master of Balliol) and Michael Brock (then Warden of Nuffield), both in the background because of inhibitions arising from Heath's honorary fellowships in their colleges; and in the foreground Alec Cairncross (ex-Master of St Peter's, Chancellor of Glasgow University, and my former Chief Economic Adviser at the Treasury, which for the purpose was a singularly happy combination of posts held); Patrick O'Brien, fellow of St Antony's and now director of the Institute of Historical Research; Celia Goodhart, who ran the London end of the campaign; Claus Moser (Warden of Wadham) and Asa Briggs (Provost of Worcester), who provided early and influential head of house support; and, above all in influence, Isaiah Berlin, the doyen of the University, who, by not hesitating to commit his prestige, encouraged a lot of others of friendly mind but cautious disposition to come into the open.

This was of particular value, for the campaign we fought was essentially one of nominations. Only two nominations were required for a valid candidature, and there was indeed a fourth candidate who practised this austerity (and got thirty-five votes), but the rest of us thought there was no harm in deploying a superfluity of force. Only the organisers of my campaign, however, came near to emulating the saturation feats of Bomber Harris. The University *Gazette* published cumulative lists of nominators in three successive weeks. In the first week (19 February) we published 120 names against Blake's 60 and Heath's 28. The next week we went up to 237. By the third and last week we had gone to 410 (almost exactly as many *votes* as Asquith's defeated candidature had received), Heath to 160, and Blake had merely made a stately shuffle to 67.

We did not go merely for tonnage of bombs unloaded. With more discrimination than Air Marshal Harris we devoted a lot of attention to spread between colleges (and between sexes) as well as to assembling different categories of influential eminence. Almost unbelievably, Heath's first list contained no one from any college other than Balliol. Ours covered thirty colleges, and we subsequently filled in the five gaps. This difference was more than a curiosity, for Balliol (only about 4 per cent of the University) had already provided four of the seven Chancellors elected this century, and to treat it as the imperial and arbitrating power was clearly rash. But this, I believe, was precisely Heath's characteristically uncompromising view. I remembered an occasion a year or two before when Robin Day (not on television) had been provocatively asking us together which was going to be Chancellor. I kept quiet. Ted jocularly but symptomatically said: 'It will be decided within *the* college.' Also his list, as indeed that of

Blake, contained not a single woman. Heath repaired this on the second round, but Blake never did. His first list was also heavily concentrated on his own colleges, Christ Church and Queen's.

Our lists contained eight heads of houses, thirteen former heads, five heads of Cambridge colleges (a bizarre touch; they were all former Oxonians of course), two Nobel Prizewinners, three members of the Order of Merit and twenty-seven Fellows of the Royal Society or of the British Academy. Altogether my promoters operated on this sector of the front, which the absence of most normal forms of campaigning made important, with imagination and efficiency.

I do not think that the campaign engendered much bitterness, at any rate between either of the Conservative candidates and me. What there was they reserved for one another, each being naturally irritated that the other did not give him a free run. This was exacerbated by the fact that the Tory whips, having encouraged Blake for the first month, then appeared to switch to Heath.

As the poll approached, no one had much idea what was going to happen. I had narrowly won a student vote (but as they were disenfranchised that was like taking a straw poll amongst the blacks in a South African election) and was also narrowly ahead in a Gallup Poll which had inevitably been taken by hit-and-miss methods. But it all looked very hazardous. Apart from anything else it was totally impossible to predict the size of the turn-out. There were probably about 80,000 entitled to vote, but the highest previous participation had been 3700.

I went to Oxford at the end of the Thursday morning, voted in the afternoon and then retired to East Hendred. It was a day of sharp cold sunlight, with mainly dons voting, although enough of them to form an hour's queue. I won an exit poll conducted for the *Daily Telegraph*, but we expected and indeed needed to be ahead amongst the resident members of the University.

The Friday was a day of lying up between the two polls (a day of fasting between the two bacchanalia was I think the medieval theory which produced the odd timetable of voting) and the sun did not waste itself upon this *dies non*. Saturday, by contrast, brought a return of Thursday's cloudlessness but with no wind and the first spring balm of the year. It was a day of magical light in which the stone of Oxford memorably glowed and there was a massive return to the University of its alumni. About six thousand came that day, which was far more than was expected. The result was not only a high poll but an heroic traffic snarl-up. Nearly all colleges gave luncheons for their old members and the atmosphere for most was nostalgic rather than partisan. But for me it was becoming a little agitated as the afternoon wore on. When we left a Wadham tea-party to go back to East Hendred there were still slow queues winding round the Sheldonian in the already fading light.

An hour after we got back the Senior Proctor telephoned to say that I had won. I remember a moment of unusual tension as I took up the instrument to receive the call. After the first seconds it was also a moment of unusual pleasure. By the standards of harsh reality it was hardly the most important election that I had fought, but it was an immensely enjoyable election to have won. Nor did it take place under a bushel. Throughout the ten weeks between Macmillan's death and the result the press and even television gave the contest considerable intermittent attention. The result was a main news item. And, most surprising of all, the world press gave it almost the treatment of a British general election. From the *New York Times* to *Le Monde* to the *Frankfurter Algemeine* it was front-page news. Voting queues for an office without power which comprised, almost cheek by jowl, the Archbishop of Canterbury, the Lord Chancellor, two former Prime Ministers, Isaiah Berlin, A. J. Ayer and Iris Murdoch were by any standards remarkably good copy on British idiosyncrasy.

The mocking note in the subsequent comment was devoted to pointing out that, while vigorously advocating proportional representation, I had been a major beneficiary of a first-past-the-post system. The figures were: Jenkins 3249, Blake 2674, and Heath 2348. Superficially they suggest that an alternative-vote system, the nearest approach to proportional representation that can be achieved in an election for a single position, would have united the Conservative vote and defeated me on the second count. I doubt if this would have been the outcome. Heath would have been eliminated and his second preferences distributed between Blake and me. In order to win I would have needed to get a minimum of 887 of them while allowing Blake to receive up to 1461. Given the combination in Heath's vote of an appreciable left-wing element, a large Balliol contingent and an unidentifiable number of those who preferred to stick to Oxford's long tradition of electing a supernumerary officer of state (or 'failed politician' as the Blake partisans liked to refer to Heath and me during the campaign) rather than move to an internal academic candidate, I think I would probably have got this necessary 37 per cent. That is unprovable, but I am in favour of moving to such a system for the future and would have been willing to take its risks in the past. But I did not see it as reasonable that, being about to be defeated by the absence of an alternative vote system in Hillhead, I should reject a favourable election not based upon it in Oxford.

There was indeed a certain ironic even-handedness of fate in the conjuncture of defeating Edward Heath and Robert Blake on the banks of the Thames in March and then succumbing to George

Galloway on the banks of the Clyde in June. By winning in Oxford I at least avoided an exact emulation of the fate of my favourite biographical subject; Asquith lost both the University election and a Clydeside constituency (Paisley) within the same twelve months.

I have greatly enjoyed the chancellorship. It is often the case that a position which has been vigorously sought proves a disappointment when it comes to the performance of the duties. This has emphatically not been the case with Oxford, which is fortunate, for the duties for such an honorific post have proved surprisingly heavy. In 1989 when the specifically inaugural occasions were all behind me my diary shows that I did forty-three engagements in Oxford and another thirty 'Oxford' engagements outside the city, some in London but also in places scattered from Chicago to Frankfurt to Athens. Most of them involved the preparation of a speech, or at least the titivation of an old text in order to make it seem more suited to the particular occasion. As a result Oxford involves a good quarter of my time and energy. But as it has come to provide something more like a half of my interest the balance is a favourable one.

The pace of activity has been increased by the need for major fund-raising, which did not much involve my predecessors. I approached this with more determination than enthusiasm, for I do not regard the extraction of money from benefactors as the highest of the intellectual arts. Nor do I wish John Henry Newman's phrase 'the idea of a university' to assume a new meaning of being the sighting and pursuit of the nearest rich man. There is also danger of the new concentration upon fund-raising being divisive between universities with rich alumni and those who are on the whole without. But these considerations are outweighed by my conviction that, unless Oxford raises substantial private funds, it will not, for all the splendour of its buildings and the glory of its history, be able to maintain its position as one of the handful of universities of pre-eminent world class, and that if Oxford does not do so it is doubtful whether any university outside the United States will. This would be a state of affairs highly undesirable, not merely for Oxford, but for Britain, Europe and world academic balance as a whole. Fortunately the five-year Oxford Appeal for £220 million, which was a bold throw when it was launched in 1988, now looks likely to be achieved, for which the main credit must lie with the successive Vice-Chancellors, Patrick Neill and Richard Southwood.

The Chancellor does retain some non-fund-raising functions and prerogatives. He starts with the fine but unrepeatable patronage of being able to compile a large list of honorary graduands entirely of his own choosing. Lord Cave had managed to achieve one of no less than twenty-six. I decided to be more restrained than any of my predecessors and settled for one of only twelve. The theory was that, provided they had some claim to achievement and repute, they should roughly represent different aspects of my life. It was the only occasion on which those within the University could be honoured, for except on the Chancellor's inaugural list they are excluded in order to prevent mutual back-scratching. With these considerations in mind, I had three European men of state (the King of the Belgians, President Cossiga of Italy and Garret Fitzgerald, who had just ceased to be Irish Prime Minister), two Americans (Robert McNamara and the historian Arthur Schlesinger), five resident members of the University (Isaiah Berlin OM, Dorothy Hodgkin, also OM, Iris Murdoch, my old adversary in the 1940 dispute about the funds or liabilities of the Oxford Labour Club who had become a friend in the 1970s, the Master of my own college Anthony Kenny and the Vice-Chancellor of the day Patrick Neill), plus one outside academic (Alwyn Williams, the Principal of Glasgow University) and one diplomat (Nicholas Henderson, who it could be said with only a touch of hyperbole had been in charge of more embassies than anyone since Talleyrand).

The Chancellor also retains the rights which Bagehot saw as appropriate for a constitutional sovereign: the right to be consulted, the right to encourage and the right to warn. And, it should perhaps be added, the right to bear some of the responsibility and incur some of the odium when things go wrong or the University appears to make an ass of itself.

Nineteen-eighty-seven was not only the year in which I plunged from victory in Oxford to defeat in Glasgow. As a result of the latter event it was also the year in which I finally disappeared from the House of Commons and, after six months, reappeared in the House of Lords. I had not previously given a great deal of thought to the question of whether or not I was likely to finish as a peer. I had rejected Callaghan's offers of the late 1970s, not because of a principled objection to politicians ending up in the House of Lords, but because I was not then in an ending-up mood. Nineteen-eighty-seven was different in that respect from 1979. I had made a throw at recasting British politics, with the degree of near success which I have described in the previous chapter, and after defeat at Hillhead there was obviously no sense in fighting again there at the age of over seventy, while I certainly had no taste for fighting anywhere else. *Mr Balfour's Poodle* could be regarded as a slightly mocking book about the House of Lords, and in its epilogue I had written satirically of the increasing appropriateness of the words of the old hymn: 'There is room for new creations/In that upper place of bliss.' But I had never spoken or written any words which made it less appropriate for me to go to the House of Lords than other radical politicians from Asquith and Lloyd George to Attlee and Morrison.

Nevertheless I admired those who had not done so, and thought, 'Mr Pitt', 'Mr Gladstone', 'Mr Joseph Chamberlain' and even 'Sir Winston Churchill' (although the last weakened by the knighthood handle which a Garter imposes upon a commoner) to be more impressive final designations than, say, the Earl of Iddesleigh or of Avon. As a result I regretted ceasing to be officially 'Mr Roy Jenkins'. There is a dining club, founded by Dr Johnson, which simply calls itself The Club (the Other Club being a counterpoise to it) in which I had graduated over twenty years or so to being one of the eight or ten senior members, and it gave me mild pleasure that I was alone in the first two (out of three) columns of the membership list in being neither 'Lord' nor 'Sir'. But I need not have worried unduly, for the majority of the semi-strangers who address me in chance encounters still bestow upon me a 'Mr' rather than a 'Lord'.

There were, however, compelling arguments the other way. There have only been two periods in my adult life when I have had no working base in London, and have been entirely dependent upon Kensington Park Gardens with my secretary there installed in a simulacrum of an office. The first was the three months after I came back from Brussels and before I joined Morgan Grenfell. The second was in 1987 between the House of Commons and the House of Lords. Neither was satisfactory. So, given my propensity not to attract commercial offers, and indeed by this time my lack of desire for them, the House of Lords was attractive as a base as well as a platform.

The offer came at the end of June, within three weeks of the Hillhead defeat. David Owen, still then leader of an unsplit SDP, passed it on with courtesy and speed. The only curious suggestion he made was that I might prefer to hold out for an hereditary viscountcy in the New Year list. I could not decide whether or not that was a joke. I decided against, for he was not in general a very jokey man. In any event a barony in the hand seemed better than a viscountcy in the bush, and I accepted with alacrity. Correctly, I think, I could not regard a peerage as being an honour. This was in accordance with the fact that it cannot be removed, however disgraceful one's conduct. A knighthood went from Blunt, privy councillorships from Profumo and Stonehouse, even a Garter from the Emperor of Japan. But a peerage, because it is a station in life and not 'a riband to stick on [one's] coat', is inviolate. And it was a station in life which had come to suit me well by the middle of 1987.

I then had to decide, with the assistance of Garter King of Arms, what I should be called. Some people claimed to have had a terrible time with him, or his predecessor, or his Scottish equivalent Lyon King of Arms. George Brown had typically engaged in some storming sessions with Garter and Noel Annan had found his right to call himself by his own name disputed by Lyon on the ground that the Provost and Corporation of the Dumfriesshire town had not been consulted. I remembered Asquith's trouble about becoming Earl of Oxford and being required to tack on a redundant 'and Asquith', in the hope that this might take out the resonance. Duff Cooper, however, had been allowed to take the equally grand title of Norwich without remonstrance. Herbert Morrison had been told he could not be Morrison of London, which was too big for him, in spite of his six years of highly effective government of the whole capital, and that he must confine himself to Morrison of Lambeth, which might have been expected to cause as much upset to the Archbishop as London would have done to the Lord Mayor.

I had none of these troubles, as I had no intention of cloaking myself in the senile anonymity of a territorial title. This displeased Lord Jenkins of Putney, who wrote urging me to do this, or at least to follow George Brown and call myself Lord Roy-Jenkins. I told him I was equally unprepared to masquerade as the younger son of a duke. However, my preference satisfied Garter and left him with only the geographical handle, which he assured me would have to be part of the so-called *nomen dignitatus* to distinguish me from Putney, about which to argue. He opened by saying that, as the surname came first, I could be of more or less anywhere I liked, provided 'it was not abroad'. This aroused my historico-argumentative instincts and I said, 'Why not abroad? What about Kitchener of Khartoum, Alexander of Tunis, Montgomery of Alamein, and indeed Samuel of Mount Carmel and Toxteth?' He said, 'But they won great battles abroad' (hardly true of Samuel). I said, 'And do you not think that I won great battles in Brussels, Strasbourg and Luxembourg?' By this time we were on good terms, and settled quickly on Hillhead. He decided that, as his atlas index showed there were also several Hillheads in England, we need not trouble Lyon, particularly as I did not wish to follow a Glasgow path for the territorial designation itself, which is not part of the title as such and lives only a vestigial life. I thought I could get the best of both worlds by becoming *Jenkins of Hillhead*, of Pontypool in the County of Gwent. This piece of Cymro-Scottish miscegenation was surprisingly permissible. In my experience, therefore, the dreaded Garter was both teasable and amenable.

The choice of Hillhead was easy. The only attractive alternative was Oxford. But my memory of Asquith's troubles over that contentious name (although I would have been using it in a much more modest way) was too vivid. I did not want a latterday Lady Cranborne writing to me, as that then very young lady had done to Asquith, and saying 'it is like a suburban villa calling itself Versailles'. I thought it was enough to be *Chancellor* of Oxford, and that the custard should not be over-egged. In any event I much valued my Hillhead connection. It was a good, clear, easily pronounceable name, and the choice even seemed to give some local pleasure.

There was a queue to get into the House of Lords that autumn. I was not in a hurry, and so, although my peerage had been announced in July, I did not arrive until 1 December. I was then conducted through the somewhat over-elaborate introduction ceremony under the joint sponsorship of Jo Grimond and Jack Diamond, the latter still the leader of the SDP peers. I was doing my best, ineffective though it proved, to hold the old Alliance together. As 1987 came to an end, I felt that with this and the two Oxford Encaenias I had had enough ceremonies for the time being, and also that it had been a swooping roller-coaster of a year.

I did not make a speech in the House of Lords until late February 1988, and that, in a somewhat abstract debate on the principles of taxation, was more a paving exercise than an event of its own. In the following week we had an Alliance day on which we proposed to debate the excessive concentration of power in Mrs Thatcher's Britain. The desire was that I should move the motion, but as it was intended to be a hard-hitting debate (by House of Lords standards) it was inappropriate that the opener should be hobbled by the conventional restrictions on a maiden speech. That had therefore to be out of the way first. The result of the conjuncture was that I remember the second speech more than the first as my House of Lords baptism of fire. 'Baptism of fire' is a rather ludicrous cliché for the polite quietness of the Lords and the obligatory tributes, some delivered in anticipation, which echo throughout the debate when a maiden speech is taking place. This does not mean that the underlying atmosphere is not at best keenly appraising and at worst sharply critical in thoughts if not in words. No doubt, and reasonably, this applies particularly to the speeches of those who come with a reputation for ministerial offices held and House of Commons orations delivered.

Many of these, including curiously some with the most 'senatorial' styles, never properly found their feet in the House of Lords. Asquith and Baldwin were both in this category. On the other hand, Attlee's laconicism probably went as well in the Lords as in the Commons, Macmillan's brief parliamentary resurrection as Earl of Stockton was theatre with high box-office appeal, and Willie Whitelaw's imitation of the Duke of Devonshire (ex-Hartington) of the 1890s made him more effective in the Lords than he had been in the Commons, and equally well liked in both.

The differences between the styles of the two Houses are considerable but elusive. In most circumstances debates in the Lords are, as they should be on any proper theory of democracy, less important. Great careers can be founded on mastery over the House of Commons. From F. E. Smith to Iain Macleod reputations have been made by a single speech. I can recollect no career, at any rate since Brougham, based on oratorical prowess in the House of Lords. Nothing follows from an exceptional speech other than agreeable congratulations, and nothing seems to follow either from examples of manifest incompetence, even on the government front bench. Sometimes if the Lords has an interesting debate, and the Commons a dull day, there can be an approach to equality of newspaper coverage. But if the two are debating the same subject on the same day, as with the Gulf crisis debates in 1990–1, the Lords cannot hold a candle to the Commons.

The exceptions to the rule of relative unimportance are when an amendment to a bill is being debated. Then a speech of unusual persuasiveness (debating pyrotechnics will not do) can swing votes and maybe determine whether or not the proposition is carried. Many cross-bench peers will not vote unless they have heard the debate, and their votes are often determining. This is different from the Commons, where a lost debate may damage the standing of a minister but has no effect on the whipped cohorts who trudge in for the division from dining room or library with their minds unsullied by the arguments.

Judged purely as a receptive forum for a speech the Lords has both advantages and disadvantages compared with the Commons. The Lords audience is not only more polite (although it can mutter and its attention can certainly slip away) but is frequently larger. The tensely packed chamber of a 1960s Commons wind-up cannot be found, but there is a better chance of getting a listening 150/200 for the opening stages of a debate of general interest than there is in the Commons. Yet the House of Lords is more difficult to get hold of as a whole than is the Commons in favourable circumstances. It is a curiously compartmentalised chamber, in the way that Westminster Abbey is a compartmentalised church. The Commons, appropriately, is more like St Margaret's, less grand but easier to weld into a whole.

The Lords is also slow to laugh. Sometimes it reminds me of the European Parliament in this respect. There the response, if any, comes in a series of delayed ripples, the Danish translation for some reason or other usually taking the longest to get through. The Commons is much readier both to laugh against you, which is disagreeable, and to laugh with you, which is agreeable. This does not however lead me to the view of Robert Lowe (later Lord Sherbrooke) that speaking in the Lords is like 'a corpse addressing a charnel house' or even to Disraeli's description of himself as 'dead, but in the Elysian fields', when he became Beaconsfield. My subjective view of the House of

Lords is that it is rather like Adlai Stevenson's comment on flattery: it is all right provided you do not inhale. In other words it is a satisfactory place to end up provided you do not take it too seriously, do not succumb to its cosseting charm, but treat its mixture of archaic pageantry and Puginesque extravagance of décor with a touch of polite mockery. My objective view is that it remains schematically indefensible, although a two-chamber legislature is certainly desirable, but that after a topsy-turvy decade dominated by Mrs Thatcher's harshly untraditionalist Conservative Party it joins with the ancient universities, the established Church and, indeed, the monarchy in providing a few islands of countervailing liberal urbanity in a sea of brashly selfish materialism with little sense of continuity.

In terms of the question posed in the title of this chapter this obviously sounds more compatible with a whig than a radical answer. In my own mind I am not so sure. I have no desire to claim a political position more left-wing than that which I instinctively feel. As I recorded earlier I had given up describing myself as a socialist for several years before I left the Labour Party. Yet I see myself as being somewhat to the left of James Callaghan, maybe of Denis Healey and certainly of David Owen. Owen may be more at personal odds with established institutions than I am, but for the rest I do not share his nuclear fixation, his free-market enthusiasm, his instinctive nationalism or his respect for Mrs Thatcher's style of government. With Callaghan, the difference would be most sharp on libertarian issues. He did not like my reforms of the 1960s, and in the 1970s we clashed sharply on my desire to change the Official Secrets Act, and in general I think I have more iconoclasm, about, say, the police, the TUC (despite his scars of 1979) or the intelligence services than he has. With Denis Healey the difference is more difficult to pinpoint. He has long carried light ideological baggage on a heavy gun carriage.

My broad position remains firmly libertarian, sceptical of official cover-ups and uncompromisingly internationalist, believing sovereignty to be an almost total illusion in the modern world, although both expecting and welcoming the continuance of strong differences in national traditions and behaviour. I distrust the deification of the enterprise culture. I think there are more limitations to the wisdom of the market than were dreamt of in Mrs Thatcher's philosophy. I believe that levels of taxation on the prosperous, having been too high for many years (including my own period at the Treasury), are now too low for the provision of decent public services. And I think the privatisation of near monopolies is about as irrelevant as (and sometimes worse than) were the Labour Party's proposals for further nationalisation in the 1970s and early 1980s.

As I come to what should be the end of this book I become aware for the first time of a technical problem relating to autobiography. The way to finish a biography is to follow the advice which Lewis Carroll made the King give: 'Begin at the beginning, and go on till you come to the end; then stop.' And the way to stop is to describe the end of the subject's life, put him in his grave and, if you can think of a succinct epitaph to put upon it, give it a headstone. That, by definition, is not possible with an autobiography. As a result there is no obvious *terminus ad quem*.

Yet I believe that even the meanest work requires something of a *finale*, as opposed to just subsiding in mid-passage. So I conclude in two ways. First I pose the question whether I would rather have lived a life away from politics, and second I ask whether, in politics, I regret not having devoted myself more unconditionally to climbing to the top of the greasy pole.

On the first question I believe that I was too politically concentrated between the ages of, say, eighteen and thirty-two, although my four army years necessarily constituted something of a diversion. I devoted too much attention to politics at Oxford. I was too eager to get into the House of Commons, for anywhere, almost anyhow, and when I got there I was too much of a party loyalist, thinking more about the game than about the merits of issues. I also neglected equipping myself with any money-earning qualifications, so that, but for the unpredictable chance that I found I could increasingly write for profit, I would have been exposed to the vagaries, penuries and ingrowing narrowness of being a full-time politician.

I am strongly against the current fashion for full-time MPs. Of course being a minister or a leading member of a party in opposition is almost exclusively demanding. But no one can guarantee to command such positions, and so long as we insist on having one of the biggest legislatures in the world (450 would be better than 650) the majority of members are not going to get near to them. Being a full-time back-bench MP is not in my view a satisfactory occupation. The time can obviously be filled in, but not with work of sufficient intellectual stimulus. Constituency problems and constituency experiences can be rewarding and enjoyable, but not as a staple diet. And excessive attendance at the House of Commons, with the too many hours spent hanging around in tearoom or smoking room which this implies, either atrophies the brain or obsesses it with the minutiae of political gossip and intrigue. If the electorate or (more likely) the local party caucuses insist upon this sort of member they will get and deserve a House of Commons which will be increasingly a grey shadow of its former self. There are times when an effective politician must be prepared to throw every ounce of his commitment and every moment of his working capacity into a struggle for causes which fully engage him.

But these times do not occur often over a lifetime in politics, and he also needs the resources to lie fallow in the House of Commons without stultifying himself.

In my first four or five years as an MP I was short of the resources with which to do this, but the gap luckily filled itself in the mid-1950s and, once it had done so, not exactly causally but by a process of spontaneous harmony, I also escaped from the party-apparatchik syndrome which had shown signs of engulfing me. From 1955 onwards my parliamentary interests – Europe and, for a time, the campaign against literary censorship – were almost excessively free of party orthodoxy. This new balance gave me both the material and the intellectual detachment to treat party machines with scepticism, and once I had achieved that I began a long phase of feeling that I had politics and life in much better balance with each other.

From this time onwards I believe that politics, not always taken in excessive doses, has given me more satisfaction than I could have obtained from any other way of life. It has inevitably produced its ration of boredom, pettiness, frustration, exhaustion and dismay, but less I think than I would have found in any profession or other occupation. And to offset these low points there has been greater variety and stimulus, a more frequent sense of widening horizons, at least as many friends, and a wider acquaintanceship both with people and with places than I would have been likely to find elsewhere.

How much pleasure have I derived from relative fame, from most people (although this has only been so for the second half of my time in politics) knowing vaguely who I am? Fame is a mixed blessing, evoking contradictory emotions well illustrated by a tendency to be equally displeased if one is over-accosted in the street or if one is aware of a declining recognition factor and greeted with blankness when it might be nice to be more positively received. Then there is the blend of pleasure and pain which comes from newspaper exposure. A flat and disappointed: 'Nothing much in the papers today' is a frequent politician's reaction after a quick and unavailing search for his own name. On the other hand I can recollect several periods when I was having a bad press, when it was sheer misery to bring myself to open the wretched journals, and when, if for once I was ignored, it was nothing but relief.

Parents' fame also has a tendency to make life difficult for their children. This view certainly seems to be supported by the experiences of the offspring of many of those who have achieved the foremost position. Happily I do not think my family has suffered unduly from this, but perhaps this was simply because I did not achieve enough success for the issue to be put to the full test. I therefore do not regard the lure of fame with all its fickleness as one of the unmitigated benefits of politics. But it would be hypocritical to pretend that its pull plays no part. I suspect that we all (all politicians at least) have in us something of the 'having one's cake and eating it' spirit which is reputed to have afflicted the well-known Labour peer who wrote a book on Humility, walked down Piccadilly without seeing it in Hatchard's bookshop, went in, sent for the manager and demanded to know why it was not in the window.

The more serious question is whether the opportunity to influence the course of events which politics gives to a minority of those who participate has in my case produced significant results. To this I answer hesitantly yes. The Home Office reforms of the 1960s were well within this category. The next period at the Treasury is more marginal. The stringency of the policy I pursued was right, was important at the time and, within its own terms of reference, was a success. Its objective was fully achieved. But economic management by its very nature leaves only footprints in the sand. The tide of the next Chancellor washes them away.

Paradoxically my subsequent period in opposition, with the possibility which it brought of leading a decisive adjunct to the majority for Britain going into Europe, particularly when fortified by the referendum campaign a few years later, has had a longer-term effect. Normally opposition is sterile, made worthwhile by the period of power and opportunity to which it may lead. In my case this was by no means sharply so.

During my four years in Brussels by far the most significant development was the creation of the European Monetary System. This has so far proved not merely durable but seminal. The SDP must I fear be judged less durable, although not necessarily less seminal. In sum therefore I feel that I have had substantially more influence on the course of events than I could have done in any other way of life, and at least as much as I could have realistically hoped for when I so eagerly embraced politics nearly fifty years ago. I hope this capacity to influence events has done more good than harm, and on the whole believe this to be so. But I do not feel certainty about this, for my beliefs have become much less dogmatic and my outlook far more relativist than at the beginning.

I turn to the second question, which is whether I wish I had been a more whole-hearted party politician, rolling with the punch of policies I did not like and subordinating everything to being in position to succeed to the Labour Party leadership and (probably) to the premiership. There is obviously a qualitative difference between being Prime Minister and occupying other great offices but not attaining the highest. It is not exactly a question of influence, for some non-prime ministerial politicians – Joseph Chamberlain, Ernest

Bevin and R. A. Butler for example – put more imprint on British politics than did, say, Campbell-Bannerman, Anthony Eden or Alec Home. But there is nonetheless something in Melbourne's remark that 'it is a damned fine thing to have been, even if it only lasts for two months'. It puts one in a sort of apostolic succession of forty-nine men and one woman descending from Walpole, for which no amount of explaining how narrowly or even honourably it was missed is a compensation. Gaitskell was a considerably greater man than either of his two immediate Labour successors, yet there is no contesting the fact that because he was out of that list and they are in he has become more quickly forgotten by those who did not know him.

The prime ministership seemed at times within my grasp. Had the Labour Party won the 1970 general election, as for once it on the whole deserved to do, there can be little doubt in view of his 1976 decision that Wilson would have stuck to his privately stated intention and resigned within two or three years, with a strong presumption that I would then have succeeded him. Even with that election lost, I had the option of finessing the European issue, maintaining my deputy leader's position and being well placed for the 1976 contest. That I did not follow that course I do not regret. The inheritance had by then become a tawdry one, and I would have been through so many humiliating compromises that I would have lost any capacity to preside over a government with verve. There was also the possibility of attempting a pre-emptive strike, first in 1968 and then in 1972 or 1973. On the first occasion it was my primary duty to get on with the job of being a beleaguered Chancellor, and again I do not regret that I was not diverted. In 1972–3 it might have been better for the future health of the Labour Party had I challenged, but had I done so I might well have achieved just about the outcome that Michael Heseltine did in 1990. I half regret I did not do that, but not on ground of ambition.

The last appearance of the will o' the wisp was in 1981–2. Such was the success of the SDP that there was a brief flickering moment when Ladbrokes' odds made me the most likely person to be the next Prime Minister. Few horses have been both the favourite and an outsider to the system at the same time. So that was heady, and it would then have been still more satisfactory to have succeeded with a whole style of government to be made afresh than after a victorious 1970 election, even though, unlike 1976, there would on both occasions have been no need to stoop to conquer. But that early 1980s prospect faded away, not this time through lack of ruthless resolution, but because of the resilience, behind the fortifications of the British electoral system, of the Conservative/Labour duopoly.

One reason that I was not more tantalised by these more or less near misses is that I always sensed that I would enjoy being Prime

Minister more when it was over than while it was taking place. This thought set a limit to the thrust of my ambition. No doubt, also, it raises the question of how much I was truly at ease with power. It is not a thought which I suspect much troubled the minds of the great determined leaders of history. Napoleon was not secretly looking forward to writing his memoirs, whether at St Helena or elsewhere. And even those multi-volume memorialists and politicians of genius, Lloyd George and Churchill, never doubted that they were happier in 10 Downing Street even in the darkest days of war than they ever could be on the hills of Wales or in the painting groves of the South of France.

So, although I think that I was a decisive and even an adventurous politician at various stages in my life, and had more sensible views about how to lead a government than many of those who have actually done it, I nonetheless lacked at least one of the essential ingredients of a capacity to seize power. I may have avoided doing too much stooping, but I also missed conquering. However, I do not feel retrospectively deprived, except that I wish I could have produced more of a promised land for those who have followed me. But at a personal level looking around does not lead me to feel envy of those who have been Prime Minister.

I have a lot of friends and a lot of interests. I have at the time of writing been married for forty-six years to the same wife, and her preoccupations with the chairmanships successively of the Consumers' Association, the Historic Buildings Council and the National Trust have not prevented her from being engaged in all the major decisions and enterprises of my life. With each of our three children we are on good and even close terms. These are not negligible fixed points. There are also seven grandchildren who have so far brought much more pleasure than pain. I have tried to write truthfully in this book of events pleasant and otherwise, but it seems to me that I would be inexcusably churlish if I concluded with any note of complaint against fate, or events, or almost anyone with whom I have been closely associated.

# References

### Chapter One: A Late and Only Child
1 Thomas Jones, *Whitehall Diary* (Oxford University Press, 1969), vol. II, p. 95.

### Chapter Five: The Evolution of a Gaitskellite
1 Alan Bullock, *Ernest Bevin* (Heinemann, 1983), vol. III, p. 834.
2 *New Fabian Essays* (Turnstile, 1952), pp. 69–88.

### Chapter Seven: Almost Out of Politics
1 *The Political Diary of Hugh Dalton, 1918–40 and 1945–60*, ed. Ben Pimlott (Jonathan Cape, 1986), pp. 694–5.
2 Douglas Jay, *Change and Fortune* (Hutchinson, 1980), pp. 271–8
3 Quoted in Philip Williams, *Gaitskell* (Jonathan Cape, 1979), p. 736.

### Chapter Nine: A Young Home Secretary
1 James Callaghan, *Time and Chance* (Collins, 1987), p. 203.
2 Barbara Castle, *The Castle Diaries, 1964–70* (Weidenfeld & Nicolson, 1984), p. 172.
3 Richard Crossman, *The Diaries of a Cabinet Minister*, vol. I: *Minister of Housing, 1964–66* (Hamish Hamilton and Jonathan Cape, 1975), p. 574.
4 Castle, *Castle Diaries*, p. 172.
5 Richard Crossman, *The Diaries of a Cabinet Minister*, vol. II: *Lord President of the Council and Leader of the House of Commons, 1966–68* (Hamish Hamilton and Jonathan Cape, 1976), p. 87.

### Chapter Ten: The Liberal Hour
1 Harold Wilson, *The Labour Government, 1964–70: A Personal Record* (Weidenfeld & Nicolson/Michael Joseph, 1971), p. 385.
2 Crossman, *Diaries*, vol. II, p. 433.

### Chapter Twelve: A Budget Born in a Crisis
1 Wilson, *Labour Government*, p. 513.
2 Castle, *Diaries, 1964–70*, p. 407.
3 Crossman, *Diaries*, vol. II, p. 723.
4 Tony Benn, *Diaries, 1968–72* (Hutchinson, 1988), pp. 48–9.
5 *Spectator*, 5 April 1968.

### Chapter Thirteen: Rough Times with Sterling and with Wilson
1 Castle, *Diaries, 1964–70*, pp. 419–20.
2 Richard Crossman, *The Diaries of a Cabinet Minister*, vol. III: *Secretary of State for Social Services, 1968–70* (Hamish Hamilton and Jonathan Cape, 1977), p. 97.

### Chapter Fifteen: The Sun Climbs Slow, How Slowly
1 Kenneth Rose, *King George V* (Weidenfeld & Nicolson, 1983), p. 174.
2 Castle, *Diaries, 1964–70*, pp. 632–3.
3 Crossman, *Diaries*, vol. II, p. 778.
4 Castle, *Diaries, 1964–70*, p. 659.

### Chapter Sixteen: Defeat Out of the Jaws of Victory
1 Crossman, *Diaries*, vol. III, pp. 838–9.

### Chapter Seventeen: European Unity and Labour Party Schism
1 Benn, *Diaries, 1968–72*, pp. 315–16, 353 (entries for 30 May and 29 June 1971).

### Chapter Eighteen: The Road to Resignation
1 Benn, *Diaries, 1968–72*, p. 377.

### Chapter Nineteen: A More Comfortable Life?
1 See my *European Diary, 1977–1981* (Collins, 1989), pp. 407–8.

### Chapter Twenty-One: A Recidivist Home Secretary
1 Barbara Castle, *The Castle Diaries, 1974–76* (Weidenfeld & Nicolson, 1980), pp. 69–70.
2 Ibid., p. 116.

### *Chapter Twenty-Three: Goodbye to Whitehall*

1 Jenkins, *European Diary*, p. 243.
2 Ibid., pp. 3–4.
3 Ibid., p. 5.


### *Chapter Twenty-Four: Cross-Channel Packet*

1 Callaghan, *Time and Chance*, p. 399.
2 Jenkins, *European Diary*, p. 2.


### *Chapter Twenty-Five: Monetary Union Reproclaimed*

1 Jenkins, *European Diary*, pp. 193, 194.
2 Ibid., p. 49.
3 Ibid., pp. 49–50.
4 Ibid., p. 50.
5 Ibid., p. 152.
6 Unpublished section of my diary for 4 November 1977.
7 Jenkins, *European Diary*, p. 224.


### *Chapter Twenty-Six: The Creation of the EMS*

1 Jenkins, *European Diary*, p. 246.
2 Denis Healey, *The Time of My Life* (Michael Joseph, 1989), pp. 438–40.
3 Jenkins, *European Diary*, p. 325.
4 Ibid., p. 313.
5 Ibid., pp. 324–5.
6 Ibid., p. 337.
7 Ibid., p. 334.
8 Ibid., p. 341.
9 Ibid., p. 347.
10 Ibid., pp. 364–5.


### *Chapter Twenty-Seven: Bloody British Question*

1 Jenkins, *European Diary*, p. 333.
2 Ibid., p. 593.
3 Ibid., pp. 602–3.


### *Chapter Twenty-Eight: The Twitch Upon the Political Thread*

1 Jenkins, *European Diary*, p. 425.
2 Ibid., p. 460.

3 David Steel, *Against Goliath* (Weidenfeld & Nicolson, 1989), pp. 215–16.
4 Jenkins, *European Diary*, p. 489.
5 Ibid., p. 509.
6 Ibid., p. 517.
7 Ibid., pp. 525, 526.
8 Ibid., p. 528.
9 Ibid., pp. 642–3.
10 Ibid., pp. 608–9.
11 Ibid., p. 609.
12 Ibid., pp. 553, 587 and 625.
13 Ibid., pp. 619–20.
14 Ibid., p. 492.
15 Ibid., p. 626.
16 Ibid., p. 632.
17 Ibid., p. 635.
18 Ibid., p. 650.

### Chapter Twenty-Nine: The Annus Mirabilis of the SDP

1 Kenneth Harris, *David Owen: Personally Speaking* (Weidenfeld & Nicolson, 1987), p. 214.

### Chapter Thirty: The Path Grows Steeper: Hillhead to Ettrick Bridge

1 Steel, *Against Goliath*, p. 238.
2 Lecture on 'Glasgow's Place in the Cities of the World', given to the Royal Philosophical Society of Glasgow to mark the city's year as European City of Culture, 11 April 1990.
3 Harris, *David Owen*, p. 219.

### Chapter Thirty-One: What Went Wrong?

1 Steel, *Against Goliath*, pp. 282–5.

# Index

# Picture Acknowledgements

*Plate section I*: Central Press Photos Ltd page 3. Hulton Picture Company page 6 above.

*Plate section II*: *Daily Express* page 2 below. Popperfoto page 1. *Daily Telegraph* page 6 below. *The Times* page 6 above. White House Official Photograph page 8.

*Plate section III*: *Birmingham Post and Mail* page 7 below. Camera Press page 4 above. Crown Copyright Reserved page 1. Hulton Picture Company page 4 below. *Daily Mail* page 6 above. *The Times* page 7 above. Press Association page 8 below.

*Plate section IV*: Associated Newspapers Limited page 6. Bundesbildstelle, Bonn page 2 above. Department of State, Washington page 1 above. *Guardian* page 5 above. Press Association page 4 above. *Daily Telegraph* page 5 below. White House Official Photograph page 1 below.

Every effort has been made to trace all copyright holders but if any has been inadvertently overlooked, the publishers will be pleased to make the necessary arrangement at the first opportunity.